PROFESSIONAL BAKING

Photography
by
J. Gerard Smith

■ **Third Edition**

Professional
BAKING

Wayne Gisslen

**Featuring recipes from
Le Cordon Bleu** • *L'Art Culinaire* • **Paris—1895**

with a foreword
by
André J. Cointreau,
President, Le Cordon Bleu

JOHN WILEY & SONS, INC.

NEW YORK · CHICHESTER · WEINHEIM
BRISBANE · SINGAPORE · TORONTO

Library of Congress Cataloging-in-Publication Data:

Gisslen, Wayne, 1946–
      Professional baking / by Wayne Gisslen.—3rd ed.
         p. cm.
      Includes index.
      ISBN 0-471-34646-2 (cloth : college: alk. paper). — ISBN
  0-471-34647-0 (cloth : trade: alk. paper)
        1. Baking. 2. Food presentation. I. Title.
  TX763 .G47 2000
  641.8'15—dc21
                                00-038202
                                00-035180

Printed in the United States of America.

10 9 8 7 6

This

book

is

dedicated

to

Anne and Jim Smith and their family.

Contents

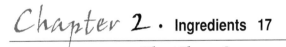

Chapter 1 • Basic Principles   3

Chapter 2 • Ingredients   17

Chapter 3 • Understanding Yeast Doughs   49

Recipe Contents

Recipes in blue type were
developed and tested by
Le Cordon Blue.

Chapter 6 / Quick Breads

Chapter 7 / Doughnuts, Fritters, Pancakes, and Waffles

Chapter 8 / Basic Syrups, Creams, and Sauces

Chapter 9 / Pies

Chapter 10 / Pastry Basics

Chapter 11 / Tarts and Special Pastries

Chapter 12 / Cake Mixing and Baking

Chapter 13 / Assembling and Decorating Cakes

Chapter 14 / Specialty Cakes, Gâteaux, and Torten

Chapter 15 / Cookies

Chapter 16 / Custards, Puddings, Mousses, and Soufflés

Chapter 17 / Frozen Desserts

Chapter 18 / Fruit Desserts

Chapter 19 / Dessert Presentation

Chapter 20 / Chocolate

Chapter 21 / Decorative Work: Marzipan, Pastillage, and Nougatine

Chapter 22 / Decorative Work: Sugar Techniques

About Le Cordon Bleu

With schools on five continents, in France, Great Britain, Japan, Australia and the Americas, and a student body made up of fifty different nationalities, Le Cordon Bleu is well known and highly regarded around the globe. Le Cordon Bleu, with its team of over 50 Masterchefs, has a tradition of excellence in the culinary arts and is committed to furthering the appreciation of fine food and fine living. Already involved in consulting and in promotion of a variety of culinary products, Le Cordon Bleu has successfully developed partnerships with major hospitality and culinary institutions, professional organizations, and one of the top luxury cruise lines.

Le Cordon Bleu Addresses

Paris
8 rue Léon Delhomme
Paris 75015
France
Telephone: 33-1-53-68-22-50
Fax: 33-1-48-56-03-96
Email: infoparis@cordonbleu.net

London
114 Marylebone Lane
London W1M 6HH
Great Britain
Telephone: 44-20-7935-3503
Toll Free in
 Great Britain: 44-800-980-3503
Fax: 44-20-7935-7621
Email: london@cordonbleu.net

Tokyo
ROOB-1, 28-113 Saragaku-cho, Daikanyama
Shibuya-ku, Tokyo 150
Japan
Telephone: 81-3-54-89-01-41
Fax: 81-3-54-89-01-45
Email: tokyoinfo@cordonbleu.net

Ottawa
453 Laurier Avenue East
Ottawa, Ontario K1N 6R4
Canada
Telephone: 1-613-236-CHEF (2433)
Fax: 1-613-236-2460
Email: ottawa@cordonbleu.net

Sydney
250 Blaxland Road, Ryde
Sydney, NSW 2112
Australia
Telephone: 61-2-9808-8307
Fax: 61-2-9807-6541

Le Cordon Bleu Restaurant, Business and Management - Australia
163 Days Road, Regency Park
Adelaide SA 5010
Australia
Telephone: 61-8-8348-4659
Fax: 61-8-8348-4661
Email: degree@cordonbleu.net

New York Corporate Office
404 Airport Executive Park
Nanuet, New York NY10954
USA
Telephone: 1-914-426-7400
Fax: 1-914-426-0104
Toll Free in the US
 and Canada: 1-800-457-CHEF (2433)
Email: lcbinfo@cordonbleu.net
Website: http://www.cordonbleu.net

Brazil
Universidade de Brasilia-UNB Centro de Excelencia em Turismo
Campus Universitario Darcy Ribeiro, Av L3 Norte, ED. Finatec
CEP 70910-900 D.F
Brazil
Telephone: 55-61-307-1110
Fax: 55-61-307-3201

Mexico
Universidade Anahuac
Av. Lomas Anahuac s/n,
Lomas Anahuac
Mexico 57260
Mexico
Telephone: 52-5-328-8047
Fax: 52-5-596-1938

Peru
Escuela Superior de Administracion Hoteleria y Turismo
Av Nunez de Balboa 530
Miraflores
Lima 18
Peru
Telephone: 51-1-447-0437
Fax: 51-1-242-9209

XIX

Foreword

Le Cordon Bleu-*L'Art Culinarie* is proud to continue its collaboration with author Wayne Gisslen on the third edition of *Professional Baking*. This collaboration underlines the importance of French pastry and baking technique through the talented guidance of an American educator considered one of the best of his generation. It has always been the view of Le Cordon Bleu that through mastering and understanding the importance of French pâtisserie techniques, process, and methods, students gain the skills and confidence with which to create their own masterpieces. Le Cordon Bleu envisions the third edition of *Professional Baking* as one of those tools.

Founded in Paris in 1895, Le Cordon Bleu now includes schools and restaurant and hospitality management programs spanning five continents. It has established academic alliances and partnerships as well as an extensive culinary product line. Le Cordon Bleu's team of over 50 Master Chefs share their knowledge with students from over fifty countries, and the school maintains close links with the culinary industry by attending and participating in over 30 festivals per year. Le Cordon Bleu is dedicated to promoting the advancement of education, training, and the appreciation of gastronomy worldwide.

Le Cordon Bleu's teaching skills are recognized by prestigious organizations around the world. The Ministry of Tourism of Shanghai selected Le Cordon Bleu to train their elite chefs in the French culinary arts. In 1997, Le Cordon Bleu opened its fifth school in Sydney, which led to a joint venture with the Australian government to train and advise cuisine and pâtisserie chefs for the Olympic Games of 2000. Recently, developments in Le Cordon Bleu's curriculum have led to the establishment of the bachelor's degree in Restaurant Business, an intensive qualification for future restaurant professionals and the perfect complement to skills learned during the renowned Grand Diploma courses at Le Cordon Bleu.

Professional Baking has been a mainstay in universities, community colleges, and technical schools throughout North America specializing in restaurant management and the culinary arts. It has been used to train tens of thousands of pastry chefs and bakers! Created by the talented Wayne Gisslen, the text teaches, through its lucid writing style, photographs, and recipes, how to understand and then perform in a working kitchen or bakery. Gisslen has balanced his practical knowledge with a clean pedagogical approach to make this a reference of a lifetime. In the third edition of *Professional Baking*, Wayne Gisslen and Le Cordon Bleu pastry chefs and staff combine their knowledge to introduce students to recipes including classic French boulangerie, elaborate pâtisserie items, and European specialties such as gâteaux and tortes. Students also learn the art of perfecting dessert presentations using marzipan, pastillage, nougatine, and pulled and blown sugar. *Professional Baking* is devoted to step-by-step procedures and production techniques. This is supported with basic theory and ingredient information, so students learn both the hows and whys of baking and pastry techniques.

This second collaboration with Wayne Gisslen has resulted in a strong partnership and friendship that has strengthened this edition and will continue with future projects.

André J. Cointreau
President
Le Cordon Bleu—*L'Art Culinaire*

Preface

This new third edition of *Professional Baking* has been planned to appeal especially to two groups of readers: those who are looking for something new in a baking text, and those who liked the second edition of *Professional Baking* because it met their needs so well. In other words, nearly every student of the baking and pastry arts will find this new text to be the ideal manual.

Approximately 350 new color photographs and more than 230 new recipes, in addition to a redesigned page style to make it even clearer and easier to use, make this a genuinely new, state-of-the-art work. At the same time, the revised edition retains virtually all the material from the popular second edition. This means that it is the same trusted text that students, teachers, and readers interested in baking have relied on for more than 15 years.

The most exciting advance made in this revision is the participation of Le Cordon Bleu. This distinguished international organization has been devoted to the highest standards of training for chefs, cooks, and pastry chefs for more than 100 years. With schools and culinary centers on five continents, Le Cordon Bleu is a dynamic force in modern culinary education. More than three-fourths of the new recipes were developed and tested by master pastry chefs at Le Cordon Bleu, and the majority of the new photographs were taken in their classrooms. This new material will add immeasurable value to students' learning experiences.

What's New

Dialog with instructors in schools large and small has been crucial in planning the changes in this edition. As a result, *Professional Baking* is now even more useful and adaptable to nearly every need. Among the most prominent additions and changes are the following:

- More than 230 new recipes, including more than 175 from the chefs at Le Cordon Bleu, bringing the total number to nearly 700

- Approximately 350 new color photographs illustrating step-by-step techniques as well as finished breads, cakes, pastries, and desserts

- More ingredient information, including a new section on fresh fruits

- A greatly expanded, profusely illustrated section on advanced decorative work, including a complete chapter on working with chocolate, a chapter on marzipan, pastillage, and nougatine, and a chapter on pulled sugar and other sugar work

- More information on artisan breads and other specialty yeast products, including popular sourdoughs

- Expanded sections on pastries and cakes, with special attention to modern decorative techniques

- A more detailed chapter on restaurant-style plating of desserts

- Revised quantities for major recipes, including small-quantity formulas and, in a new appendix, large-quantity formulas

- A new section on the historical background of the arts of baking and pastry

- This red logo indicates recipes that I have developed and tested

- This blue logo indicates recipes that were developed and tested by Le Cordon Bleu

The Goals of This Text

The goal of this book is to provide students with a solid theoretical and practical foundation in baking practices, including selection of ingredients, proper mixing and baking techniques, careful makeup and assembly, and skilled and imaginative decoration and presentation. With its attention to both theory and practice, it is designed as a primary text for use in colleges and vocational-technical schools, for baking courses within broader food service curricula, and for on-the-job training programs. It is also valuable as a manual for cooks and bakers, both professional and amateur.

The methods and procedures in this book are primarily those of small bakeshops and food service organizations. The emphasis is on producing high-quality handcrafted items. Development of manual skills is stressed. Such skills are a valuable asset even to students who eventually move on to more industrialized, automated production like that found in large commercial bakeries.

The focus of the text is two fold: understanding and performing. The practical material is supported by a systematic presentation of basic theory and ingredient information, so that students learn not only what techniques work but also why they work. Procedures for basic bread and pastry doughs, cake mixes, creams, and icings form the core of the material, as in previous editions. A major portion of the text is devoted to step-by-step procedures and production techniques. These techniques are reinforced with straightforward recipes that allow students to develop their skills while working with large or small quantities.

This new edition strengthens the focus on fine handmade pastries, cakes, breads, and desserts, so that the book is evenly balanced between basic and advanced techniques. Those students who have developed a good understanding and mastery of basic techniques are usually eager to progress to fine pastries and other advanced work. The new recipes have been selected to give students practice with a broad range of advanced techniques for fine pastries, cakes, and decorative pieces. Emphasis here is on developing manual skills for careful detailed work rather than on producing large quantities.

The Organization of the Text

Two factors strongly influence the arrangement and organization of this book. The first is the dual emphasis already mentioned—the emphasis on both understanding and performing. It is not enough merely to present students with a collection of recipes, nor is it enough to give them only a summary of baking theory and principles. They must be presented together, and the connections between them must be clear. Thus, when students practice preparing specific items, their study of theory helps them to understand what they are doing, why they

are doing it, and how to get the best results. At the same time, each recipe they prepare helps to reinforce their understanding of the basic principles so that knowledge builds upon knowledge.

The second factor is that most of a baker's activities fall naturally into two categories: (1) mixing, baking, and/or cooking doughs, batters, fillings, creams, and icings, and (2) assembling these elements (for example, baked cake layers, fillings, and icings) into finished pieces. The first category of tasks requires careful selection of ingredients, accurate measurements, and close attention to mixing and baking procedures. Naturally, most of the detailed guidelines and procedures in this book are devoted to these kinds of tasks. The second category, assembly of prepared components, is not so much a matter of scientific accuracy as it is of manual skills and artistic abilities.

This division of tasks is so well known to the practicing baker that it is usually taken for granted. Consequently, it is often neglected in written materials. As far as possible, the arrangement of subjects in this text reflects the working practices of bakeshops and kitchens. In a typical facility, operations such as mixing pie doughs, cooking fillings, preparing icings, and mixing and baking cake layers are done separately and in advance. Then, depending on demand, finished products can be assembled quickly. In this book, procedures for mixing and baking cakes, for example, are discussed separately from the procedures for assembling, icing, and decorating them. These are very different techniques, and it is helpful for students to approach them in a realistic context. Similarly, basic creams and icings are fundamental elements required for making a wide range of pastries, cakes, and other desserts; hence, they are treated early in the text.

Although the arrangement of chapters represents a logical grouping of products and procedures, it is not intended to dictate the order in which each instructor should teach the units. Every curriculum has different requirements and constraints, so that the sequence of instruction varies from school to school and instructor to instructor. The arrangement of material in this text is designed to encourage flexibility. Of course, baking techniques are highly interdependent; frequent cross-references help students understand these connections.

An important element in the text is the participation of the instructor, whose ideas and professional experience are invaluable. There is no substitute for firsthand seeing and doing under the guidance and supervision of experienced teachers. Baking is an art as much as a skill, and there are many points on which bakers and pastry chefs differ in their preferences. The text frequently explains possible variations in theory and procedure, and students are encouraged to consult the instructor for the techniques he or she prefers. Throughout the book, the instructor's input is encouraged. Exposure to a variety of formulas and techniques can only enrich the students' education and enhance the flexibility of their skills.

The text is designed for readability and practicality. Discussions of baking theory are presented in easy-to-read, point-by-point explanations. Techniques and makeup methods are detailed in concise yet complete step-by-step procedures. The format emphasizes and highlights key points in bold type, italics, and numbered sequences, so that basic information can be located and reviewed at a glance.

The Recipes

Nearly 700 formulas and recipes are included for the most popular breads, cakes, pastries, and desserts. These recipes are not selected at random, merely for the sake of having recipes in the book. Rather, they are carefully chosen and developed to teach and reinforce the techniques the students are learning and to strengthen their understanding of basic principles. The goal is that the students will understand and use not only the formulas in this book but any formula they encounter.

The recipes in this book are instructional recipes—that is, their purpose is not merely to give directions for producing baked goods but also to provide an opportunity to practice, with specific ingredients, the general principles being studied. Directions within recipes are often abbreviated. For example, instead of spelling out the straight dough method for breads in detail for each dough mixed in this way, this book refers the student to the preceding discussion of the procedure. By thinking and reviewing, the students derive a stronger learning experience from their lab work.

Many recipes are followed by variations. These are actually whole recipes given in abbreviated terms. This encourages students to see the similarities and differences among preparations. For example, there seems little point in giving a recipe for cream pie filling in the pie chapter, a recipe for custard filling for éclairs and napoleons in a pastry chapter, and separate recipes for each flavor of cream pudding in a pudding chapter, and never point out that these are all basically the same preparation. Skill as a baker depends on understanding and being able to exercise judgment, not just on following recipes. The ability to exercise judgment is essential in all branches of cookery, but especially in baking, where the smallest variation in procedures can produce significant changes in the baked product. The recipes in this text will help students develop judgment by requiring them to think about the relationships between general procedures and specific products.

Many of the new recipes in this edition illustrate more advanced techniques, which will enable readers to develop the skills required to produce sophisticated pas-

tries and other decorative dessert items. The recipes contributed by Le Cordon Bleu are regularly used by their chefs to train students to work in fine kitchens around the world.

Students are encouraged to study chapter 1 before actually proceeding with any of the recipes. The second section of the chapter explains the principles of measurement, the various formats used for the recipes in this book, the techniques for converting yield, and the usage of U.S. and metric measurements and bakers' percentages.

Acknowledgements

The participation of internationally renowned Le Cordon Bleu in the development of my texts began with the fourth edition of *Professional Cooking* and has continued with this new edition of *Professional Baking*. I must begin by expressing my deep gratitude to André J. Cointreau, president of Le Cordon Bleu and a great leader in culinary education worldwide, for making possible the contribution of Le Cordon Bleu. Second, my thanks to two remarkable pastry chefs, Julie Walsh and Laurent Duchêne, whose brilliant work graces this text, and who spent countless hours developing and testing a series of new recipes for *Professional Baking* and demonstrating

Julie Walsh, Wayne Gisslen, and Laurent Duchêne

their skills for the camera. Alison Oakervee and Deepika Sukhwani performed invaluable services in many capacities, especially in coordinating the chefs' contributions. I thank them heartily. The following students at Le Cordon Bleu in London assisted chefs Walsh and Duchêne during photography: Saori Matsunuma, Yuka Eguchi, Kaori Tsuboi, Erica Kahn, Michele Perle, Townley Morrison, James Rizzo, Daniel Schumer, and Benjamin Coffin.

The hundreds of new color photographs are the most immediately apparent enhancement to this revised edition. Photographer Jim Smith has worked with me for 20 years with creativity, patience, and stamina, as his work has become an increasingly important part of the texts. As ever, I'm grateful for the contribution of both Jim and Anne Smith, as well as for the work of Ryan Basten in Jim's studio. For our photography work at Le Cordon Bleu Culinary Institute in London, I would like to acknowledge the contribution of Pierre Deux—French Country and Le Cordon Bleu for the use of their accessories and designs.

Suggestions and input from instructors is essential in the development of a useful textbook, and many instructors have made important contributions by reviewing all or part of the manuscripts and by answering survey questions. A list of reviewers follows these acknowledgments. My thanks to all of them as well as to many other instructors with whom I have been privileged to share ideas, either in person or via letter and e-mail.

None of this work would have been possible without the critical judgment and support of my wife, Mary Ellen Griffin; my deepest thanks to her.

Finally, I wish to thank everyone at John Wiley & Sons who worked so hard on this project: Jennifer Mazurkie, Diana Cisek, Karin Kincheloe, and, especially, my indefatigable editor and friend, JoAnna Turtletaub.

Reviewers

Robert L. Anderson, Des Moines Area Community College, Ankeny, Iowa

Mark S. Cole, Del Mar College, Corpus Christi, Texas

John R. Farris, Lansing Community College, Lansing, Michigan

Joseph D. Ford, New York Food and Hotel Management, New York, New York

Robert J. Galloway, Dunwoody Industrial Institute, Minneapolis, Minnesota

David Gibson, Niagara College of Applied Arts and Technology, Niagara Falls, Ontario, Canada

Jean Hassell, Youngstown State University, Youngstown, Ohio

Iris A. Helveston, State Department of Education, Tallahassee, Florida

Nancy A. Higgins, Art Institute of Atlanta, Atlanta, Georgia

George Jack, The Cooking and Hospitality Institute of Chicago, Chicago, Illinois

Mike Jung, Hennepin Technical College, Brooklyn Park, Minnesota

Frederick Glen Knight, The Southeast Institute of Culinary Arts, St. Augustine, Florida

Paul Krebs, Schenectady County Community College, Schenectady, New York

Jeffrey C. LaBarge, Central Piedmont Community College, Charlotte, North Carolina

Fred LeMeisz, St. Petersburg Vocational Technical Institute, St. Petersburg, Florida

Laurel Leslie, Kapiolani Community College, Honolulu, Hawaii

Janet Lightizer, Newbury College, Brookline, Massachusetts

Valeria S. Mason, State Department of Education, Gainesville, Florida

Philip Panzarino, New York City Technical College, Brooklyn, New York

Richard Petrello, Withlacoochee Vocational-Technical Center, Inverness, Florida

William H. Pifer, Bellingham Technical College, Bellingham, Washington

Gunter Rehm, Orange Coast College, Costa Mesa, California

Kent R. Rigby, Baltimore International College, Baltimore, Maryland

Kimberly Schenk, Diablo Valley College, Pleasant Hill, California

Peter Scholtes, George Brown College, Toronto, Ontario, Canada

Patrick Sweeney, Johnson County Community College, Overland Park, Kansas

F. H. Waskey, University of Houston, Houston, Texas

J. William White, Pinellas County School System, St. Petersburg, Florida

Ronald Zabkiewicz, South Technical Education Center, Boynton Beach, Florida

PROFESSIONAL BAKING

1

Basic
Principles

When you consider that most bakery products are made of the same few ingredients—flour, shortening, sugar, eggs, water or milk, and leavenings—you should have no difficulty understanding the importance of accuracy in the bakeshop, as slight variations in proportions or procedures can mean great differences in the final product.

In this chapter, you are introduced to bakeshop production through a discussion of the kinds of measurements and mathematical calculations necessary for baking and of the basic processes common to nearly all baked goods.

BAKING— HISTORICAL BACKGROUND

After reading this chapter, you should be able to:

- ■ Explain the importance of weighing baking ingredients.

- ■ Use a baker's balance scale.

- ■ Use formulas based on bakers' percentages.

- ■ Explain the factors that control the development of gluten in baked products.

- ■ Explain the changes that take place in a dough or batter as it bakes.

- ■ Prevent or retard the staling of baked items.

Grains have been the most important staple food in the human diet since prehistoric times, so it is only a slight exaggeration to say that baking is almost as old as the human race.

Because of the lack of cooking utensils, it is probable that one of the earliest grain preparations was made by toasting dry grains, pounding them to a meal, and mixing the meal to a paste with water. Eventually, it was discovered that some of this paste, if laid on a hot stone next to a fire, turned into a flatbread that was a little more appetizing than the plain paste. Unleavened flatbreads are still important foods in many cultures.

A grain paste left to stand for a period of time eventually collects wild yeasts and begins to ferment. This was, no doubt, the beginning of leavened bread, although for most of history the presence of yeast was mostly accidental. Not until relatively recent times did bakers learn to control yeast with any accuracy.

By the time of the ancient Greeks, about five or six hundred years BCE, enclosed ovens, heated by wood fires, were in use. People took turns baking their breads in a large communal oven, unless they were wealthy enough to have their own ovens.

Several centuries later, ancient Rome saw the first mass production of breads, so the baking profession can be said to have started at that time. Many of the products made by the professional bakers contained quantities of honey and oil, so these foods might be called *pastries* rather than *breads.*

After the collapse of the Roman Empire, baking as a profession almost disappeared. Not until the latter part of the Middle Ages did baking and pastry making begin to reappear as important professions in service of the nobility. Bakers and pastry chefs in France, with the permission of the king, formed guilds in order to protect and further their art.

The discovery of the Americas in 1492 sparked a revolution in pastry making. Sugar and cocoa, brought from the New World, were available for the first time; up until this time, the only significant sweetener was honey. Once the new ingredients became widely available, baking and pastry making became more and more sophisticated, with many new recipes being developed.

By the 17th and 18th centuries, there was a definite split between bread bakers and pastry makers. First of all, the controlled use of yeast made bread baking a profession unto itself. Second, pastry and bread making usually required different oven temperatures. Because ovens were heated by building fires in them, it was not easy to change temperatures. Bakers and pastry chefs found that it was easier to use separate ovens.

The French Revolution in 1789 freed bakers and pastry chefs, who had been the servants of royalty and nobility, to start independent businesses. This was the beginning of modern baking as we know it. Artisans competed for customers with the quality of their products. For the first time, the general public, not just aristocrats, could buy fine pastries. Many of the pastries that we still enjoy today were first developed in the 19th century. Some of the pastry shops started during that time still serve Parisians today.

The most famous chef of the period was Marie-Antonin Carême, also called Antoine Carême, who lived from 1784 to 1833. His spectacular constructions of sugar and pastry earned him great fame, and he elevated the jobs of cook and pastry chef to respected professions. Carême's book, *Le Pâtissier Royal,* was one of the first systematic explanations of the pastry chef's art.

Modern advances in technology, from refrigeration to sophisticated ovens to air transportation that brings us fresh ingredients from around the world, have contributed immeasurably to baking and pastry making. Today, the popularity of fine breads and pastries is growing even faster than new chefs can be trained. At the beginning of the 21st century, young bakers and pastry chefs continue to refine their crafts and develop new techniques, building on centuries of progress.

FORMULAS AND MEASUREMENT

Bakers generally talk about *formulas* rather than *recipes.* If this sounds to you more like a chemistry lab than a food production facility, it is with good reason. The bakeshop is very much like a chemistry laboratory, both in the scientific accuracy of the procedures and in the complex reactions that take place during mixing and baking.

MEASUREMENT

Ingredients are almost always weighed in the bakeshop, rather than measured by volume, because measurement by weight is more accurate. Accuracy of measurement, as we have said, is essential in the bakeshop. Unlike home baking recipes, a professional baker's formula will not call for 6 cups of flour, for example.

To demonstrate to yourself the importance of weighing rather than measuring by volume, measure a cup of flour in two ways: a) Sift some flour and lightly spoon it into a dry measure. Level the top and weigh the flour. b) Scoop some unsifted flour into the same measure and pack it lightly. Level the top and weigh the flour. Note the difference. No wonder home recipes can be so inconsistent!

The baker's term for weighing ingredients is *scaling.*

The following ingredients, and only these ingredients, may sometimes be measured by volume, at the ratio of *one pint per pound* or *one liter per kilogram:*

- water
- milk
- eggs

Volume measure is often used when scaling water for small or medium-sized batches of bread. Results are generally good. However, whenever accuracy is critical, it is better to weigh. This is because a pint of water actually weighs slightly more than a pound, or approximately 16.7 ounces. (This figure varies with the temperature of the water.)

For convenience, volume measures of liquids are frequently used when products other than baked flour goods—such as sauces, syrups, puddings, and custards—are being made.

Units of Measure

The system of measurement used in the United States is very complicated. Even those who have used the system all their lives still sometimes have trouble remembering things like how many fluid ounces are in a quart and how many feet in a mile.

The first table below lists equivalents among the units of measure used in the bakeshop and kitchen. You should memorize these thoroughly so you don't lose time making simple calculations. The second table below lists the abbreviations used in this book.

Units of Measure—U.S. System

Weight	
1 pound	= 16 ounces
Volume	
1 gallon	= 4 quarts
1 quart	= 2 pints
	or
	4 cups
	or
	32 (fluid) ounces
1 pint	= 2 cups
	or
	16 (fluid) ounces
1 cup	= 8 (fluid) ounces
1 (fluid) ounce	= 2 tablespoons
1 tablespoon	= 3 teaspoons
Length	
1 foot	= 12 inches

Note: One fluid ounce (often simply called *ounce*) of water weighs one ounce. One pint of water weighs approximately one pound.

Abbreviations of U.S. Units of Measure Used in This Book

Pound	lb
Ounce	oz
Gallon	gal
Quart	qt
Pint	pt
Fluid ounce	fl oz
Tablespoon	tbsp
Teaspoon	tsp
Inch	in.

The Metric System

The United States is the only major country that uses the complex system of measurement we have just described. Other countries use a much simpler system called the *metric system.*

Basic Units

In the metric system, there is one basic unit for each type of measurement:

The *gram* is the basic unit of weight.

The *liter* is the basic unit of volume.

The *meter* is the basic unit of length.

The *degree Celsius* is the basic unit of temperature.

Larger or smaller units are simply made by multiplying or dividing by 10, 100, 1000, and so on. These divisions are expressed by *prefixes*. The ones you need to know are:

kilo- = 1000

deci- = $\frac{1}{10}$ or 0.1

centi- = $\frac{1}{100}$ or 0.01

milli- = $\frac{1}{1000}$ or 0.001

Once you know these basic units, you do not need complicated tables such as the first table on page 6. The table below summarizes the metric units you need to know in the bakeshop.

Metric Units

Basic units		
Quantity	**Unit**	**Abbreviation**
Weight	gram	g
Volume	liter	L
Length	meter	m
Temperature	degree Celcius	°C
Divisions and multiples		
Prefix/Example	**Meaning**	**Abbreviation**
kilo-	1000	k
kilogram	1000 grams	kg
deci-	$\frac{1}{10}$	d
deciliter	0.1 liter	dL
centi-	$\frac{1}{100}$	c
centimeter	0.01 meter	cm
milli-	$\frac{1}{1000}$	m
millimeter	0.001 meter	mm

Converting to Metric

Most people think that the metric system is much harder to learn than it really is. This is because they think about metric units in terms of U.S. units. They read that there are 28.35 grams in an ounce and are immediately convinced that they will never be able to learn metrics.

Do not worry about being able to convert U.S. units into metric units and vice versa. This is a very important point to remember, especially if you think that the metric system might be hard to learn.

The reason for this is simple. You will usually be working in either one system or the other. You will rarely, if ever, have to convert from one to the other. (An exception might be if you have equipment based on one system and you want to use a formula written in the other.) Many people today own imported cars and repair them with metric tools without ever worrying about how many millimeters are in an inch. Similarly, if and when American bakeshops and kitchens change to the metric system, you will use scales that measure in grams and kilograms, volume measures that measure in liters and deciliters, and thermometers that measure in degrees Celsius, and you will use formulas that indicate these units. You will not have to worry about how many grams are in an ounce. All you will have to remember is the information in the table on page 7.

To become accustomed to working in metric units, it is helpful to have a feel for how large the units are. The following rough equivalents may be used to help you visualize metric units. They are not exact conversion factors. (When you need exact conversion factors, see Appendix 1.)

A *kilogram* is slightly more than 2 pounds.

A *gram* is about $\frac{1}{30}$ ounce. A half teaspoon of flour weighs a little less than a gram.

A *liter* is slightly more than a quart.

A *deciliter* is slightly less than a half cup.

A *centiliter* is about 2 teaspoons.

A *meter* is slightly more than 3 feet.

A *centimeter* is about $\frac{3}{8}$ inch.

0°C is the freezing point of water (32°F).

100°C is the boiling point of water (212°F).

An increase or decrease of *1 degree Celsius* is equivalent to about 2 degrees Fahrenheit.

Metric Recipes

American industry will probably adopt the metric system someday. Many recipe writers are already eager to get a head start and are printing metric equivalents. As a result, you will see recipes calling for 454 grams of flour, 28.35 grams of butter, or a baking temperature of 191°C. No wonder people are afraid of the metric system!

Kitchens in metric countries do not work with such impractical numbers, any more than we normally use figures like 1 lb 1¼ oz flour, 2.19 oz butter, or a baking temperature of 348°F. That would defeat the whole purpose of the metric system, which is to be simple and practical. If you have a chance to look at a French cookbook, you will see nice, round numbers such as 1 kg, 200 g, and 4 dL.

The metric measures in the formulas in this book are NOT equivalent to the U.S. measures given alongside them. You should think of the metric portion of the formulas as separate recipes with yields that are close to but not the same as the yields of the U.S. recipes. To give exact equivalents would require using awkward, impractical numbers. If you have metric equipment, use the metric units, and if you have U.S. equipment, use the U.S. units. You should rarely have to worry about converting between the two.

For the most part, the total yield of the metric recipes in this book is close to the yield of the U.S. recipes while keeping the ingredient proportions the same. Unfortunately, it is not always possible to keep the proportions *exactly* the same because the U.S. system is not decimal-based like the metric system. In some cases, the metric quantities produce slightly different results due to the varying proportions, but these differences are usually extremely small.

Procedure for Using a Baker's Balance Scale

The principle of using a baker's scale is simple: The scale must balance before setting the weights, and it must balance again after scaling. The following procedure applies to the most commonly used type of baker's scale.

1. Set the scale scoop or other container on the left side of the scale.

2. Balance the scale by placing counterweights on the right side and/or by adjusting the ounce weight on the horizontal bar.

3. Set the scale for the desired weight by placing weights on the right side and/or by moving the ounce weight.

   For example, to set the scale for 1 lb 8 oz, place a 1-pound weight on the right side, and move the ounce weight to the right 8 ounces. If the ounce weight is already over 8 ounces, so that you cannot move it another 8, add 2 pounds to the right side of the scale and subtract 8 ounces by moving the ounce weight 8 places to the left. The result is still 1 lb 8 oz.

4. Add the ingredient being scaled to the left side until the scale balances.

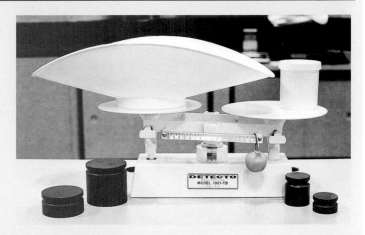

A good balance scale should be accurate to ¼ ounce (0.25 oz) or, if metric, to 5 grams. Dry ingredients weighing less than ¼ ounce can be scaled by physically dividing larger quantities into equal portions. For example, to scale ¹⁄₁₆ ounce (0.06 oz), first weigh out ¼ ounce, then divide this into four equal piles using a small knife.

For fine pastry work, a small battery-operated digital scale is often more useful than a large balance scale. A good digital scale is relatively inexpensive. It can instantly measure quantities to the nearest ⅛ ounce or the nearest 2 grams. Most digital scales have a zero or tare button that sets the indicated weight to zero. For example, you may set a container on the scale, set the weight to zero, add the desired quantity of the first ingredient, again set the weight to zero, add the second ingredient, and so on. This speeds the weighing of dry ingredients that are to be sifted together, for example.

When very small quantities of items such as spices are required in formulas in this book, an approximate volume equivalent (usually in fractions of a teaspoon) is also included. However, remember that careful weighing on a good scale is more accurate. Approximate volume equivalents of selected ingredients are given in Appendix 3.

British bakers have a convenient method for measuring baking powder when small quantities are needed. They use a mixture called *scone flour*. To make a pound of scone flour, combine 15 ounces of flour and 1 ounce of baking powder; sift together three times. One ounce (¹⁄₁₆ lb) of scone flour thus contains ¹⁄₁₆ ounce (0.06 oz) baking powder. For each ¹⁄₁₆ ounce of baking powder you need in a formula, substitute one ounce of scone flour for one ounce of the flour called for in the formula.

In order to make formula conversions and calculations easier, fractions of ounces that appear in the ingredient tables of the formulas in this book are written as decimals. Thus, 1½ oz is written as 1.5 oz and ¼ oz is written as 0.25 oz. A list of decimal equivalents is included in Appendix 2.

BAKER'S PERCENTAGES

Bakers use a simple but versatile system of percentages for expressing their formulas. Baker's percentages express the amount of each ingredient used as a percentage of the amount of flour used.

To put it differently, the percentage of each ingredient is its total weight divided by the weight of the flour, multiplied by 100%, or:

$$\frac{\text{total weight of ingredient}}{\text{total weight of flour}} \times 100\% = \% \text{ of ingredient}$$

Thus, flour is always 100%. If two kinds of flour are used, their total is 100%. Any ingredient that weighs the same as the amount of flour used is also given as 100%. The cake formula ingredients listed on page 11 illustrate how these percentages are used. Check the figures with the above equation to make sure you understand them.

The advantages of using baker's percentages is that the formula is easily adapted for any yield, and single ingredients may be varied and other ingredients added without changing the whole formulation. For example, you can add raisins to a muffin mix formula, while keeping the percentages of all the other ingredients the same.

Please remember that these numbers do not refer to the percentage of the total yield. They are simply a way of expressing *ingredient proportions*. The total yield of these percentage numbers will always be greater than 100%.

Clearly, a percentage system based on the weight of flour can be used only when flour is a major ingredient, as in breads, cakes, and cookies. However, this principle can be used in other formulas as well by selecting a major ingredient and establishing it as 100%. In this book, *whenever an ingredient other than flour is used as the base of 100%, this is indicated at the top of the formula above the percentage column.* See, for example, the formulas for Almond Filling on page 118. These recipes indicate "almond paste at 100%" and the weights of the sugar, eggs, and other ingredients are expressed as percentages of the weight of the almond paste. (In some of the formulas in this book, especially those without a predominant ingredient, percentages are not included.)

FORMULA YIELDS

Yields for the formulas in this book are indicated in one of two ways. In most cases, the yields are given as a total of the ingredient quantities. For example, in the sample formula on page 11, the yield tells us how much cake batter the formula makes. This is the figure we need to know for the purpose of scaling the batter into pans. The actual weight of baked cake will vary depending on pan size and shape, oven temperature, and so on.

Other formulas of this type, in which the yield is the total weight of the ingredients, include formulas for bread doughs, coffee cake fillings, pastry doughs, and cookie doughs.

On the other hand, in some formulas, the yield is not the same as the total weight of ingredients. For example, see the recipe for French Buttercream, page 336. When sugar and water are boiled to make a syrup, about half of the water evaporates. Thus, the actual yield is less than the total weight of the ingredients.

In this book, when the yield is not the same as the total weight of the ingredients, the yield is indicated above the ingredients list rather than below it.

Also, please note that all yields, including percentage totals, are rounded off to the next lower whole number. This eliminates insignificant fractions and makes reading easier.

Procedure for Calculating the Weight of an Ingredient When the Weight of Flour Is Known

1. Change the ingredient percentage to decimal form by moving the decimal point two places to the left.
2. Multiply the weight of the flour by this decimal figure to get the weight of the ingredient.

   Example: A formula calls for 20% sugar and you are using 10 pounds of flour. How much sugar do you need?

   20% = 0.20

   10 lb × 0.20 = 2 lb sugar

   Note: In the U.S. system, weights must normally be expressed all in one unit, either ounces or pounds, in order for the calculations to work. Unless quantities are very large, it is usually easiest to express weights in ounces.

   Example: Determine 50% of 1 lb 8 oz.

   1 lb 8 oz = 24 oz

   0.50 × 24 oz = 12 oz

   Example (metric): A formula calls for 20% sugar and you are using 5000 g (5 kg) of flour. How much sugar do you need?

   20% = 0.20

   5000 g × 0.20 = 1000 g sugar

Procedure for Converting a Formula to a New Yield

1. Change the total percentage to decimal form by moving the decimal point two places to the left.
2. Divide the desired yield by this decimal figure to get the weight of flour needed.
3. If necessary, round off this number to the next highest figure. This will allow for losses in mixing, makeup, and panning, and it will make calculations easier.
4. Use the weight of flour and remaining ingredient percentages to calculate the weights of the other ingredients, as in the previous procedure.

   Example: In the sample cake formula in the table, how much flour is needed if you require 6 pounds (or 3000 grams) of cake batter?

   377.5% = 3.775

   6 lb = 96 oz

   96 oz/3.775 = 25.43 oz or, rounded off, 26 oz (1 lb 10 oz)

   3000 g/3.775 = 794.7 g or, rounded off, 800 g

Ingredients	U.S. Weight		Metric Weight	%
Cake flour	5 lb		2500 g	100
Sugar	5 lb		2500 g	100
Baking powder		4 oz	125 g	5
Salt		2 oz	63 g	2.5
Emulsified shortening	2 lb	8 oz	1250 g	50
Skim milk	3 lb		1500 g	60
Egg whites	3 lb		1500 g	60
Total weight:	*18 lb 14 oz*		*9438 g*	*377.5%*

SELECTION OF INGREDIENTS

In addition to measuring, there is another basic rule of accuracy in the bakeshop: *Use the exact ingredients specified.*

As you will learn in the next chapter, different flours, shortenings, and other ingredients do not function alike. Bakers' formulas are balanced for specific ingredients. For example, do not substitute bread flour for pastry flour or regular shortening for emulsified shortening. They won't work the same way.

Occasionally, a substitution may be made, such as active dry yeast for compressed yeast (see p. 37), but not without adjusting the quantities and rebalancing the formula.

MIXING AND GLUTEN DEVELOPMENT

Gluten is a substance made up of proteins present in wheat flour; it gives structure and strength to baked goods.

In order for gluten to be developed, the proteins must first absorb water. Then, as the dough or batter is mixed or kneaded, the gluten forms long, elastic strands. As the dough or batter is leavened, these strands capture the gases in tiny pockets or cells, and we say the product *rises.*

When proteins are heated, they coagulate. This means they become firm or solidify. You are familiar with this process in the case of eggs, which are liquid when raw but firm when cooked.

This process is also important in baking. When dough or batter is baked, the gluten, like all proteins, coagulates or solidifies and gives structure to the product.

CONTROLLING GLUTEN

Flour is mostly starch, as you know, but it is the protein or gluten content, not the starch, that concerns the baker most. Gluten proteins are needed to give structure to baked goods. Bakers must be able to control the gluten, however. For example, we want French bread to be firm and chewy, which requires much gluten. On the other hand, we want cakes to be tender, which means we want very little gluten development.

Ingredient proportions and mixing methods are determined, in part, by how they affect the development of gluten. The baker has several methods for adjusting gluten development:

1. *Selection of flours* Wheat flours are classified as *strong* or *weak,* depending on their protein content.

    Strong flours come from *hard wheat* and have a high protein content.

    Weak flours come from *soft wheat* and have a low protein content.

    Thus, we use strong flours for breads and weak flours for cakes. (The protein content of flours is discussed in greater detail in the next chapter.)

    Only wheat flour develops enough gluten to make bread. To make bread from rye or other grains, the formula must be balanced with some high-gluten flour, or the bread will be heavy.

2. *Shortening* Any fat used in baking is called a *shortening* because it shortens gluten strands. It does this by surrounding the particles and lubricating them so they do not stick together. Thus, *fats are tenderizers.* A

cookie or pastry that is very crumbly, which is due to high fat content and little gluten development, is said to be *short*.

You can see why French bread has little or no fat, while cakes contain a great deal.

3. *Liquid*   Because gluten proteins must absorb water before they can be developed, the amount of water in a formula can affect toughness or tenderness. Pie crusts and crisp cookies, for instance, are made with very little liquid in order to keep them tender.

4. *Mixing methods*   In general, the more a dough or batter is mixed, the more the gluten develops. Thus, bread doughs are mixed or kneaded for a long time to develop the gluten. Pie crusts, muffins, and other products that must be tender are mixed for a short time.

    It is possible to overmix bread dough, however. Gluten strands will stretch only so far. They will break if the dough is overmixed.

THE BAKING PROCESS

The changes to a dough or batter as it bakes are basically the same in all baked products, from breads to cookies and cakes. You should know what these changes are so that you can learn how to control them.

The stages in the baking process are as follows:

1. *Formation and expansion of gases*   The gases primarily responsible for leavening baked goods are *carbon dioxide,* which is released by the action of yeast and by baking powder and baking soda; *air,* which is incorporated into doughs and batters during mixing; and *steam,* which is formed during baking.

    Some gases—such as carbon dioxide in proofed bread dough and air in sponge cake batters—are already present in the dough. As they are heated, the gases expand and leaven the product.

    Some gases are not formed until heat is applied. Yeast and baking powder form gases rapidly when first placed in the oven. Steam is also formed as the moisture of the dough is heated.

    Leavening agents are discussed in greater detail in the next chapter.

2. *Trapping of the gases in air cells*   As the gases are formed and expand, they are trapped in a stretchable network formed by the proteins in the dough. These proteins are primarily gluten and sometimes egg protein.

    Without gluten or egg protein, most of the gases would escape, and the product would be poorly leavened. Breads without enough gluten are heavy.

3. *Gelatinization of starches*   The starches absorb moisture, expand, and become firmer. This contributes to structure. Gelatinization of starches begins at about 140°F (60°C).

4. *Coagulation of proteins*   Like all proteins, gluten and egg proteins coagulate or solidify when they reach high enough temperatures. This process gives most of the structure to baked goods. Coagulation begins when the temperature of the dough reaches about 165°F (74°C).

    Correct baking temperature is important. If the temperature is too high, coagulation starts too soon, before the expansion of gases reaches its peak. The resulting product has poor volume or a split crust. If the temperature is too low, the proteins do not coagulate soon enough, and the product may collapse.

5. ***Evaporation of some of the water*** This takes place throughout the baking process. If a baked product of a specific weight is required, allowance must be made for moisture loss when scaling the dough. For example, to get a 1-pound loaf of baked bread, it is necessary to scale about 18 ounces of dough. The percentage of weight loss varies greatly, depending on such factors as proportion of surface area to volume, baking time, and whether the item is baked in a pan or directly on the oven hearth.

6. ***Melting of shortenings*** Different shortenings melt and release trapped gases at different temperatures, so the proper shortening should be selected for each product.

7. ***Crust formation and browning*** A crust is formed as water evaporates from the surface and leaves it dry. Browning occurs when sugars caramelize and starches and sugars undergo certain chemical changes caused by heat. This contributes to flavor. Milk, sugar, and egg increase browning.

STALING

Staling is the change in texture and aroma of baked goods due to a change of structure and a loss of moisture by the starch granules. Stale baked goods have lost their fresh-baked aroma and are firmer, drier, and more crumbly than fresh products. Prevention of staling is a major concern of the baker, because most baked goods lose quality rapidly.

Staling begins almost as soon as the baked items are taken from the oven. There are, apparently, two factors in staling. The first is loss of moisture or drying. This is apparent, for example, when a slice of fresh bread is left exposed to air. It soon becomes dry to the touch.

The second factor is a chemical change in the structure of the starch. This process, called *starch retrogradation,* occurs even when little or no moisture is lost. This means that even a well-wrapped loaf of bread will eventually stale.

Chemical staling is very rapid at refrigerator temperatures, but it nearly stops at freezer temperatures. Thus, bread should not be stored in the refrigerator. It should be left at room temperature for short-term storage or frozen for long-term storage.

Chemical staling, if it is not too great, can be partially reversed by heating. Breads, muffins, and coffee cakes, for example, are frequently refreshed by placing them briefly in an oven. Remember, however, that this also results in more loss of moisture, so the items should be reheated only just before they are to be served.

Loss of crispness is caused by absorption of moisture, so, in a sense, it is the opposite of staling. The crusts of hard-crusted breads absorb moisture from the crumb and become soft and leathery. Reheating these products to refresh them not only reverses chemical staling of the crumb but also recrisps the crusts.

Loss of crispness is also a problem with low-moisture products such as cookies and pie crusts. The problem is usually solved by proper storage in airtight wraps or containers to protect the products from moisture in the air. Prebaked pie shells should be filled as close to service time as possible.

In addition to refreshing baked goods in the oven, three main techniques are used to slow staling:

1. ***Protecting the product from air*** Two examples of protecting baked goods are wrapping bread in plastic and covering cakes with icing, especially icing that is thick and rich in fat.

Hard-crusted breads, which stale very rapidly, should not be wrapped, or the crusts will quickly become soft and leathery. These bread products should always be served very fresh.

2. ***Adding moisture retainers to the formula*** Fats and sugars are good moisture retainers, so products high in these ingredients keep best.

   Some of the best French bread has no fat at all, so it must be served within hours of baking or it will begin to stale. For longer keeping, bakers often add a very small amount of fat and/or sugar to the formula.

3. ***Freezing*** Baked goods frozen before they become stale maintain quality for longer periods. For best results, freeze soon after baking in a blast freezer at −40°F (−40°C), and maintain at or below 0°F (−18°C) until ready to thaw. Breads should be served very quickly after thawing. Frozen breads may be reheated with excellent results if they are to be served immediately.

   Refrigeration, on the other hand, speeds staling. Only baked goods that could become health hazards, such as those with cream fillings, are refrigerated.

▶ TERMS FOR REVIEW

scaling	meter	centi-	strong flour
metric system	degree Celsius	milli-	weak flour
gram	kilo-	gluten	shortening
liter	deci-	coagulate	staling

▶ QUESTIONS FOR REVIEW

1. Below are ingredients for a white cake. The weight of the flour is given, and the proportions of other ingredients are indicated by percentages. Calculate the weights required for each.

Cake flour	3 lb (100%)
Baking powder	4%
Shortening	50%
Sugar	100%
Salt	1%
Milk	75%
Egg whites	33%
Vanilla	2%

2. In the formula in question 1, how much of each ingredient is needed if you want a total yield of $4\frac{1}{2}$ lb of batter?

3. Why are baking ingredients usually weighed rather than measured by volume?

4. Make the following conversions in the U.S. system of measurement:

   $3\frac{1}{2}$ pounds = _____ ounces

   6 cups = _____ pints

   $8\frac{1}{2}$ quarts = _____ fluid ounces

   $\frac{3}{4}$ cup = _____ tablespoons

   46 ounces = _____ pounds

   $2\frac{1}{2}$ gallons = _____ fluid ounces

   5 pounds 5 ounces divided by 2 = _____

   10 teaspoons = _____ fluid ounces

5. Make the following conversions in the metric system:

   1.4 kilograms = _____ grams

   53 deciliters = _____ liters

   15 centimeters = _____ millimeters

   2590 grams = _____ kilograms

   4.6 liters = _____ deciliters

   220 centiliters = _____ deciliters

6. Discuss four factors that affect the development of gluten in batters and doughs.

7. Why do some cakes fall if they are removed from the oven too soon?

8. Which kind of cake would you expect to have better keeping qualities—a sponge cake, which is low in fat, or a high-ratio cake, which is high in both fat and sugar?

2

Ingredients

The following introduction to baking ingredients is necessarily simplified. Hundreds of pages could be written—and have been—on wheat flour alone. Much of the available information, however, is technical and of concern primarily to large industrial bakers. In this chapter, you will find the information you need to produce a full range of baked items in a small bakeshop or a hotel or restaurant kitchen.

WHEAT FLOUR

Wheat flour is the most important ingredient in the bakeshop. It provides bulk and structure to most of the baker's products, including breads, cakes, cookies, and pastries. While the home cook depends almost exclusively on a product called *all-purpose flour,* the professional baker has available a wide variety of flours with different qualities and characteristics. In order to select the proper flour for each product and to handle each correctly, you should understand the different types of flour and how they are milled.

After reading this chapter, you should be able to:

- Understand the characteristics and functions of the major baking ingredients.

- Make appropriate adjustments in formulas when substituting ingredients, such as dry milk for liquid milk and dry yeast for cake yeast.

- Identify the main types of wheat flours by sight and feel.

HARD AND SOFT WHEATS

The characteristics of flour depend on the variety of wheat from which it is milled, the location in which the wheat is grown, and its growing conditions. Types of wheat grown in North America include Hard Red Spring, Hard Red Winter, Soft Red Winter, Durum, and White. Different varieties are grown in Europe. For example, four principal wheat strains grown in France—Recital, Scipion, Soissons, and Textel—are softer—that is, lower in protein—than most North American varieties.

For our purposes, it is enough to know that some wheats are classified as *hard* and some as *soft.* Hard wheats contain greater quantities of the proteins called *glutenin* and *gliadin,* which together form gluten when the flour is moistened and mixed.

You will recall from chapter 1 that gluten development is one of the baker's major concerns when mixing doughs and batters. *Strong flours*—that is, flours from hard wheats with high protein content—are used primarily to make breads and other yeast products. *Weak flours*—that is, flours from soft wheats with low protein content—are important in the production of cakes, cookies, and pies.

THE MILLING OF HARD WHEAT

The wheat kernel consists of three main parts:

1. The *bran* is the hard outer covering of the kernel. It is present in whole wheat flour as tiny brown flakes, but it is removed in the milling of white flour.

2. The *germ* is the part of the kernel that becomes the new wheat plant if the kernel is sprouted. It has a high fat content, which can quickly become rancid. Therefore, whole wheat flour containing the germ has poor keeping qualities.

3. The *endosperm* is the starchy part of the kernel that remains when the bran and germ are removed. It is the portion of the wheat kernel that is milled into white flour.

Depending on its source, the wheat endosperm contains about 63 to 73% starch and 7 to 15% protein, plus small amounts of moisture, fat, sugar, and minerals.

Modern milling of wheat into flour is accomplished by a fairly complex and highly refined system that uses grooved steel rollers. In what is called the *break system,* the rollers are set so that the space between them is slightly smaller than the width of the kernels, and the rollers rotate at different speeds. When the wheat is fed between them, the rollers flake off the bran layers and germ and crack the endosperm into coarse pieces. Approximately 72% of the wheat kernel can be separated as endosperm, to be milled into flour. The remaining 28% consists of bran (about 14%), germ (about 3%), and other outer portions called *shorts* (about 11%).

The inner parts of the endosperm tend to break into smaller pieces than the outer parts. Therefore, by repeatedly sifting and breaking the wheat, different grades of flour can be extracted from one type of wheat. The term *extraction* means the portion of the endosperm that is separated into a particular grade of flour. For example, a flour with an extraction rate of 90% consists of all but 10% of the endosperm. (Confusingly, the term *extraction* may also be used to indicate what portion of the whole wheat grain is left after the bran and germ are removed. In this book, we do not use the term *extraction* in this sense, but you may see it elsewhere.)

TYPES OF WHEAT FLOUR

The most important characteristic of flour for the baker is its protein content. As we have said, the protein content depends primarily on the type of wheat used and its growing conditions. In other words, to make high-protein flour, you must start with high-protein wheat. Secondarily, the milling process has a slight effect on the protein content, depending on the extraction rate. Flour available to professional bakers always indicates the protein content, ranging from about 8% for cake flours to 12% for bread flour and 14% for high-gluten flour.

Another number available to bakers is the *ash content,* which is an indication of the flour's mineral content. Soft white cake and pastry flours may have an ash content as low as 0.4% or even 0.3%, while dark whole wheat flours may have an ash content as high as 1.5% or greater.

In much of Europe, a grading system based on the ash content is dominant. For example, the grades T45 and T55 are white wheat flours for breads and pastries with low ash, T65 includes high-gluten flours, and T80, T110, and T150 are whole wheat flours of increasing darkness. Other flours are included in this grading system. For example, T170 is dark rye flour.

Within each of these grades, the protein content varies, depending on the variety of wheat the flour was made from.

The most important North American types of wheat flour can be summarized as follows. No exact parallels can be made to European flours.

Straight flour   Straight flour is 100% extraction flour. In other words, it is made from the entire wheat kernel after the bran and germ are removed. Straight flour from a hard wheat has a high protein content and can be used for making breads.

Patent flour   Patent flour is milled from the inner part of the endosperm, which breaks into finer particles than the part nearer the bran. Patent flour made from a hard wheat is a strong flour of excellent quality and is somewhat lighter in color than straight flour. When a formula calls for *bread flour,* patent flour is the flour of choice, although a strong straight flour could also be used.

The extraction rate of patent flour can be varied depending on specific needs and on the quality of the wheat. Fancy or extra-short patent has an extraction rate of less than 60%. It comes from the innermost part of the kernel and is the whitest of all strong flours. Long patent may be as high as 90 or 95% extraction.

Clear flour   The portion of the endosperm that remains after the patent flour is removed is called *clear flour*. Because this portion of the wheat is closest to the bran, it is darker in color than patent flour. Clear flour may be separated into more than one grade, such as first clear (lighter in color) and second clear (darker, poorer grade).

Because of its color, clear flour is not suitable for making white breads. Its primary use is in making rye breads, where its color is not noticed and its gluten content contributes strength. Clear flour can also be used in combination with whole wheat flour.

High-gluten flour   Flour that has an especially high protein content is sometimes used in hard-crusted breads and in such specialty products as pizza dough and bagels. It is also used to strengthen doughs made from flours that contain little or no gluten. See, for example, the recipe for Chestnut Bread on page 87.

Aging and Bleaching

Freshly milled flour is not good for bread making. The gluten is somewhat weak and inelastic, and the color may be yellowish. When the flour is aged for several months, the oxygen in the air matures the proteins so that they are stronger and more elastic, and it bleaches the color.

Aging flour is costly and haphazard, however, so millers add small quantities of certain chemicals to accomplish the same results quickly. Bromates, added to bread flours, mature the gluten but do not bleach the flour a great deal. Chlorine is added to cake flour because not only is it a maturing agent but it also bleaches the flour to pure white.

Enzymes in Flour

A small but important component of wheat flour is a group of enzymes called *diastase*. These enzymes break down some of the starch into sugars that can be acted on by yeast. If a particular flour is low in diastase, these enzymes can be added by the miller.

SOFT WHEAT FLOURS

In addition to bread flour (patent) and clear flour, both of which are strong, formulas in this book call for two types of weak flours.

Cake flour is a weak or low-gluten flour made from soft wheat. It has a very soft, smooth texture and a pure white color. Cake flour is used for cakes and other delicate baked goods that require low gluten content.

Pastry flour is also a weak or low-gluten flour, but it is slightly stronger

Pastry Flour

than cake flour. It has the same creamy white color as bread flour rather than the pure white of cake flour. Pastry flour is used for pie doughs and for some cookies, biscuits, and muffins.

Cake or pastry flour may be blended with bread flour in order to weaken it slightly for use in some rich, sweet yeast doughs.

Hand Test for Flour Strength

You should be able to identify bread flour, cake flour, and pastry flour by sight and touch, because sooner or later someone will dump a bag of flour into the wrong bin or label it incorrectly, and you will need to be able to recognize the problem.

Bread flour feels slightly coarse when rubbed between the fingers. If squeezed into a lump in the hand, it falls apart as soon as the hand is opened. Its color is creamy white.

Cake flour feels very smooth and fine. It stays in a lump when squeezed in the hand. Its color is pure white.

Pastry flour feels smooth and fine like cake flour and can also be squeezed into a lump. It has the creamy color of bread flour, not the pure white color of cake flour.

OTHER WHEAT FLOURS

All-purpose flour, seen in retail markets, is not often found in bakeshops. This flour is formulated to be slightly weaker than bread flour so that it can be used for pastries as well. A professional baker, however, prefers to use flours that are formulated for specific purposes, because these give the best results.

Self-rising flour is a white flour to which baking powder and, sometimes, salt has been added. Its advantage is that the baking powder is blended in uniformly. However, its use is limited by two factors. First, different formulas call for different proportions of baking powder. No single blend is right for all purposes. Second, baking powder loses its aerating or leavening power with time, so the quality of baked goods made from this flour can fluctuate.

Whole wheat flour is made by grinding the entire wheat kernel, including the bran and germ. The germ, as you have learned, is high in fat, which can become rancid, so whole wheat flour does not keep as well as white flour.

Because it is made from wheat, whole wheat flour contains gluten, so it can be used alone in bread making. However, bread made with 100% whole wheat flour is heavier than white bread because the gluten strands are cut by the sharp edges of the bran flakes. Also, the fat from the wheat germ contributes to the shortening action. This is why most whole wheat breads are strengthened with white bread flour.

Bran flour is flour to which bran flakes have been added. The bran may be coarse or fine, depending on specifications.

OTHER FLOURS, MEALS, AND STARCHES

Rye Flour

RYE FLOUR

Next to white and whole wheat, rye is the most popular flour for bread making. Although rye flour contains some proteins, these do not form gluten. Therefore, breads made with 100% rye flour are heavy and dense. To make a lighter rye loaf, it is necessary to use a mixture of rye and hard wheat flours. Typical formulas call for 25 to 40% rye flour and 60 to 75% hard wheat flour.

Rye flour is milled much like wheat flour. The lightest rye flours, from the inner part of the kernel, have a low extraction rate, corresponding to patent flour. The following grades and types are generally available:

Light rye The lightest is nearly white. It has a very fine texture and a high percentage of starch, with little protein.

Medium rye This is a straight flour, milled from the whole rye grain after the bran is removed. Thus, it is darker than light rye and has a higher protein content.

Dark rye Like clear flour milled from wheat, dark rye comes from the part of the rye grain closest to the bran. Thus, it is darker than other rye flours and has a lower percentage of fine starch particles.

Rye meal or pumpernickel flour Rye meal is a dark, coarse meal made from the entire rye grain, including the bran. It looks somewhat like oatmeal. Rye meal is used for pumpernickel bread and similar specialty products.

Rye blend This is a mixture of rye flour (generally about 25 to 40%) and a strong wheat flour, such as clear flour.

Yellow Cornmeal

MISCELLANEOUS FLOURS AND MEALS

Products milled from other grains are occasionally used to add variety to baked goods. These include cornmeal, rice flour, buckwheat flour, soy flour, potato flour, oat flour, and barley flour. The term *meal* is used for products that are not as finely ground as flour.

All of these products are normally used in combination with wheat flour because they do not form gluten.

STARCHES

In addition to flours, other starch products are used in the bakeshop. Unlike flour, they are used primarily to thicken puddings, pie fillings, and similar products. The most important starches in dessert production are as follows:

1. *Cornstarch* has a special property that makes it valuable for certain purposes. Products thickened with cornstarch set up almost like gelatin when cooled. For this reason, cornstarch is used to thicken cream pies and other products that must hold their shape.

2. **Waxy maize** and other **modified starches** also have valuable properties. Because they do not break down when frozen, they are used for products that are to be frozen. Also, they are very clear when cooked and give a brilliant, clear appearance to fruit pie fillings.

 Waxy maize does not set up firm like cornstarch but makes a soft paste that has the same consistency hot and cold. Thus, it is not suitable for cream pie fillings.

3. **Instant starches** are precooked or pregelatinized so they thicken cold liquids without further cooking. They are useful when heat will damage the flavor of the product, as in fresh fruit glazes, such as strawberry.

SUGARS

Sugars or sweetening agents have the following purposes in baking:

- They add sweetness and flavor.
- They create tenderness and fineness of texture, partly by weakening the gluten structure.
- They give crust color.
- They increase keeping qualities by retaining moisture.
- They act as creaming agents with fats and as foaming agents with eggs.
- They provide food for yeast.

 We customarily use the term *sugar* for regular refined sugars derived from sugarcane or beets. The chemical name for these sugars is *sucrose*. However, other sugars of different chemical structure are also used in the bakeshop.

 Sugars belong to a group of substances called *carbohydrates,* a group that also includes starches. There are two basic groups of sugars: *simple sugars* (or *monosaccharides,* which means "single sugars") and *complex sugars* (or *disaccharides,* meaning "double sugars"). Starches, or polysaccharides, have more complex chemical structures than sugars. Sucrose is a disaccharide, as are maltose (malt sugar) and lactose (the sugar found in milk). Examples of simple sugars are glucose and fructose.

 All these sugars have different degrees of sweetness. For example, lactose is much less sweet than regular table sugar (sucrose), while fructose (or fruit sugar, one of the sugars in honey) is much sweeter than sucrose.

INVERT SUGAR

When a sucrose solution is heated with an acid, some of the sucrose breaks down into equal parts of two simple sugars, dextrose and levulose. A mixture of equal parts of dextrose and levulose is called *invert sugar.* It is about 30% sweeter than regular sucrose.

 Invert sugar has two properties that make it interesting to the baker. First, it holds moisture especially well and, therefore, helps keep cakes fresh and moist. Second, it resists crystallization. Thus, it promotes smoothness in candies, icings, and syrups. This is why an acid such as cream of tartar is often added to sugar syrups. The acid inverts some of the sugar when it is boiled, thus preventing graininess in the candy or icing.

 Invert sugar is produced commercially and it is also present in honey.

REGULAR REFINED SUGARS, OR SUCROSE

Refined sugars are classified by the size of the grains. However, there is no standardized system of labeling, so the names of the various granulations vary depending on the manufacturer.

Granulated Sugar

Regular granulated sugar, also called *fine granulated* or *table sugar,* is the most familiar and the most commonly used.

Very fine and **ultra fine sugars** (also called *caster sugar*) are finer than regular granulated sugar. They are prized for making cakes and cookies because they make a more uniform batter and can support higher quantities of fat.

Sanding sugars are coarse and are used for coating cookies, cakes, and other products.

In general, finer granulations are better for mixing into doughs and batters because they dissolve relatively quickly. Coarse sugars are likely to leave undissolved grains, even after long mixing. These show up after baking as dark spots on crusts, irregular texture, and syrupy spots. Also, fine sugars are better for creaming with fats because they create a finer, more uniform air cell structure and better volume.

Coarse sugar, on the other hand, can be used in syrups, where its mixing properties are not a factor. Even a very coarse sugar dissolves readily when boiled with water. In fact, coarse crystalline sugar is often purer than fine sugar and makes a clearer syrup.

Confectioners' or Powdered Sugars

These sugars are ground to a fine powder and mixed with a small amount of starch (about 3%) to prevent caking. They are classified by coarseness or fineness.

10X is the finest sugar. It gives the smoothest textures in icings.

6X is the standard confectioners' sugar. It is used in icings, toppings, and cream fillings.

Coarser types (*XXXX* and *XX*) are used for dusting and for any purposes for which 6X and 10X are too fine.

Confectioners' sugar is also known as *icing sugar* because of its importance in making many kinds of icings.

Dehydrated Fondant

Dehydrated fondant is not a powdered sugar, though its appearance is similar. It is a dried form of fondant icing. During the manufacture of fondant, part of the sucrose is changed to invert sugar. This helps keep the sugar crystals tiny, which makes for a very smooth, creamy icing with a good shine.

Fondant is discussed with other icings in chapter 13.

Brown Sugar

Brown sugar is mostly sucrose (about 85 to 92%), but it also contains varying amounts of caramel, molasses, and other impurities, which give it its characteristic flavor. The darker grades contain more of these impurities. Basically, brown sugar is regular cane sugar that has not been completely refined. However, it can also be made by adding measured amounts of these impurities to refined white sugar.

Brown sugar was, at one time, available in 15 grades, ranging from very dark to very light. Today, only two to four grades are generally available.

Because it contains a small amount of acid, brown sugar can be used with baking soda to provide some leavening (see p. 37). It is used in place of regular white sugar when its flavor is desired and its color will not be objectionable. Of course, it should not be used in white cakes.

Keep brown sugar in an airtight container to prevent it from drying out and hardening.

Demerara sugar is a crystalline brown sugar. It is dry rather than moist like regular brown sugar. Demerara sugar is sometimes used in baking, but it is more often served as a sweetener with coffee and tea.

SYRUPS

Molasses

Molasses is concentrated sugarcane juice. *Sulfured molasses* is a byproduct of sugar refining. It is the product that remains after most of the sugar is extracted from cane juice. *Unsulfured molasses* is not a byproduct but a specially manufactured sugar product. It has a less bitter taste than sulfured molasses.

Molasses contains large amounts of sucrose and other sugars, including invert sugar. It also contains acids, moisture, and other constituents that give it its flavor and color. Darker grades are stronger in flavor and contain less sugar than lighter grades.

Molasses retains moisture in baked goods and, therefore, prolongs freshness. Crisp cookies made with molasses can become soft quickly because the invert sugars absorb moisture from the air.

Corn Syrup

Corn syrup is a liquid sweetener consisting of water, a vegetable gum called *dextrin,* and various sugars, primarily *dextrose* (also called *glucose*). Corn syrup is made by converting cornstarch into simpler compounds through the use of enzymes.

Corn syrup aids in retaining moisture and is used in some icings and candies. It has a mild flavor and is not as sweet as granulated sugar (sucrose).

Glucose Syrup

While corn syrup contains sugars in addition to glucose, pure glucose syrup is also available. It resembles corn syrup but is colorless and nearly tasteless. It has the same uses as corn syrup in the pastry shop but is often preferred by pastry chefs because of its purity. If a recipe calls for glucose syrup and none is available, substitute light corn syrup.

Honey

Honey is a natural sugar syrup consisting largely of the simple sugars glucose and fructose, in addition to other compounds that give it its flavor. Honeys vary considerably in flavor and color, depending on their source. Flavor is the major reason for using honey, especially as it can be expensive.

Because honey contains invert sugar, it helps retain moisture in baked goods. Like molasses, it contains acid, which enables it to be used with baking soda as a leavening.

Malt Syrup

Malt syrup, also called *malt extract,* is used primarily in yeast breads. It serves as food for the yeast and adds flavor and crust color to the breads. Malt is extracted from barley that has been sprouted (malted) and then dried and ground.

There are two basic types of malt syrup, *diastatic* and *nondiastatic.* Diastatic malt contains a group of enzymes called *diastase,* which breaks down starch into sugars that can be acted on by yeast. Thus, diastatic malt, when added to bread dough, is a powerful food for yeast. It is used when fermentation times are short. It should not be used when fermentation times are long because too much starch will be broken down by the enzyme. This results in bread with a sticky crumb.

Diastatic malt is produced with high, medium, or low diastase content.

Nondiastatic malt is processed at high temperatures that destroy the enzymes and give the syrup a darker color and stronger flavor. It is used because it contains fermentable sugar and contributes flavor, crust color, and keeping qualities to breads.

Whenever malt syrup is called for in formulas in this book, nondiastatic malt should be used. No formulas require diastatic malt. If malt syrup is not available, you may substitute regular granulated sugar.

Malt is available in two other forms. *Dried malt extract* is simply malt syrup that has been dried. It must be kept in an airtight container to keep it from absorbing moisture from the air. *Malt flour* is the dried, ground, malted barley that has not had the malt extracted from it. It is obviously a much less concentrated form of malt. When used in breadmaking, it is blended with the flour.

FATS

The major functions of fats in baked items are:

- To tenderize the product and soften the texture.
- To add moistness and richness.
- To increase keeping quality.
- To add flavor.
- To assist in leavening when used as creaming agents or when used to give flakiness to puff pastry, pie dough, and similar products.

Many fats are available to the baker. These fats have different properties that make them suitable for different purposes. Among the properties a baker must consider when selecting a fat for a specific use are its melting point, its softness or hardness at different temperatures, its flavor, and its ability to form emulsions.

FAT EMULSIONS

Most bakery ingredients mix easily with water and other liquids and actually undergo a change in form. For example, salt and sugar dissolve in water; flour and starch absorb water and the water becomes bound up with the starch and protein molecules. Fat, on the other hand, does not change form when it is mixed with liquids or other bakery ingredients. Instead, it is merely broken down into smaller and smaller particles during mixing. These small fat particles eventually become more or less evenly distributed in the mix.

A uniform mixture of two unmixable substances, such as a fat and water, is called an *emulsion.* Mayonnaise is a familiar example of an emulsion from outside the bakeshop—in this case, an emulsion of oil and vinegar. There are also emulsions of air and fat, such as that formed when shortening and sugar are creamed together in the production of cakes and other products (see p. 38).

Fats have differing abilities to form emulsions. For example, if the wrong shortening is used in certain cakes, the emulsion may fail because the batter contains more water than the fat can hold. We then say that the batter curdles or breaks.

SHORTENINGS

Any fat acts as a shortening in baking, because it shortens gluten strands and tenderizes the product. However, we generally use the word *shortening* to mean any of a group of solid fats, usually white and tasteless, that are especially formulated for baking. Shortenings generally consist of nearly 100% fat.

Shortenings may be made from vegetable oils, animal fats, or both. During manufacturing, the fats are *hydrogenated*. This process turns liquid oils into solid fats. Because shortenings are used for many purposes, manufacturers have formulated different kinds of fats with different properties. There are two main types: regular shortenings and emulsified shortenings.

Regular Shortenings

These shortenings have a fairly tough, waxy texture, and small particles of the fat tend to hold their shape in a dough or batter. These shortenings can be manufactured to varying degrees of hardness. Regular shortenings have a good creaming ability. This means that a good quantity of air can be mixed into them to give a batter lightness and leavening power (see p. 38). Also, this type of shortening melts only at a high temperature.

Because of their texture, regular shortenings are used for flaky products such as pie crusts and biscuits. They are also used in many other pastries, breads, and products mixed by creaming, such as certain pound cakes, cookies, and quick breads.

Unless another shortening is specified in a formula, regular shortening is generally used.

Emulsified Shortenings

These are soft shortenings that spread easily throughout a batter and quickly coat the particles of sugar and flour. Because they contain added emulsifying agents, they can hold a larger quantity of liquid and sugar than regular shortenings can. Thus, they give a smoother and finer texture to cakes and make them moister.

On the other hand, emulsified shortening does not cream well. When recipe instructions call for creaming shortening and sugar, regular shortening rather than emulsified shortening should be used.

Emulsified shortening is often used when the weight of sugar in a cake batter is greater than the weight of flour. Because this shortening spreads so well, a simpler mixing method can be used, as explained in chapter 12. Such cakes are referred to as *high-ratio cakes,* and emulsified shortening is sometimes called *high-ratio shortening.*

In addition, emulsified shortening is often used in icings because it can hold more sugar and liquid without curdling.

The term *emulsified shortenings* is not, strictly speaking, an accurate one. Pure fat cannot be emulsified, because an emulsion is a mixture of at least two substances. It would, perhaps, be more accurate to call them *emulsifier shortenings.* However, the term *emulsified shortenings* is the more widely recognized and commonly used term.

BUTTER

Fresh butter consists of about 80% fat, about 15% water, and about 5% milk solids. (Many European butters have a higher fat content—about 82% or even more—and a lower moisture content.)

Butter is graded according to United States Department of Agriculture (USDA) standards, although grading is not mandatory. Grades are AA, A, B, and C. Most operations use grades AA and A because flavors of the lower grades may be off.

Butter is available *salted* and *unsalted.* Unsalted butter is more perishable, but it has a fresher, sweeter taste and is thus preferred in baking. If salted butter is used, the salt in the formula may have to be reduced.

Shortenings are manufactured to have certain textures and hardnesses so that they will be particularly suited to certain uses. Butter, on the other hand, is a natural product that doesn't have this advantage. It is hard and brittle when cold, very soft at room temperature, and it melts easily. Consequently, doughs made with butter are much harder to handle. Also, butter is more expensive than shortening.

On the other hand, butter has two major advantages:

1. *Flavor*   Shortenings are intentionally flavorless, but butter has a highly desirable flavor.
2. *Melting qualities*   Butter melts in the mouth. Shortenings do not. After eating pastries or icings made with shortening, one can be left with an unpleasant film of shortening coating the mouth.

For these reasons, many bakers and pastry chefs feel that the advantages of butter outweigh its disadvantages for many purposes. Shortening is not often used in fine French pastries. Frequently, you may blend 50% butter and 50% shortening to get both the flavor of butter and the handling qualities of shortening.

MARGARINE

Margarine is manufactured from various hydrogenated animal and vegetable fats, plus flavoring ingredients, emulsifiers, coloring agents, and other ingredients. It contains 80 to 85% fat, 10 to 15% moisture, and about 5% salt, milk solids, and other components. Thus, it may be considered a sort of imitation butter consisting of shortening, water, and flavoring.

Unlike the margarines sold by retail grocers, bakers' margarines are formulated in different ways for different purposes. Following are the two major categories.

Cake Margarines or Bakers' Margarines

These types of margarine are soft and have good creaming ability. They are used not only in cakes but in a wide variety of products.

Pastry Margarines

These margarines are tougher and more elastic and have a waxy texture. They are especially formulated for doughs that form layers, such as Danish dough and puff pastry.

Puff pastry margarine, the toughest of these fats, is sometimes called *puff pastry shortening.* Puff pastry made with this margarine generally rises higher than pastry made with butter. However, as the fat doesn't melt in the mouth like butter, many people find the pastry unpleasant to eat.

OILS

Oils are liquid fats. They are not often used as shortenings in baking because they spread through a batter or dough too thoroughly and shorten too much. Some breads and a few cakes and quick breads use oil as a shortening. Beyond this, the usefulness of oil in the bakeshop is limited primarily to greasing pans, deep-frying doughnuts, and serving as a wash for some kinds of rolls.

LARD

Lard is the rendered fat of hogs. Because of its plastic quality, it was once highly valued for making flaky pie crusts. Since the development of modern shortenings, however, it is not often used in the bakeshop.

STORAGE OF FATS

All fats become rancid if exposed to the air too long. Also, they tend to absorb odors and flavors from other foods. Highly perishable fats, such as butter, should be stored, well wrapped, in the refrigerator. Other fats and oils should be kept in tightly closed containers in a cool, dry, dark place.

MILK AND MILK PRODUCTS

Next to water, milk is the most important liquid in the bakeshop. As we discussed in chapter 1, water is essential for the development of gluten. Fresh milk, being 88 to 91% water, fulfills this function. In addition, milk contributes to the texture, flavor, crust color, keeping quality, and nutritional value of baked products.

In this section, we discuss milk products in two parts: first, an explanation and definition of the various products available; second, guidelines for using milk products in baking.

The table below lists the water, fat, and milk solids content of the most important milk products. Milk solids include protein, lactose (milk sugar), and minerals.

Composition of Milk Products

	Water (%)	Fat (%)	Milk Solids (%)
Fresh, whole	88	3.5	8.5
Fresh, skim	91	trace	9
Evaporated, whole	72	8	20
Evaporated, skim	72	trace	28
Condensed, whole[a]	31	8	20
Dried, whole	1.5	27.5	71
Dried, skim	2.5	trace	97.5

[a]Condensed milk also contains 41% sugar (sucrose).

CATEGORIES AND DEFINITIONS

Fresh Liquid Milk

Whole milk is fresh milk as it comes from the cow, with nothing removed and nothing added (except when fortified with vitamin D). It contains $3\frac{1}{2}$% fat (known as *milkfat* or *butterfat*), $8\frac{1}{2}$% nonfat milk solids, and 88% water. Fresh whole milk is available in several forms:

Pasteurized milk has been heated to kill disease-producing bacteria and then cooled. Most milk and cream products on the market have been pasteurized.

Raw milk is milk that has not been pasteurized. It is not often used and, in fact, is generally not allowed to be sold.

Certified milk is produced by disease-free herds under strict sanitary conditions. It may be raw or pasteurized.

Homogenized milk has been processed so that the cream doesn't separate. This is done by forcing the milk through very tiny holes, which breaks up the fat into particles so small that they stay distributed in the milk.

The above terms apply not only to whole milk but also to other forms. *Skim or nonfat milk* has had most or all fat removed. Its fat content is 0.5% or less. Other forms available to food service and to retail outlets include *low-fat milk* (0.5 to 3% milkfat), *fortified nonfat* or *low-fat milk,* and *flavored milk.* However, these products are generally not used in bakeshops.

Cream

Various types of fresh cream, differing primarily in fat content, are available:

Whipping cream has a fat content of 30 to 40%. Within this category, you may find *light whipping cream* (30 to 35%) and *heavy whipping cream* (36 to 40%). Light whipping cream has about the same fat content as the product called *single cream* in England. *Double cream,* on the other hand, is much richer than most heavy whipping cream. With a fat content of about 48%, double cream is easy to whip and, after whipping, less likely to weep or to separate into liquid and foam.

Whipping cream labeled *ultrapasteurized* keeps longer than regular pasteurized cream, but it does not whip as well. Ultrapasteurized cream often contains vegetable gums or other stabilizers to partially compensate for this decreased whipping ability.

Light cream, also called *table cream* or *coffee cream,* contains 16 to 22% fat, usually about 18%.

Half-and-half has a fat content of 10 to 12%, too low for it to be called cream.

Crème fraîche is a slightly aged, cultured heavy cream, thick but pourable, with a pleasant, somewhat tangy flavor. It is widely used in saucemaking in the savory kitchen. In the bakeshop, it is not often mixed into doughs or batters, but it is used for whipping and for incorporating into dessert sauces and Bavarian creams. If crème fraîche is not available, you can make a close approximation by warming 1 qt (1 L) of heavy cream to about 100°F (38°C), adding $1\frac{1}{2}$ oz (50 mL) buttermilk, and letting the mixture stand in a warm place until slightly thickened, about 6 to 24 hours.

Fermented Milk Products

Buttermilk is fresh, liquid milk, usually skim milk, that has been cultured or soured by bacteria. It is usually called *cultured buttermilk* to distinguish it from the original buttermilk, which was the liquid left after buttermaking. Buttermilk is generally used in recipes calling for *sour milk*.

Sour cream has been cultured or fermented by adding lactic acid bacteria. This makes it thick and slightly tangy in flavor. It has about 18% fat.

Yogurt is milk (whole or low-fat) cultured by special bacteria. It has a custardlike consistency. Most yogurt has additional milk solids added, and some of it is flavored and sweetened.

Evaporated and Condensed Milk

Evaporated milk is milk, either whole or skim, with about 60% of the water removed. It is then sterilized and canned. Evaporated milk has a somewhat cooked flavor.

Condensed milk is whole milk or low-fat milk that has had about 60% of the water removed and is heavily sweetened with sugar. It is available canned and in bulk.

Dried Milk

Dried whole milk is whole milk that has been dried to powder. It has poor keeping qualities because it contains the original butterfat, which can become rancid. Therefore, it should be purchased in small quantities and always stored in a cool place.

Nonfat dry milk, also known as *nonfat milk solids,* is skim milk that has been dried to a powder. It is available in regular form and in instant form, which dissolves in water more easily.

Cheese

Two types of cheese are used in the bakeshop, primarily in the production of cheese fillings and cheesecakes.

Baker's cheese is a soft, unaged cheese with a very low fat content. It is dry and pliable and can be kneaded somewhat like a dough. Generally available in 30-lb and 50-lb packs, it can be frozen for longer storage.

Cream cheese is also a soft, unaged cheese, but it has a higher fat content, about 35%. It is used mainly in rich cheesecakes and in a few specialty products.

Two other cheeses are occasionally used for specialty products. *Mascarpone* is a type of Italian cream cheese with a tangier flavor than American-style cream cheese. It is used to make the filling for Tiramisu (p. 384). Another Italian cheese, *ricotta,* was originally made from the whey left over from making cheese out of cow's milk or sheep's milk, although now it is more often made from whole milk rather than whey. It has many uses in the kitchen and bakeshop. A smooth, relatively dry ricotta called *ricotta impastato* is used to make a filling for cannoli (p. 163). Regular ricotta has too much moisture for this purpose.

GUIDELINES FOR USING MILK PRODUCTS IN BAKING

Fresh Liquid Milk

Whole milk contains fat, which must be calculated as part of the shortening in a dough. For this reason, whole and skim milk are not interchangeable in a formula, unless adjustments are made for the fat. Refer to the table on page 29 for the fat content of milk products.

Acid ingredients, such as lemon juice, cream of tartar, and baking powder, normally should not be added directly to milk, as they will curdle it.

Buttermilk

When buttermilk is produced, the lactose in the milk is converted to lactic acid. When buttermilk is used in place of regular milk in baked goods such as cakes or muffins, this acidity must, in most cases, be neutralized by adding baking soda to the formula. Then, because the soda and acid together release carbon dioxide, this extra leavening power must be compensated for by reducing the baking powder, as follows:

For each quart (2 lb) of buttermilk:

1. Add 0.5 oz baking soda
2. Subtract 1 oz baking powder

For each liter (1 kg) of buttermilk:

1. Add 15 g baking soda.
2. Subtract 30 g baking powder

Cream

Cream is not often used as a liquid in doughs and batters, except in a few specialty products. In these instances, because of its fat content, it functions as a shortening as well as a liquid.

Cream is more important in the production of fillings, toppings, dessert sauces, and cold desserts such as mousses and Bavarian creams. For detailed instructions on whipping heavy cream into a foam, see chapter 8, page 180.

Dried Milk

1. Dried milk is often used because of its convenience and low cost. In many formulas, it is not necessary to reconstitute it. The milk powder is included with the dry ingredients and water is used as the liquid. This practice is common in bread making and in no way reduces quality.

2. Proportions for reconstituting dry milk can be calculated from the table on page 29. For easy use, the equivalents in the table below can be used.

3. *Heat-treated* dry milk, not low-heat-processed dry milk, should be purchased by the bakeshop. In the heat-treated product, certain enzymes that can break down gluten have been destroyed.

Substituting Dry Milk for Liquid Milk

To substitute for	Use
1 lb skim milk	14.5 oz water + 1.5 oz nonfat dry milk
1 lb whole milk	14 oz water + 2 oz dried whole milk
1 lb whole milk	14 oz water + 1.5 oz nonfat dried milk + 0.5 oz shortening *or* 0.7 oz butter
1 kg skim milk	910 g water + 90 g nonfat dry milk
1 kg whole milk	880 g water + 120 g dried whole milk
1 kg whole milk	880 g water + 90 g nonfat dry milk + 30 g shortening *or* 40 g butter

STORAGE OF MILK PRODUCTS

Fresh milk and cream, buttermilk and other fermented milk products, and cheese must be kept refrigerated at all times.

Evaporated milk in unopened cans may be kept in a cool storage area. After opening, store it in the refrigerator.

Condensed milk in large containers keeps for a week or more after opening if kept covered and in a cool place. The sugar acts as a preservative. Stir before using because the sugar tends to settle to the bottom and sides.

Dried milk should be kept in a cool, dark place. It does not need refrigeration, although you should store it well away from ovens and other heat sources. Keep the container tightly closed to prevent the milk from absorbing moisture from the air.

EGGS

Eggs should be well understood by the baker because they are used in large quantities in the bakeshop and are more expensive than many of the other high-volume ingredients, such as flour and sugar. For example, half or more of the ingredient cost of the average cake batter is for the eggs.

COMPOSITION

A whole egg consists primarily of a yolk, a white, and a shell. In addition, it contains a membrane that lines the shell and forms an air cell at the large end, and two white strands called *chalazae* that hold the yolk centered.

- The yolk is high in both fat and protein, and it contains iron and several vitamins. Its color ranges from light to dark yellow, depending on the diet of the chicken.

- The white is primarily albumin protein, which is clear and soluble when raw but white and firm when coagulated. The white also contains sulfur.

- The shell is *not* the perfect package, in spite of what you may have heard. It is not only fragile but also porous, allowing odors and flavors to be absorbed by the egg, and allowing the egg to lose moisture even if unbroken.

The table below lists the water, protein, and fat content of whole eggs, whites, and yolks.

Average Composition of Fresh Liquid Eggs

	Whole eggs (%)	Whites (%)	Yolks (%)
Water	73	86	49
Protein	13	12	17
Fat	12	—	32
Minerals and other components	2	2	2

GRADES AND QUALITY

Grades

Eggs are graded for quality by the U.S. Department of Agriculture. There are three grades: AA, A, and B. The best grade has a firm white and yolk that stand up high when broken onto a flat surface and do not spread over a large area. As eggs age, they become thinner and are graded lower.

As a baker, you will not be concerned so much with the firmness of yolks and white. Rather, you will want eggs that are clean and fresh-tasting, free of bad odors and tastes caused by spoilage or absorption of foreign odors. One bad-smelling egg can ruin an entire batch of cakes.

Maintaining Quality

Proper storage is essential for maintaining quality. Eggs keep for weeks if held at 36°F (2°C) but lose quality quickly if held at room temperature. In fact, they can lose a full grade in one day at warm bakeshop temperatures. There's no point in paying for Grade AA eggs if they are Grade B by the time you use them. Store eggs away from other foods that might pass on undesirable flavors or odors.

Size

Eggs are also graded by size. The table below gives the minimum weight per dozen (including shell) of each size category. Note that each size differs from the next by 3 ounces per dozen. European eggs are also graded by size, with size 1 being the largest (70 g each, or about 2.5 oz) and 7 being the smallest (45 g each, or about 1.6 oz). This weight includes the shell.

Large eggs are the standard size used in baking and in food service. Shelled large whole eggs, yolks, and whites have the following approximate weights.

Average Large Eggs, Approximate Weights Without Shell

One whole egg = 1.67 oz	47 g
One egg white = 1 oz	28 g
One yolk = 0.67 oz	19 g

9½ whole eggs = 1 lb	21 whole eggs = 1 kg
16 whites = 1 lb	36 whites = 1 kg
24 yolks = 1 lb	53 yolks = 1 kg

To measure small quantities or odd quantities of whole egg, such as ½ oz or 15 g, beat the whole egg or eggs and then measure by weight.

Egg Size Classifications

	Minimum Weight per Dozen	
Size	**U.S.**	**Metric**
Jumbo	30 oz	850 g
Extra large	27 oz	765 g
Large	24 oz	680 g
Medium	21 oz	595 g
Small	18 oz	510 g
Peewee	15 oz	425 g

MARKET FORMS

1. *Fresh eggs* or *shell eggs*

2. *Frozen eggs*   Frozen eggs are usually made from high-quality fresh eggs and are excellent for use in baking. They are pasteurized and are usually purchased in 30-lb tins.

   To thaw, place them unopened in refrigerator and hold for two days, or place in a defrosting tank containing running water at 50° to 60°F (10° to 15°C) for about 6 hours. Do not defrost at room temperature or in warm water. Stir well before using.

   > Whole eggs
   >
   > Whole eggs with extra yolks
   >
   > Whites
   >
   > Yolks

   Frozen yolks may contain a small amount of sugar (usually about 10%; check the label) to keep the components from separating while frozen.

   When these sugared yolks are used in products such as cakes, you should allow for this sugar content by reducing the sugar in the formula by the same amount. For example, if you are using 20 oz yolks with 10% sugar, subtract 2 oz (20 oz × .10) from the sugar in the formula.

3. *Dried eggs*

   > Whole
   >
   > Yolks
   >
   > Whites

   Dried eggs are sometimes used in the bakeshop, though less often than frozen eggs. The whites are frequently used for making meringue powders. Dried egg products are also used by commercial manufacturers of cake mixes.

   Dried eggs are incorporated in baked goods in two ways: by reconstituting them with water to make liquid eggs, or by mixing them with the dry ingredients and by adding the extra water to the liquid portion of the formula.

   It is important to follow manufacturers' instructions for the ratio of egg to water because egg products vary. After mixing, let the eggs stand to allow time for the water to be absorbed. This takes 1 hour for whole eggs and yolks, and sometimes 3 hours or more for whites. Mix again before using. The following are typical ratios for reconstituting eggs:

Product	Ratio of egg to water by weight
Whole eggs	$1 : 2\frac{1}{2}$
Yolks	$1 : 1$ to $1 : 1\frac{1}{2}$
Whites	$1 : 5\frac{1}{2}$ to $1 : 6$

   Unlike most dried products, dried eggs do not keep well. Keep refrigerated or frozen, tightly sealed.

FUNCTIONS

Eggs perform the following functions in baking:

1. *Structure*   Like gluten protein, egg protein coagulates to give structure to baked products. This is especially important in high-ratio cakes, in which the high content of sugar and fat weakens the gluten.

If used in large quantities, eggs make baked products more tough or chewy unless balanced by fat and sugar, which are tenderizers.

2. *Emulsifying of fats and liquids* Egg yolks contain natural emulsifiers, which help produce smooth batters. This action contributes to volume and to texture.

3. *Leavening* Beaten eggs incorporate air in tiny cells or bubbles. In a batter, this trapped air expands when heated and aids in leavening.

4. *Shortening action* The fat in egg yolks acts as a shortening. This is an important function in products that are low in other fats.

5. *Moisture* Eggs are mostly water (see the table on p. 33). This moisture must be calculated as part of the total liquid in a formula. If yolks are substituted for whole eggs, for example, or if dried eggs are used, adjust the liquid in the formula to allow for the different moisture content of these products.

6. *Flavor*

7. *Nutritional value*

8. *Color* Yolks impart a yellow color to doughs and batters. Also, eggs brown easily and contribute to crust color.

LEAVENING AGENTS

Leavening is the production or incorporation of gases in a baked product to increase volume and to produce shape and texture. These gases must be retained in the product until the structure is set enough (by the coagulation of gluten and egg proteins and the gelatinization of starches) to hold its shape.

Exact measurement of leavening agents is important because small changes can produce major defects in baked products.

YEAST

Yeast is the leavening agent in breads, dinner rolls, Danish pastries, and similar products. This section discusses the characteristics of yeast. The handling of yeast and its use in yeast doughs are discussed in chapter 3.

Fermentation is the process by which yeast acts on sugars and changes them into carbon dioxide gas and alcohol. This release of gas produces the leavening action in yeast products. The alcohol evaporates completely during and immediately after baking.

Fermentable sugar in bread dough comes from two sources:

1. It is added to the dough by the baker.

2. It is produced from flour by enzymes that break down the wheat starch into sugar. These enzymes are present in the flour and/or are added by the baker in the form of diastatic malt (see p. 26).

Yeast is a microscopic plant that accomplishes this fermentation process by producing enzymes. Some of these enzymes change complex sugars (sucrose and maltose) into simple sugars. Others change the simple sugars into carbon dioxide gas and alcohol. The following formula describes this reaction in chemical terms:

$$C_6H_{12}O_6 \quad \rightarrow \quad 2CO_2 \quad + \quad 2C_2H_5OH$$

| simple sugar | carbon dioxide | alcohol |

Because yeast is a living organism, it is sensitive to temperatures.

34°F (1°C)	Inactive (storage temperature)
60° to 70°F (15° to 20°C)	Slow action
70° to 90°F (20° to 32°C)	Best growth (fermentation and proofing temperatures for bread doughs)
Above 100°F (38°C)	Reaction slows
140°F (60°C)	Yeast is killed

Yeast is available in two forms: compressed and active dry. The formulas in this book call for compressed yeast, which is preferred by professional bakers. *To convert recipes to use active dry yeast, use only 40% of the weight of compressed yeast specified.* In other words, in place of 1 pound of compressed yeast, use 6.5 oz dry yeast (.40 × 16 oz). Dry yeast must be dissolved in 4 times its weight of warm water (at about 110°F/43°C) before use.

Yeast contributes flavor in addition to leavening action.

CHEMICAL LEAVENERS

Chemical leaveners are those that release gases produced by chemical reactions.

Baking Soda

Baking soda is the chemical *sodium bicarbonate.* If *moisture* and an *acid* are present, soda releases carbon dioxide gas, which leavens the product.

Heat is not necessary for the reaction (though the gas is released faster at high temperatures). For this reason, products leavened with soda must be baked at once or gases will escape and leavening power will be lost.

Acids that react with soda in a batter include honey, molasses, buttermilk, fruit juices and purées, and chocolate. Sometimes cream of tartar is used for the acid. The amount of soda used in a formula is generally the amount needed to balance the acid. If more leavening power is needed, baking powder, not more soda, is used.

Baking Powder

Baking powders are mixtures of baking soda plus an acid to react with it. They also contain starch, which prevents lumping and brings the leavening power down to a standard level. Because baking powders do not depend for their leavening power on acid ingredients in a formula, they are more versatile.

Single-acting baking powders require only moisture to be able to release gas. Like baking soda, they can be used only if the product is to be baked immediately after mixing.

Double-acting baking powders release some gas when cold, but they require heat for complete reaction. Thus, cake batters made with these can incorporate the leavening agent early in the mixing period and can stand for some time before being baked.

Do not include more baking powder than necessary in a formula because undesirable flavors may be created. Also, excess leavening may create an undesirably light, crumbly texture. Cakes may rise too much and then fall before they become set.

Baking Ammonia

Baking ammonia is a mixture of ammonium carbonate, ammonium bicarbonate, and ammonium carbamate. It decomposes rapidly during baking to form carbon dioxide gas, ammonia gas, and water. Only heat and moisture are necessary for it to work. No acids are needed.

Because it decomposes completely, it leaves no residue that could affect flavor when it is properly used. However, it can be used only in small products that are baked until dry, such as cookies. Only in such products can the ammonia gas be completely driven off.

Because ammonia releases gases very quickly, it is sometimes used in products in which rapid leavening is desired, such as cream puffs. Use of ammonia enables the baker to lower the cost of such products by reducing the quantity of eggs. However, the quality of the resulting goods is lowered.

Storage of Chemical Leaveners

Baking soda, powder, and ammonia must always be kept tightly closed when not in use. If left open, they can absorb moisture from the air and lose part of their leavening power. They must be stored in a cool place, because heat also causes them to deteriorate.

AIR

Air is incorporated into a batter primarily by two methods: creaming and foaming. This air expands during baking and leavens the products.

1. *Creaming* is the process of beating fat and sugar together to incorporate air. It is an important technique in cake and cookie making. Some pound cakes and cookies are leavened almost entirely by this method.

2. *Foaming* is the process of beating eggs, with or without sugar, to incorporate air. Foams made with whole eggs are used to leaven sponge cakes, while angel food cakes, meringues, and soufflés are leavened with egg white foams.

STEAM

When water turns to steam, it expands to 1100 times its original volume. Because all baked products contain some moisture, steam is an important leavening agent.

Puff pastry, cream puffs, popovers, and pie crusts use steam as their primary or only leavening agent. If the starting baking temperature for these products is high, steam is produced rapidly and leavening is greatest.

JELLING AGENTS

GELATIN

Gelatin is a water-soluble protein extracted from animal connective tissue. When a sufficient quantity of gelatin is dissolved in hot water or other liquid, the liquid will solidify when cooled or chilled.

Weight-Volume Equivalents for Powdered Gelatin

U.S.		Metric	
Weight	Approximate volume	Weight	Approximate volume
0.1 oz	1 tsp	1 g	1.75 mL
0.12–0.13 oz	1¼ tsp	2 g	3.5 mL
0.16–0.17 oz	1⅔ tsp	3 g	5 mL
0.2 oz	2 tsp	4 g	7 mL
0.25 oz	2½ tsp	6 g	10 mL
0.33 oz	3⅓ tsp	8 g	14 mL
0.4 oz	4 tsp	10 g	18 mL
0.5 oz	5 tsp	12 g	21 mL
0.75 oz	7½ tsp	14 g	25 mL
1 oz	10 tsp	16 g	28 mL
		20 g	36 mL
		30 g	54 mL

Culinary gelatin is available in a powdered form and in sheets. Powdered gelatin is most widely available to North American kitchens, although sheet gelatin, also called leaf gelatin, is also available and is often preferred by pastry chefs. The sheet form is especially easy to use as it is premeasured (the sheets are of uniform weights). Also, when using sheet gelatin, it is not necessary to measure the liquid for soaking it. This is explained below.

By weight, powdered gelatin has the same jelling power as sheet gelatin. One teaspoon of powdered gelatin weighs about 2.8 g or ¹⁄₁₀ oz. Ten teaspoons equal 1 oz. The reference table above lists volume equivalents for a range of weights of gelatin.

Sheet gelatin is available in various sizes, ranging from 1.7 g to 3 g.

Powdered gelatin and sheet gelatin can be used interchangeably, but they are handled differently. Guidelines for handling the two products and for substituting one for the other are described below.

Using Gelatin in Recipes

Using gelatin in a recipe requires three main steps:

1. The gelatin is softened in water or other liquid. It absorbs 5 times its weight in water.

2. The softened gelatin is added to hot ingredients, or it is heated with other ingredients, until it dissolves.

3. The mixture is chilled until it sets.

Most of the recipes in this book that require gelatin were developed using powdered gelatin (others were developed using sheet gelatin). The following guidelines will help you use recipes requiring gelatin:

• When a recipe was developed using sheet gelatin, no soaking liquid is indicated in the ingredient list. In the procedure, the instructions direct you to soften the gelatin in cold water. To use sheet gelatin, add the indicated weight of gelatin to a generous quantity of cold water and soak until soft. Remove the soaked sheets from the water, drain well, and incorporate into the recipe. (See p. 189 for an illustration of using sheet gelatin to make Chiboust Cream.)

- Always use very cold water to soak sheet gelatin. If the water is warm, some gelatin will dissolve and be lost.

- To substitute powdered gelatin when no quantity of soaking liquid is given, measure the gelatin, then add 5 times its weight of cold water. Let stand until the water is absorbed.

- When a recipe was developed using powdered gelatin, the quantity of water for soaking is usually indicated. Either powdered gelatin or sheet gelatin can be used in these recipes. Add the measured gelatin to the measured water and soak. Then add the gelatin and the soaking liquid to the mixture in the recipe.

- For an example of a recipe developed using sheet gelatin, in which no soaking liquid is indicated in the ingredient list, see Fruit Glaçage, page 345. For an example of a recipe developed using powdered gelatin, in which the quantity of soaking liquid is indicated, see Vanilla Bavarian Cream, page 441.

Bavarian creams and many mousses depend on gelatin for their texture. More information on the use of gelatin in these products is included in chapter 16.

PECTIN

Pectin is a soluble fiber present in many fruits. In general, unripe fruits have more pectin than ripe fruits. One of the reasons fruits get softer as they ripen is that the pectin breaks down.

Pectin is extracted from fruits and used to thicken or jell fruit preserves, jams, and jellies. It can also be used to make fruit glazes, because the pectin thickens or sets fruit juices and purées.

Several fruit preparations in chapter 18 require the use of pectin.

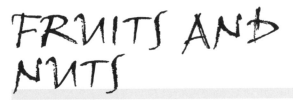

FRUITS AND NUTS

FRUIT PRODUCTS

Nearly any kind of fresh fruit can be used in the production of desserts. In addition, a wide variety of dried, frozen, canned, and processed fruit products are important ingredients in the bakeshop. The following is a list of some of the most important fruit products. Use of these products is covered in appropriate chapters throughout the book. You will find more detailed information on fresh fruits in chapter 18.

Fresh

apples	kiwi	papayas
apricots	kumquats	passion fruit
bananas	lemons	peaches
berries	limes	pears
cherries	mangoes	pineapples
figs	melons	plums
grapefruit	nectarines	rhubarb (actually not a fruit, but a stem)
grapes	oranges	

Canned and frozen	Dried	Candied and glacé	Other processed fruits
apples, sliced	apricots	cherries	apricot glaze or coating
apricots, halves	currants (actually very small raisins)	citron	jams, jellies, and preserves
blueberries		figs	prepared pie fillings
cherries, both sour and sweet	dates	fruitcake mix	
peaches, slices and halves	figs	lemon peel	
pineapple, rings, chunks, nibs, crushed, juice	raisins, light and dark	orange peel	
strawberries	prunes	pineapple	

NUTS

Most nuts are available whole, halved, or broken or chopped. Because they are high in oil, all nuts can become rancid. Store them tightly closed in a cool, dark place.

Almonds   The most important nut in the bakeshop. Available natural (skin on) and blanched (skin off) in many forms: whole, split, slivered, chopped, ground (almond flour).

Brazil nuts

Cashews

Chestnuts   Must be cooked. Forms used in bakeshops are purée and glacé (in syrup).

Coconut   Sweetened coconut is used primarily for cake decoration.

Unsweetened coconut is used as an ingredient in a great variety of goods, such as cookies, macaroons, cakes, and fillings. Many types are available, based on the size of the individual grains, flakes, or shreds. The smallest types are *extra fine,* which is about the texture of granulated sugar, and *macaroon,* about the texture of cornmeal. Large sizes include *short* and *long shred, chip,* and *flake.*

Hazelnuts   Best if toasted before use. Also available ground (hazelnut flour or meal).

Macadamia nuts

Pecans   More expensive than walnuts. Used in premium goods.

Peanuts

Pine nuts or *pignoli*   A small kernel that is usually toasted to enhance flavor. Especially important in Italian pastries.

Pistachios   Often used in decorations because of the attractive green color of the kernel.

Walnuts   One of the most important nuts in the bakeshop, along with almonds and hazelnuts.

NUT PRODUCTS

Almond paste   An expensive but highly versatile nut paste used in a variety of cakes, pastries, cookies, and fillings. It is made from two parts finely ground almonds and one part sugar, plus enough moisture to bring it to the proper consistency.

Kernel paste   A product similar to almond paste, but less expensive. It is made from apricot kernels, which have a strong almondlike flavor.

Macaroon paste   This product stands between almond paste and kernel paste in that it is made from a blend of almonds and apricot kernels.

Marzipan   Essentially a sweetened almond paste, used in decorative and confectionery work. This product can be purchased or made in the bakeshop from almond paste.

Praline paste   A confectionery paste made from almonds and/or hazelnuts and caramelized sugar, all ground to a paste. It is used as a flavoring for icings, fillings, pastries, and creams.

CHOCOLATE AND COCOA

Chocolate and cocoa are derived from cocoa or cacao beans. When the beans are fermented, roasted, and ground, the resulting product is called *chocolate liquor,* which contains a white or yellowish fat called *cocoa butter.*

Much more information on the characteristics of chocolate and on handling chocolate can be found in chapter 20, which is completely devoted to this specialty. The brief summary of chocolate products in this chapter is an overview of those used in the bakeshop.

Cocoa

Cocoa is the dry powder that remains after part of the cocoa butter is removed from chocolate liquor. *Dutch process cocoa,* or *dutched cocoa,* is processed with an alkali. It is slightly darker, smoother in flavor, and more easily dissolved in liquids than is natural cocoa.

Natural cocoa is somewhat acidic. When it is used in such products as cakes, it is possible to use baking soda (which reacts with acid) as part of the leavening power.

Dutched cocoa, on the other hand, is generally neutral or even slightly alkaline. Therefore, it does not react with baking soda (see table below). Instead, baking powder is used as the sole leavening agent. If you are substituting dutched for natural cocoa, you must increase the baking powder by 1 oz (30 g) for each ½ oz (15 g) of soda omitted.

If not enough soda is used in chocolate products, the color of the finished product may range from light tan to dark brown, depending on the quantity used. If too much is used, the color will be reddish brown. This color is desired in devil's-food cakes, but it may not be wanted in other products. When switching from one kind of cocoa to another, you may have to adjust the soda in your recipes.

Baking Soda Needed to Balance the Acidity of Typical Cocoa Products

	Amount of Baking Soda per lb	Amount of Baking Soda per kg
Natural cocoa	1.25 oz	80 g
Dutched cocoa	0	0
Bitter chocolate	0.8 oz	50 g
Sweet chocolate	0.4 oz	25 g

Bitter Chocolate

Bitter or unsweetened chocolate is straight chocolate liquor. It contains no sugar and has a strongly bitter taste. Because it is molded in blocks, it is also referred to as *block cocoa* or *cocoa block.* It is used to flavor items that have other sources of sweetness.

In some less expensive brands, some of the cocoa butter may be replaced by another fat.

Sweet Chocolate

Sweet chocolate is bitter chocolate with the addition of sugar and cocoa butter in various proportions. If the percentage of sugar is low, sweetened chocolate may be called *semisweet* or, with even less sugar, *bittersweet.* Both of these products must contain at least 35% chocolate liquor, and their sugar content ranges from 35 to 50%. A product labeled *sweet chocolate* may contain as little as 15% chocolate liquor. Do not confuse sweet chocolate with milk chocolate (described below). In this book, when sweet chocolate is specified in a recipe, any sweetened chocolate may be used, although the results will, of course, vary. Bittersweet chocolate is specified if a good grade of chocolate with a high chocolate liquor content is essential for the best results.

Because sweet chocolate has only half the chocolate content of bitter chocolate, it is usually not economical to add it to products that are already highly sweetened because twice as much will be needed. For example, it is better to use bitter chocolate when making chocolate fondant from plain white fondant.

Good-quality chocolate products—including not only dark chocolate but also milk chocolate and white chocolate (see below)—are often called *couverture,* which means "coating" in French. When couverture is used to coat candies, cookies, and other products, the chocolate must be prepared by a process called *tempering.* This involves carefully melting the chocolate without letting it get too warm, then bringing the temperature back down to a certain level. The process requires a fair amount of skill. See page 537 for procedures.

Less expensive chocolates, which have part of the cocoa butter replaced by other fats, are easier to handle and don't require tempering. However, they do not have the flavor and eating qualities of good chocolate. These products are sold under such names as *cookie coating, cake coating, baking chocolate,* and *coating chocolate.* Do not confuse coating chocolate with couverture. These two products are entirely different, even though couverture means "coating." It would be less confusing if this lower-quality chocolate were referred to only as *baking chocolate,* without using the word *coating.*

Milk Chocolate

Milk chocolate is sweet chocolate to which milk solids have been added. It is usually used as a coating chocolate and in various confections. It is seldom melted and then incorporated in batters because it contains a relatively low proportion of chocolate liquor.

Cocoa Butter

Cocoa butter is the fat that is pressed out of chocolate liquor when cocoa is processed. Its main use in the bakeshop is to thin melted couverture to a proper consistency.

White Chocolate

White chocolate consists of cocoa butter, sugar, and milk solids. It is used primarily in confectionery. Some inexpensive brands, in which another fat is substituted for the cocoa butter, don't deserve the name chocolate at all, as they contain neither chocolate nor any of its components.

SUBSTITUTING COCOA AND CHOCOLATE

Because cocoa is the same as bitter chocolate, only with less cocoa butter, it is often possible to substitute one product for the other. Shortening is usually used to take the place of the missing fat. However, various fats behave differently in baking. Regular shortening, for example, has about twice the shortening power of cocoa butter, so only half as much is needed in many products, such as cakes. The procedures below take this difference into account.

Because of these varying factors, as well as the different baking properties of cakes, cookies, and other products, it is recommended that you test-bake a small batch when making a substitution in a formula. You can then make additional adjustments, if necessary. *No single substitution ratio is adequate for all purposes.*

ᚱrocedure for Substituting Natural Cocoa in Place of Bitter Chocolate

1. Multiply the weight of the chocolate by ⅝. The result is the amount of cocoa to use.

2. Subtract the weight of the cocoa from the original weight of chocolate. Divide this difference by 2. The result is the amount of shortening to add to the formula.

Example: Replace 1 lb chocolate with natural cocoa.

$$\tfrac{5}{8} \times 16 \text{ oz} = 10 \text{ oz cocoa}$$

$$\frac{16 \text{ oz} - 10 \text{ oz}}{2} = \frac{6 \text{ oz}}{2} = 3 \text{ oz shortening}$$

ᚱrocedure for Substituting Bitter Chocolate for Natural Cocoa

1. Multiply the weight of the cocoa by ⅘. The result is the amount of chocolate to use.

2. Subtract the weight of cocoa from the weight of chocolate. Divide by 2. Reduce the weight of shortening in the mix by this amount.

Example: Substitute bitter chocolate for 1 lb natural cocoa.

$$\tfrac{8}{5} \times 16 \text{ oz} = 26 \text{ oz chocolate (rounded off)}$$

$$\frac{26 \text{ oz} - 16 \text{ oz}}{2} = \frac{10}{2} = 5 \text{ oz } \textit{less} \text{ shortening}$$

Starch Content of Cocoa

Cocoa contains starch, which tends to absorb moisture in a batter. Consequently, when cocoa is added to a mix—for example, to change a yellow cake to a chocolate cake—the quantity of flour is reduced to compensate for this added starch. Exact adjustments will vary depending on the product. However, the following may be used as a rule of thumb:

Reduce the flour by ⅜ (37.5%) of the weight of cocoa added.

Thus, if 1 lb of cocoa is added, the flour is reduced by 6 oz. Or, if 400 g cocoa is added, reduce the flour by 150 g.

Chocolate, of course, also contains starch. When melted chocolate is added to fondant, for example, the fondant gets stiffer because of this starch and usually requires thinning. Often, however, the drying effect of the starch is balanced by the tenderizing effect of the cocoa butter. Methods of incorporating both chocolate and cocoa in various products are discussed in appropriate chapters.

SALT, SPICES, AND FLAVORINGS

SALT

Salt plays a very important role in baking. It is more than just a seasoning or flavor enhancer. It also has these functions:

- Salt strengthens gluten structure and makes it more stretchable. Thus, it improves the texture of breads.
- Salt inhibits yeast growth. It is therefore important for controlling fermentation in bread doughs and preventing the growth of undesirable wild yeasts.

For these reasons, the quantity of salt in a formula must be carefully controlled. If too much salt is used, fermentation and proofing are slowed down. If not enough salt is used, fermentation proceeds too rapidly. The yeast uses up too much of the sugar in the dough and, consequently, the crust doesn't brown well. Other results of overfermentation are described in chapter 3.

Because of the effect of salt on yeast, never add salt directly to the water in which yeast is softened.

SPICES

Spices are plant or vegetable substances used to flavor foods. Plant parts used as spices include seeds, flower buds (such as cloves), roots (such as ginger), and bark (such as cinnamon). Spices are generally whole or ground. Ground spices lose their flavor rapidly, so it is important to have fresh spices always on hand. Keep them tightly sealed in a cool, dark, dry place.

Because a small amount of spice usually has a great deal of flavoring power, it is important to weigh spices carefully and accurately. A quarter ounce too much of nutmeg, for example, could make a product inedible. In most cases, it is better to use too little than too much.

The following are the most important spices and seeds in the bakeshop:

- allspice
- anise
- caraway
- cardamom
- cinnamon
- cloves
- ginger

- mace
- nutmeg
- poppy seeds
- sesame seeds
- zest of lemon and orange (the colored, outer part of the peel)

VANILLA

Vanilla is the most important flavoring in the pastry shop. The source of the flavor is the ripened, partially dried fruit of a tropical orchid. This fruit, called *vanilla bean* or *vanilla pod,* is readily available, but at a high price. In spite of their cost, vanilla beans are valued by pastry chefs for making the finest quality pastries and dessert sauces and fillings.

There are several ways of flavoring products directly with vanilla beans. The simplest is simply to add one to a liquid when the liquid is heated, allowing the flavors to be extracted. The bean is then removed. For a stronger flavor, split the bean lengthwise before adding it. Then, when the bean is removed, scrape out the tiny black seeds from the inside of the pod and return them to the liquid.

Vanilla beans can also be used to flavor items that are not heated, such as whipped cream. Simply split the bean lengthwise, scrape out the seeds, and add them to the preparation.

A more common and economical way of flavoring with vanilla is to use *vanilla extract.* Vanilla extract is made by dissolving the flavoring elements of vanilla beans in an alcohol solution. To use, simply add the indicated quantity of the liquid as directed in the recipe.

If a recipe calls for vanilla beans, there is no exact equivalent if you must substitute vanilla extract. This is because the strength of the flavor that is extracted from the bean depends on many factors, such as how long it was left in the liquid, whether or not it was split, and so on. However, a rule of thumb is to substitute $\frac{1}{2}$ to 1 teaspoon (2.5 to 5 mL) of extract for each vanilla bean.

EXTRACTS AND EMULSIONS

Extracts are flavorful oils and other substances dissolved in alcohol. These include vanilla, lemon, bitter almond, cinnamon, and coffee. Coffee extract can be approximated if it is not available. Dissolve 5 oz (150 g) instant coffee powder in 12 oz (360 g) water.

Emulsions are flavorful oils mixed with water with the aid of emulsifiers such as vegetable gums. Lemon and orange are the most frequently used emulsions. Their flavor is strong. For example, it takes less lemon emulsion than lemon extract to give the same flavor.

Flavorings in general may be divided into two categories: natural and artificial. Natural flavorings are usually more expensive but have a superior flavor. Because flavorings and spices are used in small quantities, it is not much more expensive to use the best quality. Trying to save a few pennies on a cake by using inferior flavorings is false economy.

ALCOHOLS

Various alcoholic beverages are useful flavoring ingredients in the pastry shop. These include sweet alcohols, often called *liqueurs,* nonsweet alcohols, and wines.

Many liqueurs are fruit flavored. The most important of these are orange (including Cointreau, Grand Marnier, and Triple Sec) and cassis or blackcurrant. Other important flavors are bitter almond (amaretto), chocolate (crème de cacao), mint (crème de menthe), and coffee (crème de café, Kahlúa, Tía Maria).

Nonsweet alcohols include rum, cognac, kirschwasser (a colorless brandy made from cherries), and Calvados (a brandy made from apples).

The two most important wines are both sweet wines, Marsala (from Sicily) and Madeira (from the Portuguese island of the same name).

▶ TERMS FOR REVIEW

hard wheat	cake flour	glucose	creaming
soft wheat	pastry flour	malt syrup	foaming
strong flour	whole wheat flour	emulsion	gelatin
weak flour	bran flour	regular shortening	pectin
bran	rye meal	emulsified shortening	almond paste
germ	rye blend	margarine	kernel paste
endosperm	sucrose	crème fraîche	chocolate liquor
extraction rate	invert sugar	leavening	couverture
straight flour	granulated sugar	fermentation	cocoa butter
patent flour	confectioners' sugar	chemical leavener	cocoa
bread flour	brown sugar	single- and double-acting	dutched cocoa
clear flour	molasses	baking powder	extract
diastase	corn syrup	baking ammonia	emulsion

▶ QUESTIONS FOR REVIEW

1. Why is white wheat flour used in rye breads? In whole wheat breads? Some bakeries in Europe produce a kind of pumpernickel bread with 100% rye flour. What would you expect its texture to be like?

2. Describe how to distinguish bread, pastry, and cake flours by touch and sight.

3. Why does white flour have better keeping qualities than whole wheat flour?

4. What is the importance of aging in the production of flour? How is this accomplished in modern flour milling?

5. What is clear flour? What products is it used for?

6. List four functions of sugars in baked foods.

7. What is invert sugar? What properties make it useful in baking?

8. True or false: 10X sugar is one of the purest forms of sucrose. Explain your answer.

9. What is the difference between regular and emulsified shortening? Between cake margarine and pastry margarine?

10. What are some advantages and disadvantages in using butter as the fat in pie dough?

11. List six functions of eggs in baked goods.

12. What is the difference between single-acting and double-acting baking powders? Which is most frequently used, and why?

13. Explain how to use sheet gelatin in a recipe. Explain how to substitute powdered gelatin for sheet gelatin.

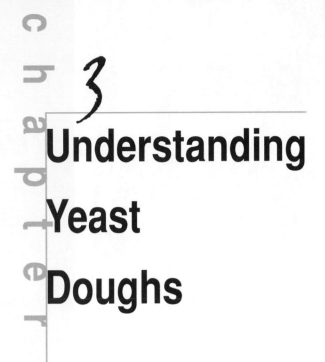

chapter 3

Understanding Yeast Doughs

In its simplest form, bread is nothing more than a baked dough made of flour and water and leavened by yeast. In fact, some hard-crusted French breads contain only these ingredients, plus salt. Other kinds of bread contain additional ingredients, including sugar, shortening, milk, eggs, and flavorings. But flour, water, and yeast are still the basic building blocks of all breads.

Yet, for something that seems so simple, bread can be one of the most exacting and complex products to make. Success in bread making depends largely on your understanding of two basic principles: gluten development, which was discussed in chapter 1, and yeast fermentation, which has already been touched on and is described in greater detail here.

This chapter focuses on the basic procedures in the production of many kinds of yeast products. Special attention is given to mixing methods and to control of fermentation. In chapter 4, these procedures are applied to specific formulas.

After reading this chapter, you should be able to:

■ List and describe the twelve basic steps in the production of yeast goods.

■ Explain the three basic mixing methods used for yeast doughs.

■ Understand and control the factors affecting dough fermentation.

■ Recognize and correct faults in yeast products.

YEAST PRODUCT TYPES

Although all yeast doughs are made according to essentially the same basic principles, it is useful to divide yeast products into categories such as the following:

LEAN DOUGH PRODUCTS

A lean dough is one that is low in fat and sugar.

- Hard-crusted breads and rolls, including French and Italian breads, kaiser rolls and other hard rolls, and pizza. These are the leanest of all bread products.

- Other white and whole wheat breads and dinner rolls. These have a higher fat and sugar content and sometimes also contain eggs and milk solids. Because they are slightly richer, they generally have soft crusts.

- Breads made with other grains. Rye breads are the most common. Many varieties of rye breads are produced, with light or dark flours or with pumpernickel flour, and with various flavorings, especially molasses and caraway seeds.

RICH DOUGH PRODUCTS

There is no exact dividing line between rich and lean doughs but, in general, rich doughs are those that contain higher proportions of fat, sugar, and sometimes eggs.

- Nonsweet breads and rolls, including rich dinner rolls and brioche. These have a high fat content, but their sugar content is low enough to allow them to be served as dinner breads. Brioche dough, made with a high proportion of butter and eggs, is especially rich.

- Sweet rolls, including coffee cakes and many breakfast and tea rolls. These have high fat and sugar content and usually contain eggs. They generally have a sweet filling or topping.

ROLLED-IN YEAST DOUGH PRODUCTS

Rolled-in doughs are those in which a fat is incorporated into the dough in many layers by using a rolling and folding procedure. The alternating layers of fat and dough give the baked product a flaky texture.

- Nonsweet rolled-in dough: croissants
- Sweet rolled-in doughs: Danish pastry

STEPS IN YEAST DOUGH PRODUCTION

There are twelve basic steps in the production of yeast breads. These steps are generally applied to all yeast products, with variations depending on the particular product.

1. Scaling ingredients   **7.** Benching

2. Mixing   **8.** Makeup and panning

3. Fermentation   **9.** Proofing

4. Punching   **10.** Baking

5. Scaling   **11.** Cooling

6. Rounding   **12.** Storing

As you can see, mixing ingredients into a dough is only one part of a complex procedure.

This section describes each of these twelve steps, including the basic procedures. In the next sections, dough making and fermentation are discussed in greater detail. Specific makeup procedures are included with the formulas in chapters 4 and 5.

SCALING INGREDIENTS

All ingredients must be weighed accurately.

Water, milk, and eggs may be measured by volume. They are scaled at one pint per pound, or one kilogram per liter. However, if quantities are large, it is more accurate to weigh these liquids (see p. 5).

Special care must be taken when measuring spices and other ingredients used in very small quantities. This is particularly important with salt, which affects the rate of fermentation (see p. 45).

MIXING

Mixing yeast doughs has three main purposes:

* To combine all ingredients into a uniform, smooth dough.
* To distribute the yeast evenly throughout the dough.
* To develop the gluten.

Three principal mixing methods are used for yeast doughs: the straight dough method, the modified straight dough method, and the sponge method (also called the sponge-and-dough method).

Straight Dough Method

In its simplest form, the straight dough method consists of only one step: Combine all ingredients in the mixing bowl and mix. Many bakers make good-quality products by using this procedure. However, the yeast may not be evenly distributed in the dough. It is therefore safer to mix the yeast separately with a little of the water.

Procedure: Straight Dough Mixing Method for Yeast Products

1. Soften the yeast in a little of the water.

    Fresh yeast: Mix with about twice its weight in water, or more.

    Ideal water temperature: 100°F (38°C).

    Active dry yeast: Mix with about four times its weight in water.

    Ideal water temperature: 105°F (40°C).

2. Combine the remaining ingredients, including the rest of the water, in the mixing bowl. Add the dissolved yeast, taking care not to let it come in contact with the salt.

3. Mix to a smooth, developed dough.

Modified Straight Dough Method

For rich sweet doughs, the straight dough method is modified to ensure even distribution of the fat and sugar.

Procedure: Modified Straight Dough Method

1. Soften the yeast in part of the liquid, using a separate container.

2. Combine the fat, sugar, salt, milk solids, and flavorings and mix until well combined, but do not whip until light.

3. Add the eggs gradually, as fast as they are absorbed.

4. Add the liquid and mix briefly.

5. Add the flour and yeast. Mix to a smooth dough.

Procedure: Sponge Method

1. Combine the liquid, the yeast, and part of the flour (and, sometimes, part of the sugar). Mix into a thick batter or soft dough. Let ferment until double in bulk.

2. Punch down and add the rest of the flour and the remaining ingredients. Mix to a uniform, smooth dough.

Sponge Method

Sponge doughs are prepared in two stages. This procedure gives the yeast action a head start.

There are many variations of this procedure. Part of the liquid is occasionally reserved for step 2. The sponge sometimes incorporates a sour starter, which is, essentially, an older sponge. Frequently, the sponge is fermented until it expands as much as possible and falls back upon itself. Sourdoughs are discussed in more detail later in this chapter.

Mixing Times and Speeds

The first two purposes of mixing—combining the ingredients into a dough and distributing the yeast—are accomplished during the first part of this step. The remaining time is necessary to develop the gluten. Overmixed and undermixed doughs have poor volume and texture (review Gluten Development, p. 12).

Mixing times given in formulas in this book are *guidelines only.* You must learn to tell by sight and feel when a dough is thoroughly mixed. This can be done only through experience. A properly developed dough feels smooth and elastic. A lean dough should not be sticky.

Mixing speeds, too, should be taken as guidelines rather than as firm instructions. Small mixers, whose motors and gears are not as strong as those of larger mixers, can be damaged if they are run at too high a speed with stiff bread doughs. In such cases, a lower speed than the one indicated in the formula should be used. For the same reason, batches of stiff dough should be kept small. Too large a batch puts excessive strain on the machine.

Follow the recommendations of the mixer manufacturer with regard to mixing times and batch sizes; manufacturers' recommendations should take priority over the instructions in this book. If a slower speed is used, extend the mixing time as necessary to obtain a properly mixed dough. Depending on the mixer, developing a dough at first or slow speed requires approximately twice as much time as at second speed.

Rich doughs are generally undermixed slightly because a greater tenderness is desired for these products. Rye breads are also mixed less because of their weaker gluten, which tears easily.

Overmixing is a common error in bread making. Gluten that is developed too long has stretched nearly as far as it can and loses its elasticity. Then it tears instead of stretches, and molding is more difficult. The texture and volume of overmixed products are less desirable.

Salt, used in proper quantities, helps alleviate this problem because it makes gluten stronger and more elastic.

FERMENTATION

Fermentation is the process by which yeast acts on the sugars and starches in the dough to produce carbon dioxide gas (CO_2) and alcohol. The action of the yeast is described in chapter 2 (p. 36).

Gluten becomes smoother and more elastic during fermentation, so it stretches farther and holds more gas. An underfermented dough will not develop proper volume and the texture of the product will be coarse. A dough that ferments too long or at too high a temperature becomes sticky, hard to work, and slightly sour. An underfermented dough is called a *young dough.* An overfermented dough is called an *old dough.*

Doughs with weak gluten, such as rye doughs and rich doughs, are usually underfermented or "taken to the bench young."

Yeast action continues until the yeast cells are killed when the temperature of the dough reaches 140°F (60°C) in the oven. It is important to be aware that fermentation continues during the next steps in yeast dough production—punching, scaling, rounding, benching, and makeup or molding. Failure to allow for this time may result in overfermented doughs. Doughs that are to be made into rolls and loaves requiring a great deal of makeup time should be slightly underfermented to prevent the dough from being too old by the time makeup is completed.

More detailed information on dough making and on controlling fermentation is given in the sections beginning on page 59.

PUNCHING

Punching is *not* hitting the dough with your fist. It is a method of deflating the dough that *expels carbon dioxide, redistributes the yeast* for further growth, *relaxes the gluten,* and *equalizes the temperature* throughout the dough.

Additional fermentation and punching may or may not be necessary, depending on the product.

Procedure for Fermenting Yeast Dough

Place the dough in a container large enough to allow for expansion of the dough. Cover the container and let the dough rise at a temperature of about 80°F (27°C) or at the temperature indicated in the specific formula. Ideally, the fermentation temperature is the same as the temperature of the dough when it is taken from the mixer.

If proper containers are not available or if humidity is too low to prevent a crust from forming on the dough, you may oil the surface of the dough lightly.

Fermentation is complete when the dough is doubled in volume. A dent remains or fills very slowly after the fingers are pressed lightly into the top of the dough if fermentation is complete. If the dough springs back, fermentation is not complete.

Procedure for Punching Dough

Pull up the dough on all sides, fold it over the center, and press down. Then turn the dough upside down in the container.

SCALING

Using a baker's scale, divide the dough into pieces of the same weight, according to the product being made.

During scaling, allowance is made for weight loss due to evaporation of moisture in the oven. This weight loss is approximately 10 to 13% of the weight of the dough. Allow an extra $1\frac{1}{2}$ to 2 ounces of dough for each 1 pound of baked bread, or 50 to 65 grams per 500 grams.

Actual baking loss depends on baking time, size of the unit, and whether it is baked in a pan or freestanding.

Scaling should be done rapidly and efficiently to avoid overfermenting the dough.

If a dough divider is used to make rolls, the dough is scaled into *presses,* which are then divided into 36 equal pieces (see p. 90). For example, if $1\frac{1}{3}$-ounce rolls are desired, the presses should be scaled at 3 lb ($36 \times 1\frac{1}{3}$ oz), plus 6 oz to allow for baking loss. Presses are rounded, relaxed, and divided; the divided units may or may not be rounded again, depending on the product.

ROUNDING

After scaling, the pieces of dough are shaped into smooth, round balls. This procedure forms a kind of skin by stretching the gluten on the outside of the dough into a smooth layer. Rounding simplifies the later shaping of the dough and also helps retain gases produced by the yeast.

Your instructor will demonstrate rounding techniques. Machines are also available that divide and round portions of dough automatically.

BENCHING, BENCH PROOFING, OR INTERMEDIATE PROOFING

Rounded portions of dough are allowed to rest for 10 to 20 minutes. This relaxes the gluten to make shaping the dough easier. Also, fermentation continues during this time.

In large operations, the rounded dough is placed in special proofers for this rest. Smaller operations place the dough in boxes that are stacked on one another to keep the dough covered. Or the dough may simply be placed on the workbench and covered—hence the term *benching.*

MAKEUP AND PANNING

The dough is shaped into loaves or rolls and then placed in pans or on baking sheets. *Hearth breads*—breads that are baked directly on the bottom of the oven—may be placed in floured baskets or other molds after makeup.

Proper makeup or molding is of critical importance to the finished baked product. All gas bubbles should be expelled during molding. Bubbles left in the dough will result in large air holes in the baked product.

For both pan breads and hearth breads, the seam must be centered on the bottom to avoid splitting during baking. For units baked in pans, the pan size must be matched to the weight of the dough. Too little or too much dough will result in a poorly shaped loaf.

Breads and rolls take a great many forms. Many shapes and techniques are presented in the next two chapters.

PROOFING

Proofing is a continuation of the process of yeast fermentation that increases the volume of the shaped dough. Bakers use two different terms so they can distinguish between fermentation of the mixed dough and proofing of the made-up product before baking. Proofing temperatures are generally higher than fermentation temperatures.

Underproofing results in poor volume and dense texture. Overproofing results in coarse texture and some loss of flavor.

French bread is generally given a long proof to create its characteristic open texture. Its strong gluten withstands the extra stretching of a long proof.

Rich doughs are slightly underproofed because their weaker gluten structure does not withstand too much stretching.

BAKING

As you recall from chapter 1, many changes take place in the dough during baking. The most important changes are:

1. *Oven spring,* which is the rapid rising in the oven due to production and expansion of trapped gases as a result of the oven heat. The yeast is very active at first but is killed when the temperature inside the dough reaches 140°F (60°C).

2. Coagulation of proteins and gelatinization of starches. In other words, the product becomes firm and holds its shape.

3. Formation and browning of the crust.

In order to control the baking process, the following factors should be considered.

Oven Temperature and Baking Time

Temperatures must be adjusted for the product being baked. At the proper temperature, the inside of the unit becomes completely baked at the same time that the crust achieves the desired color. Therefore:

1. Large units are baked at a lower temperature and for a longer time than small rolls spaced apart.

2. Rich doughs and sweet doughs are baked at a lower temperature because their fat, sugar, and milk content makes them brown faster.

3. French breads made with no added sugar and a long fermentation require very high temperatures to achieve the desired crust color.

- Popular American lean breads are baked at 400° to 425°F (205° to 220°C).
- Some French breads are baked at 425° to 475°F (220° to 245°C).
- Rich products are baked at 350° to 400°F (175° to 205°C).

A golden-brown crust color is the normal indication of doneness. Loaves that are done sound hollow when thumped.

Washes

Many, if not most, yeast products are brushed with a liquid, called a *wash,* just before baking. The most common washes are as follows:

Procedure for Proofing Yeast Dough Items

1. For lean yeast doughs, place the panned products in a proof box at 80° to 85°F (27° to 30°F) and 70 to 80% humidity, or as indicated in the formula. Proof until double in bulk.

   Rich doughs, especially rolled-in doughs, are usually proofed at a lower temperature (77°F or 25°C) so that the butter does not melt out of the dough.

   Avoid using too much steam. This weakens the surface of the dough and causes uneven proofing.

   If a proof box is not available, come as close to these conditions as you can by covering the products to retain moisture and setting them in a warm place.

2. Test proof by sight (the unit doubles in bulk) and by touch. When touched *lightly,* properly proofed dough springs back slowly. If it is still firm and elastic, it needs more proofing. If the dent remains in the dough, the dough is probably overproofed.

1. *Water* is used primarily for hard-crusted products, such as French bread. Like steam in the oven (see below), the water helps keep the crust from drying too quickly and thus becoming too thick.

2. *Starch paste* is used primarily for rye breads. In addition to keeping the crust from drying too quickly, the starch paste helps give a shine to the crust.

   To make a starch paste, mix 1 ounce of light rye flour with 1 quart of water (60 g rye per 500 mL water). Bring to a boil while stirring. Cool. If necessary, thin with water to the consistency of cream.

3. *Egg wash* is used to give a shiny brown crust to soft breads and rolls and to rich doughs and Danish. It is made by mixing beaten eggs with water or, sometimes, with milk. Proportions may vary greatly depending on how strong a wash is desired.

Cutting or Scoring

A break on the side of the loaf is caused by continued rising after the crust is formed. To allow for this expansion, the tops of hard-crusted breads are cut before baking. Slashes are made on the top of the loaf with a sharp knife or razor immediately before it is put into the oven. The pattern created by the cuts also contributes to the appearance of the bread.

Small rolls often bake completely without a break, so they are usually cut for the sake of appearance only.

Note: The term *docking* is often used for this procedure. However, many bakers feel that this term should be reserved for a different process—namely, the piercing or perforating of pastry and pie doughs. To avoid confusion, this book uses the terms *cutting* and *scoring* for the slashing of bread crusts, but you should be aware of the other term because you will hear it used.

Loading the Ovens

Proofed doughs are fragile until they become set by baking. They should be handled carefully when being loaded into the ovens, and they should not be disturbed during the first part of baking.

Breads and rolls are baked either directly on the bottom of the oven (hearth breads) or in pans.

1. *Hearth breads*   To load ovens, place the proofed units on a peel that is well dusted with cornmeal. Slide the peel into the oven. Then, with a quick snap, remove the peel, leaving the loaves or rolls in place. To remove baked items, quickly slide the peel under them and pull them out.

2. *Pan breads and rolls*   Freestanding items may be baked on sheet pans instead of on the hearth. Bakers generally refer to such breads and rolls as *hearth breads* even if they are not baked directly on the bottom of the oven. Sprinkle the pans with cornmeal to keep the units from sticking and to simulate the appearance of hearth-baked items. Pans may also be lined with silicone paper. Perforated sheet pans or screens are also available. These allow better air circulation and therefore permit more even browning.

   Sandwich loaves and other pan breads are, of course, baked in loaf pans or other appropriate pans. Details are given in the makeup section of chapter 4.

Steam

Hard-crusted breads are baked with steam injected into the ovens during the first part of the baking period. Rye breads also benefit from baking with steam for the first 10 minutes.

The steam helps keep the crust soft during the first part of baking so that the bread can expand rapidly and evenly. If steam were not used, the crust would begin forming earlier and thus would become thick and heavy. The steam also helps distribute the heat in the oven, further aiding oven spring. When the moisture of the steam reacts with the starches on the surface, some of the starches form dextrins. Then, when the steam is withdrawn, these dextrins, along with sugars in the dough, caramelize and turn brown. The result is a thin, crisp, glazed crust.

Rich doughs, those with higher fat or sugar content, do not form crisp crusts and are usually baked without steam.

COOLING

After baking, bread must be removed from pans and cooled on racks to allow the escape of the excess moisture and alcohol created during fermentation.

Small rolls spaced on baking sheets are often cooled on the pans when air circulation is adequate. On the other hand, if condensation is likely to make the bottoms of the rolls soggy, it is better to cool them on racks.

If soft crusts are desired, breads may be brushed with melted shortening before cooling.

Do not cool bread in a draft because the crust may crack.

STORING

Breads to be served within 8 hours may be left on racks. For longer storage, wrap cooled breads in moisture-proof bags to retard staling. Bread must be thoroughly cool before wrapping or moisture will collect inside the bags.

Wrapping and freezing maintains quality for longer periods. Refrigeration, on the other hand, increases staling.

Hard-crusted breads should not be wrapped (unless frozen) because the crusts will soften and become leathery.

TYPES OF DOUGH-MAKING PROCESSES

STRAIGHT DOUGH

In the typical small retail shop, most breads are mixed by the straight dough method—that is, all ingredients are mixed in one operation, as described on page 52. The dough is then given a bulk fermentation time (that is, until molding and proofing) of 1 to 2½ hours. This is called a *short-fermentation straight dough.*

A *no-time dough* is made with a large quantity of yeast, taken from the mixer at a higher temperature (up to 90°F/32°C), and given only a few minutes' rest before being scaled and made up. It is also given a shorter proof. This process should be used only in emergencies because the final product does not have a good texture and flavor.

Long-fermentation doughs are fermented for 5 or 6 hours or longer, sometimes overnight, at a temperature of 75°F (24°C) or lower. The advantage of this method is that the long, slow fermentation greatly enhances the flavor of the product. Some of the best European breads are made this way. The major disadvantage—beside being harder on the work schedule—is that the fermentation is harder to control because of fluctuations in temperature and other factors. Doughs often become overfermented. Therefore, this process is used much less today than in the past.

To avoid the problems of a long-fermentation straight dough but achieve the flavor created by a long fermentation, one can use the sponge method.

Sponge Processes

The sponge process involves a two-stage mixing method, as described on page 52. First, a sponge is made of water, flour, and yeast and is allowed to ferment. Then the dough is made by mixing in the remaining ingredients. The finished dough may be given a short fermentation or, if the sponge has had a long fermentation, it may be scaled immediately, like a no-time dough.

Advantages of the Sponge Method

- Shorter fermentation time for the finished dough.
- Scheduling flexibility. Sponges can usually be held longer than finished dough.
- Increased flavor, developed by the long fermentation of the sponge.
- Stronger fermentation of rich doughs. High sugar and fat content inhibits yeast growth. When the sponge method is used, most of the fermentation is completed before the fat and sugar are incorporated.
- Less yeast is needed, because it multiplies greatly during the sponge fermentation.

SOURDOUGHS

Before commercially prepared yeast was widely available, bread was often started by mixing flour and water and letting this mixture stand until wild airborne yeasts settled on it and began to ferment it. This *starter* was then used to leaven bread. A portion of the starter was saved, mixed with more flour and water, and set aside to leaven the next day's bread.

This starter is called a *natural sour* or *natural starter*. It is still widely used today. Because varieties of natural yeast differ from region to region, and because the characteristics of a natural sour depend on the variety of yeast, no two natural sours are alike. Even if a sour is brought from one region to another (for example, many visitors to San Francisco like to bring a sample of one of that city's famed natural sours back home), the sour will gradually change character because the yeasts in the new location apparently take over.

The sour is actually a kind of sponge, except that it is allowed to ferment until it becomes strongly acidic. It may be used in two ways:

- The sour is "built" by mixing in more flour and water and allowing it to ferment. The amounts of flour and water are determined by how much bread is to be produced. This building process may be repeated more than once in a production day, if a large quantity is needed. The completed sour is then used like a sponge in the production of the bread dough, except that a portion is saved for the next day's production. Additional yeast may or may not be added to the bread dough, depending on the desired fermentation time and the proportion of sour used.
- A small portion of sour may be added to a straight dough. In this case, it contributes little leavening power. Its purpose is primarily flavoring.

Chapter 4 includes three recipes for natural starters: Potato Sour, Yogurt Sour, and Apple Sour. The success of these recipes depends, in part, on local conditions. If the bakeshop or kitchen where they are made does not have sufficient natural yeast in the air, they won't work well.

Because it may be difficult to get a good sourdough starter going, a quicker approach is to start a sour with baker's yeast. This type of sour is called a *yeast starter.* Once the sour starter has fermented, it is maintained the same way as a natural sour—that is, some of the starter is used for each day's production and the remaining starter is refreshed with additional flour and water.

Alternatively, a fresh batch of yeast starter can be made for the following day's production. Although the starter will not become very sour in less than 24 hours, the long fermentation contributes to flavor.

Chapter 4 contains two recipes for yeast starters. Basic Yeast Starter (p. 77) uses white wheat flour, while Rye Sour III is a similar formula using rye flour. These starters may be made fresh each day, or they may be maintained the same way as a natural sour, as described above. Chapter 4 also contains two additional formulas for rye sours.

Still another process used by many bakers is to simply save a small piece of dough from the day's production and mix it into the next day's dough. Although this, of course, is not a sour, it does contribute to the flavor of the bread by incorporating a piece of dough that has had long fermentation. This process is, for all practical purposes, the same process as making a fresh yeast starter each day for the next day's bread. When a bread formula in this book calls for a yeast starter, the same quantity of old dough may be used instead.

Commercial sour cultures are available for bakers who do not wish to maintain sour cultures. Although these cultures do not add the same flavor as a naturally fermented sour, they have the advantage of convenience. They may be added as a flavoring ingredient to straight doughs or they may be used in place of, or in addition to, yeast to leaven a sponge. This sponge is then used like a fermented sour.

CONTROLLING FERMENTATION

Proper fermentation—that is, fermentation that produces a dough that is neither underripe (young) nor overripe (old)—requires a balance of time, temperature, and yeast quantity.

TIME

Fermentation times vary, so the time to punch the dough is indicated not by clock but by the appearance and feel of the dough. Fermentation times given in the formulas in this book are guidelines only.

To vary the fermentation time, you must control the dough temperature and the amount of yeast.

TEMPERATURE

Ideally, dough is fermented at the temperature at which it is taken from the mixer. Large bakeries have special fermentation rooms for controlling temper-

Procedure for Determining Water Temperature

1. Multiply the desired dough temperature by 3.

2. Add together the flour temperature and room temperature, plus 20°F (11°C) to allow for the friction caused by mixing (see *note*).

3. Subtract the result of step 2 from that of step 1. The difference is the required water temperature.

   Example: Dough temperature needed = 80°F

   > Flour temperature = 68°F
   >
   > Room temperature = 72°F
   >
   > Machine friction = 20°F
   >
   > Water temperature = ?
   >
   > 1. 80° × 3 = 240°
   >
   > 2. 68° + 72° + 20° = 160°
   >
   > 3. 240° − 160° = 80°

   Therefore, the water temperature should be 80°F.

   Note: This procedure is precise enough for most purposes in the small bakeshop. However, there are other complications, such as variations in machine friction, that you may want to consider if you wish to be even more exact. To make these calculations, see appendix 4.

ature and humidity, but small bakeshops and restaurant kitchens seldom have this luxury. If a short-fermentation process is used, however, the fermentation is completed before the dough is greatly affected by changes in shop temperature.

Water Temperature

Dough must be at the proper temperature, usually 78° to 80°F (25.5° to 26.7°C), in order to ferment at the desired rate. The temperature of the dough is affected by several factors:

- Shop temperature
- Flour temperature
- Water temperature

Of these, the water temperature is the easiest to control in the small bakeshop. Therefore, when the water is scaled, it should be brought to the required temperature. On cold days, it may have to be warmed, and on hot days, it may be necessary to use a mixture of crushed ice and water. Also, if a long fermentation is used, the dough temperature must be reduced in order to avoid overfermenting.

YEAST QUANTITY

If other conditions are constant, the fermentation time may be increased or decreased by decreasing or increasing the quantity of yeast (see procedure on page 61).

Small Batches

When very small quantities of dough—only a few pounds—are made, the dough is more likely to be affected by shop temperature. Thus, it may be necessary to slightly increase the yeast quantity in cool weather and slightly decrease it in hot weather.

OTHER FACTORS

The salt in the formula, the minerals in the water, and the use of dough conditioners or improvers affect the rate of fermentation. See page 45 for a discussion of salt and its effect on fermentation.

Water that is excessively soft lacks the minerals that ensure proper gluten development and dough fermentation. On the other hand, water that is very hard—that is, has high mineral content and, as a result, is alkaline—also inhibits the development of the dough. These conditions are more of a problem for lean doughs than for rich doughs. In most localities, small bakeshops can overcome these problems with the proper use of salt or, in areas with alkaline water, by adding a very small amount of a mild acid to the water. Various dough conditioners, buffers, and improvers that can correct these conditions are available from bakers' suppliers. Their use should be determined by local water conditions.

The richness of the dough must also be considered. Doughs high in fat or sugar ferment more slowly than lean doughs. This problem can be avoided by using a sponge instead of a straight dough.

Procedure for Modifying Yeast Quantities

1. Determine a factor by dividing the old fermentation time by the fermentation time desired.

2. Multiply this factor by the original quantity of yeast to determine the new quantity.

$$\frac{\text{old fermentation time}}{\text{new fermentation time}} \times \text{old yeast quantity} = \text{new yeast quantity}$$

Example: A formula requiring 12 oz yeast has a fermentation time of 2 hours at 80°F. How much yeast is needed to reduce the fermentation time to $1\frac{1}{2}$ hours?

$$\frac{\text{2 hours}}{\text{1.5 hours}} \times \text{12 oz yeast} = \text{16 oz yeast}$$

Caution: This procedure should be used within narrow limits only. An excessive increase or decrease in yeast quantities introduces many other problems and results in inferior products.

RETARDING

Retarding means slowing down the fermentation or proof of yeast doughs by refrigeration. This may be done in regular refrigerators or in special retarders that maintain a high humidity. If regular refrigerators are used, the product must be covered to prevent drying and the formation of a skin.

Retarded Fermentation

Dough to be retarded in bulk is usually given partial fermentation. It is then flattened out on sheet pans, covered with plastic wrap, and placed in the retarder. The layer of dough must not be too thick because the inside will take too long to chill and will overferment. When needed, the dough is allowed to warm before molding. Some doughs high in fat are made up while chilled so that they do not become too soft.

Retarded Proof

Made-up units to be retarded are made from young dough. After makeup, they are immediately placed in the retarder. When needed, they are allowed to warm and finish their proof, if necessary. They are then baked.

A valuable labor-saving tool for medium to large bakeshops is the *retarder-proofer.* As the name suggests, this equipment is a combination of freezer/retarder and proofer, with thermostats for both functions and with timers to automate the process. For example, the baker can make up a batch of rolls in the afternoon or evening and place them in the retarder-proofer with the controls set for retarding or freezing. The baker sets the timer for the proper hour the following morning and the machine automatically begins to raise the temperature, proofing the rolls so that they are ready to bake in time for breakfast.

BREAD FAULTS AND THEIR CAUSES

Because of the complexity of bread production, many things can go wrong. To remedy common bread faults, check the following troubleshooting guide for possible causes and correct your procedures.

Fault	Causes
Shape	
Poor volume	Too much salt
	Too little yeast
	Too little liquid
	Weak flour
	Under- or overmixing
	Oven too hot
Too much volume	Too little salt
	Too much yeast
	Too much dough scaled
	Overproofed
Poor shape	Too much liquid
	Flour too weak
	Improper molding or makeup
	Improper fermentation or proofing
	Too much oven steam
Split or burst crust	Overmixing
	Underfermented dough
	Improper molding—seam not on bottom
	Uneven heat in oven
	Oven too hot
	Insufficient steam
Texture and crumb	
Too dense or close-grained	Too much salt
	Too little liquid
	Too little yeast
	Underfermented
	Underproofed
Too coarse or open	Too much yeast
	Too much liquid
	Incorrect mixing time
	Improper fermentation
	Overproofed
	Pan too large
Streaked crumb	Improper mixing procedure
	Poor molding or makeup techniques
	Too much flour used for dusting

Fault	Causes
Poor texture or crumbly	Flour too weak
	Too little salt
	Fermentation time too long or too short
	Overproofed
	Baking temperature too low
Gray crumb	Fermentation time or temperature too high
Crust	
Too dark	Too much sugar or milk
	Underfermented dough
	Oven temperature too high
	Baking time too long
	Insufficient steam at beginning of baking
Too pale	Too little sugar or milk
	Overfermented dough
	Overproofed
	Oven temperature too low
	Baking time too short
	Too much steam in oven
Too thick	Too little sugar or fat
	Improper fermentation
	Baked too long or at wrong temperature
	Too little steam
Blisters on crust	Too much liquid
	Improper fermentation
	Improper shaping of loaf
Flavor	
Flat taste	Too little salt
Poor flavor	Inferior, spoiled, or rancid ingredients
	Poor bakeshop sanitation
	Under- or overfermented

▶ TERMS FOR REVIEW

lean dough	natural starter	punching	no-time dough
rich dough	yeast starter	rounding	sourdough
rolled-in dough	fermentation	oven spring	retarding
straight dough method	young dough	wash	retarder-proofer
sponge method	old dough	hearth bread	

▶ QUESTIONS FOR REVIEW

1. What are the main differences in ingredients between French bread and white sandwich bread?

2. Why is Danish pastry dough flaky?

3. What are the 12 steps in the production of yeast products? Explain each briefly.

4. What are the three major purposes of mixing yeast doughs?

5. Explain the differences in procedure between the straight dough method and the sponge method. How is the straight dough method sometimes modified for sweet doughs, and why is this necessary?

6. What are the purposes of punching a fermented dough?

7. How much French bread dough will you need if you want to make 16 loaves that weigh 12 oz each after baking?

8. List four advantages of the sponge method for mixing bread doughs.

9. What is the importance of water temperature in mixing yeast doughs?

10. Explain the difference between a natural starter and a yeast starter.

Lean Yeast Doughs

*T*he basic yeast dough production methods discussed in chapter 3 apply to the formulas presented in this chapter. Therefore, the methods are not repeated in detail for each formula. The basic procedures are indicated, and you should refer to the preceding chapter if you need to refresh your memory of the details.

The discussion of yeast doughs is divided into two chapters. This chapter presents a variety of lean dough products, representing a complete range of formula types, from basic white loaves and dinner rolls to sourdoughs to unusual artisan breads to popular specialty items like bagels, pita, focaccia, and crumpets. Chapter 5 completes the study of yeast products with a range of rich doughs, including Danish, brioche, and sweet roll doughs.

Large bakeries have machinery that automatically forms loaves and rolls of many types. In a small bakeshop, however, the baker still makes up most products by hand. Learning how to shape loaves, rolls, and pastries is an important part of the art and craft of fine baking.

INTRODUCTION TO HANDCRAFTED BREADS

After reading this chapter, you should be able to:

- Prepare lean straight doughs and sponge doughs.

- Prepare natural starters and yeast starters, and mix sourdoughs using them.

- Make up a variety of loaf and roll types using lean doughs.

- Prepare a variety of specialty bread items with nonstandard makeup and baking techniques, including English muffins, crumpets, and bagels.

Not many years ago, bread was somewhat of an afterthought in most restaurants, and there was not much variety or even attention to quality. In many cities today, however, fine restaurants vie with one another to serve the most interesting selections of fresh artisanal breads. Customers are often given a choice from among four, five, or even more types of bread. Handcrafted specialty breads are appearing in neighborhood bakeries, and everyone seems to have discovered the delights of sourdough.

Traditional formulas such as hard rolls, soft rolls, Italian bread, white and whole wheat loaf breads, and American-style rye bread form the core of this chapter. It is important to learn the basics of yeast dough production well, and this is easiest to do when you are working on familiar recipes without unusual techniques and exotic ingredients. Not only will you learn how mix basic yeast doughs but you will also practice making up a variety of loaf and roll types by hand to develop your manual skills. Then you can proceed with confidence to the specialty handcrafted items in this chapter. Working with sourdoughs, in particular, is more challenging than working with straight doughs, so your earlier practice and experience will benefit you.

The classic yeast dough formulas in this chapter are augmented in this edition with nearly 20 new formulas for a variety of specialty items. These include newly popular breads, such as olive bread, prosciutto bread, ciabatta, multigrain breads, and focaccia, and are joined by several new sourdough bread formulas, including a traditional French country bread or *pain de campagne.*

Making and fermenting dough is a craft distinct from making up rolls and loaves using these doughs. Each dough may be made into many types of loaves and rolls, and each makeup method may be applied to many formulas. Therefore, most makeup techniques—except for a few unique procedures for specialty items—are described in a section at the end of the chapter rather than repeated after every formula.

CRISP-CRUSTED BREAD FORMULAS

The crisp, thin crusts of French, Italian, and Vienna breads and of hard rolls are achieved by using formulas with little or no sugar and fat and by baking with steam. Because the crust is part of the attraction of these items, they are often made in long, thin shapes that increase the proportion of crust.

These breads are usually baked freestanding, either directly on the hearth or on sheet pans. The water content must be low enough that the units hold their shape in the oven.

There is no clear difference between French bread dough and Italian bread dough. Some sources say that French bread contains a little fat and sugar, while Italian bread does not. Other sources give Italian bread formulas that contain fat and sugar. Furthermore, breads containing neither of these ingredients are common in both France and Italy. Also, both Italy and France produce breads in many shapes, not only in the long, thin loaf shape familiar here.

In practice, French and Italian bread formulas in the United States are widely interchangeable. The best practice is to follow regional preferences and to produce good-quality products that are appealing to your customers.

To create the open-cell structure characteristic of French bread, give the loaves a very full proof before baking.

Two unusual breads are included in this section. Fougasse is a traditional shape from the French countryside. It is made with a basic French bread dough but is formed into a large, flat, ladder-shaped loaf and coated with olive oil. Ciabatta (its Italian name refers to its resemblance to a beat-up old slipper) is made with a very slack dough. Because it is so sticky, it is handled as little as possible and is simply deposited on sheet pans without being shaped into loaves. This gives it a very light, open texture.

Hard Rolls

For large-quantity measurements, see page 581.

Ingredients	U.S.		Metric	%
Water	12	oz	350 g	55
Yeast, fresh	0.75	oz	22 g	3.5
Bread flour	1 lb 6	oz	625 g	100
Salt	0.5	oz	14 g	2.25
Sugar	0.5	oz	14 g	2.25
Shortening	0.5	oz	14 g	2.25
Egg whites	0.5	oz	14 g	2.25
Total weight:	*2 lb 4*	*oz*	*1053 g*	*167%*

■ P r o c e d u r e

Mixing
Straight dough method
10 minutes at second speed (see p. 52)
Fermentation
About 1 hour at 80°F (27°C)
Makeup
See pages 91–94.
Baking
425°F (218°C) for loaves; 450°F (230°C) for rolls. Steam for first 10 minutes.

Vienna Bread

For large-quantity measurements, see page 581.

Ingredients	U.S.		Metric	%
Water	12	oz	350 g	55
Yeast, fresh	0.75	oz	22 g	3.5
Bread flour	1 lb 6	oz	625 g	100
Salt	0.5	oz	14 g	2.25
Sugar	0.6	oz	18 g	3
Malt syrup	0.25	oz	6 g	1
Oil	0.6	oz	18 g	3
Eggs	0.9	oz	25 g	4
Total weight:	*2 lb 5*	*oz*	*1078 g*	*171%*

■ P r o c e d u r e

Mixing
Straight dough method
10 minutes at second speed (see p. 52)
Fermentation
About 1 hour at 80°F (27°C)
Makeup
See pages 91–94.
Baking
425°F (218°C) for loaves; 450°F (230°C) for rolls. Steam for first 10 minutes.

Italian Bread

For large-quantity measurements, see page 581.

Ingredients	U.S.		Metric	%
Water	1 lb		425 g	57
Yeast, fresh		0.75 oz	20 g	2.75
Bread flour	1 lb 12	oz	750 g	100
Salt		0.5 oz	12 g	1.75
Malt syrup		0.13 oz (¾ tsp)	4 g	0.5
Total weight:	*2 lb 13*	*oz*	*1211 g*	*162%*

■ P r o c e d u r e

Mixing
Straight dough method
8–10 minutes at second speed (see p. 52).
Fermentation
1½ hours at 80°F (27°C) or 2 hours at 75°F (24°C)
Makeup
See pages 91–94.
Baking
425°F (218°C) for loaves; 450°F (230°C) for rolls.
Steam for first 10 minutes.

Variations

Whole Wheat Italian Bread
For large-quantity measurements, see page 581.

Use the following proportions of flour in the above formula.

Ingredients	U.S.	Metric	%
Whole wheat flour	12 oz	325 g	43
Bread flour	1 lb	425 g	57

Increase the water to 59–60% to allow for the extra absorption
by the bran. Mix 8 minutes.

Pizza
Add 2.5% vegetable oil or olive oil (0.63 oz/18 g) to Italian Bread formula. For dough to be retarded, also add
1% sugar (0.25 oz/8 g). Ferment, scale (see the table below), and round. After bench rest, sheet or roll out and
apply tomato sauce, cheese, and toppings. Bake without proofing.
Baking temperature: 550°F (290°C).

Scaling Guidelines for Pizza

	12-inch	14-inch	16-inch
Dough	10–12 oz	13–15 oz	18–20 oz
Tomato sauce	3 oz	4.5 oz	5.5 oz
Cheese	4 oz	5.5 oz	7.5 oz

French Bread (Straight Dough)

For large-quantity measurements, see page 582.

Ingredients	U.S.		Metric	%
Water	1 lb		425 g	57
Yeast, fresh		0.75 oz	20 g	2.75
Bread flour	1 lb 12	oz	750 g	100
Salt		0.5 oz	12 g	1.75
Malt syrup		0.13 oz	4 g	0.5
Sugar		0.5 oz	12 g	1.75
Shortening		0.5 oz	12 g	1.75
Total weight:	*2 lb 14*	*oz*	*1235 g*	*165%*

■ P r o c e d u r e

Mixing
Straight dough method
8–10 minutes at second speed (see p. 52)
Fermentation
1½ hours at 80°F (27°C) or 2 hours at 75°F (24°C)
Makeup
See pages 91–94.
Baking
425°F (218°C) for loaves; 450°F (230°C) for rolls. Steam for first 10 minutes.

Variations

Whole Wheat French Bread
For large-quantity measurements, see page 582.

Use the following proportions of flour in the above formula.

Ingredients	U.S.	Metric	%
Whole wheat flour	12 oz	325 g	43
Bread flour	1 lb	425 g	57

Increase the water to 59–60% to allow for the extra absorption by the bran. Mix 8 minutes.

French Bread (Sponge)

For large-quantity measurements, see page 582.

Ingredients	U.S.		Metric	%
Sponge				
Bread flour	8	oz	250 g	33
Water	8	oz	250 g	33
Yeast, fresh	0.5	oz	15 g	2
Malt syrup	0.25	oz	8 g	1
Dough				
Bread flour	1 lb		500 g	67
Water	6.5	oz	202 g	27
Salt	0.44	oz (2¼ tsp)	13 g	1.75
Total weight:	*2 lb 7*	*oz*	*1238 g*	*164%*

■ P r o c e d u r e

Mixing
Sponge method
Fermentation
Sponge: 4 hours at 75°F (24°C) or overnight at 65°F (18°C)
Dough: 30 minutes at 80°F (27°C)
Makeup
See pages 91–94.
Baking
425°F (218°C)

Variations

Country-Style French Bread
For large-quantity measurements, see page 582.

Use the following proportions of flour and water in the dough stage of the above formula.

Ingredients	U.S.		Metric	%
Clear or bread flour	6	oz	200 g	25
Whole wheat flour	10	oz	300 g	42
Water	7.25 oz		225 g	30

Make up the dough into round loaves.

Baguette

For large-quantity measurements, see page 582.

Ingredients	U.S.		Metric	%
Bread flour	2 lb 2	oz	1000 g	100
Salt	0.67	oz	20 g	2
Yeast, fresh	0.75	oz	25 g	2.5
Water	1 lb 4	oz	600 g	60
Total weight:	*3 lb 7*	*oz*	*1645 g*	*164%*

■ P r o c e d u r e

Mixing
Straight dough method
3–5 minutes at first speed
15 minutes at second speed (see p. 52)
Fermentation
1 hour at 80°F (27°C)
Makeup
See page 93. Scale at 11 oz (320 g).
Baking
475°F (250°C) for 20 minutes with steam

Variation

Fougasse
Scale dough at 18 oz (540 g). See page 94 for makeup.

An assortment of hearth breads: in back, ciabatta and fougasses; in center, two differently formed pains de camagne; in front, baguettes, French rye, and assorted dinner rolls

Cuban Bread

For large-quantity measurements, see page 582.

Ingredients	U.S.		Metric	%
Water	15	oz	465 g	62
Yeast, fresh	1	oz	30 g	4
Bread flour	1 lb 8	oz	750 g	100
Salt	0.5	oz	15 g	2
Sugar	1	oz	30 g	4
Total weight:	*2 lb 9*	*oz*	*1290 g*	*172%*

■ P r o c e d u r e

Mixing
Straight dough method
12 minutes at first speed
Fermentation
60 minutes at 80°F (27°C)
Makeup
Scale at 20 oz (625 g).
Round loaves (p. 93).
Score top with a cross.
Baking
400°F (200°C)

Ciabatta

For large-quantity measurements, see page 583.

Ingredients	U.S.		Metric	%
Sponge				
Water	1 lb 1	oz	480 g	72
Yeast, fresh	1	oz	30 g	4
Bread flour	1 lb		450 g	67
Virgin olive oil	6	oz	180 g	27
Dough				
Salt	0.5 oz		15 g	2
Bread flour	8	oz	220 g	33
Total weight:	*3 lb*		*1375 g*	*205%*

a.

b.

■ P r o c e d u r e

Mixing

Sponge method

1. Warm the water to about 100°F (37°C). Dissolve yeast in the warm water.

2. Add the yeast mixture to the flour for the sponge. Add the oil.

3. Mix to form a soft dough. Beat well for approximately 5 minutes or until the sponge starts to become smooth.

4. Cover and leave at room temperature until doubled in size, approximately 1 hour.

5. Stir down and add the ingredients for the dough. Beat for a few minutes to form a smooth dough, which will be very soft and sticky.

Fermentation

Cover and allow to ferment at room temperature until doubled in size, approximately 1 hour.

Makeup and Baking

1. Lightly oil sheet pans. Handling the fermented dough as little as possible, scale it into portions weighing about 18 oz (550 g). This is usually done by approximation to avoid having to handle the dough. Deposit the dough on a greased and floured sheet pan (a).

2. Shape very lightly into rough ovals or rectangles on the oiled pans (b). The dough will be very sticky; handle as little as possible.

3. Dust tops with extra flour. Proof at room temperature until the dough doubles in volume and the flour on the top starts to crack slightly.

4. Bake at 425°F (220°C) for about 30 minutes, until golden. Cool on a wire rack.

SOFT-CRUSTED BREAD AND RYE BREAD FORMULAS

This category includes sandwich-type breads baked in loaf pans, soft rolls, braided breads, and straight-dough rye (sour rye breads are in the next section). Many of these formulas incorporate milk, eggs, and higher percentages of sugar and fat.

White Pan Bread

For large-quantity measurements, see page 583.

Ingredients	U.S.		Metric	%
Water	12	oz	300 g	60
Yeast, fresh	0.75	oz	18 g	3.75
Bread flour	1 lb 4	oz	500 g	100
Salt	0.5	oz	12 g	2.5
Sugar	0.75	oz	18 g	3.75
Nonfat milk solids	1	oz	25 g	5
Shortening	0.75	oz	18 g	3.75
Total weight:	*2 lb 3*	*oz*	*891 g*	*178%*

■ P r o c e d u r e

Mixing
Straight dough method
10 minutes at second speed (see p. 52).
Fermentation
1½ hours at 80°F (27°C)
Makeup
See page 98.
Baking
400°F (200°C)

Variations

Whole Wheat Bread
For large-quantity measurements, see page 583.

Use the following proportions of flour in the above formula.

Ingredients	U.S.	Metric	%
Bread flour	**8 oz**	**200 g**	**40**
Whole wheat flour	**12 oz**	**300 g**	**60**

White Pan Bread (Sponge)

For large-quantity measurements, see page 583.

Ingredients	U.S.		Metric	%
Sponge				
Flour	1 lb		500 g	67
Water	11	oz	340 g	45
Yeast, fresh	0.6	oz	18 g	2.5
Malt syrup	0.13	oz	4 g	0.5
Dough				
Flour	8	oz	250 g	33
Water	3.5	oz	112 g	15
Salt	0.5	oz	15 g	2
Nonfat milk solids	0.75	oz	22 g	3
Sugar	1.25	oz	38 g	5
Shortening	0.75	oz	22 g	3
Total weight:	*2 lb 10*	*oz*	*1319 g*	*176%*

■ P r o c e d u r e

Mixing
Sponge method
Fermentation
Sponge: about 4 hours at 75°F (24°C)
Dough: about 15 minutes at 80°F (27°C)
Makeup
See page 98. Especially suitable for pull-man loaf.
Baking
400°F (200°C)

Soft Rolls

For large-quantity measurements, see page 583.

Ingredients	U.S.			Metric	%
Water	12	oz		360 g	57
Yeast, fresh	0.75	oz		22 g	3.5
Bread flour	1 lb 5	oz		625 g	100
Salt	0.4	oz	(2 tsp)	12 g	1.75
Sugar	2	oz		60 g	9.5
Nonfat milk solids	1	oz		30 g	4.75
Shortening	1	oz		30 g	4.75
Butter	1	oz		30 g	4.75
Total weight:	*2 lb 7*	*oz*		*1165 g*	*186%*

Egg Bread and Rolls

For large-quantity measurements, see page 584.

Ingredients	U.S.			Metric	%
Water	10.5	oz		312 g	50
Yeast, fresh	0.75	oz		22 g	3.5
Bread flour	1 lb 5	oz		625 g	100
Salt	0.4	oz	(2 tsp)	12 g	1.75
Sugar	2	oz		60 g	9.5
Nonfat milk solids	1	oz		30 g	4.75
Shortening	1	oz		30 g	4.75
Butter	1	oz		30 g	4.75
Eggs	2	oz		60 g	9.5
Total weight:	*2 lb 7*	*oz*		*1181 g*	*188%*

100% Whole Wheat Bread

For large-quantity measurements, see page 584.

Ingredients	U.S.		Metric	%
Water	1 lb		465 g	62
Yeast, fresh	0.75	oz	22 g	3
Whole wheat flour	1 lb 10	oz	750 g	100
Sugar	0.5	oz	15 g	2
Malt syrup	0.5	oz	15 g	2
Nonfat milk solids	0.75	oz	22 g	3
Shortening	1	oz	30 g	4
Salt	0.5	oz	15 g	2
Total weight:	*2 lb 14*	*oz*	*1334 g*	*178%*

■ P r o c e d u r e

Mixing
Straight dough method
10–12 minutes at second speed (see p. 52)
Fermentation
1½ hours at 80°F (27°C)
Makeup
See pages 94–97.
Baking
400°F (200°C)

Variations

Raisin Bread
Scale 75% raisins (1 lb/470 g). Soak in warm water to soften; drain and dry. Add to Soft Roll Dough 1–2 minutes before end of mixing.

Cinnamon Bread
Make up Soft Roll Dough as for loaves (p. 98) but, after flattening out each unit brush with melted butter and sprinkle with cinnamon sugar. After baking, while still hot, brush tops of loaves with melted butter or shortening and sprinkle with cinnamon sugar (p. 116).

■ P r o c e d u r e

Mixing
Straight dough method
10–12 minutes at second speed (see p. 52)
Fermentation
1½ hours at 80°F (27°C)
Makeup
See pages 94–102.
Baking
400°F (200°C)

■ P r o c e d u r e

Mixing
Straight dough method
10 minutes at second speed (see p. 52)
Fermentation
1½ hours at 80°F (27°C)
Makeup
See pages 94–98.
Baking
400°F (200°C)

Challah

For large-quantity measurements, see page 584.

Ingredients	U.S.		Metric	%
Water	8	oz	200 g	40
Yeast, fresh	0.75	oz	20 g	3.75
Bread flour	1 lb 4	oz	500 g	100
Egg yolks	4	oz	100 g	20
Sugar	1.5	oz	38 g	7.5
Malt syrup	0.13	oz	2 g	0.6
Salt	0.4	oz (2 tsp)	10 g	1.9
Vegetable oil	2	oz	62 g	10
Total weight:	*2 lb 4*	*oz*	*482 g*	*183%*

■ P r o c e d u r e

Mixing
Straight dough method
10 minutes at second speed (see p. 52).
Fermentation
1½ hours at 80°F (27°C)
Makeup
See pages 99–102.
Baking
400°F (200°C)

Milk Bread (Pain au Lait)

For large-quantity measurements, see page 584.

Ingredients	U.S.		Metric	%
Bread flour	2 lb 4	oz	1000 g	100
Sugar	3.5	oz	100 g	10
Salt	0.75	oz	20 g	2
Yeast, fresh	1	oz	30 g	3
Eggs	3.5	oz	100 g	10
Milk	1 lb 2	oz	500 g	50
Butter or margarine	5	oz	150 g	15
Malt syrup	0.33	oz	10 g	1
Total weight:	*4 lb 4*	*oz*	*1910 g*	*191%*

■ P r o c e d u r e

Mixing
Straight dough method.
10–15 minutes at medium speed (see p. 52)
Fermentation
60–90 minutes at 77°F (25°C)
Makeup
Any method for soft rolls, pages 94–97. Glaze with egg wash.
Baking
425°F (220°C)

Assorted rolls made with milk bread (pain au lait) dough

Light American Rye Bread and Rolls

For large-quantity measurements, see page 584.

Ingredients	U.S.		Metric	%
Water	12	oz	350 g	60
Yeast, fresh	0.75	oz	22 g	3.75
Light rye flour	8	oz	250 g	40
Bread or clear flour	12	oz	350 g	60
Salt	0.4	oz (2 tsp)	12 g	2
Shortening	0.5	oz	15 g	2.5
Molasses or malt syrup	0.5	oz	15 g	2.5
Caraway seeds (*optional*)	0.25	oz	8 g	1.25
Rye flavor	0.25	oz	8 g	1.25
Total weight:	2 lb 2	oz	1030 g	173%

■ P r o c e d u r e

Mixing
Straight dough method
5–6 minutes at second speed (see p. 52)
Fermentation
1½ hours at 80°F (27°C)
Makeup
See pages 91–93.
Baking
400°F (200°C). Steam for first 10 minutes.

Variations

Add up to 10% Rye Sour (pp. 77–78) to the formula to contribute flavor.

Onion Rye

For large-quantity measurements, see page 585.

Ingredients	U.S.		Metric	%
Water	12	oz	300 g	60
Yeast, fresh	0.75	oz	18 g	3.75
Light rye flour	7	oz	175 g	35
Clear flour	13	oz	325 g	65
Dried onions, scaled, soaked in water, and well drained	1	oz	25 g	5
Salt	0.4	oz (2 tsp)	10 g	1.9
Caraway seeds	0.25	oz	6 g	1.25
Rye flavor	0.25	oz	6 g	1.25
Malt syrup	0.5	oz	12 g	2.5
Total weight:	1 lb 3	oz	877 g	175%

■ P r o c e d u r e

Mixing
Straight dough method
5 minutes at second speed (see p. 52)
Fermentation
**1½ hours at 76°F (24°C), punch down, then
1 more hour**
Makeup
See pages 91–93.
Baking
400°F (200°C). Steam for first 10 minutes.

Variations

Onion Pumpernickel (Nonsour)
For large-quantity measurements, see page 585.
Use the following proportions of flour in the above formula.

Ingredients	U.S.	Metric	%
Rye meal (pumpernickel flour)	4 oz	100 g	20
Medium rye flour	3 oz	75 g	15
Clear flour	13 oz	325 g	65

Dough may be colored with caramel color or cocoa powder.

Seven-Grain Bread

Ingredients	U.S.			Metric	%
Water	1 lb	10	oz	815 g	62
Yeast, fresh		1	oz	30 g	2.4
Bread flour	1 lb	8	oz	750 g	57
Rye flour		6	oz	185 g	14
Barley flour		2	oz	65 g	5
Cornmeal		3	oz	90 g	7
Rolled oats		3	oz	90 g	7
Flax seeds		2	oz	65 g	5
Millet		2	oz	65 g	5
Salt		0.75	oz	24 g	1.8
Total weight:	*4 lb*	*5*	*oz*	*2179 g*	*166%*

Note　For the purposes of calculating with percentages, all seven grains are included as part of the total flour, even though three of them are not ground.

■ **P r o c e d u r e**

Mixing
Straight dough method
Sift together the bread flour, rye flour, barley flour, and cornmeal; add the oats, flax seeds, and millet and mix well. This ensures even distribution of the flours.
Mix 10 minutes at first speed.
Fermentation
1½ **hours at 75°F (24°C)**
Makeup
See pages 93 and 98. Make up as desired for loaf pans or round loaves.
Baking
425°F (220°C)

 ## Four-Grain Bread

Ingredients	U.S.			Metric	%
Water	1 lb 10		oz	770 g	63
Yeast, fresh		0.5	oz	15 g	1.25
Bread flour	1 lb	4	oz	600 g	49
Rye flour		14	oz	415 g	34
Barley flour		3	oz	85 g	7
Oat flour		4	oz	125 g	10
Salt		0.75	oz	24 g	2
Basic Yeast Starter (p. 77) or fermented dough	1 lb			490 g	40
Total weight:	*5 lb*	*4 oz*		*2524 g*	*206%*

■ **P r o c e d u r e**

Mixing
Straight dough method
Sift together the four flours and mix well to ensure even distribution.
Mix 10 minutes at first speed. Punch down halfway through the fermentation.
Fermentation
1½ **hours at 75°F (24°C)**
Makeup
See pages 93 and 98. Make up as desired for loaf pans or round loaves.
Baking
425°F (220°C)

SOURDOUGH FORMULAS

The purposes of a sour are to provide *flavor* and *leavening power.* If a large proportion of active sour is used, it can provide all the leavening, so that little or no additional yeast is needed. If a small percentage of sour is used, it functions primarily as a flavoring ingredient, and additional yeast is generally required for the dough.

Sourdoughs are introduced in detail in chapter 3 (p. 58). You should reread this section, if necessary, before beginning work on the formulas in this section.

The first recipes in this section are for sour starters, both natural starters and yeast starters (see p. 58 for an explanation of these terms). The natural starters are difficult to control because they depend on the yeast in the environment for their success. In addition, they take longer to develop than yeast starters. Apple Sour, in fact, takes up to 10 days to develop enough to be used in a bread dough. Make sure your production planning takes these long lead times into consideration. Once the sours are developed, maintain them by adding more flour and water to them each day in the same proportion as in the original formula.

Sour rye doughs are stickier than regular doughs, so handling of the dough and makeup of loaves requires more skill and practice. Care should be taken not to overmix the dough. Use low speed to avoid damaging the gluten.

Underproof sourdough breads, especially if a high percentage of sour is used. Proofed units are very fragile. Steam should be used in baking to allow the crust to expand without breaking.

Basic Yeast Starter

For large-quantity measurements, see page 585.

Ingredients	U.S.		Metric	%
Bread flour	15	oz	450 g	100
Water	9	oz	270 g	60
Yeast, fresh	0.03	oz	1 g	0.2
Salt	0.3	oz	9 g	2
Total weight:	*1 lb 8*	*oz*	*730 g*	*162%*

■ P r o c e d u r e

Mixing
Straight dough method
Fermentation
12–14 hours at 80°F (27°C) or 18 hours at 70°F (21°C)

Rye Sour I

For large-quantity measurements, see page 585.

Ingredients	U.S.		Metric	%
Rye flour	1 lb		400 g	100
Water	12	oz	300 g	75
Yeast, fresh	0.8	oz	2 g	5
Onion, halved (*optional*)	1		1	
Total weight:	*1 lb 12*	*oz*	*702 g*	*180%*

■ P r o c e d u r e

1. Dissolve yeast in water.
2. Add rye flour and mix until smooth.
3. Bury the onion in the mix.
4. Let stand 24 hours. Desired temperature: 70°F (21°C)
5. Remove onion.

To use
1. Add to doughs as needed.
2. Save some of the sour as starter for next batch of starter. Add flour and water in same proportions as formula (75% water to 100% flour) and let ferment until next day. Additional yeast is not needed as long as the sour is active.

Variations

Wheat Sour
Prepare as in the basic recipe but, in place of the rye flour, use 85% bread flour and 15% whole wheat flour.

Rye Sour II

Ingredients	U.S.		Metric	%
Starter				
Light rye flour	1 lb		500 g	100
Water		12 oz	375 g	75
Yeast, fresh		2 oz	60 g	12.5
First build				
Light rye flour	4 lb		2000 g	100
Water	3 lb		1500 g	75
Second build				
Light rye flour	4 lb		2000 g	100
Water	3 lb		1500 g	75
Third build				
Light rye flour	up to 24 lb		up to 10,000 g	100
Water	up to 18 lb		up to 7500 g	75
Total weight:	*up to 57 lb*		*25,000 g*	

■ P r o c e d u r e

Mixing

1. Mix starter ingredients. Let stand at shop temperature 24 hours.

2. Add first build ingredients. Ferment at 80°F (27°C) until the mixture falls back, about 3 hours.

3. Repeat with remaining builds. Second build may be omitted if schedule does not permit. Amounts added in last build depend on production requirements.

4. Save about 2 lb (1 kg) sour as starter for next day's production.

Rye Sour III

For large-quantity measurements, see page 585.

Ingredients	U.S.	Metric		%
Rye flour	1 lb	500	g	100
Water, warm (85-90°F or 30-35°C)	1 lb	500	g	100
Yeast, fresh	0.25 oz	7.5	g	1.5
Total weight:	*2 lb*	*1007*	*g*	*201%*

■ P r o c e d u r e

1. Mix together all ingredients.

2. Cover and let ferment at room temperature for about 15 hours.

Yogurt Sour

Ingredients	U.S.	Metric	%
Skim milk	7 oz	225 g	180
Plain yogurt	3 oz	90 g	72
Bread flour	4 oz	125 g	100
Total weight:	*14 oz*	*440 g*	*352%*

■ P r o c e d u r e

1. Warm the milk to about 98°F (37°C), or body temperature.

2. Stir in the yogurt.

3. Mix in the flour until smooth.

4. Pour into a sterile container, cover with a damp cloth, then cover tightly with plastic film.

5. Allow to stand in a warm place for 2–5 days, until bubbles form.

Potato Sour

Ingredients	U.S.		Metric	%
Bread flour	8	oz	225 g	100
Water, warm	6.5	oz	185 g	82
Salt	0.16 oz (1 tsp)		5 g	2
Sugar	0.16 oz (1 tsp)		5 g	2
Large potato, peeled	1		1	
Total weight (without potato):	*14*	*oz*	*420 g*	*186%*

■ P r o c e d u r e

1. Mix together the flour, water, salt, and sugar into a soft, smooth dough. Add the potato.

2. Place into a sterilized bowl. Cover tightly with muslin or other clean fabric so that the starter can breathe. Rest in a warm place for up to 24 hours, until the mixture becomes frothy.

3. Stir well and cover with plastic film. Leave to stand for 2–3 days in a warm place, until the mixture becomes light and foamy. Stir thoroughly each day.

4. Pour the fermented starter into a glass jar and store in the refrigerator for approximately 3 days or until a clear liquid collects on top of the mixture. This indicates that the mixture is ripened enough for use. Carefully pour all the liquid that has collected on the surface into a measuring jug, discarding the solid mixture that remains on the bottom. The weight of the liquid should be greater than the weight of the water used, because some of the flour will be poured off with the liquid.

Apple Sour

Yield: 2 lb (900 g)

Ingredients	U.S.			Metric
Starter				
Whole apple, cored		12	oz	360 g
Sugar		2	oz	60 g
Water		1.33	oz	40 g
First build				
Honey		0.67	oz	20 g
Water, warm		4	oz	120 g
Apple starter (above)		5	oz	160 g
Bread flour (see *note*)		13	oz	390 g
Second build				
Honey		0.2	oz	6 g
Water, warm		3	oz	85 g
Starter from first build	1 lb	6	oz	650 g
Bread flour		6	oz	195 g

Note For best results, use unbleached, organic bread flour. The total weight is less than the summed weights of the ingredients due to losses from evaporation and from skimming and other mixing losses.

■ P r o c e d u r e

1. Leaving the skin on, grate the cored apple.

2. Combine the ingredients for the starter. Cover with a damp cloth and plastic film. Keep in a warm place for 8–10 days.

3. Each day, dampen the cloth, but do not mix the starter. Once the mixture starts to give off gases, it is ready. Remove any crust that may have formed on the surface.

4. For the first build, dissolve the honey in warm water. Mix in the apple starter and mash to a paste. Mix in the flour. Knead by hand for 5–10 minutes to form a dough.

5. Place in a clean bowl and cover with a damp cloth and plastic film. Allow to ferment for 8–10 hours.

6. Repeat step 3 with the ingredients for the second build.

7. Allow to ferment for 5–8 hours. The dough should be well risen.

Sour Rye Bread

For large-quantity measurements, see page 585.

Ingredients	U.S.		Metric	%
Water	8	oz	200 g	50
Yeast, fresh	0.16 oz		4 g	1
Fermented rye sour	9.5 oz		240 g	60
Clear flour	1 lb		400 g	100
Salt	0.33 oz		8 g	2
Total weight:	*2 lb 1*	*oz*	*852 g*	*213%*
Optional ingredients				
Caraway seeds	up to 0.25 oz		up to 6 g	up to 1.5
Molasses or malt syrup	up to 0.5 oz		up to 12 g	up to 3
Caramel color	up to 0.25 oz		up to 6 g	up to 1.5

■ P r o c e d u r e

Mixing
1. Dissolve yeast in water.
2. Add the sour and mix to break up the sour.
3. Add the flour, salt, and optional flavoring ingredients. Develop the dough 5 minutes at low speed. Do not overmix.

Fermentation
Rest 15 minutes, then scale.

Makeup
See pages 91–93. Give only ¾ proof.

Baking
425°F (218°C) with steam for first 10 minutes.

Variations

Sourdough White Bread
Prepare a white sour using either of the sour formulas but substituting patent flour for the rye flour. Prepare the bread using the formula for sour rye, but use white sour in place of the rye sour and use either clear flour, patent flour, or a mixture of 85% patent and 15% whole wheat flour. The water quantity may need some adjustment depending on the flour used. Allow a 2-hour fermentation and a full proof.

 ## Pumpernickel

For large-quantity measurements, see page 586.

Ingredients	U.S.		Metric	%
Water	12	oz	375 g	50
Yeast, fresh	0.25 oz		8 g	1
Fermented rye sour	10	oz	315 g	42
Rye meal (pumpernickel)	5	oz	150 g	20
Clear flour	1 lb 3	oz	600 g	80
Salt	0.5 oz		15 g	2
Malt syrup	0.25 oz		8 g	1
Molasses	0.5 oz		15 g	2
Caramel color (*optional*)	0.38 oz		12 g	1.5
Total weight:	*2 lb 15*	*oz*	*1498 g*	*199%*

■ P r o c e d u r e

Mixing
1. Dissolve the yeast in water.
2. Add the sour and mix to break up the sour.
3. Add the rye meal, flour, salt, malt, molasses, and color. Develop the dough 5 minutes at low speed. Do not overdevelop the dough.

Fermentation
Rest 15 minutes, then scale.

Makeup
See pages 91–93. Give only ¾ proof.

Baking
425°F (218°C) with steam for first 10 minutes

French Rye

For large-quantity measurements, see page 586.

Ingredients	U.S.			Metric	%
Rye Sour III (p. 78)	1 lb	8	oz	750 g	600
Bread flour		4	oz	125 g	100
Salt		0.33	oz	10 g	8
Total weight:	*1 lb 12*		*oz*	*985 g*	*708%*

■ **P r o c e d u r e**

Mixing

1. Place the sour in a mixing bowl. Add the flour and salt.

2. Mix at low speed for 10 minutes. The dough will be soft and somewhat sticky, and therefore a little difficult to handle.

Fermentation

30 minutes at warm room temperature

Makeup

Scale at 1 lb (500 g). Shape into round or slightly oval loaves.

Brush or spray with water and dust heavily with flour. Proof 30–60 minutes at 85°F (27°C) until about double in volume. Score the tops of the loaves.

Baking

450°F (230°C) with steam, 40–45 minutes

Pain de Campagne (Country-Style Bread)

For large-quantity measurements, see page 586.

Ingredients	U.S.			Metric	%
Rye Sour III (p. 78)		6	oz	200 g	20
Bread flour	1 lb 8		oz	800 g	80
Rye flour		6	oz	200 g	20
Salt		0.6	oz	20 g	2
Yeast, fresh		0.5	oz	15 g	1.5
Water	1 lb 4		oz	650 g	65
Lard or goose fat (*optional*)		0.6	oz	20 g	2
Total weight:	*3 lb 9*		*oz*	*1905 g*	*190%*

■ **P r o c e d u r e**

Mixing

Straight dough method

12 minutes at first speed

Fermentation

1 hour at warm room temperature

Makeup

Scale at 1 lb 12 oz (950 g). Round into tight, round loaves. Dust with flour before proofing. Before baking, score in a crosshatch or grid pattern.

Baking

425°F (218°C) with steam, about 45 minutes

Apple Sourdough

Yield: 5 lb 10 oz (2400 g)

Ingredients	U.S.		Metric	%
Granny Smith apples	15	oz	450 g	64
Butter	2.5	oz	80 g	11
Cinnamon	0.25	oz	8 g	1
Yeast, dry	0.25	oz	8 g	1
Water, warm	12	oz	360 g	51
Honey	0.2	oz	6 g	0.85
Salt	0.5	oz	15 g	2
Apple Starter (p. 79)	1 lb 14	oz	900 g	129
Bread flour (see *note*)	1 lb 2	oz	525 g	75
Rye flour	6	oz	175 g	25
Raisins or dried cranberries	7	oz	200 g	29

Note   For best results, use unbleached, organic flour for this bread.

The dough yield is less than the summed weights of the ingredients due mostly to trimming and cooking loss of the apples.

■ P r o c e d u r e

Mixing

1. Peel, core, and chop the apple into ¼ inch (5 mm) pieces. Sauté in the butter with the cinnamon until tender. Pour onto a tray and allow to cool.

2. Dissolve the yeast with half of the warm water. Mix to dissolve. Dissolve the honey and salt in the remaining water.

3. Cut up Apple Starter into pieces and place in the bowl of a mixer fitted with the dough hook. Add the yeast liquid and then the honey, salt, and water, adding slowly to make a smooth paste. Add in the flour slowly until a soft dough is formed. Add the sautéed apples and raisins. Mix until combined.

4. Turn the dough out onto a light floured work surface and knead gently to form a smooth dough.

Fermentation
2½–3 hours at 80°F (27°C)

Makeup
Scale at 1 lb 6 oz (600 g).

Make up into long loaves like Italian or Vienna loaves (p. 93).

Allow 2–3 hours for proofing.

Baking
425°F (220°C) for 20 minutes. Reduce the temperature to 375°F (190°C) for another 20 minutes.

Whole Wheat, Rye, and Nut Sourdough

Ingredients	U.S.		Metric	%
Sponge				
Yogurt Sour (p.78)	10	oz	290 g	27
Water, warm	13	oz	375 g	35
Whole wheat flour	12	oz	350 g	32
Dough				
Water	8.5	oz	250 g	23
Yeast, dry	0.5	oz	15 g	1.4
Salt	0.33	oz	10 g	0.9
Whole wheat flour	11	oz	325 g	30
Rye flour	8	oz	225 g	21
Bread flour	6	oz	180 g	17
Walnuts, chopped and lightly toasted	2.5	oz	70 g	6.5
Pecans, chopped and lightly toasted	2.5	oz	70 g	6.5
Total weight:	*4 lb 10*	*oz*	*2160 g*	*200%*

■ **P r o c e d u r e**

Mixing
Sponge method
Fermentation
Sponge: 8 hours or overnight at room temperature
Dough: 1 hour at warm room temperature
Makeup
Scale at 2 lb 4 oz (1050 g) for large loaves, 1 lb 8 oz (700 g) for medium loaves. Shape into round or elongated oval loaves. Spray tops with water and dust heavily with flour. Proof until double in volume. Score tops with desired pattern.
Baking
425°F (220°C) for 30 minutes. Reduce to 350°F (180°C) until done.

Variations

The nuts used may be varied—as, for example, all walnuts, all pecans, all hazelnuts, or all almonds. Raisins may be added in addition to the nuts.

Potato Sourdough

Ingredients	U.S.		Metric	%
Sponge				
Potato Sour (p. 79)	8	oz	250 g	29
Bread flour	6	oz	180 g	21
Sugar	1.75	oz	50 g	6
Water	4	oz	120 g	14
Boiled potato, grated	5	oz	150 g	17
Sautéed onions	5.25	oz	160 g	18
Salt	0.33	oz	10 g	1
Dough				
Water, warm	4	oz	120 g	14
Milk powder	3	oz	90 g	10
Bread flour	1 lb 7	oz	690 g	79
Baking soda	0.4	oz (2½ tsp)	12 g	1.4
Cream of tartar	0.4	oz (5 tsp)	12 g	1.4
Butter	2.67	oz	80 g	9
Salt	0.33	oz	10 g	1
Total weight:	*4 lb 6*	*oz*	*1934 g*	*221%*

■ **P r o c e d u r e**

Mixing

Sponge method

1. For the sponge, mix together the sour and flour to make a very soft dough. Allow to rest for 2 hours.

2. Combine the sugar, water, potato, onions, and salt. Pour this mixture over the starter dough. Stir lightly. Cover tightly and allow to ferment overnight or until the dough is risen and foamy.

3. For the dough, combine the sponge, water, milk powder, flour, baking soda, and cream of tarter. Add just enough of the flour to make a soft dough and mix about 2 minutes.

4. Beat in the butter, salt, and remaining flour. Knead by hand or with the machine at first speed for 10 minutes.

Fermentation and Makeup

This dough is not fermented because the baking soda and cream of tartar begin to generate gas at once. Scale the dough at 1 lb (450 g). Shape into elongated oval loaves. Slash the tops of the loaves with diagonal slashes. Bake without proofing.

SPECIALTY BREADS

Some of the items in this section are produced by methods unlike those of other breads. English muffins and crumpets are made on a griddle rather than baked in an oven. Both of these items are toasted before being eaten. English muffins are split in half before toasting and crumpets are toasted whole.

Bagels are boiled in a malt solution before being baked. As bagels have become more popular, there has been a proliferation of bagel-like rolls that are really only ordinary bread shaped like bagels. True bagels are dense, chewy rolls made with high-gluten flour and a low proportion of water. Also, flavorings for true bagels are generally limited to toppings, such as poppy seeds, sesame seeds, coarse salt, and chopped onion or garlic.

Production methods for these items are modified for use in a small bakeshop. Large producers have special equipment for bagels, English muffins, and crumpets.

Additional formulas in this chapter include two popular recipes for focaccia, which is closely related to pizza dough; an unusual and flavorful bread made with chestnut flour; a flatbread called *pita,* which puffs up when baked to form a hollow center; an Amish-style soft pretzel; and two rustic crisp-crusted breads, one containing olives and the other containing chunks of prosciutto.

English Muffins

For large-quantity measurements, see page 586.

Ingredients	U.S.		Metric	%
Water (see mixing instructions)	12	oz	375 g	75
Yeast, fresh		0.25 oz	8 g	1.5
Bread flour	1 lb		500 g	100
Salt		0.25 oz	8 g	1.5
Sugar		0.25 oz	8 g	1.5
Nonfat milk solids		0.4 oz (2 tsp)	12 g	2.3
Shortening		0.25 oz	8 g	1.5
Total weight:	*1 lb 13*	*oz*	*919 g*	*183%*

■ P r o c e d u r e

Mixing
Straight dough method
20–25 minutes at second speed (see p. 52). This dough is intentionally overmixed to develop its characteristic coarse texture. Because of this long mixing time, use twice your normal machine friction factor (see p. 60) when calculating water temperature. For this reason, and because of the low fermentation temperature, it is usually necessary to use very cold water or part crushed ice.

Fermentation
Dough temperature: 70°F (21°C). Ferment 2½ to 3 hours.

Scaling and makeup
Because this dough is very soft and sticky, you must use plenty of dusting flour. Scale at 1.5 oz (45 g) per unit. Round and relax the units, then flatten with the palms of the hands. Place on cornmeal-covered trays to proof.

Baking
Bake on both sides on a griddle at low heat.

Bagels

For large-quantity measurements, see page 586.

Ingredients	U.S.		Metric	%
Water	8	oz	250 g	50
Yeast, fresh	0.5	oz	15 g	3
High-gluten flour	1 lb		500 g	100
Malt syrup	1	oz	30 g	6
Salt	0.25	oz	8 g	1.5
Oil	0.13	oz	4 g	0.8
Total weight:	*1 lb 9*	*oz*	*807 g*	*161%*

■ P r o c e d u r e

Mixing
Straight dough method
8–10 minutes at low speed
Fermentation
1 hour at 80°F (27°C)
Makeup and baking

1. Scale at 1¾ to 2 oz (50 to 55 g) per unit.

2. One of two methods may be used for shaping bagels by hand:

   • Roll with the palms of the hands into ropes (as for knotted or tied rolls). Loop around palms into doughnut shape. Seal the ends together well by rolling under the palms on the bench.

   • Round the scaled unit and flatten into a thick disk. Press a hole in the center and tear open with the fingers. Pull the hole open and smooth the edges.

3. Give half proof.

4. Boil in a malt solution (⅓ qt malt syrup per 4 gal water, or 3 dL malt per 15 L water) about 1 minute.

5. Place on sheet pans about 1 inch apart. Bake at 450°F (230°C) until golden brown, turning them over when they are half baked.

Total baking time is about 20 minutes.

If desired, bagels may be sprinkled with sesame seeds, poppy seeds, diced onion, or coarse salt before baking.

Olive Focaccia

For large-quantity measurements, see page 587.

Ingredients	U.S.		Metric	%
Water	14.5	oz	450 g	60
Yeast, fresh	0.33	oz	10 g	1.5
Bread flour	1 lb 8	oz	750 g	100
Salt	0.25	oz	7.5 g	1
Olive oil	1	oz	25 g	3.5
Chopped, pitted oil-cured black olives	8	oz	250 g	33
Total weight:	*3 lb*		*1492 g*	*198%*

■ P r o c e d u r e

Mixing
Straight dough method
Add the olives after the other ingredients have formed a dough.
12 minutes at first speed
Fermentation
1½ hours at 80°F (27°C)
Makeup and baking
See Herb Focaccia.

Herb Focaccia (Sponge Method)

For large-quantity measurements, see page 587.

Ingredients	U.S.		Metric	%
Sponge				
Flour	8	oz	225 g	29
Water	6	oz	175 g	21
Yeast, fresh	0.12	oz	4 g	0.5
Flour	1 lb 4	oz	575 g	71
Water	14	oz	400 g	50
Yeast, fresh	0.12	oz	4 g	0.5
Salt	0.5	oz	15 g	1.75
Olive oil	1	oz	30 g	3.5
Rosemary and salt (see Makeup)				
Total weight:	*3 lb 1*	*oz*	*1428 g*	*177%*

■ P r o c e d u r e

Mixing
Sponge method
Fermentation
Sponge: 8–16 hours at 70°F (21°C)
Dough: 30 minutes at 80°F (27°C)
Makeup and Baking

1. Scale at 3 lb (1400 g) for each half-size sheet pan.
2. Oil pans heavily with olive oil.
3. Roll and stretch dough into a rectangle to fit pans and place in pans (a).
4. Proof until doubled in thickness.
5. Top each unit with 2 oz (60 mL) olive oil. With fingertips, poke holes heavily at regular intervals (b).
6. Top each unit with 2 tbsp (30 mL) fresh rosemary and with coarse salt to taste (c).
7. Bake at 400°F (200°C) for 30 minutes.

a.

b.

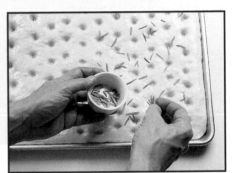

c.

Chestnut Bread

For large-quantity measurements, see page 587.

Ingredients	U.S.		Metric	%
Water	12	oz	360 g	60
Yeast, fresh	1.2	oz	36 g	6
High-gluten flour	15	oz	450 g	75
Chestnut flour	5	oz	150 g	25
Salt	0.5	oz	15 g	2.5
Butter	0.6	oz	18 g	3
Total weight:	*2 lb 2*	*oz*	*1029 g*	*171%*

■ P r o c e d u r e

Mixing
Straight dough method
10 minutes at first speed
Fermentation
40 minutes at 80°F (27°C)
Makeup
Scale at 10–11 oz (300–330 g).
Oval-shaped loaves
Baking
450°F (230°C)

Variations

For a more developed flavor, add 30% Basic Yeast Starter (p. 77)

Prosciutto Bread

For large-quantity measurements, see page 587.

Ingredients	U.S.		Metric	%
Water	9	oz	285 g	57
Yeast, fresh	0.33	oz	10 g	2
Bread flour	1 lb		500 g	100
Salt	0.33	oz	10 g	2
Rendered lard or prosciutto fat	1	oz	30 g	6
Basic Yeast Starter (p. 77) or fermented dough	3.25	oz	100 g	20
Prosciutto, chopped or diced into small pieces	3.25	oz	100 g	20
Total weight:	*2 lb 1*	*oz*	*1035 g*	*207%*

■ P r o c e d u r e

Mixing
Straight dough method
1. Mix the water, yeast, flour, salt, and fat 6 minutes at first speed.
2. Add Basic Yeast Starter and mix another 4 minutes.
3. Add the prosciutto and mix another 1–2 minutes.

Fermentation
1 hour at 80°F (27°C)

Makeup
Scale at 12–18 oz (360–540 g) as desired. Shape like long Italian loaves. See page 93.

Baking
425°F (220°C) with steam

Olive Bread

For large-quantity measurements, see page 588.

Ingredients	U.S.		Metric	%
Water	12.5	oz	370 g	62
Yeast, fresh	0.3	oz	9 g	1.5
Bread flour	15	oz	450 g	75
Whole wheat flour	2	oz	60 g	10
Rye flour	3	oz	90 g	15
Salt	0.4	oz	12 g	2
Olive oil	1	oz	30 g	5
Basic Yeast Starter (p. 77) or fermented dough	2	oz	60 g	10
Pitted black olives, whole or halved (see *note*)	6	oz	180 g	30
Total weight:	*2 lb 10*	*oz*	*1261 g*	*210%*

■ P r o c e d u r e

Mixing
Straight dough method
1. Mix all ingredients except the olives 10 minutes at first speed.
2. Add the olives and mix another 4–5 minutes.

Fermentation
90 minutes at 75°F (24°C)

Makeup
Same as Prosciutto Bread

Baking
425°F (220°C) with steam

Note   Use a flavorful brined olive such as Greek kalamata. Do not use canned, water-packed olives, as they have little flavor.

Crumpets

For large-quantity measurements, see page 588.

Ingredients	U.S.			Metric		%
Water, warm	1 lb	4	oz	550	g	110
Yeast, fresh		1	oz	30	g	5.5
Bread flour	1 lb	2	oz	500	g	100
Salt		0.33	oz	10	g	2
Sugar		0.13 oz (¾ tsp)		3.5	g	0.7
Baking soda		0.06 oz (⅜ tsp)		1.5	g	0.3
Water, cold		5	oz	140	g	28
Total weight:	*2 lb 12*		*oz*	*1235*	*g*	*246%*

■ P r o c e d u r e

1. Mix the first five ingredients to form a soft dough or batter. Ferment 1½ hours at room temperature.

2. Dissolve the baking soda in the second quantity of water. Mix into the flour mixture until smooth.

3. Lightly grease crumpet rings or any round cutters. Place on a moderately hot griddle. Using a ladle or dropping funnel, fill the rings with the batter to a depth of about ½ inch (12 mm). The amount of batter for each crumpet varies from 1½ to 2 oz depending on the size of the rings.

4. As the crumpets bake, they will develop bubbles on the surface. When the bubbles become holes and the batter is set, remove the rings and turn the crumpets over with a spatula. Continue to bake until the second side just begins to color.

Amish-Style Soft Pretzels

Ingredients	U.S.		Metric	%
Water	10.5	oz	325 g	65
Yeast, fresh	0.33	oz	11 g	2.25
Bread flour	12	oz	375 g	75
Pastry flour	4	oz	125 g	25
Salt	0.1	oz	3 g	0.6
Sugar	0.3	oz	10 g	2
Soda wash				
Water, warm	8	oz	250 g	
Baking soda	1	oz	30 g	
Pretzel salt or coarse salt				
Total dough weight:	*31*	*oz*	*849 g*	*170%*

■ P r o c e d u r e

Mixing
Straight dough method
Makeup

1. *Scaling:* With a bench scraper, cut off a long piece of dough 5 oz (150 g) in weight.

2. With the palms of the hands, roll on the bench to a uniform strip 30 inches (75 cm) long. Twist into a pretzel shape.

3. Dip in a solution of 2 oz (60 g) baking soda in 1 pt (500 mL) water. Arrange on baking sheets lined with parchment. Stretch out and reform the pretzel shapes as necessary. (*Note:* After dipping in soda solution, the units are difficult to handle. If desired, pan the pretzels first, then brush thoroughly with the soda solution.)

4. Sprinkle with pretzel salt.

5. Bake at 500°F (260°C) for 8–9 minutes or until well browned.

6. *Optional:* Dip in melted butter immediately after baking and drain on racks.

Pita

Ingredients	U.S.			Metric	%
Water		14	oz	435 g	58
Yeast, fresh		1	oz	30 g	4
Bread flour	1 lb	4	oz	625 g	83
Whole wheat flour		4	oz	125 g	17
Salt		0.5	oz	15 g	2
Sugar		0.67	oz	22 g	3
Yogurt, plain low-fat		3	oz	90 g	12.5
Oil, preferably olive		1	oz	30 g	4
Total weight:	2 lb	12	oz	1372 g	183%

■ **P r o c e d u r e**

Mixing
Straight dough method
Fermentation
Until doubled in bulk, about 1½ hours at 80°F (27°C)
Makeup and Baking
1. Scale at 3 oz (90 g). Round the units and bench-rest.

2. With a rolling pin, roll out into circles about 4–5 inches (10–12 cm) in diameter.

3. Bake on oven hearth or on dry sheet pans at 500°F (260°C) until lightly golden around edges, about 5 minutes. Do not overbake or the pitas will be dry and stiff. They should be soft when cool.

MAKEUP TECHNIQUES

The object of yeast dough makeup is to shape the dough into rolls or loaves that bake properly and have an attractive appearance. When you shape a roll or loaf correctly, you stretch the gluten strands on the surface into a smooth skin. This tight gluten surface holds the item in shape. This is especially important for loaves and rolls that are baked freestanding, not in pans. Units that are not made up correctly will develop irregular shapes and splits and may flatten out.

USE OF DUSTING FLOUR

In most cases, the bench and the dough must be dusted lightly with flour to prevent the dough from sticking to the bench and to the hands. Some bakers use light rye flour for dusting. Others prefer bread flour.

Whichever flour you use, one rule is very important: *Use as little dusting flour as possible.* Excessive flour makes seams difficult to seal and shows up as streaks in the baked product.

Procedure for Scaling and Dividing Dough for Rolls

This procedure involves the use of a dough divider. A dough divider cuts a large unit of dough, called a *press,* into small units of equal weight. If this equipment is not available, you must scale individual roll units.

1. Scale the dough into presses of desired weight. One press makes 36 rolls.

2. Round the presses and allow them to relax.

3. Divide the dough using a dough divider. Separate the pieces, using a little dusting flour to prevent sticking.

4. Make up the rolls as desired. In some cases, the pieces are rounded first. In other cases, the rolls are made up without rounding, just as they come from the divider.

CRISP-CRUSTED PRODUCTS AND RYE PRODUCTS

Round Rolls

1. Scale the dough as required, such as 3½ lb (1600 g) per press or 1½ oz (45 g) per roll. Divide presses into rolls.

2. Holding the palm of the hand fairly flat, roll the dough in a tight circle on the workbench (a). Do not use too much flour for dusting, as the dough must stick to the bench a little in order for the technique to work.

3. As the ball of dough takes on a round shape, gradually cup the hand (b, c).

4. The finished ball of dough should have a smooth surface, except for a slight pucker on the bottom.

5. Place rolls 2 inches (5 cm) apart on sheet pans sprinkled with cornmeal.

6. Proof, wash with water, and bake with steam.

a.   b.   c.

Oval Rolls

1. Scale and round the rolls as indicated above for round rolls.

2. Roll the rounded units back and forth under the palms of the hands so that they become slightly elongated and tapered.

3. Proof and wash with water. Slash with one lengthwise cut or three diagonal cuts.

4. Bake with steam.

Split Rolls

1. Round up the rolls as for round rolls. Let them rest a few minutes.

2. Dust the tops lightly with rye flour. Using a lightly oiled ¾-in. (2 cm) thick wooden pin, press a crease in the center of each roll.

3. Proof upside down in boxes or on canvas dusted with flour. Turn right side up and place on pans or peels dusted with cornmeal. Do not slash. Bake as for other hard rolls.

Crescent Rolls

1. Scale the dough into 16–20-oz (450–575 g) units. Round and relax the units.

2. Flatten the dough and roll out into 12-in. (30 cm) circles.

3. With a pastry wheel, cut each dough circle into 12 equal wedges or triangles, (Alternative method: For large quantities of dough, roll out into a rectangle and cut like croissant dough; see p. 122).

4. Roll the triangles into crescents using the same technique as for croissants (see p. 122). The rolls may be either left as straight sticks or bent into crescents.

5. Proof. Wash with water and, if desired, sprinkle with poppy seeds, caraway seeds, sesame seeds, or coarse salt. Bake with steam.

Club Rolls

Rather than being rounded, these units are molded as they come from the divider.

a.

1. Flatten the piece of dough roughly into a rectangle (a).

2. Begin to roll up the dough by folding over the back edge of the rectangle. Press the seam firmly with the fingertips (b).

3. Continue to roll the dough, always pressing the seam firmly after each turn. As you roll up the dough, the front edge will appear to shrink. Stretch the front corners as shown by the arrows, to keep the width uniform (c).

b.

4. When the roll is finished, seal the seam well so that the roll is tight (d).

5. Docking the proofed roll with a single slash gives the baked roll this appearance (e).

6. Place units 2 in. (5 cm) apart on sheet pans sprinkled with cornmeal.

7. Proof, wash with water, and slash with one cut lengthwise. Bake with steam.

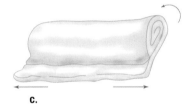

c.

d.

e.

Onion Rolls (for Rye or Hard Roll Dough)

1. Prepare onion mixture:
   a. Cover 1 lb (500 g) dried onions with water and soak until soft. Drain.
   b. Mix with 2 oz (60 g) oil and ½ oz (15 g) salt.
   c. Place on a flat pan. Keep covered until ready to use.

2. Divide and round the dough for rolls. Let rest 10 minutes.

3. Place the rolls face down on top of the onions and flatten well with the hands. Place the flattened rolls onion-side up on paper-lined pans.

4. Proof. Press the center of each roll with two fingers to make an indentation. Bake with steam.

Kaiser Rolls

1. Scale Vienna dough to produce rolls of desired size. 5-lb (2300 g) presses yield 2-oz (60 g) baked rolls, large enough for sandwiches.

2. Press the dough in the divider and separate the pieces, dusting them with light rye flour.

3. Round the units and let them rest.

4. Flatten the pieces lightly with the hands.

Kaiser Roll Tool

5. Stamp each roll with a kaiser roll tool. The cuts should go about halfway through the rolls. Do not cut all the way through.

6. Place the rolls upside down on boxes or trays sprinkled generously with poppy seeds or lined with canvas cloth. Proof.

7. Place right-side up on cornmeal-dusted baking sheets or peels. Place in oven and bake with steam.

a.

French, Italian, and Vienna Loaves

These loaves vary in shape from thick, elongated ovals to long, thin French baguettes.

1. Flatten the rounded, relaxed dough into an oval with the hands or with a rolling pin. Stretch the oval with the hands to lengthen it (a). Roll up tightly and seal the seam well (b, c). Roll the loaf on the bench under the palms of the hands to even out the shape. This will produce an elongated, oval-shaped loaf. The ends should be tapered and rounded, not pointed.

b.

2. If a longer, thinner loaf is desired, relax these units again for a few minutes. Flatten them with the palms of the hands and stretch the dough lightly to increase its length. Once again, roll up tightly and seal the seam well. Roll on the bench under the palms of the hands to even it out and to stretch it to the desired shape and length.

3. Place seam-side down on pans dusted with cornmeal. Proofing the baguettes in these special pans (d) maintains their shape. Proof. Wash with water. Slash with diagonal cuts or one lengthwise cut; this can be done before or after proofing. Bake with steam for first 10 minutes.

c.

Round Loaves and Oval Loaves

These techniques are used for many types of breads, including Pain de Campagne and French Rye.

For round loaves, like Pain de Campagne:

1. Flatten the rounded, relaxed dough into a circle. Fold the sides over the center, then round again. Shape the dough into a seam-free ball (a).

2. Place on pans sprinkled with cornmeal or flour. Proof, wash the tops with water, and slash the tops in a crosshatch pattern (b, c). Bake with steam.

d.

a.

b.

c.

For oval loaves, like French Rye:

1. As for round loaves, flatten the rounded, relaxed dough into a circle. Fold the sides over the center, then round again. Roll the dough under the palms of the hands into a smooth oval loaf (a).

2. Place on pans sprinkled with cornmeal or flour. Proof, wash the tops with water, and dredge with flour. Score as shown (b).

As an alternative to proofing on pans, proof upside down in special baskets called *bannetons*. Dust the inside of the banneton with flour and push the dough firmly into the basket (c). When the dough is proofed, turn out onto a sheet pan or a peel and slide into the oven.

a.

b.

c.

Fougasse

1. Roll out the dough into a large, thin oval, letting it rest at intervals to allow the gluten to relax.

2. Oil a sheet pan with olive oil. Place the dough on the sheet pan and brush the dough well with olive oil.

3. Press the fingertips into the dough at regular intervals, as for focaccia (see p. 87).

4. Cut slits in the dough (a). Stretch the dough to open the slits (b).

5. Proof for 30 minutes at room temperature.

a.

b.

SOFT ROLL DOUGHS, PAN LOAVES, AND BRAIDED BREADS

Tied or Knotted Rolls

1. Scale the dough into presses of desired size. Divide the presses.

2. With the palms of the hands, roll each unit on the workbench into a strip or rope of dough.

3. Tie the rolls as shown on this page.

4. Place rolls 2 in. (5 cm) apart on greased or paper-lined baking sheets.

5. Proof, egg wash, and bake without steam.

Single-knot rolls

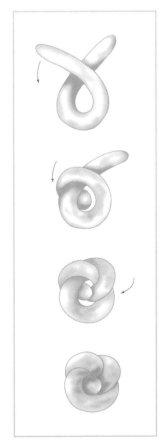

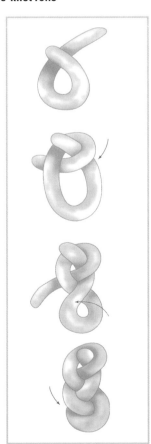

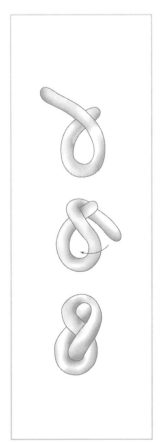

Double-knot rolls　　　　**Braided rolls**　　　　**Figure-eight rolls**

Sawtooth Rolls

1. Prepare elongated oval rolls.
2. With a scissors, cut a row of snips down the tops of the rolls.

Crescent Rolls

1. Make up as for hard crescent rolls, except brush the triangles with melted butter before rolling up.
2. Proof, egg wash, and sprinkle with poppy seeds. Bake without steam.

Pan Rolls

1. Scale dough into presses of desired size. Divide.
2. Make up as for round hard rolls.
3. Place on greased pans $\frac{1}{2}$ in. (1 cm) apart.

Parker House Rolls

1. Scale dough into presses of desired size. Divide.
2. Round the scaled piece of dough (a).
3. Flatten the center of the dough with a narrow rolling pin (b).
4. Fold the dough over and press down on the folded edge to make a crease (c).
5. Place on greased baking sheet $\frac{1}{2}$ in. (1 cm) apart. The baked rolls have a seam that splits open easily (d).

a.

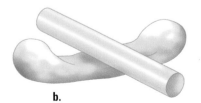

b.

c.

d.

Cloverleaf Rolls

1. Scale dough into presses of desired size. Divide each piece of dough into 3 equal parts and shape them into balls.

2. Place 3 balls in the bottom of each greased muffin tin (a). The balls merge as they bake to form a cloverleaf shape (b).

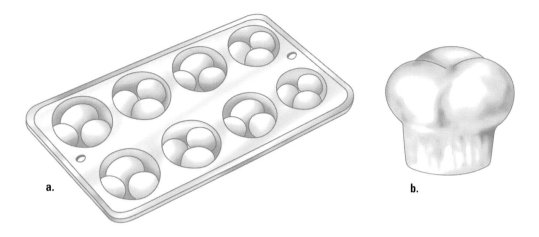

a.

b.

Butterflake Rolls

1. Roll the dough out into a very thin rectangular shape. Brush it with melted butter. Cut it into strips 1 in. (2.5 cm) wide (a).

2. Stack up 6 strips. Cut into $1\frac{1}{2}$-in. ($3\frac{1}{2}$ cm) pieces (b).

3. Place the pieces on end in greased muffin tins (c). Proof. The baked rolls have a flaky appearance (d).

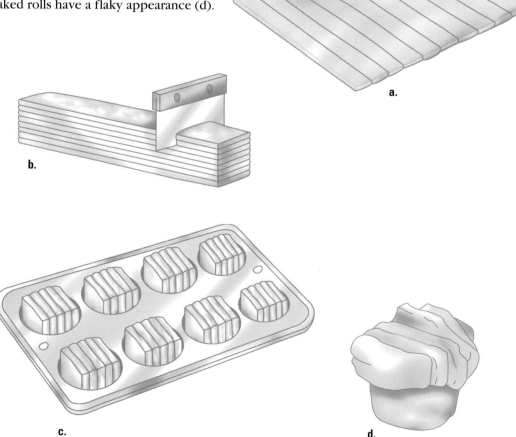

a.

b.

c.

d.

Pan Loaves

1. Start with the rounded, benched dough (a).
2. Stretch it out into a long rectangle (b).
3. Fold into thirds (c, d).

a.

b.

c.

d.

4. Roll the dough up into a tight roll that has the same length as the pan it is to be baked in (e). Seal the seam very well and place the dough seam-side down in the greased pan.

   For split-top loaves, make one cut from end to end in top of loaf after proofing.

e.

Pullman Loaf

Pullman loaves are baked in loaf pans with sliding lids so that slices from the loaf are square, ideal for sandwiches. Pans are usually of standard sizes to make 1-lb (450 g), 1½-lb (675 g), 2-lb (900 g), and 3-lb (1350 g) loaves.

1. Scale the dough to fit the loaf pans. Add an extra 2 oz (50 g) of dough per pound (450 g) to allow for baking loss.
2. Make up loaves in one of two ways:

   • Make up as standard pan loaves as in the preceding technique.
   • Divide each scaled unit into two pieces. Roll out into strips and twist the two strips together. Seal the ends well. This method is preferred by many bakers because it gives extra strength to the loaf structure. The sides of the loaf are less likely to collapse.

3. Place the made-up loaves in lightly greased pans. Put on the lids (greased on the underside), but leave them open about 1 in. (2.5 cm).
4. Proof until the dough has risen almost to the lids.
5. Close the lids. Bake at 400° to 425°F (200° to 218°C) without steam.

6. Remove the lids after 30 minutes. The bread should be taking on color by this time. If the lid sticks, it may be because the bread requires a few more minutes of baking with the lid. Try again after a few minutes.

7. Complete baking with lid off to allow moisture to escape.

Braided Loaves

Egg-enriched soft roll dough and challah dough are the most appropriate for braided loaves. The dough should be relatively stiff so that the braids hold their shape.

Braids of one to six strands are commonly made. More complicated braids of seven or more strands are not presented here because they are rarely made.

Braided breads are egg-washed after proofing. If desired, they may also be sprinkled with poppy seeds after washing.

One-Strand Braid

1. Roll the dough into a smooth, straight strip with the palms of the hands. The strip should be of uniform thickness from end to end.

2. Tie or braid the strip the same way as for a braided roll (see p. 95).

Two-, Three-, Four-, Five-, and Six-Strand Braids

1. Divide the dough into equal pieces, depending on how many strips are required.

   For a double three-strand braid, divide the dough into 4 equal pieces, then divide one of these pieces into three smaller pieces, so that you have three large and three small pieces.

2. Roll the pieces with the palms of the hands into long, smooth strips. The pieces should be thickest in the middle and gradually tapered toward the ends.

3. Braid the strips as shown in the illustrations. Please note that the numbers used in these descriptions refer to the *positions* of the strands (numbered from left to right). At each stage in the braiding, number 1 always indicates the first strand on the left.

Two-Strand Braids

1. Cross the 2 strands in the middle (a).
2. Fold the two ends of the bottom strand over the upper one (b).
3. Now fold the ends of the other strand over in the same way (c).
4. Repeat steps 2 and 3 until the braid is finished (d).

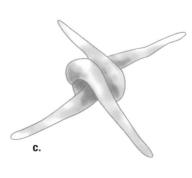

b.

c.

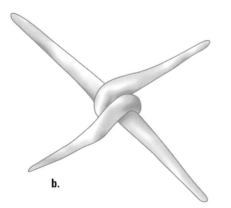

d.

a.

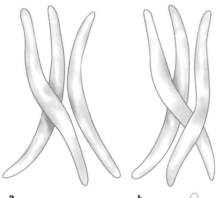

a.

b.

Three-Strand Braids

1. Lay the 3 strands side by side. Starting in the center, fold the left strand over the center one (1 over 2) (a).

2. Now fold the right strand over the center (3 over 2) (b).

3. Repeat the sequence (1 over 2, 3 over 2) (c).

4. When you reach the end of the strands, turn the braid over (d).

5. Braid the other half (e).

6. If desired, a smaller three-strand braid can be placed on top (f).

c.

d.

e.

f.

Four-Strand Braids

1. Start with 4 strands, fastened at the end (a).

2. Move 4 over 2 (b).

3. Move 1 over 3 (c).

4. Move 2 over 3 (d).

5. Repeat steps 2, 3, 4 until the braid is finished (e, f).

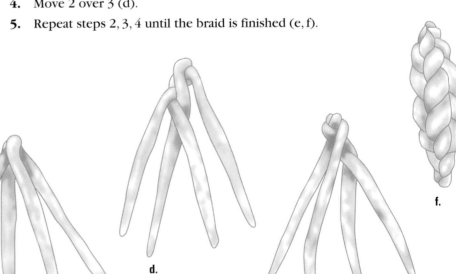

a.

b.

c.

d.

e.

f.

Five-Strand Braids

1. Start with 5 strands, fastened at the end (a).
2. Move 1 over 3 (b).
3. Move 2 over 3 (c).
4. Move 5 over 2 (d).
5. Repeat steps 2, 3, 4 until the braid is finished (e, f).

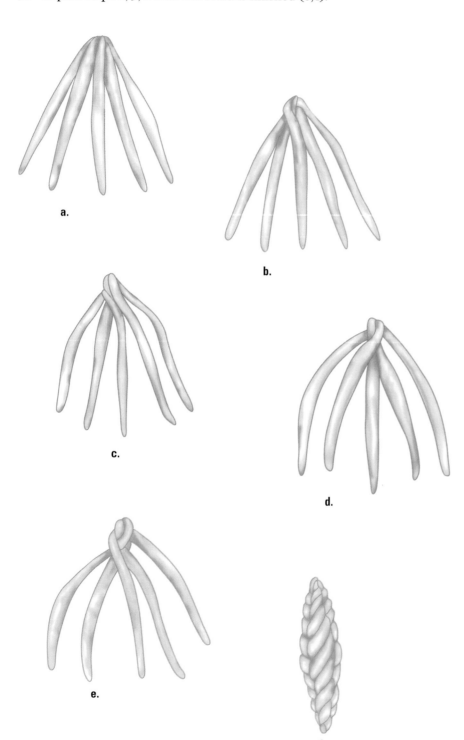

a.

b.

c.

d.

e.

f.

Six-Strand Braids

1. Start with 6 strands, fastened at the end (a).
2. The first step, 6 over 1, is *not* part of the repeated sequence (b).
3. The repeated sequence begins with 2 over 6 (c).
4. Move 1 over 3 (d).
5. Move 5 over 1 (e).
6. Move 6 over 4 (f).
7. Repeat steps 3–6 until braid is finished (g).

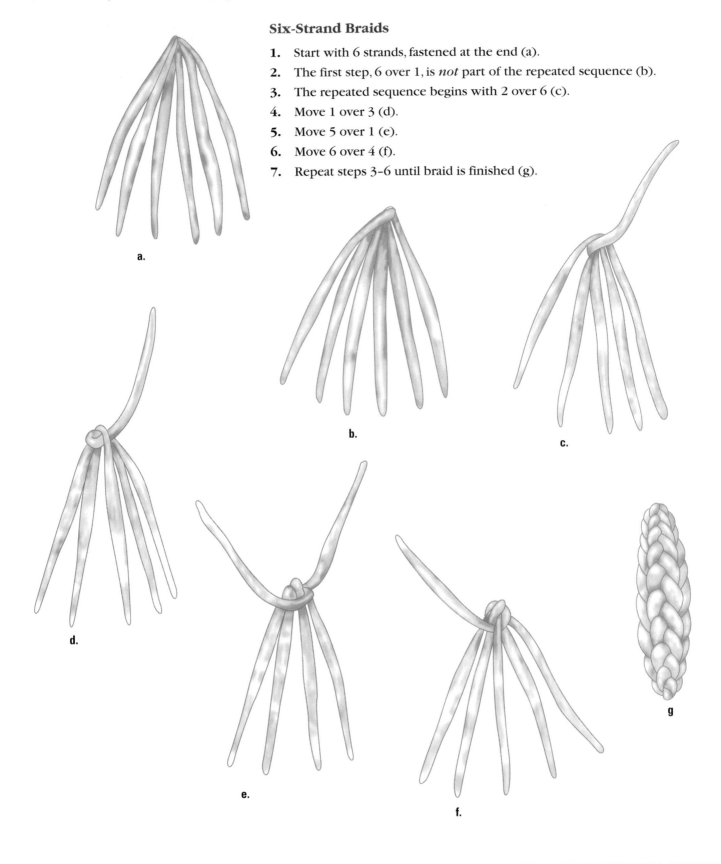

a.

b.

c.

d.

e.

f.

g

▶ TERMS FOR REVIEW

French bread	sour	press	pain de campagne
bagel	pumpernickel	ciabatta	fougasse
English muffin	pullman loaf	focaccia	

▶ QUESTIONS FOR REVIEW

1. How would the baked loaves be different if you increased the shortening in the French bread formula (p. 69) to 7%?

2. Why is the baking temperature for Italian bread (p. 68) higher than that for challah (p. 74)?

3. How could you modify the formula for Vienna bread (p. 67) if you didn't have any malt?

4. Why is it important not to use too much dusting flour when making up breads and rolls?

5. Describe the procedure for makeup of focaccia.

6. Describe the procedure for using a dough divider.

7. Describe the procedure for rounding rolls.

8. Describe the procedure for makeup of baguettes.

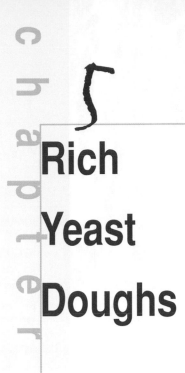

5

Rich Yeast Doughs

*T*his chapter completes the study of yeast doughs with a survey of the most important rich yeast doughs. As explained in chapter 3, rich doughs are those with higher proportions of fat and, sometimes, sugar and eggs as well.

Simple sweet-roll doughs are the easiest of these products to handle. Even these, however, require care, as they are usually softer and stickier than bread doughs. Because their gluten structure is not as strong as that of lean doughs, more care must be taken in proofing and baking sweet dough products.

Rolled-in doughs, such as those for Danish pastries and croissants, are especially rich in fat because they consist of layers of butter between layers of dough. Like other sweet doughs, these yeast-leavened doughs are usually considered the pastry chef's department rather than the bread baker's department. Considerable practice and skill are required for the makeup of fine Danish products.

As in chapter 4, the dough formulas and makeup techniques are given in separate sections of the chapter because each dough can be made up into a great many different items. This chapter also includes a selection of fillings and toppings suitable for rich yeast-dough products. Review chapter 3 with respect to the basic mixing methods and other production procedures for yeast doughs.

SWEET DOUGH AND RICH DOUGH FORMULAS

It must be remembered that high percentages of fat and sugar in a yeast dough inhibit fermentation. For this reason, most of the doughs in this section are mixed by the sponge method so that most of the fermentation can take place before the sugar and fat are added. The major exception here is the regular sweet dough or bun dough, which is low enough in fat and sugar that it can be mixed by the modified straight dough method. The quantity of yeast is also increased. Refer to pages 51–52 to review the basic mixing methods.

High levels of fat and eggs make rich doughs very soft. The amount of liquid is reduced to compensate for this.

Because they are so tender, rich doughs are generally underfermented and underproofed. About three-quarters proof is best for rich doughs. Overproofed units may collapse in baking.

Bun pans should be lined with silicone paper whenever there is danger of sticking. This is especially true in items with fruit fillings or other sugary fillings or toppings.

Note that the recipes exemplify two ways of mixing rich sponge doughs. Rich sweet dough and kugelhopf dough are high in sugar. To ensure even distribution in the dough, the sugar is creamed with the fat, just as in the modified straight dough method. In brioche and baba doughs there is little sugar, so this method is not used. The fat is mixed into the dough last.

After reading this chapter, you should be able to:

- Produce simple sweet doughs.
- Produce rolled-in yeast doughs.
- Produce a variety of toppings and fillings for rich yeast doughs.
- Make up a variety of products using sweet doughs and rolled-in doughs, including Danish pastry and croissants.

Sweet Roll Dough

For large-quantity measurements, see page 588.

Ingredients	U.S.		Metric	%
Water	8	oz	200 g	40
Yeast, fresh	1.5	oz	38 g	7.5
Butter, margarine, or shortening (see *note*)	4	oz	100 g	20
Sugar	4	oz	100 g	20
Salt	0.25	oz	6 g	1.25
Nonfat milk solids	1	oz	25 g	5
Eggs	3	oz	75 g	15
Bread flour	1 lb		400 g	80
Cake flour	4	oz	100 g	20
Total weight:	*2 lb 9 oz*		*1044 g*	*208%*

Note Any of the fats listed may be used alone or in combination.

■ P r o c e d u r e

Mixing
Modified straight dough method
Develop the dough 4 minutes at second speed (see p. 52).

Fermentation
1½ hours at 80°F (27°C)

Makeup
See pages 123–131.

Baking
375°F (190°C)

Rich Sweet Dough

For large-quantity measurements, see page 588.

Ingredients	U.S.		Metric	%
Milk, scalded and cooled	8	oz	200 g	40
Yeast, fresh	1	oz	50 g	5
Bread flour	10	oz	250 g	50
Butter	8	oz	200 g	40
Sugar	4	oz	100 g	20
Salt	0.25	oz	6 g	1.25
Eggs	5	oz	125 g	25
Bread flour	10	oz	250 g	50
Total weight:	*2 lb 14*	*oz*	*1181 g*	*231%*

Note Any of the fats listed may be used alone or in combination.

For large-quantity measurements, see page 588.

■ P r o c e d u r e

Mixing
Sponge method

1. Make a sponge with the first 3 ingredients. Ferment until double.

2. Cream butter, sugar, and salt until well blended. Blend in eggs.

3. Add the sponge. Mix to break up the sponge.

4. Add the flour and develop the dough. Mixing time: about 3 minutes

Fermentation

30–40 minutes or retard immediately. Retarding makes it easier to handle the dough, which is very soft.

Variations

Stollen

For large-quantity measurements, see page 588.

Ingredients	U.S.	Metric	%
Almond extract	0.12 oz (¾ tsp)	2 g	0.5
Lemon rind, grated	0.12 oz (1½ tsp)	2 g	0.5
Vanilla extract	0.12 oz (¾ tsp)	2 g	0.5
Raisins (light, dark, or a mixture)	4 oz	150 g	30
Mixed glacéed fruit	7 oz	175 g	35

Add almond extract, lemon rind, and vanilla extract to the butter and sugar during the blending stage. Knead raisins and mixed glacéed fruit into the dough.

Makeup

1. Scale, round, and let rest. Scaling weights may range from 12 oz to 2 lb (350 g to 1 kg), depending on individual needs.

2. With hands or a rolling pin, flatten out slightly into an oval shape.

3. Wash the top with butter.

4. Make a crease down the length of the oval about ½ in. (1 cm) off center. Fold one side (the smaller side) over the other, as though you are making a large, wide Parker House roll (see p. 96).

5. Give three-quarters proof. Wash the tops with melted butter.

6. Bake at 375°F (190°C).

7. Cool. Dredge heavily with 4X or 6X sugar.

Babka

For large-quantity measurements, see page 588.

Ingredients	U.S.	Metric	%
Vanilla extract	0.12 oz (¾ tsp)	2 g	0.5
Cardamom	0.06 oz (¾ tsp)	1 g	0.25
Raisins	4 oz	100 g	20

Add vanilla and cardamom to the butter during blending. Knead raisins into the dough.

Makeup

Loaf-type coffee cake (p. 131). May be topped with streusel.

Baking

350°F (175°C). Be sure to bake thoroughly; underbaked units will have sticky crumb and may collapse.

Kugelhopf

Ingredients	U.S.		Metric	%
Milk, scalded and cooled	6	oz	190 g	30
Yeast, fresh	1	oz	30 g	5
Bread flour	6	oz	190 g	30
Butter	8	oz	250 g	40
Sugar	4	oz	125 g	20
Salt	0.25	oz	8 g	1.25
Eggs	7	oz	220 g	35
Bread flour	14	oz	440 g	70
Raisins	2.5	oz	75 g	12.5
Total weight:	*3 lb*		*1522 g*	*243%*

■ **P r o c e d u r e**

Mixing
Sponge method
1. Make a sponge with the first 3 ingredients. Ferment until double.
2. Cream the butter, sugar, and salt until well blended. Blend in the eggs.
3. Add the sponge. Mix to break up the sponge.
4. Add the flour and develop the dough. Mixing time: about 3 minutes. Dough will be very soft and sticky.
5. Carefully blend in the raisins.

Fermentation
Needs only 15–20 minutes bench rest before scaling and panning. Or retard immediately.

Makeup
Heavily butter kugelhopf molds or tube pans. Line with sliced almonds (which will stick to the buttered sides). Fill molds halfway with dough (each quart of volume requires about 1 lb of dough, or each liter requires about 500 g). Give three-quarters proof.

Baking
375°F (190°C)
Unmold and cool completely. Dust with confectioners' sugar.

Hot Cross Buns

For large-quantity measurements, see page 589.

Ingredients	U.S.			Metric	
Sweet Roll Dough (p. 106)	2 lb	8	oz	1250	g
Dried currants		4	oz	125	g
Golden raisins		2	oz	60	g
Mixed candied peel, diced		1	oz	30	g
Ground allspice		0.07 oz (1 tsp)		2.5	g
Total weight:	*2 lb 15*		*oz*	*1467*	*g*

■ **P r o c e d u r e**

1. Undermix the Sweet Roll Dough. Mix together the fruits and spice until thoroughly mixed, then work into the dough until well incorporated.
2. See Sweet Roll Dough formula for fermentation and baking.

Makeup
Scale into 2-oz (60 g) units and round. Place in greased or parchment-lined sheet pans, just touching. Egg wash. After baking, brush with Clear Glaze (p. 116). Pipe Flat Icing (p. 342) into a cross shape on each roll.

Variation

For a more traditional cross on top of the buns, mix together the ingredients for Cross Paste (below) until smooth. Pipe crosses onto the buns after they are proofed but before they are baked.

Cross Paste

Ingredients	U.S.		Metric	%
Water	10	oz	300 g	111
Pastry flour or cake flour	9	oz	270 g	100
Shortening	2	oz	60 g	22
Milk powder	1	oz	30 g	11
Baking powder	0.06 oz (¹/₃ tsp)		2 g	0.7
Salt	0.06 oz (¹/₃ tsp)		2 g	0.7

Baba/Savarin Dough

For large-quantity measurements, see page 589.

Ingredients	U.S.		Metric	%
Milk	4	oz	125 g	40
Yeast, fresh	0.5	oz	15 g	5
Bread flour	2.5	oz	75 g	25
Eggs	5	oz	150 g	50
Bread flour	7.5	oz	225 g	75
Sugar	0.25	oz	8 g	2.5
Salt	0.4	oz (2 tsp)	4 g	1.25
Butter, melted	4	oz	125 g	40
Total weight:	*1 lb 8*	*oz*	*727 g*	*238%*

■ P r o c e d u r e

Mixing

Sponge method

1. Scald milk and cool to lukewarm. Dissolve yeast. Add flour and mix to make a sponge. Let rise until double.

2. Gradually mix in eggs and then dry ingredients (using the paddle attachment) to make a soft dough.

3. Beat in butter a little at a time until it is completely absorbed and the dough is smooth. Dough will be very soft and sticky.

Makeup and Baking

1. Fill greased molds half full. Average baba molds require about 2 oz (60 g). For savarin molds (ring molds), the following are averages:

5-in. ring: 5–6 oz	13-cm ring: 140–170 g
7-in. ring: 10–12 oz	18-cm ring: 280–340 g
8-in. ring: 14–16 oz	20-cm ring: 400–450 g
10-in. ring: 20–24 oz	25-cm ring: 575–675 g

2. Proof until dough is level with top of mold.

3. Bake at 400°F (200°C).

4. While still warm, soak in Dessert Syrup (p. 178) flavored with rum or kirsch. Drain.

5. Glaze with Apricot Glaze (p. 117). If desired, decorate with candied fruits.

Variation

Add 25% raisins (10 oz/300 g) to baba dough.

Panettone

Ingredients	U.S.		Metric	%
Raisins	2.5	oz	75 g	11
Golden raisins or sultanas	2.5	oz	75 g	11
Mixed candied peel	5	oz	150 g	21
Blanched almonds, chopped	2.5	oz	75 g	11
Grated lemon zest	0.12 oz (1½ tsp)		4 g	0.6
Grated orange zest	0.12 oz (1½ tsp)		4 g	0.6
Lemon juice	2	oz	60 g	9
Orange juice	2	oz	60 g	9
Rum	4	tsp	20 g	3
Nutmeg	½	tsp	2 mL	
Bread flour	1 lb 8	oz	700 g	100
Milk	10	oz	285 g	41
Yeast, fresh	1.5	oz	40 g	6
Egg yolks	4	oz	120 g	17
Salt	0.17 oz (1 tsp)		5 g	0.7
Sugar	4	oz	125 g	17
Butter	8	oz	225 g	32
Total weight:	*3 lb 12*	*oz*	*2025 g*	*289%*

■ Procedure

Mixing and Fermentation

1. *Prepare the marinated fruit mixture:* Combine the raisins, peel, almonds, zest, juice, rum, and nutmeg in a bowl. Cover and allow to marinate several hours or, refrigerated, overnight.

2. Sift the flour into bowl and make a well in the center.

3. Warm the milk to 100°F (37°C) and mix with the yeast. Pour this mixture into the well in the flour. Sprinkle a little flour from the sides of the bowl on top of the yeast liquid. Cover bowl and allow to stand at room temperature until the flour starts to appear cracked on top and the mixture bubbles, approximately 45 minutes.

4. Add the egg yolks, salt, and sugar to the flour mixture. Mix lightly to form a soft dough. Turn out onto a floured work surface and knead for 10 minutes, until smooth.

5. Place the dough in a lightly floured bowl, cover with a damp cloth, and let ferment at room temperature until doubled in size.

6. Drain the marinated fruit. Add the fruit and the butter, softened, into the dough until smooth and well incorporated. Put back into the bowl and let ferment a second time at room temperature until doubled in size.

Pan Preparation and Baking

1. (Note: This procedure makes one large loaf weighing about 3 lbs (1500 g) after baking. For smaller loaves, divide the dough into two, three, or four equal parts and bake in smaller molds.) Cut a double layer of parchment paper, long enough to line a 6-inch (15 cm) cake tin with an overlap of 1 in. (2 cm) and approximately 9 in. (23 cm) tall. Place into a buttered cake tin. Place on a baking sheet. Fold a sheet of foil several times to form a stiff collar on the outside of the tin. The foil should be the same height as the baking paper inside. Secure with string. Line the bottom of the tin with a double layer of paper cut into a 6-in. (15 cm) circle.

2. Punch down the dough and round into a smooth ball.

3. Place the dough in the prepared cake tin and press down lightly with the knuckles.

4. Cover and proof at room temperature until doubled in volume.

5. Cut a cross in the top of the dough and brush with melted butter.

6. Bake in a preheated oven at 375°F (190°C) until lightly colored. Place a piece of butter (about 4 tsp [20 g]) in the center of cross and continue to bake for 1 hour. Cover top of panettone with foil when golden in order to prevent excessive browning.

7. Reduce oven temperature to 325°F (160°C). Continue baking until a skewer inserted in the center comes out clean, approximately 1¾ to 2 hours in all.

8. Remove from the oven and brush with melted butter.

9. Once cold, dust top with confectioners' sugar.

Brioche

For large-quantity measurements, see page 589.

Ingredients	U.S.		Metric	%
Milk	2	oz	60 g	20
Yeast, fresh	0.5	oz	15 g	5
Bread flour	2	oz	60 g	20
Eggs	5	oz	150 g	50
Bread flour	8	oz	240 g	80
Sugar	0.5	oz	15 g	5
Salt	0.13 oz (¾ tsp)		4 g	1.25
Butter, softened (see *note*)	7	oz	210 g	70
Total weight:	*1 lb 9*	*oz*	*758 g*	*251%*

Note   To make dough less sticky and less difficult to handle, the butter may be reduced to 50% (5 oz/150 g) or as low as 35% (3.5 oz/105 g). However, the product will not be as rich and delicate.

■ P r o c e d u r e

Mixing
Sponge method
1. Scald milk and cool to lukewarm. Dissolve yeast. Add flour and mix to make a sponge. Let rise until double.
2. Gradually mix in eggs and then dry ingredients (using the paddle attachment) to make a soft dough.
3. Beat in butter a little at a time until it is completely absorbed and the dough is smooth. Dough will be very soft and sticky.

Fermentation
1. If the dough will require much handling in makeup, as for small brioche rolls, it is easiest to retard the dough overnight. Making it up while chilled reduces stickiness.
2. If the dough is to be simply deposited in pans, its stickiness and softness is not a problem, so it need not be retarded. Ferment 20 minutes, then scale and pan.

Makeup
See page 123. Egg wash after proofing.
Baking
400°F (200°C) for small rolls; 375°F (190°C) for large units

ROLLED-IN DOUGH FORMULAS

Rolled-in doughs contain many layers of fat sandwiched between layers of dough. These layers create the flakiness that you are familiar with in Danish pastry.

Rolling-In Procedure for Danish and Croissant Dough

The rolling-in procedure has two major parts: enclosing the fat in the dough and rolling out and folding the dough to increase the number of layers.

In these doughs, we use a *simple fold,* or *three-fold,* which means that we fold the dough in thirds. Each complete rolling and folding step is called a *turn.* We give Danish dough three turns. Rest the dough in the refrigerator for 30 minutes after the first turn to allow the gluten to relax.

After each turn, use the fingertips to press indentations in the dough near the edge—one indentation after the first turn, two after the second, three after the third. This helps you keep track of your production if you have several batches in progress, and it is essential if you have several people working on the same dough.

1. Roll out the dough into a rectangle. Smear softened butter over two-thirds of the dough, leaving a margin around the edges.

2. Fold the unbuttered third of the dough over the center.

3. Fold the remaining third on top.

4. Rotate the dough 90 degrees on the countertop. This step is necessary before each rolling-out of the dough so that the dough is stretched in all directions, not just lengthwise. In addition, always place the worse side up before rolling so it will be hidden after folding and the better side will be on the outside. Roll out the dough into a long rectangle.

5. Fold the dough into thirds by first folding the top third over the center.

6. Then fold over the remaining third. This is the first turn or first fold (enclosing the butter doesn't count as a turn). Let the dough rest in the refrigerator 30 minutes to relax the gluten. Repeat this rolling and folding two more times for a total of three turns.

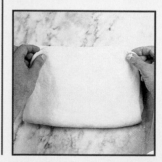

In the classical pastry shop, there are two basic rolled-in yeast doughs:

1. *Croissant dough* (also called *Danish pastry dough, croissant-style*) resembles a puff pastry (see chapter 10) with the addition of yeast. It is based on a dough made of milk, flour, a little sugar, and, of course, yeast. The rolled-in butter gives the dough its flaky texture.

2. *Danish dough, brioche-style,* is a richer dough containing eggs, although it is not as rich in eggs as regular brioche. This dough is also called *brioche feuilletée,* or flaky brioche.

Both these doughs are used in making Danish pastries, although only the first one is generally used for croissants. In addition to the classic French recipes for these two pastry doughs, this section also includes two formulas similar to those widely used in North American bakeshops.

Take care not to overmix rolled-in doughs. The rolling-in procedure continues to develop the gluten. Overmixing the dough results in inferior baked products.

Butter is the preferred fat because of its flavor and melt-in-the-mouth qualities. The highest-quality products use butter for at least part of the rolled-in fat. However, butter is difficult to work because it is hard when cold and soft when a little too warm. Specially formulated shortenings and margarines can be used when lower cost and greater ease of handling are important considerations.

a.

Danish Pastry Dough (Croissant-Style)

Ingredients	U.S.		Metric	%
Water	7	oz	200 g	18
Yeast, fresh	1.25	oz	40 g	3.5
Bread flour	5	oz	150 g	14
Sugar	2.5	oz	80 g	7
Salt	0.75	oz	25 g	2
Milk	12	oz	350 g	32
Water	1.5	oz	50 g	4.5
Bread flour	2 lb		950 g	86
Butter	1 lb 4	oz	600 g	55
Total weight:	*5 lb 2*	*oz*	*2445 g*	*222%*

b.

c.

■ P r o c e d u r e

Mixing and Fermentation
Modified straight dough method
1. In a bowl, mix the yeast and water (a). Sprinkle the first quantity of flour over the mixture. Let stand about 15 minutes.

2. In another bowl, mix the sugar, salt, milk, and water until the solids are dissolved.

3. Sift the flour and add it to the yeast mixture. Add the liquid mixture. Begin mixing to form a dough (b).

4. Mix just until a uniform dough is formed. Continue mixing by hand; avoid overmixing (c).

5. Finish by kneading the dough on the countertop (d).

6. Cover and allow to ferment for 40 minutes at room temperature.

7. Punch down and place in refrigerator for 1 hour.

Rolling in
Incorporate the butter and give three 3-folds (see p. 112 for rolling-procedure).

d.

Danish Pastry Dough (Brioche-Style)

For large-quantity measurements, see page 589.

Ingredients	U.S.		Metric	%
Milk	7	oz	225 g	28
Yeast, fresh	1.33	oz	40 g	5
Bread flour	1 lb 10	oz	800 g	100
Eggs	3.25	oz	100 g	12.5
Butter, melted	1.5	oz	50 g	6
Salt	0.33	oz (2 tsp)	10 g	1.25
Sugar	1.5	oz	50 g	6
Milk	2.5	oz	75 g	9
Butter, softened	1 lb		500 g	62
Total weight:	*3 lb 11*	*oz*	*1850 g*	*229%*

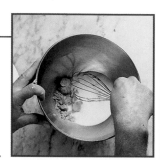

a.

■ P r o c e d u r e

Mixing and Fermentation

1. In a bowl, mix the first quantity of milk with the yeast (a).
2. Sift the flour on top of the yeast mixture. Add the eggs and melted butter (b).

b.

3. Dissolve the salt and sugar in the second quantity of milk. Add to the bowl.
4. Mix for 1½ minutes with the dough hook to form a dough (c).
5. Place the dough in a mixing bowl, cover, and let ferment 30 minutes at room temperature or overnight in the refrigerator.
6. Punch down the dough and rest in the refrigerator for 45 minutes.

Rolling in

Incorporate the last quantity of butter and give three 3-folds (see p. 112 for rolling-in procedure).

c.

Croissants

For large-quantity measurements, see page 589.

Ingredients	U.S.		Metric	%
Milk	8	oz	225 g	57
Yeast, fresh	0.5	oz	15 g	4
Sugar	0.5	oz	15 g	4
Salt	0.25	oz	8 g	2
Butter, softened	1.5	oz	40 g	10
Bread flour	14	oz	400 g	100
Butter	8	oz	225 g	57
Total weight:	*2 lb*		*928 g*	*234%*

■ P r o c e d u r e

Mixing
Straight dough method. Scald milk, cool to lukewarm, and dissolve yeast. Add remaining ingredients except last quantity of butter. Mix into a smooth dough, but do not develop the gluten. Gluten development will take place during rolling-in procedure.
Fermentation
1 hour at 80°F (27°C)
Punch down, spread out on a flat pan, and rest in retarder 30 minutes.
Rolling in
Incorporate the last amount of butter and give three 3-folds (see p. 112). Rest in retarder overnight.
Makeup
See p. 122.
Proof at 80°F (27°C) and 65% humidity. Egg wash before baking.
Baking
400°F (200°C)

Danish Pastry

For large-quantity measurements, see page 590.

Ingredients	U.S.		Metric	%
Water	8	oz	200 g	40
Yeast, fresh	1.25	oz	32 g	6.25
Butter	2.5	oz	62 g	12.5
Sugar	3	oz	75 g	15
Nonfat milk solids	1	oz	25 g	5
Salt	0.25	oz	6 g	1.25
Cardamom or mace (optional)	0.04 oz (½ tsp)		1 g	0.2
Whole eggs	4	oz	100 g	20
Egg yolks	1	oz	25 g	5
Bread flour	1 lb		400 g	80
Cake flour	4	oz	100 g	20
Butter (for rolling in)	10	oz	250 g	50
Total weight:	*3 lb 3*	*oz*	*1276 g*	*255%*

■ P r o c e d u r e

Mixing
Modified straight dough method
Develop dough 3–4 minutes at second speed (see p. 52).
Rest in retarder 30 minutes.
Roll in last quantity of butter. Give four 3-folds (see p. 112).
Makeup
See pages 123–133.
Proof at 90°F (32°C) with little steam. Egg wash before baking.
Baking
375°F (190°C)

FILLINGS AND TOPPINGS

The formulas in this section include many of the most popular fillings and toppings for Danish pastry, coffee cakes, and other sweet yeast products. Several of these items, such as cinnamon sugar, streusel topping, almond filling, and clear glaze, are used for many other bakery products, including cakes, cookies, puff pastries, pies, and tarts. However, their primary use is in the production of yeast goods.

Many of these and similar fillings are available ready-made from bakery supply houses. For example, good-quality prune, poppy, apricot, and other fruit and nut fillings can be purchased in No. 10 cans.

 ## Cinnamon Sugar

For large-quantity measurements, see page 590.

Ingredients	U.S.		Sugar at 100% Metric	%
Sugar	8	oz	250 g	100
Cinnamon	0.25 oz (4 tsp)		8 g	3
Total weight:	*8*	*oz*	*258 g*	*103%*

■ **P r o c e d u r e**

Stir together thoroughly.

 ## Streusel or Crumb Topping

For large-quantity measurements, see page 590.

Ingredients	U.S.		Metric	%
Butter and/or shortening	4	oz	125 g	50
Granulated sugar	2.5	oz	75 g	30
Brown sugar	2	oz	60 g	25
Salt	0.04	oz (¼ tsp)	1 g	0.5
Cinnamon or mace	0.02–0.04 oz (¼—½ tsp)		0.6–1 g	0.25–0.5
Pastry flour	8	oz	250 g	100
Total weight:	*1 lb*		*514 g*	*206%*

■ **P r o c e d u r e**

Rub all ingredients together until the fat is thoroughly blended in and the mixture appears crumbly.

Variation

Nut Streusel
Add 25% chopped nuts (2 oz/60 g).

 ## Clear Glaze

Ingredients	U.S.	Corn syrup at 100% Metric	%
Water	8 oz	250 g	50
Light corn syrup	1 lb	500 g	100
Granulated sugar	8 oz	250 g	50
Total weight:	*2 lb*	*1000 g*	*200%*

■ **P r o c e d u r e**

1. **Mix ingredients together and bring to a boil. Stir to ensure that sugar is completely dissolved.**

2. **Apply while hot, or reheat before use.**

Apricot Glaze I

For large-quantity measurements, see page 590.

Yield: 1 lb 10 oz (1880 g)

Ingredients	U.S.		Metric	Fruit at 100% %
Apricots, canned	1 lb		500 g	50
Apples	1 lb		500 g	50
Sugar	1 lb 14	oz	950 g	95
Water	1	oz	25 g	2.5
Sugar	2	oz	50 g	5
Pectin	0.67	oz	20 g	2

■ P r o c e d u r e

1. Cut the fruit into small pieces, including the skins and seeds. Place in a heavy saucepan.

2. Add the first quantity of sugar and water. Cook slowly, covered, over medium heat until the fruit is soft.

3. Pass through a food mill.

4. Bring back to a boil.

5. Mix the second quantity of sugar and pectin together and add to the fruit. Cook another 3–4 minutes.

6. Strain, skim, and pour into a plastic container. Cool, then refrigerate.

Apricot Glaze II

For large-quantity measurements, see page 590.

Yield: 7 oz (220 g)

Ingredients	U.S.	Metric	%
Apricot preserves	8 oz	250 g	100
Water	2 oz	60 g	25

■ P r o c e d u r e

1. Combine the preserves and water in a heavy saucepan. Bring to a simmer. Stir and cook until the preserves are melted and well mixed with the water. Simmer until reduced and thickened slightly.

2. Pass the mixture through a fine sieve.

3. Test the mixture by placing a small spoonful on a plate and refrigerating for a few minutes to see if it gels. If necessary, cook down for a few more minutes to make it thicker.

Lemon Cheese Filling

For large-quantity measurements, see page 590.

Ingredients	U.S.	Cheese at 100% Metric	%
Cream cheese	5 oz	150 g	100
Sugar	1 oz	30 g	20
Grated lemon zest	0.1 oz (1¼ tsp)	3 g	2
Total weight:	*6 oz*	*183 g*	*122%*

■ P r o c e d u r e

Mix together the cheese, sugar, and zest until well blended.

Date, Prune, or Apricot Filling

For large-quantity measurements, see page 591.

Yield: 1 lb 8 oz (750 g)

Ingredients	U.S.	Fruit at 100% Metric	%
Dates, prunes (pitted), or dried apricots	1 lb	500 g	100
Sugar	3 oz	100 g	20
Water	8 oz	250 g	50

■ **P r o c e d u r e**

1. Pass the fruit through a grinder.
2. Combine all ingredients in a saucepan. Bring to a boil. Simmer and stir until thick and smooth, about 10 minutes.
3. Cool before using.

Variations

1. Date or prune filling may be flavored with lemon and/or cinnamon.
2. Add 12.5% (8 oz/250 g) chopped walnuts to date or prune filling.

 ## Almond Filling I (Frangipane)

For large-quantity measurements, see page 591.

Ingredients	U.S.	Almond paste at 100% Metric	%
Almond paste	8 oz	250 g	100
Sugar	8 oz	250 g	100
Butter and/or shortening	4 oz	125 g	50
Pastry or cake flour	2 oz	62 g	25
Eggs	2 oz	62 g	25
Total weight:	*1 lb 8 oz*	*750 g*	*300%*

■ **P r o c e d u r e**

1. With paddle attachment, mix almond paste and sugar at low speed until evenly mixed.
2. Mix in fat and flour until smooth.
3. Beat in eggs, a little at a time, until smooth.

Almond Filling II (Frangipane)

Ingredients	U.S.	Almond paste at 100% Metric	%
Almond paste	8 oz	200 g	100
Sugar	1 oz	25 g	12.5
Butter	4 oz	100 g	50
Cake flour	1 oz	25 g	12.5
Eggs	4 oz	100 g	50
Total weight:	*1 lb 2 oz*	*450 g*	*225%*

■ **P r o c e d u r e**

1. With the paddle attachment, mix almond paste and sugar at low speed until evenly blended.
2. Blend in the butter.
3. Blend in the flour.
4. Blend in the eggs until smooth.

Almond Cream (Crème d'Amande)

For large-quantity measurements, see page 591.

Ingredients	U.S.		Metric
Butter	3	oz	90 g
Fine granulated sugar	3	oz	90 g
Grated lemon zest	0.03 oz (⅜ tsp)		1 g
Whole egg	1.67 oz (1 egg)		50 g
Egg yolk	0.67 oz (1 yolk)		20 g
Vanilla extract	2	drops	2 drops
Powdered almonds	3	oz	90 g
Cake flour	1	oz	30 g
Total weight:	*12*	*oz*	*370 g*

■ **P r o c e d u r e**

1. Cream together the butter, sugar, and zest until pale and light.

2. Add the eggs, egg yolks, and vanilla a little at a time, beating well after each addition.

3. Stir in the powdered almonds and flour.

Lemon Filling

Ingredients	U.S.		Pie filling at 100%	
			Metric	%
Lemon Pie Filling (p. 221)	1 lb		500 g	100
Cake crumbs		8 oz	250 g	50
Lemon juice		2 oz	62 g	12.5
Total weight:	*1 lb 10 oz*		*812 g*	*162%*

■ **P r o c e d u r e**

Mix ingredients together until smooth.

Apple Compote Filling

For large-quantity measurements, see page 591.

Yield: about 1 lb (500 g) or 9 oz (275 g) drained

Ingredients	U.S.		Apple at 100%	
			Metric	%
Apples, peeled and cored	9	oz	275 g	100
Butter	2.5	oz	75 g	27
Sugar	4	oz	120 g	44
Water	2	oz	60 g	22

■ **P r o c e d u r e**

1. Cut the apple into ¼-in. (5–6 mm) dice.

2. Combine all ingredients. Simmer, covered, over low heat about 15 minutes, until the apple dice are tender but still hold their shape.

Cinnamon Raisin Filling

For large-quantity measurements, see page 591.

Ingredients	U.S.		Almonds at 100%	
			Metric	%
Powdered almonds	3.5	oz	100 g	100
Sugar	2	oz	60 g	60
Maple syrup	1	oz	30 g	30
Egg whites	2	oz	60 g	60
Cinnamon	0.33 oz		10 g	10
Raisins, golden	1.67 oz		50 g	50
Total weight:	*10.5*	*oz*	*310 g*	*310%*

■ **P r o c e d u r e**

1. Using a wire whip (if mixing by hand) or the paddle attachment (if mixing by machine), mix together the almonds, sugar, syrup, egg whites, and cinnamon until smooth.

2. The raisins may be mixed in at this point. For more even distribution, however, sprinkle them evenly over the filling after it has been spread.

Pecan Maple Filling

For large-quantity measurements, see page 591.

Ingredients	U.S.	Hazelnuts at 100% Metric	%
Powdered hazelnuts	3.5 oz	100 g	100
Sugar	2 oz	60 g	60
Egg whites	2 oz	60 g	60
Maple syrup	1 oz	30 g	30
Pecans, finely sliced or chopped	2 oz	60 g	60
Total weight:	*10 oz*	*310 g*	*310%*

■ **P r o c e d u r e**

Mix all ingredients together.

Cheese Filling

Ingredients	U.S.	Cheese at 100% Metric	%
Baker's cheese	1 lb	500 g	100
Sugar	5 oz	150 g	30
Salt	0.12 oz	4 g	0.7
Eggs	3 oz	100 g	20
Butter and/or shortening, softened	3 oz	100 g	20
Vanilla	0.25 oz	8 g	1.5
Grated lemon zest (*optional*)	0.12 oz (1½ tsp)	4 g	0.7
Cake flour	1.5 oz	50 g	10
Milk	3–5 oz	100–150 g	20–30
Raisins (*optional*)	4 oz	125 g	25
Total weight:	*2 lb*	*1012 g*	*203%*
	to	*to*	*to*
	2 lb 6 oz	*1191 g*	*228%*

■ **P r o c e d u r e**

1. **Using the paddle attachment, cream the cheese, sugar, and salt until smooth.**
2. **Add the eggs, fat, vanilla, and zest. Blend in.**
3. **Add the flour. Blend just until absorbed. Add the milk a little at a time, adding just enough to bring the mixture to a smooth, spreadable consistency.**
4. **Stir in the raisins, if desired.**

Hazelnut Filling

For large-quantity measurements, see page 592.

Ingredients	U.S.	Nuts at 100% Metric	%
Hazelnuts, toasted and ground	4 oz	125 g	100
Sugar	8 oz	250 g	200
Cinnamon	0.12 oz (2 tsp)	4 g	3
Eggs	1.5 oz	50 g	37.5
Cake crumbs	8 oz	250 g	200
Milk	4–8 oz	125–250 g	100–200
Total weight:	*1 lb 9 oz*	*804 g*	*640%*
	to	*to*	*to*
	1 lb 13 oz	*927 g*	*740%*

■ **P r o c e d u r e**

1. **Blend together all ingredients except milk.**
2. **Mix in enough milk to bring the mixture to a spreadable consistency.**

Poppy Seed Filling

Ingredients	U.S.		Poppy seeds at 100% Metric	%
Poppy seeds	8	oz	200 g	100
Water	4	oz	100 g	50
Butter, softened	3	oz	75 g	38
Honey	2	oz	50 g	25
Sugar	3	oz	75 g	38
Cake crumbs	8	oz	200 g	100
Eggs	1.5	oz	40 g	19
Lemon rind, grated	0.12	oz (1½ tsp)	3 g	1.5
Cinnamon	0.006	oz (¾ tsp)	1 g	0.75
Water (*as needed*)				
Total weight:	*1 lb 13*	*oz*	*744 g*	*372%*

or more, depending on amount of water added

■ **P r o c e d u r e**

1. Soak the seeds in the water overnight. Grind to a paste.

2. Add remaining ingredients and blend until smooth.

3. Add water as needed to bring to a spreadable consistency.

Chocolate Filling

For large-quantity measurements, see page 592.

Ingredients	U.S.		Cake crumbs at 100% Metric	%
Sugar	4	oz	100 g	33
Cocoa	1.25	oz	40 g	12
Cake crumbs	12	oz	300 g	100
Eggs	1	oz	25 g	8
Butter, melted	1.25	oz	40 g	12
Vanilla	0.25	oz	6 g	2
Water (*as needed*)	3	oz	75 g	25
Total weight:	*1 lb 6*	*oz*	*582 g*	*192%*

■ **P r o c e d u r e**

1. Sift together the sugar and cocoa.

2. Mix in the cake crumbs.

3. Add the eggs, butter, vanilla, and a little of the water. Blend in. Add enough additional water to bring to a smooth, spreadable consistency.

Variation

Mix 50% (6 oz/150 g) miniature chocolate chips into the filling.

Honey Pan Glaze (For Caramel Rolls)

For large-quantity measurements, see page 592.

Ingredients	U.S.		Brown sugar at 100% Metric	%
Brown sugar	10	oz	25 g	100
Butter, margarine, or shortening	4	oz	100 g	40
Honey	2.5	oz	60 g	25
Corn syrup (or malt syrup)	2.5	oz	60 g	25
Water (*as needed*)	1	oz	25 g	10
Total weight:	*1 lb 4*	*oz*	*274 g*	*200%*

■ **P r o c e d u r e**

1. Cream together the sugar, fat, honey, and corn syrup.

2. Add enough water to bring the mixture to a spreadable consistency.

MAKEUP TECHNIQUES

Just as for lean doughs, the object of rich dough makeup is to shape the dough into items that bake properly and have an attractive appearance. Most of the guidelines for making up lean yeast breads also hold true for rich doughs. In particular, review the use of dusting flour, discussed on page 90.

While lean doughs usually can be handled vigorously, rich doughs require more care. In particular, temperature control is important when handling rolled-in doughs so that the butter is neither too hard nor too soft and so that the dough does not become overproofed while you are making it up. Study the procedures for these doughs carefully.

Many sweet dough products, including most Danish pastries, are glazed with a clear glaze or apricot glaze after baking, preferably while they are still warm. After cooling, they may also be decorated with Flat Icing (p. 342). Flat icing is drizzled over the products; it doesn't cover them completely.

CROISSANT DOUGH

Plain Croissants

1. Roll the dough out into a rectangle 10 in. (25 cm) wide and about ⅛ in. (3 mm) thick. The length depends on the amount of dough used (a).

2. Cut the rectangle into triangles (b). Special roller cutters that do this quickly are available.

3. Place one of the triangles on the bench in front of you. Stretch the back corners outward slightly, as shown by the arrows (c).

4. Begin to roll up the dough toward the point (d).

5. Stretch out the point of the triangle slightly as you roll it up (e).

6. Finish rolling up the dough (f).

7. Bend the roll into a crescent shape. The point of the triangle must face the inside of the crescent and be tucked under the roll so that it won't pop up during baking (g).

a.

b.

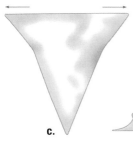

c.

d.

e.

f.

g.

Filled Croissants

Make up as for plain croissants, except place a small amount of desired filling on the base of each triangle before rolling up.

The technique used for petits pains au chocolat (which follows) can also be used to create filled croissant-dough products with a variety of fillings. These rolls are often called *croissants,* but this term is not accurate because the rolls are not crescent-shaped. (*Croissant* is the French word for crescent).

Petits Pains au Chocolat (Chocolate Rolls)

1. Roll out croissant dough into a sheet as for croissants.

2. Cut into rectangles 6 × 4 in. (15 × 10 cm).

3. Arrange a row of chocolate chips about 1½ inches (4 cm) from the narrow end of each rectangle. Use ⅓ oz (10 g) chocolate per roll.

4. Egg wash the opposite end of each rectangle so that the rolls will seal.

5. Roll up the dough tightly around the chocolate.

6. Proof, egg wash, and bake as for croissants.

BRIOCHES

The traditional brioche shape is shown here. Brioches may also be baked as pan loaves in many sizes and shapes.

1. For a small brioche, roll the dough into a round piece (a).

2. Using the edge of the hand, pinch off about one-fourth of the dough without detaching it. Roll the dough on the bench so that both parts are round (b).

3. Place the dough in the tin, large end first. With the fingertips, press the small ball into the larger one (c).

4. For a large brioche, separate the two parts of the dough. Place the large ball in the tin and make a hole in the center. Form the smaller ball into a pear shape and fit it into the hole (d). The baked loaf has the traditional brioche shape (e).

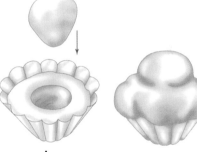

SWEET ROLLS AND DANISH ROLLS

Note: Many sweet dough products, including most Danish products, are glazed with Clear Glaze (p. 116) after baking, while still hot. After cooling, they may also be decorated with Flat Icing (p. 342). Flat icing is drizzled over the products; it doesn't cover them completely.

Crumb Buns

1. With a rolling pin, roll out sweet dough about ½-in. (12 mm) thick.

2. Cut into 2-in. (5 cm) squares.

3. Arrange the squares in rows on paper-lined sheet pans so that they touch each other.

4. Wash with egg wash or milk.

5. Sprinkle the tops heavily with Streusel Topping (p. 116).

6. Proof. Bake at 400°F (200°C).

7. When the buns are cool, they may be dusted lightly with 6X sugar.

Filled Buns

1. Scale the sweet dough into presses of desired size. Suggested size: 3 lb (1400 g) for 36 rolls. Round the presses, relax, and divide.

2. Round up the units and place them on paper-lined sheet pans in one of two ways:

   • Place them 2 in. (5 cm) apart so that they bake without touching.

   • Place them in rows so that they are just touching each other. Rolls baked in this way will rise higher and must be broken apart before being served.

3. Give the rolls a half proof.

4. Using either the fingers or a small, round object, press a round 1-in. (2.5 cm) indentation in the center of each roll.

5. Egg wash the tops of the rolls.

6. Fill the centers with desired filling, using about $\frac{1}{2}$ oz (15 g) per roll.

7. Continue proofing to about three-quarters proof. Bake at 400°F (200°C).

8. When cool, drizzle Flat Icing over the rolls.

Cinnamon Raisin Rolls

1. Prepare Cinnamon Raisin Filling (p. 119), leaving the raisins separate for now; you will need 1 small batch or about 10 ounces (300 g) for each unit of dough, as scaled in step 2.

2. Scale Danish Pastry Dough (Brioche-Style) into 22-oz (615 g) units. Roll out each unit into a rectangle 20 × 10 in. (50 × 25 cm). For the neatest results, roll slightly larger and trim to size with a knife or pastry wheel.

3. Spread the filling evenly over the dough with a palette knife, sprinkling the raisins over the dough after the filling has been spread. Leave a narrow band of dough uncovered along the top edge.

4. Roll up tightly from the bottom edge into a cylinder 20 in. (50 cm) long (a).

5. Cut into 8 slices $2\frac{1}{2}$ in. (6 cm) thick (b).

6. Place on a baking sheet lined with parchment and tuck the loose edge of the roll underneath. With the palm of the hand, flatten each roll to about 1 in. (2.5 cm) thick (c).

7. Proof for 25 minutes at 85°F (30°C).

8. Bake at 350°F (180°C) for 15 minutes.

9. Brush with Clear Glaze or Apricot Glaze when cool.

a.

b.

c.

Cinnamon Rolls

1. Scale sweet dough into 20-oz (570 g) units or as desired. On a floured bench, roll each piece of dough into a 9 × 12-in. rectangle about ¼-inch thick (23 × 30 × 0.5 cm). Brush off excess flour.

2. Brush with butter and sprinkle with 2 oz (60 g) cinnamon sugar (a). **a.**

3. Roll up like a jelly roll 12 in. (30 cm) long (b).

4. Cut into 1-in. (2.5 cm) rolls (c).

5. Place cut-side down in greased muffin tins or on greased sheet pans. One full-size 18 × 26-inch (46 × 66 cm) pan holds 48 rolls arranged in 6 rows of 8.

b.

c.

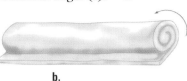
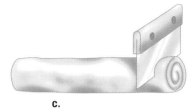

Pecan Maple Rolls

1. Prepare Pecan Maple Filling (p. 120); you will need 1 small batch or about 10 ounces (300 g) for each unit of dough, as scaled in step 2.

2. Scale Danish Pastry Dough (Brioche-Style) into 22-oz (615 g) units. Roll out each unit into a rectangle 20 × 10 in. (50 × 25 cm). For the neatest results, roll slightly larger and trim to size with a knife or pastry wheel.

3. Spread the filling evenly over the dough with a palette knife. Leave a narrow band of dough uncovered along the top edge.

4. Roll up from the bottom edge into a cylinder 20 in. (50 cm) long.

5. Cut into 20 slices 2 in. (5 cm) thick (a).

6. Butter and sugar 10 small brioche molds.

7. Place one slice of the dough roll cut-side up in each mold, tucking the loose end of the roll underneath. Press lightly into molds (b).

8. Egg wash the tops.

9. Proof for 25 minutes at 85°F (30°C).

10. Egg wash a second time.

11. Bake at 350°F (180°C) for 20 minutes.

12. Brush with Clear Glaze when cool.

**Clockwise from top left:
Pecan Maple Rolls,
Cinnamon Raisin Rolls,
Lemon Cheese Pastries**

a.

b.

Caramel Rolls

1. Prepare like cinnamon rolls.
2. Before panning, spread the bottoms of the pans with Honey Pan Glaze (p. 121). Use about 1 oz (30 g) per roll.

Caramel Nut Rolls or Pecan Rolls

Prepare like caramel rolls, but sprinkle the pan glaze with chopped nuts or pecan halves before placing the rolls in the pans.

Danish Spirals

1. Roll out Danish dough into a rectangle as for cinnamon rolls. The width of the roll may vary, depending on the desired size of the finished units. A wider rectangle will produce a thicker roll and, therefore, larger finished units.
2. Spread or sprinkle the rectangle with the desired filling. For example:

    Butter, cinnamon sugar, chopped nuts, and cake crumbs

    Butter, cinnamon sugar, and raisins

    Almond filling

    Prune filling

    Chocolate filling

    Loose fillings, such as chopped nuts, should be pressed on gently with a rolling pin.
3. Roll up like a jelly roll.
4. Slice to desired size.
5. Place the rolls on paper-lined pans and tuck the loose ends underneath.
6. Proof, egg wash, and bake at 400°F (200°C).

Variations Made from Filled Dough Roll or Danish Spiral

The filled dough roll is the starting point for a variety of sweet dough and Danish products.

1. *Filled Spirals.*   Make up like Danish Spirals, above. Give half proof, then press an indentation in the center and fill with desired filling. Complete the proof and bake as above.
2. *Combs and Bear Claws*   Make the Danish Spiral roll thinner and cut it into longer pieces. Flatten the pieces slightly and cut partway through each in three to five places. Leave straight or bend into a curve to open up the cuts (a).
3. *Figure-Eight Rolls*   Cut the Danish spiral rolls almost through. Open them up and lay them flat on the baking sheet (b).

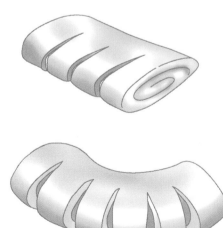

a.

b.

4. ***Three-Leaf Rolls***   Cut Danish spiral pieces in two places and spread the three segments apart (c).

c.

5. ***Butterfly Rolls***   Cut off slightly larger pieces from the Danish spiral roll. Crease them by pressing the center firmly with a wooden rod (d).

d.

Filled Danish Crescents

Make up like filled croissants (p. 123).

Danish Twists or Snails

1. Roll out the dough into a rectangle 16 in. (40 cm) wide and less then $\frac{1}{4}$ in. (5 mm) thick. (The length of the rectangle depends on the quantity of dough.) Brush the dough with melted butter. Sprinkle half of it with cinnamon sugar (a).

2. Fold the unsugared half over the sugared half. You now have a rectangle 8 in. (20 cm) wide. Roll the dough very gently with a rolling pin to press the layers together (b).

3. Cut the dough into strips $\frac{1}{2}$ in. (1 cm) wide (c).

4. Place one strip crosswise in front of you on the bench (d).

5. With the palms of your hands on the ends of the strip, roll one end toward you and the other end away from you, so that the strip twists. Stretch the strip slightly as you twist it (e).

6. Curl the strip into a spiral shape on the baking sheet. Tuck the end underneath and pinch it against the roll to seal it in place (f). If desired, press a hollow in the center of the roll and place a spoonful of filling in it.

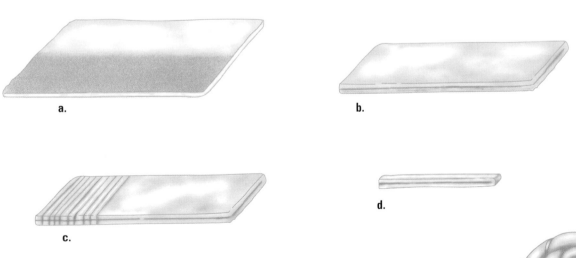

a.

b.

c.

d.

e.

f.

Danish Pockets

1. Roll out the dough less than ¼ in. (5 mm) thick. Cut it into 5-in. (13-cm) squares. Place desired filling in the center of each square (a). Brush the four corners lightly with water to help them seal when pressed together.

2. Fold two opposite corners over the center. Press down firmly to seal them together. (If desired, rolls may be left in this shape.) (b).

3. Fold the other two corners over the center and, again, press them firmly together (c).

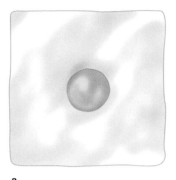
a.

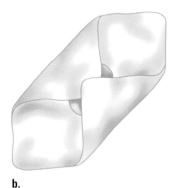
b.

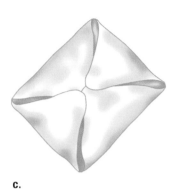
c.

a.

b.

Lemon Cheese Pastries

1. Prepare Lemon Cheese Filling (p. 117); you will need 3 oz (90 g) filling for each unit of dough, as scaled in step 2. Fill a pastry bag with a small plain tip with the filling.

2. Scale Danish Pastry Dough (Brioche-Style) into 22-oz (615 g) units. Roll out each unit into a rectangle 20 × 10 in. (50 × 25 cm). For the neatest results, roll slightly larger and trim to size with a knife or pastry wheel.

3. Roll out the dough into a rectangle 16 × 12 in. (40 × 30 cm). Cut 4 by 3 into 12 squares 4 in. (10 cm) on each side.

4. Egg wash the surface of each square.

5. Pipe the cheese mixture in a line down the center of each square (a).

6. Fold in half to make a rectangle. Press the edges well to seal (b).

7. Turn upside down and arrange on sheet pans lined with parchment. Egg wash the tops.

8. Proof for 15 minutes at 85°F (30°C).

9. Egg wash a second time. Sprinkle with sugar.

10. Bake at 350°F (180°C) for 12 minutes.

11. If desired, decorate the tops with slices of poached lemon.

Apricot Pinwheels

1. Scale Danish Pastry Dough (Croissant-Style) into 14-oz (400 g) units.

2. Roll out into a rectangle about ⅛ in. (3 mm) thick and approximately 8 × 12 inches (20 × 30 cm). (For the neatest results, roll slightly larger and trim to size with a knife or pastry wheel.)

3. Cut into 6 squares 4 in. (10 cm) on a side.

4. Make a cut about 1½ in. (4 cm) long from the corner of each square toward the center (a).

5. Brush each square with egg wash. Fold alternating corner flaps toward the center to make a pinwheel (b).

6. Proof for 20 minutes at 85°F (30°C).

7. Egg wash again.

8. With a pastry bag or spoon, deposit about 2 tsp (10 g) of Pastry Cream at the center of each pinwheel. Place an apricot half on top of the pastry cream, cut-side down (c).

9. Bake at 350°F (180°C) for 15 minutes.

10. Cool and brush with Clear Glaze or Apricot Glaze.

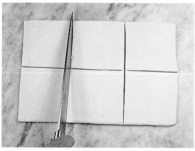

a.

b.

c.

**Left to right:
Apple Rosettes,
Cherry Vol-au-Vents,
Apricot Pinwheels**

Apple Rosettes

1. Scale Danish Pastry Dough (Croissant-Style) into 14-oz (400 g) units.
2. Roll out into a rectangle about ⅛ in. (3 mm) thick and approximately 8 × 12 in. (20 × 30 cm).
3. With a 4-in. (10 cm) round cutter, cut into 6 circles.
4. Make four equidistant cuts about 1½ in. (4 cm) long from the outside edge of each circle toward the center (a).
5. Brush each circle with egg wash. Fold alternating corner flaps toward the center to make a pinwheel. Press corners down to seal (b, c).
6. Proof for 20 minutes at 85°F (30°C).
7. Egg wash again.
8. With a pastry bag or spoon, deposit about 2 tsp (10 g) of Pastry Cream at the center of each pinwheel (d). Top the pastry cream with about an ounce (25 g) of Apple Compote Filling (e). Carefully press each mound of apple into place by hand.
9. Bake at 350°F (180°C) for 15 minutes.
10. Cool and brush with Clear Glaze or Apricot Glaze.

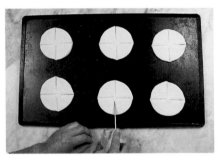

a.

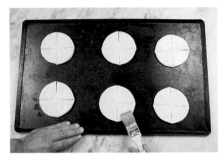

b.

c.

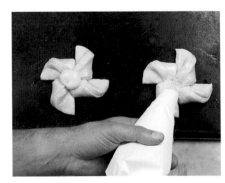

d.

e.

Cherry Vol-au-Vents

1. Scale Danish Pastry Dough (Croissant-Style) into 14-oz (400 g) units.

2. Roll out into a rectangle 7 × 11 in. (18 × 27 cm) in size.

3. Cut into 2 strips 3½ × 11 in. (9 × 27 cm), then cut each strip into 3½-inch (9 cm) squares.

4. Fold each square in half diagonally to form a triangle.

5. With a chef's knife, cut a strip ½ in. (1 cm) wide along the two short sides of the triangle, starting at the folded edge and stopping about ¾ inch (2 cm) from the opposite corner (a).

6. Unfold the square. Brush with egg wash.

7. Fold each cut strip to the opposite side to make a diamond-shaped pastry with a raised border all around. Press corners to seal (b).

8. Proof for 20 minutes at 85°F (30°C) for 15 minutes.

9. Egg wash again.

10. With a pastry bag or spoon, deposit about 2 tsp (10 g) of pastry cream in the center of each pastry. Fill with cherries. You will need about 1 oz (25 g) of cherries for each pastry (c).

11. Bake at 350°F (180°C) for 15 minutes.

12. Cool and brush with Apricot Glaze.

a.

b.

c.

COFFEE CAKES

Coffee cakes can be made up into many different sizes and shapes. The weight of the dough required and the size of the cake can be varied greatly according to the needs of the bakeshop. Except when a specific dough is indicated, the following can be made with either a sweet dough or Danish dough.

Wreath Coffee Cake

1. Using a sweet dough or Danish dough, make a filled dough roll as for cinnamon rolls, but do not cut into separate pieces. Other fillings, such as prune or date, may be used instead of butter and cinnamon sugar.

2. Shape the roll into a circle (a). Place on a greased baking sheet. Cut partway through the dough at 1-in. (2.5 cm) intervals (b). Twist each segment outward to open the cuts (c).

3. Egg wash after proofing.

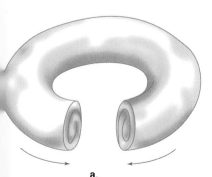

a.

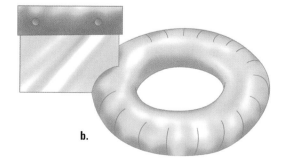

b.

c.

Filled Coffee Cake

1. Scale sweet dough or Danish dough into 12-oz (340 g) units.
2. Roll each unit into a rectangle 9 × 18 in. (23 × 46 cm).
3. Spread half of each rectangle with desired filling, using about 6 oz (170 g) filling.
4. Fold the unspread half over the spread half to make a 9-in. (23 cm) square.
5. Place in greased 9-in. (23 cm) square pan.
6. Sprinkle with streusel topping, about 4 oz (110 g) per pan.
7. Proof. Bake at 375°F (190°C).

Loaf Coffee Cake

1. Using babka dough, make a filled dough roll as for cinnamon rolls, using desired filling.
2. Fold the roll in half, then twist it up.
3. Place the twisted roll in a greased loaf pan, or coil the twist like a snail and place in a round pan.
4. Proof, wash with melted butter, and bake at 350°F (175°C).

Danish Pretzel

1. Using almond filling, make up Danish dough into a long, thin dough roll as for cinnamon rolls.
2. Twist the roll into a pretzel shape. Place on a sheet pan.
3. Proof, egg wash, and bake at 375°F (190°C).

Strip Coffee Cake or Danish Strip

1. Roll the Danish dough out about ¼ in. (6 mm) thick into a rectangle the length of the desired strip and about twice as wide.
2. Spread the desired filling lengthwise down the center of the dough, leaving a ½-in. (1 cm) margin at both ends.
3. Brush both ends and one edge of the rectangle with egg wash (in order to seal the seams).
4. Fold the side of the rectangle without the egg wash over the center of the filling. Fold the other side over the center, overlapping the first side by ½ in. (1 cm).
5. Turn the strip over and place it seam-side down on a paper-lined pan. Make five or six diagonal slashes in the top of the dough; cut through to the filling but not to the bottom layer of dough.
6. Proof, egg wash, and bake at 375°F (190°C).

Danish Ring

1. Using desired filling, make up Danish dough into a filled dough roll as for cinnamon rolls, but make it longer and thinner.
2. Flatten the roll slightly with a rolling pin. Make two parallel cuts lengthwise through the dough; cut through the bottom layer, but leave about 1 in. (2.5 cm) uncut at both ends.
3. Twist the strip as for Danish Twists (p. 127). Form the twist into a ring and seal the ends together.
4. Proof and egg wash. Ring may also be sprinkled with chopped or sliced nuts. Bake at 375°F (190°C).

▶ TERMS FOR REVIEW

brioche   panettone
baba   simple fold
croissant

▶ QUESTIONS FOR REVIEW

1. What mixing method is used for brioche dough and kugelhopf dough? Why?

2. Butter is hard when cold and melts easily at room temperature. What precautions do you think are necessary when using butter as the rolling-in fat for Danish pastry dough?

3. Explain the difference between Danish dough, croissant-style, and Danish dough, brioche-style.

4. Describe the rolling-in procedure for Danish dough.

Quick Breads

Quick breads are the perfect solution for food service operations that want to offer their patrons fresh, homemade bread products but can't justify the labor cost of making yeast breads. Retail bakeries have discovered a great demand for such items as fresh muffins. Also, quick breads have the advantage of being easily made in almost unlimited varieties using such ingredients as whole wheat flour, rye flour, cornmeal, bran, oatmeal, and many kinds of fruits, nuts, and spices. Even breads made with vegetables have become popular.

As their name implies, quick breads are quick to make. Because they are leavened by chemical leaveners and steam, not by yeast, no fermentation time is necessary. And because they are usually tender products with little gluten development, mixing them takes just a few minutes.

Although prepared biscuit and muffin mixes are available, the only extra work that making these products from scratch requires is the time to scale a few ingredients. With a careful and imaginative selection of ingredients and an understanding of basic mixing methods, you can create superior products.

After reading this
chapter, you should be
able to:

■ Prepare baking powder biscuits
and variations of them.

■ Prepare muffins, loaf breads, coffee cakes, and corn breads.

■ Prepare popovers.

MIXING AND PRODUCTION METHODS

Dough mixtures for quick breads are generally of two types:

- *Soft doughs* are used for biscuits. They are, with a few exceptions, rolled out and cut into desired shapes.

- *Batters* may be either *pour batters,* which are liquid enough to be poured, or *drop batters,* which are thick enough to be dropped from a spoon in lumps.

GLUTEN DEVELOPMENT IN QUICK BREADS

Only slight gluten development is desirable in most quick breads. Tenderness is a desirable quality, rather than the chewy quality of many yeast breads.

In addition, chemical leavening agents do not create the same kind of texture that yeast does, and they are not strong enough to create a light, tender product if the gluten is too strong.

Muffin, loaf bread, and pancake batters are mixed as little as possible, only until the dry ingredients are moistened. This, plus the presence of fat and sugar, keeps gluten development low. Overmixing muffin batter produces not only toughness but also irregular shapes and large, elongated holes inside the muffins. This last condition is called *tunneling.*

Biscuit dough is often lightly kneaded, enough to help develop some flakiness but not enough to toughen the product.

Popovers are the exception among quick breads. They are made with a thin batter and leavened only by steam. Very large holes develop inside the product during baking, and the structure must be strong enough to hold up without collapsing. Thus, bread flour is used and the batter is mixed well to develop the gluten. The high percentage of egg in popovers also helps build structure.

MIXING METHODS

Most quick-bread doughs and batters are mixed by one of three mixing methods.

- The *biscuit method* is used for biscuits, scones, and similar products. It is sometimes called the *pastry method* because it is like that used for mixing pie pastry.

- The *muffin method* is used for muffins, pancakes, waffles, and many loaf-type or sheet-type quick breads. This method is fast and easy. However, the danger is that the dough can quickly become overmixed, resulting in toughness. *Muffin batter should be mixed only until the dry ingredients are just moistened.* Do not attempt to achieve a smooth batter. Some loaf breads and coffee cakes are higher in fat and sugar than muffins, so they can withstand a little more mixing without becoming tough.

- The *creaming method* is a cake mixing method that is sometimes applied to muffins and loaf breads. Actually, there is no exact dividing line between muffin products and cakes, and if they are rich enough, muffin products may be considered cakes rather than breads.

The creaming method is a more time-consuming procedure than the muffin method. However, it produces fine-textured goods and there is less danger of overmixing. The creaming method is especially useful for products with high fat and sugar content because it helps mix the ingredients more uniformly.

Some biscuits are also mixed by the creaming method. These have a texture that is more cakelike and less flaky than that produced by the biscuit method.

Procedure—Biscuit Method

1. Scale all ingredients accurately.

2. Sift the dry ingredients together into a mixing bowl.

3. Cut in the shortening, using the paddle attachment or the pastry knife attachment; if you prefer, cut in the fat by hand, using a pastry blender or your fingers. Continue until the mixture resembles a coarse cornmeal.

4. Combine the liquid ingredients.

5. Add the liquid to the dry ingredients. Mix just until the ingredients are combined and a soft dough is formed. Do not overmix.

6. Bring the dough to the bench and knead it lightly by pressing it out and folding it in half. Rotate the dough 90 degrees between folds.

7. Repeat this procedure about 10 to 20 times, or for about 30 seconds. The dough should be soft and slightly elastic, but not sticky. Overkneading toughens the biscuits.

   The dough is now ready for makeup.

Variations

Changes in the basic procedure produce different characteristics in the finished product:

1. Using slightly more shortening and cutting it in less—only until the pieces are the size of peas—produces a flakier biscuit.

2. Omitting the kneading step produces very tender, crustier biscuits, but with less volume.

a.

b.

Procedure—Muffin Method

1. Sift together the dry ingredients (a).

2. Combine all liquid ingredients, including melted fat or oil.

3. Add the liquids to the dry ingredients and mix just until all the flour is moistened. The batter will look lumpy. Be careful not to overmix (b).

4. Pan and bake immediately (c). The dry and liquid mixtures may be prepared in advance, but once the mixtures are combined, the batter should be baked without delay, or loss of volume may result.

c.

*P*rocedure—Creaming Method for Biscuits

1. Combine the fat, sugar, salt, and milk powder (if used) in the bowl of a mixer fitted with the paddle attachment.
2. Blend to a smooth paste.
3. Add the eggs and blend in thoroughly.
4. Add the water or milk (liquid) and mix in.
5. Sift together the flour and baking powder. Add to the bowl and mix to a smooth dough.

*P*rocedure—Creaming Method for Muffins, Loaves, and Coffee Cakes

1. Combine the fat, sugar, salt, spices, and milk powder (if used) in the bowl of a mixer fitted with the paddle attachment.
2. Cream the ingredients together until light.
3. Add the eggs in two or three stages. Cream well after each addition before adding more eggs.
4. Add the liquid ingredients and stir lightly.
5. Sift together the flour and baking powder. Add and mix just until smooth.

MAKEUP METHODS

Makeup of Biscuits

1. Roll the biscuit dough out into a sheet about ½ in. (1 cm) thick, being careful to roll it evenly and to a uniform thickness.

   Biscuits approximately double in height during baking.

2. Cut into desired shapes.

   When using round hand cutters, cut straight down. Do not twist the cutter. Space the cuts as closely as possible to minimize scraps. Reworked scrap dough produces tougher biscuits.

   Cutting into squares or triangles with a pastry cutter knife eliminates scraps that would have to be rerolled. Roller cutters also eliminate or reduce scraps.

3. Place the biscuits ½ in. (1 cm) apart on greased or paper-lined baking sheets. For softer biscuits without crusty sides, arrange the units so that they touch each other; these must be broken apart after baking.

4. If desired, brush the tops with egg wash or milk to aid browning.

5. Bake as soon as possible.

Makeup and Panning of Muffin Products

Muffin tins and loaf pans should be greased with shortening and dusted with flour or greased with a commercial pan grease preparation. Sheet pans for corn breads and other sheet products may be lined with silicone paper.

Paper liners may be used for muffin tins. However, because the muffins do not stick to greased tins, they rise more freely and take a better shape without paper liners.

When portioning batter into muffin tins, be careful not to stir the mix and toughen it. Scoop the batter from the outside edge for best results.

Batters for muffins and quick loaf breads are generally interchangeable. In other words, formulas for banana bread or date-nut bread, for example, may be baked as muffins instead of as loaves. Similarly, standard muffin batters may also be baked as loaves or sheets.

Please note that the muffin and loaf bread recipes included here should be thought of as breads rather than as tea cakes. In particular, their fat and sugar contents are intentionally kept lower than some of the rather rich, oily muffins sometimes sold today. Formulas for richer, more cakelike muffins are included later in the chapter. If you wish to experiment with the two basic muffin recipes to make them richer in fat and sugar, first read the section on cake formula balance beginning on page 292.

FORMULAS

Biscuits I

Ingredients	U.S.			Metric	%
Bread flour	1 lb	4	oz	600 g	50
Pastry flour	1 lb	4	oz	600 g	50
Salt		0.75	oz	24 g	2
Sugar		2	oz	60 g	5
Baking powder		2.5	oz	72 g	6
Shortening (regular) and/or butter		14	oz	420 g	35
Milk	1 lb	10	oz	800 g	65
Total weight:	*5 lb*	*5*	*oz*	*2576 g*	*213%*

■ Procedure

Mixing
Biscuit method
Scaling
Approximately 1 lb (450 g) per dozen 2-in. (5 cm) biscuits
Baking
425°F (218°C), about 15–20 minutes

Variations

Buttermilk Biscuits
Use buttermilk in place of regular milk.

Cheese Biscuits

Ingredients	U.S.	Metric	%
Grated cheddar cheese	12 oz	360 g	30

Add cheese to dry ingredients.

Currant Biscuits

Ingredients	U.S.	Metric	%
Sugar	4 oz	120 g	10
Dried currants	6 oz	180 g	15

Increase sugar to the above amount. Add currants to the dry ingredients. Sprinkle tops with cinnamon sugar before baking.

Herb Biscuits

Ingredients	U.S.	Metric	%
Fresh chopped parsley	2 oz	60 g	5

Add parsley to the dry ingredients.

Biscuits II

Ingredients	U.S.			Metric		%
Shortening		6	oz	150	g	15
Sugar		4	oz	100	g	10
Salt		0.5	oz	12.5	g	1.25
Nonfat milk solids		2	oz	50	g	5
Eggs		3	oz	75	g	7.5
Water	1 lb	8	oz	600	g	60
Bread flour	1 lb	12	oz	700	g	70
Cake flour		12	oz	300	g	30
Baking powder		2	oz	50	g	5
Total weight:	*5 lb*	*1*	*oz*	*2037*	*g*	*203%*

■ P r o c e d u r e

Mixing
Creaming method
Baking
425°F (218°C)

Variation

Ingredients	U.S.	Metric	%
Butter	7.5 oz	190 g	19

Substitute butter for the shortening.

Plain Muffins

Ingredients	U.S.			Metric	%
Pastry flour	2 lb	8	oz	1200 g	100
Sugar		12	oz	360 g	30
Baking powder		2.5	oz	72 g	6
Salt		0.5	oz	15 g	1.25
Eggs, beaten		8	oz	240 g	20
Milk	2 lb			950 g	80
Butter or shortening, melted		12	oz	360 g	30
Total weight:	*6 lb*	*11*	*oz*	*3197 g*	*267%*

■ P r o c e d u r e

Mixing
Muffin method
Panning
Grease and flour muffin tins. Fill tins one-half to two-thirds full. Exact weight depends on pan size. Average sizes are 2 oz (60 g) for small muffins, 4 oz (110 g) for medium muffins, and 5–6 oz (140–170 g) for large muffins.
Baking
400°F (200°C), about 20–30 minutes

Muffins, clockwise from top: blueberry, corn, bran

Variations

Raisin Spice Muffins

Ingredients	U.S.	Metric	%
Raisins	8 oz	240 g	20
Cinnamon	0.17 oz (2½ tsp)	5 g	0.4
Nutmeg	0.08 oz (1 tsp)	2.5 g	0.2

Add raisins, cinnamon, and nutmeg to dry ingredients.

Blueberry Muffins

Ingredients	U.S.	Metric	%
Blueberries (well drained)	1 lb	480 g	40

Fold blueberries into finished batter.

Whole Wheat Muffins

Ingredients	U.S.	Metric	%
Pastry flour	1 lb 12 oz	840 g	70
Whole wheat flour	12 oz	360 g	30
Baking powder	1.5 oz	50 g	4
Baking soda	0.3 oz (2 tsp)	10 g	0.75
Molasses	4 oz	120 g	10

Adjust the flour and leavening as listed above. Add molasses to liquid ingredients.

Corn Muffins

Ingredients	U.S.	Metric	%
Pastry flour	1 lb 10 oz	800 g	65
Cornmeal	14 oz	400 g	35

Adjust the flour as listed above. (See also the Corn Bread formula on p. 143.)

Corn Cheese Muffins

Ingredients	U.S.	Metric	%
Grated cheddar cheese	1 lb 4 oz	600 g	50

Add cheese to the dry ingredients in the above Corn Muffin formula. Use half the amount of sugar.

Bran Muffins

Ingredients	U.S.	Metric	%
Pastry flour	12 oz	360 g	30
Bread flour	1 lb	480 g	40
Bran	12 oz	360 g	30
Eggs	12 oz	360 g	30
Raisins	6 oz	180 g	15
Molasses	6 oz	180 g	15

Adjust flour and increase eggs as listed above. Add raisins to the dry ingredients and molasses to the liquid ingredients.

Crumb Coffee Cake

Ingredients	U.S.	Metric	%
Sugar	1 lb 4 oz	600 g	50
Butter or shortening	1 lb 4 oz	600 g	50
Streusel (p. 116)	2 lb	1000 g	80

Increase sugar and fat as listed above. Pour into a greased, paper-lined sheet pan and spread smooth. Top with Streusel. Bake at 360°F (182°C), about 30 minutes.

Muffins

Ingredients	U.S.			Metric	%
Shortening and/or butter	1 lb			400 g	40
Sugar	1 lb	4	oz	500 g	50
Salt		0.5	oz	12 g	1.25
Nonfat milk solids		3	oz	70 g	7
Eggs		12	oz	300 g	30
Water	1 lb	14	oz	750 g	75
Cake flour	2 lb	8	oz	1000 g	100
Baking powder		2	oz		5
Total weight:	*7 lb*	*11*	*oz*	*3082 g*	*308%*

■ **P r o c e d u r e**

Mixing
Creaming method
Scaling
Fill tins one-half to two-thirds full.
Baking
400°F (200°C), about 20–30 minutes

Variations

Chocolate Chip Muffins

Ingredients	U.S.		Metric		%
White granulated sugar	1 lb		400	g	40
Brown sugar		4 oz	100	g	10
Vanilla extract		0.5 oz	12.5 g		1.25
Chocolate chips		12 oz	300	g	30

Adjust the sugar as listed above. Add vanilla and chocolate chips to the formula. Top with Cinnamon Sugar (p. 116) before baking.

Blueberry Muffins

Ingredients	U.S.	Metric	%
Blueberries (well drained)	1 lb 4 oz	500 g	50

Fold blueberries into finished batter.

Raisin Spice Muffins

Ingredients	U.S.	Metric		%
Raisins	10 oz	250	g	25
Cinnamon	0.2 oz (3½ tsp)	5	g	0.5
Nutmeg	0.1 oz (1¼ tsp)	2.5	g	0.25

Add raisins, cinnamon, and nutmeg to dry ingredients.

Corn Bread, Muffins, or Sticks

Ingredients	U.S.			Metric	%
Pastry flour	1 lb	4	oz	600 g	50
Cornmeal	1 lb	4	oz	600 g	50
Sugar		6	oz	180 g	15
Baking powder		2	oz	60 g	5
Nonfat milk solids		3	oz	90 g	7.5
Salt		0.75	oz	24 g	2
Eggs, beaten		8	oz	240 g	20
Water	2 lb	2	oz	1000 g	85
Corn syrup		2	oz	60 g	5
Butter or shortening, melted		12	oz	360 g	30
Total weight:	6 lb 11		oz	3214 g	269%

■ Procedure

Mixing
Muffin method
Scaling
60 oz (1700 g) per half-size sheet pan (13 × 18 in./33 × 46 cm)
24 oz (680 g) per 9-in. (23 cm) square pan or per dozen muffins
10 oz (280 g) per dozen corn sticks
Baking
400°F (200°C) for corn bread, 25–30 minutes
425°F (218°C) for muffins or sticks, 15–20 minutes

Variation

Use buttermilk instead of water and omit nonfat milk solids. Reduce baking powder to 2.5% (1 oz/30 g) and add 1.25% (0.5 oz/15 g) baking soda.

Zucchini Carrot Nut Muffins

Ingredients	U.S.			Metric		%
Pastry flour	2 lb			960	g	80
Bran		8	oz	240	g	20
Salt		0.5	oz	15	g	1.25
Baking powder		0.6	oz (3½ tsp)	18	g	1.5
Baking soda		0.4	oz (2¼ tsp)	12	g	1
Cinnamon		0.17	oz (2½ tsp)	5	g	0.4
Nutmeg		0.08	oz (1 tsp)	2.5 g		0.2
Ginger		0.04	oz (½ tsp)	1	g	0.1
Pecans or walnuts, chopped		10	oz	300	g	25
Shredded, unsweetened coconut		4	oz	120	g	10
Eggs	1 lb			480	g	40
Sugar	1 lb 14		oz	900	g	75
Zucchini, grated		12	oz	360	g	30
Carrot, grated		12	oz	360	g	30
Vegetable oil	1 lb			480	g	40
Total weight:	8 lb 13		oz	4253	g	354%

■ Procedure

Mixing
Modified muffin method
1. Sift the flour, leavenings, and spices. Stir in the bran, nuts, and coconut.
2. Beat the eggs and sugar until well mixed, but do not whip into a foam. Stir in the grated vegetables and the oil.
3. Add the egg mixture to the dry ingredients and mix just until combined.

Scaling
Fill tins two-thirds full.
Baking
400°F (200°C), about 30 minutes.

Scones

Ingredients	U.S.			Metric	%
Bread flour	1 lb	8	oz	600 g	50
Pastry flour	1 lb	8	oz	600 g	50
Sugar		6	oz	150 g	12.5
Salt		0.5	oz	12 g	1
Baking powder		3	oz	72 g	6
Shortening and/or butter	1 lb			400 g	33
Eggs		10	oz	240 g	20
Milk	1 lb	10	oz	650 g	54
Total weight:	*6 lb*	*13*	*oz*	*2724 g*	*226%*

■ **P r o c e d u r e**

Mixing
Biscuit method
Makeup Variations
- **Scale at 1 lb (450 g), round up, and flatten to ½ in. (12 mm) thick. Cut into 8 wedges.**
- **Roll out into a rectangle ½ in. (12 mm) thick and cut into triangles as for croissants (see p. 122).**
- **Roll out into a rectangle ½ in. (12 mm) thick and cut out with cutters like biscuits.**
Place on greased or paper-lined sheet pans. Egg wash tops.
Baking
425°F (218°C), about 15–20 minutes

Variation

Ingredients	U.S.	Metric	%
Raisins or currants	12 oz	300 g	25

Add raisins or currants to the dry ingredients after cutting in fat.

 Cranberry Scones

For large-quantity measurements, see page 592.

Ingredients	U.S.			Metric	%
Butter		6	oz	185 g	25
Sugar		5	oz	150 g	21
Salt		0.25	oz	8 g	1
Egg yolks		1.33 oz (2 yolks)		40 g	5.5
Milk		14	oz	435 g	58
Pastry flour	1 lb	8	oz	750 g	100
Baking powder		1.5	oz	45 g	6
Dried cranberries		4	oz	125 g	17
Total weight:	*2 lb*	*10*	*oz*	*1303 g*	*175%*

■ **P r o c e d u r e**

Mixing
Creaming method
Makeup and Baking
See Scones formula above.

Steamed Brown Bread

Ingredients	U.S.		Metric	%
Bread flour	8	oz	250 g	28.5
Whole wheat flour	4	oz	125 g	14
Light rye flour	8	oz	250 g	28.5
Cornmeal	8	oz	250 g	28.5
Salt	0.75	oz	10 g	1
Baking soda	1.25	oz	20 g	2
Raisins	8	oz	250 g	28.5
Buttermilk	2 lb		1000 g	114
Molasses	15	oz	475 g	54
Total weight:	*5 lb 5 oz*		*2630 g*	*299%*

■ Procedure

Mixing
Muffin method
Scaling and Cooking
Fill well-greased molds one-half full, about 16 oz for each quart of capacity (500 g per liter). Cover molds and steam for 3 hours.

Orange Nut Bread

Ingredients	U.S.		Metric	%
Sugar	12	oz	350 g	50
Orange zest, grated	1	oz	30 g	4
Pastry flour	1 lb 8	oz	700 g	100
Nonfat milk solids	2	oz	60 g	8
Baking powder	1	oz	30 g	4
Baking soda	0.3 oz (2 tsp)		10 g	1.4
Salt	0.3 oz (2 tsp)		10 g	1.4
Walnuts, chopped	12	oz	350 g	50
Eggs	5	oz	140 g	20
Orange juice	6	oz	175 g	25
Water	1 lb		450 g	65
Oil or melted butter or shortening	2.5 oz		70 g	10
Total weight:	*5 lb 2 oz*		*2375 g*	*329%*

■ Procedure

Mixing
Muffin method. Blend the sugar and orange zest thoroughly before adding remaining ingredients to ensure even distribution.
Scaling
1 lb 4 oz (575 g) per $7^3/_8 \times 3^5/_8$-in. (19 × 9 cm) loaf pan
1 lb 10 oz (750 g) per $8^1/_2 \times 4^1/_2$-in. (22 × 11 cm) loaf pan
Baking
375°F (190°C), about 50 minutes

Variation

Lemon Nut Bread
Substitute grated lemon zest for the orange zest. Omit the orange juice and add 8% (2 oz/60 g) lemon juice. Increase the water to 83% (1 lb 4 oz/580 g).

Banana Bread

Ingredients	U.S.		Metric	%
Pastry flour	1 lb 8	oz	700 g	100
Sugar	10	oz	280 g	40
Baking powder	1.25	oz	35 g	5
Baking soda	0.14 oz (1 tsp)		4 g	0.6
Salt	0.33 oz (2 tsp)		9 g	1.25
Walnuts, chopped	6	oz	175 g	25
Eggs	10	oz	280 g	40
Ripe banana pulp, puréed	1 lb 8	oz	700 g	100
Oil or melted butter or shortening	8	oz	230 g	33
Total weight:	*5 lb 4*	*oz*	*2413 g*	*344%*

■ P r o c e d u r e

Mixing
Muffin method
Scaling
1 lb 4 oz (575 g) per 7³/₈ × 3⁵/₈-in. (19 × 9 cm) loaf pan
1 lb 10 oz (750 g) per 8¹/₂ × 4¹/₂-in. (22 × 11 cm) loaf pan
Baking
375°F (190°C), about 50 minutes

Variation

For a more delicate, cakelike product, make the following adjustments:
1. Fat: Increase to 40% (10 oz/280 g). Use shortening and/or butter, not oil.
2. Sugar: Increase to 60% (15 oz/420 g).
3. Flour: Use cake flour.
4. Mixing: Mix by the creaming method.

Date Nut Bread

Ingredients	U.S.		Metric	%
Shortening and/or butter	8	oz	200 g	40
Brown sugar	8	oz	200 g	40
Salt	0.25 oz		6 g	1.25
Nonfat milk solids	1.5	oz	35 g	7
Eggs	6	oz	150 g	30
Water	15	oz	375 g	75
Cake flour	1 lb		400 g	80
Whole wheat flour	4	oz	100 g	20
Baking powder	0.75 oz		20 g	3.75
Baking soda	0.25 oz		6 g	1.25
Dates (see *note*)	10	oz	250 g	50
Walnuts, chopped	6	oz	3150 g	30
Total weight:	*4 lb 11*	*oz*	*1891 g*	*378%*

Note After scaling the dates, soak them in water until very soft. Drain and chop.

■ P r o c e d u r e

Mixing
Creaming method. Fold dates and nuts into finished batter.
Scaling
1 lb 4 oz (575 g) per 7³/₈ × 3⁵/₈-in. (19 × 9 cm) loaf pan
1 lb 10 oz (750 g) per 8¹/₂ × 4¹/₂-in. (22 × 11 cm) loaf pan
Baking
375°F (190°C), about 50 minutes

Variations

Substitute other nuts, or a mixture, for the walnuts. For example:
 pecans
 hazelnuts, toasted
 almonds, toasted
Substitute other dried fruits for the dates. For example:
 prunes
 raisins
 dried apricots
 dried apples
 dried figs

Plum Cake

Ingredients	U.S.			Metric	%
Pastry flour	1 lb	4	oz	600 g	100
Baking powder		0.5	oz	15 g	3
Salt		0.25	oz	8 g	1.5
Cinnamon		0.06	oz (1 tsp)	2 g	0.3
Brown sugar		10	oz	300 g	50
Butter		10	oz	300 g	50
Eggs		9	oz	270 g	45
Milk	1 lb	2	oz	540 g	
Topping					
Italian-style prune plums, halved and pitted	3 lb	12	oz	1800 g	300
Cinnamon Sugar (p. 116)		4	oz	120 g	20
Total weight:	*8 lb*	*3*	*oz*	*3955 g*	*659%*

■ P r o c e d u r e

Mixing
Biscuit method. Because of the moisture in the brown sugar, the dry ingredients must be rubbed through the sieve when sifted.
Scaling and Makeup
One recipe is enough for one half-size sheet pan, three 9-in. (23 cm) square pans, or four 8-in. (20 cm) square pans. Spread the dough in greased and floured pans. Arrange plum halves, cut-side up, on top of the dough. Sprinkle with Cinnamon Sugar.
Baking
400°F (200°C), 35 minutes

Variations

For a more cakelike texture, mix the dough using the creaming method.

Top the cake with Streusel (p. 116) instead of cinnamon sugar before baking.

Almond–Poppy Seed Muffins

Ingredients	U.S.			Metric	%
Butter		14	oz	450 g	60
Sugar	1 lb	2	oz	560 g	75
Eggs		12	oz	375 g	50
Almond extract		0.16	oz (1 tsp)	5 g	0.7
Buttermilk	1 pt			500 g	67
Pastry flour	1 lb	8	oz	750 g	100
Baking powder		0.25	oz (1½ tsp)	8 g	1
Baking soda		0.16	oz (1 tsp)	5 g	0.7
Salt		0.2	oz (1 tsp)	6 g	0.8
Poppy seeds		1	oz	30 g	4
Total weight:	*5 lb*	*5*	*oz*	*2689 g*	*359%*

■ P r o c e d u r e

Mixing
Creaming method. Mix the poppy seeds with the dry ingredients after sifting.
Scaling
Fill tins two-thirds full.
Baking
375°F (190°C), about 30 minutes

Variation

Lemon–Poppy Seed Muffins
Flavor the muffins with lemon extract instead of almond extract.

Apple Spice Muffins

Ingredients	U.S.		Metric		%
Butter		14 oz	435	g	60
Brown sugar	1 lb 2	oz	540	g	75
Salt		0.25 oz (1½ tsp)	7	g	1
Cinnamon		0.15 oz (2 tsp)	4	g	0.6
Nutmeg		0.05 oz (¾ tsp)	1.5	g	0.2
Eggs		8 oz	240	g	33
Buttermilk		12 oz	360	g	50
Applesauce	1 lb 2	oz	540	g	75
Pastry flour	1 lb 4	oz	600	g	83
Whole wheat flour		4 oz	120	g	17
Baking powder		0.5 oz	15	g	2
Baking soda		0.25 oz (1½ tsp)	7	g	1
Total weight:	5 lb 14	oz	2869	g	397%

■ **P r o c e d u r e**

Mixing
Creaming method
Scaling
Fill tins two-thirds full.
Baking
400°F (200°C), about 30 minutes

Pumpkin Muffins

Ingredients	U.S.		Metric		%
Butter		12 oz	375	g	50
Brown sugar	1 lb		500	g	67
Ginger		0.05 oz (¾ tsp)	1.5	g	0.2
Cinnamon		0.04 oz (½ tsp)	1.25	g	0.17
Nutmeg		0.03 oz (⅓ tsp)	0.75	g	0.1
Allspice		0.05 oz (¾ tsp)	1.5	g	0.2
Salt		0.14 oz (¾ tsp)	4.5	g	0.6
Eggs		6 oz	190	g	25
Buttermilk		12 oz	375	g	50
Pumpkin purée, canned	10	oz	300	g	40
Pastry flour	1 lb 8	oz	750	g	100
Baking powder		0.33 oz (2 tsp)	10	g	1.4
Baking soda		0.33 oz (2 tsp)	10	g	1.4
Total weight:	5 lb		2519	g	336%

■ **P r o c e d u r e**

Mixing
Creaming method
Scaling
Fill tins two-thirds full.
Baking
400°F (200°C), about 30 minutes

Double Chocolate Muffins

Ingredients	U.S.			Metric		%
Butter		10	oz	300	g	40
Sugar		11	oz	340	g	45
Semisweet chocolate	1 lb			500	g	67
Eggs		5	oz	150	g	20
Buttermilk	1 pt	4	oz	625	g	83
Flour	1 lb	8	oz	750	g	100
Baking soda		0.5	oz	15	g	2
Salt		0.14 oz (¾ tsp)		4.5	g	0.6
Chocolate chips		12	oz	375	g	50
Total weight:	*6 lb*	*2*	*oz*	*3059*	*g*	*407%*

■ P r o c e d u r e

Mixing
Creaming method. Melt the chocolate, cool it to room temperature, and cream it into the butter and sugar mixture. Add the chocolate chips to the batter at the same time as the dry ingredients. (Note that there is no baking powder in this formula, only baking soda.)

Scaling
Fill tins two-thirds full.

Baking
400°F (200°C), about 30 minutes

Soda Bread

Ingredients	U.S.			Metric		%
Pastry flour	2 lb	8	oz	1200	g	100
Baking powder		2	oz	60	g	5
Baking soda		0.5	oz	15	g	1.25
Salt		0.5	oz	15	g	1.25
Sugar		2	oz	60	g	5
Shortening or butter		4	oz	120	g	10
Currants		8	oz	240	g	20
Buttermilk	2 lb	4	oz	1080	g	90
Total weight:	*5 lb 13*		*oz*	*2790*	*g*	*232%*

■ P r o c e d u r e

Mixing
Biscuit method. Stir in currants after cutting in fat.

Scaling
1 lb (450 g) per unit

Makeup
Round into a ball-shaped loaf. Place on sheet pan. Cut a deep cross into the top.

Baking
400°F (200°C), about 40–50 minutes

Variation

Add 1.25% (0.5 oz/15 g) caraway seeds. Omit currants or leave them in, as desired.

Popovers

Ingredients	U.S.			Metric		%
Eggs	1 lb	4	oz	625	g	125
Milk	2 lb			1000	g	200
Salt		0.25	oz	8	g	1.5
Butter or shortening, melted		2	oz	60	g	12.5
Bread flour	1 lb			500	g	100
Total weight:	*4 lb 6*		*ozs*	*2193*	*g*	*439%*

■ P r o c e d u r e

Mixing
1. Beat eggs, milk, and salt together with whip attachment until well blended. Add melted fat.
2. Replace whip with paddle. Mix in flour until completely smooth.

Scaling and Panning
Grease every other cup of muffin tins (to allow room for expansion). Fill cups about one-half full, about 1½ oz (45 g) batter per unit.

Baking
425°F (218°C) for 30–40 minutes. Before removing them from the oven, be sure popovers are dry and firm enough to avoid collapsing. Remove from pans immediately.

Gingerbread

Ingredients	Old-Fashioned Gingerbread						Pain d'Épices (French Gingerbread)					
	U.S.			Metric		%	U.S.			Metric		%
Pastry flour	2 lb 8		oz	1100 g		100	1 lb 4		oz	550 g		50
Rye flour	—			—		—	1 lb 4		oz	550 g		50
Salt	0.25		oz	7 g		0.6	0.25 oz			7 g		0.6
Baking soda	1.25		oz	33 g		3	1.25 oz			33 g		3
Baking powder	0.6		oz	16 g		1.5	0.6 oz			16 g		1.5
Ginger	0.5		oz	14 g		1.25	0.5 oz			14 g		1.25
Cinnamon	—			—		—	0.25 oz			7 g		0.6
Cloves, ground	—			—		—	0.12 oz			3.5 g		0.3
Anise, ground	—			—		—	0.5 oz			14 g		1.25
Orange rind, grated	—			—		—	0.5 oz			14 g		1.25
Currants	—			—		—	8 oz			220 g		20
Molasses	2 lb 8		oz	1100 g		100	—			—		—
Honey	—			—		—	1 lb 14		oz	825 g		75
Hot water	1 lb 4		oz	550 g		50	1 lb 4		oz	550 g		50
Butter or shortening, melted	10		oz	275 g		25	10		oz	275 g		25
Total weight:	*7 lb 1*		*oz*	*3095 g*		*281%*	*6 lb 15*		*oz*	*3078 g*		*279%*

■ P r o c e d u r e

Mixing
Muffin method
Panning
Old-Fashioned Gingerbread: greased, paper-lined sheet pans, about 6.5 to 7 lb per sheet (one recipe per sheet).
Pain d'Épices (pronounced "pan day peece"): greased loaf pans. Fill about one-half full of batter.
Baking
375°F (190°C)

▶ **TERMS FOR REVIEW**

pour batter	tunneling	muffin method
drop batter	biscuit method	creaming method

▶ **QUESTIONS FOR REVIEW**

1. If you made a batch of muffins that came out of the oven with strange, knobby shapes, what would you expect to be the reason?

2. What is the most important difference between the biscuit method and the muffin method?

3. Why do popovers require more mixing than other quick breads?

7

Doughnuts, Fritters, Pancakes, and Waffles

$\mathcal{U}$nlike the products we have discussed so far, those included in this chapter are cooked not by baking in ovens but by deep-frying, by cooking in greased fry pans or on griddles, or, in the case of waffles, by cooking in specially designed griddles that heat the product from both sides at once.

There are several types of doughs or batters for these products. To produce the two most popular types of doughnuts, you will need to understand the principles of yeast dough production (chapters 3–5) and the creaming method used for mixing some quick breads (chapter 6). French doughnuts are a fried version of the same pastry used to make cream puffs and éclairs (chapter 10). American pancakes are made from chemically leavened batters mixed by the muffin method, while French pancakes or crêpes are made from thin, unleavened batters made of milk, eggs, and flour.

After reading this
chapter, you should be
able to:

■ Prepare doughnuts and other
deep-fried desserts and pastries.

■ Prepare pancakes and waffles.

■ Prepare crêpes and crêpe
desserts.

DOUGHNUTS

YEAST-RAISED DOUGHNUTS

The mixing method used to prepare yeast-raised doughnuts is the modified straight dough method (p. 52). Review this procedure before beginning doughnut production. In addition, the following points will help you understand and produce high-quality doughnuts. Makeup and finishing procedures follow the formula.

1. The dough used for yeast doughnuts is similar to regular sweet dough or bun dough, except that it is often not as rich—that is, doughnuts are made with less fat, sugar, and eggs (compare the formulas on pp. 106 and 156). Doughs that are too rich will brown too fast and will absorb too much frying fat. The finished products will be greasy and either too dark on the outside or insufficiently cooked inside. Also, a leaner dough has stronger gluten, which can better withstand the handling involved in proofing and frying.

2. Punch the dough and bring it to the bench in sufficient time to allow for makeup. Remember that fermentation continues during makeup. If the dough gets too old, the doughnuts will require longer frying to become browned and thus will be greasier. When you are preparing a large quantity of doughnuts, it may be necessary to place some of the dough in the retarder so that it doesn't become old.

3. Watch the dough temperature carefully, especially in warm weather. If the dough is much above 80°F (24°C), it will become old more quickly.

4. Proof the doughnuts at a lower temperature and humidity than those used for breads. Some bakers proof them at room temperature. Doughnuts proofed this way are less likely to be deformed or dented when handled or brought to the fryer.

5. Handle fully proofed units carefully, as they are soft and easily dented. Many bakers give doughnuts only three-quarters proof. This makes a denser doughnut, but one that is more easily handled.

6. Heat the frying fat to the proper temperature. Fat temperature for raised doughnuts varies from 365° to 385°F (185° to 195°C), depending on the formula. Richer formulas require a lower temperature to avoid excessive browning. The formulas in this book require a frying temperature of 375° to 380°F (190° to 193°C).

7. Arrange the proofed units on screens on which they can be lowered into fat. (For small quantities, you can place them by hand in the fryer, but be careful not to burn yourself.) Frying time is about $2\frac{1}{2}$ minutes. The doughnuts must be turned over when they are half done in order to brown evenly on both sides.

CAKE-TYPE DOUGHNUTS

Operations that produce cake doughnuts in volume use equipment that forms the dough and drops it directly into the hot fat. This equipment is usually automatic, although small hand-operated depositors are also available. Automatic depositors use a relatively slack dough that is generally made from prepared mixes. To use these mixes and depositors, follow two important guidelines:

• Follow manufacturers' directions closely when preparing the mix.

- Keep the depositor head 1½ in. (4 cm) above the fat. If the doughnut must drop much farther than this into the fat, poor shapes may result.

Operations that make cake doughnuts by hand use a stiffer mix that is rolled out and cut with cutters. Two formulas for this type of mix are included in this chapter. Follow these guidelines when preparing cake doughnuts:

1. Scale ingredients carefully. Even small errors can result in products with unsatisfactory texture or appearance.

2. Mix the dough until smooth, but do not overmix. Undermixed doughs result in a rough appearance and excessive fat absorption. Overmixed doughs result in tough, dense doughnuts.

3. Dough temperature should be about 70° to 75°F (21° to 24°C) when the units are fried. Be especially careful of dough temperature during hot weather.

4. Let the cut-out units rest about 15 minutes before frying in order to relax the gluten. Failure to relax the dough results in toughness and poor expansion.

5. Fry at proper temperature. Normal fat temperature for cake doughnuts is 375° to 385°F (190° to 195°C). Frying time is about 1½ to 2 minutes. Doughnuts must be turned over when half done.

PREPARATION AND CARE OF FRYING FAT

Properly fried doughnuts absorb about 2 oz of fat per dozen. Therefore, frying fat should be of good quality and be properly maintained; otherwise, the quality of the doughnuts will suffer. Observe the following guidelines for care of frying fat:

1. Use good-quality, flavorless fat. The best fat for frying has a high smoke point (the temperature at which the fat begins to smoke and to break down rapidly).

   Solid shortenings are popular for frying because they are stable and because they congeal when the doughnuts cool, making them *appear* less greasy. However, such doughnuts can have an unpleasant eating quality because the fat does not melt in the mouth.

2. Fry at the proper temperature. Using too low a temperature extends frying time, causing excessive greasiness.

   If you do not have automatic equipment with thermostatic temperature controls, keep a fat thermometer clipped to the side of the frying kettle.

3. Maintain the fat at the proper level in the fryer. When additional fat must be added, allow time for it to heat up.

4. Do not fry too many doughnuts at a time. Overloading will lower the fat temperature, will not allow room for expansion of the doughnuts, and will make it difficult to turn them over.

5. Keep fat clean. Skim out food particles as necessary. After each day's use, cool the fat until it is warm, strain it, and clean the equipment.

6. Discard spent fat. Old fat loses frying ability, browns excessively, and imparts a bad flavor.

7. Keep fat covered when not in use. Try to aerate the fat as little as possible when filtering.

Yeast-Raised Doughnuts

Ingredients	U.S.		Metric	%
Water	1 lb		410 g	55
Yeast	1.5	oz	38 g	5
Shortening	3	oz	75 g	10
Sugar	4	oz	105 g	14
Salt	0.5	oz	13 g	1.75
Mace	0.09 oz (½ tsp)		2 g	0.3
Nonfat milk solids	1.5	oz	38 g	5
Eggs	4	oz	105 g	14
Bread flour	2 lb 2	oz	750 g	100
Total weight:	*3 lb 1*	*oz*	*1536 g*	*205%*

■ P r o c e d u r e

Mixing

Modified straight dough method

Develop the dough completely, about 6–8 minutes at second speed.

Fermentation

About 1½ hours at 80°F (24°C)

Scaling

1.5 oz (45 g) per unit

See below for makeup.

Frying

375°F (190°C)

When doughnuts are fried, lift them from fat and let excess fat drip off. Place doughnuts in one layer on absorbent paper. Cool.

Variations

Makeup of Yeast-Raised Doughnuts

Ring Doughnuts

1. Roll out dough ½ in. (12 mm) thick. Make sure dough is of even thickness. Let the dough relax.

2. Cut out doughnuts with a doughnut cutter. Cut as close together as possible to minimize the quantity of scrap.

3. Combine the scrap dough and let it relax. Roll out and let it relax again. Continue cutting doughnuts.

Jelly-Filled Doughnuts or Bismarcks

Method 1

1. Scale the dough into 3½ lb (1600 g) presses. Let them relax for 10 minutes.

2. Divide the dough. Round the small units.

3. Let them relax a few minutes, then flatten lightly.

Method 2

1. Roll out the dough ½ in. (12 mm) thick, as for ring doughnuts.

2. Cut out with round cutters (biscuit cutters, or doughnut cutters with the "hole" removed).

    After frying and cooling, use a doughnut pump or jelly pump to fill the doughnuts. Using a sharp, straight nozzle, pierce the side of the doughnut and inject the jelly into the *center*.

    Other fillings besides jelly may be used, such as lemon, custard (see Pastry Cream, p. 187), and cream. If a filling containing egg, milk, or cream is used, the doughnuts must be kept refrigerated.

Long Johns

1. Roll out the dough ½ in. (12 mm) thick, as for ring doughnuts.

2. With a pastry wheel, cut into strips 1½ in. (4 cm) wide and 3½ in. (9 cm) long.

Fried Cinnamon Rolls

1. Make up like baked Cinnamon Rolls (p. 124), except omit the butter in the filling.

2. Make sure the edges are well sealed so the rolls don't unwind during frying.

Twists

1. Scale into presses, divide the dough, and round the units, as for filled doughnuts.

2. Roll each unit on the bench with the palms of the hands to a strip about 8 in. (20 cm) long.

3. Place one hand over each end of the strip. Roll one end toward you and the other away from you to twist the strip.

4. Holding it by the ends, lift the strip off the bench and bring the two ends together. The strip will twist around itself.

5. Seal the ends together.

Cake Doughnuts

Ingredients	U.S.		Metric	%
Shortening	3	oz	90 g	9
Sugar	7	oz	220 g	22
Salt	0.25	oz	8 g	0.8
Nonfat milk solids	1.5	oz	45 g	4.7
Mace	0.12	oz ($1\frac{3}{4}$ tsp)	4 g	0.4
Vanilla	0.5	oz	15 g	1.5
Whole eggs	3	oz	90 g	9
Egg yolks	1.5	oz	30 g	3
Water	1 lb		500 g	50
Cake flour	1 lb 4	oz	750 g	62.5
Bread flour	12	oz	250 g	37.5
Baking powder	1.25 oz		40 g	4
Total weight:	*4 lb 4*	*oz*	*2042 g*	*204%*

■ P r o c e d u r e

Mixing

Creaming method (p. 138)

Mix the dough until it is smooth, but do not overmix.

Makeup

1. Place the dough on the bench and form into a smooth rectangular shape with the hands; rest 15 minutes.

2. Roll out to about $\frac{3}{8}$ in. (1 cm) thick. Make sure the dough is of even thickness and is not sticking to the bench.

3. Cut out doughnuts with cutters.

4. Collect the scrap dough and let it relax. Roll it out again and continue cutting doughnuts.

5. Place the doughnuts on lightly floured pans and let them relax 15 minutes.

Frying

380°F (193°C)

Lift doughnuts from fat, let excess fat drip off, and place them in one layer on absorbent paper. Cool.

Chocolate Cake Doughnuts

For large-quantity measurements, see page 592.

Ingredients	U.S.		Metric	%
Shortening	1.5	oz	45 g	9
Sugar	4	oz	125 g	25
Salt	0.13	oz ($\frac{5}{8}$ tsp)	4 g	0.8
Nonfat milk solids	0.75	oz	24 g	4.7
Vanilla extract	0.25	oz	8 g	1.5
Whole eggs	1.5	oz	45 g	9
Egg yolks	0.5	oz	15 g	3
Water	8.5	oz	265 g	53
Cake flour	10	oz	375 g	62.5
Bread flour	6	oz	125 g	37.5
Cocoa powder	1.25 oz		40 g	7.8
Baking powder	0.25 oz		15 g	3
Baking soda	0.1	oz ($\frac{2}{3}$ tsp)	3 g	0.63
Total weight:	*2 lb 2*	*oz*	*1089 g*	*217%*

■ P r o c e d u r e

Mixing

Creaming method (p. 138)

Mix the dough until it is smooth, but do not over-mix.

Makeup and Frying

Same as for Cake Doughnuts, above. *Caution:* Watch chocolate doughnuts carefully when frying because it is harder to tell doneness by their color.

Rich Vanilla Spice Doughnuts

For large-quantity measurements, see page 593.

Ingredients	U.S.		Metric	%
Bread flour	12	oz	375 g	50
Cake flour	12	oz	375 g	50
Baking powder	0.75	oz	22 g	3
Nutmeg	0.2	oz (1 tbsp)		0.8
Cinnamon	0.06	oz (1 tsp)	2 g	0.25
Salt	0.3	oz (1 tsp)	9 g	1.25
Whole eggs	5	oz	155 g	21
Egg yolks	1	oz	30 g	4
Sugar	10	oz	315 g	42
Milk	9.5	oz	300 g	40
Vanilla extract	0.75	oz	22 g	3
Butter, melted	3	oz	95 g	12.5
Total weight:	*3 lb 6*	*oz*	*1706 g*	*227%*

Mixing

Muffin method (p. 137), modified as follows:

1. Sift together the flour, baking powder, spices, and salt

2. Whip together the eggs, egg yolks, and sugar until light. Mix in the milk, vanilla, and melted butter.

3. Fold the liquid ingredients into the dry ingredients to make a soft dough.

4. Refrigerate at least 1 hour before rolling and cutting.

Makeup

Same as for Cake Doughnuts.

Frying

375°F (190°C)

FINISHING DOUGHNUTS

Doughnuts should be well drained and cooled before finishing with sugar or other coatings. If they are hot, steam from the doughnuts will soak the coating. The following are some popular coatings and finishes for doughnuts:

• Roll in cinnamon sugar.

• Roll in 4X sugar. (To keep sugar from lumping and absorbing moisture, it may be sifted with cornstarch. Use about 2 to 3 oz of starch per pound of sugar, or about 150 g per kg.)

• Ice the tops of the doughnuts with a fondant or fudge icing (see chapter 7).

• To glaze, dip in *warm* Doughnut Glaze (recipe follows) or in a warmed, thinned simple icing or fondant. Place on screens until glaze sets.

• After glazing, while glaze is still moist, doughnuts may be rolled in coconut or chopped nuts.

Doughnut Glaze

Ingredients	U.S.		Sugar at 100% Metric	%
Gelatin	0.12	oz	3 g	0.3
Water	8	oz	200 g	20
Corn syrup	2	oz	50 g	5
Vanilla extract	0.25	oz (1½ tsp)	6 g	0.6
Confectioners' sugar	2 lb 8	oz	1000 g	100
Total weight:	*3 lb 2*	*oz*	*1259 g*	*125%*

1. Soften the gelatin in the water.

2. Heat the water until the gelatin dissolves.

3. Add the remaining ingredients and mix until smooth.

4. Dip doughnuts into warm glaze, or rewarm the glaze as necessary.

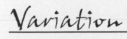

Variation

Honey Glaze

Substitute honey for the corn syrup.

FRENCH DOUGHNUTS

French doughnuts are made from Éclair Paste (p. 248) that has been piped into ring shapes and deep fried. They are included in the following section on fritters.

FRITTERS

The term *fritter* is used for a great variety of fried items, both sweet and savory, including many made with vegetables, meats, or fish. Fried items of all types are often referred to by the French term for fritter, *beignet* (pronounced "ben yay"). In the pastry shop, we are concerned with two basic types of fritters:

- *Simple fritters,* like doughnuts, are portions of dough that are deep-fried. They are usually dusted with sugar and often served with a sauce or a fruit preserve. This chapter includes recipes for four kinds of simple fritters, including the classic *beignet soufflé,* which is fried éclair paste.

- *Fruit fritters* are made by dipping pieces of fresh, cooked, or canned fruit in batter and then deep-frying. A basic procedure for making fruit fritters follows. Two recipes for fritter batters are included.

Also included in this chapter are cannoli shells. This type of fried pastry is not generally classified as a fritter. Nevertheless, cannoli shells are made in nearly the same way as two fritters in this chapter, fattigman and beignets de carnival—that is, they are made from a stiff dough that is rolled thin, cut out, and fried. Cannoli, however, are fried in a cylinder shape so that they can take various fillings.

Procedure for Preparing Fruit Fritters

1. Prepare batter (see formulas that follow).
2. Prepare the desired fruit. Popular fruits for fritters are:

   Apples   Peel, core, and slice into rings ¼ in. (6 mm) thick.

   Bananas   Peel, cut in half lengthwise, and then cut crosswise to make four quarters.

   Pinepple   Use fresh or canned rings.

   Apricots and plums   Split in half and remove the stones.

   For extra flavor, fruits may be sprinkled heavily with sugar and rum or kirsch and marinated 1 to 2 hours.
3. Drain the fruit pieces well and dip them in batter to coat completely. Dip only as much as can be fried in one batch.
4. Drop into hot fat (375°F/190°C). Fry until golden brown on all sides.
5. Remove from fat and drain well.
6. Serve warm, sprinkled with cinnamon sugar. Crème Anglaise (p. 185) or Fruit Sauce (p. 194) may be served on the side.

Fritter Batter I

For large-quantity measurements, see page 593.

Ingredients	U.S.		Metric	%
Pastry flour	9	oz	250 g	100
Sugar	0.5	oz	15 g	6
Salt	0.12 oz (⅔ tsp)		4 g	1.5
Baking powder	0.12 oz (¾ tsp)		4 g	1.5
Eggs, beaten	4.5	oz	125 g	50
Milk	8	oz	225 g	90
Oil	0.5	oz	15 g	6
Vanilla extract	0.08 oz (½ tsp)		2 g	1
Total weight:	*1 lb 7*	*oz*	*640 g*	*256%*

■ P r o c e d u r e

Mixing

Muffin method (p. 137)

1. Sift together the dry ingredients.

2. Combine the liquid ingredients.

3. Gradually stir the liquid into the dry ingredients. Mix until nearly smooth, but do not overmix.

4. Let stand at least 30 minutes before using.

French Doughnuts (Beignets Soufflés)

For large-quantity measurements, see page 593.

Ingredients	U.S.		Metric	%
Milk	10	oz	250 g	167
Butter	4	oz	100 g	67
Salt	0.18 oz (1 tsp)		5 g	3
Sugar	0.18 oz (1 tsp)		5 g	3
Bread flour	6	oz	150 g	100
Eggs	8	oz	200 g	133
Total weight:	*1 lb 12*	*oz*	*710 g*	*473%*

■ P r o c e d u r e

Mixing

1. In a saucepan, heat the milk, butter, salt, and sugar until the sugar dissolves and the butter is melted.

2. Bring to a rapid boil, then remove from the heat. Add the flour all at once and beat in vigorously with a wooden spoon.

3. Set the pan over medium heat and beat the mixture for 2–3 minutes, until the mixture pulls away from the sides of the pan.

4. Turn the mixture into a stainless-steel bowl and cool slightly.

5. Add the eggs in three stages, beating well between additions.

6. Place the dough in a piping bag fitted with a large star tip.

Frying

The doughnuts may be finished in either of two ways:

1. Pipe the mixture directly into a deep fryer heated to 340°F (170°C), cutting off the dough in 3-in. (7–8 cm) pieces using a knife dipped in the hot fat. Fry until puffed and golden. Drain on kitchen paper.

2. Pipe 2-in. circles onto parchment paper. (To make uniform shapes, mark 2-in. circles onto the paper by tracing around a 2-in. cutter with a pencil. Turn the paper over and use the outlines as a guide.) Freeze. Fry the frozen units as in method 1.

See page 527 for presentation suggestions.

Fritter Batter II

For large-quantity measurements, see page 593.

Ingredients	U.S.		Metric	%
Bread flour	6	oz	190 g	75
Cake flour	2	oz	60 g	25
Salt	0.12 oz (⅔ tsp)		4 g	1.5
Sugar	0.25 oz		8 g	3
Milk	9	oz	312 g	113
Egg yolks, beaten	1	oz	30 g	12.5
Oil	1	oz	30 g	12.5
Egg whites	2	oz	60 g	25
Total weight:	*1 lb 5*	*oz*	*694 g*	*267%*

■ P r o c e d u r e

1. Sift together the dry ingredients.
2. Combine the milk, egg yolks, and oil.
3. Stir the liquid into the dry ingredients. Mix until smooth.
4. Let rest until ready to use, at least 30 minutes.
5. Whip the egg whites until stiff but not dry.
6. Fold the egg whites into the batter. Use immediately.

Beignets de Carnival

For large-quantity measurements, see page 593.

Ingredients	U.S.		Metric	%
Bread flour	7	oz	200 g	100
Sugar	0.5	oz	15 g	8
Salt	0.18 oz (1 tsp)		5 g	2.5
Egg yolks	2	oz	60 g	30
Light cream	2	oz	60 g	30
Kirsch	0.5	oz	15 g	8
Rose water	0.33 oz (2 tsp)		10 g	5
Total weight:	*12*	*oz*	*365 g*	*183%*

■ P r o c e d u r e

Mixing

1. Sift the flour, sugar, and salt into a bowl.
2. In a separate bowl, combine egg yolks, cream, kirsch, and rose water.
3. Make a well in the dry ingredients and pour in the liquids. Combine to a stiff dough.
4. Turn out onto a lightly floured surface and knead until a smooth ball forms.
5. Place dough onto a lightly floured plate, cover tightly with plastic film, and chill overnight.

Frying

1. Bring the dough back to room temperature.
2. Cut rested dough into pieces ⅓ oz (10 g) each. Keep covered with a damp cloth or plastic film all the time you are working to prevent a crust forming.
3. Taking one piece of dough at a time, roll out very thinly until the dough starts to shrink back. Place under damp cloth or plastic film and continue rolling all the pieces of dough.
4. Go back to the first piece and begin rolling again until the dough is nearly transparent. This process gives the dough time to rest and assists very thin rolling.
5. Once they are rolled for the second time, trim the circles to uniform size using a 4½-in. (11 cm) round cutter. Place the cut pieces onto a sheet pan lined with parchment paper. Cover with plastic film.
6. Preheat the fryer to 180°C. Drop the beignets into the hot fat one at a time. Turn once when golden brown. The beignets can be either fried flat or shaped by holding them under the fat with a long-handled spoon, pressing firmly into the middle of each beignet; this causes them to cup slightly as they fry.
7. When golden, remove and drain on kitchen paper.
8. Serve with choice of poached fruit or fruit compote.

Fattigman

Ingredients	U.S.		Metric	%
Whole eggs	3.33 oz (2 eggs)		100 g (2 eggs)	24
Egg yolks	1.33 oz (2 yolks)		40 g (2 yolks)	10
Salt	0.13 oz (⅔ tsp)		4 g	1
Sugar	2.5 oz		70 g	18
Cardamom, ground	0.07 oz (1 tsp)		2 g	0.5
Heavy cream	3 oz		85 g	21
Brandy	1.5 oz		45 g	11
Bread flour	14 oz		400 g	100
Confectioners' sugar	as needed		as needed	
Total dough weight:	*1 lb 9 oz*		*746 g*	*185%*

■ P r o c e d u r e

1. Whip the eggs and yolks until foamy.

2. Beat in the salt, sugar, cardamom, and cream.

3. Add the brandy and mix well.

4. Add the flour and blend to make a dough.

5. Wrap or cover the dough and rest, refrigerated, for at least 1 hour.

6. Roll out the dough ⅛ in. (3 mm) thick.

7. Cut into small triangles about 2½ in. (6 cm) on a side.

8. Deep-fry at 375°F (190°C) until lightly browned and crisp.

9. Drain and cool.

10. Dust lightly with 10X sugar.

    See page 517 for presentation suggestion.

Viennoise

For large-quantity measurements, see page 593.

Yield: 10 pastries, 2 oz (60 g) each

Ingredients	U.S.		Metric
Brioche Dough (p. 111)	1 lb 4 oz		600 g
Egg wash	as needed		as needed
Red currant jelly	3.5 oz		100 g

■ P r o c e d u r e

1. Scale Brioche Dough into 2-oz (60 g) pieces.

2. On a lightly floured work surface, roll each piece into a 4-in. (10 cm) circle.

3. Brush the tops with egg wash.

4. Place ⅓ oz (10 g) of jelly in the center of each circle. Enclose the jelly by gathering the edges of the circle together over the jelly to form a purse. Place upside down (seam on bottom) on a sheet pan lined with parchment. Proof in a warm place until double in size, about 40 minutes.

5. Deep-fry at 340°F (170°C) until golden brown, turning once. Frying time is about 8 minutes.

6. Drain.

Cannoli Shells

For large-quantity measurements, see page 594.

Ingredients	U.S.		Metric	%
Bread flour	6	oz	175 g	50
Pastry flour	6	oz	175 g	50
Sugar	1	oz	30 g	8
Salt	0.04 oz (⅛ tsp)		1 g	0.3
Butter	2	oz	60 g	17
Egg, beaten (1 egg)	1.67 oz		50 g	14
Dry white wine or Marsala	4	oz	125 g	33
Total weight:	*1 lb 4*	*oz*	*616 g*	*172%*

■ P r o c e d u r e

1. Sift the flour, sugar, and salt together into a bowl.

2. Add the butter and work in with the hands until evenly blended.

3. Add the egg and wine and work in to make a dough. Knead it a few times on a floured workbench until it is smooth. Cover and let rest for 30 minutes.

4. Roll the pastry out into a sheet about ⅛ in. (3 mm) thick. Dock it well. For small cannoli, cut into 3½-in. (9 cm) circles; for large cannoli, cut into 5-in. (12 cm) circles. Rework the scraps to cut additional circles. 20 oz (600 g) of dough is enough for about 16–18 large cannoli or 32–36 small ones.

5. Roll the circles around cannoli tubes. Where the edges of the circle overlap, press firmly to seal.

6. Deep-fry at 375°F (190°C) until golden brown. Cool for a few seconds, then carefully slip out the tube. Cool completely before filling. Shells may be filled with a variety of fillings, including vanilla and chocolate pastry creams and other thick creams and puddings.

Variation

Sicilian Cannoli
Using a pastry bag, fill cooled cannoli shells from both ends with Ricotta Cannoli Filling (below). Sprinkle lightly with confectioners' sugar. If desired, decorate the filling at the ends of the cannoli with halved candied cherries.

Ricotta Cannoli Filling

For large-quantity measurements, see page 594.

Ingredients	U.S.		Metric	%
Ricotta impastato (see p. 31)	1 lb		500 g	100
Confectioners' sugar	8	oz	250 g	50
Cinnamon extract	0.25 oz (1½ tsp)		7 g	1.5
Candied citron, candied citrus peel, or candied pumpkin, finely diced	1.5	oz	45 g	9
Sweet chocolate, finely chopped, or tiny chocolate bits	1	oz	30 g	6
Total weight:	*1 lb 10*	*oz*	*832 g*	*166%*

■ P r o c e d u r e

1. Process the ricotta in a blender until it is very smooth.

2. Sift the sugar and fold in until well mixed.

3. Mix in the remaining ingredients.

PANCAKES AND WAFFLES

Although pancakes and waffles are rarely produced in the retail bakeshop, they are essential items on the breakfast, brunch, and dessert menus in food service operations. In addition, a French waffle formula, especially well suited for dessert, is included here. This batter is actually an éclair paste that is thinned out with cream or milk. French pancakes, or crêpes, and various desserts made from them are also presented.

AMERICAN-STYLE PANCAKES AND WAFFLES

American-style pancakes and waffles are made from pourable batters mixed by the muffin method, which is presented in chapter 6. As with muffins, it is important to avoid overmixing the batters for these products in order to prevent excessive gluten development.

Pancakes and waffles can be made in almost unlimited varieties by substituting other types of flour, such as buckwheat flour, whole wheat flour, and cornmeal, for part of the pastry flour. As some of these absorb more water than others, additional liquid may be needed to thin out the batter.

Compare the formulas for pancakes and waffles. In particular, you should notice these differences:

- Waffle batter contains more fat. This makes the waffles richer and crisper and aids in their release from the waffle iron.
- Waffle batter contains less liquid, so it is slightly thicker. This, too, makes waffles crisp, as crispness depends on low moisture content.
- Whipping the egg whites separately and folding them into the batter gives waffles added lightness.

ADVANCE PREPARATION FOR VOLUME SERVICE

1. Pancake and waffle batters leavened *only by baking powder* may be mixed the night before and stored in the cooler. Some rising power may be lost, so baking powder may have to be increased.
2. Batters leavened by *baking soda* should not be made too far ahead because the soda will lose its power. Mix dry ingredients and liquid ingredients ahead; combine just before service.
3. Batters using *beaten egg whites and baking powder* may be partially made ahead, but *incorporate the egg whites just before service.*

Pancakes and Waffles

Yield: about 1 qt (1 L)	Pancakes				Waffles			
Ingredients	U.S.		Metric	%	U.S.		Metric	%
Pastry flour	8	oz	225 g	100	8	oz	225 g	100
Sugar	1	oz	30 g	12.5	—		—	—
Salt	0.08	oz (½ tsp)	2.5 g	1	0.08	oz (½ tsp)	2 g	1
Baking powder	0.5	oz (1 tbsp)	15 g	6	0.5	oz (1 tbsp)	15 g	6
Whole eggs, beaten	3.5	oz (2 large)	100 g	44	—		—	—
Egg yolks, beaten	—		—	—	2	oz (3 large)	55 g	25
Milk	1 lb		450 g	200	12	oz	340 g	150
Butter, melted, or oil	2	oz	55 g	25	4	oz	112 g	50
Egg whites	—		—	—	3	oz (3 large)	85 g	38
Sugar	—		—	—	1	oz	30 g	12.5

■ P r o c e d u r e

Mixing

Muffin method (p. 137)

1. Sift together the dry ingredients.

2. Combine the eggs or egg yolks, milk, and fat.

3. Add the liquid ingredients to the dry ingredients. Mix until just combined. Do not overmix.

4. *For waffles:* Just before they are to be cooked, whip the egg whites until they form soft peaks, then beat in the sugar until the meringue is stiff. Fold into the batter.

Cooking Pancakes

1. Using a 2-oz (60 mL) ladle, measure portions of batter onto a greased, preheated griddle (375°F/190°C), allowing space for spreading.

2. Fry the pancakes until the tops are full of bubbles and begin to look dry, and the bottoms are golden brown.

3. Turn and brown the other side.

4. Serve hot, accompanied by butter, maple syrup, fruit syrup, jams or preserves, applesauce, or fresh berries.

Cooking Waffles

1. Pour enough batter onto a lightly greased, preheated waffle iron to almost cover the surface. Close the iron.

2. Cook the waffles until the signal light indicates they are done, or until steam is no longer emitted. The waffles should be brown and crisp.

3. Serve warm, with confectioners' sugar, syrup, jam, or fresh fruit.

Variation

Buttermilk Pancakes and Waffles

Use buttermilk instead of milk. Reduce baking powder to 2% (0.16 oz or 1 tsp/5 g) and add 1 tsp (5 g) baking soda. If the batter is too thick, thin it with milk or water as necessary (up to 50%).

Gaufres (French Waffles)

Ingredients	U.S.		Metric	%
Milk	1 lb		500 g	200
Salt		0.25 oz	8 g	3
Butter	3	oz	95 g	37.5
Bread flour	8	oz	250 g	100
Eggs	13	oz	400 g	162.5
	(about 8 large eggs)			
Cream	8	oz	250 g	100
Milk	4	oz	125 g	50
Total weight:	*3 lb 4*	*oz*	*1628 g*	*653%*

■ P r o c e d u r e

1. Combine the milk, salt, and butter in a saucepan or kettle. Carefully bring to a boil.

2. Add the flour all at once and stir vigorously. Continue to stir until the mixture forms a ball and pulls away from the sides of the kettle.

3. Remove from the heat and transfer to the bowl of a mixer. Let cool 5 minutes.

4. With the mixer on low speed, add the eggs a little at a time. Wait until each addition is absorbed before adding more.

5. With the mixer continuing to run, slowly pour in the cream, then the milk. Don't worry if the batter is slightly lumpy even after all the milk is added; this is normal. The batter should be slightly thicker than regular waffle batter. If it is much thicker, add a little more milk.

6. Bake as you would regular waffles.

CRÊPES

Crêpes are thin, unleavened pancakes. They are rarely served plain but are instead used to construct a great variety of desserts by being rolled around various fillings, layered with fillings, or served with sweet sauces. Unsweetened crêpes are used in similar ways but filled with various meat, fish, and vegetable preparations.

Unlike leavened pancakes, crêpes may be made in advance, covered and refrigerated, and used as needed. When the crêpes are filled and rolled or folded, the side that was browned first, which is the most attractive side, should be on the outside.

Crêpes

Yield: about 18 crêpes

Ingredients	U.S.		Metric	%
Cake flour	7	oz	200 g	100
Milk	1 lb		440 g	225
Perrier or other sparkling mineral water	4	oz	125 g	60
Eggs		3.5 oz	100 g	50
Sugar		3.5 oz	100 g	50
Total weight	2 lb 2	oz	*965 g*	*485%*

■ P r o c e d u r e

Mixing

1. Sift the flour into a bowl and make a well in the center.
2. Pour the milk, water, eggs, and sugar into the well. Whip to form a smooth batter.
3. Cover and refrigerate 2 hours.

Cooking Crêpes

1. Heat a crêpe pan over moderately high heat. Brush lightly with melted butter and pour off any excess (a).
2. Ladle 1½–2 oz (50 mL) batter into the pan. Swirl in the pan to coat the bottom with a thin coating and pour off any excess (b).
3. Cook until bubbles appear on the surface of the crêpe and the bottom starts to brown lightly.
4. Flip the crêpe over with a palette knife (c).
5. Cook the second side, which will not brown as much (d).
6. Turn out onto a parchment-lined tray. Cool.
7. Repeat with the remaining batter, brushing the pan as necessary with butter.
8. Use a round cutter to neaten the edges of the crêpes.
9. Cover and refrigerate until needed.

a

b

c

d

Variation

Chocolate Crêpes

Ingredients	U.S.	Metric	%
Cake flour	5 oz	150 g	75
Cocoa powder	1 oz	30 g	15

Reduce the quantity of flour in the crêpe formula and add cocoa powder in the proportions listed above. Sift the cocoa with the flour in step 1 of the mixing procedure and continue with the basic recipe.

CRÊPE DESSERTS

The following are only a few of many possible suggestions. The variety of crêpe desserts you can prepare is limited only by your imagination.

Crêpes Normande Sauté fresh sliced apples in butter and sprinkle with sugar and a dash of cinnamon. Roll up the apples in crêpes and dust with confectioners' sugar.

Banana Crêpes Sauté sliced bananas quickly in butter and sprinkle with brown sugar and a dash of rum. Roll up the filling in the crêpes. Serve with Apricot Sauce (p. 194).

Crêpes with Jam Spread apricot jam on crêpes and roll them up. Sprinkle with sugar and run under the broiler quickly to glaze the sugar.

Glazed Crêpes Fill crêpes with vanilla Pastry Cream (p. 187) and roll them up. Sprinkle with sugar and run under the broiler to glaze the sugar.

Crêpes Frangipane Spread the crêpes with frangipane filling (p. 118) and roll them up or fold them in quarters. Brush with butter and sprinkle with sugar. Place in a buttered baking dish and bake in a hot oven about 10 minutes to heat through. Serve with chocolate sauce or vanilla sauce.

Crêpes Suzette This most famous of all crêpe desserts is generally prepared at tableside by the waiter, according to the procedure in the following recipe. The crêpes, fruit, sugar, and butter are supplied by the kitchen. It can also be prepared in the kitchen or pastry department by coating crêpes with hot Sauce Suzette (p. 198).

Crêpes Suzette (Dining Room Preparation)

Yield: 4 portions

Ingredients	U.S.	Metric
Sugar	3 oz	85 g
Orange	1	1
Lemon	½	½
Butter	2 oz	60 g
Orange-flavored liqueur	1 oz	30 mL
Cognac	2 oz	60 mL
Crêpes	12	12

■ Procedure

1. In a flambé pan, heat the sugar until it melts and begins to caramelize.

2. Cut several strips of rind from the orange and one from the lemon; add them to the pan.

3. Add the butter and squeeze the juice from the orange and lemon into the pan. Cook and stir until the sugar is dissolved and the mixture is a little syrupy.

4. Add the orange liqueur. One by one, dip the crêpes in the sauce to coat them, then fold them into quarters in the pan.

5. Add the cognac and allow it to heat for a few seconds. Flame by *carefully* tipping the pan toward the burner flame until the cognac ignites.

6. Shake the pan gently and spoon the sauce over the crêpes until the flame dies down.

7. Serve three crêpes per portion. Spoon a little of the remaining sauce over each serving.

Crêpes Soufflé Suzette

Yield: 6 portions

Ingredients	U.S.	Metric
Orange juice	8 oz	250 g
Cornstarch	1 oz	25 g
Water	as needed	as needed
Sugar	1 oz	30 g
Orange liqueur, such as Grand Marnier	1.67 oz	50 g
Vanilla extract	½ tsp	2 g
Egg whites	4 oz	125 g
Sugar	2.5 oz	75 g
Crêpes	18	18
Confectioners' sugar	as needed	as needed
Sauce Suzette (p. 198)	8 oz	240 mL
Candied orange zest	as desired	as desired
Berries or other fruit garnish	as desired	as desired

■ P r o c e d u r e

1. Heat the orange juice.

2. Mix the cornstarch with enough cold water to make a smooth slurry. Stir into the orange juice and cook, stirring, until thickened.

3. Add the sugar, liqueur, and vanilla. Boil to dissolve the sugar.

4. Cool the mixture.

5. Whip the egg whites to soft peaks. Add the sugar and whip to a firm meringue.

6. Whip one-third of the meringue into the orange base, then fold in the remaining meringue.

7. Fit a pastry bag with a medium plain tip. Fill with the orange meringue mixture.

8. Fold the crêpes into quarters. Fill the folded pancakes with the orange meringue mixture using the pastry bag. The pancakes may now be frozen for later use if desired.

9. Arrange the filled pancakes on a greased baking sheet. Bake at 375°F (190°C) until well risen and firm to the touch.

10. Dust lightly with confectioners' sugar.

11. Ladle a ring of Sauce Suzette onto each plate. Arrange three crêpes on each plate. Garnish as desired with candied zest and berries.

Crêpe Gâteau with Plum Compote

Yield: 6 portions

Ingredients	U.S.	Metric
Plum Compote (p. 504)	1 lb	450 g
Crêpes (p. 167)	9	9
Garnish		
Confectioners' sugar	as needed	as needed
Quartered plum, fanned	as needed	as needed
Berries or other soft fruit	as needed	as needed

■ P r o c e d u r e

1. Place the Plum Compote in a fine strainer. Reserve the drained liquid for use as a sauce.

2. Place a crêpe on the center of an ovenproof plate that has been lightly buttered. Top with about one-eighth of the drained compote.

3. Repeat with the remaining crêpes and compote, ending with a crêpe. The stack should be about 4 in. (10 cm) high.

4. Dust the top with confectioners' sugar. With a hot skewer, mark a lattice pattern in the top to resemble grill marks.

5. Dust again with confectioners' sugar. Brown lightly under a salamander or broiler.

6. Place in an oven at 325°F (160°C) until warm, about 10 to 15 minutes.

7. Remove from the oven. Decorate with the fruit. Ladle a little of the plum sauce (from step 1) around the gateau.

8. To serve, cut into 6 wedges like a small cake.

Crêpes Georgette

Yield: 6 portions

Ingredients	U.S.		Metric
Filling			
Sugar	3.5	oz	100 g
Butter	1	oz	30 g
Vanilla bean, split (see *note*)	1		1
Cloves	2		2
Pineapple, medium dice	1 lb		500 g
Kirsch	1	oz	30 g
Crêpes (p. 167)	18		18
Passion-fruit sabayon			
Whole eggs	2		2
Egg yolks	2		2
Fine granulated sugar	2.75	oz	80 g
Kirsch	0.5	oz	15 g
Passion-fruit purée	2	oz	60 g

Note If vanilla beans are not available, add ½ tsp (2 mL) vanilla extract after step 2.

■ P r o c e d u r e

1. Heat the sugar to a golden caramel. Remove from heat and add the butter, vanilla bean, and cloves.

2. Add the diced pineapple and the kirsch. Flambé to burn off the alcohol.

3. Simmer until the pineapple is tender. Cool.

4. Place the crêpes on a tray or work surface upside down (that is, with the best side down). Place a spoonful of pineapple on each crêpe and roll up.

5. Lightly butter 6 plates. Place 3 crêpes on each plate, seam-side down.

6. Cover with foil and keep warm in an oven at 325°F (160°C).

7. *Prepare the sabayon:* Put the eggs, egg yolks, and sugar in a round-bottomed stainless-steel bowl. Whip over low heat until thick and pale, about 6 minutes.

8. Remove from the heat and continue whipping until cold.

9. Stir in the kirsch and the passion-fruit purée.

10. Spoon the sabayon over the crêpes, covering them completely.

11. Place the plates under a salamander or broiler until the sabayon is lightly browned.

12. If desired, dust lightly with confectioners' sugar and garnish with a sprig of mint, a few passion-fruit seeds, and a few red berries.

Chocolate Soufflé Crêpes

Yield: 6 portions

Ingredients	U.S.		Metric
Milk	8	oz	250 g
Bittersweet chocolate	1.67	oz	50 g
Cornstarch	1	oz	25 g
Rum	1	oz	30 g
Sugar	1.67	oz	50 g
Vanilla extract	½	tsp	2 g
Egg whites	4	oz	125 g
Sugar	2.5	oz	75 g
Chocolate Crêpes (p. 167)	18		18
Chocolate Sauce (p. 195)	8	oz	250 g
Plain yogurt	4	tsp	20 g
Candied orange zest	0.5–1	oz	20 g

■ P r o c e d u r e

1. Heat the milk and chocolate together, stirring, until the chocolate is melted and well mixed with the milk. Bring to a simmer.

2. Combine the cornstarch and rum and mix to a smooth paste. Stir into the hot milk and simmer until thickened.

3. Stir in the sugar and vanilla until the sugar is dissolved.

4. Whip the egg whites to soft peaks. Add the sugar and whip to a firm meringue.

5. Whip one-third of the meringue into the chocolate base, then fold in the remaining meringue.

6. Fit a pastry bag with a medium plain tip. Fill with the chocolate meringue mixture.

7. Fold the Chocolate Crêpes into quarters. Fill the folded pancakes with the chocolate meringue mixture using the pastry bag. The pancakes may now be frozen for later use if desired.

8. Arrange the filled pancakes on a greased baking sheet. Bake at 375°F (190°C) until well risen and firm to the touch.

9. Dust lightly with confectioners' sugar.

10. Ladle a pool of Chocolate Sauce onto each plate. Arrange 3 crêpes on each plate. Pipe a few dots of yogurt onto the sauce and feather. Garnish with candied orange zest.

► **TERMS FOR REVIEW**

modified straight dough method
glaze
French doughnut
fritter
beignet soufflé

cannoli
gaufre
crêpe
Crêpes Suzette

► **QUESTIONS FOR REVIEW**

1. Two yeast doughnut formulas have the same quantities of fat and milk, but one has more sugar than the other. Which one do you expect would require a higher frying temperature? Why?

2. Why is it important to carefully control the mixing time when making cake doughnuts?

3. List five rules for maintaining frying fat to produce good-quality fried foods.

4. What type of leavening is used in crêpes (French pancakes)? In French doughnuts?

5. Why does waffle batter often contain less liquid (water or milk) than pancake batter?

6. Which mixing method is used to make American-style pancakes? What are the steps in this method?

8

Basic
Syrups,
Creams,
and Sauces

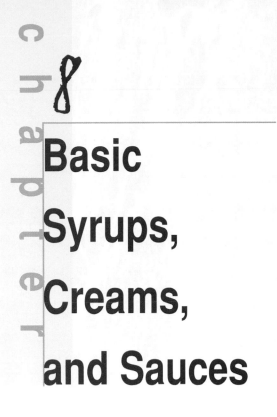

Much of the baker's craft consists of mixing and baking flour goods such as breads, cakes, and pastries. However, the baker also must be able to make a variety of other products, sometimes known as *adjuncts,* such as toppings, fillings, and sauces. These are not baked goods in themselves, but they are essential in the preparation of many baked goods and desserts.

Several of the procedures you learn in this chapter are used in many ways. For example, crème anglaise or custard sauce is used not only as a dessert sauce but is also the basis for such items as Bavarian creams and ice creams. Pastry cream, with a variety of flavorings, is also used for pie fillings, puddings, and soufflés.

After reading this chapter, you should be able to:

■ Cook sugar syrups to various stages of hardness.

■ Prepare whipped cream, meringues, custard sauces, and pastry cream variations.

■ Prepare dessert sauces.

SUGAR COOKING

Understanding sugar cooking is important in the preparation of desserts and confections because sugar syrups of various strengths are often required (see, for example, Italian Meringue, p. 183).

SYRUP STRENGTH

The principle of sugar cooking is fairly simple: A solution or syrup of sugar and water is boiled to evaporate part of the water. As the water is boiled off, the temperature of the syrup gradually rises. When all the water has evaporated, you are left with melted sugar. The sugar will then begin to *caramelize,* or turn brown and change flavor. If heating continues, the sugar will continue to darken and then burn.

A syrup cooked to a high temperature is harder when it is cooled than will a syrup cooked to a lower temperature. For example, a syrup cooked to 240°F (115°C) forms a soft ball when cooled. A syrup cooked to 300°F (150°C) is hard and brittle when cooled.

One pint (1 pound) of water is enough to dissolve up to 3 or 4 pounds of sugar. There is no point in adding more water than you need for a particular purpose because you will just have to boil it off again.

Pure, clean granulated sugar is used to make syrups. Impurities cloud the syrup and form a scum or foam on the syrup as it is being boiled. Any scum should be carefully skimmed off.

CRYSTALLIZATION AND INVERSION

Graininess is a common fault in many candies and desserts. Graininess results when cooked sugar crystallizes—that is, turns to tiny sugar crystals rather than staying dissolved in the syrup. If even one sugar crystal comes in contact with a cooked syrup, it can start a chain reaction that turns the whole thing into a mass of sugar crystals.

To avoid crystallization during the first stages of boiling sugar syrups, use one of the following techniques:

- As you boil the sugar, wash down the sides of the saucepan with a brush dipped in water. Do not let the brush touch the syrup, but let water from the brush run down the sides of the pan. This removes crystals that may seed the whole batch.

- When first bringing the syrup to a boil, cover the pan and boil for several minutes. This causes condensed steam to wash down the sides of the pan. Uncover and finish cooking without stirring.

Syrups cooked until they have a high concentration of sugar are liable to crystallize after they have been cooled. This can be controlled by a process called *inversion.* As explained in chapter 2 (p. 23), inversion is a chemical change of regular sugar (sucrose) into another form of sugar that resists crystallizing.

If an acid, such as cream of tartar or lemon juice, is added to a syrup before or during cooking, some of the sugar is inverted. The type and amount of acid used affect the amount of sugar that is inverted. Therefore, specific formulas should be followed carefully whenever acids are required in sugar boiling.

Glucose or corn syrup may also be added to control crystallization in boiling syrups. These are convenient to use and produce good results.

STAGES OF SUGAR COOKING

Testing the temperature with a candy thermometer is the most accurate way to determine the doneness of a syrup.

In the old days, a syrup was tested by dropping a little of it into a bowl of cold water and checking the hardness of the cooled sugar. The stages of doneness were given names that described their hardness.

The table below lists these stages of sugar cooking. Please note that the names for the various stages are not absolute; different sources may use slightly different names. In fact, all such tables are misleading because they suggest that the syrup jumps from one stage to the next. Actually, of course, it changes *gradually* as the water is boiled off. For this reason, it is best to rely on the thermometer and not worry too much about the names.

Stages of Doneness in Sugar Cooking

Stage	Temperature	
	°F	°C
Thread	230	110
Soft ball	240	115
Firm ball	245	118
Hard ball	250–260	122–127
Small crack	265–270	130–132
Crack	275–280	135–138
Hard crack	290–310	143–155
Caramel	320–340	160–170

BASIC SYRUPS FOR THE BAKESHOP

Two basic syrups are kept in stock in the bakeshop and used in a variety of ways. *Simple syrup,* also known as *stock syrup,* is a solution of equal weights of sugar and water. It is used for such purposes as diluting Fondant (p. 335) and for preparing a variety of dessert syrups. *Dessert syrup* is simply a flavored simple syrup. It is used to moisten and flavor sponge cakes and various desserts, such as Babas au Rum (p. 109).

The concentration of both these syrups may be varied to taste. Some chefs prefer a sweeter syrup for some purposes, such as 1 part water to 1½ parts sugar. Others use a less sweet syrup, such as 2 parts water to 1 part sugar.

Following are procedures for preparing simple syrup and a basic dessert syrup. The recipes in this section also include a variety of flavored syrups. Other flavored syrups appear throughout the book as parts of formulas for cakes and pastries.

Procedure for Preparing Simple Syrup

1. Combine the following ingredients in a saucepan:

water	1 pt	5 dL
sugar	1 lb	500 g

2. Stir and bring to a boil over moderate heat. Cook and stir until the sugar is dissolved.

3. Remove any scum. Cool syrup and store in a covered container.

Procedure for Preparing Dessert Syrup

Method 1

Prepare and cool a simple syrup. Add any desired flavoring according to taste. Extracts such as vanilla or liquors such as rum or kirsch may serve as flavorings. Flavoring should be added after the syrup has cooled, as some of the flavor may evaporate if it is added to hot syrup.

Method 2

Prepare a simple syrup, but add the rind of one orange and/or one lemon to the sugar and water before bringing it to a boil. Let the syrup simmer for 5 minutes before cooling. Remove the rind from the cooled syrup.

Vanilla Syrup

For large-quantity measurements, see page 594.

Ingredients	U.S.	Metric
Water	7 oz	200 g
Sugar	6 oz	180 g
Vanilla bean, split (see variation)	1	1
Total weight:	*13 oz (about 12 fl. oz)*	*380 g (about 325 mL)*

■ Procedure

1. Place all ingredients in a saucepan and heat gently until the sugar is dissolved.
2. Remove from the heat and allow the vanilla to infuse for 30 minutes.

Variation

If vanilla beans are not available, flavor plain syrup to taste with vanilla extract.

Coffee Rum Syrup

For large-quantity measurements, see page 595.

Ingredients	U.S.	Metric
Sugar	2.5 oz	65 g
Water	2.5 oz	65 g
Ground coffee	0.16 oz	5 g
Rum	3.5 oz	90 g
Total weight:	*8.5 oz (7-8 fl. oz)*	*225 g (185-210 mL)*

■ P r o c e d u r e

1. Boil the sugar and water until the sugar is dissolved.
2. Remove from the heat and add the coffee. Let stand 10 minutes.
3. Add the rum.
4. Strain.

Variations

Coffee Syrup

For large-quantity measurements, see page 595.

Ingredients	U.S.	Metric
Coffee liqueur	1.67 oz	40 g

Omit the rum in the basic recipe and add the coffee-flavored liqueur:

Rum Syrup

For large-quantity measurements, see page 595.

Ingredients	U.S.	Metric
Water	3 oz	75 g
Sugar	2.5 oz	65 g
Dark rum	0.5 oz	15 g

Omit the coffee in the basic recipe and adjust the ingredient quantities as listed above:

Cocoa Vanilla Syrup

For large-quantity measurements, see page 594.

Ingredients	U.S.	Metric
Water	4 oz	120 g
Sugar	4 oz	120 g
Vanilla bean (see *note*)	1	1
Cocoa powder	1 oz	30 g
Total weight:	*9 oz (about 7 1/2 fl. oz)*	*270 g (about 240 L)*

Note   If vanilla beans are not available, add 1/2 tsp vanilla extract just before straining.

■ P r o c e d u r e

1. Bring the water, sugar, and vanilla bean to a boil. Boil until the sugar is dissolved.
2. Remove from the heat and add the cocoa powder a little at a time, whipping constantly.
3. Strain through a fine strainer or chinois.

BASIC CREAMS

Many of the preparations discussed in this section are among the most important and useful in the bakeshop or pastry shop. They find their way into a great variety of desserts—as fillings or components of cakes and pastries, as ingredients of such desserts as Bavarian creams and mousses, and as sauces or toppings. Learn these techniques well because you will use them over and over again.

WHIPPED CREAM

Whipped cream is not only one of the most useful dessert toppings and fillings but also an ingredient in many desserts. Cream with a fat content of 30% or more, but preferably over 35%, can be whipped into a foam. One quart of cream produces about 2 to 2½ quarts of whipped cream.

In the classical pastry shop, sweetened, vanilla-flavored whipped cream is known as *crème chantilly* (pronounced "kremm shawn tee yee"). A recipe is included on p. 181. When making all whipped cream preparations, observe the following guidelines:

Guidelines for Whipping Cream

1. Cream for whipping should be at least 1 day old. Very fresh cream doesn't whip well.

2. Chill the cream and all equipment thoroughly, especially in hot weather. Cream that is too warm is hard to whip and curdles easily.

3. Use a wire whip for beating by hand. For machine whipping, use the whip attachment and run the machine at medium speed.

4. If the cream is to be sweetened, use extra-fine granulated sugar or, for best stability, sifted confectioners' sugar.

5. Do not overwhip. Stop beating when the cream forms peaks that hold their shape. If the cream is whipped longer, it first becomes grainy in appearance and then separates into butter and whey.

6. Cream to be folded into other ingredients should be slightly underbeaten because the action of folding whips it more and may overbeat it.

7. Fold in flavoring ingredients last, after the cream is whipped.

8. If the cream is not to be used immediately, store it, covered, in the refrigerator.

Procedure for Stabilizing Whipped Cream

During warm weather, it is sometimes helpful to add gelatin or a commercial stabilizer to whipped cream so that it will hold up. This is especially true of whipped cream–topped items displayed on a buffet.

1. To use a commercial stabilizer, sift it with the sugar used to sweeten the cream. Use about ¼ oz stabilizer per quart of cream (7 g/L). Add the sugar as in the basic procedure.

2. To use gelatin, use the following proportions:

Heavy cream	1 qt	1 L
Gelatin	0.33 oz	10 g
Cold water	2 oz	60 mL

Soften the gelatin in the cold water, then warm it until the gelatin dissolves. Cool it, but do not let it set. Beat it into the cream just as the cream begins to thicken.

Procedure for Making Chocolate Whipped Cream

1. Use the following proportions:

Heavy cream	1 qt	1 L
Sweet chocolate	12 oz	375 g

2. Whip the cream as in the basic procedure, but underwhip it slightly.

3. Grate or chop the chocolate into small pieces and place in a saucepan. Set over warm water and stir until the chocolate is melted. Let it cool to lukewarm. It must not cool too much or it will solidify before it can be mixed evenly with the cream.

4. Stir about one-fourth of the whipped cream into the chocolate until it is well mixed.

5. Fold the chocolate mixture into the rest of the cream carefully but thoroughly. Be careful not to overwhip the cream.

Crème Chantilly

For large-quantity measurements, see page 595.

Ingredients	U.S.		Cream at 100% Metric	%
Heavy cream or crème fraîche (see note)	8	oz	250 g	100
Confectioners' sugar	1.25	oz	40 g	16
Vanilla extract	½	tsp	2 mL	2
Total weight:	*9*	*oz*	*290 g*	*167%*

Note   For best results, use crème fraîche or, if it is not available, heavy cream with a fat content of 40% or more. Crème Chantilly can be made with cream having a fat content as low as 30%, but it is more likely to separate slightly or weep on standing.

■ Procedure

1. Make sure that the cream and all equipment and utensils are chilled.

2. Whip the cream by hand or machine until it forms soft peaks.

3. Add the sugar and vanilla. Continue to whip until the cream forms stiff peaks but is still smooth. Do not overwhip or the cream will become grainy and then separate to form particles of butter.

MERINGUE

Meringues are whipped egg whites sweetened with sugar. They are frequently used for pie toppings and cake icings. They are also used to give volume and lightness to buttercream icings and to such preparations as mousses and dessert soufflés.

Another excellent use for meringues is to bake them in a slow oven until crisp. In this form, they can be used as cake layers or pastry shells to make light, elegant desserts. To add flavor, chopped nuts may be folded into meringues before forming and baking. Pastries and cakes incorporating crisp meringues are discussed in chapters 10 and 14.

Basic Meringue Types

Meringues may be whipped to various degrees of stiffness as long as they are not overbeaten until they are too stiff and dry. For most purposes, they are beaten until they form stiff, or nearly stiff, moist peaks.

Common meringue, also called *French meringue,* is made from egg whites at room temperature, beaten with sugar. It is the easiest to make, and it is reasonably stable due to the high percentage of sugar.

Swiss meringue is made from egg whites and sugar that are warmed over a hot water bath while they are beaten. This warming gives the meringue better volume and stability.

Italian meringue is made by beating a hot sugar syrup into the egg whites. This meringue is the most stable of the three because the egg whites are cooked by the heat of the syrup. When flavored with vanilla, it is also known as *boiled icing.* It is also used in meringue-type buttercream icings.

The amount of sugar used in meringues may vary. *Soft meringues,* those used for pie toppings, may be made with as little as 1 pound of sugar per pound of egg whites. *Hard meringues,* those baked until crisp, are made with up to twice as much sugar as egg whites.

Guidelines for Making Meringues

1. ***Fats prevent whites from foaming properly*** This is very important. Make sure that all equipment is free of any trace of fat or grease, and that the egg whites have no trace of yolks in them.

Common Meringue or French Meringue

Ingredients	U.S.	Egg whites at 100% Metric	%
Egg whites	8 oz	250 g	100
Fine granulated sugar	8 oz	250 g	100
Fine granulated sugar or sifted confectioners' sugar	8 oz	250 g	100
Total weight:	*1 lb 8 oz*	*750 g*	*300%*

Note For soft meringue pie toppings, the second quantity of sugar may be omitted.

■ **P r o c e d u r e**

1. With the whip attachment, beat the egg whites first at medium speed, then at high speed, until they form soft peaks.

2. Add the first quantity of sugar, a little at a time, with the machine running. Whip until stiff.

3. Stop the machine. Fold in the remaining sugar with a spatula.

Variation

Chocolate Meringue

Ingredients	U.S.	Metric	%
Cocoa powder	4 oz	125 g	25

Use the confectioners' sugar in step 3 of the basic formula.
Sift the sugar twice with the cocoa powder.

2. *Egg whites foam better if they are at room temperature than if they are cold*   Remove them from the cooler 1 hour before whipping.

3. *Do not overbeat*   Beaten egg whites should look moist and shiny. Over-beaten meringues look dry and curdled; they are difficult to fold into other ingredients and have lost much of their ability to leaven cakes and souf-flés.

4. *Sugar makes egg white foams more stable*   Meringues are thicker and heavier than unsweetened egg white foams, and they are more stable. However, egg whites can hold only a limited amount of sugar without sac-rificing some volume. For this reason, when making common meringues, many cooks prefer to whip the egg whites with no more than an equal weight of sugar. Additional sugar can be folded in after the meringue is whipped.

5. *Mild acids help foaming*   A small amount of cream of tartar or lemon juice is sometimes added to egg whites for whipping in order to give them more volume and stability. This is especially helpful when the whipped whites are folded into other ingredients to provide lightness or leavening, as in the case of angel food cakes. Use about 2 teaspoons cream of tartar per pound of egg whites (15 g/kg).

Swiss Meringue

Ingredients	U.S.	Egg whites at 100% Metric	%
Egg whites	8 oz	250 g	100
Fine granulated sugar or half granulated and half confectioners'	1 lb	500 g	200
Total weight:	*1 lb 8 oz*	*750 g*	*300%*

■ P r o c e d u r e

1. Place the egg whites and sugar in a stainless steel bowl or in the top of a double boiler. Beat with a wire whip over hot water until the mixture is warm (about 120°F/50°C).

2. Transfer the mixture to the bowl of a mixing machine. Whip it at high speed until stiff peaks form and the meringue is completely cool.

Italian Meringue

Yield: about 2 qt (2 L)

Ingredients	U.S.	Egg whites at 100% Metric	%
Sugar	1 lb	500 g	200
Water	4 oz	125 mL	50
Egg whites	8 oz	250 g	100

■ P r o c e d u r e

1. Heat the sugar and water in a saucepan until the sugar dissolves and the mixture boils. Boil until a candy thermometer placed in the syrup regis-ters 243°F (117°C).

2. While the syrup is cooking, beat the egg whites in a mixing machine until they form soft peaks.

3. With the machine running, very slowly beat in the hot syrup.

4. Continue beating until the meringue is cool and forms firm peaks.

CRÈME ANGLAISE

Crème anglaise (pronounced "krem awng glezz"), also known as *vanilla custard sauce,* is a stirred custard. It consists of milk, sugar, and egg yolks stirred over very low heat until slightly thickened, then flavored with vanilla.

The recipe that follows gives the method for preparing custard sauce. Special care is necessary in preparing this sauce because the eggs can curdle easily if overcooked. The following guidelines will help you be successful:

1. Use clean, sanitized equipment and follow strict sanitation procedures. Egg mixtures are good breeding grounds for bacteria that cause food poisoning.

2. Heat the milk to scalding (just below simmering) in a double boiler before combining with the egg yolks. This makes the final cooking much shorter.

3. *Slowly* beat the hot milk into the beaten eggs and sugar. This raises the temperature of the eggs gradually and helps prevent curdling.

4. Heat the mixture slowly in a double boiler, stirring constantly, in order to prevent curdling.

5. To test for doneness, two methods are available. Keep in mind that this is a very light sauce, so you can't expect a lot of thickening.

   - Check the temperature with a thermometer. When it reaches 185°F (85°C), the sauce is cooked. Never let the temperature go above 190°F (87°C).

   - When the mixture lightly coats the back of a spoon, instead of running off it like milk, the sauce is cooked.

6. Immediately cool the sauce by setting the pan or bowl in ice water. Stir occasionally to cool it evenly.

7. If the sauce accidentally curdles, it is sometimes possible to save it. Immediately stir in 1 to 2 oz cold milk, transfer the sauce to a blender, and blend at high speed.

Crème Anglaise

Yield: about 2½ pt (1.25 L)

Ingredients	U.S.	Metric	Milk at 100% %
Egg yolks	8 oz (12 yolks)	250 g (12 yolks)	25
Sugar	8 oz	250 g	25
Milk	2 lb (1 qt)	1 L	100
Vanilla extract	0.5 oz (1 tbsp)	15 mL	1.5

■ P r o c e d u r e

1. Review the guidelines for preparing custard sauce preceding this recipe.
2. Combine the egg yolks and sugar in the bowl of a mixer. Beat with the whip attachment until thick and light.
3. Scald the milk in a double boiler.
4. With the mixer running at low speed, very gradually pour the scalded milk into the egg yolk mixture.
5. Pour the mixture back into the doubler boiler. Heat it slowly, stirring constantly, until it thickens enough to coat the back of spoon (or until it reaches 185°F/85°C).
6. Immediately remove the top part of the double boiler from the heat and set it in a pan of cold water. Stir in the vanilla. Stir the sauce occasionally as it cools.

Variations

Chocolate Crème Anglaise
Melt 6 oz (180 g/18%) sweet chocolate. Stir it into the vanilla custard sauce while it is still warm (not hot).

Coffee Crème Anglaise
Add 2 tbsp (8 g) instant coffee to the warm custard sauce.

PASTRY CREAM

Although it requires more ingredients and steps, pastry cream is easier to make than vanilla custard sauce because it is less likely to curdle. Pastry cream contains a starch thickening agent, which stabilizes the eggs. It can actually be boiled without curdling. In fact, it *must* be brought to a boil or the starch will not cook completely and the cream will have a raw, starchy taste.

Strict observance of all sanitation rules is essential when preparing pastry cream because of the danger of bacterial contamination. Use clean, sanitized equipment. Do not put your fingers in the cream; do not taste except with a clean spoon. Chill the finished cream rapidly in shallow pans. Keep the cream and all cream-filled products refrigerated at all times.

The procedure for preparing pastry cream is given in the formula that follows. Note that the basic steps are similar to those for custard sauce. In this case, however, a starch is mixed with the eggs and half the sugar to make a smooth paste. (In some recipes with lower egg content, it is necessary to add a little cold milk to provide enough liquid to make a paste.) Meanwhile, the milk is scalded with the other half of the sugar. The egg mixture is then tempered with some of the hot milk and then returned to the kettle and brought to a boil. Some chefs prefer to add the cold paste gradually to the hot milk, but the tempering procedure described here seems to give better protection against lumping.

Pastry Cream Variations

Pastry cream has many applications in the bakeshop, so it is important to master the basic technique. Pastry cream and its variations are used as fillings for cakes and pastries, as fillings for cream pies (p. 220), and as puddings (p. 429). With more liquid added, it can also be used as a custard sauce.

Cornstarch should be used as the thickening agent when the cream is to be used as a pie filling so that the cut slices hold their shape. For other uses, either cornstarch or flour may be used. Remember that twice as much flour is needed to provide the same thickening power as cornstarch.

Other variations are possible, as you will see in the recipes. Sometimes whipped cream is folded into pastry cream to lighten it and make it creamier. Adding a meringue to pastry cream and stabilizing it with gelatin makes a cream called *Chiboust* (p. 189).

Pastry Cream I

Yield: about 1⅛ qt (1.12 L)

Ingredients	U.S.	Metric	Milk at 100% %
Milk	2 lb (1 qt)	1 L	100
Sugar	4 oz	125 g	12.5
Egg yolks	2.5 oz (4 yolks)	75 g (4 yolks)	8
Whole eggs	3.5 oz (2 eggs)	110 g (2 eggs)	11
Cornstarch	2.5 oz	75 g	8
Sugar	4 oz	125 g	12.5
Butter	2 oz	60 g	6
Vanilla extract	0.5 oz (1 tbsp)	15 mL	1.5

■ P r o c e d u r e

1.   In a heavy saucepan or kettle, dissolve the sugar in the milk and bring just to a boil.

2.   With a whip, beat the egg yolks and whole eggs in a stainless-steel bowl.

3.   Sift the cornstarch and sugar into the eggs. Beat with the whip until perfectly smooth.

4.   Temper the egg mixture by slowly beating in the hot milk in a thin stream.

5.   Return the mixture to the heat and bring to a boil, stirring constantly.

6.   When the mixture comes to a boil and thickens, remove from the heat.

7.   Stir in the butter and vanilla. Mix until the butter is melted and completely blended in.

8.   Pour out into a clean, sanitized hotel pan or other shallow pan. Dust lightly with sugar and cover with waxed paper to prevent a crust from forming. Cool and chill as quickly as possible.

9.   For filling pastries such as éclairs and napoleons, whip the chilled pastry cream until smooth before using.

Variations

Deluxe Pastry Cream
Omit the whole eggs in the basic recipe and use 8–10 egg yolks (5–7 oz/150–200 g/7–10%).

Pastry Cream Mousseline
For a lighter pastry cream filling, fold whipped heavy cream into the chilled pastry cream. Quantities may be varied to taste. In general, for every 1 qt (1 L) pastry cream, use 0.5–1 cup (1.25–2.5 dL) heavy cream.

Chocolate Pastry Cream
Melt together 2 oz (60 g) sweet chocolate and 2 oz (60 g) unsweetened chocolate. Stir into the hot pastry cream.

Coffee Pastry Cream
Add 2 tbsp (8 g) instant coffee powder to the milk in step 1.

Pastry Cream II (Crème Patissière)

Ingredients	U.S.	Metric	Milk at 100% %
Milk	2 pt	1000 g	100
Vanilla bean (see *note*)	1	1	
Sugar	3.5 oz	100 g	10
Egg yolks	5.33 oz	160 g	16
Sugar	3.5 oz	100 g	10
Cake flour	1.67 oz	50 g	5
Cornstarch	1.67 oz	50 g	5
Total weight:	*1 lb 15 oz (about 2¹/₂ pt)*	*1460 g (about 1200 mL)*	*146%*

Note If vanilla beans are not available, substitute ¹/₂ tsp (2 mL) vanilla extract or to taste, for each vanilla bean.

■ P r o c e d u r e

1. In a saucepan, heat the milk with the vanilla bean and the first quantity of sugar, stirring to dissolve the sugar. Bring to a boil.

2. Whip the egg yolks with the remaining sugar.

3. Sift together the flour and cornstarch. Add the egg mixture and mix well.

4. Temper the egg mixture by slowly beating in about half the hot milk. Then pour this mixture back into the saucepan with the remaining milk. Bring to a boil, stirring constantly, until thickened.

5. Remove from heat and immediately pour the cream into a bowl set over ice water. Stir until cool.

6. Cover the surface of the cream with plastic film to prevent a crust from forming.

Variations

Chocolate Crème Patissière
For each 12 oz pastry cream, stir in 4 oz melted dark chocolate while the pastry cream is still warm (100 g chocolate for each 300 g pastry cream).

Praline Crème Patissière
For each 12 oz pastry cream, stir in 4 oz softened praline paste while the pastry cream is still warm (100 g praline paste for each 300 g pastry cream).

Chiboust Cream

Yield: about 3 lb (1500 g)

Ingredients	U.S.		Metric	%
			Milk at 100%	
			Metric	%
Milk	1 pt		500 g	100
Vanilla extract	½	tsp	2 g	0.4
Sugar	1	oz	30 g	6
Egg yolks	5.33	oz	160 g	33
Sugar	1	oz	30 g	6
Cornstarch	1.33	oz	40 g	8
Italian meringue				
Sugar	13	oz	400 g	80
Water	4	oz	120 g	24
Egg whites	8	oz	240 g	48
Gelatin	0.4	oz	12 g	2.5

a.

b.

c.

d.

■ P r o c e d u r e

1. Combine the milk, vanilla, and sugar and bring to a boil, stirring to dissolve the sugar.

2. Whip the egg yolks with the second quantity of sugar. Stir in the cornstarch.

3. Temper the egg mixture with half of the hot milk. Pour this mixture back into the pan with the re-maining milk. Return to a boil and boil for 1 minute, until thickened.

4. Turn out into a bowl and cover the surface with plastic film to prevent a skin from forming. Keep warm while making the Italian meringue.

5. Boil the sugar and water until the temperature of the syrup reaches 258°F (120°C). Whip the egg whites to firm peaks, then slowly pour the syrup into the whites, whipping constantly. Continue whipping until cool.

6. Soak the gelatin in cold water (see p. 39) and add to hot pastry cream (a).

7. Mix until the gelatin is dissolved (b). (If the pastry cream is not warm enough, rewarm it slightly.)

8. Add one-third of the meringue to the cream and mix quickly to lighten the mixture (c).

9. Gently fold in the remaining meringue until evenly mixed (d).

Variations

Chocolate Chiboust Cream

Ingredients	U.S.		Metric	%
Rum	1	oz	30 g	6
Bittersweet chocolate	3.5	oz	100 g	20

After step 3 in the basic recipe, stir in the rum and chopped bittersweet chocolate until the chocolate is melted and well blended:

Coffee Chiboust Cream

Ingredients	U.S.		Metric	%
Coffee liqueur	1	oz	30 g	6
Liquid coffee extract	1.67	oz	50 g	10

After step 3 in the basic recipe, stir in coffee liqueur and liquid coffee extract.

Praline Chiboust Cream

Ingredients	U.S.		Metric	%
Rum	1	oz	30 g	6
Praline paste	2.5	oz	75 g	15

After step 3 in the basic recipe, stir in rum and praline paste.

Chiboust Cream with Raspberries

Yield: about 3 lb (1500 g)

Ingredients	U.S.		Metric	Milk at 100% %
Milk	1 pt		500 g	100
Sugar	1.33 oz		40 g	8
Egg yolks	5.33 oz		160 g	33
Sugar	1.33 oz		40 g	8
Cornstarch	1.67 oz		50 g	10
Italian meringue				
Sugar	13	oz	400 g	80
Water	4	oz	120 g	24
Egg whites	8	oz	240 g	48
Raspberry purée (unsweetened)	6	oz	180 g	36
Gelatin	0.5	oz	16 g	

Note   The quantities of sugar, starch, and gelatin are greater in this recipe than in the basic Chiboust because the addition of raspberry purée requires additional sweetening and thickening.

■ P r o c e d u r e

1. Combine the milk and sugar and bring to a boil, stirring to dissolve the sugar.

2. Whip the egg yolks with the second quantity of sugar. Stir in the cornstarch.

3. Temper the egg mixture with half of the hot milk. Pour this mixture back into the pan with the remaining milk. Return to a boil and boil for 1 minute, until thickened.

4. Turn out into a bowl and cover the surface with plastic film to prevent a skin from forming. Keep warm while making the Italian meringue.

5. Boil the sugar and water until the temperature of the syrup reaches 258°F (120°C). Whip the egg whites to firm peaks, then slowly pour the syrup into the whites, whipping constantly. Continue whipping until cool.

6. Fold the raspberry purée into the meringue.

7. Soak the gelatin in cold water (see p. 39). Stir the gelatin into the warm pastry cream until dissolved and evenly mixed. (If the pastry cream is not warm enough, rewarm it slightly.)

8. Add one-third of the meringue to the cream and mix quickly to lighten the mixture. Gently fold in the remaining meringue.

Variation

Chiboust Cream Flavored with Alcohol

Ingredients	U.S.	Metric	%
Lemon zest, grated	½ tsp	2 g	0.4
Liqueur or other alcohol	1.67 oz	50 g	10

Omit the raspberry purée from the basic recipe. Add grated lemon zest to the egg yolk mixture in step 2, and stir choice of rum, kirsch, brandy, or orange liqueur into the warm pastry cream when adding the gelatin in step 7.

Lime or Lemon Chiboust

Yield: about 1 lb 12 oz (750 g)

Ingredients	U.S.		Metric	%
Lime or lemon juice	10	oz	250 g	100
Lime or lemon zest, grated	0.16 oz (2 tsp)		4 g	1.5
Sugar	1	oz	25 g	10
Egg yolks	3	oz	80 g	32
Sugar	1	oz	25 g	10
Cornstarch	1	oz	25 g	10.0
Gelatin	0.25 oz		6 g	2.5
Italian Meringue (p. 183)	1 lb		400 g	160

■ P r o c e d u r e

1. Heat the juice, zest, and sugar to a simmer.

2. Whip the egg yolks with the second quantity of sugar and the cornstarch. As for making pastry cream, gradually stir the juice into the egg yolk mixture, then return to the saucepan and bring to a boil. Remove from the heat.

3. Soak the gelatin in cold water (see p. 39). Add the gelatin to the egg yolk mixture and stir until dissolved. Cool.

4. Fold in the Italian Meringue.

Vanilla Crème Diplomat

For large-quantity measurements, see page 595.

Ingredients	U.S.		Metric	%
Milk	8	oz	250 g	100
Vanilla bean, split (see *note*)	½		½	
Egg yolks	1.33 oz (2 yolks)		40 g (2 yolks)	16
Fine granulated sugar	1	oz	30 g	12
Cake flour	0.67 oz		20 g	8
Cornstarch	0.5	oz	15 g	6
Orange liqueur, such as Grand Marnier	1	oz	30 g	12
Crème Chantilly (p. 181)	6.5	oz	200 g	80
Total weight:	*1 lb 3*	*oz*	*585 g*	*234%*

Note If vanilla beans are not available, flavor the finished cream with vanilla extract to taste.

■ P r o c e d u r e

1. Heat the milk and vanilla bean to just below the boiling point.

2. Whip the egg yolks and sugar until pale. Add the flour and cornstarch and mix well.

3. Temper the egg mixture by gradually stirring in about half the hot milk. Pour this mixture back into the saucepan with the remaining hot milk. Return to a boil, whipping constantly.

4. Remove from the heat and stir in the liqueur.

5. Cover with plastic film and cool the pastry cream thoroughly, then chill.

6. Once the cream is cold, beat well until perfectly smooth.

7. Fold in the Crème Chantilly.

Variations

Crème Diplomat is often stabilized with gelatin, using the same procedure as for Chiboust Cream (p. 189). For each 8 oz (250 g) milk, use ⅛ oz (4 g or 2 leaves) gelatin.

Chocolate Crème Diplomat
For large-quantity measurements, see page 595.

Ingredients	U.S.	Metric	%
Dark chocolate, finely chopped	2.25 oz	70 g	28%

Omit the orange liqueur from the basic recipe. Stir dark chocolate into the hot pastry cream in step 4. Stir until the chocolate is completely melted and well mixed.

Crème Diplomat may also be flavored with coffee extract, praline paste, or chestnut purée.

CHOCOLATE CREAMS

Ganache (pronounced "gah nahsh") is a rich chocolate cream filling with many uses. When freshly made and still warm, it can be used as a glaze or icing for cakes, much like fondant; pour it over the product to be iced and it will set into a soft icing. When cooled, ganache is used to make chocolate truffles or a filling for other candies. It can also be whipped to make a filling for cakes, tortes, and meringue pastries.

In its simplest form, ganache is a mixture of heavy cream and melted chocolate couverture. Butter can also be included, as illustrated in the second recipe in this section. The quality of a simple ganache depends primarily on the quality of the chocolate. More complex formulas for ganache can include eggs and a variety of flavoring ingredients. You might like to experiment with the recipe for Passion Fruit Ganache (p. 193), substituting other fruit purées and flavoring ingredients for the passion fruit.

Chocolate Ganache I

Ingredients	U.S.	Chocolate at 100% Metric	%
Dark chocolate	1 lb	500 g	100
Heavy cream	12 oz	375 g	75
Total weight:	*1 lb 12 oz*	*875 g*	*175%*

Variations

The proportion of chocolate and cream may be varied. For a firmer product, or if the weather is warm, decrease the cream to as little as 50%. For a very soft ganache, increase the cream to 100%. This proportion makes a ganache that is too soft to make truffles but may be whipped into a mousse.

The composition of the chocolate also affects the consistency of the ganache, and the formula may require slight adjustments depending on the chocolate used.

Chocolate Ganache II

Ingredients	U.S.	Chocolate at 100% Metric	%
Heavy cream	1 lb 2 oz	600 g	100
Vanilla powder	pinch	pinch	
Bittersweet chocolate	1 lb 2 oz	600 g	100
Butter, softened	3 oz	100 g	17
Total weight:	*2 lb 7 oz*	*1300 g*	*217%*

■ Procedure

1. Bring the cream and vanilla powder to a boil.
2. Chop the chocolate.
3. Pour the hot cream over the chocolate. Stir until the chocolate is melted.
4. When the mixture has cooled to 95°F (35°C), stir in the butter. Use the ganache at once.

■ Procedure

1. Chop the chocolate into small pieces.
2. Bring the cream just to a boil, stirring to prevent scorching. (Use very fresh cream; old cream is more likely to curdle when it is boiled.)
3. Add the chocolate. Remove from the heat, stir, and let stand for a few minutes. Stir again until the chocolate is completely melted and the mixture is smooth. If necessary, warm gently over low heat to completely melt the chocolate. At this point, the ganache is ready to be used as an icing or glaze. Apply it by pouring it over the item to be iced, like Fondant (see p. 335).
4. If the ganache is not to be used warm, let it cool at room temperature. Stir from time to time so that it cools evenly. Cooled ganache may be stored in the refrigerator and rewarmed over a water bath when needed.
5. For whipped ganache, the mixture should first be cooled thoroughly or it will not whip properly. Do not let it become too cold, however, or it will be too hard. With a wire whip or the whip attachment of a mixer, whip the ganache until it is light, thick, and creamy. Use at once. If stored, whipped ganache will become firm and hard to spread.

Chapter 13 includes a recipe for a ganache intended specifically for icing cakes, as well as other similar glazes.

The two chocolate mousse recipes included here are well suited for fillings and pastries. They can also be served by themselves as desserts. Additional chocolate mousses are included with the puddings in chapter 16.

Passion Fruit Ganache

For large-quantity measurements, see page 596.

Ingredients	U.S.		Metric	Chocolate at 100% %
Heavy cream	4	oz	120 g	56
Passion fruit juice	4	oz	120 g	56
Butter	2	oz	60 g	28
Egg yolks	1.67	oz	50 g	23
Sugar	2	oz	60 g	28
Dark chocolate, chopped	7	oz	215 g	100
Total weight:	*1 lb 4*	*oz*	*625 g*	*291%*

Procedure

1. Combine the cream, juice, and butter in a saucepan and bring to a boil.
2. Whip the egg yolks with the sugar until light.
3. Gradually beat the hot liquid into the egg mixture.
4. Return this mixture to the heat and bring quickly to a boil, then remove from heat.
5. Strain the liquid over the chopped chocolate in a bowl. Stir until all the chocolate is melted and the mixture is evenly blended.

Chocolate Mousse I

Ingredients	U.S.		Metric	Chocolate at 100% %
Dark chocolate	1 lb		500 g	100
Butter	9	oz	280 g	56
Egg yolks	5	oz	155 g	31
Egg whites	12	oz	375 g	75
Sugar	2.5	oz	80 g	16
Total weight:	*2 lb 12*	*oz*	*1390 g*	*278%*

Procedure

1. Melt the chocolate over hot water.
2. Remove from the heat and add the butter. Stir until the butter is melted and completely mixed in.
3. Add the egg yolks one at a time. Mix in each egg yolk completely before adding the next.
4. Beat the egg whites until they form soft peaks. Add the sugar and beat until the egg whites form stiff but moist peaks. Do not overbeat.
5. Fold the egg whites into the chocolate mixture.

Chocolate Mousse II

For large-quantity measurements, see page 596.

Ingredients	U.S.		Metric	Chocolate at 100% %
Egg yolks	1.5	oz	40 g	25
Fine granulated sugar	1.33	oz	35 g	22
Water	1	oz	30 g	19
Dark chocolate, melted	6	oz	160 g	100
Heavy cream	11	oz	300 g	190
Total weight:	*1 lb 4*	*oz*	*565 g*	*356%*

Procedure

1. In a round-bottomed stainless-steel bowl, whip the egg yolks until pale.
2. Make a syrup with the sugar and water and boil to 244°F (118°C). Whip the hot syrup into the yolks and continue whipping until cool.
3. Melt the chocolate and fold into the egg mixture.
4. Whip the cream until it forms soft peaks. Whip one-third of the cream into the chocolate mixture. Then fold in the remaining cream until well incorporated.

DESSERT SAUCES

In addition to the recipes presented in this section, the following types of dessert sauces are discussed elsewhere in this book or can be made easily without recipes.

Custard Sauces   Vanilla custard sauce, or crème anglaise, is presented earlier in this chapter (p. 184). It is one of the most basic preparations in dessert cookery. Chocolate or other flavors may be added to create variations.

Pastry Cream (p. 185) can be thinned with heavy cream or milk to make another type of custard sauce.

Chocolate Sauce   In addition to the three recipes that follow, chocolate sauce may be made in several other ways. For example:

Flavor vanilla custard sauce with chocolate (see p. 184).

Prepare Ganache I (p. 192) through step 3 in the procedure. Then thin to desired consistency with cream, milk, or simple syrup.

Lemon Sauce   Prepare Lemon Filling (p. 221), but use only $1\frac{1}{2}$ oz (45 g) cornstarch, or use 1 oz (30 g) waxy maize.

Fruit Sauces   Some of the best fruit sauces are also the simplest. These are of two types:

Purées of fresh or cooked fruits, sweetened with sugar. Such a purée is often called a *coulis* (pronounced "koo-lee").

Heated, strained fruit jams and preserves, diluted with simple syrup, water, or liquor.

More economical fruit sauces can be stretched by diluting them with water, adding more sugar, and thickening them with starch. Other sauces, such as those made of blueberries or pineapple, may have a more desirable texture when thickened slightly with starch. These may also be flavored with spices and/or lemon juice.

Procedures for Preparing Fruit Sauces

These procedures can be used to make apricot sauce, raspberry sauce, strawberry sauce, and other fruit sauces.

Method 1

1. Using fresh, canned, or frozen fruit, rub the fruit through a sieve or purée it in a blender.

2. Mix fruit with sugar to taste. Use as is, or bring to a boil, and let it simmer until thickened to desired consistency.

Method 2

1. Melt jam or preserves, diluted with a little water, syrup, or appropriate liquor such as kirsch.

2. Rub through a sieve. Adjust consistency by adding more liquid to it (to thin out) or by cooking it down (to thicken).

Caramel Sauces The first section of this chapter explains the stages of sugar cooking, the last stage of which is caramel. In other words, caramel is simply sugar that has been cooked until it is golden. The simplest caramel sauce is merely caramelized sugar that is diluted to sauce consistency with water. The addition of heavy cream makes a creamy caramel sauce, as shown by the recipe in this section.

A more complex type of caramel is *butter caramel*. The recipe included in this section is rarely used by itself (except to make hard toffee candies). Rather, it is a component of other preparations, such as caramelized fruits. See, for example, the recipes for Caramelized Apricots, Figs in Port Wine, and Spiced Pineapple in chapter 18. Because butter caramel is somewhat difficult to make, it is included here to give you an opportunity to study it by itself and master it before trying one of the recipes mentioned. It is necessary to follow the instructions in the recipe procedure carefully in order to make the butter and caramelized sugar form a uniform, emulsified mixture.

Chocolate Sauce I

Yield: 1 qt (1 L)

Ingredients	U.S.	Metric
Dark chocolate	1 lb	500 g
Water	1 pt	500 mL
Butter	6 oz	190 g

■ P r o c e d u r e

1. Chop the chocolate into small pieces.
2. Place the chocolate and water in a saucepan. Heat over low heat or over hot water until the chocolate is melted. Stir while cooking to make a smooth mixture.
3. Remove from the heat and add the butter. Stir until the butter is melted and mixed in.
4. Set the pan in a bowl of ice water and stir the sauce until it is cool.

Chocolate Sauce II

Yield: 1 qt (1 L)

Ingredients	U.S.	Metric
Water	1 pt	0.5 L
Sugar	2 lb	1 kg
Corn syrup	6 oz	375 g
Unsweetened chocolate	8 oz	250 g
Butter	2 oz	62 g

■ P r o c e d u r e

1. Combine the water, sugar, and syrup and bring to a boil, stirring to dissolve the sugar.
2. Boil 1 minute and remove from the heat. Let cool a few minutes.
3. Melt the chocolate and butter together over low heat. Stir until smooth.
4. Very slowly stir the hot syrup into the chocolate.
5. Place over moderate heat and bring to a boil. Boil for 4 minutes.
6. Remove from the heat and cool.

Chocolate Sauce III

Yield: 1 lb 8 oz (600 g)

Ingredients	U.S.	Metric
Water	12 oz	300 g
Sugar	7 oz	175 g
Dark chocolate couverture	3 oz	75 g
Cornstarch	1 oz	25 g
Cocoa powder	2 oz	50 g
Water, cold	as needed	as needed

■ P r o c e d u r e

1. Combine the water, sugar, and chocolate. Bring to a boil, stirring to mix the chocolate with the syrup.
2. Mix the cornstarch and cocoa powder to a thin paste with a little water.
3. Add this paste to the chocolate syrup mixture and return to a boil. Strain and cool.

Melba Sauce

Yield: about 1 pt (400 mL)

Ingredients	U.S.	Metric
Frozen, sweetened raspberries	1 lb 8 oz	600 g
Red currant jelly	8 oz	200 g

■ P r o c e d u r e

1. Thaw the raspberries and force them through a sieve to purée them and remove the seeds.

2. Combine with the jelly in a saucepan. Bring to a boil, stirring until the jelly is melted and completely blended with the fruit purée.

Variations

Raspberry Sauce

Purée and sieve frozen sweetened raspberries, or use fresh raspberries and sweeten to taste. Omit the red currant jelly. Use as is or simmer until thickened, as desired.

Other fruits can be puréed and sweetened to taste to make dessert sauces, using the same procedures. If purées from pulpy fruits (such as mangoes) are too thick, thin with water, simple syrup, or an appropriate fruit juice.

Caramel Sauce

For large-quantity measurements, see page 596.

Yield: 12 oz (375 mL)

Ingredients	U.S.	Metric
Sugar	8 oz	250 g
Water	2 oz	60 mL
Lemon juice	¾ tsp	4 mL
Heavy cream	6 oz	190 mL
Milk	4 oz	125 mL

■ P r o c e d u r e

1. Combine the sugar, water, and juice in a heavy saucepan. Bring to a boil, stirring to dissolve the sugar. Cook the syrup to the caramel stage (see p. 177). Toward the end of the cooking time, turn the heat to very low to avoid burning the sugar or letting it get too dark. It should be a golden color.

2. Remove from the heat and cool 5 minutes.

3. Bring the heavy cream to a boil. Add a few ounces of it to the caramel.

4. Stir and continue to add the cream slowly. Return to the heat and stir until all the caramel is dissolved.

5. Let cool completely.

6. Stir the milk into the cooled caramel to thin it.

Variations

Hot Caramel Sauce

Proceed as directed through step 4. Omit the milk.

Clear Caramel Sauce

Substitute 2.5–3 oz (75–90 mL) water for the heavy cream and omit the milk. If the sauce is too thick when cool, add more water.

Butterscotch Sauce

Use brown sugar instead of white granulated sugar in the basic recipe. Omit the lemon juice. In step 1, cook the syrup only to 240°F (115°C). Add 2 oz (60 g) butter before adding the heavy cream.

Caramel Cream

Prepare 2 oz Clear Caramel Sauce. Soften 0.06 oz (½ tsp/2 g) gelatin in 0.5 oz (1 tbsp/15 mL) water. Add to the warm caramel sauce and stir until dissolved (rewarm if necessary). Cool to room temperature but do not cool until set. Whip 4 oz (125 g) heavy cream to soft peaks. Mix about one-fourth of the cream into the caramel sauce, then fold in the remaining cream.

Butter Caramel

Yield: 11 oz (330 g)

Ingredients	U.S.	Metric
Sugar	8 oz	250 g
Butter	4 oz	125 g

■ P r o c e d u r e

1. Heat the sugar over moderate heat until it melts and then turns to a golden brown caramel.

2. Keeping the pan over moderate heat. Add the butter. Stir constantly over heat until the butter has melted and is blended into the caramel. It is essential to stir vigorously in order to emulsify the butter and caramel. If you do not stir well enough, the butterfat will tend to separate.

3. The caramel will hold reasonably well for a short time over heat. It should be stirred from time to time. If the caramel is allowed to cool, it will become a hard, brittle toffee. If it is reheated, the butter will separate, but it can be reincorporated by adding a few drops of water and stirring vigorously.

Sabayon I

Yield: about 1½ pt (750 mL)

Ingredients	U.S.	Metric
Egg yolks	2.67 oz (4 yolks)	80 g (4 yolks)
Simple Syrup (p. 177)	3.5 oz	100 g
Whipped cream	2 oz	60 g

■ P r o c e d u r e

1. Mix the egg yolks and syrup in a stainless-steel bowl. Place the bowl over a hot water bath and whip until light, frothy, and pale in color.

2. Remove the bowl from the hot water bath and continue to whip until cool and doubled in volume.

3. Gently fold in the whipped cream.

4. Use as a dessert sauce or topping that can be browned (gratinéed) under a salamander or broiler.

Sabayon II

Yield: about 1 qt (900 mL)

Ingredients	U.S.	Metric
Egg yolks	4 oz (6 yolks)	115 g (6 yolks)
Sugar	8 oz	225 g
Dry white wine	8 oz	225 mL

■ P r o c e d u r e

1. In a stainless steel bowl, beat the yolks until foamy.

2. Beat in the sugar and wine. Place over a hot water bath and continue beating until thick and hot.

3. Serve hot as a dessert or as a sauce for fruit or fritters. Serve without delay; it will lose some foaminess and begin to separate if it is allowed to stand.

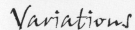

Cold Sabayon

Dissolve 0.04 oz (½ tsp/1 g) gelatin in the wine. Proceed as in the basic recipe. When the sauce is done, place the bowl over ice and whip the sauce until it is cool.

Zabaglione

This is the Italian sauce and dessert that is the origin of sabayon. Use sweet Marsala wine instead of the dry white wine, and use only half the sugar. Other wines or spirits may be used, such as port or sherry. Adjust the sugar according to the sweetness of the wine.

Sauce Suzette

Yield: about 1 pt (450 mL)

Ingredients	U.S.		Metric
Orange juice	7	oz	200 g
Lemon juice	2	oz	60 g
Orange zest, grated	0.5	oz	15 g
Sugar	7	oz	200 g
Butter	2.5	oz	80 g
Orange liqueur, such as Cointreau	7	oz	100 g
Brandy	2	oz	60 g

■ **P r o c e d u r e**

1. Warm the juice and zest in a saucepan.

2. In a separate pan, cook the sugar to a golden caramel.

3. Remove from the heat and add the butter. Stir to begin to dissolve the caramelized sugar.

4. Add the warmed juices. Reduce by one-third, stirring continuously.

5. Add the liqueur and brandy. Ignite to burn off the alcohol.

6. Serve warm.

Fruit Coulis

Yield: 10–11 oz (300 g)

Ingredients	U.S.	Metric
Berries or other soft fruit	7 oz	200 g
Fine granulated sugar	3.5 oz	100 g
Water	1.33 oz (8 tsp)	40 g
Lemon juice	0.5 oz (3 tsp)	15 g
Optional		
Kirsch or other fruit brandy or liqueur	0.67 oz (4 tsp)	20 g

■ **P r o c e d u r e**

1. Purée the fruit in a blender or food processor and pass through a fine sieve or chinois.

2. Warm the fruit purée in a saucepan.

3. Separately, make a syrup of the sugar and water and boil to 220°F (105°C). Mix into the fruit purée.

4. Return to a boil, strain, and mix in the juice and alcohol. Cool.

Dulce de Leche

Yield: about 1 pt (500 mL)

Ingredients	U.S.	Metric
Milk	2 pt	1 L
Sugar	12 oz	375 mL
Baking soda	¼ tsp	1 mL
Vanilla extract	½ tsp	2 mL

■ **P r o c e d u r e**

1. Combine the milk, sugar, and baking soda in a heavy saucepan. Set over medium heat. Bring to a slow boil *without stirring*.

2. As the mixture approaches the boil, it will foam up. Quickly remove it from the heat before it boils over; stir.

3. Turn the heat to low, set the pan back on the heat, and cook slowly, stirring frequently with a wooden spoon, for about 45 to 60 minutes. The mixture will gradually caramelize.

4. When the mixture is a rich caramel brown and thickened but still pourable, remove from the heat and stir in the vanilla.

5. Cool thoroughly.

Hard Sauce

Yield: about 1 pt (500 mL)

Ingredients	U.S.	Metric
Butter	8 oz	250 g
Confectioners' sugar	1 lb	500 g
Brandy or rum	1 oz	30 mL

■ P r o c e d u r e

1. Cream the butter and sugar until light and fluffy, as for simple buttercream.
2. Beat in the brandy or rum.
3. Serve with steamed puddings, such as English Christmas pudding.

Cream Sauce for Piping

Yield: variable

Ingredients	U.S.	Metric
Sour cream	as needed	as needed
Heavy cream	as needed	as needed

■ P r o c e d u r e

1. Stir sour cream until it is smooth.
2. As this sauce is used for marbling or decorating other sauces, the quantity of cream needed depends on the texture of the other sauces. Gradually stir in heavy cream to thin the sour cream until it is the same consistency as the sauce to be decorated.

▶ TERMS FOR REVIEW

caramelize
simple syrup
dessert syrup
crystallize

common meringue
Swiss meringue
Italian meringue

crème anglaise
pastry cream
crème Chiboust

ganache
crème Chantilly
coulis

▶ QUESTIONS FOR REVIEW

1. How can you avoid unwanted crystallization when cooking sugar syrups?

2. Why is cream of tartar or lemon juice sometimes added to a sugar syrup before or during cooking?

3. Vanilla custard sauce and pastry cream both contain eggs. Why is it possible to boil pastry cream but not custard sauce?

4. Explain the importance of sanitation in the production of pastry cream. What specific steps should you take to ensure a safe product?

5. Explain the effects of fat, sugar, and temperature on the whipping of egg whites into foams.

6. Describe two simple ways of preparing fruit sauces.

chapter

9
Pies

On the early American frontier, it was not uncommon for the pioneer housewife to bake 21 pies each week—one for every meal. Pies were so important to the settlers that in winter, when fruits were unavailable, cooks would bake dessert pies out of whatever materials were available, such as potatoes, vinegar, and soda crackers.

Few of us today eat pie at every meal. Nevertheless, pies are still a favorite American dessert. Most customers will order and pay a higher price for a piece of chocolate cream pie than for chocolate pudding, even if the pie filling is the same as the pudding and even if they leave the crust uneaten.

In this chapter, we study the preparation of pie doughs and fillings and the procedures for assembling and baking pies.

After reading this chapter, you should be able to:

- Prepare pie doughs.
- Roll pie doughs and line pie pans.
- Fill, assemble, and bake single-crust pies, double-crust pies, and lattice-topped pies.
- Form and bake pie shells for unbaked pies.
- Prepare fruit fillings.
- Prepare soft or custard-type pie fillings.
- Prepare cream fillings.
- Prepare chiffon fillings.

PIE DOUGHS

Before you begin studying this section, review the section on gluten development in chapter 1. Pie pastry is a simple product in terms of its ingredients: flour, shortening, water, and salt. Yet success or failure depends on how the shortening and flour are mixed and how the gluten is developed. The key to making pie dough is proper technique, and you will remember the techniques better if you understand why they work.

INGREDIENTS

Flour   Pastry flour is the best choice for pie doughs. It has enough gluten to produce the desired structure and flakiness, yet is low enough in gluten to yield a tender product, if handled properly. If stronger flours are used, the percentage of shortening should be increased slightly to provide more tenderness.

Fat   Regular hydrogenated shortening is the most popular fat for pie crusts because it has the right plastic consistency to produce a flaky crust. It is firm and moldable enough to make an easily workable dough. Emulsified shortening should not be used, as it blends too quickly with the flour and makes it difficult to achieve a flaky pastry.

Butter contributes excellent flavor to pie pastry, but it is frequently avoided in volume production for two reasons: it is expensive, and it melts easily, making the dough difficult to work.

It is desirable, if costs permit, to blend a quantity of butter into the shortening used for pie crusts in order to improve flavor. The large quantity of pie crust that is dumped into the garbage after customers have eaten the filling is evidence that many people are not satisfied with the taste of shortening pie crusts.

If butter is used to replace all the shortening for pie doughs, the percentage of fat in the formula should be increased by about one-fourth. (If 1 lb shortening is called for, use 1 lb 4 oz butter.) The liquid can be reduced slightly, as butter contains moisture.

In the case of richer pastries and short doughs, butter is specified as the primary fat in the formulas here. These doughs are used primarily for European-style tarts and pastries, in which the flavor of the butter is an important part of the dessert.

Lard is an excellent shortening for pies because it is firm and plastic. However, it is not widely used in food service.

Liquid   Water is necessary to develop some gluten in the flour and to give structure and flakiness to the dough. If too much water is used, the crust will become tough because of too much gluten development. If not enough water is used, the crust will fall apart.

Milk makes a richer dough that browns more quickly. However, the crust is less crisp and the production cost is higher. If dry milk is used, it should be dissolved in the water to ensure even distribution in the dough.

Whether water or milk is used, it must be added cold (40°F/4°C or colder) to maintain proper dough temperature.

Salt   Salt has some tenderizing and conditioning effect on the gluten. However, it contributes mainly to flavor. Salt must be dissolved in the liquid before being added to the mix in order to ensure even distribution.

TEMPERATURE

Pie dough should be kept cool, about 60°F (15°C), during mixing and makeup, for two reasons.

• Shortening has the best consistency when cool. If it is warm, it blends too quickly with the flour. If it is very cold, it is too firm to be easily worked.

• Gluten develops more slowly at cool temperatures than at warm temperatures.

PIE DOUGH TYPES

There are two basic types of pie dough:

• Flaky pie dough
• Mealy pie dough

The difference between the two is in how the fat is blended with the flour. Complete mixing procedures are given in the formulas that follow. First, it is important to understand the basic distinction between the two types.

Flaky Pie Dough

For flaky dough, the fat is cut or rubbed into the flour until the particles of shortening are about the size of peas or hazelnuts—that is, the flour is not completely blended with the fat, and the fat is left in pieces. (Many bakers distinguish between this crust, which they call *short-flake,* and *long-flake* crusts, in which the fat is left in pieces the size of walnuts and the flour is coated even less with shortening. Blitz puff paste, introduced in the next section, is actually a long-flake pie dough that is rolled and folded like puff paste.)

When water is added, the flour absorbs it and develops some gluten. When the dough is rolled out, the lumps of fat and moistened flour are flattened and become flakes of dough separated by layers of fat.

Mealy Pie Dough

For mealy dough, the fat is blended into the flour more thoroughly, until the mixture looks like coarse cornmeal. The more complete coating of the flour with fat has several results:

• The crust is very short and tender because less gluten can develop.
• Less water is needed in the mix because the flour won't absorb as much as in flaky dough.
• The baked dough is less likely to absorb moisture from the filling and become soggy.

Mealy dough is used for bottom crusts, especially in baked fruit pies and soft or custard-type pies, because it resists sogginess. Flaky doughs are used for top crusts and sometimes for prebaked shells.

To produce mealy doughs with even more resistance to soaking, the flour and fat can be blended together completely to make a smooth paste. Such a dough is very short when baked. It is especially appropriate for custard pies.

The formula called Enriched Pie Pastry included in this section is essentially a mealy dough, except that it contains more sugar, is enriched with egg yolks, and works especially well with butter as the only fat. Its delicate, rich flavor makes it suited for European-style tarts and single-crust pies.

Trimmings

Reworked scraps or trimmings are tougher than freshly made dough. They may be combined with mealy dough and used for bottom crusts only.

MIXING

Hand mixing is best for small quantities of dough, especially flaky dough, because you have more control over the mixing. Quantities up to 10 pounds can be mixed almost as quickly by hand as by machine.

For machine mixing, use a pastry knife or paddle attachment. Blend at low speed.

CRUMB CRUSTS

Graham cracker crusts are popular because they have an appealing flavor and are much easier to make than pastry crusts. For variations, vanilla or chocolate wafer crumbs, gingersnap crumbs, or zwieback crumbs may be used instead of graham cracker crumbs. Ground nuts may be added for special desserts.

Crumb crusts are used primarily for unbaked pies, such as cream pies and chiffon pies. They can also be used for such desserts as cheesecake. Be sure that the flavor of the crust is compatible with the filling. Lime chiffon pie with a chocolate crumb crust is not an appealing combination. Some cream fillings are so delicate in flavor that they would be overwhelmed by a crust that is too flavorful.

Baking a crumb crust before filling it makes it firmer and less crumbly, and gives it a toasted flavor.

 Pie Dough

For large-quantity measurements, see page 596.

Ingredients	Flaky Pie Dough			Mealy Pie Dough		
	U.S.	Metric	%	U.S.	Metric	%
Pastry flour	1 lb 4 oz	500 g	100	1 lb 4 oz	500 g	100
Shortening, regular	14 oz	350 g	70	13 oz	325 g	65
Water, cold	6 oz	150 g	30	5 oz	125 g	25
Salt	0.4 oz (2 tsp)	10 g	2	0.4 oz (2 tsp)	10 g	2
Sugar (*optional*)	1 oz	25 g	5	1 oz	25 g	5
Total weight:	*2 lb 9 oz*	*1035 g*	*207%*	*2 lb 7 oz*	*985 g*	*197%*

■ Procedure

1. Sift flour into a mixing bowl. Add shortening.

2. Rub or cut shortening into flour to the proper degree:

   For flaky dough, until fat particles are the size of peas or hazelnuts.

   For mealy dough, until mixture resembles cornmeal.

3. Dissolve salt and sugar (if used) in water.

4. Add water to flour mixture. Mix very gently, just until water is absorbed. Do not overwork the dough.

5. Place dough in pans, cover with plastic film, and place in refrigerator or retarder for at least 4 hours.

6. Scale portions of dough as needed.

Enriched Pie Pastry

For large-quantity measurements, see page 596.

Ingredients	U.S.		Metric	%
Pastry flour	12	oz	375 g	100
Sugar	2	oz	62 g	17
Butter	6	oz	188 g	50
Egg yolks	1	oz	30 g	8
Water, cold	3	oz	94 g	25
Salt	0.13 oz (⅞ tsp)		4 g	1
Total weight:	*1 lb 8 oz*		*753 g*	*201%*

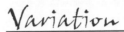 **Procedure**

This pastry is mixed somewhat like mealy pie dough, except that the quantity of sugar is too large to dissolve easily in the water.

1. Sift the flour and sugar into a mixing bowl.

2. Add the butter and rub it in until it is well combined and no lumps remain.

3. Beat the egg yolks with the water and salt until the salt is dissolved.

4. Add the liquid to the flour mixture. Mix gently until it is completely absorbed.

5. Place the dough in pans, cover with plastic film, and place in refrigerator for at least 4 hours.

6. Scale portions as needed.

Variation

For quiches and other savory pies and tarts, omit the sugar.

 Graham Cracker Crust

Yield: Enough for four 9-in. pies or five 8-in. pies

Ingredients	U.S.	Crumbs at 100% Metric	%
Graham cracker crumbs	1 lb	450 g	100
Sugar	8 oz	225 g	50
Butter, melted	8 oz	225 g	50
Total weight:	*2 lb*	*900 g*	*200%*

Procedure

1. Mix crumbs and sugar in a mixing bowl.

2. Add melted butter and mix until evenly blended; crumbs should be completely moistened by the butter.

3. Scale the mixture into pie pans:

   8 oz (225 g) for 9-in. pans

   6 oz (180 g) for 8-in. pans

4. Spread the mixture evenly on bottom and sides of pan. Press another pan on top to pack crumbs evenly.

5. Bake at 350°F (175°C) for 10 minutes.

6. Cool thoroughly before filling.

Variations

Substitute chocolate or vanilla wafer crumbs, gingersnap crumbs, or zwieback crumbs for the graham cracker crumbs.

ASSEMBLY AND BAKING

Pies may be classified into two groups, based on method of assembling and baking.

Baked Pies Raw pie shells are filled and then baked. *Fruit pies* contain fruit fillings and usually have a top crust. *Soft pies* are those with custard-type fillings—that is, liquid fillings that become firm when their egg content coagulates. They are usually baked as single-crust pies.

Unbaked Pies Prebaked pie shells are filled with a prepared filling, chilled, and served when the filling is firm enough to slice. *Cream pies* are made with pudding or boiled custard-type fillings. *Chiffon pies* are made with fillings that are lightened by the addition of beaten egg whites and/or whipped cream. Gelatin or starch gives them a firm consistency.

The two main components of pies are the dough or pastry and the filling. The production of these two components are two quite separate and distinct operations. Once the pastry and fillings are made, rolling the dough and assembling and baking the pies can proceed rapidly.

Because these operations are separate and involve different kinds of problems and techniques, it is helpful to concentrate on them one at a time. The preparation of pie dough is discussed above. This section begins with procedures for making pie pastry into pie shells and for filling and baking pies, followed by a discussion of pie fillings.

Procedure for Rolling Pie Dough and Lining Pans

1. **Select the best doughs for each purpose.**

   Mealy pie doughs are used whenever soaking is a problem, so they are mainly used for bottom crusts, especially bottom crusts for soft pie fillings such as custard and pumpkin. This is because mealy doughs resist soaking better than flaky dough does.

   Flaky pie doughs are best for top crusts. They can also be used for prebaked pie shells if the shells are filled with cooled filling just before serving. However, if the prebaked shells are filled with hot filling, it is safer to use mealy dough.

2. **Scale the dough.**

   8 oz (225 g) for 9-in. bottom crusts

   6 oz (170 g) for 9-in. top crusts

   6 oz (170 g) for 8-in. bottom crusts

   5 oz (140 g) for 8-in. top crusts

   Experienced bakers are able to use less dough when rolling out crusts because they roll the dough to a perfect circle of the right size and need to trim away little excess dough.

3. **Dust the bench and rolling pin lightly with flour.**

   Too much dusting flour toughens the dough, so use no more than needed to prevent sticking.

   Instead of rolling the dough directly on the bench, you may roll it out on flour-dusted canvas. Rolling on canvas does not require as much dusting flour.

4. *Roll out the dough.*

   Flatten the dough lightly and roll it out to a *uniform* ⅛-in. (3 mm) thickness. Use even strokes and roll from the center outward in all directions. Lift the dough frequently to make sure that it is not sticking. The finished dough should be a nearly perfect circle.

5. *Place the dough in the pan.*

   To lift the dough without breaking it, roll it lightly around the rolling pin. A second method is to fold the dough in half, place the folded dough into the pan with the fold in the center, and unfold the dough.

   Allow the dough to drop into the pans; press it into the corners without stretching the dough. Stretched dough will shrink during baking.

   There should be no air bubbles between the dough and the pan.

6. For single-crust pies, flute or crimp the edges, if desired, and trim off excess dough. For double-crust pies, fill with cold filling, brush the edge of the crust with water, and top with the second crust, as explained in the procedure for preparing baked pies (p. 208). Seal edges; crimp or flute, if desired. Trim off the excess dough.

   The simplest way to trim excess dough is to rotate the pie tin between the palms of the hands while pressing with the palms against the edge of the rim. This pinches off the excess dough flush with the rim.

7. Some bakers feel that fluted edges add to the appearance of the product. Others feel that fluting takes too much time and only produces a rim of heavy dough that most customers leave on their plates. Follow your instructor's directions on this procedure. Whether you flute the edges or not, be sure that double-crust pies are well sealed. Many bakers like to make a raised, fluted rim of dough on pie shells for soft-filled pies such as custard or pumpkin. This raised edge, as shown in the illustration at right, enables them to fill the shell quite full while reducing the chance of spillover.

Instead of being given a top crust, fruit pies are sometimes topped with Streusel (p. 116) or with a lattice crust (see the following procedure). Streusel is especially good on apple pies. Lattice crusts are best for pies with attractive, colorful fruit, such as cherry or blueberry.

Procedure for Making a Lattice Top Crust

1. Roll out fresh pie dough (not scraps) ⅛ in. (3 mm) thick.
2. Cut long strips about ⅜ in. (1 cm) wide and long enough to cross the center of the pie.
3. Egg wash the strips and the rim of the filled pie.
4. Place the strips across the pie about 1 in. (2.5 cm) apart. Be sure they are parallel and evenly spaced. Seal them well onto the rim of the pie shell and trim off excess.
5. Place additional strips across the pie at an angle to the first. They may be at a 45-degree angle to make a diamond pattern or at a 90-degree angle to make a checkerboard pattern. Seal and trim excess.

   Note: Instead of laying the strips across each other, you may interweave them, but this is usually too time-consuming for a bakeshop and is generally done only in home kitchens.

Procedure for Preparing Baked Pies

Note: For pies without a top crust, omit steps 3 to 7.

1. Line pie pans with pie dough as in the basic procedure.

2. Fill with *cooled* fillings. See the table below for scaling instructions. Do not drop filling on the rims of the pie shells; this will make it harder to seal the rims to the top crusts, and leaking may result during baking.

   To avoid spilling custard fillings, place the empty shells on the racks in the ovens, then pour in the filling.

3. Roll out dough for the top crusts.

4. Cut perforations in the top crusts to allow steam to escape during baking.

5. Moisten the rim of the bottom crusts with water or egg wash to help seal them to the top crusts.

6. Fit the top crusts in place. Seal the edges together firmly and trim excess dough. The rims may be fluted or crimped if desired. Pressing with the tines of a fork is a quick way to seal and crimp the edge. An efficient way to trim excess pastry is to rotate the pie tin while pressing on the edges with the palms of the hands.

7. Brush tops with desired wash: milk, cream, egg wash, or melted butter. Sprinkle lightly with granulated sugar, if desired.

   Egg-washed tops have a shiny appearance when baked. Tops brushed with fat, milk, or cream are not shiny but have a home-baked look.

8. Place pies on the lower level of an oven preheated to 425° to 450°F (210° to 220°C). The high initial heat helps set the bottom crust to avoid soaking. Fruit pies are baked at this high heat until done. For custard pies, reduce heat after 10 minutes to 325° to 350°F (165° to 175°C) to avoid overcooking and curdling the custard. Custard pies include all those containing large quantities of egg, such as pumpkin pie and pecan pie.

Scaling Instructions for Baked Pies

U.S.		Metric	
Pie size	Weight of filling	Pie size	Weight of filling
8 in.	26–30 oz	20 cm	750–850 g
9 in.	32–40 oz	23 cm	900–1150 g
10 in.	40–50 oz	25 cm	1150–1400 g

Note: Weights are guidelines only. Exact weights may vary, depending on the filling and the depth of the pans.

THE SOGGY BOTTOM

Underbaked bottom crusts or crusts that have soaked up moisture from the filling are common faults in pies. Soggy bottoms can be avoided in several ways:

1. Use mealy dough for bottom crusts. Mealy dough absorbs less liquid than flaky dough does.

2. Use high bottom heat, at least at the beginning of baking, to set the crust quickly. Bake the pies at the bottom of the oven.

3. Do not add hot fillings to unbaked crusts.

4. For fruit pies, line the bottom of the pie shell with a thin layer of cake crumbs before pouring in the filling. This helps absorb some juice that might otherwise soak into the crust.

5. Use dark metal pie tins, which absorb heat. (Because so many bakers use disposable aluminum pans, other methods must be relied on.)

Procedure for Preparing Unbaked Pies

1. Line pie pans with pie dough as in the basic procedure.

2. Dock the crust well with a fork to prevent blistering.

3. Place another pan inside the first one so that the dough is between two pans.

4. Place the pans upside down in a preheated oven at 450°F (230°C). Baking upside down helps keep the dough from shrinking down into the pan.

   Some bakers like to chill the crusts before baking to relax the gluten and help reduce shrinkage.

5. Bake at 450°F (230°C) for 10 to 15 minutes. One pan may be removed during the last part of baking so that the crust can brown.

6. Cool the baked crust completely.

7. Fill with cream filling or chiffon filling. Fill as close as possible to service time to prevent soaking the crust.

8. Chill the pie until it is set enough to slice.

9. Most cream pies and chiffon pies are especially good topped with whipped cream. Some cream pies, especially lemon, are popular when topped with meringue and browned (procedure follows).

Procedure for Making Meringue Pie Topping

1. Make common meringue or Swiss meringue, using 1 pound of sugar per pound of egg whites. Whip until just stiff. See page 182 for procedure.

2. Spread a generous amount of meringue on each pie. Mound it slightly and be sure to attach it to the edge of the crust all around. If this is not done, the meringue may slide around on the finished pie. Leave the meringue in ripples or peaks.

3. Bake at 400°F (200°C) until the surface is attractively browned. Do not use higher temperatures, which will cause the surface of the meringue to shrink and toughen.

4. Remove from the oven and cool.

FILLINGS

Most pie fillings require thickeners of some sort. The two most important thickeners for pies are starches and eggs.

STARCHES FOR FILLINGS

Many kinds of pie fillings, especially fruit fillings and cream fillings, depend on starch for their thickness. Some egg-thickened fillings, such as pumpkin, also sometimes contain starch. The starch acts as a stabilizer and may also reduce the cost by allowing for a lower egg content.

Cornstarch is used for cream pies because it sets up into a firm gel that holds its shape when sliced. It may also be used for fruit pies.

Waxy maize or *modified starches* are best for fruit pies because they are clear when set and make a soft paste rather than a firm gel. Waxy maize should be used for pies that are to be frozen, as this starch is not broken down by freezing.

Flour, tapioca, potato starch, rice starch, and other starches are used less frequently for fillings. Flour has less thickening power than other starches and makes fruit fillings cloudy.

Instant or *pregelatinized starch* needs no cooking because it has already been cooked. When used with certain fruit fillings, it eliminates the need to cook the filling before making up the pie. It loses this advantage, however, if the filling is made of raw fruit that must be cooked anyway. In the case of soft fillings such as pumpkin, instant starch can be used to eliminate a problem that often occurs with cornstarch: Cornstarch tends to settle out before gelatinizing. This creates a dense, starchy layer on the bottom and improperly thickened filling on top. Instant starches differ in thickening power, so follow the manufacturer's recommendations.

Cooking Starches

To avoid lumping, starches must be mixed with a cold liquid or with sugar before being added to a hot liquid.

Sugar and *strong acids,* such as lemon juice, reduce the thickening power of starch. When possible, all or part of the sugar and strong acids should be added *after the starch has thickened.*

FRUIT FILLINGS

Fruit fillings consist of solid fruit pieces bound together by a gel. The gel consists of fruit juice, water, sugar, spices, and a starch thickener. As we have explained, modified starch such as waxy maize is the preferred thickener for fruit fillings because it makes a clear, not cloudy, gel.

Of course, other starches, such as cornstarch, tapioca, or potato starch, may also be used. Cornstarch is frequently used in food service operations in which baking is only part of the food preparation, making it inconvenient to have on hand all the specialty ingredients found in a bakery.

The functions of the gel are to bind the solid fruit pieces together, to help carry the flavors of the spices and the sweetness of the sugar, and to improve appearance by giving a shine or gloss to the fruit. However, the solid fruit is the most important part of the filling. To have a good-quality pie filling, you should have 2 to 3 pounds of drained fruit for each pound of liquid (juice plus water).

The two basic methods for making pie fillings are the *cooked juice method* and the *cooked fruit method.* In the cooked juice method, the gel is made separately by cooking fruit juice, water, and sugar with a starch. The gel is then mixed with the fruit. In the cooked fruit method, the fruit, water, and juices (if any) are all cooked together and then thickened with a starch.

Fruits for Pie Fillings

Fresh fruits are excellent in pies if they are at their seasonal peak. Fresh apples are used extensively for high-quality pies. The quality of fresh fruits can vary considerably, however, and many fruits require a lot of labor.

Frozen fruits are widely used for pies because they are consistent in quality and readily available. Frozen fruits for quantity use are commonly packed with sugar in 30-pound tins. They may be defrosted in the refrigerator for 2 to 3 days, or in a water bath. A third method of thawing is to thaw the fruit just enough to free it from its container, add the water to be used in making it into a pie filling, and heat it to 185° to 195°F (85° to 90°C). Then drain the juice well and make the filling. Whatever method you use, be sure the fruit is completely thawed before preparing the filling. If it is partially frozen, you will not be able to drain the juice properly to make the gel. The frozen, undrained juice will then water down the filling later.

Some frozen fruits, especially berries, are packed without sugar. Naturally, the sugar content of any fruit must be taken into account when you are adding sugar to pie fillings.

Canned fruits are packed in four basic styles: solid pack, heavy pack, water pack, and syrup pack. *Solid pack* means that no water is added, although you will be able to drain off a small quantity of juice. *Heavy pack* means that only a small quantity of water or juice is added. *Water pack* fruits are canned with the water that was used to process them. Sour cherries are usually packed this way. *Syrup pack* fruits are packed in a sugar syrup, which may be light, medium, heavy, or extra heavy. Heavy syrup means that there is more sugar in the syrup. In general, fruits packed in heavy syrup are firmer and less broken than fruits in light syrup.

With water-pack and syrup-pack fruits, it is important to know the *drained weight* (the weight of the solid fruit without the juice). This information may be indicated on the label or available from the processor. The *net weight* is the weight of the total contents, including juice or syrup.

If the drained weight of a fruit is very low, you may need to add extra drained fruit to a batch of filling in order to get a good ratio of fruit to gel.

Dried fruits must be rehydrated by soaking and, usually, simmering before they are made into pie fillings.

Fruits must have sufficient acid (tartness) to make flavorful fillings. If they lack natural acid, you may need to add some lemon, orange, or pineapple juice to supply the acid.

Cooked Juice Method

The advantage of this method is that only the juice is cooked. The fruit retains better shape and flavor because it is subjected to less heat and handling. This method is used when the fruit requires little or no cooking before filling the pie. Most canned and frozen fruits are prepared this way. Fresh berries can also be prepared with this method: Part of the berries are cooked or puréed to provide juice, and the remaining berries are then mixed with the finished gel.

Procedure—Cooked Juice Method

1. Drain the juice from the fruit.

2. Measure the juice and, if necessary, add water or other fruit juice to bring to the desired volume.

3. Bring the juice to a boil.

4. Dissolve the starch in cold water and stir it into the boiling juice. Return to a boil and cook until clear and thickened.

5. Add sugar, salt, and flavorings. Stir until dissolved.

6. Pour the thickened juice over the drained fruit and mix gently. Be careful not to break or mash the fruit.

7. Cool.

Cooked Fruit Method

This method is used when the fruit requires cooking or when there is not enough liquid for the cooked juice method. Most fresh fruits (except berries) are prepared this way, as are dried fruits such as raisins and dried apricots. Canned fruits should not be prepared by this method because they have already been cooked and are likely to break up or turn to mush.

Procedure—Cooked Fruit Method

1. Bring the fruit and juice or water to a boil. Some sugar may be added to the fruit to draw out juices.
2. Dissolve the starch in cold water and stir into the fruit. Return to a boil and cook until clear and thickened. Stir while cooking.
3. Add sugar, salt, flavorings, and other ingredients. Stir until dissolved.
4. Cool as quickly as possible.

Variation

Some fruits, such as fresh apples, may be cooked in butter, rather than boiled in water, for better flavor.

Old-Fashioned Method

This method is commonly used for homemade apple pies and peach pies. However, it is not often used in food service operations because of its disadvantages. First, the thickening of the juices is more difficult to control. Second, because raw fruit shrinks as it cooks, it is necessary to pile the fruit high in the shell. The fruit then shrinks, often leaving a large air space between the crust and fruit, and the top crust becomes misshapen. The juices given off are more likely to boil over than when the filling is cooked and the juice thickened before filling the pie.

For these reasons, the cooked fruit method usually gives better results than the old-fashioned method. See the Apple Pie recipe and variations on page 215.

Procedure—Old-Fashioned Method

1. Mix the starch and spices with the sugar until uniformly blended.
2. Mix the fruit with the sugar mixture.
3. Fill the unbaked pie shells with the fruit.
4. Place lumps of butter on top of the filling.
5. Cover with top crust or Streusel (p. 116) and bake.

Apple Pie Filling (Canned Fruit)

Yield: About 9½ lb (4500 g)
  Five 8-in. (20 cm) pies
  Four 9-in. (23 cm) pies
  Three 10-in. (25 cm) pies

Ingredients	U.S.		Metric
Canned apples, solid pack or heavy pack (one No. 10 can)	6 lb 8	oz	3000 g
Drained juice plus water	1 pt 8	fl oz	750 mL
Water, cold	8	fl oz	250 mL
Cornstarch	3	oz	90 g
or			
Modified starch (waxy maize)	2.5	oz	75 g
Sugar	1 lb 4	oz	570 g
Salt	0.25 oz		7 g
Cinnamon	0.25 oz (4¼ tsp)		7 g
Nutmeg	0.08 oz (1 tsp)		2 g
Butter	3	oz	90 g

■ P r o c e d u r e

Use the cooked juice method.

1. Drain the apples and save the juice. Add enough water to the juice to measure 1½ pt (750 mL).

2. Mix the cold water and starch.

3. Bring the juice mixture to a boil. Stir in the starch mixture and return to a boil.

4. Add the remaining ingredients, except the drained apples. Simmer until the sugar is dissolved.

5. Pour the syrup over the apples and mix gently. Cool completely.

6. Fill the pie shells. Bake at 425°F (220°C) about 30–40 minutes.

Variations

Dutch Apple Pie Filling
Simmer 8 oz (250 g) raisins in water. Drain and add to apple pie filling.

Cherry Pie Filling
Use one No. 10 can sour cherries instead of apples and make the following ingredient adjustments:
  Increase starch to 4 oz (125 g) cornstarch *or* 3 oz (90 g) waxy maize.
  Increase sugar to 1 lb 12 oz (825 g).
  Add 1½ oz (45 ml) lemon juice in step 4.
  Omit cinnamon and nutmeg. Add almond extract to taste (optional).
  If desired, color with 2 to 3 drops red coloring.

Peach Pie Filling
Use one No. 10 can sliced peaches, preferably solid or heavy pack, instead of apples. Increase liquid in step 1 to 1 qt (1 L). Omit cinnamon and nutmeg.

Pineapple Pie Filling
Use one No. 10 can crushed pineapple instead of apples. Gently press the fruit in a sieve to squeeze out the juice. Make the following ingredient adjustments:
  Increase the liquid in step 1 to 1 qt (1 L).
  Increase the starch to 4 oz (125 g) cornstarch *or* 3 oz (90 g) waxy maize.
  Use 1 lb 8 oz (750 g) sugar and 8 oz (250 g) corn syrup.
  Omit the cinnamon and nutmeg.
  If desired, color with 2 to 3 drops yellow coloring.

Blueberry Pie Filling (Frozen Fruit)

Yield: About 7 lb 8 oz (3375 g)
   Four 8-in. (20 cm) pies
   Three 9-in. (23 cm) pies

Ingredients	U.S.		Metric
Blueberries, frozen, unsweetened	5 lb		2250 g
Drained juice plus water	12	oz	375 mL
Sugar	6	oz	175 g
Water, cold	6	oz	190 mL
Cornstarch	3	oz	90 g
or			
Modified starch (waxy maize)	2.25 oz		68 g
Sugar	14	oz	412 g
Salt	0.25 oz		8 g
Cinnamon	0.12 oz (2⅛ tsp)		4 g
Lemon juice	1.5	oz	45 mL

■ P r o c e d u r e

Use the cooked juice method.

1. Thaw the berries in their unopened original container.

2. Drain the berries. Add enough water to the juice to measure 12 oz (375 mL). Add the first quantity of sugar.

3. Mix the cold water and the starch.

4. Bring the juice mixture to a boil. Stir in the starch mixture. Return to a boil to thicken.

5. Add the remaining ingredients, except the drained berries. Stir over heat until the sugar is dissolved.

6. Pour the syrup over the drained berries. Mix gently. Cool completely.

7. Fill pie shells. Bake at 425°F (220°C) about 30 minutes.

Variations

Apple Pie Filling

Use 5 lb (2.25 kg) frozen apples instead of blueberries. Make the following ingredient adjustments:

   Reduce the starch to 1.5 oz (45 g) cornstarch *or* 1.25 oz (38 g) waxy maize.

   Reduce the second quantity of sugar to 8 oz (225 g).

   Add ½ tsp (1 g) nutmeg and 3 oz (87 g) butter in step 5.

Cherry Pie Filling

Use 5 lb (2.25 kg) frozen cherries instead of blueberries. Make the following ingredient adjustments:

   Increase the liquid in step 2 to 1 pt (500 mL).

   Reduce the starch to 2.5 oz (75 g) cornstarch *or* 2 oz (60 g) waxy maize.

   Reduce the second quantity of sugar to 10 oz (285 g).

   Omit the cinnamon.

   Reduce the lemon juice to 0.75 oz (22 mL).

Raisin Pie Filling

For large-quantity measurements, see page 597.

Yield: About 2 lb/1 kg
   One 9-in. (23 cm) pie

Ingredients	U.S.		Metric	
Raisins	13	oz	360	g
Water	13	oz	400	mL
Water, cold	2	oz	50	mL
Cornstarch	0.5	oz	15	g
or				
Modified starch (waxy maize)	0.4	oz	12	g
Sugar	4	oz	114	g
Salt	0.06	oz (⅖ tsp)	2	g
Lemon juice	0.6	oz	18	mL
Grated lemon zest	0.02	oz (⅕ tsp)	0.6	g
Cinnamon	0.012 oz (⅕ tsp)		0.4	g
Butter	0.6	oz	18	g

■ P r o c e d u r e

Use the cooked fruit method.

1. Combine the raisins and water in a saucepan. Simmer 5 minutes.

2. Mix the water and starch. Stir into the raisins and simmer until thickened.

3. Add the remaining ingredients. Stir until the sugar is dissolved and the mixture is uniform.

4. Cool thoroughly.

5. Fill the pie shells. Bake at 425°F (220°C) about 30–40 minutes.

Fresh Apple Pie Filling I

For large-quantity measurements, see page 598.

Yield: about 2 lb 6 oz (1070 g)
  One 9-in. (23 cm) pie

Ingredients	U.S.		Metric	
Apples, peeled and sliced	2 lb		900	g
Butter	1	oz	30	g
Sugar	3	oz	90	g
Water, cold	2	oz	60	g
Cornstarch	1	oz	30	g
or				
Modified starch (waxy maize)	0.75 oz		24	g
Sugar	3.5	oz	100	g
Salt	0.06 oz (⅕ tsp)		1	g
Cinnamon	0.06 oz (1 tsp)		1	g
Nutmeg	0.03 oz (¼ tsp)		0.5	g
Lemon juice	0.33 oz (2 tsp)		10	g
Butter	0.25 oz		7	g

■ P r o c e d u r e

Use this variation of the cooked fruit method.

1. Sauté the apples lightly in the first quantity of butter until they are slightly softened. Add the first quantity of sugar as the apples cook. This will draw juices out of the apples, which will then simmer in these juices.

2. Mix the water and starch until smooth. Add the starch mixture to the apples and boil until the liquid is thick and clear.

3. Remove from the heat. Add the remaining ingredients. Stir gently until the sugar is dissolved and the butter is melted.

4. Cool completely.

5. Fill the pie shells. Bake at 425°F (220°C) about 30–40 minutes.

Variations

Fresh Apple Pie Filling II

For large-quantity measurements, see page 598.

Ingredients	U.S.	Metric
Water	3.5 oz	100 g

Omit the first quantity of butter. Instead, simmer the apples in water and the first quantity of sugar as in the basic cooked fruit method, using the quantity of water listed above.

Apple Ginger Pie Filling

For large-quantity measurements, see page 598.

Ingredients	U.S.	Metric
Ground ginger	0.03 oz (¼ tsp)	0.5 g
Candied ginger, finely chopped	0.67 oz	20 g

Prepare as for Fresh Apple Pie Filling I or II, but omit the cinnamon and instead add ground and candied ginger.

Apple Pear Pie Filling

Prepare as for Fresh Apple Pie Filling I or II, but substitute slightly firm pears for half the apples.

Apple Walnut Pie Filling

For large-quantity measurements, see page 598.

Ingredients	U.S.	Metric
Chopped walnuts	2.5 oz	75 g

Mix walnuts into Fresh Apple Pie Filling I or II:

Rhubarb Pie Filling

For large-quantity measurements, see page 598.

Ingredients	U.S.	Metric
Fresh rhubarb	1 lb 6 oz	650 g

Substitute rhubarb, cut into 1-in. (2.5 cm) pieces, for the apples. Omit the cinnamon, nutmeg, and lemon juice.

Peach Sour Cream Pie Filling

For large-quantity measurements, see page 597.

Yield: 2 lb 8 oz (1250 g)
   One 9-in. (23 cm) pie

Ingredients	U.S.		Metric	
Sour cream	8	oz	250	g
Sugar	4	oz	125	g
Cornstarch	0.5	oz	15	g
Eggs, beaten	2		2	
Vanilla extract	½	tsp	2	mL
Nutmeg	⅛	tsp	0.5	mL
Fresh peaches, sliced (see *note*)	1 lb 4	oz	625	g
Streusel (p. 116)	6	oz	180	g

Note If fresh peaches are not available, substitute canned peaches packed in light syrup. Drain them well before weighing.

■ Procedure

1. Mix the sour cream, sugar, and cornstarch until smooth.
2. Add the eggs, vanilla, and nutmeg and mix in.
3. Carefully fold the peaches into the sour cream mixture.
4. Fill unbaked pie shells.
5. Top with Streusel.
6. Bake at 425°F (220°C) for about 30 minutes, until the filling is set.

Variation

Pear Sour Cream Pie
Substitute sliced pears for the sliced peaches.

Old-Fashioned Apple Pie Filling

Yield: About 11 lb (5 kg)
   Six 8-in. (20 cm) pies
   Five 9-in. (23 cm) pies
   Four 10-in. (25 cm) pies

Ingredients	U.S.		Metric
Apples, peeled and sliced	9 lb		4100 g
Lemon juice	2	oz	60 mL
Sugar	2 lb		900 g
Cornstarch	3	oz	90 g
Salt	0.25	oz	7 g
Cinnamon	0.25	oz	7 g
Nutmeg	0.08	oz (1 tsp)	2 g
Butter	3	oz	90 g

■ Procedure

Use the old-fashioned method.

1. Select firm, tart apples. Scale *after* peeling and coring.
2. Combine the apple slices and lemon juice in a large mixing bowl. Toss to coat apples with the juice.
3. Mix together with sugar, cornstarch, salt, and spices. Add to the apples and toss gently until well mixed.
4. Fill the pie shells. Dot the tops with pieces of butter before covering with top crusts. Bake at 400°F (200°C) about 45 minutes.

Fresh Strawberry Pie Filling

Yield: About 12 lb (5.5 kg)
Six 8-in. (20 cm) pies
Five 9-in. (23 cm) pies
Four 10-in. (25 cm) pies

Ingredients	U.S.		Metric
Fresh whole strawberries	9 lb		4100 g
Water, cold	1 pt		500 mL
Sugar	1 lb 12	oz	800 g
Cornstarch	4	oz	120 g
or			
Modified starch (waxy maize)	3	oz	90 g
Salt	0.17 oz (1 tsp)		5 g
Lemon juice	2	oz	60 mL

■ P r o c e d u r e

Use the cooked juice method.

1. Hull, wash, and drain the berries. Set aside 7 lb (3.2 kg) of the berries. These may be left whole, if small, or cut in halves or quarters, if large.

2. Mash or purée the remaining 2 lb (900 g) of the berries. Mix with the water. (If a clear filling is desired, this mixture may be strained.)

3. Mix together the sugar, starch, and salt. Stir into the berry-and-water mixture until no lumps remain.

4. Bring to a boil, stirring constantly. Cook until thickened.

5. Remove from the heat and stir in the lemon juice.

6. Cool to room temperature but do not chill.

7. Stir to eliminate lumps. Fold in the reserved berries.

8. Fill baked pie shells and chill (do not bake).

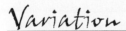

Fresh Blueberry Tart Filling

Substitute blueberries for the strawberries. This recipe works best with small berries and with cornstarch rather than modified starch. Adjust the sugar as desired, depending on the sweetness of the fruit. Force the cooked, thickened juices through a sieve (cooking the juices before straining gives more color to the gel). Fold the glaze into the berries while it is still hot.

This mixture is more suitable for tarts than for pies. Because pie shells are deeper, the filling may not hold its shape when sliced. One recipe makes enough filling for eight or nine 8-in. (20 cm) tarts, seven or eight 9-in. (23 cm) tarts, or six 10-in. (25 cm) tarts.

CUSTARD OR SOFT FILLINGS

Custard, pumpkin, pecan, and similar pies are made with an uncooked liquid filling containing eggs. The eggs coagulate during baking, which sets the filling. For more information on custards, see page 428.

The method for one pie in this section is unusual. Key Lime Pie is similar to other soft pies, except the pie is not baked. Instead, the acidity of the lime juice is sufficient to coagulate the proteins and thicken the pie filling.

Many soft fillings contain some starch in addition to eggs. Flour, cornstarch, and instant starch are frequently used. Although starch is unnecessary if enough eggs are used, many bakers prefer to add a little starch because it allows them to reduce the egg content. Also, the use of starch helps bind the liquids and reduce the chance of separating, or weeping, in the baked pie. If starch is used, be sure the mix is well stirred before filling the pies in order to reduce the danger of the starch settling out.

The greatest difficulty in cooking soft pies is cooking the crust completely without overcooking the filling. Start the pie at the bottom of a hot oven (425° to 450°F/220° to 230°C) for the first 10 to 15 minutes in order to set the crust. Then reduce the heat to 325° to 350°F (165° to 175°C) in order to cook the filling slowly.

Use one of these methods to test for doneness:

1. Shake the pie very gently. If it is no longer liquid, it is done. The center will still be slightly soft, but its own heat will continue to cook the pie after it is removed from the oven.

2. Insert a thin knife an inch from the center. If it comes out clean, the pie is done.

Custard Pie Filling

For large-quantity measurements, see page 597.

Yield: 2 lb (0.9 kg)
  One 9-in. (23 cm) pie

Ingredients	U.S.		Metric	
Eggs	8	oz	225	g
Sugar	4	oz	112	g
Salt	¼	tsp	1	g
Vanilla extract	0.25 oz (1½ tsp)		7.5	mL
Milk (see *note*)	1.25 pt		600	mL
Nutmeg	¼–½	tsp	0.5–0.75	g

Note For a richer custard, use part milk and part cream.

■ P r o c e d u r e

1. Combine the eggs, sugar, salt, and vanilla and blend until smooth. Do not whip air into the mixture.

2. Stir in the milk. Skim off any foam.

3. Place the unbaked pie shells in preheated oven (450°F/230°C) and carefully ladle in the filling. Sprinkle tops with nutmeg.

4. Bake at 450°F (230°C) for 15 minutes. Reduce heat to 325°F (165°C) and bake until set, about 20–30 minutes more.

Variation

Coconut Custard Pie Filling
Use 2.5 oz (70 g) unsweetened, flaked coconut. Sprinkle the coconut into pie shells before adding the custard mixture. The coconut may be lightly toasted in the oven before it is added to the pies. Omit the nutmeg.

Pumpkin Pie Filling

For large-quantity measurements, see page 599.

Yield: About 4.25 lb (2 kg)
Two 9-in. (23 cm) pies

Ingredients	U.S.		Metric	
Pumpkin purée,	1 lb 10.5	oz	750	g
	(one No. 2½ can)			
Pastry flour	1	oz	30	g
Cinnamon	0.12	oz	4	g
Nutmeg	¼	tsp	1	mL
Ginger	¼	tsp	1	mL
Cloves	⅛	tsp	0.5	mL
Salt	0.12 oz (⅞ tsp)		4	g
Brown sugar	10	oz	290	g
Eggs (see *note*)	6	oz	175	g
Corn syrup or half	2	oz	60	g
corn syrup and				
half molasses				
Milk	1.5	pt	750	mL

Note   Pumpkin pie filling should be allowed to stand at least 30 minutes before being poured into the pie shells. This gives the pumpkin time to absorb the liquid and makes a smoother filling that is less likely to separate after baking. If the filling is to stand for much more than an hour, do not add the eggs until the pies are to be filled. If the eggs are added earlier, the acidity of the pumpkin and brown sugar may partially coagulate the eggs.

■ P r o c e d u r e

1. Place the pumpkin in the bowl of a mixer fitted with the whip attachment.

2. Sift together the flour, spices, and salt.

3. Add the flour mixture and sugar to the pumpkin. Mix at second speed until smooth and well blended.

4. Add the eggs and mix in. Scrape down the sides of the bowl.

5. Turn the machine to low speed. Gradually pour in the syrup, then the milk. Mix until evenly blended.

6. Let the filling stand for 30–60 minutes.

7. Stir the filling to remix. Fill the pie shells. Bake at 450°F (230°C) for 15 minutes. Lower heat to 350°F (175°C) and bake until set, about 30–40 minutes more.

Variations

Sweet Potato Pie Filling
Substitute canned sweet potatoes, drained and puréed, for the pumpkin.

Squash Pie Filling
Substitute puréed squash for the pumpkin.

Pecan Pie Filling

For large-quantity measurements, see page 599.

Yield: 2 lb (0.9 kg) filling plus 5 oz (142 g) pecans
One 9-in. (23 cm) pie

Ingredients	U.S.		Metric	
Granulated sugar (see *note*)	8	oz	225	g
Butter	2	oz	60	g
Salt	¼	tsp	1.5	g
Eggs	8	oz	225	g
Dark corn syrup	14	oz	400	g
	(about 10 fl. oz)			
Vanilla extract	0.25 oz (1½ tsp)		8	g
Pecans	5	oz	142	g

Note   Brown sugar may be used if a darker color and stronger flavor are desired.

■ P r o c e d u r e

1. Using the paddle attachment at low speed, blend the sugar, butter, and salt until evenly blended.

2. With the machine running, add the eggs a little at a time until they are all absorbed.

3. Add the syrup and vanilla. Mix until well blended.

4. To assemble pies, distribute the pecans evenly in the pie shells and then fill with the syrup mixture.

5. Bake at 425°F (220°C) for 10 minutes. Reduce heat to 350°F (175°C). Bake 30–40 minutes more, until set.

Variation

Maple Walnut Pie Filling
Substitute pure maple syrup for the corn syrup. Substitute coarsely chopped walnuts for the pecans.

Key Lime Pie Filling

For large-quantity measurements, see page 599.

Yield: 1 lb 8 oz (750 g)
  One 9-in. (23 cm) pie

Ingredients	U.S.	Metric
Egg yolks	4	4
Sweetened condensed milk	14 oz	400 g
Freshly squeezed key lime juice (see *note*)	5 oz	150 g

Note If key limes are not available, substitute regular lime juice. Classic key lime pie filling is pale yellow in color, not green. However, if desired, tint the filling pale green with a few drops of food color.

■ **P r o c e d u r e**

1. Beat the egg yolks lightly, then stir in the sweetened condensed milk.

2. Add the lime juice and beat until smooth.

3. Pour the filling into a baked pie shell or a graham cracker crumb pie shell. Refrigerate overnight. The acidity of the limes will partially coagulate the egg and milk proteins so that the filling becomes firm.

4. Top with whipped cream.

CREAM PIE FILLINGS

Cream pie fillings are the same as puddings, which in turn are the same as basic pastry cream with added flavorings such as vanilla, chocolate, or coconut. Lemon filling is made by the same method, using water and lemon juice instead of milk.

There is one difference between pastry cream and pie filling that you should note: *Cream pie fillings are made with cornstarch* so that slices hold their shape when cut. Pastry cream may be made with flour, cornstarch, or other starches.

Vanilla Cream Pie Filling

For large-quantity measurements, see page 600.

Yield: About 1 1/8 pt (0.5 mL) or 13 oz (0.8 kg)
  One 9-in. (23 cm) pie

Ingredients	U.S.	Metric
Milk	1 pt	500 g
Sugar	2 oz	60 g
Egg yolks	1.25 oz (2 yolks)	38 g (2 yolks)
Whole eggs	1.67 oz (1 egg)	55 g (1 egg)
Cornstarch	1.25 oz	38 g
Sugar	2 oz	60 g
Butter	1 oz	30 g
Vanilla extract	0.25 oz (1 1/2 tsp)	8 g

■ **P r o c e d u r e**

Before beginning production, review the discussion of pastry cream on page 186.

1. In a heavy saucepan or kettle, dissolve the sugar in the milk and bring just to a boil.

2. With a whip, beat the egg yolks and whole eggs in a stainless-steel bowl.

3. Sift the starch and sugar into the eggs. Beat with the whip until perfectly smooth.

4. Temper the egg mixture by slowly beating in the hot milk in a thin stream.

5. Return the mixture to the heat and bring it to a boil, stirring constantly.

6. When the mixture comes to a boil and thickens, remove it from the heat.

7. Stir in the butter and vanilla. Mix until the butter is melted and completely blended in.

8. Pour into baked, cooled pie shells. Cool, then keep chilled. Chilled pies may be decorated with whipped cream, using a pastry bag with a star tube.

The basic principles and procedures for making pastry cream are included in chapter 8. See pages 186–188 to review this information. For your convenience, the formula for vanilla pastry cream is repeated here under the name Vanilla Cream Pie Filling. Popular flavor variations for cream pie fillings follow this basic recipe.

Opinion is divided as to whether pie shells should be filled with warm cream fillings, which are then cooled in the shell, or whether the filling should be cooled first and then added to the shell. For the best-looking slices, warm filling is best. The filling cools to a smooth, uniform mass and the slices hold sharp, clean cuts. However, you must be sure to use a good, mealy pie dough that resists soaking, or you risk having soggy bottom crusts. Enriched pie pastry (p. 205) is good for this purpose. Many food service operations prefer to fill each pie shell with cold filling shortly before the pie is to be cut and served. The slice does not cut as cleanly but the crusts are crisp and you can use flaky dough for the crusts. We use the warm filling method in this book, but you can, of course, modify the procedure to suit your needs.

Variations

Coconut Cream Pie Filling
Add 2 oz (60 g) toasted, unsweetened coconut to the basic filling.

Banana Cream Pie Filling
Using vanilla cream filling, pour half the filling into pie shells, cover with sliced bananas, and fill with remaining filling. (Bananas may be dipped in lemon juice to prevent browning.)

Chocolate Cream Pie Filling I
For large-quantity measurements, see page 600.

Ingredients	U.S.	Metric
Unsweetened chocolate	1 oz	30 g
Sweet chocolate	1 oz	30 g

Melt together unsweetened and sweet chocolate and mix into hot vanilla cream filling.

Chocolate Cream Pie Filling II
For large-quantity measurements, see page 600.

Ingredients	U.S.	Metric
Milk	14 oz	438 mL
Sugar	2 oz	60 g
Egg yolks	1.25 oz (2 yolks)	38 g (2 yolks)
Whole eggs	1.67 oz (1 egg)	55 g (1 egg)
Cold milk	2 oz	60 g
Cornstarch	1.25 oz	38 g
Cocoa	0.75 oz	22 g
Sugar	2 oz	60 g
Butter	1 oz	30 g
Vanilla extract	0.25 oz	8 mL

This variation uses cocoa instead of chocolate. The cocoa is sifted with the starch. Some of the milk must be included with the eggs in order to provide enough liquid to make a paste with the starch and cocoa. Follow the procedure in the basic recipe, but use the above ingredients.

Butterscotch Cream Pie Filling
For large-quantity measurements, see page 600.

Ingredients	U.S.	Metric
Brown sugar	8 oz	250 g
Butter	2.5 oz	75 g

Combine brown sugar and butter in a saucepan. Heat over low heat, stirring, until the butter is melted and the ingredients are blended. Prepare the basic vanilla cream filling recipe, but omit all the sugar and increase the starch to 6 oz (180 g). As the mixture comes to a boil in step 5, gradually stir in the brown sugar mixture. Finish as in the basic recipe.

Lemon Pie Filling
For large-quantity measurements, see page 600.

Ingredients	U.S.	Metric
Water	1 pt	500 mL
Sugar	4 oz	125 g
Egg yolks	1.25 oz (2 yolks)	38 g (2 yolks)
Whole eggs	1.67 oz (1 egg)	55 g (1 egg)
Cornstarch	1.5 oz	45 g
Sugar	2 oz	60 g
Lemon zest, grated	0.12 oz (1½ tsp)	4 g
Butter	1 oz	30 g
Lemon juice	2 oz	60 mL

Follow the procedure for vanilla cream filling, but use the above ingredients. Note that the lemon juice is added after the filling is thickened.

Strawberry Rhubarb Pie Filling

For large-quantity measurements, see page 601.

Yield: 3 lb 8 oz (1680 g)
  Two 9-inch (20-cm) pies

Ingredients	U.S.			Metric
Rhubarb, fresh or frozen, in 1-in. (2.5 cm) pieces	1 lb	4	oz	600 g
Sugar		12	oz	360 g
Water		4	oz	120 g
Egg yolks		4		4
Heavy cream		4	oz	120 g
Cornstarch		1.5 oz		45 g
Fresh strawberries, hulled and quartered	1 lb			480 g

■ P r o c e d u r e

1. Place the rhubarb, sugar, and water in a heavy saucepan. Cover and set over low heat. Bring to a simmer. The sugar will help to draw juices out of the rhubarb. Simmer until the rhubarb is soft and the sugar is dissolved.

2. Beat the egg yolks with the cream until well mixed. Add the cornstarch and stir until evenly blended.

3. Remove the rhubarb from the heat. Stir in the cream mixture.

4. Return the rhubarb to the heat and bring to a simmer. Simmer about 1 minute, until thickened.

5. Pour the rhubarb out into a bowl and mix in the strawberries. Let stand until slightly warm. Mix again to blend the strawberry juices with the filling, then fill baked pie shells. Chill until firm.

CHIFFON PIE FILLINGS

Chiffon fillings have a light, fluffy texture that is created by the addition of beaten egg whites and, sometimes, whipped cream. The egg whites and cream are folded into a cream or fruit base that is stabilized with gelatin. The folding-in of the egg whites and the filling of the baked pie shells must be done before the gelatin sets. After the pie is chilled to set the gelatin, the filling should be firm enough to hold a clean slice.

When chiffon filling contains both egg whites and whipped cream, most chefs and bakers prefer to fold in the egg whites first, even though they may lose some volume. The reason is that if the cream is added first, there is more danger that it will be overbeaten and turn to butter during the folding and mixing procedure.

For a review of the guidelines for beating egg whites, see page 182–183. For the guidelines for whipping cream, see page 180.

Bases for chiffons include the following three main types:

1. *Thickened with starch*   The procedure is the same as for fruit pie fillings made by the cooked juice method or cooked fruit method, except that the fruit is finely chopped or puréed. Most fruit chiffons are made this way.

2. *Thickened with egg*   The procedure is the same as for Crème Anglaise (p. 185). Chocolate chiffons and pumpkin chiffons are sometimes made this way.

3. *Thickened with egg and starch*   The procedure is the same as for pastry cream or cream pie fillings. Lemon chiffon is usually made this way.

Guidelines for Using Gelatin

Although some chiffons contain starch as their only stabilizer, most contain gelatin. Gelatin must be handled properly so that it is completely dissolved and mixed evenly throughout the filling. All references to gelatin in this book mean unflavored gelatin, not flavored, sweetened gelatin mixes.

*P*rocedure for Making Chiffon Fillings

1. Prepare base.

2. Soften gelatin in cold liquid. Stir it into the hot base until dissolved. Chill until thickened, but not set.

3. Fold in beaten egg whites.

4. Fold in whipped cream, if used.

5. Immediately pour into pie shells and chill.

1. Measure gelatin accurately. Too much gelatin makes a stiff, rubbery product. Too little makes a soft product that does not hold its shape.

2. Do not mix raw pineapple or papaya with gelatin. These fruits contain enzymes that dissolve gelatin. These fruits may be used if they are cooked or canned.

3. To dissolve unflavored gelatin, stir it into *cold* liquid to avoid lumping. Let it stand for 5 minutes to absorb water. Then heat it until it is dissolved, or combine it with a hot liquid and stir until dissolved.

4. After the gelatin is dissolved in the base, cool or chill it until it is slightly thickened, but not set. If the base starts to set, it will be difficult or impossible to fold in the egg whites uniformly.

5. Stir the base occasionally while it is cooling so that it cools evenly. Otherwise, the outside edges may start to set before the inside is sufficiently cooled, which creates lumps.

6. If the gelatin sets before you can add the egg whites, warm the base slightly by stirring it over hot water just until the gelatin is melted and there are no lumps. Cool again.

7. When folding in egg whites and whipped cream, work rapidly without pausing, or the gelatin might set before you are finished. Fill the pie shells immediately, before the filling sets.

8. Keep the pies refrigerated, especially in hot weather.
   See chapter 2 for additional information on gelatin.

In addition to the following chiffons, you may also use Bavarian creams (p. 439) as pie fillings. Although Bavarian creams contain gelatin and whipped cream, they are not, strictly speaking, chiffons, because they do not contain whipped egg whites. Nevertheless, their texture is similar to that of chiffons because of the lightening effect of the whipped cream.

Strawberry Chiffon Pie Filling

Yield: 6 lb 8 oz (3 kg)
   Six 8-in. (20 cm) pies
   Five 9-in. (23 cm) pies
   Four 10-in. (25 cm) pies

Ingredients	U.S.		Metric
Frozen sweetened strawberries (see *note*)	4 lb		1800 g
Salt	0.16 oz (1 tsp)		5 g
Cornstarch	1	oz	30 g
Water, cold	4	oz	120 mL
Gelatin	1	oz	30 g
Cold water	8	oz	240 mL
Lemon juice	1	oz	30 mL
Egg whites	1 lb		450 g
Sugar	12	oz	350 g

Note To use fresh strawberries, slice or chop 3 lb (1.4 kg) fresh, hulled strawberries and mix with 1 lb (450 g) sugar. Let stand in refrigerator for 2 hours. Drain and reserve juice and proceed as in basic recipe.

■ P r o c e d u r e

1. Thaw and drain the strawberries. Chop them coarsely.

2. Place the drained juice and salt in a saucepan. Bring to a boil.

3. Dissolve the cornstarch in the water and stir into the juice. Cook until thick. Remove from the heat.

4. Soften the gelatin in the second quantity of water. Add it to the hot, thickened juice and stir until completely dissolved.

5. Stir in the lemon juice and the drained strawberries.

6. Chill the mixture until thickened, but not set.

7. Beat the egg whites until they form soft peaks. Gradually add the sugar and continue to beat until a thick, glossy meringue is formed.

8. Fold the meringue into the fruit mixture.

9. Pour the mixture into baked pie shells. Chill until set.

Variations

Strawberry Cream Chiffon Pie Filling
For a creamier filling, reduce the egg whites to 12 oz (350 g). Whip 1 pt (500 mL) heavy cream and fold it in after the meringue.

Raspberry Chiffon Pie Filling
Substitute raspberries for strawberries in the basic recipe.

Pineapple Chiffon Pie Filling
Use 3 lb (1.4 kg) crushed pineapple. Mix the drained juice with an additional 1 pt (500 mL) pineapple juice and add 8 oz (240 g) sugar.

Chocolate Chiffon Pie Filling

Yield: 7 lb (3.2 kg)
  Six 8-in. (20 cm) pies
  Five 9-in. (23 cm) pies
  Four 10-in. (25 cm) pies

Ingredients	U.S.	Metric
Unsweetened chocolate	10 oz	300 g
Water	1 pt 8 oz	750 mL
Egg yolks	1 lb	450 g
Sugar	1 lb	450 g
Gelatin	1 oz	30 g
Water, cold	8 oz	240 mL
Egg whites	1 lb 4 oz	580 g
Sugar	1 lb 4 oz	700 g

■ P r o c e d u r e

1. Combine the chocolate and water in a heavy saucepan. Bring to a boil over moderate heat, stirring constantly until smooth.
2. With the whip attachment, beat the egg yolks and sugar together until thick and light.
3. With the mixer running, gradually pour in the chocolate mixture.
4. Return the mixture to the saucepan and stir over very low heat until thickened. Remove from heat.
5. Soften the gelatin in the second quantity of water. Add it to the hot chocolate mixture and stir until the gelatin is completely dissolved.
6. Chill until thick, but not set.
7. Beat the egg whites until they form soft peaks. Gradually beat in the last quantity of sugar. Continue beating until a firm, glossy meringue is formed.
8. Fold meringue into the chocolate mixture.
9. Pour the mixture into baked pie shells. Chill until set.

Variation

Chocolate Cream Chiffon Pie Filling
For a creamier filling, reduce the egg white to 1 lb (450 g). Whip 1 pt (500 mL) heavy cream and fold it in after the meringue.

Pumpkin Chiffon Pie Filling

Yield: 7 lb 12 oz (3.4 kg)
  Six 8-in. (20 cm) pies
  Five 9-in. (23 cm) pies
  Four 10-in. (25 cm) pies

Ingredients	U.S.		Metric
Pumpkin purée	2 lb 8	oz	1200 g
Brown sugar	1 lb 4	oz	600 g
Milk	12	oz	350 g
Egg yolks	12	oz	350 g
Salt	0.17 oz (1 tsp)		5 g
Cinnamon	0.25 oz (4 tsp)		7 g
Nutmeg	0.16 oz (2 tsp)		4 g
Ginger	0.08 oz (1 tsp)		2 g
Gelatin	1	oz	30 g
Water, cold	8	oz	240 mL
Egg whites	1 lb		450 g
Sugar	1 lb		450 g

■ P r o c e d u r e

1. Combine the pumpkin, brown sugar, milk, egg yolks, salt, and spices. Mix until smooth and uniform.
2. Place mixture in a double boiler. Cook, stirring frequently, until thickened, or until the temperature of the mix is 185°F (85°C). Remove from heat.
3. Soften the gelatin in the water. Add it to the hot pumpkin mixture and stir until dissolved.
4. Chill until very thick, but not set.
5. Beat the egg whites until they form soft peaks. Gradually add the sugar and continue to beat until a thick, glossy meringue is formed.
6. Fold the meringue into the pumpkin mixture.
7. Fill baked pie shells with mixture. Chill until set.

Variation

Pumpkin Cream Chiffon Pie Filling
For a creamier filling, reduce the egg whites to 12 oz (350 g). Whip 1 pt (500 mL) heavy cream and fold it in after the meringue.

Lemon Chiffon Pie Filling

Yield: 7 lb (3.2 kg)
  Six 8-in. (20 cm) pies
  Five 9-in. (23 cm) pies
  Four 10-in. (25 cm) pies

Ingredients	U.S.		Metric
Water	1 pt	8 oz	750 mL
Sugar		8 oz	240 g
Egg yolks		12 oz	350 g
Water, cold		4 oz	120 mL
Cornstarch		3 oz	90 g
Sugar		8 oz	240 g
Lemon zest, grated		½ oz	15 g
Gelatin		1 oz	30 g
Water, cold		8 oz	250 mL
Lemon juice		12 oz	350 mL
Egg whites	1 lb		450 g
Sugar	1 lb		450 g

■ Procedure

1. Dissolve the sugar in the water and bring to a boil.

2. Beat together the egg yolks, second quantity of water, cornstarch, sugar, and zest until smooth.

3. Gradually beat the boiling syrup into the egg yolk mixture in a thin stream.

4. Return the mixture to the heat and bring it to a boil, beating constantly with a whip.

5. As soon as the mixture thickens and boils, remove it from the heat.

6. Soften the gelatin in the third quantity of water.

7. Add in the gelatin to the hot lemon mixture. Stir until it is dissolved.

8. Stir in the lemon juice.

9. Chill it until thick, but not set.

10. Beat the egg whites until they form soft peaks. Gradually add the sugar and continue to beat until a thick, glossy meringue is formed.

11. Fold the meringue into the lemon mixture.

12. Fill baked pie shells. Chill until set.

Variations

Lime Chiffon Pie Filling
Substitute lime juice and zest for the lemon juice and zest.

Orange Chiffon Pie Filling
Make the following ingredient adjustments.
  Use orange juice instead of water in step 1.
  Omit the first 8 oz (240 g) of sugar.
  Substitute orange zest for the lemon zest.
  Reduce the lemon juice to 4 oz (120 mL).

PIE FAULTS AND THEIR CAUSES

To remedy common pie faults, check the following troubleshooting guide for possible causes and correct your procedures.

Fault	Causes
Crust	
Dough too stiff	Not enough shortening
	Not enough liquid
	Flour too strong
Tough	Overmixing
	Not enough shortening
	Flour too strong
	Too much rolling or too much scrap dough used
	Too much water
Crumbly	Not enough water
	Too much shortening
	Improper mixing
	Flour too weak
Not flaky	Not enough shortening
	Shortening blended in too much
	Overmixing or too much rolling
	Dough or ingredients too warm
Soggy or raw bottom crust	Oven temperature too low; not enough bottom heat
	Filling hot when put in shell
	Not baked long enough
	Use of wrong dough (use mealy dough for bottom crusts)
	Not enough starch in fruit fillings
Shrinkage	Dough overworked
	Not enough shortening
	Flour too strong
	Too much water
	Dough stretched when put in pans
	Dough not rested
Filling	
Filling boils out	No steam vents in top crust
	Top crust not sealed to bottom crust at edges
	Oven temperature too low
	Fruit too acidic
	Filling hot when put in shell
	Not enough starch in filling
	Too much sugar in filling
	Too much filling
Curdling of custard or soft fillings	Overbaked

► TERMS FOR REVIEW

flaky pie dough	soft pie	instant starch	heavy pack
mealy pie dough	cream pie	cooked juice method	water pack
crumb crust	chiffon pie	cooked fruit method	syrup pack
fruit pie	lattice crust	solid pack	drained weight

► QUESTIONS FOR REVIEW

1. Discuss the various factors that affect tenderness, toughness, and flakiness in pie dough. Why should emulsifier shortening not be used for pie dough?

2. What are some advantages and disadvantages of using butter in pie dough?

3. What would happen to a flaky pie dough if you mixed it too long before adding the water? After adding the water?

4. Describe the difference between mealy pie dough and flaky pie dough.

5. What kind of crust would you use for a pumpkin pie? An apple pie? A banana cream pie?

6. How can you prevent shrinkage when baking empty pie shells?

7. How can you prevent soggy or undercooked bottom pie crusts?

8. What starch would you use to thicken apple pie filling? Chocolate cream pie filling? Lemon pie filling? Peach pie filling?

9. Why is lemon juice added to lemon pie filling after the starch has thickened the water? Wouldn't this thin out the filling?

10. Why is the cooked juice method usually used when making pie fillings from canned fruits?

11. What problem might you have if you make blueberry pie filling out of blueberries that are still partially frozen?

12. How can you test a custard pie for doneness?

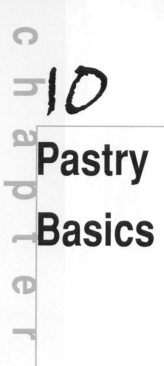

10

Pastry
Basics

*T*he term "pastry" comes from the word "paste," meaning in this case a mixture of flour, liquid, and fat. In the bakeshop, pastry refers both to various pastes or doughs and to the many products made from these doughs.

We have already discussed two fundamental types of pastry: yeast-raised pastry such as Danish dough in chapters 3 and 5, and pie doughs in chapter 9. Besides these two, the most important types of pastry are short doughs of various types, puff pastry, also known as *pâte feuilletée,* and éclair paste, also known as *pâte à choux.* These three pastries are introduced in this chapter. We also take a look at strudel and phyllo doughs, which are important for some specialty items. Finally, we look at crisp meringues and other meringue-type sponges. These are not pastries in the original sense of the word, because they are not made from a flour paste. Nevertheless, they are used like flour pastries in combination with creams, fillings, fruits, and icings to create a wide range of desserts.

This chapter concentrates on production of the doughs themselves. It is important to master the production techniques for these preparations before applying them to more complicated pastry desserts. Some simple applications of puff paste and éclair paste are included to give you practice handling these doughs. In addition, the section on strudel and phyllo includes examples of pastries made with these doughs. Once you understand the fundamentals, continue to the next chapter, where these doughs are used in specialty pastry work.

PÂTE BRISÉE AND SHORT PASTRIES

The quality of the pastry used to make tarts and tartlets is perhaps even more important than the quality of pie dough. Because tarts are generally thinner than pies, with less filling, the dough is a prominent part of the finished pastry and not just a holder for the filling, as often seems to be the case with American-style pies. The best of these doughs are made with pure butter, not shortening, and they generally are enriched with eggs and sugar.

This section includes two types of doughs, which differ in their mixing methods. Pâte brisée (pronounced "pot bree zay;" the term means "broken dough") is mixed the same way as pie dough—that is, the fat is first combined with the flour. The amount of mixing determines how flaky the dough is. Review pie dough production (pp. 202–205) if necessary. If you compare the formula for pâte brisée in this chapter with the formula for Enriched Pie Pastry on page 205, you will see that they are very similar. Pâte brisée is usually used for large tarts.

The remaining doughs in this section are mixed by the creaming method (see p.138), in which the fat and sugar are mixed first. This method is also used for cookies and cakes. In fact, these doughs can be used to make plain cookies. Because they are fragile and more difficult to handle than pâte brisée, these doughs are used primarily for small items such as tartlets and petits fours.

After reading this
chapter, you should be
able to:

■ Prepare pâte brisée and short pastries.

■ Prepare puff pastry dough, blitz puff pastry dough, and reversed puff pastry doughs, and prepare simple pastries from these doughs.

■ Prepare pâte à choux (éclair paste), and prepare simple pastries from it.

■ Prepare strudel dough, handle commercial phyllo (strudel) dough, and prepare pastries using either homemade or commercial dough.

■ Bake meringue and meringue-type sponges, and assemble simple desserts with these meringues.

Pâte Brisée

For large-quantity measurements, see page 601

Ingredients	U.S.		Metric	%
Pastry flour	12	oz	400 g	100
Salt	0.3	oz (1½ tsp)	10 g	2.5
Sugar	0.3	oz (1½ tsp)	10 g	2.5
Butter, chilled	6	oz	200 g	50
Eggs	4	oz	130 g	33
Water	0.6	oz (4 tsp)	20 g	10
Vanilla extract	4 drops		4 drops	
Lemon zest, grated	0.12	oz (1½ tsp)	4 g	1
Total weight	*1 lb 7*	*oz*	*774 g*	*199%*

■ P r o c e d u r e

1. Sift the flour, salt, and sugar into a round-bottomed bowl.

2. Cut the butter into small cubes. Rub it into the flour, using the fingertips, until the mixture looks like fine breadcrumbs. Make a well in the center.

3. Mix the eggs, water, vanilla, and lemon zest. Pour into the well into the flour. Mix to form a soft dough.

4. Turn the dough out onto a lightly floured work surface. Knead gently just until it is smooth and well mixed.

5. Wrap in plastic film and chill for at least 30 minutes before use.

Pâte Sablée

For large-quantity measurements, see page 601.

Ingredients	U.S.			Metric	%
Butter, softened	6	oz		150 g	67
Confectioners' sugar	3	oz		75 g	33
Lemon zest, grated	0.04 oz (½ tsp)			1 g	0.5
Vanilla extract	2 drops			2 drops	
Eggs, beaten	1	oz		25 g	11
Pastry flour	9	oz		225 g	100
Total weight	*1 lb 3*	*oz*		*475 g*	*211%*

■ Procedure

1. Cream together the butter, confectioners' sugar, lemon zest, and vanilla until the mixture is smooth and pale.
2. Add the eggs a little at a time and beat well between each addition.
3. Add the flour. With a plastic scraper, carefully blend into a soft dough.
4. Wrap in plastic film and flatten out. Chill until firm before use.

Variation

Chocolate Sablée

For large-quantity measurements, see page 601.

Ingredients	U.S.		Metric	%
Butter	6	oz	150 g	86
Confectioners' sugar	3	oz	75 g	43
Grated orange zest	0.08 oz (1 tsp)		2 g	0.2
Eggs, beaten	2	oz	50 g	28
Pastry flour	7	oz	175 g	100
Cocoa powder	1	oz	30 g	17

Substitute the above ingredients and follow the basic procedure.
Sift the flour with the cocoa.

Pâte Sucrée

For large-quantity measurements, see page 602.

Ingredients	U.S.			Metric	%
Butter, softened	7.5	oz		250 g	62.5
Sugar	3	oz		100 g	25
Salt	0.06 oz (⅓ tsp)			2 g	0.5
Lemon zest, grated	0.06 oz (¾ tsp)			2 g	0.5
Vanilla extract	4 drops			4 drops	
Eggs, beaten	3	oz		100 g	25
Pastry flour	12	oz		400 g	100
Total weight:	*1 lb 9*	*oz*		*854 g*	*213%*

■ Procedure

1. Cream together the butter, confectioners' sugar, salt, lemon zest, and vanilla until the mixture is smooth and pale.
2. Add the eggs a little at a time and beat well between each addition.
3. Add the flour. With a plastic scraper, carefully blend into a soft dough.
4. Wrap in plastic film and flatten out. Chill until firm before use.

Short Dough I

For large-quantity measurements, see page 602.

Ingredients	U.S.		Metric	%
Butter *or* butter and shortening	8	oz	250 g	67
Sugar	3	oz	90 g	25
Salt	0.06 oz (¼ tsp)		2 g	0.5
Eggs	2.25	oz	70 g	19
Pastry flour	12	oz	375 g	100
Total weight:	*1 lb 9*	*oz*	*787 g*	*211%*

For large-quantity measurements, see page 602.

■ P r o c e d u r e

1. Using the paddle attachment, mix the butter, sugar, and salt at low speed until smooth and evenly blended.
2. Add the eggs and mix just until absorbed.
3. Sift the flour and add it to the mixture. Mix just until evenly blended.
4. Chill several hours before using.

Almond Short Dough

For large-quantity measurements, see page 602.

Ingredients	U.S.		Metric		%
Butter	8	oz	200	g	80
Sugar	6	oz	150	g	60
Salt	0.1 oz (½ tsp)		2.5	g	1
Powdered almonds	5	oz	125	g	50
Eggs	1.6	oz	42	g	16.5
Vanilla extract	¼	tsp	1.25 g		0.5
Pastry flour	10	oz	250	g	100
Total weight:	*1 lb 14*	*oz*	*770*	*g*	*308%*

■ P r o c e d u r e

1. Using the paddle attachment, blend the butter, sugar, and salt at low speed until smooth and well mixed. Do not cream until light.
2. Add the almonds and blend in.
3. Add the eggs and vanilla. Mix just until absorbed.
4. Sift the flour and add it to the mixture. Mix just until evenly blended.
5. Chill several hours before using.

Variation

Linzer Dough

For large-quantity measurements, see page 602.

Ingredients	U.S.	Metric	%
Cinnamon	0.06 oz (1⅛ tsp)	1.5 g	0.6
Nutmeg	0.01 oz (⅛ tsp)	0.25 g	0.1

Use ground hazelnuts, ground almonds, or a mixture of the two. Mix in the cinnamon and nutmeg with the salt in the first step.

Short Dough II

For large-quantity measurements, see page 602.

Ingredients	U.S.		Metric	%
Butter	5	oz	150 g	60
Sugar	3.5	oz	100 g	40
Salt	0.07	oz	2 g	0.8
Vanilla powder	0.07	oz	2 g	0.8
Powdered almonds	1	oz	30 g	12
Eggs	1.75	oz	50 g	22
Pastry flour	8	oz	250 g	100
Total weight:	*1 lb 3*	*oz*	*584 g*	*213%*

■ P r o c e d u r e

1. Using the paddle attachment, mix the butter, sugar, salt, vanilla powder, and almonds.
2. Add the eggs and flour. Mix until just combined.
3. Chill several hours before using.

PUFF PASTRY

Puff pastry is one of the most remarkable products of the bakeshop. Although it includes no added leavening agent, it can rise to eight times its original thickness when baked.

Puff pastry is a rolled-in dough, like Danish and croissant doughs. This means that it is made up of many layers of fat sandwiched between layers of dough. Unlike Danish dough, however, puffy pastry contains no yeast. Steam, created when the moisture in the dough is heated, is responsible for the spectacular rising power of puff pastry.

Puff pastry, or puff dough, is one of the most difficult bakery products to make. Because it consists of over 1000 layers, many more than in Danish dough, the rolling-in procedure requires a great deal of time and care.

Like so many other products, there are nearly as many versions of puff pastry as there are bakers. Both formulas and rolling-in techniques vary. The formula provided here contains no eggs, for example, although some bakers add them.

Two methods for enclosing the butter and two rolling-in methods are illustrated.

Butter is the preferred fat for rolling in because of its flavor and melt-in-the-mouth quality. Special puff pastry shortening is also available. This shortening is easier to work because it is not as hard when refrigerated and because it doesn't soften and melt at warm temperatures as easily as butter does. It is also less expensive than butter. However, it can be unpleasant to eat because it tends to congeal and coat the inside of the mouth.

The quantity of rolled-in fat may vary from 50 to 100% of the weight of the flour, or 8 oz to 1 lb fat per pound of flour. If the lower quantity of fat is used, the dough should be left slightly thicker when rolled out. Puff pastry that is low in fat will not rise as high and may rise unevenly. This is because there is less fat between the dough layers, so that the layers are more likely to stick together.

The illustrations in this section show in detail the procedures for mixing the dough, enclosing the butter, and rolling. The procedure below shows one complete method for making puff pastry using the 4-fold method for rolling in. An alternative method for enclosing the butter in the dough is illustrated next. Finally, the three-fold method is shown as an alternative rolling-in procedure.

Formulas for *blitz puff pastry* and *reversed puff pastry* are also included. Blitz puff pastry is actually a very flaky pie dough that is rolled and folded like puff pastry. It is easier and quicker to make than classic puff dough (*blitz* is the German word for lightning). It does not rise as high as true puff pastry and its texture is not as fine, so it is not suitable for products in which a high, light pastry is desirable. However, it bakes up crisp and flaky and is perfectly suitable for napoleons and similar desserts that are layered with cream fillings.

Reversed puff pastry is somewhat unusual and rather difficult to work with. As the name suggests, the butter and dough are reversed—that is, the butter (which has some flour mixed into it) encloses the dough rather than the dough enclosing the butter. Although it is more difficult to prepare, it can be made up and baked without a final rest, as it shrinks less than classic puff pastry.

Procedure for Making Puff Pastry Dough

1. Make a well in the mound of flour and add the liquids.

2. Work the ingredients into a dough.

3. Knead the dough until it is smooth. Refrigerate for 30 minutes. Then roll it out into a large rectangle.

4. To prepare the butter, first soften it by beating it with a rolling pin.

5. Square off the butter. Roll it into a smooth rectangle two-thirds the size of the dough rectangle.

6. Place the butter on the dough so that it covers the bottom two-thirds of the rectangle.

7. Fold down the top, unbuttered third of the dough so that it covers half the butter.

8. Fold the bottom third over the center. The butter is now enclosed.

9. To give the dough its first 4-fold, roll the dough into a long rectangle. Before rolling, beat the dough lightly as shown so that the butter is evenly distributed.

10. Before folding, always brush off excess dusting flour.

11. Fold down the top edge of the dough to the center.

12. Fold up the bottom edge to the center.

13. Fold in half to achieve the finished 4-fold.

Alternative Method: Enclosing the Butter in Puff Pastry

1. Roll the dough into a blunt cross shape as shown, leaving the center thicker than the arms of the cross.

2. Place the square of butter in the center. Fold one of the arms of dough over the butter to cover it.

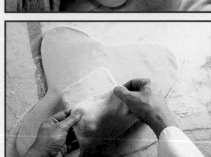

3. Fold the remaining three arms of dough over the center.

Alternative Method: Rolling-in Procedure

1. Fold the dough rectangle in thirds, as for making Danish Pastry (p. 112).

2. Square off the finished 3-fold with the rolling pin.

Classic Puff Pastry
(Pâte Feuilletée Classique)

For large-quantity measurements, see page 602.

Ingredients	U.S.		Metric	%
Bread flour	1 lb		500 g	100
Salt		0.33 oz	10 g	2
Butter, melted	2.5	oz	75 g	15
Water	8	oz	250 g	50
Butter, for rolling in	9.5	oz	300 g	60
Total weight:	*2 lb 4*	*oz*	*1135 g*	*227%*

■ P r o c e d u r e

Mixing Procedure

1. Mix the flour and the salt. Place the flour in a mound on a work surface and make a well in the center.

2. Pour the melted butter and water into the center of the well. Gradually stir from the inside outward to incorporate the flour into the liquids, making a dough.

3. Once the dough has formed, knead briefly just until it is smooth. Do not overwork or the dough will become too elastic and difficult to work. Gather the dough into a smooth ball.

4. Decide which method for enclosing the butter (below) you will use. If method 1, wrap in plastic and refrigerate for 30 minutes. If method 2, cut a cross in the top of the dough and wrap in plastic film. Allow to rest for 30 minutes in the refrigerator.

Enclosing the Butter, Method 1

1. Roll the dough out into a large rectangle.

2. Place the butter between two sheets of plastic film. Soften it and flatten it out by beating it with a rolling pin. Set aside while the dough is rolled out.

3. Keeping the butter between the plastic sheets, roll it out and square the edges using the rolling pin to make a rectangle about two-thirds the size of the dough rectangle.

4. Remove the plastic from the rectangle of butter and place it on the bottom two-thirds of the dough rectangle. Fold the top third of the dough down over the center to cover half the butter. Fold the bottom one-third over the center. The butter is now enclosed in the dough, making two layers of butter between three layers of dough.

5. Give the dough *four 4-folds.* This will give the dough 1028 layers of dough and butter. Rest the dough in a cool place between folds to allow the gluten to relax.

   Alternatively, give the dough *five 3-folds,* making a total of 883 layers. (If you wish, you can double this number of layers by simply rolling and folding it in half after the last 3-fold. This is preferable to giving the dough a sixth 3-fold—for over 2400 layers—because the dough may not rise properly when the layers become this thin.)

Enclosing the Butter, Method 2

1. With the rolling pin, spread open the four quarters of the dough made by cutting the cross and roll out the dough in the shape of a large, thick cross. Keep the dough thicker in the center than in the four arms of the cross.

2. Place the butter between two sheets of parchment or plastic film. Flatten it out and soften it slightly by beating it lightly with a rolling pin. Then roll it out into a square about ¾ inch (2 cm) thick. The size of the square of butter should be smaller than the center section of dough so that the butter will not overlap the edges of the dough in step 3.

3. Place the square of butter in the center of the dough cross. Fold the four arms of the dough over the butter to enclose it completely as in an envelope.

4. Give the dough *six 3-folds.* Rest the dough in a cool place between folds to allow the gluten to relax. This will give the dough 1459 layers of dough and butter.

Ordinary Puff Pastry

For large-quantity measurements, see page 603.

Ingredients	U.S.		Metric	%
Bread flour	12	oz	375 g	75
Cake flour	4	oz	125 g	25
Butter, softened	2	oz	60 g	12.5
Salt	0.25	oz	8 g	1.5
Water, cold	9	oz	282 g	56
Butter	1 lb		500 g	100
Bread flour (see *note*)	2	oz	60 g	12.5
Total weight:	*2 lb 13*	*oz*	*1410 g*	*282%*

Note   The purpose of the second quantity of bread flour is to absorb some of the moisture of the butter and help make the dough more manageable. Omit this flour if shop temperature is cool or if puff paste shortening is used instead of butter.

■ P r o c e d u r e

Mixing

1. Place the first quantities of flour and butter in a mixing bowl. With the paddle attachment, mix at low speed until well blended.

2. Dissolve the salt in the cold water.

3. Add the salted water to the flour mixture and mix at low speed until a soft dough is formed. Do not overmix.

4. Remove the dough from the mixer and let it rest in the refrigerator or retarder for 20 minutes.

5. Blend the last quantities of butter and flour at low speed in the mixer until the mixture is the same consistency as the dough, neither too soft nor too hard.

6. Roll the butter into the dough following the procedure shown on pages 234–235. Give the dough *four 4-folds* or *five 3-folds*.

Variation

The butter for rolling in may be reduced to 75% or even to as little as 50%. If the butter is reduced, you should also reduce the last quantity of flour (for mixing with the butter) in the same proportion, so that it is one-eighth the weight of the butter.

Blitz Puff Pastry

Ingredients	U.S.		Metric	%
Bread flour	8	oz	250 g	50
Pastry flour	8	oz	250 g	50
Butter, slightly softened	1 lb		500 g	100
Salt	0.25	oz	8 g	
Water, cold	8	oz	250 g	50
Total weight:	*2 lb 8*	*oz*	*1258 g*	*250%*

■ P r o c e d u r e

Mixing

1. Sift the two flours together into a mixing bowl.

2. Cut the butter into the flour as for pie dough, but leave the fat in very large lumps, 1 in. (2½ cm) across.

3. Dissolve the salt in the water.

4. Add the salted water to the flour/butter mixture. Mix until the water is absorbed.

5. Let the dough rest 15 minutes. Refrigerate it if the bakeshop is warm.

6. Dust the bench with flour and roll out the dough into a rectangle. Give the dough three 4-folds.

Variation

Reduce the butter to 75% (12 oz/375 g).

Reversed Puff Pastry
(Pâte Feuilletée Inversée)

Ingredients	U.S.		Metric	%
Butter	1 lb	4 oz	500 g	100
Bread flour		10 oz	250 g	50
Bread flour	1 lb	4 oz	500 g	100
Salt		1 oz	25 g	5
Water		11 oz	270 g	54
Butter, melted		7 oz	175 g	35
Total weight:	*4 lb*	*5 oz*	*1720 g*	*344%*

■ P r o c e d u r e

1. Combine the first quantities of butter and flour in a mixing bowl and mix together, either by hand or with the paddle attachment of a mixer, until completely blended.

2. Roll the butter mixture between two sheets of parchment paper to make a large rectangle ¾ in. (2 cm) thick. Refrigerate for 30 minutes.

3. Mix the remaining ingredients into a dough using the procedure described in steps 1 and 2 of the recipe for Classic Puff Pastry. Wrap and refrigerate for 30 minutes.

4. Roll out the dough to make a rectangle half the size of the butter rectangle.

5. Place the dough on the top half of the butter rectangle. Fold the butter over it to enclose completely, using the parchment to lift the butter.

6. Chill for 30 minutes.

7. Give the dough *five 3-folds.* Be sure to dust the work surface well with flour so that the butter does not stick.

GUIDELINES FOR MAKEUP AND BAKING OF PUFF DOUGH PRODUCTS

1. Dough should be cool and firm when it is rolled and cut. If it is too soft, layers may stick together at the cuts, preventing proper rising.

2. Cut with straight, firm, even cuts. Use a sharp cutting tool.

3. Avoid touching the cut edges with the fingers, or layers may stick together.

4. For best rising, place units upside down on baking sheets. Even sharp cutting tools may press the top layers of dough together. Baking upside down puts the stuck-together layers at the bottom.

5. Avoid letting egg wash run down the edges. Egg wash can cause the layers to stick together at the edges.

6. Rest made-up products for 30 minutes or more in a cool place or in the refrigerator before baking. This relaxes the gluten and reduces shrinkage.

7. Trimmings may be pressed together, keeping the layers in the same direction. After being rolled out and given a 3-fold, they may be used again, although they will not rise as high.

8. Baking temperatures of 400° to 425°F (200° to 220°C) are best for most puff dough products. Cooler temperatures will not create enough steam in the products to leaven them well. Higher temperatures will set the crust too quickly.

9. Larger products such as Pithiviers (p. 281) are harder to bake through than the small ones. To avoid underbaked, soggy interiors, start large items at a high temperature and bake until they are well risen. Then turn the temperature down to about 350°F (175°C) and finish baking until crisp.

PUFF PASTRY DESSERTS

The following recipes include instructions for simple puff pastry products, including petits fours. If any of your products do not turn out well, consult the troubleshooting guide in the table below.

Puff Pastry Faults and Their Causes

Faults	Possible Causes
Shrinkage during baking	Dough not relaxed before baking
Poor lift or rising	Too little or too much fat used
	Dough rolled out too thin or given too many turns
	Oven too hot or too cold
Uneven lift or irregular shapes	Improper rolling-in procedure
	Uneven distribution of fat before rolling
	Dough not relaxed before baking
	Uneven heat in oven
Fat running out during baking	Too much fat used
	Not enough turns given
	Oven too cool
	(Note: Some fat running out is normal, but it should not be excessive.)

 Pinwheels

Components	
Puff Pastry dough	■ **P r o c e d u r e**
Egg wash	1. Roll out the puff pastry dough ⅛ in. (3 mm) thick.
Fruit filling	2. Cut into squares 5 in. (12 cm) per side, or other size as desired.
	3. Cut diagonally from the corners to about 2 in. (5 cm) from the center. Brush the pastry with egg wash.
	4. Fold every other corner to the center and press into place, as for making Danish pinwheels (p. 129).
	5. Brush with egg wash a second time.
	6. Select a thick filling that will not run when baked (see step 9). Place a spoonful of the filling in the center of each pinwheel.
	7. Bake at 400°F (200°C) until puffed and golden.
	8. Cool. Dust with confectioners' sugar.
	9. Pinwheels may also be filled after, instead of before, baking. This method is used for fillings that might run or burn when baked.

Patty Shells

Components

Puff Pastry dough
Egg wash

■ P r o c e d u r e

1. Roll out puff pastry dough ⅛ in. (3 mm) thick.

2. Roll out a second piece of dough ¼ in. (6 mm) thick.

3. Cut the same number of circles from each piece of dough with a round 3-in. (7.5 cm) cutter.

4. With a 2-in. (5 cm) cutter, cut out the centers of the *thick* circles.

5. Wash the thin circles with water or egg wash and place one of the rings on top of each. Wash the top carefully with egg wash (do not drip wash down the edges). Let them rest 30 minutes.

6. Place a sheet of greased parchment over the tops of the shells to prevent their toppling over while baking.

7. Bake at 400°F (200°C) until brown and crisp.

Turnovers

Components

Puff Pastry dough
Fruit filling
Egg wash
   or
Milk or water and granulated sugar

■ P r o c e d u r e

1. Roll puff pastry dough ⅛ in. (3 mm) thick.

2. Cut into 4-in. (10 cm) squares. Wash the edges of each with water.

3. Place a portion of the desired filling into the center of each square.

4. Fold the squares diagonally and press the edges together. With a knife, puncture the tops in two or three places to allow steam to escape. Let them rest 30 minutes.

5. Brush the tops with egg wash, if desired, or brush with milk or water and sprinkle with sugar.

6. Bake at 400°F (200°C) until crisp and brown.

Cream Horns

Components

Puff Pastry dough
Granulated sugar
Whipped cream or Pastry Cream (pp.187–188)
Confectioners' sugar

■ P r o c e d u r e

1. Roll out puff pastry dough into a sheet ⅛ in. (3 mm) thick and about 15 in. (38 cm) wide.

2. Cut out strips 1¼ in. (3 cm) wide by 15 in. (38 cm) long.

3. Wash the strips with water.

4. Press one end of a strip, with the washed side facing outward, onto one end of a cream horn tube (a). If you are using conical tubes, start at the small end.

5. Roll the strip diagonally in a spiral by turning the tube (b). Overlap the edges by ⅜ in. (1 cm). Do not stretch the dough.

6. Roll up completely and press the end in place to seal (c)

7. Roll the horns in granulated sugar and lay them on baking sheets.
The end of the dough strip should be on the bottom so that it will not pop up during baking.

8. Bake at 400°F (200°C) until brown and crisp.

9. Slip out tubes while still warm.

10. Just before service, fill the horns from both ends with whipped cream or pastry cream, using a pastry bag with a star tip. Dust with confectioners' sugar.

a.

b.

c.

Napoleons

Components

Puff Pastry dough
Pastry Cream (pp.187–189)
  or mixture of pastry cream
  and whipped cream
Fondant (p. 335)
Chocolate fondant (p. 334)

■ P r o c e d u r e

1. Roll puff pastry dough into a very thin sheet about the size of a sheet pan. Blitz puff paste or rerolled trimmings may be used.

2. Place on sheet pan and let rest 30 minutes, preferably in the refrigerator.

3. Dock with a fork to prevent blistering.

4. Bake at 400°F (200°C) until brown and crisp.

5. Trim the edges of the pastry sheet and cut with a serrated knife into equal strips 3 to 4 in. (7.5–10 cm) wide. Set the best strip aside for the top layer. If one of the strips breaks, it can be used as the middle layer.

6. Spread one rectangle with pastry cream or with a mixture of pastry cream and whipped cream.

7. Top with a second sheet of pastry.

8. Spread with another layer of pastry cream.

9. Place third pastry rectangle on top, with the flattest side up.

10. Ice the top with fondant (see p. 335).

11. To decorate, pipe four strips of chocolate fondant lengthwise on the white fondant. Draw a spatula or the back of a knife across the top in opposite directions to feather the design.

12. Cut into strips 1½ to 2 in. (4 to 5 cm) wide.

Baked Apple Dumplings

Components

Small, tart baking apples

Puff Pastry dough

Cake crumbs (optional)

Cinnamon Sugar (p. 116)

Raisins

Egg wash

■ P r o c e d u r e

1. Peel and core as many apples as desired.

2. Roll out puff pastry dough ⅛ in. (3 mm) thick. Cut out squares large enough to cover an apple completely when the points of the square are overlapped at the top of the apple. The dough must not be stretched over the apple or it will pull away during baking. *Caution:* Cut out one square and test it to be sure it is large enough to cover the apple. Then cut out the remaining squares.

3. If the dough becomes soft, refrigerate it for 15 to 30 minutes before continuing.

4. Place a teaspoonful of cake crumbs in the center of each pastry square. The place an apple on top of the crumbs. (The crumbs are optional, but they help absorb some of the juice of the apple.)

5. Fill the center of the apples (where the cores used to be) with cinnamon sugar and raisins. Taste a small piece of apple for tartness, to help you judge how much sugar to use.

6. Brush the edges of the dough with water or egg wash. Draw up the four corners of the dough and overlap them at the top of the apple. Press the corners together to seal. Pinch the edges of the dough together to seal the seams.

7. Cut out 1-in. (2.5 cm) circles of dough. Moisten the top of each apple with egg wash and cap with a circle of dough. This covers the overlapping corners and makes the product more attractive.

8. Arrange the apples on parchment-lined pans. Brush with egg wash.

9. Bake at 400°F (200°C) until the pastry is browned and the apples are cooked through but not too soft (or they will sag and flatten out). This will take 45 to 60 minutes, depending on the apples. Test for doneness by piercing one of the apples with a thin skewer. If the pastry browns too fast, cover lightly with a sheet of parchment or foil.

Fruit Tarts

Puff pastry may be used instead of short dough to make fruit tarts. Fruit strips are fruit tarts made in the shape of long strips about 4 to 5 in. (10 to 12 cm) wide.

The procedure for assembling these desserts is the same as that for unbaked fruit tarts described in Chapter 11 (p. 270). except that baked puff pastry should be assembled only at the last minute because the pastry quickly becomes soggy.

The shells can be made in any shape, but squares and rectangles are easiest, as in this procedure.

Fruit Tarts

Components

Puff Pastry dough

Egg wash

Pastry Cream (pp. 187-188)

Fruit, as desired

Apricot Glaze (p. 117) or other glaze

■ P r o c e d u r e

1. Roll out puff pastry dough ⅛ in. (3 mm) thick.

2. Cut out squares or rectangles of desired size.

3. With the remaining dough, cut strips about ¾ in. (2 cm) wide and long enough to make borders for the tarts.

4. Brush the rims of the dough squares with water or egg wash. Lay the strips in place on the moistened edges to make borders. Egg wash the tops of the borders.

5. With a fork, knife tip, or roller docker, dock the inside of the shell (not the borders) to prevent blistering.

6. Rest in the refrigerator 30 minutes before baking.

7. Bake at 400°F (200°C) until browned and crisp. Cool.

8. Fill with a thin layer of pastry cream, arrange fruit on top, and brush with apricot glaze. See page 270 for the detailed procedure for filling fruit tarts.

Variation

Fruit Strips

Follow the above procedure, but make the rectangles 4 to 5 in. (10–12 cm) wide and as long as your sheet pans. Put borders on the two long sides, but leave the ends open.

PUFF PASTRY PETITS FOURS

Chaussons

Components

Puff Pastry dough

Egg wash

Apple Compote (p.119)

■ P r o c e d u r e

1. Roll out puff pastry dough less than ⅛ in. (2 mm) thick. Place on a sheet pan lined with parchment paper. Chill for 30 minutes.

2. With a 2½-in. (6 cm) round cutter, cut out circles of dough.

3. Brush the edges with egg wash.

4. Spoon about ½ tsp (2–3 mL) Apple Compote onto the center of each circle.

5. Fold over to make a half-moon shape. Seal the edges by pressing with the reverse edge (the dull edge) of the round cutter.

6. Brush with egg wash. Score the tops lightly with the back of a fork to make a simple decoration.

7. Bake at 375°F (190°C) until puffed and golden brown.

Variation

Use other fruit compotes (see Chapter 18) or Frangipane (p. 118) instead of the apple filling.

Palmiers

Components

Puff Pastry dough
Granulated sugar

■ P r o c e d u r e

1. Thickly butter a baking tray and chill.
2. Scale 1 lb (500 g) of puff pastry dough. Dust the work surface heavily with sugar. Roll out the pastry to a rectangle 13 × 17 in. (33 × 43 cm). Trim the edges with a sharp knife.
3. Fold the long sides into the middle so that they meet without overlapping. Brush with a little water and fold the long sides a second time to the middle so that they meet without overlapping. You should now have a rectangle about 3¼ × 17 in. (8 × 43 cm)
4. Brush with a little water again and fold together to form a 1½ × 17 in. (4 × 43 cm) rectangle.
5. Cut into ½-in. (6-mm) slices with a sharp knife and lay on the buttered tray in staggered rows (a).
6. Press down on the slices with the palm of the hand to flatten lightly (b).
7. Bake at 375°F (190°C) until golden brown. Turn the palmiers over and bake the second side until well colored. Transfer to a wire rack to cool.

a.

b.

Variations

Serve plain as a dry petit four.
Sandwich with buttercream and serve as a tea pastry.
Dip half-way in melted chocolate.

Allumettes

Components

Puff Pastry dough
Royal Icing (p. 343)

■ P r o c e d u r e

1. Roll out puff pastry dough to a rectangle ⅛ in. (3mm) thick. Place on a sheet pan.
2. Spread a thin layer of royal icing thinly over the puff pastry. Freeze until icing sets.
3. Cut the pastry with a wet knife into batons or strips approximately ⅝ × 1½ in. (1½ × 4 cm). Place on a sheet pan lined with parchment paper.
4. Bake at 375°F (190°C) until risen, then cover with a silicon mat and cook until golden and fully cooked, approximately 20 minutes.
5. Cool on a wire rack.

Papillons (Butterflies or Bow Ties)

Components

Puff Pastry dough

Granulated sugar

■ Procedure

1. Thickly butter a baking tray and chill.

2. Scale 1 lb (500) g puff pastry dough. On a work surface dusted with sugar, roll out to a rectangle 13 × 5 in. (33 × 13 cm). Trim the edges neatly.

3. Cut into 5 equal pieces, measuring about 2½ × 5 in. (6.5 × 13 cm). Brush four of them with a little water and stack one on top of the other, placing the unbrushed one on top.

4. Using the back of a knife, mark a center line down the length of the pastry, turn over and repeat in the same place on the underside. Chill.

5. Trim the edges of the stack to neaten if necessary. Using a sharp knife, cut crosswise into ¼ in. (5 mm) thick slices with an indention in the middle (a).

6. Twist the slices in the middle, which will splay the layers. Place on the tray and press down the edges lightly (b). Bake at 375°F (190°C) until golden brown

a.   b.

Variation

Add ground cinnamon or ginger to the sugar.

Conversations

Components

Puff Pastry dough

Fruit jam, such as raspberry

Frangipane Filling (p. 118)

Royal Icing (p. 343)

Puff pastry petits fours, left to right: Palmiers, Conversations, Papillons

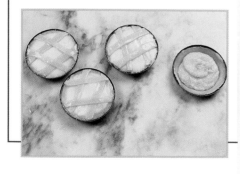

■ P r o c e d u r e

1. Roll out puff pastry dough as thin as possible. It should be nearly transparent. Chill for 30 minutes on a tray lined with parchment paper.

2. With a round cutter cut out circles of dough large enough to line 2-in. (5-cm) tartlet cases. Cut out additional circles for the tops of each pastry and set aside. Keep the trimmings flat to use for the decoration.

3. Put about ½ tsp (3 g) of jam in the bottom of each tartlet and top with a teaspoon (5 g) frangipane filling.

4. Brush the edges of the pastry with egg wash. Top with a circle of very thin puff pastry and chill.

5. Coat the top of the puff pastry with a thin layer of royal icing, using a small palette knife.

6. Cut strips of puff pastry very thinly and lay on top of the royal icing to form a lattice pattern. The small illustration at left shows one pastry without its top (right) and three ready to bake.

7. Bake at 375°F (190°C) until golden brown and cooked through.

Sacristains

Components

Puff Pastry dough

Egg wash

Granulated sugar

Almonds, chopped (optional)

■ P r o c e d u r e

1. Roll out strips of puff pastry dough ⅛ in. (3 mm) thick. Cut into long strips 4 in. (10 cm) wide.

2. Brush the dough with egg wash and sprinkle with coarse granulated sugar or a mixture of sugar and chopped almonds. Lightly press the sugar and nuts into the dough with a rolling pin.

3. Turn the strips over and coat the other side with egg wash, sugar, and almonds in the same way.

4. Cut the strips crosswise into small strips ¾ in. (2 cm) wide and 4 in. (10 cm) long.

5. Twist each strip to make a shape like a corkscrew. Place on paper-lined baking sheets and press down the ends lightly so that the twists do not unwind during baking.

6. Bake at 425°F (220°C) until brown and crisp.

ÉCLAIR PASTE

Éclairs and cream puffs are made from a dough called *éclair paste,* or *choux paste.* The French name *pâte à choux* (pronounced "pot a shoo") means "cabbage paste," referring to the fact that cream puffs look like little cabbages.

Unlike puff pastry, éclair paste is extremely easy to make. The dough itself can be prepared in just a few minutes. This is fortunate, because for best baking results the dough should not be prepared ahead of time.

The exact procedure for making éclair paste is detailed in the formula that follows. In general, the method consists of these steps:

1. Bring the liquid, fat, salt, and sugar (if used) to a boil. The liquid must be boiling rapidly so that the fat is dispersed in the liquid, not just floating on top. If this is not done, the fat will not be as well incorporated into the paste, and some of it may run out during baking.

2. Add the flour all at once and stir until the paste forms a ball and pulls away from the sides of the pan.

3. Remove the paste from the heat and let it cool to 140°F (60°C). If the paste is not cooled slightly, it will cook the eggs when they are added.

4. Beat in the eggs a little at a time. Completely mix in each addition of eggs before adding more. If the eggs are added too quickly, it will be difficult to get a smooth batter.

5. The paste is now ready to use.

In principle, éclair paste is similar to popover batter (p.149), even though the former is a thick dough and the latter a thin batter. Both products are leavened by steam, which expands the product rapidly and forms large holes in the center of the item. The heat of the oven then coagulates the gluten and egg proteins to set the structure and make a firm product. A strong flour is necessary in both for sufficient structure.

Éclair paste must be firm enough to hold its shape when piped from a pastry bag. You may occasionally find a formula that produces too slack a dough. Correct such a formula by reducing the water or milk slightly. On the other hand, éclair paste should not be too dry. It should look smooth and moist, not dry and rough. Paste that is too dry does not puff up well and is thick and heavy.

Éclair paste for cream puffs and éclairs should be piped onto parchment-lined pans, not onto greased pans. Grease causes the paste to spread and flatten when baked.

Proper baking temperatures are important. Start at a high temperature (425°F/220°C) for the first 15 minutes to develop steam. Then reduce the heat to 375°F (190°C) to finish baking and set the structure. The products must be firm and dry before being removed from the oven. If they are removed too soon or cooled too quickly, they may collapse. Some bakers like to leave them in a turned-off oven with the door ajar. However, if the oven must be heated again for other products, this may not be the best idea. It may be better to bake the products thoroughly, remove them carefully from the oven, and let them cool slowly in a warm place.

Note: French doughnuts or crullers, also made with éclair paste, are discussed in chapter 7 (p. 160).

Éclair Paste or Pâte à Choux

Ingredients	U.S.		Metric	%
Water	10	oz	250 g	167
Butter	4	oz	100 g	67
Sugar	0.18 oz (1 tsp)		5 g	3
Salt	0.18 oz (1 tsp)		5 g	3
Bread flour	6	oz	150 g	100
Eggs	6	oz	150 g	100
Total weight:	*1 lb 10*	*oz*	*660 g*	*440*

■ **P r o c e d u r e**

1. Combine the liquid, butter, sugar, and salt in a heavy saucepan or kettle. Bring the mixture to a full, rolling boil.

2. Remove the pan from the heat and add the flour all at once. Stir quickly.

3. Return the pan to moderate heat and stir vigorously until the dough forms a ball and pulls away from the sides of the pan.

4. Transfer the dough to the bowl of a mixer. If you wish to mix it by hand, leave it in the saucepan.

5. With the paddle attachment, mix at low speed until the dough has cooled slightly. It should be about 140°F (60°C), which is still very warm, but not too hot to touch.

6. At medium speed, beat in the eggs a little at a time. Add no more than a quarter of the eggs at once, and wait until they are completely absorbed before adding more. When all the eggs are absorbed, the paste is ready to use.

ÉCLAIR PASTE PRODUCTS

Cream Puffs

Components

Éclair Paste
Filling of choice
Confectioners' sugar

■ P r o c e d u r e

1. Line sheet pans with silicone paper.
2. Fit a large pastry bag with a plain tube. Fill the bag with the éclair paste.
3. Pipe out round mounds of dough about 1½ in. (4 cm) in diameter onto the lined baking sheets. Or, if preferred, drop the dough from a spoon.
4. Bake at 425°F (215°C) for 10 minutes. Lower heat to 375°F (190°C) until mounds are well browned and very crisp.
5. Remove them from the oven and let cool slowly in a warm place.
6. When cool, cut a slice from the top of each puff. Fill with whipped cream, pastry cream (pp. 187–188), or other desired filling, using a pastry bag with a star tube.
7. Replace tops and dust with confectioners' sugar.
8. Fill as close to service time as possible. If cream-filled puffs must be held, keep refrigerated.
9. Unfilled and uncut puffs, if thoroughly dry, may be held in plastic bags in the refrigerator for a week. Recrisp in oven for a few minutes before use.

Éclairs

Components

Éclair Paste
Pastry Cream (pp. 187–188)
Chocolate Fondant (p. 334)

■ P r o c e d u r e

1. Proceed as for cream puffs, except pipe the dough out into strips about ¾ in. (2 cm) wide and 3–4 in. (8–10 cm) long. Bake as for cream puffs.
2. Fill baked, cooled éclair shells with pastry cream. Two methods may be used:

    a) Make a small hole in one end and fill with a pastry bag or a doughnut filling pump.

    b) Cut a slice lengthwise from the top and fill with a pastry bag.
3. Dip the tops of the éclairs in chocolate fondant.
4. For service and holding, see Cream Puffs, above.

Variation

Frozen Éclairs or Profiteroles

1. Fill éclairs or small cream puffs (profiteroles) with softened ice cream. Keep frozen until service.
2. At service time, top with chocolate syrup.

Paris-Brest

Components

Éclair Paste
Sliced or chopped almonds
Filling of choice

■ P r o c e d u r e

1. Line a sheet pan with silicone paper. Using a round cake pan of the desired size as a guide, draw a circle on the parchment. An 8-in. (20 cm) circle is a popular size.

2. Fit a large pastry bag with a plain tube. Pipe a ring of éclair paste 1 in. (2.5 cm) thick just inside the drawn circle. Pipe a second ring inside the first one, just touching it. Then pipe a third ring on top of the other two.

3. Sprinkle the paste circles with sliced or chopped almonds.

4. Bake as for cream puffs and éclairs.

5. When cool, cut a slice off the top of the pastry. Fill with whipped cream, Vanilla Pastry Cream (pp. 187–188), Pastry Cream Mousseline (p. 187), or Chiboust Cream (p. 189). Replace the top.

Choux Pastry Lattice

Components

Éclair Paste
Poppy seeds

■ P r o c e d u r e

1. Draw lattice designs on a sheet of parchment paper. Turn the paper over and place on a sheet pan. The drawings should show through.

2. Fill a paper cone with éclair paste and cut a small opening in the tip. Pipe the pastry over the outlines. If necessary, neaten the joints with the point of a small knife.

3. Sprinkle with poppy seeds.

4. Bake at 375°F (190°C) until evenly golden, about 4–7 minutes.

Use as a garnish for various cakes and plated desserts.

CHOUX PETITS FOURS

 Paris-Brest

Components

Choux Pastry

Flaked almonds

Praline Crème Pâtissière (p. 188)

Melted chocolate

Confectioners' sugar

■ Procedure

1. On a lightly buttered sheet pan, mark circles by dipping a 1-in. (2.5 cm) pastry cutter into flour and then tapping onto the tray.

2. Following this line, pipe a continuous ring of choux pastry using a small star tip.

3. Brush lightly with egg wash. Sprinkle with flaked almonds.

4. Bake at 375°F (190°C) until golden brown and hollow-sounding when tapped. Cool on a wire rack.

5. Slice the rings in half horizontally and pipe $1/3$ oz (10 g) praline crème pâtissière in the lower half of each.

6. Flick the tops with melted chocolate, dust with confectioners' sugar, and replace the tops.

Choux petits fours,
left to right:
Paris-brest,
mini éclairs,
pralines,
mini cream puffs,
choux florentines

Pralines

Components

Choux Pastry
Praline Crème Pâtissière (p. 188)
Nuts, lightly toasted
Caramelized sugar (p. 570)

■ **P r o c e d u r e**

1. On a lightly buttered sheet pan, pipe ¾-in. (2 cm) bulbs of choux pastry. Brush lightly with egg wash.

2. Bake at 375°F (190°C) until golden and well risen. Cool on a wire rack.

3. Once cold, pipe praline crème pâtissière into small holes in the bottom of each.

4. On a lightly oiled sheet pan, place lightly toasted nuts, slightly apart and one for each pastry.

5. Dip the top of each pastry in caramelized sugar and then place downward directly on top of each nut, allowing the caramel to cool around the nut and onto the flat tray.

6. Serve in paper petit four cases with the nut upward.

Mini Cream Puffs

Components

Choux Pastry
Flaked almonds
Crème Chantilly (p. 181)
Melted chocolate
Confectioners' sugar

■ **P r o c e d u r e**

1. On a lightly sheet pan, pipe ¾-in. (2 cm) bulbs of choux pastry. Brush lightly with egg wash and sprinkle with flaked almonds.

2. Bake at 375°F (190°C) until golden and hollow-sounding when tapped. Cool on a wire rack.

3. Slice in half horizontally. Pipe crème chantilly onto the bases.

4. Flick the tops with melted chocolate, dust with confectioners' sugar, and replace the tops.

5. Serve in paper petit four cases.

Mini Éclairs

Components

Choux Pastry

Chocolate Crème Pâtissière (p. 188)

Chocolate fondant (p.334)
  or Caramelized sugar (p. 570)

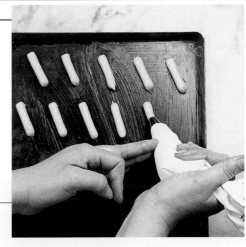

■ P r o c e d u r e

1. Pipe 2-in. (5 cm) fingers of choux pastry using a medium plain tip.

2. Brush with egg wash. Gently press down with the back of a fork.

3. Bake at 375°F (190°C) until hollow and golden. Cool on wire racks.

4. Make a hole at either end of the éclair. Pipe chocolate crème pâtissière inside, then dip the top in chocolate fondant icing or caramelized sugar.

5. Pipe designs in melted chocolate in the top of each and serve in paper petit four cases.

Choux Florentines

Components

Choux Pastry

Flaked almonds

Caramelized sugar (p. 570)

Crème Chantilly (p.181)

■ P r o c e d u r e

1. On a lightly buttered sheet pan, mark circles by dipping a 1-in. (2.5 cm) pastry cutter in flour and then tapping onto the tray.

2. Following this line, pipe a ring of Choux Pastry using a small star tip.

3. Brush lightly with egg wash.

4. Bake at 375°F (190°C) until golden brown and hollow-sounding when tapped. Cool on a wire rack.

5. Dip tops in caramelized sugar. Fill the center hole by piping a rosette of Crème Chantilly.

STRUDEL AND PHYLLO

Puff pastry dough, you will remember, consists of over 1000 layers of dough and fat. Starting with a single thick piece of dough, you fold in butter and then continue to roll out and fold until you have a very flaky pastry of extremely thin layers.

Pastries made from strudel or phyllo doughs are even flakier than puff pastries. Unlike puff pastries, these desserts start out with paper-thin layers of dough that are brushed with fat and then stacked or rolled up to make many-layered creations.

Strudel is a Hungarian pastry that begins as a soft dough made of strong flour, eggs, and water. After the dough is mixed well to develop the gluten, it is stretched by hand into a very thin, transparent sheet. This is a skilled operation that takes practice to do well.

Phyllo (pronounced "fee-lo" and sometimes spelled filo or fillo) is a Greek version of this type of paper-thin dough. Although not exactly the same as

Strudel Dough

Yield: enough for 3 sheets, each about 3 × 5 ft (1 × 1.6m)

Ingredients	U.S.		Metric	%
Bread flour	2 lb		900 g	100
Water	1 lb 2	oz	500 g	56
Salt	0.5 oz		15 g	1.5
Eggs	5	oz (3 eggs)	140 g (3 eggs)	15
Vegetable oil	2	oz	55 g	6
Total weight:	*3 lb 9*	*oz*	*1610 g*	*178%*

■ P r o c e d u r e

Mixing

1. Mix all ingredients into a smooth dough. To develop the gluten well, mix at moderate speed for about 10 minutes. The dough will be very soft.

2. Divide the dough into three equal parts. Flatten each piece into a rectangle. Place the three pieces of dough on an oiled sheet pan. Oil the top of the dough lightly and cover it with plastic film.

3. Let the dough rest at least 1 hour at room temperature, or longer in the retarder.

strudel dough, it is interchangeable with strudel dough for most of our purposes. Because it is available commercially, phyllo dough is widely used today for strudel-making. In fact, commercial phyllo is often labeled "phyllo/strudel dough."

Commercially made phyllo is almost always available frozen, and in some locations it can also be purchased fresh (refrigerated). The sheets usually measure about 11 or 12 in. × 17 in. (28 to 30 × 43 cm). A 1-pound package contains about 25 sheets.

The following recipes are for homemade strudel dough and for two popular strudel fillings, apple and cheese. Included with these are procedures for assembling and baking a strudel using both homemade dough and commercial phyllo leaves. Finally, we include a procedure for assembling and baking baklava, the popular Greek phyllo pastry filled with nuts and soaked with a honey syrup.

Procedure for Stretching Strudel Dough

1. Strudel dough stretches best if it is slightly warm, so place the dough in a warm place. Allow at least 1 to 2 hours if the dough has been refrigerated.

2. Cover a large table (at least 3 × 5 ft/1 × 1.6 m) with a cloth. Dust the cloth well with flour and rub it in lightly.

3. Using plently of dusting flour, place one piece of dough in the center of the table and, with a rolling pin, roll it out roughly into an oval or rectangle. This step is meant only to start the stretching, so don't try to roll the dough too thin.

4. Put your hands under the dough with the backs of the hands up. Carefully begin stretching the dough from the center outward, using the backs of your hands, not your fingers, to avoid poking holes in the dough. Work your way around the table, gently stretching the dough little by little in all directions. Concentrate on the thickest parts of the dough, so that it is of even thickness all around.

5. Keep on stretching the dough until it is paper thin and nearly transparent. If small holes appear, you can ignore them; if large holes appear, patch them with pieces of dough from the edges after stretching is complete. Each piece of dough should make a sheet about 3 × 5 ft (1 × 1.6 m).

6. With scissors, cut off the heavy rim of dough all around the edge and discard it.

7. Let the dough dry for about 10 minutes, then fill it and roll it according to the following procedure.

Procedure for Filling, Rolling, and Baking Strudel

Method 1, Using Homemade Dough

1. Assemble the following ingredients:

1 sheet freshly made strudel dough	3 × 5 ft	1 × 1.6 m
Melted butter	8 oz	250 g
Cake crumbs, breadcrumbs, finely chopped nuts, or a mixture of these	8 oz	250 g
Cinnamon	0.25 oz (1 tbsp)	7 g
Cheese filling	5–5½ lb	2300–2600 g
or		
Apple filling	4–4½ lb	2000–2200 g

2. Sprinkle or brush the dough all over with the melted butter. If you brush the fat on, draw the brush very lightly over the dough to avoid tearing it.

3. Mix the crumbs, nuts, and cinnamon and sprinkle them evenly over the dough.

4. Arrange the filling in a 1½-in. (4 cm) thick band along one long side of the dough. Leave a margin of about 2 in. (5 cm) between the row of filling and the edge of the dough.

5. Standing on the side where the filling is, grasp the edge of the cloth and lift it upward and forward to start the strudel rolling. Using the cloth as an aid, roll up the strudel like a jelly roll.

6. Cut the strudel in lengths to fit on a greased or paper-lined sheet, or bend the strudel to fit it on in one piece. Pinch the ends closed.

7. Brush the top with butter or egg wash. Bake at 375°F (190°C) until browned, about 45 minutes.

8. When cool, dust butter-washed strudel with confectioners' sugar, or brush egg-washed strudel with a clear syrup glaze (p. 116).

Method 2, Using Phyllo Leaves

Each unit requires 4 phyllo leaves plus one-fourth of the filling ingredients needed in Method 1.

1. Assemble the following ingredients:

Phyllo leaves	4 sheets	4 sheets
Melted butter	2 oz	60 g
Cake crumbs, breadcrumbs, finely chopped nuts, or a mixture of these	2 oz	60 g
Cinnamon	¾ tsp	2 g
Cheese filling	20–22 oz	575–625 g
or		
Apple filling	16–18 oz	500–550 g

2. Mix together the crumbs, nuts, and cinnamon.

3. Lay a cloth or a sheet of parchment on the bench. Lay a sheet of phyllo on the cloth or paper. Brush it with butter and sprinkle it with one-fourth of the crumb mixture.

4. Lay a second sheet on top of the first one. Brush with butter and sprinkle with with crumbs.

5. Repeat with the remaining two sheets.

6. Arrange the filling in a band along the wide side of the sheet, leaving a margin of about 2 in. (5 cm) between the filling and the edge.

7. Roll up and bake as in Method 1 (steps 5 to 7). Each unit will fit crosswise on a standard baking sheet, four to six units per sheet.

8. In the retail shop, it is customary to cut each of these baked units in half and display the halves with the cut edges toward the customer.

HANDLING PHYLLO DOUGH

Commercially made phyllo is so thin and delicate that it must be handled very carefully. Two guidelines are important. First, thaw frozen phyllo completely *before opening the plastic package.* Do not try to handle frozen dough; it will break.

Second, after opening the package and unfolding or unrolling the sheets of dough, keep the stack of leaves covered to prevent drying. Remove and work with one sheet at a time, keeping the rest covered. (*Note:* Instructions often say to cover the dough with a damp cloth, but this is risky because the sheets stick together if the dough becomes too damp.)

The modern trend to lighter pastries has inspired chefs to use baked layers of phyllo in place of puff pastry to make desserts such as napoleons.

Procedure for Making Crisp Phyllo Layers for Napoleons

1. On a cutting board, lay out one sheet of phyllo dough. Brush very lightly with butter. It is not necessary to cover the surface thoroughly with butter; use a light hand. Top with a second and third layer, buttering each layer lightly.
2. Cut the pastry into squares or rectangles of desired size for individual pastries—for example, squares 3 in. (8 cm) on a side. Cut two, three, or four squares for each pastry, depending on the number of layers desired. A typical napoleon requires three layers.
3. Arrange the squares on baking sheets. Bake at 400°F (200°C) until brown, about 5 minutes.
4. The pastry squares to be used for top layers may be caramelized to enhance their appearance and flavor. To caramelize, coat with confectioners' sugar by sifting the sugar over them. Place under a hot broiler until the sugar is caramelized. Watch closely so that neither the sugar nor the pastry burns or scorches.

Phyllo Tartlet Shells

Prepare squares of pastry as in steps 1 and 2, making four layers. Press each square into a tartlet shell and bake. Use as shells for unbaked fruit tartlets, following the procedure on page 270.

Apple Filling for Strudel

Yield: 4 lb (2000 g)

Ingredients	U.S.		Metric	%
Apples, peeled and cored (see *note*)	3 lb		1500 g	100
Lemon juice	1	oz	30 g	2
Sugar	8	oz	250 g	17
Sugar	8	oz	250 g	17
Raisins	4	oz	125 g	8
Walnuts, chopped	4	oz	125 g	8
Cake crumbs	2	oz	60 g	4
Lemon zest, grated	0.25	oz	8 g	0.5
Cinnamon	0.25	oz	8 g	0.5

Procedure

1. Cut the apples into thin slices or small dice. Mix with the lemon juice and the first quantity of sugar. Let stand for 30 minutes while preparing the pastry.
2. Drain the apples well. The sugar will have drawn out juice that would otherwise run out of the strudel and make the bottom soggy.
3. Mix the apples with the remaining ingredients.

Note   Canned sliced apples may be used. Weigh after draining. Omit the lemon juice and the first quantity of sugar. Omit steps 1 and 2 in the procedure.

Cheese Filling for Strudel

Yield: Enough for 4 strudels (16 inches/41 cm long each) or one 5-foot (1.6 m) strudel using homemade dough.

Ingredients	U.S.			Cheese at 100% Metric	%
Baker's cheese	2 lb	8	oz	1200 g	100
Butter		10	oz	300 g	25
Sugar		12	oz	360 g	30
Cake flour		3	oz	90 g	7.5
Salt		0.5	oz	15 g	1.25
Vanilla extract		0.5	oz	15 g	1.25
Lemon zest, grated		0.25	oz (1 tbsp)	8 g	0.6
Eggs		6	oz	180 g	15
Sour cream		8	oz	240 g	20
Raisins		8	oz	240 g	20
Total weight:	*5 lb*	*8*	*oz*	*2648 g*	*220%*

■ **P r o c e d u r e**

1. Combine the cheese and butter (at room temperature) and blend at low speed with the paddle attachment until smooth.

2. Add the sugar, flour, salt, vanilla, and zest. Blend at low speed until just smooth and completely mixed. Do not cream too much air into the mixture or it will expand when baked and may burst the pastry.

3. Add the eggs a little at a time, mixing in at low speed. Mix in the sour cream.

4. Fold in the raisins.

Variation

Cream Cheese Filling for Strudel

Ingredients	U.S.		Metric	%
Cream cheese	3 lb		1440 g	100
Sugar	12	oz	360 g	25
Cake flour	3	oz	90 g	6
Salt	0.5	oz	15 g	1
Vanilla extract	0.5	oz	15 g	1
Lemon zest	0.25	oz	8 g	0.5
Eggs	6	oz	180 g	12.5
Sour cream	8	oz	240 g	17
Raisins	8	oz	240 g	17

Substitute the above ingredients for those in the main recipe, using cream cheese instead of baker's cheese, and omitting the butter. Mix as in basic recipe.

Baklava

Yield: one 15 × 10-in. (38 × 25-cm) pan, about 48 pieces

Ingredients	U.S.		Metric	
Pastry				
Phyllo leaves	1	lb	500	g
Walnuts, chopped	1	lb	500	g
Sugar	2	oz	60	g
Cinnamon	0.06	oz (1 tsp)	2	g
Cloves, ground	0.04	oz (½ tsp)	0.5	g
Butter, melted, or mixture of butter and oil	12	oz	375	g
Syrup				
Sugar	1	lb	500	g
Water	12	oz	375	g
Honey	6	oz	190	g
Lemon peel	2 strips		2 strips	
Lemon juice	1	oz	30	g
Cinnamon stick	1		1	

■ Procedure

1. Unfold the phyllo leaves and keep them covered.

2. Mix together the nuts, sugar, cinnamon, and cloves.

3. Butter the bottom and sides of a 15 × 10-in. (38 × 25 cm) baking pan.

4. Lay one of the phyllo sheets in the bottom of the pan, letting the ends of the dough fold upward at the sides of the pan. Brush the dough with butter.

5. Repeat until there are ten buttered sheets in the pan.

6. Place one-third of the nut mixture in the pan in an even layer.

7. Put in two more phyllo leaves, buttering each one as it is placed in the pan.

8. Put in another third of the nuts, another two buttered phyllo leaves, and the rest of the nuts.

9. Finally, lay each of the remaining leaves in the pan, buttering each, including the top one.

10. There will be some excess dough sticking up around the edges of the pan. With a sharp knife, trim it off so that it is level with the top of the pastry.

11. Chill the pastry to congeal the butter. This will make cutting easier.

12. Cut the pastry into four rows of six squares, each about 2½ in. (6 cm) on a side. Then cut the squares diagonally to make triangles. (A traditional method is to cut baklava into diamond shapes, but this always leaves some small, odd-shaped pieces at the ends.)

13. Bake at 350°F (175°C) for 50–60 minutes, until golden brown.

14. While the baklava is baking, combine the syrup ingredients and bring to a boil. Simmer for 10 minutes, then cool to lukewarm. Remove the cinnamon stick and lemon peel. Skim off foam, if any.

15. When the pastry is baked, pour the warm syrup carefully over the hot baklava.

16. Let the baklava stand overnight so that the syrup can be absorbed.

BAKED MERINGUES

To refer to baked meringues as pastries may seem odd, as the term *pastry* usually refers to desserts made from flour goods such as puff pastry, short dough, or éclair paste. However, meringue that is bagged out into various shapes and baked until crisp is used in many of the same ways as flour pastry. It can be filled or iced with many kinds of creams, icings, and fruits to make an interesting variety of attractive desserts.

Basic meringue mixtures are discussed in chapter 8, along with other creams and toppings. Common meringue and Swiss meringue are the types generally used to make crisp, baked shells. The basic procedure for baking meringue is presented in this section, followed by instructions for individual desserts. Also, a special meringue mixture containing nuts is introduced. This flavorful mixture is usually made into round, crisp layers that are used somewhat like cake layers. They may be filled and iced with buttercream, chocolate mousse, whipped cream, or similar light icings and creams.

The most common use for the preparations in this section is to pipe them out into discs and use the baked meringues as bases or layers for a variety of pastries. (To make meringue or sponge layers, mark a circle on a sheet of parchment and pipe the meringue or batter in a spiral to fill the circle.) Chopped or powdered nuts, especially almonds and hazelnuts, may be folded into a meringue before baking, making flavorful, crisp layers for a variety of pastries as well as specialty cakes. Two formulas of this type are included.

Four of the recipes in this section contain some cake flour and are mixed like sponge cakes. In fact, they are sometimes called *sponges*. The flour contributes structure. The quantity of flour is low, however, and the main ingredients are egg whites and sugar, as in regular meringues. Therefore, these recipes are grouped with meringues rather than with cakes.

You will find pastry recipes using these meringues in chapter 11. Chapter 14 includes cakes that include one or more layers of meringue.

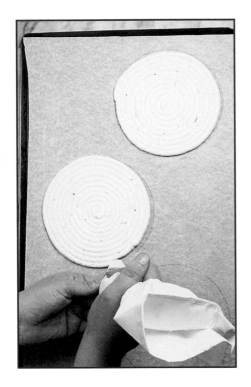

Crisp Baked Meringues

Components

Common Meringue (p. 182),
    Chocolate Meringue (p. 182),
    or Swiss Meringue (p. 183)

■ Procedure

1. Using a pastry bag, form the meringue into the desired shapes on baking sheets lined with silicone paper. Specific shapes are indicated in the procedures for specific desserts.

2. Bake at 200° to 225°F(100°C) until crisp but not browned. This will take 1 to 3 hours, depending on size.

3. Cool the meringues, then remove them from the parchment. Be careful, because they may be fragile.

Almond Meringues

For large-quantity measurements, see page 603.

Ingredients	U.S.	Egg whites at 100% Metric	%
Egg whites	4 oz	120 g	100
Fine granulated sugar	4 oz	120 g	100
Powdered almonds	4 oz	120 g	100
Total weight:	*12 oz*	*360 g*	*300%*

■ **P r o c e d u r e**

1. Whip the egg whites to soft peaks.

2. Add the sugar and continue whipping until firm and glossy.

3. Fold in the powdered almonds.

4. Prepare baking sheets by lining them with silicone paper. Draw circles of the desired size on the paper, using cake pans or other round objects as guides.

5. Using a pastry bag with a ½-in. (12 mm) plain tube, fill in the circles on the baking sheets by making spirals starting in the center of each circle, as on page 260. Each circle should be filled with a layer of meringue about ½ in. (12 mm) thick.

6. Bake at 325°F (160°C) until firm and dry, about 25 minutes.

Japonaise Meringues

Ingredients	U.S.	Egg Whites at 100% Metric	%
Egg whites	1 lb	500 g	100
Fine granulated sugar	1 lb	500 g	100
Confectioners' sugar, sifted	1 lb	500 g	100
Blanched hazelnuts or almonds, chopped very fine	1 lb	500 g	100
Total weight:	*4 lb*	*2000 g*	*400%*

■ **P r o c e d u r e**

1. Prepare baking sheets by lining them with silicone paper. Draw circles of the desired size on the paper, using cake pans or other round objects as guides.

2. With the whip attachment, beat the egg whites at medium speed until they form soft peaks.

3. Add the granulated sugar, a little at a time, with the machine running. Whip until the meringue forms stiff peaks.

4. Stop the machine. Mix together the confectioners' sugar and nuts. Fold this mixture into the meringue.

5. Using a pastry bag with a ½-in. (12 mm) plain tube, fill in the circles on the baking sheets by making spirals starting in the center of each circle, as on page 260. Each circle should be filled with a layer of meringue about ½ in. (12 mm) thick.

6. Bake at 250°F (120°C) until meringue is crisp and very lightly browned, about 1½ to 2 hours.

7. Use in place of or in addition to cake layers in assembling cakes and gâteaux (chapter 13).

Marly Sponge

Ingredients	U.S.		Egg whites at 100% Metric	%
Powdered almonds	5	oz	150 g	60
Cake flour	2.25	oz	70 g	28
Sugar	8	oz	250 g	100
Egg whites	8	oz	250 g	100
Sugar	5	oz	150 g	60
Total weight:	*1 lb 12*	*oz*	*870 g*	*248%*

■ **P r o c e d u r e**

1. Sift the almonds, flour, and first quantity of sugar.

2. Whip the egg whites to soft peaks. Add the second quantity of sugar and whip to firm peaks.

3. Fold in the almond powder mixture.

4. Line sheet pans with parchment paper. Using a pastry bag with a plain tip, pipe disks of desired size, using the technique on page 260.

5. Bake at 350°F (180°C) for 12–15 minutes.

Coconut Dacquoise

Ingredients	U.S.		Egg whites at 100% Metric	%
Powdered almonds	3	oz	90 g	60
Sugar	4	oz	120 g	80
Cake flour	1.5	oz	42 g	28
Coconut, grated	0.5	oz	15 g	10
Egg whites	5	oz	150 g	100
Sugar	4	oz	120 g	80
Total weight:	*1 lb 2*	*oz*	*537 g*	*358%*

■ **P r o c e d u r e**

1. Sift together the almond powder, first quantity of sugar, and flour. Stir in the coconut.

2. Whip the egg whites to soft peaks, add the second quantity of sugar, and continue whipping to firm peaks.

3. Add the sifted dry ingredients and fold in.

4. Line sheet pans with parchment paper. Using a pastry bag with a medium plain tip, pipe disks of the desired size, using the technique shown on page 260.

5. Bake at 350°F (180°C) for 10 minutes or until golden.

Hazelnut Coconut Sponge

Ingredients	U.S.		Egg whites at 100% Metric	%
Powdered hazelnuts	5	oz	150 g	83
Confectioners' sugar	4	oz	120 g	67
Cake flour	1	oz	30 g	17
Coconut, grated	1.16	oz	35 g	19
Egg whites	6	oz	180 g	100
Granulated sugar	3	oz	90 g	50
Total weight:	*1 lb 4*	*oz*	*605 g*	*336%*

■ **P r o c e d u r e**

1. Sift together the hazelnuts, confectioners' sugar, cake flour. Stir in the coconut.

2. Whip the egg whites and sugar to firm peaks.

3. Fold in the dry ingredients.

4. Using a medium plain tip, pipe the mixture onto parchment-lined pans into disks of desired size, as shown on page 260.

5. Bake at 350°F (180°C) for 10–12 minutes.

Succès

For large-quantity measurements, see page 603.

Ingredients	U.S.	Egg whites at 100% Metric	%
Egg whites	6 oz	180 g	100
Granulated sugar	4 oz	120 g	67
Powdered almonds	4 oz	120 g	67
Confectioners' sugar	4 oz	120 g	67
Cake flour	1 oz	30 g	17
Total weight:	*1 lb 3 oz*	*570 g*	*318%*

■ P r o c e d u r e

1. *Make a French meringue:* Whip the egg whites until they form soft peaks. Add the granulated sugar and whip until the meringue is stiff and glossy.

2. Sift together the remaining ingredients. Fold into the meringue.

3. Line sheet pans with parchment paper. Using a pastry bag with a plain tip, pipe disks of desired size, using the technique shown on page 260.

4. Bake at 350°F (180°C) until dry to the touch, but not completely hardened. About 20–30 minutes.

Variations

Progrès

This mixture can also be prepared with powdered hazelnuts, in which case it is more properly called *Progrès*. (The final *s* is not pronounced in either Succès or Progrès.)

Note that this preparation is similar to Marly Sponge (p. 262).

Pistachio Macaroon Sponge

Ingredients	U.S.		Egg whites at 100% Metric	%
Almond paste	9	oz	270 g	90
Heavy cream	2.5	oz	75 g	25
Green pistachio paste	2	oz	60 g	20
Egg whites	10	oz	300 g	100
Sugar	4	oz	120 g	40
Total weight:	*1 lb 11*	*oz*	*825 g*	*275%*

■ P r o c e d u r e

1. Soften the almond paste with the heavy cream. Heat the mixture to 105°F (40°C).

2. Mix in the pistachio paste.

3. Whip the egg whites to soft peaks. Add the sugar and whip to firm peaks.

4. Fold into the almond paste mixture.

5. Line sheet pans with parchment paper. Using a pastry bag with a medium plain tip, pipe disks of the desired size, using the technique shown on page 260.

6. Bake at 350°F (180°C) for 8 minutes.

Chocolate Heads

Components

Common Meringue (p. 182) or
 Chocolate Meringue (p. 182)

Chocolate Buttercream (p. 336)

Grated chocolate or chocolate
 sprinkles

■ P r o c e d u r e

1. Prepare shells as for Meringue Chantilly (p. 264).

2. Sandwich two shells together with chocolate buttercream.

3. Refrigerate shells until firm.

4. Spread each meringue sandwich with more chocolate buttercream so that it is completely covered.

5. Roll in grated chocolate or chocolate sprinkles.

Meringue Chantilly

Components

Common Meringue (p. 182),
Chocolate Meringue (p. 182), or
Swiss Meringue (p. 183)
Crème Chantilly (p. 181)

■ P r o c e d u r e

1. Shape the meringue into round mounds about 2 in. (5 cm) in diameter, using a ¾-in. (2 cm) plain tube in the pastry bag. Bake.

2. Optional step to allow more room for cream filling: When the shells are firm enough to handle but not completely crisp, remove them from the baking sheet; with your thumb, press a hollow in the base (the flat side). Return them to the oven to finish baking.

3. Cool shells and store them in a dry place until needed.

4. Just before serving, sandwich two shells together with crème Chantilly. Place the filled shells on their sides in paper cases.

5. Using a pastry bag with a star tube, decorate with additional whipped cream in the space between the shells.

6. If desired, the cream may be decorated with nuts or candied fruit.

Meringue Glacée

Components

Common Meringue (p. 182),
Chocolate Meringue (p. 182),
or Swiss Meringue (p. 183)
Ice cream
Whipped Cream

■ P r o c e d u r e

1. Prepare meringue shells as for **Meringue Chantilly.**

2. Sandwich two shells together with ice cream instead of crème Chantilly.

3. Decorate with whipped cream.

Meringue Mushrooms

Components

Common Meringue (p. 182)

■ P r o c e d u r e

These are used primarily for decorating Bûche de Noël (Christmas cake roll), page 387.

1. Using a pastry bag with a small, plain tube, make small mounds of meringue in the shapes of mushroom caps. Make smaller, pointed mounds to use as stems.

2. If desired, sprinkle very lightly with cocoa.

3. Bake as for Crisp Baked Meringues (p. 260).

4. When baked, make a small hole in the bottoms of the caps. Attach the stems with meringue or royal icing.

Meringue Cream Cakes

Components

Japonaise Meringues (p. 261)
Buttercream (p. 335)

■ P r o c e d u r e

1. For each cake, you will need two 2½-in. (6–7 cm) Japonaise Meringues and about 2 oz (60 g) buttercream in any flavor.

2. Spread one japonaise circle with a thin layer of buttercream. Top with a second circle.

3. Ice the top and sides smoothly.

4. If desired, iced cakes may be coated with chopped nuts, grated chocolate, toasted coconut, etc.

Vacherin

Components

Common Meringue (p. 182),
   Chocolate Meringue (p. 182),
   or Swiss Meringue (p. 183)
Sweetened whipped cream
Fruit of choice
Sponge cake, cubed, moistened
   with flavored syrup
   (*optional*)
Fresh or candied fruit

■ P r o c e d u r e

1. For a large Vacherin, draw 8-in. (20 cm) or 9-in. (23 cm) circles on sheets of parchment, using a cake pan as a guide. For individual Vacherins, draw 2½-in. (6–7 cm) circles.

2. Using a pastry bag with a plain tube, make one meringue base for each Vacherin. Do this by making a spiral starting in the center of a circle and continuing until the circle is filled in with a layer of meringue about ½ in. (12 mm) thick.

3. For the sides of the Vacherin, make rings of meringue the same size as the bases. For each large vacherin, you will need four or five rings. For each individual Vacherin, make two rings.

4. Bake as for Crisp Baked Meringues (p. 260).

5. Carefully remove the baked meringues from the parchment. Be especially careful with the rings, as they are fragile.

6. Stack the rings on the bases, using additional unbaked meringue to stick the pieces together.

7. If the rings are neatly and uniformly made, you may leave the shell as is. If the sides are not attractive, you may spread the sides of the shell smoothly with fresh meringue, or you may later ice the sides of the finished shell with buttercream.

8. Bake the shells again to dry out the fresh meringue. Cool.

9. Fill the shells with sweetened whipped cream and fruit (such as strawberries or sliced peaches). Cubes of sponge cake moistened with a flavored syrup may be used in addition to fruit.

10. Using a pastry bag, decorate the top with more whipped cream. Also, arrange pieces of fresh or candied fruit in an attractive pattern on the top.

▶ TERMS FOR REVIEW

pâte brisée	blitz puff pastry	pâte à choux	phyllo dough
short dough	reversed puff pastry	éclair	baked meringue
puff pastry	napoleon	strudel dough	japonaise
three-fold	éclair paste	strudel	meringue glacée
four-fold			

▶ QUESTIONS FOR REVIEW

1. Compare the mixing method for pâte brisée with the mixing method for short dough.

2. Describe two methods for enclosing the butter when making puff pastry.

3. Compare the mixing methods for puff pastry dough and blitz puff dough. Compare blitz puff dough and flaky pie dough.

4. What might happen to patty shells during baking if the puff dough is not relaxed before cutting and baking? What might happen to them if they are cut out of soft dough with a dull cutter?

5. Why is it important to bake cream puffs and éclairs thoroughly and to cool them slowly?

6. What precautions must you take when handling frozen commercial phyllo/strudel dough?

7. In order to bake meringue shells until crisp, should you use a hot, moderate, or cool oven? Why?

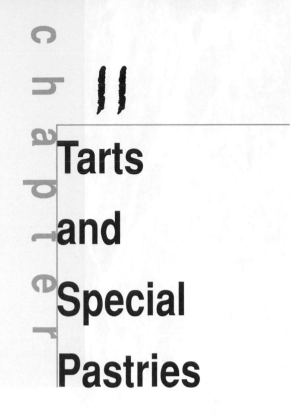

chapter 11

Tarts and Special Pastries

To many bakers, pastry work is the most exciting and challenging part of their careers. It offers unlimited scope for developing artistic creativity and it gives them opportunities for displaying their decorative skills. The basic doughs that you learned in the preceding chapter combined with the creams and icings in other chapters are the components for a nearly infinite variety of delicious and eye-appealing desserts and sweets.

Chapter 10 presented the principal pastry doughs in detail. Procedures for preparing simple items were included for all these preparations, except for short doughs, to help you become familiar with handling them. This chapter continues the study of pastries with more elaborate and advanced pastries.

The chapter is divided into two parts. The first explains the production of baked and unbaked tarts and presents a wide variety of recipes as examples. The remainder of the chapter is devoted to a selection of other special pastries, including modern creations as well as classic favorites.

TARTS AND TARTLETS

A tart is not just a pie without a top crust. Although they may resemble pies, tarts are actually more closely related to other European-style pastries. They are light, usually less than 1 inch (2.5 cm) thick, and often very colorful. Their appearance usually depends on a pattern of carefully arranged fruit. Tartlets are basically the same as tarts but prepared in small, individual-portion sizes.

Unlike pie pans, tart pans are shallow and straight-sided—that is, with sides that are perpendicular to the base. Often the sides are fluted. Because tarts are usually removed from the pans before serving, false-bottom pans are easiest to use. To remove a tart from a false-bottom pan, first remove the outside ring, then slide the tart from the flat base onto a cardboard circle or onto a serving dish. A flan ring, which is a simple metal hoop, is another form of tart pan. When a flan ring is placed on a baking sheet, it forms the side of the pan and the baking sheet serves as the bottom.

Small tartlet pans are not false-bottomed. Because the tartlets are quite small, it is easy to remove them from their tins. The tins may have straight or sloping sides, which may or may not be fluted.

Tarts need not be round. Square and rectangular tarts are also made, especially when puff pastry is used instead of short dough or pie pastry (see p. 242).

Because tarts contain less filling than pies do, the flavor of the dough is very important. Although regular pie dough can be used, the richer, buttery flavor of pâte brisée (p. 230) and short dough (p. 232) make them better choices. Short dough is a little harder to handle than enriched pie pastry, so it is used most often for individual tartlets. Almond short dough can also be used for tartlets.

The procedure on page 269 explains the method for making baked tart shells. Baked shells are most often filled with pastry cream, topped with fruit, and served without baking. The procedure for making unbaked tarts is illustrated in the recipe for Fresh Fruit Tart (p. 270). Small tartlets are made using the same procedure.

Baked tart shells may also be made of puff pastry dough, as explained on page 242.

BAKED TARTS

In its simplest form, a baked fruit tart is nothing more than an unbaked tart shell filled with a layer of fresh fruit and a little sugar and then baked. Many types of fruits may be used; the most popular are apples, pears, peaches, plums, apricots, and cherries.

A number of variations on this theme are possible, allowing you to create a wide variety of tarts. The following are among the more popular varieties:

1. When using juicy fruits, sprinkle the bottom of the tart shell with a thin layer of cake crumbs, cookie crumbs, or even breadcrumbs. These absorb some of the excess juices during baking and also contribute to the texture and flavor of the filling.

2. Chopped nuts may also be sprinkled in the bottom of the tart shell.

3. Frangipane (p. 118) may be spread on the bottom of the shell. This creates a rich, luxuriously almond-flavored fruit tart.

Procedure for Making Baked Tart Shells

This procedure is for making large tart shells. For individual tartlet shells, see the following variation.

1. Remove short dough or pâte brisée from refrigerator. Scale the dough as required.

   10–12 oz (300–340 g) for 10-in. (25 cm) tarts

   8–10 oz (225–300 g) for 9-in. (23 cm) tarts

   6–8 oz (175–225 g) for 8-in. (20 cm) tarts

   4–5 oz (115–140 g) for 6-in. (15 cm) tarts

2. Let the dough stand a few minutes or work it briefly with the hands to make it pliable. Dough should be cold, but if it is too cold and hard, it is difficult to roll out without cracking.

3. Roll out the dough on a floured surface or floured canvas. Pâte brisée should be rolled to about $\frac{1}{8}$ in. (3 mm) thick. Short dough can be a little thicker, slightly less than $\frac{1}{4}$ in. (5 mm).

4. Place the dough in the tart pan. To lift the dough without breaking it, roll it loosely around the rolling pin. Allow the dough to drop into the pan and then press it into the corners without stretching it. Stretched dough shrinks during baking.

5. Flute edges, if desired, and trim off excess dough. At this point, the dough is ready to be filled with the fillings that are to be baked in the shell. For tart shells that are to be baked empty, continue with step 6.

6. Prick the bottom of the dough all over with a fork (this is called *docking*). Line the shell with parchment and fill it with dried beans. These two steps keep the crust from puffing and blistering during baking.

7. Bake at 400°F (200°C) until shells are fully baked and lightly browned, about 20 minutes. Remove the paper liners and beans. If the centers of the shells are still slightly underbaked, return them to the oven and bake for a few minutes more.

8. Cool the shells completely.

Procedure Variation: Small Tartlet Shells

Individual tartlet molds come in many shapes, including plain round, fluted round, rectangular, and barquette (boat-shaped).

Method 1

1. Arrange the tartlet shells close together on the work surface so that there is as little space as possible between them. Different shapes may be used at the same time, as long as they are the same height.

2. Roll out the dough as in the basic procedure.

3. Lift the dough by rolling it loosely around the rolling pin. Drape it over the tartlet shells. Let the dough settle into the tins.

4. Run the rolling pin over the top of the dough to cut it off at the edges of the tins.

5. Using a small ball of scrap dough, press the pastry firmly into the shells.

6. Continue as in the basic procedure (step 5).

Method 2: For Round Shells Only

1. Roll out the dough as in the basic procedure.

2. With a round cutter about $\frac{1}{2}$ in. (1 cm) larger than the top diameter of the tartlet shells, cut the dough into circles.

3. For each shell, fit a circle of dough into a tin and press it well against the bottom and sides. If you are using fluted tins, make sure the dough is thick enough on the sides so that it won't break apart at the ridges.

4. Continue as in the basic procedure.

4. Pastry cream (pp. 187–188) may be used in place of frangipane cream, especially for small, individual tartlets. Arrange the fruit so that it covers the cream completely.

5. If the raw fruit is hard (some apples, pears, and plums, for example), it may not cook to tenderness in the time it takes to bake the pastry. This is especially true if frangipane or pastry cream is used under the fruit. In such cases, precook the fruit by poaching it in syrup (p. 491) or sautéing it in butter and sugar.

6. Before serving or displaying fruit tarts for sale, dress them up by brushing them with a glaze or by dusting them lightly with confectioners' sugar.

Quantity Notice

Ingredient quantities in the following recipes may need to be adjusted. For example, especially sour fruit may need more sugar. Also, fruit may yield more or less than average quantities after trimming (peeling, pitting, etc.).

Fresh Fruit Tart

Yield: one 10-in. (25-cm) tart

Ingredients	U.S.	Metric
Fresh fruit (see Procedure)	1.5–2 lb	750–1000 g
Pastry Cream (pp. 187–188)	14 oz	400 g
10-in. (25 cm) baked tart shell	1	1
Apricot Glaze (p. 117)	4 oz or as needed	125 g or as needed

■ P r o c e d u r e

1. Select the fruit for the tart. Fresh fruit tarts may be made from all one fruit or a colorful combination of two or more fruits. Prepare fruit as necessary. Trim and wash. Cut large fruits such as peaches or pineapples into even slices or uniform bite-size pieces. Poach hard fruits such as apples or pears (see p. 491 for poaching methods). Drain all fruits well.

2. Spread a layer of pastry cream in the baked shell. Use enough pastry cream to fill it about half full.

3. Carefully arrange the fruit on top of the pastry cream.

4. Warm the apricot glaze and, if it is too thick, dilute it with a little water or simple syrup. Brush the glaze on the fruit to coat it completely.

Most of the recipes on pages 270–276 are for 10-in. (25 cm) tarts. For smaller tarts, *multiply or divide each ingredient quantity by the factors indicated below* to get the approximate quantities needed.

Tart size	Factor
9-in. (23 cm)	multiply by 0.8 (or $\frac{4}{5}$)
8-in. (20 cm)	multiply by 0.66 (or $\frac{2}{3}$)
7-in. (18 cm)	divide by 2
6-in. (15 cm)	divide by 3
5-in. (13 cm)	divide by 4
4-in. (10 cm)	divide by 6
3-in. (7.5 cm)	divide by 10

Apple Tart

Yield: one 10-in. (25 cm) tart

Ingredients	U.S.	Metric
Firm, flavorful cooking apples	1 lb 12 oz	750 g
10-in. (25 cm) unbaked tart shell	1	1
Sugar	3 oz	90 g
Apricot Glaze (p. 117)	as needed	as needed

■ P r o c e d u r e

1. Peel, core, and cut the apples into thin slices. You should have about 1 lb 6 oz (600 g) apple slices.

2. Arrange the apple slices in the tart shell. Save the best, most uniform slices for the top; arrange them shingle-fashion in concentric rings.

3. Sprinkle the sugar evenly over the apples.

4. Bake at 400°F (200°C) about 45 minutes or until the pastry is browned and the apples are tender.

5. Cool. Brush with apricot glaze.

Variations

Saving enough of the best slices for a top layer, chop the rest of the apples and cook them with 2 oz (60 g) of the sugar and $\frac{1}{2}$ oz (15 g) butter until they make a thick applesauce. Cool and spread in the bottom of the tart shell. Arrange apple slices on top. Sprinkle with remaining sugar and bake.

If apple slices are very hard, sauté them lightly in 1 to 2 oz (30 to 60 g) butter and 1 oz (30 g) sugar until they begin to get soft and lightly browned. Turn them carefully to avoid breaking them. Proceed as in the basic recipe.

Plum, Apricot, Cherry, or Peach Tart

Follow the basic recipe, but sprinkle a thin layer of cake crumbs, cookie crumbs, or breadcrumbs in the unbaked shell before adding fruit. Adjust sugar according to the sweetness of the fruit.

Appropriate spices, such as cinnamon for plums or apples, may be added in small quantities.

Apple Custard Tart

Reduce the apples to 1 lb 4 oz/560 g (or 1 lb/450 g after peeling and coring). Reduce the sugar to 1.5 oz (45 g). Assemble and bake as in the basic recipe. When about half done, carefully pour in a custard mixture made by mixing the following ingredients.

Ingredients	U.S.	Metric
Milk	4 oz	120 mL
Heavy cream	4 oz	120 mL
Sugar	2 oz	60 g
Whole egg	1	1
Egg yolk	1	1
Vanilla extract	1 tsp	5 mL

Continue baking until set. Cool and dust with confectioners' sugar.

Pear Almond Tart

Yield: one 10-in. (25 cm) tart

Ingredients	U.S.	Metric
10-in. (25 cm) tart shell	1	1
Frangipane (p. 118) or Almond Cream (p.119)	12 oz	350 g
Pear halves, canned or poached	8	8
Apricot Glaze (p. 117)	as needed	as needed

■ P r o c e d u r e

1. Spread the frangipane filling evenly in the tart shell.

2. Drain the pears well. Cut them crosswise into thin slices, but keep the slices together in the shape of pear halves.

3. Arrange the sliced pear halves on top of the frangipane like spokes of a wheel. Do not cover all the filling with the pears. Push them gently into the cream.

4. Bake at 425°F (220°C) about 30 minutes.

5. Cool. Brush the top with apricot glaze.

Variations

Cooked or canned peaches, apples, apricots, plums, or cherries may be used instead of pears. For small fruits such as apricots, plums, and cherries, reduce the quantity of frangipane and use enough fruit to cover the top completely.

Fruit Tart with Pastry Cream
Omit the frangipane and, instead, cover the bottom of the tart shell with a ¹/₂-in. (1 cm) layer of pastry cream. Or use a mixture of 2 or 3 parts pastry cream blended smooth with 1 part almond paste. Cover the cream with a layer of fruit, arranged attractively.

Frangipane Tart
Omit the fruit. Spread the bottom of the tart shell with a thin layer of apricot jam. Fill with frangipane filling. Bake and cool. Instead of glazing, dust lightly with confectioners' sugar. This recipe is especially appropriate for small, individual tartlets.

Fruit Tartlets
The ingredients in the main recipe are the basis for all regular baked fruit tartlets. The following fresh or cooked fruits are the most commonly used: apples, pears, cherries, blueberries, pears, apricots, peaches, nectarines. Use only one type of fruit per tartlet. Approximately the following quantities will be needed for ten 3-in. (8 cm) tartlets.

Ingredients	U.S.	Metric
Short Dough (p. 232) or Pâte Sucrée (p. 231)	12 oz	350 g
Frangipane (p. 118) or Almond Cream (p. 119)	14 oz	400 g
Fruit	8–14 oz	250–400 g
Apricot Glaze (p. 117)	3–4 oz	90–120 g

Lemon Tart

Yield: one 10-in. (25 cm) tart

Ingredients	U.S.	Metric
10-in. (25 cm) tart shell	1	1
Sugar	4 oz	120 g
Lemon zest, grated	1 tbsp	15 g
Eggs	4	4
Lemon juice	6 oz	175 mL
Heavy cream	2 oz	60 mL

■ P r o c e d u r e

1. Bake the tart shell until it is golden but not too brown. Cool.

2. In a mixer with the paddle attachment, blend the sugar and zest together thoroughly.

3. Add the eggs. Mix until well combined, but do not whip.

4. Mix in first the lemon juice and then the cream. Pass the mixture through a strainer.

5. Pour the strained filling into the tart shell. Bake at 350°F (175°C) until the filling is set, about 25 minutes.

Variation

Arrange a few fresh raspberries on top of the tart. Dust lightly with confectioners' sugar.

Chocolate Tart

Yield: one 10-in. (25 cm) tart

Ingredients	U.S.	Metric
10-in. (25 cm) tart shell made with Short Dough (p. 232)	1	1
Heavy cream	6 oz	175 mL
Milk	6 oz	175 mL
Bittersweet chocolate	8 oz	240 g
Egg	1	1

■ P r o c e d u r e

1. Roll the short dough as thin as possible when making the tart shell. Bake until golden, but not too brown. Cool.

2. Combine the cream and milk. Bring to a simmer and remove from the heat.

3. Add the chocolate. Stir in until completely melted and blended uniformly with the cream.

4. Beat the egg lightly in a bowl. Gradually stir in the warm chocolate mixture.

5. Pour the chocolate into the tart shell. Bake at 375°F (190°C) until set, about 15 minutes.

Variation

Chocolate Banana Tart

In addition to the ingredients above, assemble the following:

Ingredients	U.S.	Metric
Ripe banana	1	1
Lemon juice	0.5 oz	15 g
Butter	0.5 oz	15 g
Sugar	1.5 oz	45 g

Slice the banana and toss gently with the lemon juice. Heat the butter in a nonstick sauté pan over high heat. Add the banana and then the sugar. Sauté over high heat so that the bananas brown and become coated in the caramelized sugar. Do not cook until they are soft and mushy. Transfer to a sheet pan lined with parchment and let cool. Arrange the caramelized bananas in the bottom of the tart shell before pouring in the chocolate mixture. Proceed as in the basic recipe.

Tarte Tatin

Yield: one 9-in. (23 cm) tart

Ingredients	U.S.	Metric
Apples	3 lb	1500 g
Butter	3 oz	100 g
Sugar	8 oz	250 g
Puff Pastry (pp. 236–237), Blitz Puff Pastry (p. 237), Flaky Pie Dough (p. 204), or Pâte Brisée (p. 230)	8 oz	250 g

■ Procedure

1. Peel the apples, cut them in half vertically, and remove the cores.

2. Select a heavy 10-in. (25 cm) skillet or sauté pan (a 10-in. skillet is needed to make a 9-in. tart). Melt the butter in the skillet. Cover the butter with the sugar in an even layer.

3. Arrange the apples in the pan on top of the sugar. Start by standing the apple halves on end in a circle around the sides of the pan. Fill in the center with the remaining apple halves. The pan should be completely full of apple halves standing on their edges and leaning against each other. They should protrude above the rim of the pan, but they will sink as they cook, making a tart about 1½ in. (4 cm) thick.

4. Set the pan over moderate heat and cook until the bottoms of the apples are soft and the juices are thick and syrupy, about 30 minutes. The tops of the apples will be barely cooked but will cook when the tart is baked. Remove from the heat and let cool slightly.

5. Roll out the pastry and cut a circle to fit over the top of the apples. Lay the pastry circle in place on top of the apples.

6. Bake at 425°F (220°C) about 30–40 minutes, until the pastry is brown and the apples are well caramelized.

7. Let the tart stand to cool slightly. The juices will gel or will be partially reabsorbed so that the tart can be turned out. Place a cake circle or a platter over the pan, then invert the pan and circle or platter to turn out the tart. The tops of the apples should have a rich caramel color. If more shine is desired, the top can be dusted with sugar and caramelized under a broiler. Serve warm or at room temperature.

Variations

Pear Tarte Tatin and Peach Tarte Tatin
Although these are not traditional, they may be made following the basic procedure, substituting pears or peaches for the apples.

Note on terminology: Do not call these desserts "Tatins." They are tarts. The term *Tatin* indicates what type of tart they are. *Tarte Tatin* is a shortened form of a French expression meaning, approximately, "Tart made in the style of the Tatin sisters." These ladies owned a small hotel in the Loire Valley, where they became famous for this apple tart.

Orange Brulée Tart

Yield: one 8-in. (20 cm) tart

Ingredients	U.S.		Metric
Orange juice	2.5	oz	75 g
Sugar	4	oz	125 g
Orange zest, grated	0.14	oz (1¾ tsp)	4 g
Butter	3.5	oz	100 g
Whole eggs	2		2
Egg yolks	4		4
Sugar	3.5	oz	100 g
Cornstarch	0.5	oz	15 g
Prebaked 8-in. (20 cm) tart shell made with Short Pastry II (p. 232)	1		1
Fine granulated sugar	as needed		as needed
Optional garnish			
Orange segments	as needed		as needed
Apricot Glaze (p. 117)	as needed		as needed

■ Procedure

1. Heat together the juice, first quantity of sugar, zest, and butter until the sugar is dissolved.

2. Whip the eggs, egg yolks, and remaining sugar until the sugar is dissolved.

3. Stir the cornstarch into the egg mixture.

4. Bring the juice mixture to a boil. Temper the egg mixture by gradually beating in half the orange juice mixture, then return this mixture to the pan with the rest of the orange juice.

5. Heat, stirring constantly, and bring back to a boil. Boil for 1 minute,

6. Pour the mixture into a bowl and cool in an ice-water bath, stirring.

7. Pour the mixture into the prebaked tart shell.

8. Sprinkle the surface with a thin, even layer of sugar. Heat under a salamander or with a blowtorch until the sugar is caramelized. (If using a salamander, mask the pastry rim with foil to prevent burning.)

9. Chill the tart to set the custard before cutting.

10. If desired, decorate the top with orange segments just before serving. Brush the orange segments with apricot glaze.

Caramelized Apple Tart with Vanilla

Yield: one 10-in. (25 cm) tart

Ingredients	U.S.		Metric
Firm, flavorful cooking apples	2 lb 12	oz	1300 g
Butter	2	oz	60 g
Vanilla extract	0.33	oz (2 tsp)	10 g
10-in. (25 cm) unbaked tart shell made with Pâte Brisée (p. 230)	1		
Sugar	3	oz	90 g

■ Procedure

1. Peel the apples. Cut them into quarters and remove the cores. Cut each quarter in half to make two thick wedges.

2. Heat the butter in a large sauté pan over high heat. Add the apples and sauté for about 15 minutes, until the apples are lightly golden and soft but still holding their shapes. Adjust the heat as necessary; the heat should be high enough so that the apples do not simmer in their own juices, but not so high that they become too brown.

3. Add the vanilla and sauté another 5 seconds. Remove from the heat and cool completely.

4. Arrange the apples in the tart shell. Sprinkle evenly with sugar.

5. Bake at 375°F (190°C) for 50–60 minutes, until the pastry has browned and the apples are lightly caramelized.

6. Serve warm (reheat if necessary).

Walnut Tart

Yield: one 10-in. (25 cm) tart

Ingredients	U.S.	Metric
Brown sugar	8 oz	225 g
Butter	2 oz	55 g
Eggs	3	3
Flour	1 oz	30 g
Cinnamon	½ tsp	2 mL
Walnuts, broken or coarsely chopped	12 oz	340 g
Unbaked 10-in. tart shell	1	1
Chocolate Glaçage (p. 343) or tempered chocolate	as needed	as needed

■ P r o c e d u r e

1. Cream the butter and sugar until well blended.
2. Beat in the eggs one at a time, waiting until one is absorbed before adding the next.
3. Add the flour and cinnamon. Blend in well.
4. Mix in the nuts.
5. Transfer the mixture to the tart shell. Bake at 350°F (175°C) for about 40 minutes until the pastry is golden and the filling is set.
6. Cool completely.
7. Using a paper cone (see pp. 352–353), drizzle the chocolate glaçage very lightly over the tart in a crosshatch pattern. Let stand until the chocolate is set.

Linzertorte

Yield: one 10-in. (25 cm) tart

Ingredients	U.S.	Metric
Linzer Dough (p. 232)	1 lb 8 oz	700 g
Raspberry jam	14 oz (1¼ cups)	400 g

Note   This famous Austrian pastry is called a torte but it is actually a tart filled with raspberry jam.

■ P r o c e d u r e

1. Roll out about two-thirds of the linzer dough to about ⅓–¼ in. (6–8 mm) thick.
2. Line a greased 10-in. (25 cm) tart pan with the dough.
3. Spread the jam evenly in the shell.
4. Roll out the remaining dough and cut it into strips about ⅜ in. (1 cm) wide. Arrange the strips in a lattice pattern on top of the tarts. The strips should be at an angle so that they form diamond shapes rather than squares.
5. Turn down the sides of the dough shell to make a border and to cover the ends of the lattice strips.
6. Bake at 375°F (190°C) for 35–40 minutes.

Peasant Tart

Yield: two 8-in. (20 cm) tarts

Ingredients	U.S.		Metric
Marinated prunes			
Prunes, pitted and coarsely chopped	10	oz	300 g
Raisins	1.75	oz	50 g
Sugar	3.5	oz	100 g
Cinnamon stick	1		1
Tea bag	1		1
Armagnac	1.33	oz (8 tsp)	40 g
Water	3.5	oz	100 g
Custard filling			
Milk	3.5	oz	100 g
Heavy cream	4	oz	125 g
Vanilla extract	½	tsp	2 g
Cinnamon stick	1		1
Armagnac	1.33	oz (8 tsp)	40 g
Sugar	1.17	oz (6½ tsp)	35 g
Honey	2.5	oz	75 g
Eggs	7	oz	200 g
Cornstarch	1¼	tsp	3 g
Flour	1	oz	30 g
Topping			
Pine nuts	1.67	oz	40 g
Blanched almonds, chopped	1.67	oz	40 g
Hazelnuts, whole	1.67	oz	40 g
Sugar	1.67	oz	40 g
Butter	2	tsp	10 g
Flour	5.5	oz	160 g
Cinnamon	2	tsp	4 g
Butter	3	oz	80 g
Sugar	3	oz	80 g
8-in. (20 cm) baked tart shells made with Pâte Brisée (p. 230)	2		2
Cinnamon	4	tsp	8 g
Confectioners' sugar	0.33	oz (4 tsp)	10 g

■ Procedure

Marinated Prunes

1. Combine all the ingredients for the marinated prunes in a saucepan. Heat until the sugar dissolves.

2. Poach gently for 15 minutes, until the prunes are tender. Drain. Discard the cinnamon stick.

Custard Filling

1. Heat the milk, cream, vanilla, cinnamon stick, and Armagnac to just below the simmer. Let stand for 30 minutes. Strain.

2. Whip together the sugar, honey, and eggs. Add the cornstarch and flour and mix until smooth.

3. Pour the milk into the egg mixture and mix well.

Topping

1. Lightly toast the pine nuts, almonds, and hazelnuts.

2. Cook the sugar to a golden caramel and stir in the butter.

3. Fold in the warm nuts and cook over low heat until the nuts separate.

4. Pour onto an oiled marble slab, separating the nuts as they cool.

5. Sift the flour and cinnamon. Rub in the butter until it resembles fine breadcrumbs.

6. Stir in the sugar and caramelized nuts.

Assembly and Baking

1. Place the drained prunes and raisins in the bottom of the baked tart shells.

2. Pour in the custard filling.

3. Bake at 300°F (150°C) for about 10 minutes, until the top is just set.

4. Sprinkle the topping over the top. Dust with the remaining cinnamon.

5. Bake at 350°F (180°C) for about 18–20 minutes, until the tart is golden brown and looks dry.

6. Cool. Dust with confectioners' sugar.

SPECIAL PASTRIES

This section presents a collection of pastries of many types. The first three recipes are for famous classics based on puff pastry, pâte à choux, and short dough. These are items that all pastry chefs should know how to make well. The Gâteau St-Honoré is a spectacular assembly of choux pastry, short dough, caramel, and cream fillings. It is often decorated by placing a nest of spun sugar (p. 568) on top. The rich Pithiviers and the special napoleon or millefeuille (another name for napoleon—the word means "thousand leaves") test your ability to work with puff pastry.

The remaining recipes are mostly of the type sometimes known in North America as *French pastries.* They are individual portions made up of any of a number of creams, icings, Bavarian creams (from chapter 16) and layers of meringue, pastry, and even sponge cake. The first of these recipes, Passionata, is illustrated in detail to introduce you to the basic techniques for making this type of pastry. You can then apply the same techniques to other pastries in this section.

Gâteau St-Honoré

Yield: two 8-in. (20 cm) gâteaux

Ingredients	U.S.		Metric
Pâte Brisée (p. 230)	10	oz	300 g
Pâte à Choux (p. 248)	1 lb 4	oz	600 g
Egg wash			
Egg yolks	6		6
Whole egg	1		1
Sugar	¼	tsp	1 g
Salt	¼	tsp	1 g
Water	2	tsp	10 g
Vanilla Crème Diplomat (p. 191)	12–13	oz	385 g
Chocolate Crème Diplomat (p. 191)	14	oz	425 g
Caramel			
Fine granulated sugar	7	oz	200 g
Water	2	oz	60 g
Glucose or corn syrup	0.67	oz	20 g

This chapter focuses primarily on pastries that are based on the doughs and meringue-type mixtures in chapter 10, but cake layers (chapter 12) are often used as well. Many of the cakes in chapter 14 could also be presented as French pastries, as discussed on pages 348–349. Additional pastries based on cake batters are explained in that chapter. The most common way to make French pastries from cakes is to bake the cake layers as sheets rather than as rounds, cut the sheet cakes into long strips about 4 in. (10 cm) wide, and then slice the strips crosswise into portions, as explained on page 389. In the same way, you will note that several of the desserts in chapters 16 and 18 are made in large ring molds. These, too, can be made as individual pastries by assembling them in small ring molds instead.

Finally, the chapter includes a recipe for a popular pastry called *sfogliatelle* (pronounced "sfo lee ah tell eh"), a type of filled turnover from southern Italy. It is somewhat difficult to prepare. Follow the instructions carefully.

■ P r o c e d u r e

Preparing the Pastries

1. Chill the Pâte Brisée for at least 30 minutes before use.

2. Fit a pastry bag with a medium plain tip and fill with the pâte à choux.

3. Beat together the ingredients for the egg wash. (*Note:* You will not need the total quantity of egg wash. Reserve the remainder for another use.)

4. Roll out the pâte brisée about ⅛ in. (3 mm) thick into a long oval shape (large enough to cut the circles in the next step). Place on a buttered sheet pan and dock well. Chill.

5. Cut two 8-in. (20 cm) circles from the pastry. Leave the circles on the pan and remove the excess dough.

6. Brush around the edges of the circles with egg wash.

7. Pipe a thick band of pâte à choux around the edge of the pastry circles about 1 in. (2.5 cm) from the outer edge. Brush lightly with egg wash. Press down the choux pastry lightly by running the back of a fork along the top. Pipe an additional small spiral of choux pastry in the center of each circle.

8. Onto a buttered sheet pan, pipe the remaining choux pastry into ¾-in. (2 cm) bulbs and brush with egg wash. (This will make more bulbs than necessary for the finished pastry, allowing you to select those of the best appearance.)

9. Bake all the pastries at 375°F (190°C) until risen and golden and the bulbs sound hollow when tapped. Cool on wire racks.

Assembling the Gâteaux

1. Select the best choux bulbs for the finished pastries. You will need about 12–14 for each. Make a small hole in the bottom of each bulb and fill with Vanilla Crème Diplomat, using a pastry bag.

2. Spread a layer of Chocolate Crème Diplomat in the bottom of each pastry circle.

3. Fit two pastry bags with St-Honoré tips. Fill with the remaining creams.

4. Holding the bag so that the V-shaped point of the St-Honoré tip is up, pipe alternating lines of vanilla and chocolate creams to fill the pastry circles. See the photograph of the finished gâteau, as well as page 355, for piping with the St-Honoré tip. Chill the pastries.

5. Make a caramel by heating the sugar and water gently to dissolve the sugar. Bring to a boil, add the glucose, and cook until golden. Plunge the base of the pan into ice water briefly to stop the cooking.

6. Dip the filled choux bulbs into the caramel and then place caramel-side down onto an oiled marble slab until cold.

7. Reheat the remaining caramel and use to glue the bulbs around the edges of the pastry circles, keeping the flat caramel tops of the bulbs as level as possible.

Praline Millefeuille

Yield: one pastry, about 6 × 10 in. (15 × 25 cm), weighing approximately 2½ lb (1200 g)

Ingredients	U.S.	Metric
Classic Puff Pastry (p. 236)	1 lb 4 oz	630 g
Confectioners' sugar	as needed	as needed
Praline Cream (p. 450)	1 lb	500 g
Praline Pailletine (recipe below)	5 oz	150 g
Garnish		
Caramelized nuts	as desired	as desired

■ P r o c e d u r e

1. Roll out the puff pastry to a rectangle about 13 × 20 in. (33 × 52 cm). Place on a sheet pan lined with parchment paper. Dock the dough and refrigerate for 20 minutes.

2. Bake at 400°F (200°C). When the pastry is about four-fifths baked, remove from the oven and dredge generously with confectioners' sugar.

3. Increase the oven heat to 475°F (240°C). Return the pastry to the oven and bake until the sugar caramelizes, about 2–3 minutes.

4. Remove from the oven and let cool.

5. With a serrated knife, trim the edges of the pastry so that they are straight and square. Then cut crosswise into three equal rectangles. (Exact size depends on how much the pastry shrank; approximate size is indicated above in the yield.) Select the best of the three rectangles and reserve it for the top layer.

6. Spread one of the pastry rectangles with a layer of praline cream ⅝ in. (1.5 cm) thick. Cover with a second layer of pastry.

7. Top with the praline pailletine and then another layer of the praline cream.

8. Cover with the third layer of pastry.

9. Decorate the top as desired with caramelized nuts.

Praline Pailletine

Ingredients	U.S.		Metric
Milk chocolate couverture	1	oz	25 g
Cocoa butter	0.25	oz	6 g
Almond-hazelnut praline paste	4	oz	100 g
Ice cream wafers (pailletine), crushed	1	oz	25 g
Total weight:	*6*	*oz*	*156 g*

■ P r o c e d u r e

1. Melt the chocolate and cocoa butter in a bowl over a hot water bath.

2. Mix in the praline paste.

3. Add the crushed wafers and mix in.

4. To use in Praline Millefeuille (above), spread out on a sheet pan to a thickness of about ¼ in. (5 mm), making a rectangle about 6 × 10 in. (15 × 25 cm) or the same size as the pastry rectangles.

5. Place in the refrigerator to harden.

Mirabelle Pithiviers

Yield: two 8-in. (20 cm) pastries, about 11 oz (325 g) each

Ingredients	U.S.		Metric
Classic Puff Pastry (p. 236)	1 lb		500 g
Almond Cream (p. 119)	12	oz	370 g
Canned mirabelle plums, drained, syrup reserved (see variations)	5	oz	150 g
Egg wash			
Egg yolks	4	oz	120 g
Whole egg	1.67 oz (1 egg)		50 g (1 egg)
Sugar	¼	tsp	1 g
Salt	¼	tsp	1 g
Water	2	tsp	10 g

Note This quantity of pastry allows for about 7 oz (200 g) trimmings. Each Pithiviers uses about 5 oz (150 g) pastry. Chefs who can roll pastry to accurate dimensions can get by with less pastry to start.

■ P r o c e d u r e

1. Roll out the puff pastry to ⅛ in. (3 mm) thick. Place on a sheet pan lined with parchment. Cover with plastic film and chill.

2. Cut out two 8-in. (20 cm) and two 9-in. (23-cm) circles from the pastry. Chill again.

3. Beat together the ingredients for the egg wash.

4. For each pastry, brush egg wash around the outer edge of an 8-in. (20 cm) pastry disk. Dock the center.

5. Spread with a layer of almond cream, staying about 1–1½ in. (3–4 cm) from the edge.

6. Arrange the fruit on the top of the almond cream.

7. With a pastry bag, pipe the remaining almond cream over the plums to form a dome. Smooth with a palette knife.

8. Cover with the 9-in. (23 cm) pastry circle, pressing lightly to remove any trapped air. Select a bowl slightly larger than the dome of almond cream and invert it over the pastry. Press down to seal.

9. Using a bottle cap cut in half, cut a scalloped edge around the edge. (This can also be done with a knife, but an even finish is harder to achieve.) Remove the pastry trimmings.

10. Brush the top of the pastry with egg wash. Allow to dry in the refrigerator. Repeat with another layer of egg wash and again allow to dry.

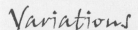

11. With a paring knife, cut a pinwheel pattern in the top, stopping short of the scalloped edge.

12. If desired, score the scalloped edge lightly to decorate.

13. Bake at 375°F (190°C) until golden brown and well risen. Reduce the oven temperature to 325°F (160°C) and bake until a knife inserted in the center comes out clean. Total baking time is about 45 minutes.

14. Use the syrup from the canned fruit to brush the hot pastry and return to the oven at 425°F (220°C) until the syrup bubbles and the top is glazed.

15. Cool on a wire rack.

Variations

Other canned fruits, such as pears or apricots, may be used.

For a classic plain Pithiviers, omit the fruit and increase the quantity of almond cream.

Passionata

Yield: 12 pastries, about 5 oz (140 g) each

Ingredients	U.S.		Metric
Canned pineapple, drained	10	oz	300 g
Vanilla Syrup (p. 178)	6	oz	175 g
Rum	0.67 oz (4 tsp)		20 g
Coconut Dacquoise disks (p. 262), 2¾ in. (7 cm) in diameter	24		24
Passion Fruit Bavarian (p. 446)	2 lb		1000 g
Gelatin	0.1	oz	3 g
Fondant (p. 334)	5	oz	150 g
Passion fruit juice	3.5	oz	100 g
Passion fruit, fresh	1		1
Coconut, grated and toasted	as needed		as needed

■ P r o c e d u r e

1. Cut the pineapple into ¼ by ¾ in. pieces (5 mm by 2 cm). Add to the Vanilla Syrup. Simmer 10 minutes. Add the rum and flambé. Cool, then chill the mixture.

2. Select 12 ring molds 2¾ in. (7 cm) in diameter and 1½ in. (4 cm) high. Place a disk of dacquoise on a cake card and set a ring mold over it so that the disk is inside the mold. Trim the disks if necessary to fit snugly (a).

3. Drain the pineapple well and arrange half of it on top of the dacquoise.

4. Fill the molds halfway with Passion Fruit Bavarian (b).

a.

b.

c.

5. Cover with a second dacquoise disk and add the remaining pineapple. Fill to the top with the remaining Bavarian and smooth with a palette knife.

6. Place in the freezer until set.

7. Prepare the passion fruit mirror for the top. Soften the gelatin in water (see p. 39). Combine the fondant and passion fruit juice and bring to a boil. Add the gelatin. Stir to dissolve. Add the seeds and juice from a fresh passion fruit.

8. Spoon a thin layer of this mixture over the tops of the cold pastries to glaze; spread it to the edges with a palette knife (c). Allow to set.

9. Remove the ring molds by heating the sides gently with a blowtorch to release them (d). Lift off the mold (e).

10. Coat the sides of the pastries with coconut (f).

d.

e.

f.

Capucine Chocolate

Yield: 12 pastries, about 3½ oz (100 g) each

Ingredients	U.S.	Metric
Marly Sponge disks (p. 262), 2¾ in. (7 cm) in diameter	24	24
Chocolate Ganache II (p. 192)	1 lb 12 oz	775 g
Chocolate shavings	as needed	as needed
Confectioners' sugar	as needed	as needed
Chocolate Ganache (*optional*)	2 oz	60 g

■ P r o c e d u r e

1. For each pastry, place a disk of sponge inside a ring mold 2¾ in. (7 cm) in diameter and 1½ in. (4 cm) high. Trim the sponge disks as necessary to fit.

2. Cover the sponge disks with a layer of ganache about ¾ in. (2 cm) thick.

3. Top with a second sponge disk.

4. Place in the freezer until set.

5. Remove the ring molds, using a blowtorch to lightly warm the molds to release them.

6. Press chocolate shavings onto the sides of the pastries.

7. Sprinkle the tops with confectioners' sugar.

8. If desired, pipe about 1 tsp (5 g) ganache onto the centers of the tops of the pastries for additional decoration.

Nougatine Parisienne

Yield: 8 pastries, about 5 oz (150 g) each

Ingredients	U.S.		Metric
Pistachio Macaroon Sponge disks (p. 263), 2¾ in. (7 cm) in diameter	24		24
Caramelized Apricots (p. 505)	10	oz	300 g
Nougatine Cream (p. 450)	1 lb 8	oz	750 g
Dark chocolate	7	oz	200 g
Apricot Glaze (p. 117)	3.5	oz	100 g
Garnish			
Apricots	as needed		as needed
Pistachios	as needed		as needed

■ P r o c e d u r e

1. For each pastry, place a sponge disk in the bottom of a ring mold 2¾ in. (7 cm) in diameter.

2. Arrange half the caramelized apricots over the sponge disks.

3. Cover with half of the nougatine cream.

4. Place another sponge disk on top of the cream.

5. Arrange the remaining apricots over the disks.

6. Fill the molds with nougatine cream, smoothing the top with a palette knife.

7. Refrigerate or freeze until set.

8. Carefully remove the ring molds by using a blowtorch to warm the rings to release them.

9. Select strips of acetate with the same width as the height of the molds. Temper the chocolate (see p. 537) and spread over the strips as shown on pages 540–541.

10. While the chocolate is still soft, wrap around the pastries, chocolate side in, and allow to set.

11. Glaze the tops with apricot glaze and decorate as desired with pieces of apricot and pistachios.

12. Peel the acetate off the chocolate just before serving.

Chocolatines

Yield: 10 pastries, about 2½ oz (75 g) each

Ingredients	U.S.	Metric
Succès disks (p. 263), 2¾ in. (7 cm) in diameter	20	20
Chocolate Mousse I (p. 193)	14 oz	400 g
Confectioners' sugar	2 oz	60 g
Cocoa powder	1 oz	30 g

■ P r o c e d u r e

1. For each pastry, place a succès disk in the bottom of a ring mold 2¾ in. (7 cm) in diameter.
2. Fill about two-thirds full with chocolate mousse.
3. Top with a second succès disk and push down gently.
4. Fill the mold with additional chocolate mousse and smooth the top.
5. Chill several hours or overnight.
6. Remove the ring mold by warming it carefully and lifting off.
7. Sift together the confectioners' sugar and cocoa. Return the mixture to the sieve and sift the mixture over the tops of the pastries.

Creole Délices

Yield: 10 pastries, about 4 oz (120 g) each

Ingredients	U.S.	Metric
Raisins	5 oz	150 g
Dessert syrup (p. 178) flavored with rum	6 oz	180 g
Almond Meringue disks (p. 261), 2¾ in. (7 cm) in diameter	20	20
Liqueur Bavarian Cream (p. 441) flavored with dark rum	1 lb 10 oz	800 g
Chocolate Glaçage (p. 343)	5 oz	150 g

■ P r o c e d u r e

1. Combine the raisins and syrup in a small saucepan. Warm slightly, then remove from heat and let stand 1 hour to allow the raisins to soften. Drain well.
2. Place half the meringue disks in the bottoms of 10 ring molds 2¾ in. (7 cm) in diameter.
3. Mix the raisins with the Bavarian cream. Fill the molds half full with the cream. Cover with the remaining cream and smooth the tops. Chill or freeze until set.
4. Coat the tops with a thin layer of chocolate glaçage. Chill again until set.
5. Warm the ring molds very gently with a blowtorch and lift off.

Variation

Chocolate Rum Délices
Prepare as in the main recipe except with the following changes. Use only half the quantity of Bavarian cream and omit the raisins and syrup. Use the cream in the bottom layer as in the main recipe. After placing the second meringue disk in the mold, fill the mold with Chocolate Mousse I (p. 193). Chill or freeze until set. Glaze the top as in the main recipe.

Financiers au Café

Yield: about 150 pastries, $^1/_7$ oz (4 g) each

Ingredients	U.S.	Metric
Raisins	1.67 oz	40 g
Rum	2 oz	60 g
Cake flour	2.25 oz	65 g
Confectioners' sugar	6.5 oz	185 g
Powdered almonds	2.25 oz	65 g
Egg whites	4.5 oz	125 g
Butter, melted	4.5 oz	125 g
Coffee extract	1 drop	1 drop
Dark rum	3.5 oz	100 g
Honey	3.5 oz	100 g
Apricot Glaze (p. 117) or Clear Glaze (p. 116)	as needed	as needed

■ P r o c e d u r e

1. Macerate the raisins and rum for as long as possible (minimum 45 minutes).

2. Butter 1-in. (2.5 cm) round or boat-shaped molds.

3. Sift flour, sugar, and almonds into a bowl and make a well.

4. Lightly froth the egg whites with a fork. Pour into the well.

5. Cook the butter to a beurre noisette and pour into the well with the coffee extract.

6. Draw all the ingredients together to form a smooth paste.

7. Place the drained, marinated raisins into the prepared molds.

8. Pipe or spoon the mixture to fill the buttered molds three-quarters full.

9. Bake at 340°F (170°C) until firm. Remove from the molds and cool on a wire rack. Turn all the pastries bottom-side up.

10. Heat the rum and honey to scalding point. Spoon the mixture over the baked financiers and brush with apricot glaze or clear glaze.

11. Place into paper petit four cases.

Praline Cake (Pralinette)

Yield: 12 individual-serving cakes, about 4 oz (110 g) each

Ingredients	U.S.	Metric
Marjolaine Sponge Cake disks (p. 325), 2¾ in. (7 cm) in diameter	24	24
Light Praline Cream (p. 339)	1 lb 8 oz	680 g
Milk chocolate couverture	1 lb 4 oz–1 lb 12 oz	600–800 g
Cocoa powder	as needed	as needed

■ P r o c e d u r e

1. For each cake, place one sponge disk in the bottom of a ring mold 2¾ in. (7 cm) in diameter and 1½ in. (4 cm) in height.

2. Using a pastry bag with a large plain tip, fill the mold with praline cream to within ½ in. (1 cm) of the top.

3. Place another sponge disk on top. Refrigerate to set.

4. Remove the ring mold.

5. Following the procedure described for Feuille d'Automne, coat the bottoms of sheet pans with melted milk chocolate (see p. 377) and, with a scraper, cut long strips of the chocolate to cover the cakes. (*Note:* For more information and further illustration of this procedure, refer to the recipe for Feuille d'Automne, p. 377.)

6. Handling the chocolate as little and as lightly as possible, wrap it around the pastry.

7. Fold the top edge of the chocolate over the top of the pastry. Decorate the top with additional narrow strips of chocolate.

8. Sprinkle very lightly with cocoa powder.

Sfogliatelle

Yield: 10 large pastries, about 3½ oz (100 g) each or 20 small pastries, about 1¾ oz (50 g) each

Ingredients	U.S.	Metric	
Dough			
Bread flour	12 oz	375	g
Pastry flour	4 oz	125	g
Salt	1 tsp	5	g
Water	7 oz	215	g
Butter	4 oz	125	g
Lard or shortening	4 oz	125	g
Filling			
Water, cold	8 oz	250	g
Sugar	3 oz	90	g
Semolina	3 oz	90	g
Ricotta cheese	12 oz	375	g
Egg yolks	2	2	
Cinnamon extract	⅛ tsp	0.5	mL
Candied orange peel, finely diced	3 oz	90	g

■ P r o c e d u r e

1. To make the dough, sift the flour and salt into a bowl. Add the water and mix to make a dry dough. Turn the mixture out onto a work surface and knead until the dough holds together.

2. Set the rollers of a pasta machine at their widest opening. Pass the dough through the rollers and fold in half. Repeat until the dough is smooth and elastic. Wrap in plastic and rest for 1–2 hours in the refrigerator.

3. Cut the dough into four equal pieces. Pass each piece through the rollers, set the rollers closer together, and repeat until you reach the narrowest setting of the rollers. You should have four long, paper-thin strips of dough.

4. Melt together the butter and shortening or lard. Cool slightly.

5. Lay one strip of dough out on the workbench and brush heavily with the melted fat. Roll up tightly from one end until only about 1 in. of the strip remains. Move the roll back to the other end of the bench and lay the second strip out so that the beginning of the first strip butts up against the end of the first strip to make a continuous roll. Again, brush heavily with the fat and continue to roll up. If you are making large pastries, repeat with the third and fourth strip. You should now have a roll of dough about 6 in. (15 cm) long and 2½ in. (6 cm) thick. If you are making small pastries, make a new roll with the third and fourth strips of dough, so that you have two rolls about 6 in. (15 cm) long and 1¾ in. (4.5 cm) thick. Refrigerate for several hours. There will be some melted fat left over. Save it for step 10.

6. Prepare the filling. Combine the water, sugar, and semolina in a saucepan and mix until smooth. Bring to a boil over moderate heat, stirring constantly, and cook until the mixture is thick. Pass the ricotta through a fine sieve and add to the pan. Cook for 2 or 3 minutes more. Remove from the heat and add the remaining filling ingredients, beating in well. Place in a bowl, cover tightly with plastic film, and chill. When the mixture is cold, beat until smooth and transfer to a pastry bag with a medium plain tip.

7. Remove the dough rolls from refrigeration and square off the ends with a sharp knife. Carefully slice each dough roll into 10 slices ½ in. (1.25 cm) thick.

8. For each pastry, place a slice of the dough on the workbench. With a small, light rolling pin, roll the circle of dough from the center outward in all directions so that the layers of dough fan outward toward the edges of the circle. At this point, if it is warm in the bakeshop, chill the rolled-out slices briefly. Remove only a few at a time from refrigeration, because they are easier to work with if the fat between the layers is firm.

9. Pick up a circle of pastry with both hands, with the thumbs underneath and the fingers above the center of the circle. (The side that was up when the circle was rolled out should be on top.) Carefully shape the circle into a cone by working the thumbs into the center of the circle and working outward so that the layers of dough slide away from each other. The side that was on top during rolling should be the outside of the cone. Hold the cone in one hand and, using the pastry bag, fill it with about 1 oz (30 g) filling for small pastries, 2 oz (60 g) for large pastries.

10. Lay the pastries on their sides on a sheet pan lined with parchment. Brush with the remaining fat.

11. Bake at 400°F (200°C) until golden, about 25–30 minutes.

Gâteau Succès

Yield: 1 gâteau, 7 in. (18 cm) in diameter

Ingredients	U.S.		Metric
Succès layers (p. 263), 7 in. (18 cm) in diameter	2		2
Praline Buttercream (p. 338)	8	oz	225 g
Nougatine (p. 562), crushed	2	oz	60 g
Sliced almonds, toasted	2.5	oz	75 g
Confectioners' sugar	as needed		as needed

■ Procedure

1. Place one succès layer on a cake card, anchoring it in place with a dab of buttercream.
2. Spread a layer of buttercream on the succès.
3. Sprinkle the crushed nougatine evenly over the buttercream.
4. Top with the second layer of succès.
5. Spread the top and sides of the cake with buttercream.
6. Coat the top and sides with the almonds. Sprinkle the top very lightly with confectioners' sugar.

Variation

Individual Succès pastries can be made using the same procedure. Use small succès disks 2³/₄ in. (7 cm) in diameter.

► TERMS FOR REVIEW

tart	Gâteau St-Honoré	Tarte Tatin	millefeuille
Linzertorte	Pithiviers	peasant tart	sfogliatelle
French pastry			

► QUESTIONS FOR REVIEW

1. What is the purpose of docking tart shells before they are baked?

2. List four or five ingredients besides fruit and sugar that are sometimes used for filling *baked* fruit tarts.

3. Describe the procedure for making baked tartlet shells.

4. Describe the procedure for making an unbaked fruit tart.

5. Describe, in as much detail as possible, the procedure for making a Gâteau St-Honoré.

6. Read the procedures for special cakes in chapter 14. Which ones do you think might be appropriate for making up as French pastries? Select one and describe how you would modify the procedure to make French pastries.

12

Cake Mixing and Baking

*C*akes are the richest and sweetest of all the baked products we have studied so far. From the baker's point of view, producing cakes requires as much precision as producing breads, but for completely opposite reasons. Breads are lean products that require strong gluten development and careful control of yeast action during the long fermentation and proofing periods.

Cakes, on the other hand, are high in both fat and sugar. The baker's job is to create a structure that supports these ingredients and yet to keep it as light and delicate as possible. Fortunately, producing cakes in quantity is relatively easy if the baker has good, well-balanced formulas, scales ingredients accurately, and understands basic mixing methods well.

Cakes owe their popularity not only to their richness and sweetness but also to their versatility. Cakes can be presented in many forms, from simple sheet cakes in cafeterias to elaborately decorated works of art for weddings and other important occasions. With only a few basic formulas and a variety of icings and fillings, the chef or baker can construct the perfect dessert for any occasion or purpose. In this chapter, we focus on the procedures for mixing and baking the basic types of cakes. In chapters 13 and 14, we discuss how to assemble and decorate many kinds of desserts, using our baked cake layers and sheets in combination with icings, fillings, and other ingredients.

After reading this chapter, you should be able to:

- Perform basic cake mixing methods.

- Produce high-fat or shortened cakes, including high-ratio cakes and cakes mixed by creaming.

- Produce foam-type cakes, including sponge, angel food, and chiffon cakes.

- Scale and bake cakes correctly.

- Correct cake failures or defects.

MIXING

The selection of high-quality ingredients is, of course, necessary to produce a good quality cake. However, good ingredients alone do not guarantee a fine cake. A thorough understanding of mixing procedures is essential. Slight errors in mixing can result in cakes with poor texture and volume.

The mixing methods presented in this chapter are the basic ones used for most types of cakes prepared in the modern bakeshop. Each of these methods is used for particular types of formulas.

- **High-fat or shortened cakes**

  Creaming method

  Two-stage method

  Flour-batter method

- **Low-fat or foam-type cakes**

  Sponge method

  Angel food method

  Chiffon method

We discuss these methods and their variations in detail beginning on page 294.

The three main goals of mixing cake batters are:

- To combine all ingredients into a smooth, uniform batter.
- To form and incorporate air cells in the batter.
- To develop the proper texture in the finished product.

These three goals are closely related. They may seem fairly obvious, especially the first one. But understanding these goals in more detail will help you avoid many errors in mixing. For example, inexperienced bakers often become impatient and turn the mixer to high speed when creaming fat and sugar, thinking that high speed will do the same job faster. But air cells do not form as well at high speed, so the texture of the cake suffers.

Let's examine these three goals one at a time.

COMBINING INGREDIENTS INTO A HOMOGENEOUS MIXTURE

Two of the major ingredients in cakes—fat and water (including the water in milk and eggs)—are, by nature, unmixable. Therefore, careful attention to mixing procedures is important if this goal is to be reached.

As you recall from chapter 2 (p. 26), a uniform mixture of two unmixable substances is called an *emulsion.* Part of the purpose of mixing is to form such an emulsion. Properly mixed cake batters contain a water-in-fat emulsion—that is, the water is held in tiny droplets surrounded by fat and other ingredients. Curdling occurs when the fat can no longer hold the water in emulsion. The mixture then changes to a fat-in-water mixture, with small particles of fat surrounded by water and other ingredients.

The following factors can cause curdling:

1. *Using the wrong type of fat* Different fats have different emulsifying abilities. High-ratio shortening contains emulsifiers that enable it to hold a

large amount of water without curdling. You should not substitute regular shortening or butter in a formula that calls specifically for high-ratio, or emulsified, shortening.

Butter has a desirable flavor but relatively poor emulsifying ability. Butter is, of course, used in many cake batters, but the formula should be specifically balanced so that it contains no more liquid than the batter can hold. Also, remember that butter contains some water.

Egg yolks, as you will recall, contain a natural emulsifier. When whole eggs or yolks are properly mixed into a batter, they help the batter hold the other liquids.

2. *Having the ingredients too cold*   Emulsions are best formed if the temperature of the ingredients is about 70°F (21°C).

3. *Mixing the first stage of the procedure too quickly*   If you do not cream the fat and sugar properly, for example, you will not form a good cell structure to hold the water.

4. *Adding the liquids too quickly*   In most cases the liquids, including the eggs, must be added in stages (that is, a little at a time). If they are added too quickly, they cannot be absorbed properly.

In batters made by the creaming method (p. 294), the liquid is often added alternately with the flour. The flour helps the batter absorb the liquid.

5. *Adding too much liquid*   This is not a problem if the formula is a good one. However, if you are using a formula that is not properly balanced, it might call for more liquid than the fat can hold in emulsion.

FORMING AIR CELLS

Air cells in cake batters are important for texture and for leavening. A fine, smooth texture is the result of small, uniform air cells. Large or irregular air cells result in a coarse texture. Also, you will recall from page 38 that air trapped in a mix helps to leaven a cake when the heat of the oven causes the air to expand. When no chemical leavener is used, this trapped air, in addition to steam, provides nearly all the leavening. Even when baking powder or soda is used, these air cells provide places to hold the gases released by the chemical leavener.

Correct ingredient temperature and mixing speed are necessary for good air cell formation. Cold fat (below 60°F/16°C) is too hard to form good air cells, and fat that is too warm (above 75°F/24°C) is too soft. Mixing speed should be moderate (medium speed). If mixing is done on high speed, friction warms the ingredients too much. Not as many air cells are formed, and those that do form tend to be more coarse and irregular.

In the case of egg-foam cakes (sponge, angel food, chiffon), the air cells are formed by whipping eggs and sugar. For the best foaming, the egg and sugar mixture should be slightly warm (about 100°F/38°C). Whipping may be done at high speed at first, but the final stages of whipping should be at medium speed in order to retain air cells.

DEVELOPING TEXTURE

Both the uniform mixing of ingredients and the formation of air cells are important to a cake's texture, as we discussed in the preceding sections. Another factor of mixing that affects texture is gluten development. For the most part, we want very little gluten development in cakes, so we use cake flour, which is low in gluten. Some sponge cake formulas call for cornstarch to replace part of the flour, so that there is even less gluten (the high percentage of eggs in sponge cakes provides much of the structure). On the other hand, some pound cake and fruit cake formulas need more gluten than other cakes, in order to give extra structure and support to the weight of the fruit. Thus, you will sometimes see such cake formulas calling for part cake flour and part bread flour.

As you will recall from chapter 1, the amout of mixing affects gluten development. In the creaming method, the sponge method, and the angel food method, the flour is added at or near the end of the mixing procedure so that there is very little gluten development in properly mixed batters. If the batter is mixed too long after the flour is added, the cakes are likely to be tough.

In the two-stage method, the flour is added in the first step. But it is mixed with high-ratio shortening, which spreads well and coats the particles of flour with fat. This coating action limits gluten development. It is important to mix the flour and fat thoroughly for the best results. Observe all mixing times closely. Also, high-ratio cakes contain a high percentage of sugar, which is also a tenderizer.

HIGH-FAT CAKES

Creaming Method

This method, also called the *conventional method,* was for a long time the standard method for mixing high-fat cakes. The development of emulsified, or high-ratio, shortenings led to the development of simpler mixing methods for

---

Procedure: Creaming Method

1. Scale ingredients accurately. Have all ingredients at room temperature (70°F/21°C).
2. Place the butter or shortening in the mixing bowl. With the paddle attachment, beat the fat slowly until it is smooth and creamy.
3. Add the sugar; cream the mixture at moderate speed until the mixture is light and fluffy. This will take about 8 to 10 minutes.

   Some bakers prefer to add the salt and flavorings with the sugar to ensure uniform distribution.

   If melted chocolate is used, it is added during creaming.
4. Add the eggs a little at a time. After each addition, beat until the eggs are absorbed before adding more. After the eggs are beaten in, mix until light and fluffy. This step will take about 5 minutes.
5. Scrape down the sides of the bowl to ensure even mixing.
6. Add the sifted dry ingredients (including the spices, if they were not added in step 3), alternating with the liquids. This is done as follows:

   Add one-fourth of the dry ingredients. Mix just until blended in.

   Add one-third of the liquid. Mix just until blended in.

   Repeat until all ingredients are used. Scrape down the sides of the bowl occasionally for even mixing.

   The reason for adding dry and liquid ingredients alternately is that the batter may not absorb all the liquid unless some of the flour is present.

Variation

A few creaming-method cakes require an extra step: Egg whites whipped to a foam with some sugar are folded into the batter to provide additional leavening.

shortened cakes containing greater amounts of sugar and liquid. The creaming method is still used for many types of butter cakes, however.

The fat specified in creaming-method formulas in this book is butter. Butter cakes are highly prized for their flavor; shortening adds no flavor to cakes. Butter also influences texture because it melts in the mouth, while shortening does not.

However, many bakers may prefer to substitute shortening for all or part of the butter in these formulas. Shortening has the advantage of being less expensive and easier to mix. In creaming recipes, use *regular shortening,* not emulsified shortening. Regular shortening has better creaming abilities.

It is usually a good idea not to substitute an equal weight of shortening for butter. Remember that butter is only 80% fat, so you will need less shortening. Also, butter contains about 15% water, so you should adjust the quantity of milk or water. The following procedures explain how to adjust formulas for these substitutions.

Procedures for Substituting Butter and Shortening in Creaming-Method Batters

To substitute regular shortening for all or part of the butter:

1. Multiply the weight of the butter to be eliminated by 0.8. This gives the weight of regular shortening to use.
2. Multiply the weight of the eliminated butter by 0.15. This gives the weight of *additional* water or milk needed.

Example: A formula calls for 3 lb butter and 3 lb milk. Adjust it so that you use 1 lb (16 oz) butter. How much shortening and milk will you need?

$$\text{Weight of butter to be eliminated} = 2 \text{ lb}$$

$$= 32 \text{ oz}$$

$$0.8 \times 32 \text{ oz} = 26 \text{ oz shortening (rounded off)}$$

$$0.15 \times 32 \text{ oz} = 5 \text{ oz extra milk (rounded off)}$$

$$\text{Total milk} = 3 \text{ lb } 5 \text{ oz}$$

Procedure for Substituting Butter for All or Part of the Regular Shortening

1. Multiply the weight of the shortening to be eliminated by 1.25. This gives the weight of the butter to use.
2. Multiply the weight of the butter by 0.15. This gives the weight of water or milk to be *subtracted* from the formula.

Example: A formula calls for 3 lb regular shortening and 3 lb milk. Adjust the formula so that you use 1 lb shortening. How much butter and milk will you need?

$$\text{Weight of shortening to be eliminated} = 2 \text{ lb}$$

$$= 32 \text{ oz}$$

$$1.25 \times 32 \text{ oz} = 40 \text{ oz butter}$$

$$0.15 \times 40 \text{ oz} = 6 \text{ oz milk to subtract from the formula}$$

$$\text{Total milk} = 2 \text{ lb } 10 \text{ oz}$$

Two-Stage Method

This mixing method was developed for use with modern high-ratio shortenings. High-ratio cakes contain a large percentage of sugar, more than 100% based on the weight of the flour. Also, they are made with more liquid than creaming-method cakes, and the batter pours freely. The mixing method is a little simpler than the creaming method, and it produces a smooth batter that bakes up into a fine-grained, moist cake. It gets its name because the liquids are added in two stages.

The first step in making high-ratio cakes is blending the flour and other dry ingredients with shortening. When this mixture is smooth, the liquids (including eggs) are added in stages. Throughout this procedure, it is important to follow two rules:

▶ Mix at low speed and observe correct mixing times. This is important to develop proper texture.

▶ Stop the machine and scrape down the sides of the bowl frequently during mixing. This is important to develop a smooth, well-mixed batter.

Note the variation following the basic procedure. Many bakers prefer this variation. It is somewhat simpler because it combines steps 2 and 3.

Procedure: Two-Stage Method

1. Scale ingredients accurately. Have all ingredients at room temperature.

2. Sift the flour, baking powder, soda, and salt into the mixing bowl and add the shortening. With the paddle attachment, mix at low speed for 2 minutes. Stop the machine, scrape down the bowl and beater, and mix again for 2 minutes.

   If melted chocolate is used, blend it in during this step.

   If cocoa is used, sift it with the flour in this step or with the sugar in step 3.

3. Sift the remaining dry ingredients into the bowl and add part of the water or milk. Blend at low speed for 3 to 5 minutes. Scrape down the sides of the bowl and the beater several times to ensure even mixing.

4. Combine the remaining liquids and lightly beaten eggs. With the mixer running, add this mixture to the batter in three parts. After each part, turn off the machine and scrape down the bowl.

   Continue mixing for a total of 5 minutes in this stage.

   The finished batter is normally quite liquid.

Variation

This variation combines steps 2 and 3 above into one step.

1. Scale ingredients as in basic method.

2. Sift all dry ingredients into the mixing bowl. Add the shortening and part of the liquid. Mix on low speed for 7 to 8 minutes. Scrape down the sides of the bowl and the beater several times.

3. Continue with step 4 in the basic procedure.

Flour-Batter Method

The following procedure is used only for a few specialty items. It produces a fine-textured cake, but there may be some toughening due to the development of gluten.

Flour-batter cakes include those made with either emulsified shortening or butter or both. There are no formulas in this book requiring this mixing method, although the batter for Old-Fashioned Pound Cake (p. 312) can be mixed by this method instead of the creaming method.

Procedure: Flour-Batter Method

1. Scale all ingredients accurately. Have all ingredients at room temperature.

2. Sift the flour and other dry ingredients *except sugar* into the mixing bowl. Add fat. Blend together until smooth and light.

3. Whip the sugar and eggs together until thick and light. Add liquid flavoring ingredients, such as vanilla.

4. Combine the flour-fat mixture and the sugar-egg mixture and mix until smooth.

5. Gradually add water or milk (if any) and mix smooth.

LOW-FAT OR EGG-FOAM CAKES

Most egg-foam cakes contain little or no shortening and depend on the air trapped in beaten eggs for most or all of their leavening. Increasing interest in fine pastries and cakes has led to new appreciation of the versatility of sponge cakes. This chapter includes formulas for a great variety of egg-foam batters. These cakes are used in many of the special desserts assembled in chapter 14.

Egg-foam cakes have a springy texture and are tougher than shortened cakes. This makes them valuable for many kinds of desserts that require much handling to assemble. Most European cakes and tortes are made with sponge or egg-foam cakes. These cakes are baked either in thin sheets or disks or in thick layers that are then sliced horizontally into thinner layers. The thin sponge layers are then stacked with a variety of fillings, creams, mousses, fruits, and icings. In addition, sponge layers in this kind of cake are usually moistened with a flavored sugar syrup to compensate for their lack of moisture.

Sponge sheets for jelly rolls and other rolled cakes are often made without any shortening so that they do not crack when rolled.

Flour for egg-foam cakes must be weak in order to avoid making the cake tougher than necessary. Cornstarch is sometimes added to cake flour for these cakes to weaken the flour further.

Sponge Method

Although there are many types of sponge cakes, they all have one characteristic in common: They are made with an egg foam that contains yolks. These are usually whole-egg foams but, in some cases, the base foam is a yolk foam, and an egg white foam is folded in at the end of the procedure.

In its simplest form, sponge cake batter is made in two basic steps: (1) eggs and sugar are whipped to a thick foam, and (2) sifted flour is folded in. Additional ingredients, such as butter or liquid, complicate the procedure slightly. It would be too confusing to try to include all the variations in one procedure, so instead we describe four separate procedures.

Procedure: Plain Sponge or Genoise Method

1. Scale ingredients accurately.

2. Combine the eggs, sugar, and salt and warm to about 110°F (43°C). This may be done in one of two ways.

   a. Stir the egg-sugar mixture over a hot water bath.

   b. Warm the sugar on a sheet pan in the oven (do not get it too hot) and gradually beat it into the eggs.

   The reason for this step is that the foam attains greater volume if warm.

3. With a wire whip or the whip attachment of a mixer, beat the eggs at high speed until they are very light and thick (a). This may take as long as 10 to 15 minutes if the quantity is large.

4. If any liquid (water, milk, liquid flavoring) is included, add it now. Either whip it in in a steady stream or stir it in, as indicated in the recipe.

5. Fold in the sifted flour in three or four stages, being careful not to deflate the foam. Many bakers do this by hand, even for large batches. Fold gently until all the flour is blended in (b). If any other dry ingredients are used, such as cornstarch or baking powder, they should first be sifted with the flour.

6. Immediately pan and bake the batter. Delays will cause loss of volume.

a.

Variation: Butter Sponge or Butter Genoise

1. Follow the plain sponge procedure through step 5.

2. Carefully fold in the melted butter after the flour has been added. Fold in the butter completely, but be careful not to overmix or the cake will be tough.

3. Immediately pan and bake.

Variation: Hot Milk and Butter Sponge

1. Scale ingredients accurately. Heat the milk and butter together until the butter is melted.

2. Whip the eggs into a foam as in the plain sponge method, steps 2 and 3.

3. Fold in the sifted dry ingredients (flour, leavening, cocoa, etc.) as in the basic procedure.

4. Carefully fold in the hot butter and milk in three stages. Fold in completely, but do not overmix.

5. Immediately pan and bake.

b.

Variation: Separated Egg Sponge

1. Follow the basic plain sponge method, but use yolks for the basic foam (steps 2 and 3). Reserve the egg whites and part of the sugar for a separate step.

2. Whip the egg whites and sugar to firm, moist peaks. Fold into the batter alternately with the sifted dry ingredients. Fold in completely, but do not overmix.

3. Immediately pan and bake.

Angel Food Method

Angel food cakes are based on egg-white foams and contain no fat. For success in beating egg whites, review the principles of egg white foams in chapter 8, p. 182. Egg whites for angel food cakes should be whipped until they form soft, not stiff, peaks. Overwhipped whites lose their ability to expand and to leaven the cake.

Procedure: Angel Food Method

1. Scale ingredients accurately. Have all ingredients at room temperature. The egg whites may be slightly warmed in order to achieve better volume.

2. Sift the flour with half the sugar. This step helps the flour mix more evenly with the foam.

3. Using the whip attachment, beat the egg whites until they form soft peaks.

   Add salt and cream of tartar near the beginning of the beating process.

4. Gradually beat in the portion of the sugar that was not mixed with the flour. Continue to whip until the egg whites form soft, moist peaks. Do not beat until stiff.

5. Fold in the flour/sugar mixture just until it is thoroughly absorbed, but no longer.

6. Deposit the mix in ungreased pans and bake immediately.

Chiffon Method

Chiffon cakes and angel food cakes are both based on egg-white foams, but here the similarities in the mixing methods end. In angel food cakes, a dry flour-sugar mixture is folded into the egg whites. In chiffon cakes, a batter containing flour, egg yolks, vegetable oil, and water is folded into the whites.

Egg whites for chiffon cakes should be whipped until they are a little firmer than those for angel food cakes, but do not whip them until they are dry. Chiffon cakes contain baking powder, so they do not depend on the egg foam for all their leavening.

Procedure: Chiffon Method

1. Scale all ingredients accurately. Have all ingredients at room temperature. Use a good-quality, flavorless vegetable oil.

2. Sift the dry ingredients, including part of the sugar, into the mixing bowl.

3. Mixing with the paddle attachment at second speed, gradually add the oil, then the egg yolks, water, and liquid flavorings, all in a slow, steady stream. While adding the liquids, stop the machine several times and scrape down the bowl and the beater. Mix until smooth, but do not overmix.

4. Whip the egg whites until they form soft peaks. Add the cream of tartar and sugar in a stream and whip to firm, moist peaks.

5. Fold the whipped egg whites into the flour-liquid mixture.

6. Immediately deposit batter in ungreased center-tube pans (like angel food cakes) or in layer pans that have had the bottoms greased and dusted, but not the sides (like sponge layers).

COMBINATION CREAMING/SPONGE METHOD

A few European-style cakes are begun by using the creaming method. In other words, butter is creamed with sugar until the mixture is light. These cakes usually contain no chemical leavening, however. Instead, whipped egg whites are folded into the batter, as for some sponge cakes. Examples of this kind of cake are Hazelnut Sponge Cake (p. 325) and Baumkuchen (p. 326). Mixing hazelnut sponge is illustrated in the procedure below.

Baumkuchen is an unusual cake that deserves extra explanation. The name means "tree cake" in German. Traditionally, it was made on a revolving wooden spit. The batter was ladled on in thin layers as the spit rotated in front of a heat source. When the cake grew thick enough, some of the batter could be cut away, the same way that wood is cut on a lathe, so that the finished cake could be made in various shapes, such as a pine tree.

Today, baumkuchen is generally made in cake pans, as illustrated on page 326. Its unusual striped interior makes it valuable for decorative lining of cake and charlotte molds.

Procedure: Combination Creaming/Sponge Method

1. Cream the butter and sugar.
2. Add the egg yolks a little at a time.
3. Mix in well after each addition.
4. Whip the egg whites and sugar to a stiff meringue.
5. Fold the meringue into the butter mixture.
6. Sift the dry ingredients together. Fold in the sifted dry ingredients.
7. Deposit the batter in prepared pans.
8. Level the top of the batter with a plastic scaper.

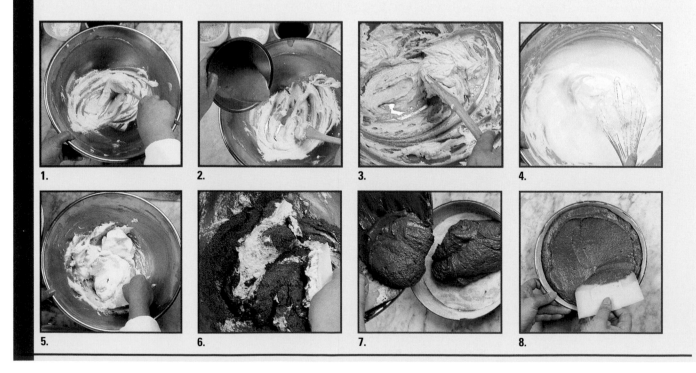

1. 2. 3. 4.
5. 6. 7. 8.

PREPARED MIXES

Many mixes are available that contain all ingredients except water and, sometimes, eggs. These products also contain emulsifiers to ensure even blending of ingredients. To use them, follow the package instructions exactly.

Most mixes produce cakes with excellent volume, texture, and tenderness. Whether or not they also taste good is a matter of opinion. On the other hand, cakes made from scratch are not necessarily better. They are better only if they are carefully mixed and baked, and prepared from good, tested formulas, using quality ingredients.

CAKE FORMULA BALANCE

It is possible to change cake formulas, either to improve them or to reduce costs. However, ingredients and quantities can be changed only within certain limits. A cake formula in which the ingredients fall within these limits is said to be in balance. Knowing these limits helps you not only modify recipes but also judge untested recipes and correct faults.

Keep in mind that new ingredients and procedures are frequently developed. Cake-balancing rules that have worked well until now may be changed as new developments come along that allow you to break the rules. A baker should be open to new ideas and willing to try them out. For example, it was once a rule that the weight of sugar in a mix should not exceed the weight of flour. But the introduction of shortenings with emulsifiers led to formulas with higher proportions of sugar.

INGREDIENT FUNCTIONS

For the purpose of balancing cake formulas, we can classify cake ingredients according to four functions: tougheners, tenderizers, driers, and moisteners. The idea of formula balancing is that tougheners should balance tenderizers and driers should balance moisteners. In other words, if we increase the amount of tougheners in a formula, for example, we must compensate by also increasing the amount of tenderizers.

Many ingredients fill more than one function, sometimes even opposite functions. Egg yolks contain protein, which is a toughener, but they also contain fat, which is a tenderizer. The major cake ingredients are classified as follows:

Tougheners provide structure: flour, eggs (whites and yolks).

Tenderizers provide softness or shortening of protein fibers: sugar, fats (including butter, shortening, and cocoa butter), chemical leaveners.

Moisteners provide moisture or water: water, liquid milk, syrups and liquid sugars, eggs.

Driers absorb moisture: flours and starches, cocoa, milk solids.

You can also use this table of ingredients as a troubleshooting guide for cake failures. A cake that fails even if mixed and baked correctly may require formula balancing. For example, if a cake is too dry, you might increase one or more of the moisteners or decrease the driers.

This takes a certain amount of experience, however. Remember that most ingredients have more than one function. If you decide to increase the eggs in a dry cake, you may wind up with an even harder, tougher cake. Although whole eggs do provide some moisture, they provide even more toughening power because of their strong protein content.

As a further complication, there are many successful cake formulas that apparently break the rules. For example, one rule for creaming-method cakes made with butter or regular shortening says that the weight of the sugar should not exceed the weight of the flour. But, in fact, there are successful recipes calling for more than 100% sugar. Many baking manuals insist on these balancing rules rather strongly. But it may be better to think of them not as ironclad laws but as guidelines that give you a starting point for judging or correcting recipes.

In summary, it takes an experienced baker to be consistently successful at adjusting cake formulas. However, even beginning bakers should have some knowledge of formula balancing. It helps you understand the formulas you are using and practicing, and it helps you understand why you assemble and mix cakes in certain ways and what makes the mixtures work.

In the following discussion of balancing rules, it is helpful to think of ingredients in terms of baker's percentages (see p. 10) rather than as specific weights. This eliminates one variable: Flour is a constant 100%, so other ingredients are increased or decreased with respect to flour.

BALANCING FAT-TYPE OR SHORTENED CAKES

A normal starting point in discussing cake balancing is old-fashioned pound cake. This cake is made of flour, sugar, butter, and eggs in equal parts. As bakers experimented with this basic recipe over the years, they reduced the quantities of sugar, fat, and eggs, and compensated by adding milk. This is the origin of the modern butter cake.

The general rules for balancing creaming-method cakes made with butter or regular shortening are as follows (all ingredient quantities are, of course, by weight):

- The sugar is equal to or less than the flour.
- The fat equals the eggs.
- The eggs and liquids (milk and water) equal the flour.

With the development of emulsified shortening, it became possible to increase the quantities of eggs and liquids. The general rules for balancing high-ratio cakes (using emulsified shortening) are as follows:

- The sugar is more than the flour (110 to 160%).
- The eggs are more than the shortening.
- The liquid (water, plus the water in the milk and eggs) is more than the sugar (see pp. 29 and 33 for the percentages of water in milk and eggs).

A common practice in balancing a formula is to decide on the sugar-flour ratio, then to balance the rest of the ingredients against these. The following guidelines are helpful:

- If liquid (water or milk) is increased, reduce the eggs and shortening.
- If eggs are increased, increase the shortening.
- If extra milk solids are added as an enrichment, add an equal weight of water.

- If cocoa is added, add water equal in weight to 75–100% of the cocoa.
- If cocoa or bitter chocolate is added, the amount of sugar may be increased to as much as 180% of the weight of the flour in high-ratio cakes and to over 100% of the weight of the flour in creaming-method cakes. This is because of the starch content of the cocoa and chocolate.
- In cakes to be baked in very large units, less liquid is needed because less water will evaporate during baking.
- If a liquid sugar is added (honey, corn syrup, etc.), reduce other liquids slightly.
- If large quantities of moist ingredients, such as applesauce or mashed bananas, are added, reduce the liquid. Extra-large additions of moist ingredients may also require increasing the flour and eggs.
- Creamed batters need less baking powder than two-stage batters because the creamed batters get more aeration in the creaming stage.

SCALING, PANNING, AND BAKING

PAN PREPARATION

Prepare pans before mixing cake batters so that cakes can be baked without delay as soon as they are mixed.

1. For high-fat cakes, layer pans must be greased, preferably with a commercial pan-greasing preparation. If this is not available, dust the greased pans with flour and tap out the excess.
2. For sheet cakes, line the pans with greased parchment. For thin layers, such as Swiss rolls, it is necessary to use level pans without dents or warps.
3. For angel food cakes and chiffon cakes baked in tube pans, do not grease the pan. The batter must be able to cling to the sides so that it doesn't sink back into the pan after rising.
4. For sponge cake layers with little or no fat, grease the bottoms but not the sides of the pans.

Procedure for Scaling Creaming-Method Batters

These batters are thick and do not pour easily.

1. Place a prepared cake pan on the left side of the balance scale. Balance the scale out by placing another pan on the right side.
2. Set the scale for desired weight.
3. Add batter to the left pan until the scale balances.
4. Remove the pan from the scale and spread the batter smooth with a spatula.
5. Repeat with remaining pans.
6. Give the pans several sharp raps on the bench to free large trapped air bubbles. Bake immediately.

Procedure for Scaling Two-Stage Batters

These batters are usually very liquid. They may be scaled like creamed batters or, for greater speed, they may be scaled as follows:

1. Place an empty volume measure on the left side of the balance scale. Balance the scale out to zero.
2. Set the scale for desired weight.
3. Pour batter into the measure until the scale balances.
4. Note the volume of batter in the measure.
5. Pour batter into the prepared pan, quickly scraping out the measure to get all the batter.
6. Scale remaining cakes with the volume measure, using the volume noted in Step 4.
7. Give the pans several sharp raps on the bench to free large trapped air bubbles. Bake immediately.

Procedure for Scaling Egg-Foam Cakes

Foam cake batters should be handled as little as possible and baked immediately in order to avoid deflating the beaten eggs. While these cakes may be scaled like creamed batters, many bakers prefer to eyeball them in order to minimize handling.

1. Have all prepared pans lined up on the bench.
2. Scale the first pan as for creamed batters.
3. Quickly fill the remaining pans to the same level as the first pan, judging the level by eye.
4. Spread the batter smooth and bake immediately.

See the table opposite for average scaling weights as well as baking temperatures and times.

Average Cake Scaling Weights, Baking Temperatures, and Times

Pan Type and Size	Scaling Weight[a]		Baking Temperature		Approximate Baking Time in Minutes
	U.S.	Metric	U.S.	Metric	
High-fat cakes					
Round layers					
6 in. (15 cm)	8–10 oz	230–285 g	375°F	190°C	18
8 in. (20 cm)	14–18 oz	400–510 g	375°F	190°C	25
10 in. (25 cm)	24–28 oz	680–800 g	360°F	180°C	35
12 in. (30 cm)	32–40 oz	900–1100 g	360°F	180°C	35
Sheets and square pans					
18 × 26 in. (46 × 66 cm)	7–8 lb	3.2–3.6 kg	360°F	180°C	35
18 × 13 in. (46 × 33 cm)	3.5–4 lb	1.6–1.8 kg	360°F	180°C	35
9 × 9 in. (23 × 23 cm)	24 oz	680 g	360°F	180°C	30–35
Loaf (pound cake)					
2¼ × 3½ × 8 in. (6 × 9 × 20 cm)	16–18 oz	450–500 g	350°F	175°C	50–60
2¾ × 4½ × 8½ in. (7 × 11 × 22 cm)	24–27 oz	680–765 g	350°F	175°C	55–65
Cupcakes					
per dozen	18 oz	510 g	385°F	195°C	18–20
Foam-type cakes					
Round layers					
6 in. (15 cm)	5–6 oz	140–170 g	375°F	190°C	20
8 in. (20 cm)	10 oz	280 g	375°F	190°C	20
10 in. (25 cm)	16 oz	450 g	360°F	180°C	25–30
12 in. (30 cm)	24 oz	700 g	360°F	180°C	25–30
Sheets (for jelly roll or sponge roll)					
18 × 26 in., ½ in. thick (46 × 66 cm, 12 mm thick)	2.5 lb	1.2 kg	375°F	190°C	15–20
18 × 26 in., ¼ in. thick (46 × 66 cm, 6 mm thick)	28 oz	800 g	400°F	200°C	7–10
Tube (angel food and chiffon)					
8 in. (20 cm)	12–14 oz	340–400 g	360°F	180°C	30
10 in. (25 cm)	24–32 oz	700–900 g	350°F	175°C	50
Cupcakes					
per dozen	10 oz	280 g	375°F	190°C	18–20

[a]The weights given are averages. Weights may be increased by 25% if thicker layers are desired. Baking times may need to be increased slightly.

BAKING AND COOLING

Cake structure is fragile, so proper baking conditions are essential for high-quality products. The following guidelines will help you avoid cake failures.

- Preheat the ovens. To conserve expensive energy, don't preheat longer than necessary.

- Make sure ovens and shelves are level.

- Do not let pans touch each other. If pans touch, air circulation is inhibited and the cakes rise unevenly.

- Bake at correct temperature.

  Too hot an oven causes the cake to set unevenly with a humped center, or to set before it has fully risen. Crusts will be too dark.

  Too slow an oven causes poor volume and texture because the cake doesn't set fast enough and may fall.

- If steam in the oven is available, use it for creamed and two-stage batters. These cakes bake with a flatter top if baked with steam because the steam delays the formation of the top crust.

- Do not open the oven or disturb cakes until they have finished rising and are partially browned. Disturbing the cakes before they are set may cause them to fall.

Tests for Doneness

- Shortened cakes shrink away slightly from sides of pan.
- Cake is springy. Center of top of cake springs back when pressed lightly.
- A cake tester or wooden pick inserted in center of cake comes out clean.

Cooling and Removing from Pans

- Cool layer cakes and sheet cakes 15 minutes in pans and turn out while slightly warm. Because they are fragile, they may break if turned out when hot.

- Turn out layer cakes onto racks to finish cooling.

- To turn out sheet cakes:

  1. Sprinkle top lightly with granulated sugar.
  2. Set an empty sheet pan on top, bottom-side down.
  3. Invert both pans.
  4. Remove top pan.
  5. Peel parchment off cake.

- Cool angel food cakes and chiffon cakes upside down in pans so that they do not fall back into the pans and lose volume. Support the edges of the pan so that the top of the cake is off the bench. When cool, loosen the cake from sides of the pan with a knife or spatula, and carefully pull out the cake.

Errors in mixing, scaling, baking, and cooling cakes cause many kinds of defects and failures. For easy reference, these various defects and their possible causes are summarized in the troubleshooting guide in the table opposite.

Common Cake Faults and Their Causes

Fault	Causes
Volume and shape	
Poor volume	Too little flour
	Too much liquid
	Too little leavening
	Oven too hot
Uneven shape	Improper mixing
	Batter spread unevenly
	Uneven oven heat
	Oven racks not level
	Cake pans warped
Crust	
Too dark	Too much sugar
	Oven too hot
Too light	Too little sugar
	Oven not hot enough
Burst or cracked	Too much flour or flour too strong
	Too little liquid
	Improper mixing
	Oven too hot
Soggy	Underbaked
	Cooling in pans or with not enough ventilation
	Wrapping before cool
Texture	
Dense or heavy	Too little leavening
	Too much liquid
	Too much sugar
	Too much shortening
	Oven not hot enough
Coarse or irregular	Too much leavening
	Too little egg
	Improper mixing
Crumbly	Too much leavening
	Too much shortening
	Too much sugar
	Wrong kind of flour
	Improper mixing
Tough	Flour too strong
	Too much flour
	Too little sugar or shortening
	Overmixing
Poor flavor	
	Poor-quality ingredients
	Poor storage or sanitation
	Unbalanced formula

ALTITUDE ADJUSTMENTS

At high altitudes, atmospheric pressure is much lower than at sea level. This factor must be taken into account in cake baking. Formulas must be adjusted to suit baking conditions more than 2000 or 3000 feet above sea level.

Although general guidelines can be given, the exact adjustments required will vary for different kinds of cakes. Many manufacturers of flour, shortening, and other bakery ingredients supply detailed information and adjusted formulas for any given locality.

In general, the following adjustments must be made. See the table below for actual adjustments.

Leavening   Leavening gases expand more when air pressure is lower, so the amounts of baking powder and baking soda must be *decreased*.

Creaming and foaming procedures should also be reduced so that less air is incorporated.

Tougheners: Flour and Eggs   Cakes require firmer structure at high altitudes. Both eggs and flour must be increased to supply adequate proteins for structure.

Tenderizers: Shortening and Sugar   For the same reasons, shortening and sugar must be decreased so that the structure will be firmer.

Liquids   At higher altitudes, water boils at a lower temperature and evaporates more easily. Liquids must be increased to prevent excess drying both during and after baking. This also helps compensate for the decrease in moisturizers (sugar and fat) and the increase in flour, which absorbs moisture.

Baking Temperatures   Increase baking temperatures by about 25°F (14°C) above 3500 feet.

Pan Greasing   High-fat cakes tend to stick at high altitudes. Grease pans more heavily. Remove baked cakes from pans as soon as possible.

Storing   To prevent drying, wrap or ice cakes as soon as they are cool.

Approximate Formula Adjustment in Shortened Cakes at High Altitude

Ingredient	Increase or Decrease	2500 ft	5000 ft	7500 ft
Baking powder	decrease	20%	40%	60%
Flour	increase	—	4%	9%
Eggs	increase	2½ %	9%	15%
Sugar	decrease	3%	6%	9%
Fat	decrease	—	—	9%
Liquid	increase	9%	15%	22%

To make adjustments, multiply the percentage indicated by the amount of ingredient and add or subtract the result as indicated.
Example: Adjust 1 lb (16 oz) eggs for 7500 ft.

$$.15 \times 16 \text{ oz} = 2.4 \text{ oz}$$
$$16 \text{ oz} + 2.4 \text{ oz} = 18.4 \text{ oz}$$

FORMULAS

The following cake mix formulas will give you practice with all major cake-mixing methods. Many popular American cake types are included, sometimes in the form of variations on the basic cake types. These variations show that by making small changes in flavoring ingredients, you can make many different cakes from the same basic recipe. Adding new flavorings sometimes requires other ingredient changes. For example, in the case of the strawberry cake (p. 316), the flavoring ingredient is high in sugar, so the amount of sugar in the formula is reduced.

Of course, many more variations are possible than there is room for here. As one example, we give a separate recipe for spice cake (made with brown sugar), but other spice cakes can be made by adding a similar spice mixture to a basic yellow cake.

The difference between chocolate cake and devil's food cake is in the amount of baking soda used. As was explained in chapter 2, an excess of soda causes a reddish color in chocolate. By reducing the amount of soda (and increasing the baking powder to make up the lost leavening power), a devil's food cake can be turned into a regular chocolate cake. Of course, both types of cake can be made with either cocoa powder or chocolate. See page 44 for instructions on substituting one type of cocoa product for another.

Because we have already discussed the mixing procedures in detail, the procedures are not repeated for each formula. If necessary, review pages 294–300 before beginning production.

 ## Chocolate Butter Cake

For large-quantity measurements, see page 603.

Ingredients	U.S.		Metric	%
Butter	8	oz	250 g	67
Sugar	14	oz	430 g	115
Salt	0.2	oz (1 tsp)	6 g	1.5
Unsweetened chocolate, melted	4	oz	125 g	33
Eggs	6	oz	188 g	50
Cake flour	12	oz	375 g	100
Baking powder	0.5	oz	15 g	4
Milk	6	oz	188 g	50
Vanilla extract	0.25	oz	8 g	2
Total weight:	*3 lb 2*	*oz*	*1585 g*	*422%*

■ P r o c e d u r e

Mixing
Creaming method. Blend in the melted chocolate after the fat and sugar are well creamed.

Scaling and Baking
See table on page 305.

Yellow Butter Cake

For large-quantity measurements, see page 603.

Ingredients	U.S.		Metric	%
Butter	9	oz	275 g	60
Sugar	12	oz	362 g	80
Salt	0.12 oz (⅔ tsp)		4 g	0.75
Eggs	6.75 oz		202 g	45
Cake flour	15	oz	450 g	100
Baking powder	0.62 oz (3¾ tsp)		18 g	4
Milk	10	oz	300 g	67
Vanilla extract	0.25 oz		8 g	1.5
Total weight:	*3 lb*	*5 oz*	*1619 g*	*358%*

■ P r o c e d u r e

Mixing
   Creaming method
Scaling and Baking
   See table on page 305.

Variations

Upside-Down Cake
Increase the eggs to 50% (7.5 oz/225 g). Decrease milk to 60% (9 oz/275 g). Add 0.75% (0.12 oz/4 g) lemon or orange flavor. Butter a sheet pan, spread with pan spread (below), and arrange desired fruit (pineapple rings, sliced peaches, etc.) on top of the pan spread. Scale batter as indicated in the table on p. 305. Bake at 360°F (180°C). Immediately after baking, turn out of pan (see p. 306). Glaze with clear glaze (p. 116) or apricot glaze (p. 117).

Pan Spread
For large-quantity measurements, see page 603.

(for 9 in. square pan)

Ingredients	U.S.		Metric
Brown sugar	4	oz	112 g
Granulated sugar	1.5	oz	42 g
Corn syrup or honey	1	oz	30 g
Water (as needed)			

Cream together the first three ingredients. Add enough water to thin out to spreading consistency.

Walnut Cake
Add 50% (7.5 oz/225 g) chopped walnuts to the batter. Bake in small loaf pans. If desired, ice with chocolate buttercream.

Brown Sugar Spice Cake

Ingredients	U.S.		Metric		%
Butter	9	oz	300	g	60
Brown sugar	15	oz	500	g	100
Salt	0.25	oz	8	g	1.5
Eggs	9	oz	300	g	60
Cake flour	15	oz	500	g	100
Baking powder	0.5	oz	15	g	3
Baking soda	0.05 oz (⅜ tsp)		1.5	g	0.3
Cinnamon	0.08 oz (1½ tsp)		2.5	g	0.5
Cloves, ground	0.05 oz (¾ tsp)		1.5	g	0.3
Nutmeg	0.03 oz (⅜ tsp)		1	g	0.2
Milk	12	oz	400	g	80
Total weight:	*3 lb 12*	*oz*	*2029*	*g*	*405%*

■ P r o c e d u r e

Mixing
   Creaming method
Scaling and Baking
   See table on page 305.

Variations

Carrot Nut Cake
Reduce the milk to 70% (10.5 oz/350 g). Add 40% (6 oz/200 g) grated fresh carrots, 20% (3 oz/100 g) finely chopped walnuts, and 1 tsp (3 g) grated orange zest. Omit the cloves.

Banana Cake
Omit the cinnamon and cloves. Reduce milk to 10% (1.5 oz/50 g). Add 125% (1 lb 3 oz/625 g) ripe, puréed bananas. If desired, add 40% (6 oz/200 g) finely chopped pecans.

Applesauce Cake
Reduce milk to 30% (4.5 oz/150 g) and add 90% (13.5 oz/450 g) applesauce. Reduce baking powder to 2% (0.3 oz or 2 tsp/10 g). Increase baking soda to 1% (0.15 oz or 1 tsp/5 g).

Old-Fashioned Pound Cake

Ingredients	U.S.	Metric	%
Butter or part butter and part shortening	1 lb	500 g	100
Sugar	1 lb	500 g	100
Vanilla extract	0.33 oz (2 tsp)	10 g	2
Eggs	1 lb	500 g	100
Cake flour	1 lb	500 g	100
Total weight:	*4 lb*	*2010 g*	*402%*

■ P r o c e d u r e

Mixing

Creaming method. After about half the eggs have been creamed in, add a little of the flour to avoid curdling.

Scaling and Baking

See table on page 305. Paper-lined loaf pans are often used for pound cakes.

Variations

Mace or grated lemon or orange zest may be used to flavor pound cake.

Raisin Pound Cake

Add 25% (4 oz/125 g) raisins or currants that have been soaked in boiling water and drained well.

Chocolate Pound Cake

Sift 25% (4 oz/125 g) cocoa and 0.8% (0.12 oz or ¾ tsp/4 g) baking soda with the flour. Add 25% (4 oz/125 g) water to the batter.

Marble Pound Cake

Fill loaf pans with alternating layers of regular and chocolate pound cake batters. Run a knife through the batter to marble the mixture.

Sheet Cake for Petits Fours and Fancy Pastries

Increase eggs to 112% (1 lb 2 oz/560 g). Bake on sheet pans lined with greased paper. Scale 4 lb (1800 g) for ¼-in. (6 mm) layers to make 3-layer petits fours. Increase the recipe and scale 6 lb (2700 g) for ⅜-in. (9 mm) layers to make 2-layer petits fours.

Fruit Cake

Use 50% cake flour and 50% bread flour in the basic recipe. Add 250–750% (2.5–7.5 lb/1.25–3.75 kg) mixed fruits and nuts to the batter. Procedure and suggested fruit mixtures follow.

1. Prepare fruits and nuts.

   Rinse and drain glazed fruits to remove excess syrup.

   Cut large fruits (such as whole dates) into smaller pieces.

   Mix all fruits and soak overnight in brandy, rum, or sherry.

   Drain well. (Reserve drained liquor for later batches or for other purposes.)

2. Mix batter as in basic procedure, using 80% of the flour. If spices are used, cream them with the butter and sugar.

3. Toss the fruits and nuts with the remaining flour. Fold them into the batter.

4. Baking: Use loaf, ring, or tube pans, preferably with paper liners. Bake at 350°F (175°C) for small cakes (1–1½ lb/450–700 g), and 300°F (150°C) for large cakes (4–5 lb/1.8–2.3 kg). Baking time ranges from about 1½ hours for small cakes to 3–4 hours or more for large cakes.

5. Cool. Glaze with Clear Glaze (p. 116), decorate with fruits and nuts, if desired, and glaze again.

Percentages in the following fruit mixes are based on the flour in the basic pound cake recipe.

Fruit Mix I (Dark)

Ingredients	U.S.			Metric		%
Dark raisins	1 lb			500	g	100
Light raisins	1 lb			500	g	100
Currants		8	oz	250	g	50
Dates	1 lb			500	g	100
Figs		8	oz	250	g	50
Glacé cherries		6.5	oz	200	g	40
Nuts (pecans, walnuts, filberts, brazil nuts)		9.5	oz	300	g	60
Spices						
Cinnamon		0.08 oz (1½ tsp)		2	g	0.5
Cloves, ground		0.04 oz (½ tsp)		1.25	g	0.25
Nutmeg		0.04 oz (½ tsp)		1.25	g	0.25
Total weight:	*5 lb*			*2500*	*g*	*700%*

Fruit Mix II (Light)

Ingredients	U.S.		Metric		%
Golden raisins	12	oz	375	g	75
Currants	8	oz	250	g	50
Mixed glacé fruit	8	oz	250	g	50
Glacé pineapple	3	oz	100	g	20
Glacé orange peel	2.5	oz	75	g	15
Glacé lemon peel	2.5	oz	75	g	15
Glacé cherries	5	oz	150	g	30
Blanched almonds	4	oz	125	g	25
Spices					
Lemon zest, grated	0.06 oz (¾ tsp)		2	g	0.4
Total weight:	*2 lb 13*	*oz*	*1400*	*g*	*280%*

Almond Cake for Petits Fours

Ingredients	U.S.		Metric	%
Almond paste	3 lb	6 oz	1500 g	300
Sugar	2 lb	8 oz	1150 g	225
Butter	2 lb	8 oz	1150 g	225
Eggs	3 lb	2 oz	1400 g	275
Cake flour		12 oz	340 g	67
Bread flour		6 oz	170 g	33
Total weight:	*12 lb*	*10 oz*	*5710 g*	*1125%*

■ **P r o c e d u r e**

Mixing
Creaming method. To soften the almond paste, blend it with a little of the egg until smooth, before adding the sugar. Proceed as for mixing pound cake.

Scaling and Panning
4 lb 3 oz (1900 g) per sheet pan. One recipe is enough for 3 pans. Pans must be level and without dents. Spread batter very smooth.

Baking
400°F (200°C)
See page 390 for makeup of petits fours.

Sacher Mix I

Ingredients	U.S.		Metric	%
Butter	10	oz	250 g	100
Sugar	10	oz	250 g	100
Sweet chocolate, melted	12.5	oz	312 g	125
Egg yolks	10	oz	250 g	100
Vanilla extract	0.33	oz (2 tsp)	8 g	3.3
Egg whites	15	oz	375 g	150
Salt	0.08	oz (½ tsp)	2 g	0.8
Sugar	7.5	oz	188 g	75
Cake flour, sifted	10	oz	250 g	100
Total weight:	*4 lb 11*	*oz*	*1885 g*	*750%*

■ **P r o c e d u r e**

Mixing
Modified creaming method
1. Cream the butter and sugar; add the chocolate; add the egg yolks and vanilla, as in the basic creaming method.
2. Whip the egg whites with the salt. Add the sugar and whip to soft peaks.
3. Fold the egg whites into the batter alternately with the flour.

Scaling
6-in. (15 cm) cake: 14 oz (400 g)

7-in. (18 cm) cake: 19 oz (540 g)

8-in. (20 cm) cake: 24 oz (680 g)

9-in. (23 cm) cake: 30 oz (850 g)

10-in. (25 cm) cake: 36 oz (1020 g)

Baking
325°F (165°C) for 45–60 minutes

Note Sachertorte is a classic Austrian chocolate cake; it originated at the Hotel Sacher in Vienna. Many recipes claim to be the authentic original. Two of them are included in this chapter.
See p. 373 for icing and decorating a Sachertorte. Layers may be iced and decorated like any other chocolate cake, but then the cake should not be called Sachertorte.

Sacher Mix II

For large-quantity measurements, see page 604.

Ingredients	U.S.		Metric	%
Butter, softened	4.5	oz	135 g	337
Fine granulated sugar	3.67	oz	110 g	275
Egg yolks	4	oz	120 g	300
Egg whites	6	oz	180 g	450
Fine granulated sugar	2	oz	60 g	150
Cake flour	1.33	oz	40 g	100
Cocoa powder	1.33	oz	40 g	100
Powdered almonds, toasted	1.75	oz	55 g	137
Total weight:	*1 lb 8*	*oz*	*740 g*	*1849%*

Note See page 373 for icing and decorating Sachertorte. Layers may be iced and decorated like other kinds of chocolate cake, but then the cake should not be called Sachertorte.

■ P r o c e d u r e

Mixing

Modified creaming method

1. Cream the butter and sugar. Add the egg yolks as in the basic creaming method.

2. Whip the egg whites and sugar to a stiff meringue.

3. Sift together the flour and cocoa powder. Mix in the almonds.

4. Fold the meringue and dry ingredients alternately into the butter mixture, starting and ending with the meringue.

Scaling

6-in. (15 cm) cake: 7 oz (200 g)

7-in. (18 cm) cake: 10 oz (280 g)

8-in. (20 cm) cake: 12 oz (370 g)

9-in. (23 cm) cake: 16 oz (470 g)

Butter pans, line bottom with parchment, and dust with flour.

Baking

325°F (160°C), 35–45 minutes, depending on size

White Cake

For large-quantity measurements, see page 604.

Ingredients	U.S.		Metric	%
Cake flour	12	oz	375 g	100
Baking powder	0.75	oz	22 g	6.25
Salt	0.25	oz	8 g	2
Emulsified shortening	6	oz	188 g	50
Sugar	15	oz	470 g	125
Skim milk	6	oz	188 g	50
Vanilla extract	0.18 oz (1⅛ tsp)		5 g	1.5
Almond extract	0.09 oz (½ tsp)		2 g	0.75
Skim milk	6	oz	188 g	50
Egg whites	8	oz	250 g	67
Total weight:	*3 lb 6*	*oz*	*1696 g*	*452%*

■ P r o c e d u r e

Mixing
   Two-stage method
Scaling and Baking
   See table on page 305.

Variations

Use water instead of milk and add 10% (0.62 oz/18 g) nonfat dry milk to the dry ingredients. Flavor with lemon extract or emulsion instead of vanilla and almond.

Yellow Cake
Make the following ingredient adjustments:
   Reduce shortening to 45% (5.5 oz/168 g).
   Substitute whole eggs for egg whites, using the same total weight (67%).
   Use 2% (0.25 oz/8 g) vanilla and omit the almond extract.

Strawberry Cake
Make the following ingredient adjustments:
   Reduce the sugar to 100% (12 oz/375 g).
   Reduce the milk in *each* stage to 33% (4 oz/125 g).
   Thaw and purée 67% (8 oz/250 g) frozen, sweetened strawberries. Mix into the batter.

Cherry Cake
Make the following ingredient adjustments:
   Reduce the milk in *each* stage to 40% (4.75 oz/150 g).
   Add 30% (3.5 oz/112 g) ground maraschino cherries, with juice, to the batter.

Devil's Food Cake

For large-quantity measurements, see page 604.

Ingredients	U.S.			Metric	%
Cake flour	12		oz	375 g	100
Cocoa	2		oz	60 g	17
Salt	0.25		oz	8 g	2
Baking powder	0.375		oz	12 g	3
Baking soda	0.25		oz	8 g	2
Emulsified shortening	7		oz	220 g	58
Sugar	1 lb			500 g	133
Skim milk	8		oz	250 g	67
Vanilla extract	0.18		oz (1 tsp)	5 g	1.5
Skim milk	6		oz	188 g	50
Eggs	8		oz	250 g	67
Total weight:	*3 lb 12*		*oz*	*1876 g*	*500%*

■ **P r o c e d u r e**

Mixing
   Two-stage method
Scaling and Baking
   See table on page 305.

 ## High-Ratio Pound Cake

Ingredients	U.S.			Metric	%
Flour	1 lb 2		oz	500 g	100
Salt		0.25	oz	8 g	2
Baking powder		0.25	oz	8 g	2
Emulsified shortening	12		oz	335 g	67
Sugar	1 lb 5		oz	585 g	117
Nonfat milk solids	1		oz	30 g	6
Water	8		oz	225 g	45
Eggs	12		oz	335 g	67
Total weight:	*4 lb 8*		*oz*	*2026 g*	*406%*

■ **P r o c e d u r e**

Mixing
   Two-stage method
Scaling and Baking
   See table on page 305.

Variations

See variations following Old-Fashioned Pound Cake, page 312.

Yellow Chiffon Cake

Ingredients	U.S.		Metric	%
Cake flour	10	oz	250 g	100
Sugar	8	oz	200 g	80
Salt	0.25	oz	6 g	2.5
Baking powder	0.5	oz	12 g	5
Vegetable oil	5	oz	125 g	50
Egg yolks	5	oz	125 g	50
Water	7.5	oz	188 g	75
Vanilla extract	0.25	oz	6 g	2.5
Egg whites	10	oz	250 g	100
Sugar	5	oz	125 g	50
Cream of tartar	0.05	oz (⅝ tsp)	1 g	0.5
Total weight:	*3 lb 3*	*oz*	*1288 g*	*515%*

■ P r o c e d u r e

Mixing
   Chiffon method
Scaling and Baking
   See table on page 305.

Variations

Chocolate Chiffon Cake
Make the following ingredient adjustments:
   Add 20% (2 oz/50 g) cocoa. Sift it with the flour.
   Increase egg yolks to 60% (6 oz/150 g).
   Increase the water to 90% (9 oz/225 g).

Orange Chiffon Cake
Make the following ingredient adjustments:
   Increase the egg yolks to 60% (6 oz/150 g).
   Use 50% (5 oz/125 g) orange juice and 25% (2.5 oz/62 g) water.
   Add 0.5 oz (1 tbsp/6 g) grated orange zest when adding the oil.

Sponge Roll I (Swiss Roll)

Ingredients	U.S.		Metric	%
Egg yolks	12	oz	350 g	100
Sugar	8	oz	235 g	67
Cake flour	12	oz	350 g	100
Egg whites	1 lb 2	oz	525 g	150
Salt	0.25	oz	7 g	2
Sugar	6	oz	175 g	50
Total weight:	*3 lb 8*	*oz*	*1642 g*	*469%*

■ P r o c e d u r e

Mixing
   Separated-egg sponge method
Scaling
   1 lb 12 oz (820 g) per sheet pan. Line pans with greased paper.
Baking
   425°F (220°C), about 7 minutes

Variations

Chocolate Sponge Roll I (Chocolate Swiss Roll)
Sift 17% (2 oz/60 g) cocoa with the flour. Add 25% (3 oz/90 g) water to the whipped egg yolks.

Dobos Mix
Blend 100% (12 oz/350 g) almond paste with the sugar. Add a little of the yolks and blend until smooth. Add the rest of the yolks and proceed as in the basic formula.
Scaling and Panning
   Seven layers are needed to make Dobos Torte (see p. 372 for assembly instructions). For a round Dobos Torte, spread a thin layer of mix onto the greased, floured bottoms of upside-down cake pans or onto circles traced on parchment. One recipe makes about seven 12-in. (30 cm) circles or fourteen 8- or 9-in. (20–22 cm) circles. For rectangular torten, spread a thin layer of mix on greased, paper-lined pans. Four times the basic recipe makes seven full-size sheets. To make only one strip, scale 20 oz (550 g) onto one sheet pan. When baked, cut into seven 3½-in. (9 cm) wide strips.
Baking
   400°F (200°C)

Genoise

Ingredients	U.S.			Metric	%
Eggs	1 lb	2	oz	562 g	150
Sugar		12	oz	375 g	100
Cake flour		12	oz	375 g	100
Butter (*optional*)		4	oz	125 g	33
Vanilla extract or lemon flavor		0.25	oz	8 g	2
Total weight:	*2 lb 14*		*oz*	*1445 g*	*385%*

■ P r o c e d u r e

Mixing
    Genoise or butter genoise method
Scaling and Baking
    See table on page 305.

Variations

Chocolate Genoise
Substitute 2 oz (60 g) cocoa powder for 2 oz (60 g) of the flour.

Sponge for Seven-Layer Cake
Add 50% (6 oz/188 g) egg yolks and 10% (1.25 oz/38 g) glucose to the first stage of mixing. Scale at 1 lb 12 oz (800 g) per sheet pan or 14 oz (400 g) per half pan.

Almond Sponge I
Make the following ingredients adjustments:
    Add 50% (6 oz/188 g) yolks to the first mixing stage.
    Increase the sugar to 150% (1 lb 2 oz/560 g).
    Add 117% (14 oz/440 g) almond powder, mixed with the sifted flour.
(For more variations, substitute other nuts for the almonds.)

Almond Sponge II
Blend 125% (15 oz/470 g) almond paste with 50% (6 oz/188 g) yolks and blend until smooth. Blend in the sugar (from the basic recipe) until smooth. Add the eggs and proceed as in the basic recipe. (*Note:* This mix does not develop as much volume as regular genoise, and it makes a layer ⅞-in. (22 mm) thick if scaled like genoise. If desired, scale 25% heavier to make a thicker layer.)

Sponge Roll II
Omit butter from the basic recipe.

Chocolate Sponge Roll II
Omit butter from chocolate genoise mix.

Genoise Mousseline

For large-quantity measurements, see page 605.

Ingredients	U.S.		Metric	%
Whole eggs	10	oz	300 g	167
Egg yolks	1.33 oz (2 yolks)		40 g (2 yolks)	22
Sugar	6	oz	180 g	100
Cake flour, sifted	6	oz	180 g	100
Total weight:	*1 lb 7*	*oz*	*700 g*	*389%*

■ P r o c e d u r e

Mixing
    Plain sponge method
Scaling and Baking
    See table on page 305.

Jelly Roll Sponge

Ingredients	U.S.			Metric	%
Sugar	11	oz		325 g	100
Whole eggs	10	oz		292 g	90
Egg yolks	2	oz		65 g	20
Salt	0.25	oz		8 g	2
Honey or corn syrup	1.5	oz		45 g	14
Water	1	oz		30 g	10
Vanilla extract	0.12 oz (⅜ tsp)			4 g	1
Water, hot	4	oz		118 g	36
Cake flour	11	oz		325 g	100
Baking powder	0.16 oz (1 tsp)			5 g	1.5
Total weight:	*2 lb*	*7*	*oz*	*1217 g*	*374%*

■ **P r o c e d u r e**

Mixing

Plain sponge method. Add the honey or syrup, the first quantity of water, and the vanilla to the sugar and eggs for the first mixing stage.

Scaling and Baking

See the table on page 305. One recipe makes two sheet pans. Line the pans with *greased* paper. Immediately after baking, turn out of pan onto a sheet of parchment and remove the paper from the bottom of the cake. Spread with jelly and roll up tightly. When cool, dust with confectioners' sugar.

Milk and Butter Sponge

For large-quantity measurements, see page 605.

Ingredients	U.S.			Metric	%
Sugar	10	oz		312 g	125
Whole eggs	6	oz		188 g	75
Egg yolks	2	oz		60 g	25
Salt	0.12 oz (⅜ tsp)			4 g	1.5
Cake flour	8	oz		250 g	100
Baking powder	0.25 oz			8 g	3
Skim milk	4	oz		125 g	50
Butter	2	oz		60 g	25
Vanilla extract	0.25 oz			8 g	3
Total weight:	*2 lb*	*4*	*oz*	*1015 g*	*407%*

■ **P r o c e d u r e**

Mixing

Hot milk and butter sponge method

Scaling and Baking

Cake layers; see table on page 305.

Variation

Instead of vanilla, add 1.5% (0.5 oz/15 g) lemon flavor.

Angel Food Cake

Ingredients	U.S.	Metric	%
Egg whites	2 lb	1000 g	267
Cream of tartar	0.25 oz	8 g	2
Salt	0.17 oz (1 tsp)	5 g	1.5
Sugar	1 lb	500 g	133
Vanilla extract	0.33 oz (2 tsp)	10 g	2.5
Almond extract	0.17 oz (1 tsp)	5 g	1.25
Sugar	1 lb	500 g	133
Cake flour	12 oz	375 g	100
Total weight:	*4 lb 12 oz*	*2403 g*	*640%*

■ P r o c e d u r e

Mixing
  Angel food method
Scaling and Baking
  See table on page 305.

Variations

Chocolate Angel Food Cake
Substitute 3 oz (90 g) cocoa for 3 oz (90 g) of the flour.

Coconut Macaroon Cupcakes
Increase the first quantity of sugar to 167% (1 lb 4 oz/625 g). Mix 350% (2 lb 10 oz/1300 g) macaroon coconut with the flour/sugar mixture. Scale at 20 oz (575 g) per dozen cupcakes. Bake at 375°F (190°C) about 25 minutes.

Chocolate Fudge Cake

Ingredients	U.S.	Metric	%
Unsweetened chocolate	1 lb	500 g	400
Butter	1 lb	500 g	400
Eggs	1 lb 4 oz	625 g	500
Sugar	1 lb 4 oz	625 g	500
Bread flour	4 oz	125 g	100
Total weight:	*4 lb 12 oz*	*2375 g*	*1900%*

■ P r o c e d u r e

Mixing
  Plain sponge method. Melt the chocolate and butter together over a hot water bath. Fold the chocolate mixture into the egg-sugar foam before folding in the flour.
Scaling
  7-in. (18 cm) round pan: 19 oz (550 g)
  8-in. (20 cm) round pan: 25 oz (750 g)
  10-in. (25 cm) round pan: 38 oz (1100 g)
  Butter pans heavily before panning.
Baking
  350°F (175°C) until slightly under-baked, 20–30 minutes. Set cake pans on sheet pans to avoid scorching bottoms.
  Cool and glaze with warm ganache (p. 344).

Variations

Chocolate Surprise Cake
Fill large muffin tins or similar pans three-quarters full of batter. Insert a 1-oz (30 g) ball of cold ganache (p. 192) into the center of each. Bake at 350°F (175°C) about 15 minutes. Turn out and serve warm with whipped cream or ice cream. The melted ganache will run out when the cake is cut open.

Joconde Sponge Cake (Biscuit Joconde)

For large-quantity measurements, see page 605.

Ingredients	U.S.		Metric	%
Powdered almonds	3.5	oz	85 g	340
Confectioners' sugar	3	oz	75 g	300
Cake flour	1	oz	25 g	100
Whole eggs	4.75	oz	120 g	480
Egg whites	3.25	oz	80 g	320
Sugar	0.4	oz (2½ tsp)	10 g	40
Butter, melted	1.25	oz	30 g	120
Total weight:	*1 lb 1*	*oz*	*425 g*	*1700%*

■ P r o c e d u r e

Mixing

1. Mix together the almonds, confectioners' sugar, and flour in a bowl.

2. Add the eggs a little at a time. Mix well after each addition. Mix until smooth and light.

3. Whip the egg whites with the sugar until they form firm, glossy peaks.

4. Gently fold the egg mixture into the whipped egg whites.

5. Fold in the melted butter.

Scaling and Baking

Spread ¼ in. (5 mm) thick in half-size sheet pans lined with parchment. Allow 1 lb (425 g) per half sheet pan. Bake at 400°F (200°C) for 15 minutes, until golden and firm to the touch. Remove from pan and cool on a rack.

Variation

Hazelnut Joconde Sponge Cake

Substitute powdered hazelnuts for the powdered almonds. Omit the melted butter.

Ribbon Sponge

Yield: two half-size sheet pan

Ingredients	U.S.		Metric
Stencil paste			
Butter	7	oz	200 g
Confectioners' sugar	7	oz	200 g
Egg whites	7	oz	200 g
Cake flour	7.75	oz	220 g
Powdered food coloring (see variation)	as needed		as needed
Joconde Sponge batter (p. 322)	2 lb		850 g

Note This cake is used for decorative linings for cake molds and charlotte molds. Chapter 13 includes instructions for using the baked ribbon sponge. The stencil paste used to make the designs is another version of the batter used for Tuile cookies (pp. 418–419).

It is advisable to bake this sponge on a silicone mat so that the bottom of the cake doesn't brown. If a mat is not available, double-pan (set one sheet pan on top another) and bake on the top shelf of the oven.

■ P r o c e d u r e

a.

1. Beat the butter until soft. Add the sugar and mix well.

2. Add the egg whites, beating continuously.

3. Sift the flour into the mixture. Mix until smooth.

4. Color the paste with food coloring if desired.

5. Spread a thin layer of the paste onto a silicon mat with a palette knife (a).

6. Comb with a plastic pastry comb to make stripes, as shown here, or zigzags, wavy lines, or other patterns (b). Alternatively, an abstract "finger-painted" design can be applied by depositing dabs of colored stencil paste (c), and spreading them thin with a palette knife (d). If desired, make abstract "finger-painted" designs with the fingers (e).

b.

c.

d.

e.

7. Place the mat in the freezer until the paste is firm.

8. Cover the stencil paste with joconde sponge cake batter, spreading it to an even layer ¼ in. (5 mm) thick (f).

9. Bake in a 475°F (250°C) oven for about 15 minutes.

10. Transfer to a baking rack to cool.

11. Cut the strip to the desired length and use to line ring molds.

f.

Variations

For chocolate stencil paste to make brown and white ribbon sponge, substitute cocoa powder for *one-fifth* of the cake flour.

Plain genoise may be used instead of joconde sponge.

Ladyfinger Sponge

Ingredients	U.S.	Metric	%
Egg yolks	6 oz	180 g	60
Sugar	3 oz	90 g	30
Egg whites	9 oz	270 g	90
Sugar	5 oz	150 g	50
Lemon juice	¼ tsp	1 mL	0.4
Pastry flour	10 oz	300 g	100
Total weight:	*2 lb 1 oz*	*990 g*	*340%*

■ P r o c e d u r e

Mixing
Separated-egg sponge

Panning and Baking
One recipe is enough for one full-size sheet pan.
Use one of two methods for sponge sheets:

1. Using a pastry bag with a medium plain tip, pipe the sponge mix in diagonal lines on a sheet pan lined with parchment. Pipe the strips of batter so that they touch each other and so that the entire pan is filled with the sponge batter.

2. Alternatively, simply spread with a palette knife.

   Bake at 375°F (190°F) for about 10 minutes.

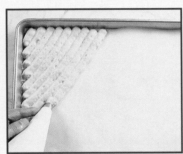

Variation

Ladyfinger Cookies
Pipe batter as in method 1 above, but pipe strips of batter 3½ in. (9 cm) long and keep them separate, not touching. Dredge the pan generously with confectioners' sugar. Grasp the parchment by two adjacent corners and lift, letting excess sugar fall off. Bake as above. One recipe makes about 100 ladyfingers.

Almond Pound Cake (Pain de Gênes)

Ingredients	U.S.		Metric	%
Almond paste	7.5	oz	225 g	167
Confectioners' sugar	5	oz	150 g	111
Egg yolks	4	oz	120 g	89
Whole eggs	1.67	oz	50 g	37
Vanilla extract	0.07	oz	2 g	1.5
	(½ tsp)			
Egg whites	6	oz	180 g	133
Sugar	2.5	oz	75 g	56
Cake flour	4.5	oz	135 g	100
Butter, melted	2.33	oz	70 g	52
Sliced almonds	2	oz	50 g	37
Total weight:	*2 lb 1*	*oz*	*1057 g*	*783%*

■ P r o c e d u r e

Mixing
Separated-egg sponge

1. Mix the almond paste and confectioners' sugar to a sand-like consistency.

2. Mix in the egg yolks, a little at a time. Then add the whole egg and vanilla. Beat well until smooth and light.

3. Whip the egg whites to soft peaks. Add the sugar and whip to stiff peaks.

4. Fold the meringue into the almond paste mixture.

5. Fold in the flour and melted butter.

Pan Preparation, Scaling, and Baking

1. Butter the bottom and sides of round or square cake pans. Line the insides of the pans with the sliced almonds.

2. For scaling, use the figures for high-fat cakes in table on page 305 at the high end of the weight range.

3. Bake at 340°F (170°C) for 20–25 minutes.

Marjolaine Sponge Cake

For large-quantity measurements, see page 605.

Ingredients	U.S.		Metric	%
Confectioners' sugar	4	oz	120 g	133
Powdered almonds	4	oz	120 g	133
Egg yolks	3.33	oz	100 g	111
Egg whites	2	oz	60 g	67
Egg whites	5	oz	150 g	167
Sugar	3	oz	90 g	100
Pastry flour, sifted	3	oz	90 g	100
Total weight:	*1 lb 8*	*oz*	*730 g*	*811%*

■ P r o c e d u r e

Mixing

Sponge method variation

1. Combine the confectioners' sugar, almonds, and egg yolks. Beat well.

2. Add the first quantity of egg whites. Whip until thick and light.

3. Whip the second quantity of egg whites with the sugar to make a common meringue. Fold into the egg yolk mixture.

4. Fold in the flour.

Makeup and Baking

Line sheet pans with parchment paper. Fit a pastry bag with a medium plain tip. Pipe disks of desired size using the technique shown on p. 260. Bake for 10 minutes at 350°F (180°C).

Hazelnut Sponge Cake

For large-quantity measurements, see page 605.

Ingredients	U.S.		Metric	%
Butter, softened	4.5	oz	135 g	337
Sugar	3.67	oz	110 g	275
Egg yolks	4	oz	120 g	300
Egg whites	6	oz	180 g	450
Sugar	2	oz	60 g	160
Cake flour	1.33	oz	40 g	100
Cocoa powder	1.33	oz	40 g	100
Ground hazelnuts, toasted	1.75	oz	55 g	138
Total weight:	*1 lb 8*	*oz*	*740 g*	*1860%*

■ P r o c e d u r e

Mixing

Combination creaming/sponge

1. Cream the butter and first quantity of sugar.

2. Add the egg yolks in several stages, beating well after each addition.

3. Whip the egg whites and second quantity of sugar to a stiff meringue.

4. Sift together the flour and cocoa. Mix in the hazelnuts.

5. Fold the meringue and the dry ingredients alternately into the butter mixture, starting and finishing with the meringue.

Scaling

12 oz (370 g) per 8-in. (20-cm) round pan. Grease pans and line bottoms with parchment. Flour the sides of the pan.

Baking

325°F (160°C), about 40 minutes.

Baumkuchen

Ingredients	U.S.		Metric	%
Butter	7	oz	200 g	114
Sugar	5	oz	150 g	85
Vanilla extract	0.07 oz (½ tsp)		2 g	1
Lemon zest, grated	0.03 oz (½ tsp)		1 g	0.5
Egg yolks	2.5	oz	80 g	43
Egg whites	7	oz	210 g	120
Sugar	5	oz	150 g	85
Cornstarch	6	oz	175 g	100
Powdered almonds	2.25 oz		65 g	37
Salt	0.07 oz (⅓ tsp)		2 g	1
Total weight:	*2 lb 2*	*oz*	*1035 g*	*586%*

■ P r o c e d u r e

Mixing

Combination creaming/sponge

1. Cream the butter, sugar, vanilla, and zest until light.

2. Beat in the egg yolks a little at a time.

3. Whip the egg whites until they form soft peaks. Add the sugar and whip until they form stiff, glossy peaks.

4. Fold the cornstarch into the egg whites.

5. Mix together the almonds and salt.

6. Fold the meringue and the almonds alternately into the butter mixture, starting and finishing with meringue.

Baking

1. Line the bottom of an 8-in. (20 cm) square cake pan with parchment.

2. Put about 1 oz (30 g) batter in the pan and spread it smooth with a small offset palette knife (a).

3. Place under a salamander or broiler until well and evenly browned (b).

4. Repeat steps 2 and 3 until the cake is about 1½ in. (4 cm) thick (c).

5. Chill.

6. The cut cake reveals a pattern of layers (d). It is used to line charlotte molds (see p. 367). It can also be cut into small pieces and served plain or iced with fondant (p. 334) as petits fours.

a.

b.

c.

d.

Almond Chocolate Sponge

For large-quantity measurements, see page 605.

Ingredients	U.S.	Metric	%
Marzipan	4.33 oz	130 g	325
Egg yolks	2.67 oz (4 yolks)	80 g (4 yolks)	200
Egg whites	4 oz (4 whites)	120 g (4 whites)	300
Sugar	1.67 oz (4 tbsp)	50 g	125
Cake flour	1.33 oz	40 g	100
Cocoa powder	1.33 oz	40 g	100
Butter, melted	1.33 oz	40 g	100
Total weight:	*1 lb*	*500 g*	*1250%*

■ **P r o c e d u r e**

Mixing

Separated-egg sponge

1. Beat the marzipan and egg yolks together until smooth and light.

2. Whip the egg whites and sugar to a stiff meringue.

3. Sift the flour and cocoa together. Fold the meringue and dry ingredients alternately into the egg yolk mixture, starting and ending with the meringue.

4. Fold in the butter.

Scaling and Baking

See table on page 305. For sponge circles (as for Monte Carlo Cake, p. 382), draw circles of desired size on parchment. Turn paper over and spread batter to fill the circles. Alternatively, pipe the batter using the technique shown in on page 260. One 7-in. (18 cm) circle requires about 8 oz (250 g) batter. Bake at 425°F (220°C) for 10–12 minutes.

Chocolate Sponge Layers

For large-quantity measurements, see page 606.

Ingredients	U.S.	Metric	%
Egg whites	5 oz	150 g	150
Sugar	4 oz	120 g	120
Egg yolks	3.5 oz	100 g	100
Cake flour	3.5 oz	100 g	100
Cocoa powder	1 oz	30 g	30
Total weight:	*1 lb 1 oz*	*500 g*	*500%*

■ **P r o c e d u r e**

Mixing

1. Whip the egg whites until foamy, then add the sugar and whip to soft peaks.

2. Whip the egg yolks until they are light and pale.

3. Fold the yolks into the whites.

4. Sift the flour with the cocoa powder. Fold into the egg mixture.

Makeup and Baking

Using a pastry bag with a plain tip, pipe circles of batter on parchment as shown on p. 260. Bake at 350°F (175°C) for 15 minutes.

Chocolate Velvet Cake (Moelleux)

For large-quantity measurements, see page 606.

Ingredients	U.S.		Metric	%
Almond paste	2.5	oz	75 g	188
Confectioners' sugar	1.67	oz	50 g	125
Egg yolks	2	oz	60 g	150
Egg whites	2	oz	60 g	150
Sugar	0.83	oz (5 tsp)	25 g	63
Cake flour	1.33	oz	40 g	100
Cocoa powder	0.33	oz	10 g	25
Butter, melted	0.67	oz	20 g	50
For baking				
Almonds, chopped	1	oz	30 g	
Total batter weight:	*11*	*oz*	*340 g*	*851%*

■ P r o c e d u r e

Mixing

    Modified separated-egg sponge

1.   Mix the almond paste and confectioners' sugar until the mixture has a sandy consistency.

2.   Mix in the egg yolks a little at a time. Beat until the mixture is smooth and light.

3.   Whip the egg whites and sugar to a stiff meringue. Fold into the almond paste mixture.

4.   Sift together the flour and cocoa. Fold into the batter.

5.   Fold in the melted butter.

Scaling and Baking

7-in. (18 cm) square pan: 11 oz (340 g)

8-in. (20 cm) square pan: 14 oz (425 g)

9-in. (23 cm) square pan: 19 oz (600 g)

    Butter the pans and line with the almonds before filling with batter.
    340°F (170°C), 20–25 minutes

Lemon Madeleines

For large-quantity measurements, see page 606.

Ingredients	U.S.		Metric	%
Egg yolks	2	oz	60 g	67
Demerara sugar (see *note*)	0.33	oz	10 g	11
Lemon zest, grated	0.13 oz (1½ tsp)		4 g	4.5
Honey	0.5	oz	15 g	17
Egg whites	2	oz	60 g	67
Extra-fine granulated sugar	2.5	oz	75 g	83
Salt	0.03 oz (⅙ tsp)		1 g	1
Baking powder	0.1 oz (½ tsp)		3 g	3
Cake flour	3	oz	90 g	100
Butter, melted	3	oz	90 g	100
Total weight:	*13*	*oz*	*408 g*	*453%*

Note   If Demerara sugar is not available, use regular white granulated sugar.

■ P r o c e d u r e

Mixing

Separated-egg sponge method. Fold the meringue and the sifted dry ingredients alternately into the whipped egg yolk mixture. Finish by folding in the melted butter. Chill the batter for 20 minutes.

Panning and Baking

1. Double-butter madeleine pans and dust with flour. Pipe batter into the pans using a pastry bag with a medium plain tip. Each small or petit four–size madeleine (1½ × 1 in. or 4 × 2.5 cm) requires about ⅙ oz (5 g) batter; a large madeleine (2½ × 1½ in. or 6.5 × 4 cm) requires about ⅔ oz (20 g) batter.

2. Bake at 350°F (180°C) until golden but still soft to the touch, about 6–7 minutes for small, at least twice as long for large madeleines.

3. Unmold onto wire racks to cool.

Variation

Chocolate and Orange Madeleines

For large-quantity measurements, see page 606.

Ingredients	U.S.		Metric	%
Egg yolks	2	oz	60 g	100
Demerara sugar (see *note*)	0.33 oz		10 g	17
Orange zest, grated	0.25 oz		8 g	13
Honey	0.5	oz	15 g	25
Egg whites	2	oz	60 g	100
Extra-fine granulated sugar	2.5	oz	75 g	125
Salt	0.03 oz (⅙ tsp)		1 g	1.7
Baking powder	0.13 oz (¾ tsp)		4 g	7
Cocoa powder	0.8 oz (4 tbsp)		25 g	42
Cake flour	2	oz	60 g	100
Butter, melted	3	oz	90 g	150

Follow the basic procedure, but make change the ingredients as listed above.

Marronier (Chestnut Cake Petits Fours)

Ingredients	U.S.		Metric	%
Sweetened chestnut purée	3.5	oz	100 g	133
Rum	0.33	oz (2 tsp)	10 g	13
Egg whites	8	oz	240 g	320
Granulated sugar	1.67	oz	50 g	67
Confectioners' sugar, sifted	5	oz	150 g	200
Powdered almonds	2	oz	60 g	80
Cake flour	2.5	oz	75 g	100
Butter, melted	3.5	oz	100 g	133
Garnish				
Confectioners' sugar	as needed		as needed	
Sugar-glazed chestnut halves	48		48	
Total batter weight:	*1 lb*	*10 oz*	*785 g*	*1046%*

■ P r o c e d u r e

Mixing

1. Soften the chestnut purée by mixing in the rum.

2. Whip the egg whites and granulated sugar to a stiff meringue. Fold into the chestnut purée.

3. Fold in the confectioners' sugar, almonds, and flour.

4. Fold in the melted butter.

Scaling and Baking

1. Butter and flour 2-in. (5 cm) tartlet molds.

2. Fill each mold with ½ oz (15 g) batter.

3. Bake at 375°F (190°C) for 8 minutes.

4. Remove from molds immediately after baking. Cool on racks.

5. When completely cool, dust the tops with confectioners' sugar. Top each cake with a half chestnut.

▶ TERMS FOR REVIEW

air cell	egg-foam cake	pound cake
emulsion	angel food method	fruit cake
creaming method	chiffon method	sponge roll
two-stage method	sponge method	ribbon sponge
flour-batter method	genoise	baumkuchen
high-fat cake	hot milk and butter sponge method	

▶ QUESTIONS FOR REVIEW

1. What are the three main goals of mixing cake batter?

2. How are the following concepts related to the goals in question 1: emulsion? creaming of fat and sugar? gluten development?

3. What are four precautions you should take to prevent a cake batter from curdling or separating?

4. List the steps in the creaming method of cake mixing.

5. List the steps in the two-stage, or high-ratio, mixing method.

6. List the steps in the sponge method. What extra steps are needed in the butter sponge or genoise method? In the hot milk and butter sponge method? In the separated-egg sponge method?

7. What are the advantages and disadvantages of using butter in high-fat cakes?

8. Why is there a lot of emphasis on scraping down the sides of the bowl and the beater in both the creaming method and the two-stage method?

9. How is mixing a creaming-method cake different from mixing a combination creaming/sponge method cake?

10. Which of the following cake ingredients are considered tougheners, which are tenderizers, which are driers, and which are moisteners?

   flour

   butter

   sugar

   egg whites

   egg yolks

   whole eggs

   milk (liquid)

   cocoa

   water

11. Why should angel food cake pans not be greased?

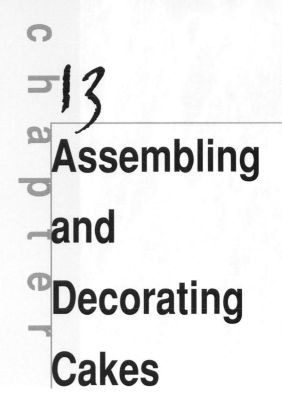

13

Assembling

and

Decorating

Cakes

$\mathcal{M}$uch of the appeal of cakes is due to their appearance. Cakes are a perfect medium with which a baker can express artistry and imagination.

A cake need not be elaborate or complex to be pleasing. Certainly, a simple but neatly finished cake is better than a gaudy, overdecorated cake that is done carelessly or without any plan for a harmonious overall design.

There are, of course, many styles of cake decorating, and within each style, hundreds or thousands of different designs are possible. This chapter is, in part, an introduction to some of the basic techniques for finishing cakes. The most important requirements for making effective desserts is hours and hours of practice with the pastry bag and paper cone—the decorator's chief tools. Even the simplest designs (such as straight lines) require a lot of practice and should be mastered. Only then should you proceed to the more advanced techniques presented in style manuals and cake decorating books.

A cake must be assembled and iced before it can be decorated. In this chapter, we begin with a study of icings, including recipes for many variations. Then we discuss the procedures for assembling basic layer cakes, sheet cakes, and other simple products. Examples of more elaborate cakes, including French and other European-style gâteaux and torten, are introduced in chapter 14.

ICINGS

Icings, also called *frostings,* are sweet coatings for cakes and other baked goods. Icings have three main functions:

- They contribute flavor and richness.
- They improve appearance.
- They improve keeping qualities by forming protective coatings around cakes.

There are seven basic types of icings:

- Fondant
- Buttercreams
- Foam-type icings
- Fudge-type icings
- Flat-type icings
- Royal or decorator's icing
- Glazes

Use top-quality flavorings for icings so that they enhance the cake rather than detract from it. Use moderation when adding flavors and colors. Flavors should be light and delicate. Colors should be delicate pastel shades—except chocolate, of course.

FONDANT

Fondant is a sugar syrup that is crystallized to a smooth, creamy white mass. It is familiar as the icing for napoleons, eclairs, petits fours, and some cakes. When applied, it sets up into a shiny, nonsticky coating.

Because it is difficult to make in the bakeshop, fondant is almost always purchased already prepared, either in the ready-to-use moist form or in the dry form, which requires only the addition of water. In an emergency (for instance, if you run out of fondant and there is no time to get more from your supplier), flat icing can be substituted for fondant, although it will not perform as well.

For those who wish to try making fondant in the bakeshop, a recipe is included here. The purpose of the glucose or the cream of tartar in the recipe is to invert some of the sugar in order to get the right amount of crystallization. If none is used, the syrup will set up to be too unworkable, and it will not be smooth and white. When an excess of glucose or cream of tartar is added, not enough crystallization will take place and the fondant will be too soft and syrupy. Also, if the hot syrup is disturbed before it cools sufficiently (step 6 in the procedure), large crystals will form and the fondant will not be smooth and shiny.

After reading this chapter, you should be able to:

- Prepare icings.
- Assemble and ice simple layer cakes, sheet cakes, and cupcakes.
- Make and use a paper decorating cone.
- Use a pastry bag to make simple icing decorations.

Procedure and Guidelines for Using Fondant

1. Heat fondant over a warm water bath, stirring constantly, to thin out the icing and make it pourable. *Do not heat it over 100° F (38° C) or it will lose its shine.*

2. If it is still too thick, thin it out with a little simple sugar syrup or water.

3. Flavorings and colorings may be added as desired.

4. To make *chocolate fondant,* stir melted bitter chocolate into warm fondant until the desired color and flavor are reached (up to about 3 oz bitter chocolate per lb of fondant, or 190 g per kg). Chocolate will thicken the fondant, so the icing may require more thinning with sugar syrup.

5. Apply the warm fondant by pouring it over the item or by dipping items into it.

Fondant

Yield: 6–7 lb (3–3.5 kg)

Ingredients	U.S.	Metric	Sugar at 100% %
Sugar	6 lb	3000 g	100
Water	1 lb 8 oz	750 g	25
Glucose	1 lb 2 oz	570 g	19
or			
Cream of tartar	0.5 oz	15 g	0.5

■ P r o c e d u r e

1. Clean a marble slab well and moisten it with water. Set four steel bars on the slab in the shape of a square to hold the hot syrup when it is poured onto the marble.

2. Combine the sugar and water in a heavy kettle and heat to dissolve the sugar. Boil until the temperature reaches 225°F (105°C).

3. If glucose is used, warm it. If cream of tartar is used, disperse it in a little warm water. Add the glucose or the cream of tartar to the boiling syrup.

4. Continue to boil the syrup until it reaches 240°F (115°C).

5. Pour the boiling syrup onto the marble slab and sprinkle it with a little cold water to prevent crystallization.

6. Let the syrup cool undisturbed to about 110°F (43°C).

7. Remove the steel bars and work the sugar with a steel scraper, turning it from the outside to the center. It will turn white and begin to solidify.

8. Continue to work the fondant, either by hand or by putting it in a mixing bowl and working it slowly with the paddle attachment, until it is smooth and creamy.

9. Keep the fondant in a tightly covered container.

BUTTERCREAMS

Buttercream icings are light, smooth mixtures of fat and sugar. They may also contain eggs to increase their smoothness or lightness. These popular icings for many kinds of cakes are easily flavored and colored to suit a variety of purposes.

There are many variations of buttercream recipes. We cover five basic kinds in this chapter:

1. *Simple buttercreams* are made by creaming together fat and confectioners' sugar to the desired consistency and lightness. A small quantity of egg whites, yolks, or whole eggs may be whipped in. Some formulas also include nonfat milk solids.

   Decorator's buttercream (sometimes called *rose paste*) is used for making flowers and other cake decorations. It is creamed only a little, as too much air beaten into it would make it unable to hold delicate shapes.

2. *Meringue-type buttercreams* are a mixture of butter and meringue. These are very light icings.

3. *French buttercreams* are prepared by beating a boiling syrup into beaten egg yolks and whipping to a light foam. Soft butter is then whipped in. These are very rich, light icings.

4. *Pastry cream–type buttercream,* in its simplest form, is made by mixing together equal parts thick pastry cream and softened butter. If more sweetness is desired, mix in sifted confectioners' sugar. The recipe included in this chapter (Vanilla Cream, p. 338) contains a lower proportion of butter. To give it the necessary body, a little gelatin is added.

5. *Fondant-type buttercream* is simple to make with only a few ingredients on hand. Simply cream together equal parts fondant and butter. Flavor as desired.

Butter, especially sweet unsalted butter, is the preferred fat for buttercreams because of its flavor and melt-in-the-mouth quality. Icings made only with shortening can be unpleasant because the fat congeals and coats the inside of the mouth, where it does not melt. However, butter makes a less stable icing because it melts so easily. There are two ways around this problem:

▶ Use buttercreams only in cool weather.
▶ Blend a small quantity of emulsifier shortening with the butter to stabilize it.

Buttercreams may be stored, covered, in the refrigerator for several days. However, they should always be used at room temperature in order to have the right consistency. Before using, remove buttercream from the refrigerator at least 1 hour ahead of time and let it come to room temperature. If it must be warmed quickly, or if it curdles, warm it gently over warm water and beat it well until smooth.

Flavoring Buttercreams

Because buttercreams may be combined with many flavorings, they are versatile and adaptable to many kinds of cakes and desserts.

The quantities given in the following variations are *suggested* amounts for each 1 lb (500 g) buttercream. In practice, flavorings may be increased or decreased to taste, but avoid flavoring icings too strongly.

Unless the instructions say otherwise, simply blend the flavoring into the buttercream.

1. *Chocolate* Use 3 oz (90 g) sweet chocolate.

   Melt chocolate and cool slightly (chocolate must not be too cool or it will solidify before completely blending with the buttercream). Blend with about one-quarter of the buttercream, then blend this mixture into the rest.

   For very sweet buttercreams, use 1½ oz (45 g) unsweetened chocolate instead of the sweet chocolate.

2. *Coffee* Use 1½ tbsp (5 g) instant coffee dissolved in ½ oz (15 mL) water.

3. *Marron (chestnut)* Use 8 oz (250 g) chestnut purée.

   Blend with a little of the buttercream until soft and smooth, then blend this mixture into the remaining buttercream. Flavor with a little rum or brandy, if desired.

French Buttercream

For large-quantity measurements, see page 607.

Yield: 1 lb 6 oz (688 g)

Ingredients	U.S.		Metric	Sugar at 100% %
Sugar	8	oz	250 g	100
Water	2	oz	60 mL	25
Egg yolks	3	oz	90 g	37.5
Butter, softened	10	oz	300 g	125
Vanilla extract	0.12 oz (¾ tsp)		4 mL	1.5

Variations

For flavored buttercreams, see pages 336–337.

■ P r o c e d u r e

1. Combine the sugar and water in a saucepan. Bring to a boil while stirring to dissolve the sugar.

2. Continue to boil until the syrup reaches a temperature or 240°F (115°C).

3. While the syrup is boiling, beat the yolks with a wire whip or the whip attachment of a mixer until they are thick and light.

4. As soon as the syrup reaches 240°F, pour it *very slowly* into the beaten yolks while whipping constantly.

5. Continue to beat until the mixture is *completely cool* and the yolks are very thick and light.

6. Whip in the butter a little at a time. Add it just as fast as it can be absorbed by the mixture.

7. Beat in the vanilla. If the icing is too soft, refrigerate it until it is firm enough to spread.

4. *Praline* Use 2 to 3 oz (60 to 90 g) praline paste.

Blend with a little of the buttercream until soft and smooth, then blend this mixture into the remaining buttercream.

5. *Almond* Use 6 oz (180 g) almond paste.

Soften almond paste with a few drops of water. Blend in a little of the buttercream until soft and smooth, then blend this mixture into the remaining buttercream.

6. *Extracts and emulsions (orange, lemon, etc.)* Add according to taste.

7. *Spirits and liqueurs* Add according to taste. For example: kirsch, orange liqueur, rum, brandy.

 ## Simple Buttercream

For large-quantity measurements, see page 607.

Ingredients	U.S.			Sugar at 100% Metric	%
Butter		8	oz	250 g	50
Shortening		4	oz	125 g	25
Confectioners' sugar	1 lb			500 g	100
Egg whites		1.25	oz	38 g	7.5
Lemon juice		0.08 oz (½ tsp)		2 g	0.5
Vanilla extract		0.12 oz (¾ tsp)		4 g	0.8
Water (*optional*)		1	oz	30 g	6.25
Total weight:	*1 lb 14*		*oz*	*949 g*	*190%*

■ P r o c e d u r e

1. Using the paddle attachment, cream together the butter, shortening, and sugar until well blended.

2. Add the egg whites, lemon juice, and vanilla. Blend in at medium speed. Then mix at high speed until light and fluffy.

3. For a softer buttercream, blend in the water.

Variations

For flavored buttercreams, see pages 336–337.

Simple Buttercream with Egg Yolks or Whole Eggs
Instead of the egg whites in the above recipe, substitute an equal weight of egg yolks or whole eggs. These substitutions make slightly richer icings. Also, the egg yolks help make a better emulsion.

Decorator's Buttercream or Rose Paste
Use 6 oz (190 g) regular shortening and 3 oz (90 g) butter. Omit lemon juice and vanilla. Add 0.75 oz (22 g) of either water or egg whites. Blend at low speed until smooth; do not whip.

Cream Cheese Icing
Substitute cream cheese for the butter and shortening. Omit egg whites. If necessary, thin the icing with cream or milk. If desired, flavor with grated lemon or orange zest instead of vanilla and use orange juice and/or lemon juice instead of milk for thinning the icing.

Meringue-Type Buttercream

For large-quantity measurements, see page 607.

Yield: 1 lb 7 oz (725 g)

Ingredients	U.S.		Metric	Sugar at 100% %
Italian meringue				
Sugar	8	oz	250 g	100
Water	2	oz	60 mL	25
Egg whites	4	oz	125 g	50
Butter	8	oz	250 g	100
Emulsified shortening	2	oz	60 g	25
Lemon juice	0.08 oz (½ tsp)		2 mL	1
Vanilla extract	0.12 oz (¾ tsp)		4 mL	1.5

■ **P r o c e d u r e**

1. Make the meringue (procedure on p. 183). Whip until *completely* cool.

2. Cream the butter, shortening, lemon juice, and vanilla until soft and light.

3. Add the meringue, a little at a time, blending it in well.

Variations

For flavored buttercreams, see pages 336–337.

Praline Buttercream

For large-quantity measurements, see page 607.

Yield: 1 lb 2 oz (550 g)

Ingredients	U.S.		Metric	Sugar at 100% %
Water	1.5	oz	40 g	33
Sugar	4	oz	120 g	100
Egg yolks	3.33 oz (5 yolks)		100 g	83
Butter, softened	6	oz	180 g	150
Praline paste	5	oz	150 g	125

■ **P r o c e d u r e**

1. Combine the water and sugar in a saucepan, bring to a boil to dissolve the sugar, and cook the syrup to 248°F (120°C).

2. Whip the egg yolks until light. Gradually add the hot syrup to the yolks, whipping constantly. Whip until cool.

3. Whip in the butter and the praline paste.

Vanilla Cream

For large-quantity measurements, see page 607.

Ingredients	U.S.		Metric
Pastry Cream II (p. 188)	1 lb		450 g
Gelatin	0.25	oz	6 g
Rum	4	tsp	20 g
Butter, softened	7	oz	200 g
Total weight:	*1 lb 7*	*oz*	*676 g*

■ **P r o c e d u r e**

1. Whip the pastry cream until smooth.

2. Soften the gelatin in cold water (see p. 39). Heat the rum. Add the gelatin and stir until dissolved, warming as necessary.

3. Beat the gelatin mixture into the pastry cream.

4. Beat in the butter a little at a time.

Caramel Buttercream

For large-quantity measurements, see page 607.

Yield: 1 lb (500 g)

Ingredients	U.S.		Metric	Sugar at 100% %
Water	1	oz	25 g	14
Sugar	6.5	oz	185 g	100
Water	1.75	oz	50 g	27
Heavy cream	1.25	oz	35 g	19
Coffee extract	0.2	oz (1 tsp)	5 g	2.7
Egg yolks	2	oz	60 g	32
Butter, softened	6.75	oz	190 g	103

■ **P r o c e d u r e**

1. Cook the first quantity of water and the sugar to the caramel stage.

2. Let the caramel cool to 250°F (120°C) and add the second quantity of water and the heavy cream. Cook until dissolved.

3. Add the coffee extract.

4. Whip the egg yolks until light, then whip in the hot caramel. Whip until light and continue whipping until the mixture has cooled to about 85°F (30°C).

5. Whip in one-third of the butter. When this has been uniformly incorporated, whip in the remaining butter.

Light Praline Cream

For large-quantity measurements, see page 607.

Ingredients	U.S.		Metric	Butter at 100% %
Butter, softened	8	oz	200 g	100
Praline paste	4	oz	100 g	50
Cognac	1.5	oz	40 g	20
Italian Meringue (p. 183)	14	oz	340 g	170
Total weight:	*1 lb 11*	*oz*	*680 g*	*340%*

■ **P r o c e d u r e**

1. Whip together the butter and praline paste until smooth and light.

2. Whip in the cognac.

3. Mix in the Italian Meringue.

FOAM-TYPE ICINGS

Foam icings, sometimes called *boiled icings,* are simply meringues made with a boiling syrup. Some also contain stabilizing ingredients like gelatin.

Foam icings should be applied thickly to cakes and left in peaks and swirls.

These icings are not stable. Regular boiled icing should be used the day it is prepared. Marshmallow icing should be made just before using and applied while still warm, before it sets.

Plain Boiled Icing

Follow the recipe for Italian meringue (p. 183), but include 2 oz (60 g) corn syrup with the sugar and water for the boiled syrup. Flavor the icing to taste with vanilla.

Marshmallow Icing

Soak ¼ oz (8 g) gelatin in 1.5 oz (45 mL) cold water. Warm the water to dissolve the gelatin. Prepare plain boiled icing. Add the dissolved gelatin to the icing after adding the hot syrup. Scrape down the sides of the bowl to make sure that the gelatin is evenly mixed in. Use while still warm.

Chocolate Foam Icing and Filling

Prepare boiled icing. After the syrup has been added, blend in 5 oz (150 g) melted, unsweetened chocolate.

FUDGE-TYPE ICINGS

Fudge-type icings are rich and heavy. Many of them are made somewhat like candy. They may be flavored with a variety of ingredients and are used on cupcakes, layer cakes, loaf cakes, and sheet cakes.

Fudge icings are stable and hold up well on cakes and in storage. Stored icings must be covered tightly to prevent drying and crusting.

To use stored fudge icing, warm it in a double boiler until it is soft enough to spread.

Caramel Fudge Icing

Yield: 2 lb (1 kg)

Ingredients	U.S.		Sugar at 100% Metric	%
Brown sugar	1 lb 8	oz	750 g	100
Milk	12	oz	375 g	50
Butter or part butter and part shortening	6	oz	188 g	25
Salt	0.1	oz (½ tsp)	2 g	0.4
Vanilla extract	0.25	oz	8 mL	1

■ Procedure

1. Combine the sugar and milk in a saucepan. Bring to a boil, stirring to dissolve the sugar. Boil the mixture until it reaches 240°F (115°C).

2. Pour the mixture into the bowl of a mixer. Let it cool to 110°F (43°C).

3. Turn on the machine and mix at low speed with the paddle attachment.

4. Add the butter, salt, and vanilla and continue to mix at low speed until cool. Beat the icing until it is smooth and creamy in texture. If it is too thick, thin it with a little water.

Quick White Fudge Icing I

Ingredients	U.S.		Sugar at 100% Metric	%
Water	4	oz	125 mL	12.5
Butter	2	oz	60 g	6
Emulsified shortening	2	oz	60 g	6
Corn syrup	1.5	oz	45 g	4.5
Salt	0.1	oz (½ tsp)	2 g	0.25
Confectioners' sugar	2 lb		1000 g	100
Vanilla extract	0.25 oz		8 mL	0.75
Total weight:	*2 lb 9*	*oz*	*1300 g*	*129%*

■ P r o c e d u r e

1. Place the water, butter, shortening, syrup, and salt in a saucepan. Bring to a boil.

2. Sift the sugar into the bowl of a mixer.

3. Using the paddle attachment and with the machine running on low speed, add the boiling water mixture. Blend until smooth. The more the icing is mixed, the lighter it will become.

4. Blend in the vanilla.

5. Use while still warm, or rewarm in a double boiler. If necessary, thin with hot water.

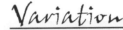

Variation

Quick Chocolate Fudge Icing
Omit the butter in the basic recipe. After step 3, blend in 6 oz (188 g) melted unsweetened chocolate. Thin the icing with hot water as needed.

Quick Fudge Icing II

Ingredients	U.S.		Fondant at 100% Metric	%
Fondant	1 lb 4	oz	500 g	100
Corn syrup	2	oz	50 g	10
Butter, softened	2	oz	50 g	10
Emulsified shortening	3	oz	75 g	15
Salt	0.12	oz	3 g	0.6
Flavoring (see procedure)				
Liquid, to thin (see procedure)				
Total weight:	*1 lb 11*	*oz*	*678 g*	*135%*
	or more		*or more*	*or more*

■ P r o c e d u r e

1. Warm the fondant to 95°F (35°C).

2. Combine the fondant, corn syrup, butter, shortening, and salt in the bowl of a mixer. Blend with the paddle attachment until smooth.

3. Blend in the desired flavoring (see below).

4. Thin to spreading consistency with appropriate liquid (see below).

Flavoring Variations

Add desired flavoring to taste, such as vanilla, almond, maple, lemon or orange (extract, emulsion, or grated zest), or instant coffee dissolved in water. Crushed fruit, such as pineapple, strawberries, or ground maraschino cherries, may be used.

For *chocolate icing,* add 6 oz (188 g) melted unsweetened chocolate.

Liquids for Adjusting Consistency

With fruit flavorings such as orange or lemon, use lemon juice and/or orange juice. With other flavors, use simple syrup or evaporated milk.

Cocoa Fudge Icing

Yield: 2 lb 6 oz (594 g)

Ingredients	U.S.		Granulated Sugar at 100% Metric	%
Granulated sugar	1 lb		500 g	100
Corn syrup	5	oz	150 g	30
Water	4	oz	125 mL	25
Salt	0.1	oz (½ tsp)	2 g	0.5
Butter or part butter and part emulsified shortening	4	oz	125 g	25
Confectioners' sugar	8	oz	250 g	50
Cocoa	3	oz	90 g	18
Vanilla extract	0.25	oz	8 mL	1.5
Water, hot	as needed		as needed	

■ P r o c e d u r e

1. Combine the granulated sugar, syrup, water, and salt in a saucepan. Bring to a boil, stirring to dissolve the sugar. Boil the mixture until it reaches 240°F (115°C).

2. While the sugar is cooking, mix the fat, confectioners' sugar, and cocoa until evenly combined, using the paddle attachment of the mixer.

3. With the machine running at low speed, slowly pour in the hot syrup.

4. Mix in the vanilla. Continue to beat until the icing is smooth, creamy, and spreadable. If necessary, thin with a little hot water.

5. Use while still warm, or rewarm in a double boiler.

Variation

Vanilla Fudge Icing

Use evaporated milk or light cream instead of water for the syrup. Omit cocoa. Adjust consistency with additional confectioners' sugar (to thicken) or water (to thin out). Other flavorings, such as almond, maple, peppermint, or coffee, may be used in place of vanilla.

FLAT ICINGS

Flat icings, also called *water icings,* are simply mixtures of confectioners' sugar and water, sometimes with corn syrup and flavoring added. They are used mostly for coffee cakes, Danish pastry, and sweet rolls.

Flat icings are warmed to 100°F (38°C) for application and are handled like fondant.

Flat Icing

For large-quantity measurements, see page 608.

Ingredients	U.S.		Sugar at 100% Metric	%
Confectioners' sugar	1 lb		500 g	100
Water, hot	3	oz	90 mL	19
Corn syrup	1	oz	30 g	6
Vanilla extract	0.12	oz (¾ tsp)	4 g	0.8
Total weight:	*1 lb 4 oz*		*630 g*	*125%*

■ P r o c e d u r e

1. Mix all ingredients together until smooth.

2. To use, place the desired amount in a double boiler. Warm to 100°F (38°C) and then apply to the product to be iced.

ROYAL ICING

This icing, also called *decorating* or *decorator's icing,* is similar to flat icings except that it is much thicker and made with egg whites, which make it hard and brittle when dry. It is used almost exclusively for decorative work.

Procedure for Preparing Royal Icing

1. Place desire amount of confectioners' sugar in a mixing bowl. Add a small quantity of cream of tartar (for whiteness), about ⅛ teaspoon per pound of sugar (1 gram per kilogram).

2. Beat in egg whites, a little at a time, until the sugar forms a smooth paste. You will need 2 to 3 ounces of egg whites per pound of sugar (125 grams per kilogram).

3. Keep unused icing covered with a damp cloth or plastic film at all times to prevent hardening.

GLAZES

Glazes are thin, glossy, transparent coatings that give a shine to baked products and help prevent drying.

The simplest glaze is a sugar syrup or diluted corn syrup brushed onto coffee cakes or Danish pastries while it is hot (see p. 116 for recipe). Syrup glazes may also contain gelatin or waxy maize starch.

Fruit glazes for pastries, the most popular of which are apricot and red currant, are available commercially prepared. They are melted, thinned with a little water, syrup, or liquor, and brushed on while hot. Fruit glazes may also be made by melting apricot or other preserves and forcing them through a strainer. It helps to add some melted, strained preserves to commercial glazes because the commercial products usually have little flavor.

Glaze recipes included in this chapter are of two types: *chocolate glazes* and *gelatin-based glazes.* Chocolate glazes are usually melted chocolate containing additional fats or liquids, or both. They are applied warm and set up to form a thin, shiny coating. Gelatin-based glazes, which include many fruit glazes, are usually applied only to the tops of cakes and charlottes made in ring molds. There are several recipes in this chapter, and chapters 14 and 16 both contain examples of products finished with gelatin-based glazes.

Chocolate Glaçage or Sacher Glaze

Ingredients	U.S.	Chocolate at 100% Metric	%
Heavy cream	6 oz	150 g	100
Dark chocolate, chopped	6 oz	150 g	100
Butter	2 oz	50 g	33
Total weight:	*14 oz*	*350 g*	*233%*

Procedure

1. Prepare a ganache (p. 192) with the cream and chocolate: Heat the cream to boiling and pour over the finely chopped chocolate. Stir until the chocolate is melted and the mixture is uniformly blended.

2. Add the butter and stir to mix in. Use as soon as possible.

Ganache Icing (Ganache à Glacer)

Ingredients	U.S.	Chocolate at 100% Metric	%
Heavy cream	10 oz	250 g	100
Sugar	2 oz	50 g	20
Glucose	2 oz	50 g	20
Dark chocolate couverture	10 oz	250 g	100
Total weight:	*1 lb 6 oz*	*600 g*	*240%*

■ **P r o c e d u r e**

1. Heat the cream, sugar, and glucose to the boiling point. Remove from the heat.

2. Finely chop the chocolate and stir into the hot cream mixture until melted.

3. Allow to cool slightly before use. This makes a thin, shiny coating when poured over cakes and charlottes.

Opera Glaze

For large-quantity measurements, see page 608.

Ingredients	U.S.	Metric
Coating chocolate (p. 43)	8 oz	250 g
Dark chocolate couverture	3.5 oz	100 g
Peanut oil	1.33 oz	40 g
Total weight:	*12 oz*	*390 g*

■ **P r o c e d u r e**

1. Melt both chocolates in a hot water bath.

2. Stir in the oil.

3. Allow to cool slightly before use. Makes a thin coating that sets solid but that can be cut with a hot knife.

Variation

If only couverture is used instead of part coating chocolate and part couverture, the quantity of oil must be increased so that the icing has the proper texture and can easily be cut with a cake knife.

For large-quantity measurements, see page 608.

Ingredients	U.S.	Metric
Dark chocolate couverture	11.5 oz	350 g
Peanut oil	2 oz	60 g

Cocoa Jelly

For large-quantity measurements, see page 608.

Ingredients	U.S.	Fondant at 100% Metric	%
Water	4 oz	100 g	67
Fondant	6 oz	150 g	100
Glucose	1 oz	25 g	17
Gelatin	0.25 oz	7 g	4.7
Cocoa powder	1.2 oz (6 tbsp)	30 g	20
Total weight:	*12 oz*	*312 g*	*208%*

■ **P r o c e d u r e**

1. Combine the water, fondant, and glucose. Bring to a boil and skim if necessary.

2. Soften the gelatin in cold water (see p. 39).

3. Add the gelatin and cocoa powder to the hot fondant mixture. Mix quickly and strain through a chinois or fine strainer.

4. This mixture is ready to use once the temperature has dropped to 95°F (35°C).

Fruit Glaçage

Ingredients	U.S.		Metric
Gelatin	0.5	oz	12 g
Sugar	3	oz	90 g
Water	2	oz	60 g
Glucose	1	oz	30 g
Fruit purée	5	oz	150 g
Total weight:	*11*	*oz*	*342 g*

■ P r o c e d u r e

1. Soften the gelatin in cold water (see p. 39).

2. Heat the sugar, water, and glucose until dissolved. Remove from the heat and stir in the gelatin until dissolved.

3. Add the fruit purée.

4. Strain through a chinois or fine strainer.

5. To use, rewarm if necessary. Pour over the top of a cake or charlotte and quickly spread to the edges of the cake with a palette knife. One small batch makes enough glaze for a 7- or 8-in. (18–20 cm) cake.

Two charlottes in this book, Passion Fruit Charlotte (p. 449) and Charlotte au Cassis (p. 448) use fruit glaçage. Passion fruit purée or juice and black currant or cassis purée, respectively, are used to make the glaçage. For other uses, most fruit purées can be used.

Coffee Marble Glaze

For large-quantity measurements, see page 608.

Yield: approximately 11 oz (350 g)

Ingredients	U.S.		Metric
Gelatin	0.33	oz	8 g
Water	8	oz	250 g
Sugar	1.33	oz	40 g
Glucose	1.33	oz	40 g
Vanilla bean, split (see *note*)	1		1
Coffee liqueur	4	tsp	20 g
Coffee extract	2	tsp	10 g

Note If vanilla beans are not available, add ½ tsp vanilla extract.

■ P r o c e d u r e

1. Soften the gelatin in cold water (see p. 39).

2. Simmer the water, sugar, glucose, and vanilla bean until the sugar and glucose are completely dissolved.

3. Remove from the heat, cool slightly, and add the gelatin. Stir until dissolved. Scrape the seeds from the vanilla bean and add to the syrup.

4. When ready to use, rewarm the glaze if necessary. Add the coffee liqueur and extract and swirl them in slightly, but do not mix them in. Swirl it over the surface of the cake so that the coffee extract gives a marbled effect (see the photo of Julianna on p. 383).

ASSEMBLING AND ICING SIMPLE CAKES

This section deals with simple, American-style cakes. Typical examples of this type are cupcakes, sheet cakes, and layer cakes made of two or three high-ratio or butter-cake layers. These are popular items in bakeshops and are standard desserts in many food service operations. They may be iced but otherwise undecorated, or they may be given some decorative touches.

SELECTION OF ICING

The flavor, texture, and color of the icing must be compatible with the cake.

In general, use heavy frostings with heavy cakes and light frostings with light cakes. For example, ice angel food cakes with a simple flat icing, fondant, or a light, fluffy, boiled icing. High-ratio cakes go well with buttercreams and fudge-type icings. Sponge layer cakes are often combined with fruits or fruit

Procedure for Assembling Layer Cakes

This is the basic procedure for assembling popular American-style layer cakes made with high-fat (that is, creaming method and two-stage method) batters. Layered sponge cakes are assembled slightly differently, as shown on page 364.

1. Cool cake layers completely before assembling and icing.

2. Trim layers if necessary.

    Remove any ragged edges.

    Slightly rounded tops are easily covered by icing, but excessively large bumps may have to be cut off.

    If desired, layers may be split in half horizontally. This makes the cake higher and increases the proportion of filling to cake (see p. 364).

3. Brush all crumbs from cakes. Loose crumbs make icing difficult.

4. Place the bottom layer upside down (to give a flat surface for the filling) on a cardboard cake circle of the same diameter. Place the cake in the center of a cake turntable. If a cake circle or turntable is not available, place the cake on a serving plate; slip sheets of wax paper or parchment under the edges of the cake to keep the plate clean.

5. Spread filling on bottom layer out to the edges. If the filling is different from the outside frosting, be careful not to spread the filling over the edges.

    Use the proper amount of filling. If applied too heavily, filling will ooze out when top layer is put in place.

6. Place top layer on bottom layer, right-side up.

7. Ice the cake:

    If a thin or light icing is used, pour or spread the icing onto the center of the cake. Then spread it to the edges and down the sides with a spatula.

    If a heavy icing is used, it may be necessary to spread the sides first, then place a good quantity of icing in the center of the top and *push* it to the edges with the spatula.

    Pushing the icing rather than pulling or dragging it with the spatula prevents pulling up crumbs and getting them mixed with the icing.

    Use enough icing to cover the entire cake generously, but not excessively, with an even layer.

    Smooth the icing with the spatula, or leave it textured or swirled, as desired.

    The finished, iced cake should have a perfectly level top and perfectly straight, even sides.

fillings, light French or meringue-type buttercreams, whipped cream, or flavored fondants.

Use the best quality flavorings and use them sparingly. The flavor of the frosting should not be stronger than that of the cake. Fudge-type icings may be flavored most strongly, as long as the flavor is of good quality.

Use color sparingly. Light, pastel shades are more appetizing than loud colors. Paste colors give the best results. To use either paste or liquid colors, mix a little color with a small portion of the icing, then use this icing to color the rest.

SHEET CAKES

Sheet cakes are ideal for volume service because they require little labor to bake, ice, and decorate, and they keep well as long as they are uncut.

For special occasions, sheet cakes are sometimes decorated as a single unit with a design or picture in colored icing, and a "Happy Special Occasion" message. It is more common, however, to ice them for individual service, as in the following procedure.

Procedure for Icing Sheet Cakes

1. Turn out the cake onto the bottom of another sheet pan or tray, as described on page 306. Cool the cake thoroughly.

2. Trim the edges evenly with a serrated knife.

3. Brush all crumbs from the cake.

4. Place a quantity of icing in the center of the cake and, with a spatula, push the icing to the edges. Smooth the top with the spatula, giving the entire cake an even layer of icing.

5. With a long knife or spatula, mark the entire cake off into portions, by pressing the back of the knife lightly into the icing. Do not cut the cake.

Cake-cutting guides for sheet cakes and round layer cakes. For half-size sheets (13 × 18 in./33 × 46 cm), simply halve the diagrams for full-size sheet cakes below.

18 x 26 in. (46 x 67 cm) sheets

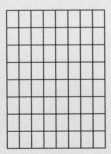

8 × 8 = 64 portions

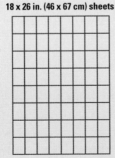

8 × 8 = 64 portions

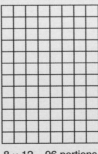

8 × 12 = 96 portions

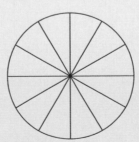

8–10 in. (20–25 cm) layers
12 portions

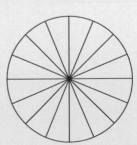

10–12 in. (25–30 cm) layers
16 portions

6. Using a paper cone or pastry bag fitted with a star tube, pipe a rosette or swirl onto the center of each marked-off portion. Or select another kind of decoration, as desired. Whatever decorations you use, keep them simple and make them the same for every portion.

7. Cut portions as close as possible to service time to keep the cake from drying.

CUPCAKES

There are three main methods for icing cupcakes. The first of these, dipping, is used for soft icings. The other methods are used when the icing is too stiff for dipping.

1. Dip the tops of the cupcakes in the icing. Do not dip them too deeply; only the tops should touch the icing.

    If the icing is reasonably stiff, not flowing, twist the cakes slightly and pull them out quickly in one smooth motion.

    If the icing is flowing (such as flat icing or fondant), pull the cakes straight out of the icing. Hold them sideways for a moment so that the icing runs to one edge. Then turn them upright and wipe the icing from the edge of the cakes with the finger. Do not let icing run down the sides.

2. Spread the icing with a spatula. Take enough icing for one cake on the tip of a bowl knife and cover the top of the cake in a smooth, neat motion, twisting the cake in one hand. Practice is necessary to develop speed and efficiency.

3. With a pastry bag fitted with a star tube, apply a swirl of icing to each cake.

    Before the icing dries, cupcakes may be decorated with glazed fruit, coconut, nuts, colored sugar, chocolate sprinkles, etc.

SPECIALTY ITEMS

A number of popular cake items don't fit in the above categories (layer cake, sheet cake, or cupcake). Among them are the following:

Boston Cream Pie

This is not a pie at all but a simple layer cake. Bake sponge cake in standard layer pans or pie tins. When cool, split each cake into two layers. Fill with Pastry Cream (p. 187) and ice the tops with chocolate fondant or sprinkle with confectioners' sugar.

Cake Rolls

Besides the popular jelly rolls (p. 320), sponge rolls can be made with a variety of fillings, such as whipped cream, vanilla or chocolate boiled icing or marshmallow icing, or buttercream. Cake rolls are discussed in more detail in the section on European-style cakes (p. 386).

Ice Cream Cakes

Ice cream may be used in place of icing to fill layer cakes or cake rolls. If the bakeshop is cool, or if you have a walk-in refrigerator to work in, you can spread slightly softened ice cream on the layers or inside the rolls. If the temperature is warm, however, it is better to cut slices of hard-frozen ice cream to fill the cakes. Work quickly; do not allow the ice cream to melt and drip out of the cake.

As soon as the layers are stacked or the rolls tightly rolled, return them to the freezer until they are firm. Then quickly frost the tops and sides with whipped cream. Store in the freezer until needed.

French Pastry

In parts of North America, the term *French pastry* is used for a wide range of decorated pastry and cake products usually made in single-portion pieces. The simplest of the cake-based varieties are tiny, decorated layer cakes made in a variety of shapes. They are assembled as follows:

1. Using thin (½–¾-in./1–2 cm) sheet cakes, stack two or three sheets with filling or icing between them. The filled cake layers together should be about 1½–2 in. (4–5 cm) thick.

   Buttercream is the most popular filling. Fruit jams and fudge icings may also be used.

2. Press the layers together firmly and chill briefly.

3. Using a sharp knife dipped in hot water before each cut, cut the sheet into desired shapes, such as squares, rectangles, or triangles. Circles may be cut out using large cutters. Pieces should be the size of a single portion.

4. Ice the sides and top of each piece with buttercream or fondant. After icing, sides may be coated with chopped nuts, coconut, chocolate sprinkles, etc.

5. Decorate the tops neatly.

French pastries are discussed further in the section on European-style cakes (p. 389).

BASIC DECORATING TECHNIQUES

A number of simple decorating techniques are discussed in this section. Of these, perhaps the most difficult ones to learn are those using the pastry bag and paper cone. Some other techniques don't require as much practice but instead rely simply on your steady hand and your sense of neatness and symmetry.

TOOLS

The following are needed for assembling and decorating cakes.

Palette knife or steel spatula A spatula with a long, flexible blade for spreading and smoothing icings and fillings.

Offset palette knife A palette knife with an angled blade that enables the chef to spread batters and creams inside pans.

Serrated knife A scalloped-edge knife for cutting cakes and for splitting cake layers horizontally into thinner layers.

Icing screens or grates Open-mesh screens for holding cakes that are being iced with a flow-type icing such as fondant. Excess icing drips off the cake and is collected on a tray under the rack.

Turntable A pedestal with a flat, rotating top, which simplifies the job of icing cakes.

Icing comb A plastic triangle with toothed or serrated edges; used for applying a grooved or ridged pattern to the sides of iced cakes. The edge of the comb is held stationary in a vertical position against one side of the cake while the turntable is rotated.

Plastic or steel scraper The flat edge is easily used to make the icing on the sides of cake perfectly smooth. The technique is the same as the technique for using the icing comb (see above).

Brushes   Used to remove crumbs from a cake, to apply dessert syrups to sponge cake layers, and to glaze the surfaces of cakes with apricot glaze and other coatings.

Sugar dredger   Looks like a large metal saltshaker. Used to dust cakes with confectioners' sugar.

Cake rings or charlotte rings   Stainless-steel rings of varying diameters and heights. Cakes are assembled inside these rings when they include soft fillings, such as Bavarian creams and other gelatin-based fillings, that must be held in place while the filling sets. Also used for charlottes (chapter 16).

Cake cards and doilies   Layer cakes are placed on cardboard circles (same diameter as the cake) when being assembled. This makes them easy to ice and to move after icing. For easy, attractive display, place a paper doily 4 in. (10 cm) larger than the cake on a cake card 2 in. (5 cm) larger than the cake. For example, to assemble, ice, and display a 10-in. cake, use a 10-in. circle, a 12-in. circle, and a 14-in. doily.

Parchment paper   For making paper cones.

Pastry bag and tips   For making borders, inscriptions, flowers, and other designs out of icing. The basic tips are described below.

 Plain (round) tips—for writing and for making lines, beads, dots, and so forth. Also used to pipe sponge batters, creams, and choux paste and to fill choux pastries and other items.

 Star tips—for making rosettes, shells, stars, and various borders.

 Rose tip—for making flower petals. These tips have a slit-shaped opening that is wider at one end than at the other.

 Leaf tips—for making leaves.

 Ribbon or basketweave tips—for making smooth or ridged stripes or ribbons. These have a slit opening that is ridged on one side.

 St-Honoré tip—for filling Gâteau St-Honoré (p. 278). This tip has a round opening with a V-shaped slit on one side.

Many other specialized tips are used for unusual shapes. However, the plain and star tips are by far the most important. It is probably best for the beginner to concentrate on these. They make a wide variety of decorations. With the exception of roses and other flowers, the majority of cake decorations are made with the plain and star tips.

The usual way of using a pastry tip is simply to fit it inside the pastry bag. When you need to use more than one tip with the same icing, you must use a separate bag for each one or you must empty out the bag to change the tip. However, special *couplers* are available that allow you to attach the tip to the outside of the bag. It is then a simple matter to change tips even when the pastry bag is full of icing.

USING THE PAPER CONE

The paper cone is widely used in decorative work. It is inexpensive, easy to make, and it can simply be discarded after use. It is especially valuable if you are working with different colors; simply make a separate cone for each color icing.

Although it is possible to fit metal decorating tubes inside paper cones, the cones are usually used without metal tubes, for writing inscriptions and for making line drawings and patterns. In other words, they are used the same way you would use a pastry bag fitted with a small plain tube. Because paper cones can be made rather small and are easy to control, pastry chefs generally prefer them to pastry bags when they are doing delicate work. For the most delicate work, a special type of plastic or cellophane is available that makes finer lines than paper because a smaller, cleaner opening can be cut on the tip.

Two factors are important if you are to be successful with both the paper cone and the pastry bag.

1. *Consistency of the icing.* Icing must be neither too thick nor too thin. With the paper cone or the writing tube, the icing must be thin enough to flow freely from the opening but not too thin to form a solid thread. Stiff icing is difficult to force through the opening and tends to break off. For flowers and large decorations, the icing must be stiffer so that it holds its shape.

2. *Pressure on the cone or bag.* Pressure control is necessary for neat, exact decorations. As described below, sometimes you must keep the pressure steady and even. For other types of decorations, such as shell borders, you must vary the pressure from heavy to light, and then stop the pressure at the right time. Learning to control the pressure with which you squeeze the decorator's cone or pastry bag takes a lot of practice.

Two methods are used to make decorations: the ***contact method*** and the ***falling method.***

The *falling method* is so called because the cone is held above the surface, and the icing is allowed to fall or drop from the tip of the cone onto the surface being decorated. This method is used to make lines of even thickness on horizontal surfaces. Much, if not most, paper-cone work is done this way, generally with royal icing, fondant, chocolate fondant, melted chocolate, or piping chocolate (p. 543).

Hold the cone vertically. Touch the tip of the cone to the surface to attach the icing to the point where you want the line to start. Then, as you begin to squeeze the cone, lift the tip of the cone from the surface and start your line. Hold the cone about 1 in. ($2\frac{1}{2}$ cm) from the surface as you trace your pattern. The thread of icing is suspended in air between the tip of the cone and the surface being decorated. Keep the pressure light and constant. To finish a line, lower the tip of the cone and touch the surface at the point where you want the line to end. At the same time, stop squeezing the cone.

This method allows you to make very fine, delicate lines and patterns while keeping the thickness of the line perfectly even. The opening in the tip of the cone should be cut quite small. At first, it may seem difficult to control the line while holding the cone an inch above the surface, but with practice, you will be able to make very precise patterns.

The *contact method* is used in two cases: (1) when you want to vary the thickness of the line, and (2) when you want to decorate a vertical surface, such as the side of a cake.

Hold the cone as you would hold a pen, with the tip in contact with the surface and at an angle of about 30 to 45 degrees. Draw lines as though you were drawing on paper with a pen. Control the thickness of the line by adjusting the pressure of your thumb. Squeezing harder makes a thicker line.

It takes a fair amount of practice to control the thickness of the line. Normally, it is best to practice the falling method first, until you can make simple lines and patterns easily. Then, when you practice the contact method, you can

Procedure for Decorating with a Paper Cone

1. Make the paper cone as shown at right.

2. Fill the cone about half full of icing. If the cone is too full, it is hard to squeeze, and icing is likely to come out the top.

3. Fold down the top of the cone to close the open end.

4. With scissors, cut off a very small piece of the tip of the cone. It is better to make the opening too small than too large. Squeeze out a little of the icing to test the cone. If necessary, cut off a little more of the tip to enlarge the opening.

5. Hold the top end of the cone between the thumb and the first two fingers of the right hand (if you are right-handed). The fingers should be positioned so that they hold the folded end closed and at the same time apply pressure to squeeze the icing from the cone.

6. The left hand does *not* squeeze the cone. Lightly hold the index finger of the left hand against the thumb of the right hand or against the cone in order to steady your right hand and help guide it.

7. Use either the contact method or the falling method (discussed on p. 351) to create different types of decorations and inscriptions.

Make a single cone out of a small triangle of parchment paper. Hold the cone with the fingertip in the center of the long side and curl one side

Curl the other side around to complete the cone.

Fold over the peak at the open end of the cone to secure it.

concentrate on controlling pressure. In addition to royal icing, fondant, and chocolate, buttercream is also used for decorating with the contact method.

The following instructions for using the cone and pastry bag are written for right-handed people. If you are left-handed, simply reverse the hands in the instructions.

For a sturdier double cone, cut a longer triangle. Start as for a single cone.

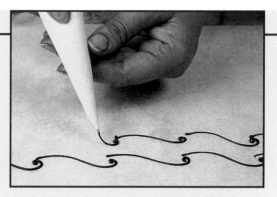

Note how the tip of the cone is held above the surface, allowing the icing to drop into place.

Twist the long end around twice to complete the cone.

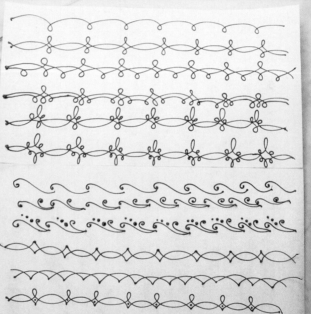

An assortment of borders made with the paper cone.

Complete single and double cones.

Paper-cone designs made by the contact method

USING THE PASTRY BAG

An advantage of the pastry bag is that it makes it easy to use different metal tips to create a wide variety of designs. Also, a pastry bag holds more icing than a paper cone. This is important when you are decorating with whipped cream or meringue. Buttercream flowers, shell borders, and many other decorations are made with the pastry bag.

Most pastry bags are made of one of the following four materials. *Disposable plastic* bags are designed to be thrown away after use. As a result, they

Procedure for Filling and Using a Pastry Bag

1. Fit the desired metal tip into the pastry bag.

2. If the filling or icing is thin, twist the bag just above the tip and force it into the tip. This prevents the filling from running out of the bag while the bag is being filled.

3. Turn down the top of the bag into a sort of collar. Slip your hand under this collar and hold the top open with your thumb and forefinger.

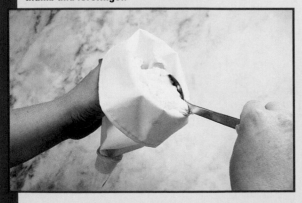

4. Fill the bag half to three-quarters full. Remember that stiff icings are relatively hard to force from the bag, so the bag should be filled less. With meringue and whipped cream, the bag can be fuller.

5. Turn the top of the bag up again. Gather the loose top together and hold it shut with the thumb and forefinger of your right hand (if you are right-handed).

6. To force out the icing or cream, squeeze the top of the bag in the palm of your right hand.

7. The fingers of the left hand are used to lightly guide the tip of the bag, *not* to squeeze the bottom of the bag. The left hand is sometimes used to hold the item being filled or decorated.

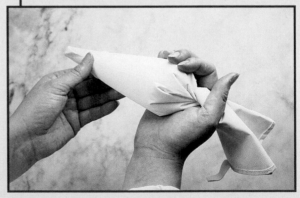

are hygienic. *Reusable plastic* bags are made of a soft, reinforced plastic, making them durable and easy to use. They must be thoroughly cleaned after use, but they do not easily absorb odors and flavors. *Nylon* bags are soft and flexible. They must be cleaned thoroughly after use, but because they are made of a synthetic fabric, they are easier to clean than cotton. *Cotton* is the traditional material for pastry bags, but because it is so absorbent, they are harder to clean. It is important to wash them well and sterilize them after use.

Piping basic shells and shell borders.

Simple bulbs, bead borders, and rosettes.

Scrolls and borders made with a star tip.

Additional scrolls and borders made with a star tip plus, at the bottom, an example of piping with a St. Honoré tip.

OTHER DECORATING TECHNIQUES

There are many dozens of techniques for decorating cakes. Below are some of the simpler, more commonly used techniques. In the next chapter and in the accompanying illustrations, you will see examples of these and other techniques.

A frequently used way of organizing the decoration of a cake is to divide the cake into portions by marking the icing on top with the back of a long knife. First mark the cake in quarters. Then divide each quarter in half, thirds, or fourths, depending on the size of the cake and the number of pieces desired.

Decorate the cake in a repetitive pattern so that each slice has the same decorations. For example, you might decorate a Black Forest Cake (p. 370) with a rosette of cream at the wide end of each wedge, then place a cherry on each rosette.

The advantage of marking the cake into wedges is that it provides portion control. Thus, this approach is often used in restaurants and in retail shops that sell cakes by the slice. Each slice, when cut and served, retains an attractive decoration.

Masking the Sides

Apply a coating of chopped or sliced nuts, coconut, chocolate sprinkles, chocolate shavings, cake crumbs, or another material to the sides of the cake. Hold the freshly iced cake (on a cardboard circle) in your left hand over the tray of nuts or other material. With your right hand, lightly press a handful of the material against the side of the cake, and let the excess fall back onto the tray. Turn the cake slightly and repeat until the coating is complete. You can coat the sides completely or just the bottom edge.

Stenciling

Designs can be made on a cake by masking part of the top with paper cutouts or paper doilies and then sprinkling the top of the cake with confectioners' sugar, cocoa, ground nuts, shaved chocolate, cake crumbs, praline powder, or another fine material. Alternatively, spray the top of the cake with a chocolate sprayer, as shown on page 543. Carefully remove the paper pattern to reveal the design. A simple type of stenciling that is effective on chocolate icings is to place parallel strips of paper on the cake and dust with confectioners' sugar.

Marbling

This technique is most frequently used with fondant. Ice the top of the cake with one color fondant, then pipe lines or spirals in a contrasting color. Quickly, before the icing sets, draw the back of the knife through the icing to marble it. This is the same technique used to ice napoleons (p. 241). More elab-

Examples of marbled icing patterns

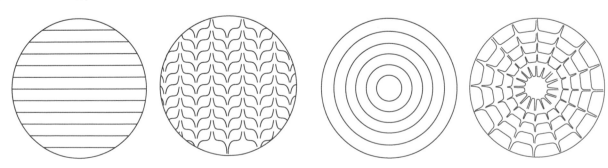

orate marbled icing patterns are made by piping lines, circles, or spirals of a contrasting color fondant onto an iced cake top, then drawing the back of a knife or spatula across the lines before the icing sets.

Palette Knife Patterns

Icing can be textured quickly and easily with a palette knife as soon as the cake is iced. To make a spiral pattern, leave the cake on the turntable and press the rounded end of the blade lightly into the icing at the center of the cake. Slowly turn the turntable and, at the same time, gradually draw the tip of the palette knife to the outer edge of the cake.

If you wish, this spiral can be marbled with the edge of the knife the same way you would marble fondant stripes. Other patterns, such as straight, parallel ridges, can be made with the palette knife and then marbled.

Piping Jelly

Piping jelly is a transparent, sweet jelly used for decorating cakes. It is available in various colors and in a clear, colorless form that you can color yourself. Piping jelly can be piped directly onto a cake with a paper cone. For example, you can add a touch of color to borders by first decorating them with one of the designs on page 353 and then filling in some of the small loops with colored piping jelly.

Another way to use piping jelly is to make jelly transfers. These are colored pictures that are made ahead of time and applied to cakes as needed. Their advantage is that they can be made during slack hours and stored until called for.

Procedure for Making Piping Jelly Transfers

1. Trace the desired drawing onto a sheet of tracing paper or, if you wish, draw a picture freehand.

2. Turn the drawing over so that the tracing is underneath and can be seen through the paper. (The paper is turned over so that the pen or pencil marks don't come off with the jelly.)

3. Outline the drawing with brown piping jelly.

4. Fill in the outlines with piping jelly of appropriate colors.

5. Let the jelly dry. This takes a day.

6. Turn the transfer over and place it, jelly-side down, on the iced cake.

7. Moisten the back of the paper lightly with a brush dipped in water.

8. Let the cake and paper stand a few minutes. Then carefully peel off the paper, leaving the jelly picture on the cake.

Adding Fruits, Nuts, and Other Items

Arranging fruits, nuts, and other items on a cake in an attractive pattern is an easy and effective way to decorate a cake while adding to its flavor and its appeal to the customer. This technique is especially appropriate for cakes that are marked off into portions, as described at the beginning of this section. Each portion can be topped with an appropriate item, such as cherries on the black forest cake.

Naturally, you should use items appropriate to the flavor of the cake. For example, you might place candy coffee beans on a mocha cake or mandarin orange segments on an orange-flavored cake.

Following are examples of items that can be arranged decoratively on cakes:

- whole strawberries
- sweet cherries
- mandarin orange segments
- pineapple wedges
- glacéed fruits
- candied chestnuts
- pecan halves
- walnut halves
- small, crisp meringues
- chocolates, such as chocolate truffles
- chocolate curls or other chocolate decorations
- small candies (except hard candies, because a customer might break a tooth)
- marzipan cutouts (cut from colored marzipan (p. 552) rolled out in sheets) and marzipan figures

DECORATING SEQUENCE

Although the order in which decorations are placed on the cake depends on the cake and the baker's preferences, many pastry chefs prefer the following sequence:

1. The sides of the cake are coated with nuts, crumbs, or other coatings, either before or after decorating. If the top decorations are delicate and might be damaged if the cake is handled, mask the sides first. However, if you are marbling the top of the cake or using some other technique that disturbs the icing on the sides of the cake, then mask the sides afterwards.

2. If the cake is to have an inscription or message, such as a person's name or a holiday or birthday greeting, put this on first.

3. Add borders and paper-cone designs.

4. Add flowers, leaves, and similar decorations made with a pastry bag.

5. Add additional items such as fruits, nuts, or candies.

► TERMS FOR REVIEW

fondant	flat icing	French pastry	paper cone
buttercream	royal icing	icing screen	marbling (icing)
boiled icing	glaze	turntable	piping jelly
marshmallow icing	Boston cream pie	icing comb	gâteau

► QUESTIONS FOR REVIEW

1. What is the most important rule to consider when using fondant? Why?

2. What are the advantages and disadvantages of using butter and using shortening in buttercream icings?

3. What are the steps for assembling and icing a two-layer cake?

4. What method would you use to ice cupcakes with fondant? With buttercream?

5. Why is the consistency of the icing important when you are decorating with a paper cone or pastry bag?

6. True or false: If you are right-handed, you should hold the top of the pastry bag shut with your right hand and squeeze the bag with your left hand. Explain your answer.

7. Name four techniques you can use for partially or completely decorating a cake without using a pastry bag or paper cone.

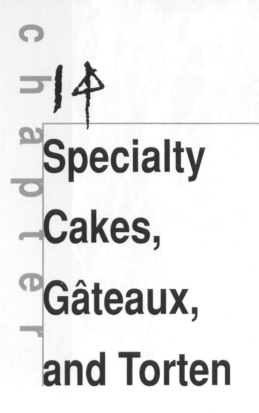

Specialty Cakes, Gâteaux, and Torten

A typical American layer cake consists of two components—cake layers and icing. The cake has two or sometimes three fairly thick layers and is often a high-ratio or creaming-method cake. The iced cake may be 3 or 4 in. high or higher.

A typical European cake, on the other hand, can be described as follows: sponge cake, such as genoise, split into thin layers, moistened with a flavored syrup, filled and iced, and frequently set on a base of baked meringue, japonaise, or short dough. It is sometimes filled with fruit between the layers, and is almost always decorated on top. A European-style cake is usually less than 3 in. (7.5 cm) high, and its broad, flat top provides an excellent medium for pastry chefs to display their decorating skills.

The above descriptions of American and European cakes are, of course, generalizations, so there are many exceptions to both descriptions. Nevertheless, they do give you some idea of the common differences and serve to introduce the subject of European-style cake assembly.

PLANNING AND ASSEMBLING SPECIALTY CAKES

After reading this chapter, you should be able to:

■ Select from a variety of components to plan cakes that have well-balanced flavors and textures.

■ Line charlotte rings or cake rings for specialty cakes.

■ Coat a cake with marzipan.

■ Assemble a variety of European-style cakes, Swiss rolls, small cakes, and petits fours.

As we have suggested several times in this book, much of a pastry cook's job is assembly work—that is, starting with a number of basic elements such as creams, fillings, and baked doughs and batters, the pastry cook builds desserts by putting these elements together in different and attractive ways. This is especially true of the construction of European-style cakes.

Although the number of ingredients that can go into a cake is nearly limitless, the most commonly used components are listed below. Following this list is a general procedure for assembling a basic European-style cake. Following that are procedures for making specific desserts, most of which are popular classics. However, once you are familiar with the general procedure, you should be able to go beyond those included here and put together your own cakes. Just make sure that the flavors of the cake layers, fillings, icings, and syrups that you choose go well together.

A cake that comprises too many flavors is less pleasing than one with a few flavors that blend well or have a pleasing contrast. Texture, too, is an important consideration. A mixture of creamy, crisp, and cakelike textures is more interesting to the palate than a cake that consists mostly of mousse. Ingredients such as fruits, nuts, nougatine, caramel, chocolate, crisp meringue, and puff pastry add textural interest.

Two words you will see often in connection with European-style cakes are *gâteau* and *torte*. Gâteau is the French word for cake (the plural is *gâteaux;* both singular and plural are pronounced "ga-toe"). The term is nearly as general as the English word *cake* and is used for a wide range of products. For example, in chapter 11 you can find Gâteau Pithiviers, made of puff pastry and almond filling, and Gateau St-Honoré, made of short dough and éclair paste and filled with a type of pastry cream. *Gâteaux* can also refer to more conventional layer cakes.

The German word *torte* (plural *torten*) is generally used for layer cakes. Its many definitions often contradict each other. According to a British definition, a torte is a sponge layer cake that is marked off into individual wedges that are then individually decorated. Another entirely different definition says that a torte is a cake baked from a batter that contains nuts and/or crumbs and little or no flour. Yet there are classic tortes that fit neither definition.

Rather than try to decide the issue or add to the confusion, we will simply use the words *torte* and *gâteau* when they are parts of a generally accepted name of a classic dessert, such as Sachertorte and Gâteau St-Honoré.

BASIC CAKE COMPONENTS

Following are some of the more important types of components that pastry chefs use to construct specialty cakes.

Optional bottom layer	Baked short dough circle (p. 232)
	Baked meringue or japonaise (pp. 260–263)
Optional cake ring linings	(p. 366)
Cake layers	Genoise, other plain sponge (p. 319)
	Almond sponge or other nut sponge (pp. 319, 325)
	Chocolate sponge (pp. 319, 327)
Additional specialty layers	Puff paste disks (pp. 236–237)
	Japonaise or meringue discs (pp. 260–263)
For moistening and flavoring cake layers	Dessert syrup (p. 178)
Fillings	Jam or jelly (especially apricot and raspberry)
	Buttercream (pp. 335–339)
	Crème Chantilly (p. 181)
	Ganache (p. 192)
	Chocolate mousse (p. 193)
	Pastry cream and variations (pp. 185–191)
	Bavarian cream (pp. 441–443)
	Fruits (fresh, poached, or canned)
Icings and coatings	Buttercream (pp. 335–339)
	Fondant (p. 334)
	Whipped cream (p. 181)
	Marzipan (p. 552)
	Glazes (pp. 343–345)

Because there are so many types of specialty cakes, some of which can be quite complex, we introduce the methods for making them in two stages. The first procedure below is for assembling a basic layered sponge cake from baked cake layers and icing. Notice that this procedure is somewhat different than the procedure used for high-fat cakes explained in chapter 13. The most important difference is the use of flavored syrups.

The second introduces many of the techniques used for some of the more elaborate cakes later in this chapter. Please note that this is only a general procedure. Some of the same steps appear in both procedures.

Procedure for Assembling a Basic Layered Sponge Cake

1. Trim the edges of the cake as necessary.

2. Cut a notch in the edge of the cake so that the layers can be lined up again after cutting.

3. Split in half horizontally.

4. Place one half on a cake card and moisten with a flavored syrup.

5. Applying the filling with a pastry bag is an easy way to get a layer of uniform thickness.

6. Top with the second layer and mask the top and sides with the desired icing.

7. Smooth the sides with a plastic scraper.

8. With a palette knife, smooth the top. The cake is now ready for glazing, if desired, and decorating.

9. Most glazes are applied by pouring the warm glaze over the cake. If necessary, spread quickly with a palette knife before the glaze sets.

General Procedure for Assembling European-Style Specialty Cakes

1. Assemble all ingredients and equipment.

2. Place a cake card on a turntable or on the work surface. The cake will be assembled on top of the card.

3. Split sponge cake horizontally into two or three layers, depending on the thickness of the cake. Alternatively, use a sponge that is baked in a thin layer, cutting it to the desired shape and size if necessary.

4. If using a charlotte ring (cake ring), line the ring as desired (see p. 366).

5. If using a japonaise, meringue, or short-dough base, place it on the cake card. Stick it down with a dab of icing or jam so that it doesn't slide off the card. (If you are using a cake ring, place the base inside the ring.) Spread with a thin layer of filling or jam. Raspberry or apricot jam is often used on short-dough bases.

6. Place one sponge layer on top of the base or, if you are not using a base layer, place the sponge layer directly on the card.

7. Brush the cake layer with dessert syrup. Use enough to moisten the cake well, but not so much that it is soggy.

8. If fruit pieces are being used, arrange them either on top of the base or on top of the filling after the next step.

9. Apply a layer of the desired filling. Either spread it on with a palette knife or, to quickly apply an even layer, pipe it on as shown in step 5 of the procedure on assembling a basic layered sponge cake.

10. Top with another sponge layer and again brush with syrup.

11. If a third sponge layer is being used, repeat steps 9 and 10.

12. It is sometimes recommended that the top sponge layer be placed cut-side up, not crust-side up. This is especially helpful if a light, translucent icing such as fondant is being used. A dark crust will show through a thin fondant layer and detract from the appearance of the cake.

13. Ice the cake with the desired icing or glaze.

14. Decorate.

RECTANGULAR CAKES OR STRIPS

Most popular cakes can also be made in a rectangular shape or strip about $2\frac{1}{2}$ to $3\frac{1}{2}$ in. (6 to 9 cm) wide and 16 to 18 in. (40 to 46 cm) long (the width of a sheet pan) or any fraction of that length. A cake baked in a standard sheet pan can be cut crosswise into seven pieces this size.

To produce one cake, cut strips of desired size from sheet cakes and layer with fillings as in basic procedure. Ice the top and sides. Ends may be iced, or they may be left uniced to show an attractive pattern of cake layers and fillings. Trim a thin slice off each end for a more attractive appearance. Use a sharp serrated knife, wiped clean and dipped in hot water before cutting each slice.

To produce rectangular or strip cakes in quantity, use full cake sheets and layer as in basic procedure. Cut into strips of desired width, then ice the top and sides of each strip.

Strip cakes are divided into portions by cutting off rectangular slices about $1\frac{1}{2}$ in. (4 cm) wide. The tops may be marked off into portions and decorated in a regular pattern, just as round cakes are often marked off into wedges.

LINING CHARLOTTE RINGS OR CAKE RINGS

Sometimes a soft filling or mousse, such as Bavarian cream or other gelatin-based filling, is used in a layer cake. In these cases, it is necessary to use a ring mold to hold the filling in place until the cake has been chilled enough to set the filling. These ring molds are often called *charlotte rings* because they are used to make charlottes, which are molded desserts made of Bavarian cream (see chapter 16). They may also be called *cake rings*.

Using a charlotte ring allows the pastry chef to create a decorative edge for the cake. The cake is finished by applying an icing or glaze only to the top, and the decorated sides of the cake are revealed when the ring is removed.

Four popular linings for charlotte rings are sponge strips, sliced sponge, chocolate, and fruit.

Sponge Strips

Sponge used to line a ring must be thin (about $\frac{1}{4}$ in. or $\frac{1}{2}$ cm) and flexible enough to bend without breaking. Sponges made with almond powder are good for this purpose because they stay moist and flexible. Joconde sponge (p. 322) is especially suitable. Ladyfinger sponge (p. 324) is another good choice, even though it does not contain nut powder, because it is strong and flexible.

Procedure for Lining a Ring Mold with a Sponge Strip

1. Use the ring as a guide to measure the width and length of the strip of sponge to be cut (a). The strip may be cut slightly narrower than the ring so that some of the filling can show above it. It should be slightly longer than the circumference of the ring so that it will fit snugly against it.

2. Brush the sponge with dessert syrup before placing it in the mold to prevent discoloration by juices seeping through from the filling.

3. Place the ring on a cake card and fit the strip of sponge into the ring (b).

4. Trim the end of the strip with a small knife (c).

a.

b.

c.

For a decorative edge, Ribbon Sponge (p. 323) is popular. Using colored stencil paste allows the chef to make many different designs for different cakes. In chapter 16, Passion Fruit Charlotte (p. 449) and L'Exotique (p. 452) are made with ribbon sponge. Caramelized sponge also makes an attractive lining and is suitable for cakes made with caramelized fruit or other caramel flavor, such as Bananier (p. 385). The procedure for making caramelized sponge follows.

Procedure for Caramelizing Sponge

1. Cut a strip of joconde sponge to the desired size for lining the mold.

2. Spread the sponge with a thin coating of Sabayon I (p. 197) and then sprinkle evenly with confectioners' sugar, using a fine sieve.

3. Brown the top of the sponge. For best results, use a hand-held electric salamander iron. If this is not available, brown under a salamander or broiler, but watch it closely to prevent it from scorching.

4. Repeat steps 2 and 3 for a second coat.

5. Turn the strip over and caramelize the other side in the same way.

Sliced Sponge

Baumkuchen (p. 326) makes an attractive lining for molds because of the striped pattern of its cut surfaces. For a recipe using baumkuchen, see Caramelized Pear Charlotte (p. 500).

Another way to make a sliced sponge lining with attractive vertical stripes is to sandwich together thin layers of sponge with jam, ganache, or other filling. The procedure for cutting the slices and lining the mold is the same as for baumkuchen. Chocolate Indulgence (p. 456) and Charlotte au Cassis (p. 448) are made this way.

Procedure for Lining a Mold with Slices of Baumkuchen

1. Cut a piece of baumkuchen into a strip that is just as wide as the desired height of the cake border. Then cut this strip crosswise into slices ¼ in. (½ cm) (a).

2. Fit these slices against the inside of the mold so that the stripes are vertical (b).

a.   b.

Chocolate

Chocolate is an especially popular lining for cake molds. Tempered chocolate is spread on a strip of acetate and placed inside the ring mold. The acetate can remain around the cake for display, but it is removed before the cake or charlotte is sliced and served. The procedure is illustrated on pages 540–541. Plain chocolate can be used, but chocolate with a pattern—such as wood grain or marble—is even more attractive. These techniques are illustrated in chapter 20. See the procedure for Julianna (p. 383) for an example of a cake made in a ring lined with chocolate.

Ganache (p. 192) may be used in the same way as tempered chocolate. Spread warm ganache on a strip of acetate and fit it inside the mold.

Fruit

Fruits can be used to line a mold, as in the procedure for Strawberry Cake (p. 375). When using fresh fruits such as strawberries, remember that the finished dessert cannot be frozen because the texture of the fruit will be ruined and the fruit will lose juices when thawed, marring the appearance of the cake.

Lining the mold with a strip of acetate gives the best results. (Use parchment if acetate is not available.) Take precautions so that the filling does not run between the fruit and the mold, which would detract from the cake's appearance. In the case of halved strawberries or similar fruit, press the cut surface firmly against the side of the mold, but not so firmly as to crush the fruit. Also, thick fillings and gelatin-based fillings that are about to set are less likely to run between the fruit and mold.

FONDANT

Fondant provides a thin, smooth, shiny coating for cakes and serves an excellent base for paper-cone decorations. Also, it is a good substitute for buttercream in hot weather, especially for cakes that, for one reason or another, may not be kept in a refrigerated case at all times.

When fondant is used to ice a cake, especially a sponge cake, it is a good idea to first brush the top and sides of the cake with hot apricot glaze. Let the glaze set before applying the fondant. This provides a moisture barrier between the fondant and the cake, and it reduces the chances of the fondant's drying out and losing its shine. Also, it reduces the problem of loose crumbs that might spoil the smoothness of the icing layer.

Guidelines for using fondant are on page 334. To ice a cake with fondant, set it on an icing screen, then pour the warm fondant over the cake, using a bowl knife to guide the fondant evenly over the sides.

This method can be used for coating products with melted chocolate.

APPLYING MARZIPAN COATINGS

A thin layer of marzipan, a confection or paste made of almonds and sugar, can be used to coat cakes. It can be colored and used in place of icing, or it can be used under fondant or other icing. When used under fondant, marzipan, like apricot coating, serves as a moisture barrier to protect the fondant. The production of marzipan is explained in chapter 15 (see p. 553).

The following are guidelines for using marzipan as a cake coating:

1. To make a sheet of marzipan, work the paste in the hands to make it pliable, if necessary. Using confectioners' sugar to dust the bench and rolling pin, roll the marzipan out into a thin sheet as though you are rolling out pastry.

2. If the marzipan is to be on the outside of the cake (that is, not covered with icing), the sheet can be textured with a ridged rolling pin. Roll the ridged pin over the sheet of marzipan once to make a ridged texture. To make a checked or dimpled texture, roll the pin across the sheet a second time at a right angle to the first.

3. For a round layer cake, it is easiest to coat only the top with marzipan. Before putting the top layer on the cake, brush it with apricot coating so that the marzipan will stick. Place it upside down on a sheet of marzipan and press it on lightly. Trim off the excess marzipan. Set the layer right-side up on the cake.

    The sides of the cake can then be iced in a conventional manner.

4. To coat the sides of a round layer cake after coating the top, first ice the sides so that the marzipan will stick. Roll out a strip of marzipan as wide as the cake is high and as long as three times the width of the cake. Roll up the strip loosely, then unroll it against the sides of the cake.

    The cake can now be coated with fondant or another light icing.

5. An alternative method for coating a cake is to roll out a sheet of marzipan large enough to cover the top and sides. Lift it with the rolling pin and drape it over the cake. With the hands, carefully mold the marzipan against the sides of the cake.

    This method produces a seamless coating for the cake, unlike the method above in step 3. However, it is more difficult to do. The sides must be molded carefully to avoid making ripples or folds in the marzipan.

6. To cover a strip cake or a sponge roll (Swiss roll) with marzipan, roll out a sheet of marzipan large enough to cover the strip or roll. Brush the marzipan with apricot glaze. Set the cake on the marzipan at one edge and roll it up in the sheet.

    As an alternative, you can first coat the cake with the apricot glaze rather than brushing the glaze onto the marzipan.

PROCEDURES FOR POPULAR CAKES

The first half of this chapter concentrated on explaining general procedures and techniques for assembling specialty cakes. This second half is devoted to specific procedures for assembling a variety of cakes and cake-based desserts, including Swiss rolls and small cakes.

The instructions for specialty cakes in this chapter are assembly procedures rather than recipes, even though they may resemble recipes with their lists of ingredients or components. These procedures may be used for cakes of any size. In many cases they can be used not only for round cakes, but also for square cakes and rectangular strips. Consequently, the quantities of fillings and icings needed will vary considerably. Presenting the procedures in this way reflects the normal working practices of a bakeshop. In a typical operation, cakes are baked ahead of time and fillings, icings, and other components are prepared separately and in advance. Depending on demand or sales, individual desserts can be quickly assembled as needed using the materials on hand.

For a few of the more complex cakes, approximate quantities for the major components are given as guidelines. These quantities apply only to the size of cake indicated in the procedure. This does not prevent you, however, from using the procedures to make any size cake, changing the quantities as necessary.

LARGE CAKES

Most of the procedures in this section are for round cakes. Many of these, except for those made in ring molds, could also be made as rectangles or strips, as explained on page 365.

Black Forest Torte

Components

Chocolate sponge (pp. 319, 327), split into three layers
Dessert syrup flavored with kirsch
Whipped cream flavored with kirsch
Sweet dark pitted cherries, drained
Chocolate shavings

■ **P r o c e d u r e**

1. Moisten one chocolate sponge layer with syrup.

2. Spread with a thin layer of whipped cream.

3. With a pastry bag fitted with a large, plain tube, pipe a circle of cream in the center of the layer. Pipe a ring of cream around the edge. Then pipe another ring in the space between these two.

4. Fill the two spaces between these rings with well-drained cherries.

5. Top with a second sponge layer. Moisten with syrup.

6. Spread with a layer of whipped cream.

7. Top with a third sponge layer, moistened with syrup.

8. Ice the top and sides with whipped cream.

9. With the back of a knife, mark off the top of the cake into the desired number of wedges.

10. Mask the sides of the cake with chocolate shavings. Sprinkle chocolate shavings in the center of the cake.

11. With a star tube, pipe rosettes of whipped cream around the top edge of the cake so that there is one on each wedge. Place a cherry on each rosette.

In addition, most of these cakes can be made in any size. Therefore, specific quantities of the individual components are not given in many cases; you have the freedom to make the cake in any size you wish. Also, bakeshops generally make cakes from the components they have on hand in larger quantities, so chefs simply use the quantities they feel they need without measuring specific amounts.

Later in this section are a number of cakes that are more complex, so quantities are included as guidelines to help you visualize the cakes a little more easily. You should feel free to modify these quantities as necessary.

Finally, many molded desserts and pastries are made in the shape of cakes and decorated like cakes. For example, molded and decorated Bavarian creams, called *charlottes,* are often made in ring molds, as some cakes are. These are included with basic Bavarians in chapter 16 if they are made without cake layers. Other desserts made in the shape of cakes are found in chapters 11 and 18. Some of these are mentioned in the section above called "Lining Charlotte Rings or Cake Rings."

Mocha Torte

Components

Genoise (p. 319), split into three or four layers

Buttercream flavored with coffee (p. 336)

Dessert syrup, flavored with coffee or coffee liqueur

■ Procedure

1. Moisten the cake layers with syrup. Sandwich them together with buttercream.

2. Ice top and sides smoothly with buttercream.

3. Decorate as desired with a pastry bag filled with additional buttercream. Chocolate decorations are also appropriate. Sides may be masked with toasted, sliced almonds, if desired.

Variation

Use two thin layers of vanilla genoise alternating with two thin layers of chocolate genoise.

Fruit Torte

Components

Short dough (p. 232) or almond short dough (p. 232) circle

Genoise (p. 319) or almond sponge (p. 319), split into two layers

Raspberry or apricot jam

Dessert syrup flavored with vanilla or kirsch

Buttercream flavored with vanilla or kirsch (p. 337)

Small fruits, preferably three or four kinds, in contrasting colors (such as mandarin orange slices, cherries, grapes, banana slices, strawberries, apricot halves, and pineapple wedges)

Apricot glaze (p. 117)

Almonds, sliced or chopped

■ Procedure

1. Spread the short dough base with jam.

2. Top with a sponge layer. Moisten with syrup.

3. Spread with a thin layer of buttercream.

4. Top with second sponge layer.

5. Moisten with syrup.

6. Ice top and sides with buttercream.

7. Arrange the fruits on the top of the cake in neat, concentric circles, as though you were making an unbaked fruit tart (p. 270).

8. Glaze the fruits with apricot glaze.

9. Mask the sides of the cake with almonds.

Variation

Instead of buttercream, used whipped cream or pastry cream.

Dobos Torte

Components

Seven Dobos layers (p. 318)

Chocolate buttercream (p. 336)

Chopped almonds

Sugar, cooked to the light caramel stage (p. 177)

■ P r o c e d u r e

1. Set aside the best dobos layer for the top.

2. Sandwich the other six layers together with chocolate buttercream.

3. Ice the top and sides completely. Mask the sides with chopped almonds.

4. Cook the sugar to the light caramel stage. Pour the hot caramel over the reserved dobos layer to coat the top completely with a thin layer.

5. With a heavy, buttered knife, immediately cut the caramel layer into portion-size wedges. This must be done before the caramel hardens.

6. Top the cake with the layer of caramel-covered wedges.

Seven-Layer Cake

Seven-layer cake is a variation of the Dobos Torte, except that it is generally made as a strip or rectangle (see p. 365 for an explanation) rather than as a round cake. Use dobos mix (p. 318), seven-layer mix (p. 319), or any thin sponge layers. Sandwich together seven layers of cake with chocolate buttercream. Coat the top and sides with chocolate buttercream, chocolate fondant, or melted chocolate.

Napoleon Gâteau

Components

Blitz Puff Paste (p. 237) or scrap puff paste

Pastry cream (p. 185)

White fondant

Chocolate fondant

Chopped almonds or puff paste crumbs

Note   This is the same as a regular napoleon, but made in the shape of a cake.

■ P r o c e d u r e

1. Roll out puff paste ⅛ in. (3 mm) thick. Cut out three circles 1 in. (2.5 cm) larger in diameter than the desired cake (this allows for shrinkage during baking). Dock the pastry well. Let rest 30 minutes.

2. Bake the puff paste at 400°F (200°C) until browned and crisp. Cool. With a serrated knife, carefully trim the circles, if necessary, so that they are perfectly round and uniform.

3. Sandwich the three layers together with generous layers of pastry cream. Use the best pastry layer for the top and place it upside down so that the top is flat and smooth.

4. Ice the top with white fondant and marble it with chocolate fondant (see p. 334).

5. Carefully smooth the sides, using additional pastry cream if necessary. Mask with almonds or pastry crumbs.

Sachertorte

Ingredients

1 baked Sacher cake (p. 315)

Dessert syrup flavored with kirsch

Apricot jam

Ganache (p. 192), made with equal parts chocolate and cream

Chocolate Glaçage (p. 343)

Grated dark chocolate

■ P r o c e d u r e

1. Trim the cake, if necessary, and cut into two layers. Moisten both layers with kirsch syrup.

2. Sandwich the layers together with a layer of apricot jam.

3. Mask the top and sides of the cake with ganache, spreading it perfectly smooth.

4. Chill the cake until the ganache is firm.

5. Place the cake on a wire rack on a tray. Ice the cake by pouring warm Chocolate Glaçage over it. Run a palette knife over the top and tap the tray to make the icing smooth. Chill until set.

6. Remove from the wire rack, neaten the bottom edge with a knife, and place on a cake board.

7. Using additional ganache, pipe the word *Sacher* across the middle of the cake. Coat the bottom of the sides with grated chocolate.

Kirsch Torte

Components

2 baked meringue or japonaise
 disks (pp. 260 and 261)

1 baked genoise layer (p. 319) about
 1 in. (2.5 cm) thick

Dessert syrup flavored with kirsch

Buttercream flavored with kirsch (p. 337)

Confectioners' sugar

Chopped almonds or meringue crumbs

■ P r o c e d u r e

1. Moisten the genoise with enough kirsch syrup to saturate it well.

2. Place one meringue or japonaise layer upside down (smooth-side up) on a cake circle.

3. Spread it with a layer of buttercream.

4. Place the genoise on top and spread it with buttercream.

5. Top with the second meringue layer, smooth-side up.

6. Spread the sides smoothly with buttercream and coat them with nuts or meringue crumbs.

7. Dust the top heavily with confectioners' sugar. With the back of a knife, mark the sugar in a diamond pattern.

Orange Cream Cake

Components

1 meringue disk (p. 260)

Genoise (p. 319), split into two layers

Orange-flavored dessert syrup

Whipped cream lightly flavored with orange liqueur

Mandarin orange segments

Note This procedure can be used with any appropriate fruit, such as strawberries, pineapple, apricots, and cherries. The flavor of the syrup and the cream should be appropriate to the fruit.

■ P r o c e d u r e

1. Spread the meringue layer with whipped cream.

2. Top with one genoise layer and brush it with syrup.

3. Spread with whipped cream.

4. Arrange a layer of orange segments, well drained, on the cream.

5. Top with a second genoise layer. Moisten with syrup.

6. Ice the top and sides of the cake with whipped cream.

7. Mark off the top of the cake into the desired number of wedges.

8. Decorate with rosettes of whipped cream around the top edge of the cake. Top each rosette with an orange segment.

Abricotine

Components

Genoise (p. 319), split into two layers

Dessert syrup flavored with kirsch

Apricot preserves

Italian meringue (p. 183)

Sliced almonds

Confectioners' sugar

■ P r o c e d u r e

1. Place a layer of genoise on a cake card and brush it with syrup.

2. Spread with a layer of apricot preserves.

3. Top with the second genoise layer and brush with syrup.

4. Coat the top and sides of the cake with Italian meringue.

5. Using a pastry bag with a star tip, pipe a decorative border of Italian meringue on top of the cake.

6. Fill the center of the top of the cake with a layer of sliced almonds and dust with confectioners' sugar.

7. Place in a hot oven (500°F/250°C) until lightly browned.

Strawberry Cake

Components

2 genoise layers (p. 319), ½ in. (1 cm) thick each

Dessert syrup flavored with kirsch

Fresh strawberries

Vanilla Bavarian cream (p. 441)

Buttercream, flavored with vanilla (p. 337)

Piping chocolate

■ P r o c e d u r e

1. Line a charlotte ring with a strip of acetate and set the ring on a cake card.

2. Place a genoise layer in the ring and brush it with syrup.

3. Select the best-looking, most uniformly sized strawberries to line the ring and cut them in half vertically. Place them on the sponge evenly spaced around the edge, with the stem end down and the cut surface against the acetate. Distribute the remaining strawberries evenly on the sponge.

4. Cover the strawberries with the Bavarian cream, which has been cooled until it is thick and just about to set, filling the ring to within ½ in. (1 cm) of the top, making sure there are no air spaces around the berries.

5. Place the second genoise layer on top, pressing down gently. Brush the top with syrup.

6. Spread the top with a thin layer of buttercream.

7. Using a paper cone, decorate the top of the cake with piping chocolate, making desired patterns (see chapter 13).

8. Chill until set. Remove the ring, but leave the acetate around the cake until ready to serve.

Chocolate Ganache Torte

Components

1 plain or chocolate meringue disk (p. 260) (*optional*)

Chocolate genoise (p. 319), split into three layers

Dessert syrup flavored with rum or vanilla

Whipped ganache (p. 192)

Chocolate buttercream (p. 336)

■ P r o c e d u r e

1. Spread the meringue disk with ganache.

2. Top with a genoise layer. Moisten with syrup and spread with a layer of ganache.

3. Repeat with a second genoise layer and more syrup and ganache.

4. Top with the remaining cake layer, moistened with syrup.

5. Ice the top and sides with buttercream.

6. Decorate as desired.

Chocolate Mousse Cake

Components

3 chocolate meringue disks (p. 260)

Chocolate mousse (p. 193)

Shaved chocolate

■ P r o c e d u r e

1. Sandwich together the chocolate meringue disks with chocolate mousse.

2. Ice the top and sides completely with chocolate mousse.

3. Coat the top and sides of the cake with shaved chocolate.

Almond Gâteau

Components

Almond Sponge (p. 319), split into 2 layers

Dessert syrup flavored with rum

Apricot jam

Apricot glaze (p. 117)

Almond macaroon mixture (pp. 414, 415)

■ P r o c e d u r e

1. Moisten the sponge layers with syrup and sandwich them together with apricot jam.

2. Coat the sides of the cake with the macaroon mixture. Using a star tube or basketweave tube, cover the top of the cake with macaroon mix in a basketweave pattern.

3. Let stand for at least 1 hour.

4. Brown quickly in a hot oven (450°F/230°C), about 10 minutes.

5. While still warm, glaze with apricot glaze.

Bavarian Cream Torte

Components

Genoise (p. 319) or other sponge cut into 3 very thin layers (about ¼ in. 6 mm)

Bavarian Cream in any flavor (pp. 441–443)

Whipped cream flavored to be compatible with the flavor of the Bavarian cream (use chocolate whipped cream with chocolate Bavarian torte)

Dessert syrup, flavored appropriately

■ P r o c e d u r e

1. Line the bottom of a cake pan or springform pan with a thin sponge layer. Moisten with syrup.

2. Prepare the Bavarian cream. Pour enough of the mixture into the cake pan to make a layer about ¾ in. (2 cm) thick.

3. Place a second layer of sponge cake on top of the cream. Moisten with syrup.

4. Fill with another layer of Bavarian cream.

5. Top with the remaining sponge layer.

6. Chill until set.

7. Unmold.

8. Ice the top and sides with whipped cream.

9. Decorate as desired.

Feuille d'Automne

Components

Almond Meringues (p. 261), three 6½-in. (16 cm) disks

Chocolate Mousse IV (p. 454) about 16–20 oz (450–550 g)

Dark chocolate couverture, about 14 oz (400 g)

Cocoa powder

Confectioners' sugar

■ P r o c e d u r e

1. Place a 7-inch charlotte ring on a cake board. Place one of the meringue disks in the bottom.

2. Fill the ring slightly less than half full of mousse.

3. Place a second meringue on top and press down lightly. Fill nearly to the top with mousse, then place the third meringue on top. Press down lightly.

4. Spread the top with a thin layer of mousse.

5. Chill until firm.

6. Remove the charlotte ring, using a blowtorch to help release the sides. Chill again to firm the sides.

7. Melt the chocolate couverture.

8. Heat three clean half-size sheet pans at 325°F (160°C) for 4 minutes. Spread the melted chocolate over the bottoms of the trays. Let cool at room temperature until the chocolate begins to get cloudy. (The purpose of warming the pans is to enable you to spread a thinner coat of chocolate; be careful, however, not to get the pans too hot. Some chefs prefer to use cold trays.)

The procedure used here is illustrated and explained in more detail in chapter 20 (see p. 542). An experienced chef may need as little as 1 or 1½ pans of chocolate to coat the cake, but it is a good idea to prepare extra to allow for mistakes.

9. Refrigerate to set completely.

10. Bring back to room temperature. The chocolate must be pliable but not soft. Use a metal scraper to lift strips of chocolate off the trays, as shown on p. 542. Wrap these around the sides of the cake. Use the same technique to make ruffles for the top of the cake. Chill.

11. Dust the top with a little cocoa powder. (The cake in the illustration is additionally decorated with chocolate leaves, made by brushing a leaf mold—real leaves could also be used—with tempered chocolate and letting the chocolate set before peeling off.)

Alhambra

Components

Hazelnut Sponge Cake (p. 325), one 8-in. (20-cm) round

Coffee Rum Syrup (p. 179)

Ganache I (p. 192), made with equal parts cream and
chocolate, about 8 oz (250 g)

Chocolate Glaçage (p. 343), 5–6 oz (150–175 g)

Decoration
  Chopped pistachios
  Marzipan rose   *Note*   Assembly of this cake is illustrated on page 364.

■ P r o c e d u r e

1. Turn the sponge cake upside down, trimming the top, if necessary, to level. Cut horizontally in half and brush both pieces with syrup to moisten.

2. Pipe the ganache, using a medium plain tip, in a spiral from the center to the edge of one sponge, place the second on top and press lightly to secure. Use remaining ganache to mask sides and top of cake. Chill.

3. Place cake onto a wire rack over a tray and pour over the glaçage. Run a palette knife over the top and tap the tray to ensure it is perfectly smooth. Chill.

4. Once chilled and set, remove from wire rack. Neaten bottom edge with a knife.

5. Press chopped pistachios around the bottom ½ in. (1 cm) of the sides. Place onto a cake board.

6. Using the remaining ganache, pipe the word *Alhambra* across the middle of the cake.

7. Make a marzipan rose and two leaves and brush with cocoa powder to highlight. Place next to writing on the top of the cake.

Genoise à la Confiture Framboise
(Genoise with Raspberry Filling)

Components

Genoise (p. 319), split into 2 layers

Dessert syrup, flavored with framboise (raspberry alcohol)

Raspberry preserves or jam (p. 502)

Italian meringue (p. 183)

Sliced almonds

Fresh raspberries

Confectioners' sugar

■ Procedure

1. Moisten one genoise layer with the syrup. Spread the top with an even layer of raspberry preserves.

2. Moisten the bottom of the second layer with syrup and place on top of the first layer. Brush the top with additional syrup.

3. Coat the top and sides with the Italian meringue and spread smooth with a palette knife. Using a pastry bag, decorate the top with additional meringue.

4. Press the almonds around the bottom edge of the sides of the cake.

5. Brown the meringue with a blowtorch.

6. Garnish the top of the cake with fresh raspberries and sprinkle with a little confectioners' sugar.

Brasilia

Components

Hazelnut Joconde Sponge Cake (p. 322), 1 half-size sheet pan

Nougatine (p. 562), freshly prepared, 10 oz (300 g)

Dark chocolate, melted, about 2 oz (50 g)

Dessert syrup flavored with rum

Caramel Buttercream (p. 339), 1 lb (500 g)

Tempered white chocolate for decoration

■ P r o c e d u r e

1. Cut the sponge into three equal rectangles, about 6 × 12 in. (15 × 30 cm).

2. Prepare the nougatine. Roll out into a thin rectangle slightly larger than the sponge rectangles. While it is still warm, trim the edges with a sharp knife so that they are straight and the rectangle is about ½ in. smaller on a side than the sponge (to allow for later trimming of the sponge). (If you rolled the nougatine on a silicon mat, remove it from the mat before cutting.) Cut portions of desired size, but leave them together. Let cool.

3. Spread one sponge layer with a thin layer of melted chocolate. Refrigerate to set.

4. Remove from the refrigerator, turn chocolate-side down, and brush with the rum syrup.

5. Spread with a layer of buttercream about ¼ in. (5 mm) thick.

6. Place a second sponge layer on top, brush with syrup, and again spread with buttercream.

7. Repeat with the third layer and spread with buttercream.

8. Trim the edges and top with the nougatine.

9. Put the tempered white chocolate in a paper cone and decorate the top of the cake with a fancy border.

10. If desired, this large cake can be cut in half to make two 6-in. (15 cm) square cakes.

Russian Cake

Components

Joconde Sponge Cake (p. 322), 1 half-size sheet pan

Dark chocolate, melted, about 2 oz (50 g)

Dessert syrup flavored with cognac

Praline Buttercream (p. 338), 1 lb (500 g)

Apricot glaze (p. 117)

Toasted sliced almonds

Confectioners' sugar

■ P r o c e d u r e

1. Cut the sponge into three equal rectangles, about 6 × 12 in. (15 × 30 cm).

2. Spread one sponge layer with a thin layer of melted chocolate. Refrigerate to set.

3. Remove from the refrigerator, turn chocolate-side down, and brush with the cognac syrup.

4. Spread with a layer of buttercream about ¹/₂ inch (1 cm) thick.

5. Place a second sponge layer on top, brush with syrup, and again spread with buttercream.

6. Top with the third layer of sponge and brush with syrup. Trim the sides of the cake neatly.

7. Heat apricot glaze and thin with water to a consistency that can be poured and spread. Glaze the top of the cake.

8. With the remaining buttercream, decorate the top of the cake with a scroll border, using a pastry bag with a star top.

9. Garnish the top of the cake with the almonds and dust them very lightly with confectioners' sugar.

Opera Cake

Components

Joconde Sponge Cake (p. 322), 1 half-size sheet pan

Dark chocolate, melted, about 2 oz (50 g)

Dessert syrup flavored with coffee extract

French Buttercream (p. 336)
 flavored with coffee
 (p. 336), 12 oz (350 g)

Ganache, 5–6 oz (150 g)

Opera Glaze (p. 344)

■ P r o c e d u r e

1. Cut the sponge into three equal rectangles, about 6 × 12 in. (15 × 30 cm).

2. Spread one sponge layer with a thin layer of melted chocolate. Refrigerate to set.

3. Remove from the refrigerator, turn chocolate-side down, and brush with the coffee syrup.

4. Spread with a layer of buttercream about ¹/₄ in. (5 mm) thick.

5. Place a second sponge layer on top, brush with syrup, and spread with a thin layer of ganache.

6. Top with the third layer of sponge and brush with syrup. Spread with a layer of the buttercream. Smooth the top carefully with a palette knife. Refrigerate or freeze until firm. The cake must be quite cold so that the warm glaze does not melt the buttercream.

7. Set the cake on a rack over a tray. Pour warm opera glaze over the cake. Pass a palette knife over the top of the cake and tap the tray to smooth the glaze.

8. Chill until set. Remove from the rack and trim the sides of the cake neatly and squarely with a hot knife.

9. With additional ganache in a paper cone, pipe the word *Opera* on top of the cake.

Monte Carlo

Components

Common meringue (p. 182), 8 oz (225 g)

Almond Chocolate Sponge (p. 327), one circle 5, 6, or 7 in. (13–18 cm) in diameter

Jelled Spiced Apricot Compote (recipe opposite)

Almond Cream (p. 446), 14 oz (400 g)

Decoration
> Crème Chantilly (p. 181)
> Apricot halves
> Cocoa powder
> Red currants

■ P r o c e d u r e

1. Pipe 7-in. (18 cm) circles of Common Meringue onto parchment paper (see p. 260 for technique). Use all the meringue—you will need two circles for the cake, plus crumbled meringue for decoration. Bake at 325°F (160°C) until firm. Using a 7-inch charlotte ring like a cookie cutter, trim two of the circles to fit inside the ring.

2. Trim the Almond Chocolate Sponge, if necessary, to fit inside a 5-in. (13 cm) cake pan. Brush generously with the reserved syrup from the apricot compote. Pour warm apricot compote on top of the sponge in the tin. Chill until set.

3. Place one of the meringue layers on a cake card. Turn out the sponge and apricot compote from the tin upside down on top of the meringue so that the almond sponge layer is on top. Be sure that this 5-in. circle is centered on the meringue.

4. Place a 7-in. (18 cm) charlotte ring on the cake card enclosing the meringue layer.

5. Fill to just below the top of the ring with the Almond Cream. Top with the second meringue layer, pressing down gently. Chill until set.

6. Remove the charlotte ring, carefully using a blowtorch to release the ring from the sides.

7. Mask the top and sides of the cake by spreading on a thin layer of almond cream.

8. Crumble the remaining baked meringue and press the crumbs onto the sides and top of the cake.

9. Using a pastry bag with a star tip, pipe 8 rosettes of Crème Chantilly around the top edge of the cake. Top each with a fanned apricot half. Dust the center lightly with cocoa powder. If desired, add a few red currants for additional decoration.

Jelled Spiced Apricot Compote

Components

Canned apricots with syrup, 12 oz (350 g)

Cinnamon stick, 1

Lemon peel, strips from 1 lemon

Gelatin, ⅙ oz (4 g or 2 leaves)

Amaretto liqueur, 2 oz (60 mL)

■ P r o c e d u r e

1. Drain and reserve the syrup from the apricots. Add the cinnamon stick and lemon peel to the syrup and bring to a boil. Add the apricots and simmer until the fruit is beginning to fall apart (if necessary, remove the apricots and chop them). Remove the cinnamon stick and lemon peel. Drain and reserve the syrup to moisten the cake layer in step 2 above.

2. Soften the gelatin in cold water (see p. 39).

3. Add the gelatin to the hot apricots and stir until it is dissolved. Stir in the amaretto.

4. Rewarm, if necessary, to use in the Monte Carlo above.

Julianna

Components

Wood-grain chocolate strip

Plain genoise (p. 319), two 7-in. (18 cm) disks, ¼–⅜ in. (1 cm) thick

Coffee Syrup (p. 179)

Praline Cream II (p. 450), 10 oz (300 g)

Vanilla Cream (p. 338), 10 oz (300 g)

Coffee Marble Glaze (p. 345), 3–4 oz (100–110 g)

Decoration
    Chocolate fan
    Chocolate cigarettes
    Caramelized hazelnuts

■ P r o c e d u r e

1. Line a 7-in. (18 cm) charlotte ring with a strip of acetate coated with wood-grain chocolate. (see p. 541). Set the ring on a cake card.

2. Place a disk of genoise sponge in the base of the ring. (*Note:* The sponge circles may be cut from a thin sheet of sponge or cut horizontally from a thicker sponge layer.)

3. Brush the sponge with coffee syrup.

4. Fill the ring halfway with praline cream.

5. Top with a second sponge layer and press down gently and evenly. Brush the sponge with coffee syrup.

6. Fill the ring to the top with vanilla cream. Smooth with a palette knife. Chill until firm.

7. Add the coffee extract to the marble glaze (see p. 345) and swirl in lightly. Spread over the surface of the cake, swirling to give a marbled pattern. Chill well.

8. Remove the ring and peel away the acetate. Neaten the edge of the glaze with a small knife.

9. Decorate the top of the cake with a chocolate fan dusted with confectioners' sugar, a few chocolate cigarettes, and caramelized hazelnuts.

Tiramisu

Components

Ladyfinger Sponge (p. 324), 1 sheet

Strong espresso coffee, 1 pt (500 mL)

Dessert syrup, 8 oz (250 mL)

Mascarpone Filling (recipe below)

Cocoa powder

Note This recipe is easily cut in half. Start with a half-size sponge sheet and use half the filling and coffee syrup. Alternatively, use ready-prepared ladyfinger cookies in place of the sponge sheet.

■ P r o c e d u r e

1. Cut the sponge sheet in half crosswise.

2. Combine the espresso and syrup. Brush the sponge sheets generously with this syrup, using it all.

3. Place one sponge sheet on a tray. Spread half the filling evenly over the sponge.

4. Top with the second layer of sponge, followed by the remaining filling. Smooth the top. Chill.

5. Dust the top with cocoa powder.

6. Cut 6 × 4 into 24 portions.

 ## Mascarpone Filling

Ingredients	U.S.	Metric
Egg yolks	2 yolks	2 yolks
Sugar	6 oz	180 g
Water	4 oz	120 g
Glucose or corn syrup	2 oz	60 g
Mascarpone	1 lb	500 g
Heavy cream	1 lb 8 oz	740 g
Approximate weight:	*3 lb*	*1600 g*

■ P r o c e d u r e

1. Whip the egg yolks until light.

2. Make a syrup of the sugar, water, and glucose, and cook to 248°F (120°C). Gradually pour into the egg yolks while whipping constantly. Continue whipping until cool.

3. In a mixer with the paddle attachment, mix the mascarpone until soft. Mix in the egg yolk mixture.

4. Whip the cream to soft peaks. Fold into the mascarpone mixture.

 ## Caramelized Banana Slices for Bananier (opposite)

Ingredients

Banana, 1

Brown sugar, 1 oz (30 g)

Butter, 2 tsp (10 g)

■ P r o c e d u r e

1. Cut the banana into slices ½ in. (1 cm) thick.

2. Heat the sugar in a small sauté pan and add the banana slices. Heat them quickly until caramelized on both sides but not soft.

3. Swirl in the butter.

4. Place the banana slices on a sheet of parchment paper to cool.

Bananier

Components

Joconde Sponge (p. 322)

Rum Syrup (p. 179)

Lime Chiboust (p. 191), 7 oz (200 g)

Caramelized Banana Slices (recipe opposite)

Banana Mousse (p. 451), 7 oz (200 g)

Chocolate spray (p. 543)

Apricot glaze (p. 117)

Decoration

   Chocolate fans

   Slices of lime and banana

■ Procedure

1. Line a 6¹/₂-in. (16 cm) ring mold with a strip of acetate.

2. Cut two 6-in. (15 cm) circles from a sheet of Joconde Sponge. Cut one strip of Joconde to line the side of the ring mold, making it slightly narrower than the height of the ring so that the filling will show above it. Caramelize the sponge strip and circles according to the procedure on p. 367.

3. Brush the caramelized sponge strip and circles with rum syrup. Line the mold with the strip of sponge and place it on a cake card. Place one sponge circle in the bottom.

4. Prepare the lime chiboust. Before it sets, use it to fill the ring nearly half full, then place the second sponge circle on top and press down gently.

5. Arrange the banana slices on top of the sponge.

6. Prepare the banana mousse. Before it sets, fill the mold to the top and level with a palette knife.

7. Place in freezer for 45 minutes to set.

8. Place a decorative stencil on top of the cake and spray with a chocolate sprayer (p. 117).

9. Coat the top with apricot glaze.

10. Garnish as desired. The cake in the illustration is garnished with two chocolate fans and slices of lime and banana coated with apricot glaze.

SWISS ROLLS

Swiss rolls are made up in much the same way as American jelly rolls, except that Swiss rolls are usually more delicate. They can be made with a great variety of fillings and are often iced and decorated on the outside.

General Procedure for Making Swiss Rolls

1. Bake Swiss roll sponge as directed in the recipe (pp. 318 or 319). Turn out onto a sheet of parchment and carefully peel the paper off the back of the sponge. Cool it partially covered so that the cake retains moisture and does not dry out. (The cake may also be moistened with dessert syrup.)

2. Trim off the edges with a sharp knife. Crusty edges do not roll well.

3. Spread with desired filling, such as:

    Jam or jelly

    Buttercream (pp. 335–339)

    Ganache (p. 192)

    Chocolate mousse (p. 193)

    Pastry cream variation (pp. 185–191)

    Whipped cream

    Lemon filling (p. 119)

    Chopped fruits or nuts may be mixed with buttercream or pastry cream.

4. If any items—such as fruit pieces or a thin rope of marzipan—are to be rolled into the center of the roll, place these along one edge of the sheet on top of the filling. Begin rolling from this edge.

5. Roll up the cake tightly with the aid of the sheet of parchment under the sponge.

6. Ice or cover the outside of the roll as desired. For example:

    Brush with apricot glaze then ice with fondant.

    Coat with melted chocolate.

    Coat with a sheet of marzipan (see p. 369), using apricot jam or glaze to make the marzipan stick.

    Spread with a thin layer of buttercream, then coat with marzipan.

    Spread with buttercream, then roll in coconut or chopped nuts.

7. Swiss rolls may be sold as whole cakes or cut into individual slices.

Variation: Half Rolls

1. Before icing the outside of the roll, chill the roll to make it firmer.

2. Cut a sheet of baked short pastry or sponge cake into two strips, each as long and as wide as the sponge roll. Spread the strips with a thin layer of icing or jam.

3. With a sharp knife, carefully cut the chilled sponge roll in half lengthwise.

4. Mount each half cut-side down on one of the prepared sponge or short dough bases.

5. Ice and decorate as in the basic procedure.

Almond Swiss Rolls

Components

Swiss roll sponge (p. 318)

Apricot jam

Almond pastry cream

Apricot glaze (p. 117)

White fondant

Toasted almonds

■ P r o c e d u r e

1. Spread plain Swiss roll sponge with apricot jam, then with almond pastry cream.

2. Roll up.

3. Brush with apricot glaze and ice with white fondant.

4. While fondant is soft, place a row of toasted almonds along the top of the roll.

Black Forest Roll

Components

Whipped cream fortified with gelatin (p. 180) and flavored with kirsch

Chocolate Swiss roll sponge (p. 318)

Dark sweet cherries, well drained

Chocolate shavings

■ P r o c e d u r e

1. Fit a pastry bag with a plain tube and fill it with the whipped cream.

2. Pipe strips of cream about $^3/_8$ in. (1 cm) apart on a sheet of chocolate Swiss roll so that the strips run the length of the roll.

3. Fill in the spaces between the strips with cherries.

4. Roll up.

5. Coat with additional cream and then with chocolate shavings.

Bûche de Noël
(Chocolate Christmas Roll)

Components

Plain or chocolate swiss roll sponge (p. 318)

Chocolate buttercream (p. 336)

Vanilla buttercream (p. 336)

Meringue mushrooms

■ P r o c e d u r e

1. Spread plain or chocolate Swiss roll sponge with chocolate buttercream.

2. Roll up.

3. Spread the ends with white buttercream and, with a paper cone, pipe on a spiral of chocolate buttercream or other chocolate icing to look like the end grain of wood.

4. Ice the rest of the roll with chocolate buttercream to resemble bark, either by using a pastry bag with a flattened star tube or by spreading on the cream and then texturing it with an icing comb.

5. Decorate with meringue mushrooms (p. 264).

Harlequin Roll

Components

Plain Swiss roll sponge (p. 318)

Vanilla buttercream (p. 336)

Chocolate buttercream (p. 336)

Melted chocolate, chocolate fondant,
   or marzipan colored with cocoa

■ P r o c e d u r e

1. On a sheet of plain Swiss roll sponge, pipe alternating rows of vanilla and chocolate buttercream so that the roll is completely covered with stripes of buttercream running the length of the roll.

2. Roll up.

3. Cover with melted chocolate, chocolate fondant, or marzipan colored with cocoa.

Mocha Roll

Components

Plain Swiss roll sponge (p. 318)

Coffee buttercream (p. 336)

Chocolate shavings

Chocolate for drizzling

■ P r o c e d u r e

1. Spread plain Swiss roll sponge with buttercream and sprinkle with chocolate shavings.

2. Roll up.

3. Ice with more buttercream. Decorate with chocolate drizzled over the icing.

Praline Ganache Roll

Components

Plain Swiss roll sponge (p. 318)

Praline buttercream (p. 337)

Ganache (p. 192)

Chopped or sliced hazelnuts

■ P r o c e d u r e

1. Spread plain Swiss roll sponge with praline buttercream.

2. Using a large plain tube, pipe a strip of ganache along one edge.

3. Roll up so that the ganache is in the center.

4. Cover with more buttercream. Roll in chopped or sliced hazelnuts.

Strawberry Cream Roll

Components

Plain Swiss roll sponge (p. 318)

Pastry cream (p. 185) flavored with orange flavor
   or orange liqueur

Fresh strawberries

Confectioners' sugar

■ P r o c e d u r e

1. Spread plain Swiss roll sponge with flavored pastry cream.

2. Place a row of fresh strawberries along one edge.

3. Roll up so that the strawberries are in the center. Dust with confectioners' sugar.

SMALL CAKES

Small fancy cakes in individual portion sizes can be made in many shapes and flavors. In some American bakeshops, these small cakes are known as *French pastries*. Using a variety of cakes, icings, fillings, and decorations, a baker can make an unlimited variety of small, attractive cakes. This section briefly discusses some of the more popular varieties.

Slices

These are simply portion-size slices of rectangular strip cakes (p. 365), Swiss rolls (p. 386), and half rolls (p. 386). An important part of the appearance of slices is the pattern of the icing and filling layers. Therefore, it is important to cut the slices carefully and neatly.

For best results, chill the rolls or strips before slicing so that the fillings and icings are firm. Use a sharp knife. Wipe the knife clean and dip it into hot water before each cut.

Slices may be lined up on trays or placed in individual paper cases for display.

Triangles

Sandwich together four or five layers of ¼-in. (6 mm) thick sponge (such as Swiss roll sponge or seven-layer sponge) with buttercream in a contrasting color. Press the layers together firmly. Chill to solidify the cream. Cut the cake into strips 2 to 2½ in. (5 to 6 cm) wide.

Place a strip at the edge of the bench and, using a sharp knife, cut diagonally into triangles. Turn the triangles so that the layers are vertical. Attach them back to back with a layer of buttercream to form a larger triangle.

Coat with marzipan, chocolate glaçage, or icing. Cut into slices.

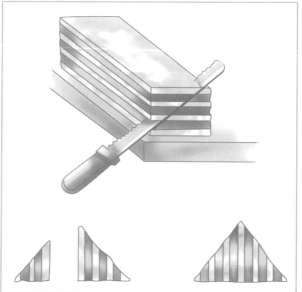

Squares

Layer two or three sheets of cake and icing or filling so that the assembled layers are 1½ to 1¾ in. (4 cm) high. Press the layers together firmly. Chill to make the filling firm.

Cut the cake into small squares, 2 in. (5 cm) across or less. Ice the sides, then the top, with buttercream. Decorate as desired.

Cutting strip layer cake to make triangles

Othellos

Othellos are small, round cakes made with a special sponge mixture. Prepare the mix for Sponge Roll I (p. 318), but reduce the first quantity of sugar to 25% (3 oz/90 g). Using a pastry bag with a plain tube, pipe 2 inch (5 cm) mounds onto silicone paper. Bake at 400°F (200°C). Cool. Scoop out a little of the cake from the flat side of each Othello base to make more room for the filling. Select half the cakes to be bottom halves and slice a little off the top of each to make a flat surface.

Sandwich two cakes together (one top and one bottom half) with appropriate filling (see below). Brush with apricot glaze. Set on screens and ice with fondant. To decorate, use a paper cone to pipe a spiral of fondant in the same color on the top of each Othello.

Although the term *Othello* is used for this whole category of pastries, it is traditional to use specific names for cakes of different flavors as follows:

Othellos	*Filling:* chocolate pastry cream *Icing:* chocolate fondant
Iagos	*Filling:* coffee-flavored pastry cream *Icing:* coffee fondant
Desdemonas	*Filling:* whipped cream flavored with vanilla *Icing:* white fondant flavored with kirsch
Rosalinds	*Filling:* whipped cream flavored with rose water *Icing:* pink fondant flavored with rose water

PETITS FOURS

The term *petit four* can be used for almost any small cake or pastry item that is small enough to be eaten in one or two bites. "Petit" in French means "little" and "four" means "oven." Most petits fours are small baked items, although there are a few that are not baked.

Petits four are divided into two categories. *Petits fours secs* ("sec" means "dry") include a variety of small, dainty cookies, baked meringues, macaroons, and puff pastry products. These will be discussed further in the next chapter.

Procedure for Making Fondant-Iced Petits Fours

1. Select a firm, close-grained cake. Cake that is too coarse, soft, or crumbly is difficult to cut evenly into small shapes. Of the formulas in this book, Almond Cake (p. 314) is recommended. Other suitable choices are Almond Sponge II (p. 319) and Pound Cake (see the variation for petits fours on p. 312). For one sheet of petits fours you will need three sheets of cake, ¼ in. (6 mm) thick each. The finished, iced petits fours should be no more than 1 in. (2.5 cm) high.

2. Lay one sheet of cake on a sheet pan and spread with a *thin* layer of hot apricot jam or of buttercream. Top with the second sheet.

3. Repeat with the third sheet. Spread the top with a thin layer of jam or whatever filling is used between the layers.

4. Roll out a thin sheet of marzipan the same size as the cake sheet. Roll it up loosely on the rolling pin and unroll it to cover the cake. Run the rolling pin over the top to make sure that the layers are stuck together firmly, or press the layers together with a second sheet pan placed on top.

5. Chill the cake for 1 hour or more.

6. Cut out small squares, rectangles, diamonds, ovals, circles, or other shapes with a knife or cutter. Remember to keep them small, no more than 1 inch (2.5 cm) across.

   Note: The marzipan layer is sometimes difficult to cut through neatly. If this is the case, turn the cake upside down before cutting.

7. Prepare some fondant for icing. The fondant should be thinned with simple syrup so that it will coat the cakes with a very thin layer. Fondant may be colored *very lightly.*

8. Place the petits fours 1 in. (2.5 cm) apart on an icing grate over a tray. Pour the fondant over each one, making sure that the top and sides are completely covered.

   Alternatively, you may dip each cake in warm fondant. Push the cake upside down into the fondant until the bottom is level with the icing. With a fork, invert the cake, lift it out, and set it on an icing grate to drain.

9. When the icing is set, use chocolate, piping gel, or colored fondant to decorate the tops of the petits fours.

10. As an interesting variation, before icing the petits fours, pipe a small bulb of buttercream on top of each cake. Refrigerate to harden the buttercream. Then coat the petits fours with fondant.

Petits fours glacés are iced petits fours ("glacé" means, in this case, "iced"). This category includes such items as tiny éclairs, tartlets, filled meringues, and cakes. In fact, nearly any iced or creamed pastry or cake item can be called a petit four as long as it is small enough to be eaten in one or two bites.

In North America, the usual type of petit four is a cake cutout iced with fondant. In fact, most people are probably not aware that there are any kinds of petit four other than this. Because of its popularity, the fondant-glazed petit four should be in the repertoire of every pastry cook. A general procedure is given here.

▶ TERMS FOR REVIEW

gâteau	black forest torte	kirsch torte	tiramisu
torte	fruit torte	Sachertorte	Othello
charlotte ring	dobos torte	opera cake	petit four glacé
Swiss roll			

▶ QUESTIONS FOR REVIEW

1. Briefly list the steps in assembling a typical, basic European-style cake or gâteau.

2. Describe how to cut cake slices to achieve the neatest results.

3. Describe four ways to line a ring mold for a cake.

4. What precautions must be taken when using fruit to line a ring mold?

5. Describe the procedure for caramelizing a strip of sponge.

6. Describe the procedure for covering a cake with marzipan.

chapter 15
Cookies

*T*he word *cookie* means "small cake," and that's more or less what a cookie is. In fact, some cookies are made from cake batter. For some products, such as certain kinds of brownies, it's difficult to know whether to classify them as cakes or cookies.

Most cookie formulas, however, call for less liquid than cake formulas do. Cookie doughs range from soft to very stiff, unlike the thinner batters for cakes. This difference in moisture content means some differences in mixing methods, although the basic procedures are much like those for cakes.

The most obvious differences between cakes and cookies are in makeup. Because most cookies are individually formed or shaped, there is a great deal of hand labor involved. Learning the correct methods and then practicing diligently are essential for efficiency.

After reading this chapter, you should be able to:

■ Understand the causes of crispness, moistness, chewiness, and spread in cookies.

■ Prepare cookie doughs by using the three basic mixing methods.

■ Prepare eight basic types of cookies: dropped, bagged, rolled, molded, icebox, bar, sheet, and stencil.

■ Bake and cool cookies properly.

COOKIE CHARACTERISTICS AND THEIR CAUSES

Cookies come in an infinite variety of shapes, sizes, flavors, and textures. Characteristics that are desirable in some types are not desirable in others. For example, we want some cookies to be crisp, others to be soft. We want some to hold their shape, others to spread during baking. In order to produce the characteristics we want and to correct faults, it is useful to know what causes these basic traits.

CRISPNESS

Cookies are crisp if they are low in moisture. The following factors contribute to crispness:

1. Low proportion of liquid in the mix. Most crisp cookies are made from a stiff dough.

2. High sugar and fat content. A large proportion of these ingredients make it possible to mix a workable dough with low moisture content.

3. Baking long enough to evaporate most of the moisture.

4. Small size or thin shape, so that the cookie dries faster during baking.

5. Proper storage. Crisp cookies can become soft if they absorb moisture.

SOFTNESS

Softness is the opposite of crispness, so it has the opposite causes, as follows:

1. High proportion of liquid in the mix.

2. Low sugar and fat.

3. Honey, molasses, or corn syrup included in the formulas. These sugars are hygroscopic, which means they readily absorb moisture from the air or from their surroundings.

4. Underbaking.

5. Large size or thick shape, so that they retain more moisture.

6. Proper storage. Soft cookies can become stale and dry if not tightly covered or wrapped.

CHEWINESS

Moisture is necessary for chewiness, but other factors are also important. In other words, all chewy cookies are soft, but not all soft cookies are chewy. The following factors contribute to chewiness:

1. High sugar and liquid content, but low fat content.

2. High proportion of eggs.

3. Strong flour or gluten developed during mixing.

SPREAD

Spread is desirable in some cookies, while others must hold their shape. Several factors contribute to spread or the lack of it.

1. *Sugar* High sugar content increases spread. Coarse granulated sugar increases spread, while fine sugar or confectioners' sugar reduces spread.

2. *Leavening* High baking soda or baking ammonia content encourages spread.

3. *Creaming* The creaming together of fat and sugar contributes to leavening by incorporating air. Creaming a mixture until light increases spread. Blending fat and sugar just to a paste (without creaming in a lot of air) reduces spread.

4. *Temperature* Low oven temperature increases spread. High temperature decreases spread because the cookie sets up before it has a chance to spread too much.

5. *Liquid* A slack batter—that is, one with a high liquid content—spreads more than a stiff dough.

6. *Flour* Strong flour or activation of gluten decreases spread.

7. *Pan grease* Cookies spread more if baked on heavily greased pans.

MIXING METHODS

Cookie mixing methods are much like cake mixing methods. The major difference is that less liquid is usually incorporated, so that mixing is somewhat easier. Less liquid means that gluten is less developed by the mixing. Also, it is a little easier to get a smooth, uniform mix.

There are three basic cookie mixing methods:

- One-stage
- Creaming
- Sponge

These methods are subject to many variations due to differences in formulas. The general procedures are as follows, but always be sure to follow the exact instructions with each formula.

ONE-STAGE METHOD

This method is the counterpart of the two-stage cake mixing method. There is more liquid in cake batters, so it must be added in two or more stages in order to blend uniformly. Low-moisture cookies, on the other hand, can be mixed all in one stage.

Because all the ingredients are mixed at once, the baker has less control over the mixing with this method than with other methods. Therefore, the one-stage method is not frequently used. When overmixing is not a great problem, as with some chewy cookies, it can be used.

Procedure for One-Stage Method

1. Scale ingredients accurately. Have all ingredients at room temperature.

2. Place all ingredients in mixer. With the paddle attachment, mix these ingredients at low speed until uniformly blended. Scrape down the sides of the bowl as necessary.

CREAMING METHOD

This is nearly identical to the creaming method for cakes. Because cookies require less liquid, it is not necessary to add the liquid alternately with the flour. It can be added all at once.

Note the importance of step 2, the creaming stage. The amount of creaming affects the texture of the cookie, the leavening, and the spread. Only a small amount of creaming is desired when the cookie must retain its shape and not spread too much. Also, if the cookie is very short (high in fat and low in gluten development), or if it is thin and delicate, too much creaming will make the cookie too crumbly.

Procedure for Creaming Method

1. Scale ingredients accurately. Have all ingredients at room temperature.

2. Place the fat, sugar, salt, and spices in the mixing bowl. With the paddle attachment, cream these ingredients at low speed.

    For light cookies, cream until the mix is light and fluffy, in order to incorporate more air for leavening. For denser cookies, blend to a smooth paste, but do not cream until light.

3. Add the eggs and liquid, if any, and blend in at low speed.

4. Sift in the flour and leavening. Mix until just combined. Do not overmix, or gluten will develop.

SPONGE METHOD

This method is similar to the egg-foam methods for cakes. The procedure varies considerably, depending on the ingredients. Batches should be kept small because the batter is delicate.

Procedure for Sponge Method

1. Scale all ingredients accurately. Have all ingredients at room temperature, or warm the eggs slightly for greater volume, as for sponge cakes.

2. Following the procedure given in the formula used, whip the eggs (whole, yolks, or whites) and the sugar to the proper stage: soft peaks for whites, thick and light for whole eggs or yolks.

3. Fold in the remaining ingredients as specified in the recipe. Be careful not to overmix or to deflate the eggs.

TYPES AND MAKEUP METHODS

We can classify cookies by their makeup methods as well as by their mixing methods. Grouping them by makeup method is perhaps more useful, from the point of view of production, because their mixing methods are relatively simple, while their makeup procedures vary considerably. In this section, you will learn the basic procedures for producing eight cookie types:

- Bagged
- Rolled
- Icebox
- Sheet
- Dropped
- Molded
- Bar
- Stencil

No matter what makeup method you use, follow one important rule: Make all cookies of uniform size and thickness. This is essential for even baking. Because baking times are so short, small cookies may burn before large ones are done.

If the tops of the cookies are to be garnished with fruits, nuts, or other items, place the garnishes on the cookies as soon as they are panned; press them on gently. If you wait until the surface of the dough begins to dry, the garnish may not stick and will fall off after baking.

BAGGED

Bagged or pressed cookies are made from soft doughs. The dough must be soft enough to be forced through a pastry bag but stiff enough to hold its shape.

1. Fit a pastry bag with a tip of the desired size and shape. Fill the bag with the cookie dough. Review p. 354 for tips on the use of the pastry bag.

2. Press out cookies of the desired shape and size directly onto prepared cookie sheets.

DROPPED

Like bagged cookies, dropped cookies are made from a soft dough. Actually, this method can be considered the same as the bagged method, and many bakers use the term *drop* for both bagging out cookies and for depositing dough with a spoon or scoop. Usually, a pastry bag is faster, and it gives better control over the shape and size of the cookies. However, in the following situations, using a scoop to drop cookies may be preferred:

- When the dough contains pieces of fruit, nuts, or chocolate that would clog the pastry tube.

- When you want the cookies to have a rough, homemade look.

1. Select the proper size scoop for accurate portioning.

   A No. 30 scoop makes a large cookie, about 1 oz (30 g).

   A No. 40 scoop makes a medium cookie.

   A No. 50, 60, or smaller scoop makes a small cookie.

2. Drop the cookies onto the prepared baking sheets. Allow enough space between cookies for spreading.

3. Rich cookies spread by themselves, but if the formula requires it, flatten the mounds of batter slightly with a weight dipped in sugar.

ROLLED

Cookies rolled and cut from a stiff dough are not made as often in bakeshops and food service operations as they are made in homes because they require excessive labor. Also, there are always scraps left over after cutting. When rerolled, these scraps make inferior, tough cookies.

The advantage of this method is that it allows you to make cookies in a great variety of shapes for different occasions.

1. Chill dough thoroughly.
2. Roll dough out ⅛ in. (3 mm) thick on a floured canvas. Use as little flour as possible for dusting because this flour can toughen the cookies.
3. Cut out cookies with cookie cutters. Place cookies on prepared baking sheets. Cut as close together as possible to reduce the quantity of scraps. Roll scraps into fresh dough to minimize toughness.
4. Baked cutout cookies are often decorated with colored icing (royal icing, flat icing, or fondant) for holidays or special occasions.

MOLDED

The first part of this procedure (steps 1 and 2) is simply a fast and fairly accurate way of dividing the dough into equal portions. Each piece is then molded into the desired shape. This usually consists of simply flattening the pieces out with a weight. For some traditional cookies, special molds are used to flatten the dough and, at the same time, stamp a design onto the cookie.

The pieces may also be shaped by hand into crescents, fingers, or other shapes.

1. Refrigerate the dough if it is too soft to handle. Roll it out into long cylinders about 1 in. (2½ cm) thick, or whatever size is required.
2. With a knife or bench scraper, cut the roll into ½ oz. (15 g) pieces, or whatever size is required.
3. Place the pieces on prepared baking sheets, leaving 2 in. (5 cm) space between each.
4. Flatten the cookies with a weight, such as a can, dipped in granulated sugar before pressing each cookie.

    A fork is sometimes used for flattening the dough, as for peanut butter cookies.
5. *Alternative method:* After Step 2, shape the dough by hand into desired shapes.

ICEBOX

The icebox or refrigerator method is ideal for operations that wish to have freshly baked cookies on hand at all times. The rolls of dough may be made up in advance and stored. Cookies can easily be cut and baked as needed.

This method is also used to make multicolored cookies in various designs, such as checkerboard and pinwheel cookies. The procedures for making these designs are included with the recipes in this chapter (p. 403).

1. Scale the dough into pieces of uniform size, from 1½ lb (700 g), if you are making small cookies, to 3 lb (1400 g) for large cookies.
2. Form the dough into cylinders 1–2 in. (2½–5 cm) in diameter, depending on the cookie size desired.

    For accurate portioning, it is important to make all the cylinders of dough the same thickness and length.

3. Wrap the cylinders in parchment or wax paper, place them on sheet pans, and refrigerate overnight.

4. Unwrap the dough and cut into slices of *uniform thickness.* The exact thickness required depends on the size of the cookie and how much the dough spreads during baking. The usual range is ⅛–¼ in. (3–6 mm).

    A slicing machine is recommended for ensuring even thickness. Doughs containing nuts or fruits, however, should be sliced by hand with a knife.

5. Place the slices on prepared baking sheets, allowing 2 in. (5 cm) between cookies.

BAR

This procedure is called the *bar method* because the dough is baked in long, narrow strips and later cut crosswise into bars. It should not be confused with *sheet cookies* (see next procedure), which are sometimes called *bars* by home cooks.

1. Scale the dough into 1¾-lb (800 g) units. 1-lb (450 g) units may be used for smaller cookies.

2. Shape the pieces of dough into cylinders the length of the sheet pans. Place three strips on each greased pan, spacing them well apart.

3. Flatten the dough with the fingers into strips about 3–4 in. wide and about ¼ in. thick (8–10 cm wide, 6 mm thick).

4. If required, brush with egg wash.

5. Bake as directed in the formula.

6. After baking, while cookies are still warm, cut each strip into bars about 1¾ in. (4½ cm) wide.

7. In some cases, as with Italian-style *biscotti* (meaning "baked twice"), the strips are cut into thinner slices, placed on sheet pans, and baked a second time until dry and crisp. See p. 423 for an example.

SHEET

Sheet cookies vary so much that it is nearly impossible to give a single procedure for all of them. Some of them are almost like sheet cakes, only denser and richer; they may even be iced like sheet cakes. Others consist of two or three layers added and baked in separate stages. The following procedure is only a general guide.

1. Spread cookie mixture into prepared sheet pans. Make sure the thickness is even.

2. If required, add topping or brush with an egg wash.

3. Bake as directed. Cool.

4. Apply icing or topping, if desired.

5. Cut into individual squares or rectangles.

STENCIL

The stencil method is a specialized technique used with a particular type of soft dough or batter. This batter is often called *stencil paste.* It is used not only for making this type of cookie but also for making ribbon sponge cake (p. 323) for decorative work. The recipe for Almond Tuiles (p. 418) illustrates the stencil method using a simple round stencil, but it is possible to cut a stencil in nearly any shape for making decorative pieces or special desserts. For example, the recipe for Sesame Tuiles (p. 419) calls for a triangular stencil, because the cookie is used in a special dessert plating (p. 530).

1. Line a sheet pan with a silicone mat, or if a mat is not available, a sheet of parchment paper.
2. Use a ready-made stencil, or make a stencil by cutting a hole of the desired pattern in a sheet of thick plastic or thin cardboard (the cardboard used for cake boxes is suitable).
3. Place the stencil on the silicone mat or parchment. With an offset palette knife, spread the batter across the stencil to make a thin layer that completely fills in the hole.
4. Lift off the stencil and repeat to make additional cookies.

PANNING, BAKING, AND COOLING

PREPARING THE PANS

1. Use clean, unwarped pans.
2. Lining the sheets with parchment or silicone paper is fast, and it eliminates the necessity of greasing the pans.
3. A heavily greased pan increases the spread of the cookie. A greased and floured pan decreases spread.
4. Some high-fat cookies can be baked on ungreased pans.

BAKING

1. Most cookies are baked at a relatively high temperature for a short time.
2. Too low a temperature increases spreading and may produce hard, dry, pale cookies.
3. Too high a temperature decreases spreading and may burn the edges or bottoms.
4. Even a minute of overbaking can burn cookies, so watch them closely. Also, the heat of the pan continues to bake the cookies if they are left on it after being removed from the oven.
5. Doneness is indicated by color. The edges and bottom should just be turning a light golden color.
6. Excessive browning is especially undesirable if the dough has been colored. The browning of the surface hides the color.
7. With some rich doughs, burnt bottoms may be a problem. In these cases, *double-pan* the cookies by placing the sheet pan on a second pan of the same size.

COOLING

1. For most cookies baked without silicone paper, remove them from the pans while they are still warm, or they may stick.
2. If cookies are very soft, do not remove them from the pans until they are cool enough and firm enough to handle.

Some cookies are soft when hot but become crisp when cool.

Cookie Faults and Their Causes

Fault	Causes
Too tough	Flour too strong
	Too much flour
	Not enough shortening
	Incorrect amount of sugar
	Mixed too long or improper mixing
Too crumbly	Improper mixing
	Too much sugar
	Too much shortening
	Too much leavening
	Not enough eggs
Too hard	Baked too long or baking temperature too low
	Too much flour
	Flour too strong
	Not enough shortening
	Not enough liquid
Too dry	Not enough liquid
	Not enough shortening
	Baked too long or baking temperature too low
	Too much flour
Not browned enough	Baking temperature too low
	Underbaked
	Not enough sugar
Too brown	Baking temperature too high
	Baked too long
	Too much sugar
Poor flavor	Poor ingredients
	Flavoring ingredients left out
	Dirty baking pans
	Ingredients improperly measured
Surface or crust sugary	Improper mixing
	Too much sugar
Too much spread	Baking temperature too low
	Not enough flour
	Too much sugar
	Too much leavening
	Too much liquid
	Pans greased too much
Not enough spread	Baking temperature too high
	Too much flour or flour too strong
	Not enough sugar
	Not enough sugar
	Not enough leavening
	Not enough liquid
	Insufficient pan grease
Stick to pans	Pans improperly greased
	Too much sugar

3. Do not cool too rapidly or in cold drafts, or cookies may crack.

4. Cool completely before storing.

    After the cookies have been baked, check them for defects. Use the troubleshooting guide in the table above to help correct problems.

PETITS FOURS SECS

In the previous chapter, the subject of petits fours was introduced with a discussion of petits fours glacés, or iced petits fours (p. 390). Petits fours secs, or dry petits fours, are, by contrast, more properly discussed with cookies than with cakes.

As you may recall, nearly any pastry or cake item that is small enough to be eaten in one or two bites can be considered a petit four. The term *sec* or *dry* means that these pastries have no icing or cream filling, although they may be dipped in chocolate. In practice, small quantities of creams or jellies are sometimes used—for example, in sandwich-type cookies.

Petits fours secs are usually served with after-dinner coffee or as an accompaniment for such cold desserts as ice cream, mousses, and Bavarian creams.

The following items from this chapter may be served as petits fours secs, provided that they are quite small. In addition, petits fours secs made from puff pastry and pâte à choux are presented in chapter 10 and madeleines can be found in chapter 12.

Butter Tea Cookies

Almond Macaroons

Coconut Macaroons (Meringue Type)

Pistachio Macaroons

Shortbread and Short Dough Cookies

Fancy Icebox Cookies

Nut Squares

Spritz Cookies

Langues de Chat

Almond Tuiles

Florentines

Florentine Squares

Almond Slices

Batons Marechaux and Eponges

Diamonds

FORMULAS

Icebox Cookies

Ingredients	U.S.		Metric	%
Butter, or half butter and half shortening	1 lb		500 g	67
Granulated sugar	8	oz	250 g	33
Confectioners' sugar	8	oz	250 g	33
Salt	0.25	oz	8 g	1
Eggs	4	oz	125 g	17
Vanilla extract	0.25	oz	8 g	1
Pastry flour	1 lb 8	oz	750 g	100
Total weight:	*3 lb 12*	*oz*	*1891 g*	*252%*

■ P r o c e d u r e

Mixing
  Creaming method
Makeup
  Icebox method. Scale dough strips 1$^1/_2$ (750 g) each. Slice cookies $^1/_4$ in. (6 mm) thick. Bake on ungreased pans.
Baking
  375°F (190°C) for 10–12 minutes

Variations

To reduce spread, use all confectioners' sugar.

Butterscotch Icebox Cookies
Make the following ingredient adjustments:
  In place of the sugars in the basic recipe, use 67% (1 lb/500 g) brown sugar.
  Use only butter, no shortening.
  Increase the eggs to 20% (5 oz/150 g)
  Add $^1/_2$ tsp (2 g) baking soda with the flour.

Nut Icebox Cookies
Add 25% (6 oz/188 g) finely chopped nuts to the sifted flour in the basic recipe or the butterscotch cookie recipe.

Chocolate Icebox Cookies
Add 17% (4 oz/125 g) melted, unsweetened, chocolate to the creamed butter and sugar.

Fancy Icebox Cookies
These are small cookies with designs in two colors. To make them, prepare white and chocolate icebox dough with only the 33% confectioners' sugar; omit the granulated sugar. This reduces the spread of the cookies and preserves the designs. Make the designs as follows:

Pinwheel Cookies
Roll out a sheet of white dough about $^1/_8$ in. (3 mm) thick. Roll out a sheet of chocolate dough the same size and thickness. Brush the white sheet lightly and evenly with egg wash, being careful not to leave any puddles. Lay the chocolate sheet on top and brush with egg wash. Roll up like a jelly roll until the roll is 1 in. (2.5 cm) thick (a). Cut off the dough evenly. Continue making rolls with the rest of the sheet. Refrigerate the rolls. Slice and bake as in the basic procedure.

a.

Checkerboard Cookies
Roll out one sheet of white dough and one sheet of chocolate dough $^1/_4$ in. (6 mm) thick. Egg wash one sheet lightly and lay the second sheet on top. Cut the double sheet of dough in half. Egg wash one sheet and lay the second on top so that you have four alternating colors. Chill until firm. Roll out another sheet of white dough very thin (less than $^1/_8$ in.) and brush with egg wash. From the chilled four-layer sheet, cut off four slices $^1/_4$ in. (6 mm) thick (b). Lay one of these strips on the rolled-out sheet of dough along one edge. Egg wash the top. Lay a second strip on top with the colors reversed, so that chocolate dough is on top of white dough and white is on top of chocolate. Egg wash the top. Repeat with the remaining two strips (c). Wrap in the thin sheet of dough (d). Chill, slice, and bake as in the basic procedure.

b.

c.

d.

Bull's-Eye Cookies
Roll out a cylinder of dough $^1/_2$ in. (12 mm) thick. Roll out a sheet of contrasting-color dough $^1/_4$ in. (6 mm) thick. Egg wash the top. Wrap the cylinder in the sheet of dough (e). Chill, slice, and bake as in the basic procedure.

e.

Oatmeal Raisin Cookies

Ingredients	U.S.		Metric	%
Butter or part butter and part shortening	8	oz	250 g	67
Brown sugar	1 lb		500 g	133
Salt	0.16 oz (1 tsp)		5 g	1.5
Eggs	4	oz	125 g	33
Vanilla extract	0.33 oz (2 tsp)		10 g	3
Milk	1	oz	30 g	8
Pastry flour	12	oz	375 g	100
Baking powder	0.5	oz	15 g	4
Baking soda	0.25	oz	8 g	2
Rolled oats (quick cooking)	10	oz	312 g	83
Raisins (see *note*)	8	oz	250 g	67
Total weight:	*3 lb 12*	*oz*	*1880 g*	*500%*

Note If raisins are hard and dry, soak them in hot water until soft, then drain them and dry them well before adding them to the cookie batter.

■ P r o c e d u r e

Mixing
Creaming method. Combine oats with other dry ingredients after they are sifted. Blend raisins in last.

Makeup
Drop method. Use greased or parchment-lined baking sheets.

Baking
375°F (190°C) for 10–12 minutes, depending on size

Chocolate Chip Cookies

Ingredients	U.S.		Metric	%
Butter or half butter and half shortening	6	oz	180 g	60
Granulated sugar	5	oz	150 g	50
Brown sugar	5	oz	150 g	50
Salt	0.12 oz		4 g	1.25
Eggs	3	oz	90 g	30
Vanilla extract	0.16 oz (1 tsp)		5 g	1.5
Water	1	oz	30 g	10
Pastry flour	10	oz	300 g	100
Baking soda	0.12 oz		4 g	1.25
Chocolate chips	10	oz	300 g	100
Chopped walnuts or pecans	4	oz	120 g	40
Total weight:	*2 lb 12*	*oz*	*1333 g*	*444%*

■ P r o c e d u r e

Mixing
Creaming method. Blend in chocolate chips and nuts last.

Makeup
Drop method. Use greased or parchment-lined baking sheets.

Baking
375°F (190°C) for 8–12 minutes, depending on size

Variation

Brown Sugar Nut Cookies
Make the following ingredient adjustments:
Omit the granulated sugar and use 100% (10 oz/300 g) brown sugar.
Omit the chocolate chips and increase the nuts to 100% (10 oz/300 g).

Double Chocolate Macadamia Chunk Cookies

Ingredients	U.S.			Metric	%
Semisweet chocolate	1 lb 8	oz		750 g	200
Butter	8	oz		250 g	67
Sugar	4	oz		125 g	33
Eggs	5	oz		150 g	42
Salt	0.2	oz (1 tsp)		5 g	1.5
Bread flour	12	oz		375 g	100
Cocoa powder	1	oz		30 g	8
Baking powder	0.33	oz (2 tsp)		10 g	3
White chocolate, cut into small bits	8	oz		250 g	67
Macadamia nuts, coarsely chopped	4	oz		125 g	33
Total weight:	*4 lb 2*	*oz*		*2070 g*	*554%*

■ P r o c e d u r e

Mixing

Modified sponge method

1. Melt the semisweet chocolate and the butter together in a double boiler. Let the mixture cool to room temperature.

2. Mix the sugar, eggs, and salt together until well blended, but do not whip. Whipping to a foam creates more leavening, resulting in a more crumbly cookie. If the eggs are not at room temperature, stir the mixture over a hot water bath just until the mixture is at a slightly warm room temperature.

3. Blend in the chocolate mixture.

4. Sift the flour, cocoa, and baking powder and fold in.

5. Fold in the white chocolate pieces and nuts.

Makeup

Dropped method. Use greased or parchment-lined baking sheets. Make up without delay, as the dough hardens as it sets. If it becomes too hard, let stand in a warm place for a few minutes to soften.)

Baking

350°F (175°C) for 10–15 minutes, depending on size

Variation

Chocolate Chocolate Chunk Cookies

Substitute dark chocolate for the white chocolate. Omit the macadamia nuts or substitute pecans.

Sugar Cookies

Ingredients	U.S.		Metric	%
Butter and/or shortening	8	oz	250 g	40
Sugar	10	oz	310 g	50
Salt	0.16	oz (1 tsp)	5 g	0.8
Eggs	2	oz	60 g	10
Milk	2	oz	60 g	10
Vanilla extract	0.25	oz	8 g	1.25
Cake flour	1 lb 4	oz	625 g	100
Baking powder	0.625	oz	18 g	3
Total weight:	*2 lb 11*	*oz*	*1336 g*	*215%*

■ P r o c e d u r e

Mixing
   Creaming method
Makeup
   Rolled method. Before cutting the rolled-out dough, wash with milk and sprinkle with granulated sugar. Use greased or parchment-lined baking sheets.
Baking
   375°F (190°C) for 8–10 minutes

Variations

Lemon zest, extract, or emulsion may be used in place of vanilla.

Brown Sugar Rolled Cookies
Make the following ingredient adjustments:
   Increase butter to 50% (10 oz/310 g)
   Omit granulated sugar and use 60% (12 oz/375 g) brown sugar.

Chocolate Rolled Cookies
Substitute 2 oz (60 g) cocoa for 2 oz (60 g) of the flour.

Almond Slices

Ingredients	U.S.		Metric	%
Butter	6	oz	175 g	40
Brown sugar	12	oz	350 g	80
Cinnamon	0.07	oz (1¼ tsp)	2 g	0.5
Egg yolks	3	oz	90 g	20
Pastry flour	15	oz	440 g	100
Slivered almonds	6	oz	175 g	40
Total weight:	*2 lb 10*	*oz*	*1232 g*	*280%*

■ P r o c e d u r e

Mixing
   Creaming method. Blend each stage of mixing until smooth, but do not cream until light.
Makeup
   Icebox method. Scale the dough into 12 oz (350 g) units. Roll into round strips about 1½ in. (4 cm) in diameter, or into rectangular strips about 1¼ × 1¾ in. (3.5 × 4.5 cm). Chill until very firm. Slice about 1/16 in. (4 mm) thick, using a sharp knife. Take care to slice through the almonds and not pull them out of the dough. Place slices on greased or paper-lined sheets.
Baking
   375°F (190°C)

Rich Shortbread

Ingredients	U.S.		Metric	%
Butter	12	oz	375 g	75
Sugar	8	oz	250 g	50
Salt	0.12 oz (¾ tsp)		4 g	0.75
Egg yolks	4	oz	125 g	25
Optional flavoring (see *note*)				
Pastry flour	1 lb		500 g	100
Total weight:	*2 lb 8*	*oz*	*1254 g*	*250%*

Note Traditional Scottish shortbread is made with butter, flour, and sugar only—no eggs, flavoring, or liquid. Because this dough is very crumbly, it is usually not rolled out but is pressed into pans or molds and baked. For the recipe given here, you may make the cookies without added flavoring, or flavor to taste with vanilla, almond, or lemon.

■ **P r o c e d u r e**

Mixing
   Creaming method
Makeup
   Rolled method. Roll the dough ¼ in. (6 mm) thick (this is thicker than most rolled cookies). Use greased or parchment-lined pans.
Baking
   350°F (175°C) for about 15 minutes

Basic Short Dough for Cookies

Ingredients	U.S.		Metric	%
Butter or half butter and half shortening	1 lb		500 g	67
Sugar	8	oz	250 g	33
Salt	0.25 oz		8 g	1
Eggs	3	oz	95 g	12.5
Vanilla extract	0.25 oz		8 g	1
Pastry flour	1 lb 8	oz	750 g	100
Total weight:	*3 lb 3*	*oz*	*1611 g*	*214%*

■ **P r o c e d u r e**

Mixing
   Creaming method
Makeup
   Rolled method. Roll out ⅛ in. (3 mm) thick and cut out with cutters of various shapes. See variations below.
Baking
   375°F (190°C)

Short dough is a versatile mixture that can be made up in many ways to provide variety in the bakeshop. Some of the many possible variations are described here.

Flavoring the dough: During mixing, vary the dough by flavoring to taste with lemon, cinnamon, mace, maple, almond extract, or other flavoring. Fine coconut or chopped nuts may be mixed with the dough.

Garnishing before baking: Decorate the tops with chopped or whole nuts, colored sugar, chocolate sprinkles, coconut, glacéed fruits, or almond macaroon mixture. Tops may be egg washed first to help the toppings stick.

Garnishing after baking: Some examples of materials for garnishing cookies are fondant, royal icing, pecan halves on dabs of fudge or fondant icing, and melted chocolate (to coat completely or to drizzle on with a paper cone).

Jam Tarts

Cut out dough with large, round cutters. With a ½-in. (12 mm) cutter, cut out the centers of half the rounds. These will be the tops of the sandwiched cookies. When baked, cool completely. Dust the tops (the ones with the cutout centers) with confectioners' sugar. Sandwich tops and bottoms together with a small dab of jam, so that the jam shows through the hole on top.

Almond Crescents

Cut out crescent shapes from rolled-out dough. Spread tops with a layer of almond macaroon mixture (p. 414). Dip tops in chopped almonds. Bake at 350°F (175°C). When cooled, dip the tips of the crescents in melted chocolate.

Peanut Butter Cookies

Ingredients	U.S.		Metric	%
Butter or part butter and part shortening	12	oz	375 g	75
Brown sugar	8	oz	250 g	50
Granulated sugar	8	oz	250 g	50
Salt	0.16 oz (1 tsp)		5 g	1
Peanut butter	12	oz	375 g	75
Eggs	4	oz	125 g	25
Pastry flour	1 lb		500 g	100
Baking soda	0.16 oz (1 tsp)		5 g	1
Total weight:	*3 lb 12 oz*		*1885 g*	*377%*

■ P r o c e d u r e

Mixing

Creaming method. Cream the peanut butter with the fat and sugar.

Makeup

Molded method. Use a fork instead of a weight to flatten the cookies. Use greased or parchment-lined pans.

Baking

375°F (190°C) for 8–12 minutes, depending on size

Cinnamon Cookies

Ingredients	U.S.		Metric	%
Butter or part butter and part shortening	1 lb		500 g	80
Granulated sugar	8	oz	250 g	40
Brown sugar	8	oz	250 g	40
Salt	0.17 oz (1 tsp)		5 g	0.8
Cinnamon	0.33 oz (2 tbsp)		10 g	1.7
Eggs	3	oz	90 g	15
Milk	1	oz	30 g	5
Pastry flour	1 lb 4	oz	625 g	100
Total weight:	*3 lb 8*	*oz*	*1760 g*	*282%*

■ P r o c e d u r e

Mixing

Creaming method

Makeup

Molded method. Roll out pieces in cinnamon sugar before placing on greased baking sheets and pressing flat.

Baking

375°F (190°C) for about 10 minutes.

Variations

Chocolate Cinnamon Cookies

Substitute 4 oz (125 g) cocoa for 4 oz (125 g) of the flour.

Nut Cookies

Ingredients	U.S.		Metric	%
Butter	14	oz	440 g	87.5
Confectioners' sugar	5	oz	155 g	31
Brown sugar	2	oz	60 g	12.5
Salt	0.08 oz (⅜ tsp)		2 g	0.5
Vanilla extract	0.33 oz (2 tsp)		10 g	2
Bread flour	1 lb		500 g	100
Ground nuts (hazelnuts, pecans, walnuts, almonds, etc.)	12	oz	375 g	75
Total weight:	*3 lb 1*	*oz*	*1542 g*	*308%*

■ **P r o c e d u r e**

Mixing
Creaming method

Makeup
Molded method. Mold cookies by hand into desired shape, such as balls, fingers, or crescents.

Baking
350°F (175°C) for about 25 minutes

Finish
Dust cooled cookies heavily with confectioners' sugar.

Speculaas

Ingredients	U.S.		Metric	%
Butter or half butter and half shortening	1 lb		500 g	67
Confectioners' sugar	13	oz	412 g	55
Fine granulated sugar	4	oz	125 g	17
Grated lemon zest	0.16 oz (2 tsp)		5 g	0.7
Cinnamon	0.25 oz (4 tsp)		8 g	1
Cloves	0.05 oz (¾ tsp)		2 g	0.2
Cardamom	0.05 oz (¾ tsp)		2 g	0.2
Eggs	2.5	oz	75 g	10
Pastry flour	1 lb 8	oz	750 g	100
Total weight:	*3 lb 12*	*oz*	*1879 g*	*251%*

■ **P r o c e d u r e**

Mixing
Creaming method. Blend at each stage until smooth, but do not cream until light.

Makeup
The classic way to make these cookies is by the molded method. The dough is pressed into special wooden speculaas molds, then removed and placed on baking sheets. Or it is stamped with special tools to emboss a design in the dough.

If these molds are not available, make up the cookies either as icebox cookies or as rolled cookies cut with cookie cutters. They can be made small or large as desired. Large cookies should be about ¼ in. (6 mm) thick.

Optional: Press sliced or whole blanched almonds onto the cookies after makeup.

Baking
375°F (190°C) for medium to large cookies: 400°F (200°C) for small, thin cookies

Diamonds

For large-quantity measurements, see page 608.

Ingredients	U.S.		Metric	%
Butter, cut in small pieces	5	oz	140 g	70
Cake flour	7	oz	200 g	100
Confectioners' sugar	2	oz	60 g	30
Salt	0.04 oz (⅕ tsp)		1 g	0.5
Grated orange zest	0.08 oz (1 tsp)		2 g	1
Vanilla extract	0.08 oz (½ tsp)		2 g	1
For rolling				
Crystal sugar	2	oz	50 g	25
Total dough weight:	*14*	*oz*	*407 g*	*202%*

For large-quantity measurements, see page 608.

■ P r o c e d u r e

Mixing
> One-stage method

Makeup and Baking

1. Shape the dough into cylinders 1¼ in. (3 cm) in diameter, making sure that the dough is very tight and that there are no air pockets.

2. Refrigerate the dough for 30 minutes.

3. Brush the cylinders with water. Roll in crystal sugar.

4. Cut into rounds ½ in. (1 cm) thick.

5. Bake on buttered sheet pans at 325°F (160°C) for 20 minutes.

Butter Tea Cookies

Ingredients	U.S.		Metric	%
Butter or half butter and half shortening	12	oz	335 g	67
Granulated sugar	6	oz	165 g	33
Confectioners' sugar	3	oz	85 g	17
Eggs	4.5	oz	125 g	25
Vanilla extract	0.16 oz (1 tsp)		4 g	0.9
Cake flour	1 lb 2	oz	500 g	100
Total weight:	*2 lb 11*	*oz*	*1214 g*	*242%*

■ P r o c e d u r e

Mixing
> Creaming method

Makeup
> Bagged method. Make small cookies about the size of a quarter, using a plain tube or star tube. Bag out onto ungreased or parchment-lined baking sheets.

Baking
> 375°F (190°C), about 10 minutes

Variations

Flavor with almond extract instead of vanilla.

Fancy Tea Cookies
Add 17% (3 oz/85 g) almond paste to the first mixing stage.

Sandwich-Type Cookies
Select cookies all of the same size and shape. Turn half of them over and dot the centers of the flat sides with a small amount of jam or fudge icing. Sandwich with the remaining cookies.

Chocolate Tea Cookies
Substitute 3 oz (85 g) cocoa for 3 oz (85 g) of the flour.

Gingerbread Cookies

Ingredients	U.S.			Metric	%
Butter or part butter and part shortening	11	oz		340 g	45
Brown sugar	8	oz		250 g	33
Baking soda	0.16 oz (1 tsp)			5 g	0.7
Salt	0.12 oz (¾ tsp)			4 g	0.5
Ginger	0.16 oz (2¼ tsp)			5 g	0.7
Cinnamon	0.12 oz (1 tsp)			2 g	0.25
Cloves, ground	0.03 oz (½ tsp)			1 g	0.12
Eggs	3.5	oz		110 g	15
Molasses	11	oz		340 g	45
Pastry flour	1 lb 8	oz		750 g	100
Total weight:	*3 lb 10*	*oz*		*1807 g*	*240%*

Gingersnaps

Ingredients	U.S.		Metric	%
Shortening	6	oz	190 g	38
Sugar	6	oz	190 g	38
Salt	0.08 oz (1 tsp)		2 g	0.5
Ginger	0.25 oz (1 tbsp)		8 g	1.5
Molasses	10	oz	300 g	63
Baking soda	0.25 oz (1½ tsp)		8 g	1.5
Water	2	oz	60 g	13
Pastry flour	1 lb		500 g	100
Total weight:	*2 lb 8*	*oz*	*1268 g*	*256%*

■ **P r o c e d u r e**

Mixing
    Creaming method. Blend the molasses into the creamed fat-sugar mixture first. Then dissolve the soda in the water and blend in. Add the flour last.
Makeup
    Bagged method. With a plain tube, bag out the size of a quarter. Flatten lightly. May also be chilled and made up by molded or rolled methods. Use paper-lined or greased and floured pans.
Baking
    375°F (190°C) for about 12 minutes.

Spritz Cookies

Ingredients	U.S.		Metric	%
Almond paste	12	oz	375 g	100
Sugar	6	oz	190 g	50
Salt	0.12 oz (¾ tsp)		4 g	1
Butter	12	oz	375 g	100
Eggs	4.5	oz	145 g	38
Vanilla extract	0.16 oz (1 tsp)		5 g	1.5
Cake flour	6	oz	190 g	50
Bread flour	6	oz	190 g	50
Total weight:	*2 lb 14*	*oz*	*1474 g*	*390%*

■ **P r o c e d u r e**

Mixing
    Creaming method. Blend the almond paste to a smooth, soft paste with a little of the egg. Add the butter and sugar, and cream as in basic procedure.
Makeup
    Bagged method. Bag out with star tube to desired shapes (small) on parchment-lined sheets. If desired, garnish tops with pieces of fruit or nuts.
Baking
    375°F (190°C)

Lemon Cookies

Ingredients	U.S.			Metric	%
Butter	1 lb			500 g	67
Sugar	1 lb 8	oz		750 g	100
Lemon zest, grated		0.75 oz (3 tbsp)		25 g	3
Salt		0.25 oz (1½ tsp)		8 g	1
Baking soda		0.25 oz (1½ tsp)		8 g	1
Eggs		4	oz	125 g	17
Milk		2	oz	60 g	8
Lemon juice		1	oz	30 g	4
Pastry flour	1 lb 8		oz	750 g	100
Total weight:	*4 lb 8*		*oz*	*2256 g*	*301%*

Mixing
  Creaming method. Cream at each stage just until smooth; do not cream until light.
Makeup
  Bagged method. With a plain tube, bag out small mounds the size of a quarter on paper-lined pans. Flatten slightly.
Baking
  375°F (190°C)

Variation

Lime Cookies
Substitute lime zest and juice for the lemon. This is an unusual and tasty cookie.

Raisin Spice Bars

Ingredients	U.S.			Metric	%
Granulated sugar	1 lb 8	oz		700 g	100
Butter and/or shortening		8	oz	230 g	33
Eggs		8	oz	230 g	33
Molasses		4	oz	115 g	17
Pastry flour	1 lb 8	oz		700 g	100
Cinnamon		0.12 oz (2 tsp)		3 g	0.5
Cloves, ground		0.04 oz (½ tsp)		1 g	0.16
Ginger		0.07 oz (1 tsp)		2 g	0.3
Baking soda		0.12 oz (¾ tsp)		3 g	0.5
Salt		0.17 oz		5 g	0.75
Raisins (see *note*)	1 lb			470 g	67
Total weight:	*5 lb 4*	*oz*		*2459 g*	*352%*

Note If raisins are hard and dry, soak them in hot water until soft, then drain them and dry them well before adding them to the cookie batter.

Mixing
  One-stage method
Makeup
  Bar method. Egg wash strips with whole egg or egg whites.
Baking
  350°F (175°C) for about 15 minutes

Nut Squares

Yield: 150–300 cookies, depending on size

Ingredients	U.S.	Metric
Old-fashioned Pound Cake batter (p. 312)	2 lb	900 g
Chopped pecans, chopped walnuts or sliced almonds	8 oz	225 g
Cinnamon sugar	as needed	

■ P r o c e d u r e

Makeup

Sheet method

1. Spread batter evenly onto a greased and floured full-size sheet pan (18 × 26 in./46 × 66 cm).

2. Sprinkle with nuts, then with cinnamon sugar.

Baking

375°F (190°C)

As soon as the sheet is baked, cut into small squares.

Langues de Chat

Ingredients	U.S.		Metric	%
Butter	14	oz	350 g	88
Extra-fine granulated sugar	7	oz	175 g	44
Confectioners' sugar	7	oz	175 g	44
Egg whites	10	oz	250 g	63
Vanilla extract	0.25	oz (1½ tsp)	6 g	1.6
Cake flour	12	oz	300 g	75
Bread flour	4	oz	100 g	25
Total weight:	*3 lb 6*	*oz*	*1356 g*	*340%*

■ P r o c e d u r e

Mixing

Creaming method

Makeup

Bagged method. Using a ¼ in. (6 mm) plain tube, bag out onto silicone paper in the shape of small fingers 2 in. (5 cm) long. Allow at least 1 in. between cookies to allow for spreading. Double-pan for more even baking.

Baking

400°F (200°C) for about 10 minutes

Finishing

Langues de chat may be served plain as petits fours sec. They may be used as decorations for ice cream, Bavarian cream, or other desserts. They may also be sandwiched together with ganache, buttercream, fudge, or jam. Sandwich cookies may be partially dipped in melted chocolate.

Coconut Macaroons (Meringue Type)

Ingredients	U.S.		Sugar at 100% Metric	%
Egg whites	8	oz	250 g	40
Cream of tartar	0.06 oz (1 tsp)		2 g	0.3
Sugar	1 lb 4	oz	625 g	100
Vanilla extract	0.5	oz	15 g	2.5
Macaroon coconut	1 lb		500 g	80
Total weight:	*2 lb 12*	*oz*	*1392 g*	*222%*

■ **P r o c e d u r e**

Mixing
Sponge method
1. Whip the egg whites with the cream of tartar until they form soft peaks. Gradually whip in the sugar. Continue to whip until stiff and glossy.
2. Fold in the coconut.

Makeup
Bagged method. Bag out with a star tube onto parchment-lined baking sheets.

Baking
300°F (150°C) for about 30 minutes

Almond Macaroons I

Yield: Enough for about 150 1½-in. (4 cm) cookies

Ingredients	U.S.	Almond Paste at 100% Metric	%
Almond paste and/or macaroon paste	1 lb	500 g	100
Granulated sugar	1 lb	500 g	100
Egg whites	6 oz	190 g	37.5
Total weight:	*2 lb 6 oz*	*1190 g*	*237 %*

■ **P r o c e d u r e**

Mixing
One-stage method. Blend the almond paste with a little of the egg whites to soften it, then blend together all ingredients. If the mixture is too stiff for a pastry bag, add a little extra egg white.

Makeup
Bagged method. Using a plain tube, deposit the mix on silicone paper in mounds the size of a quarter. Double-pan.

Baking
350°F (175°C). Let cool before removing from the paper. To make it easier to remove the macaroons from the paper, turn the sheets over and brush the bottoms of the sheets with water.

Variation

Amaretti
Make the following ingredient adjustments:
Use kernel paste instead of almond paste for a stronger flavor (*optional*).
Reduce the granulated sugar to 85% (13.5 oz/425 g).
Add 85% (13.5 oz/425 g) brown sugar.

Almond Macaroons II

For large-quantity measurements, see page 609.

Ingredients	U.S.		Confectioners' Sugar at 100% Metric	%
Powdered almonds	2	oz	60 g	48
Confectioners' sugar	4	oz	125 g	100
Egg whites	2	oz	60 g	48
Fine granulated sugar	0.83 oz (5½ tsp)		25 g	20
Vanilla extract	2 drops		2 drops	
Total weight:	*8*	*oz*	*270 g*	*216%*

■ P r o c e d u r e

Mixing

Sponge method

1. Process the almonds and confectioners' sugar in a food processor for 5 minutes. Sift into a bowl.

2. Whip the egg whites to soft peaks. Add the sugar and whip to stiff, glossy peaks.

3. Fold the dry ingredients and the vanilla into the egg whites, adding the dry ingredients a third at a time.

Makeup

Bagged method. Using a plain tip, deposit the mix on parchment paper in mounds the size of a quarter. Dust with confectioners' sugar and allow to stand for 10–15 minutes.

Baking

350°F (175°C), until golden and well risen. Remove from oven and drizzle a little water between the hot pan and the paper so that the steam helps release the macaroons. Cool completely before removing the macaroons from the paper.

Variations

Cocoa Almond Macaroons

For large-quantity measurements, see page 609.

Prepare as in the basic recipe, using the following ingredients and quantities.

Process the cocoa and cake flour with the almonds and sugar in step 1.

Ingredients	U.S.		Metric
Powdered almonds	3	oz	75 g
Confectioners' sugar	4	oz	100 g
Cocoa powder	1	oz	25 g
Cake flour	0.8 oz		20 g
Egg whites	5	oz	120 g
Fine granulated sugar	2	oz	50 g

Pistachio Macaroons

Ingredients	U.S.		Metric
Confectioners' sugar	10.5	oz	260 g
Powdered almonds	5	oz	150 g
Egg whites	2	oz	50 g
Green food coloring	2 drops		2 drops
Egg whites	3	oz	75 g
Cream of tartar	¼	tsp	1 g
Fine granulated sugar	2	oz	50 g
Pistachio Filling (recipe follows)	1 lb		400 g
Batter weight (not including filling):	*1 lb 6*	*oz*	*585 g*

■ P r o c e d u r e

Mixing

1. **Blend the confectioners' sugar and almonds in a food processor for 5 minutes. Sift into a bowl.**

2. **Mix in the first quantity of egg whites and the coloring until smooth and evenly blended.**

3. **Whip the remaining egg whites and cream of tartar to soft peaks. Add the sugar and whip until stiff.**

4. **Fold the egg whites one-third at a time into the sugar mixture until smooth. The mixture should look slightly wet.**

Makeup and Baking

Bagged method. Using a medium plain tip, pipe 1-in. (2½–3 cm) bulbs onto a parchment-lined sheet pan. Bake at 350°F (180°C) for 8–10 minutes. Remove from oven and trickle water between the hot tray and parchment (the steam helps release of the macaroons). Allow to cool completely before removing from the paper. Sandwich 2 macaroons together with pistachio filling.

Pistachio Filling for Macaroons

Ingredients	U.S.	Metric
Heavy cream	3 oz	75 g
Butter	1 oz	25 g
Glucose	1 oz	25 g
Pistachio paste	3 oz	75 g
Vanilla extract	¼ tsp	1 g
Kirsch	1 oz	25 g
Marzipan	8 oz	200 g
Total weight:	*1 lb 1 oz*	*426 g*

■ P r o c e d u r e

1. **Combine the cream, butter, and glucose. Bring to a boil. Remove from heat and cool.**

2. **Mix in the pistachio paste, vanilla, and kirsch.**

3. **Using a mixer with the paddle attachment, soften the marzipan, then add the cooked ingredients gradually to make a smooth paste.**

4. **For filling macaroons, place in a pastry bag with a small plain tip.**

Chocolate Macaroons I

Ingredients	U.S.	Almond Paste at 100% Metric	%
Almond paste	12 oz	350 g	100
Sugar	1 lb 5 oz	600 g	175
Cocoa	2 oz	60 g	17
Macaroon coconut	3 oz	90 g	25
Egg whites	8 oz	225 g	67
Total weight:	*2 lb 14 oz*	*1325 g*	*384%*

■ P r o c e d u r e

Mixing

One-stage method. Blend the almond paste with a little of the egg whites until smooth. Mix in the remaining ingredients. If the mixture is still too stiff for a pastry bag, add a little extra egg white.

Makeup

Bagged method. Using a plain tube, deposit the mix on silicone paper in mounds the size of a quarter. Double-pan.

Baking

350°F (175°C). Let cool before removing from the paper. To make it easier to remove the macaroons from the paper, turn the sheets over and brush the bottoms of the sheets with water.

Variation

Use ground nuts in place of the macaroon coconut.

Coconut Macaroons (Chewy Type)

Ingredients	U.S.	Sugar at 100% Metric	%
Sugar	1 lb 8 oz	700 g	100
Macaroon coconut	1 lb 8 oz	700 g	100
Corn syrup	3 oz	90 g	13
Vanilla extract	0.33 oz (2 tsp)	10 g	1.5
Pastry flour	1.5 oz	42 g	6
Salt	0.12 oz (¾ tsp)	4 g	0.5
Egg whites	11 oz	315 g	45
Total weight:	*3 lb 15 oz*	*1861 g*	*266%*

■ P r o c e d u r e

Mixing

One-stage method. Blend all ingredients together. Place in a kettle or stainless-steel bowl and set over a hot water bath. Stir constantly until the mixture reaches 120°F (50°C).

Makeup

Using a star tube or plain tube, bag out onto paper-lined sheet pans. Make the cookies about 1 in. (2½ cm) across.

Baking

375°F (190°C)

Variation

Chocolate Macaroons II

Add 1½ oz (45 g) cocoa to the basic recipe. Thin out with an additional ½–1 oz (15–30 g) egg white, if necessary.

Almond Tuiles I

For large-quantity measurements, see page 609.

Yield: Enough to make about 90 cookies, 2½ in. (6 cm) in diameter

Ingredients	U.S.		Metric	%
Butter	3	oz	90 g	86
Confectioners' sugar	4	oz	120 g	114
Egg whites	3	oz	90 g	86
Cake flour	3.5	oz	105 g	100
Garnish				
Sliced almonds	2.5	oz	75 g	70
Batter weight:	*13*	*oz*	*405 g*	*386%*

Note   This batter is also known as *stencil paste.* Instead of the simple round stencils for tuiles, stencils of any shape or size can be cut and used for various decorative effects. This stencil paste is interchangeable with the slightly different stencil paste included in the Ribbon Sponge recipe on page 323.

    This recipe is not interchangeable with Almond Tuiles II, which is a very different batter, even though the makeup is similar.

■ P r o c e d u r e

Mixing
Creaming method
1. **Soften the butter to a creamy consistency. Add the sugar and whip until thoroughly mixed.**
2. **Whip in the egg whites.**
3. **Sift the flour over the mixture and mix in well.**

Makeup
    Stencil method. Line a sheet pan with a silicone mat or, if a mat is not available, a sheet of parchment paper. Make a stencil by cutting a round hole in a sheet of thick plastic or thin cardboard (the cardboard used for cake boxes is suitable). For petit-four-size tuiles, make the circle 2½ in. (6 cm) in diameter. Using an offset palette knife, spread the batter across the stencil, then lift off the stencil (a). Sprinkle with a few sliced almonds (b).

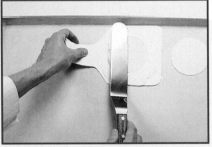
a.

b.

Baking
    350°F (175°C) about 5 minutes, until lightly browned. Remove the baked cookies from the baking sheet and immediately curve over a rolling pin or in a tuile rack (c) and allow to cool.

c.

Variation

Tulipes
Omit the almonds in the basic recipe. Immediately after baking, shape the cookies by molding them around the upturned bottom of a small glass or similar mold. Cup-shaped tulipes are used as edible containers for portions of ice cream and other desserts.

Almond Tuiles II

Ingredients	U.S.		Metric	%
Sugar	8	oz	240 g	533
Sliced, blanched almonds	9	oz	270 g	600
Bread flour	1.5	oz	45 g	100
Egg whites, lightly beaten	4.5	oz	135 g	300
Butter, melted	1.5	oz	45 g	100
Total weight:	*1 lb 8*	*oz*	*735 g*	*1633%*

■ P r o c e d u r e

Mixing

1. Mix the sugar, almonds, and flour in a bowl.

2. Add the egg whites and melted butter. Stir until well mixed.

Makeup

Dropped method. Drop by the tablespoonful 2 in. apart onto a greased and floured baking sheet. Use about ⅓–½ oz (10–15 g) per cookie. Flatten with a fork dipped in water, spreading out the mixture so that it is very thin and flat. It will not spread during baking, and the cookies must be thin.

Baking

375°F (190°C) until browned. Immediately remove one by one from the baking sheet with a spatula and drape them over a rolling pin to given them a curved shape. They will become crisp when cool. If they do not become crisp, they are underbaked; return them to the oven for 1 minute. If they become crisp before they can be curved, return them to the oven to soften them.

Sesame Tuiles

Ingredients	U.S.		Metric	%
Confectioners' sugar	7	oz	210 g	100
Cake flour	7	oz	210 g	100
Nutmeg	large pinch		large pinch	
Egg whites	5	oz	150 g	71
Butter, melted	5	oz	150 g	71
Lemon zest, grated	1	tsp	3 g	1.5
Sesame seeds	1	oz	30 g	15
Garnish				
Sesame seeds	0.5	oz	15 g	7
Total weight:	*1 lb 9*	*oz*	*753 g*	*358%*

■ P r o c e d u r e

1. Sift the sugar, flour, and nutmeg into a bowl. Make a well in the center.

2. Lightly beat the egg whites and add to the well. Also add the butter and lemon zest.

3. Mix to make a soft batter. Add the first quantity of sesame seeds and mix in. Chill.

4. Cut a triangle-shaped stencil and use it to spread the batter onto buttered, chilled sheet pans, using the procedure for making almond tuiles (p. 418). Sprinkle with the remaining sesame seeds.

5. Bake at 375°F (190°C) until golden.

6. Remove from pan and immediately curve into an *S*-shape (see p. 530).

Coconut Tuiles

For large-quantity measurements, see page 609.

Ingredients	U.S.		Sugar at 100% Metric	%
Confectioners' sugar	4	oz	130 g	100
Egg, lightly beaten	3	oz	100 g	77
Dessicated coconut	4	oz	130 g	100
Butter, melted	0.75	oz	25 g	19
Total weight:	*11*	*oz*	*385 g*	*296%*

■ P r o c e d u r e

1. Sift the sugar.
2. Mix in the egg, followed by the coconut and the butter.
3. Rest in refrigerator for 12 hours.
4. Divide the mixture into portions of the desired size and place on a silicon mat on a sheet pan. Cover with a sheet of dampened silicon paper and run a rolling pin over it to flatten the mixture.
5. Remove the paper. Bake at 350°F (180°C) until golden, about 8 minutes. Shape as required while still hot.

Brownies

For large-quantity measurements, see page 609.

Ingredients	U.S.		Metric	%
Unsweetened chocolate	3	oz	85 g	75
Bittersweet chocolate	5	oz	145 g	125
Butter	10	oz	290 g	250
Eggs	6	oz	175 g	150
Sugar	9	oz	260 g	225
Salt	0.06 oz (¼ tsp)		2 g	1.5
Vanilla extract	0.25 oz (1½ tsp)		7 mL	6
Bread flour	4	oz	115 g	100
Walnuts or pecans, chopped	4	oz	115 g	100
Total weight:	*2 lb 9*	*oz*	*1194 g*	*1032%*

■ P r o c e d u r e

Mixing

Modified sponge method

1. Melt the two chocolates and the butter together in a double boiler. Let the mixture cool to room temperature.
2. Mix the eggs, sugar, salt, and vanilla together until well blended, but do not whip. Whipping to a foam creates more leavening, resulting in a more crumbly, less fudgy brownie. If the eggs are not at room temperature, stir the mixture over a hot water bath just until the mixture is at a slightly warm room temperature.
3. Blend in the chocolate mixture.
4. Sift the flour and fold in.
5. Fold in the nuts.

Makeup

Sheet method. For 2 lb. 9 oz (1194 g) batter, use one 9 × 13 in. (23 × 33 cm) pan or two 8-in. (20 cm) square pans. Grease and flour the pans or line them with parchment.

Baking

325°F (190°C) for about 45 to 50 minutes

For 2-in. (5 cm) square brownies, cut sheet pan into 4 rows of 6 to yield 24 pieces.

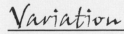

Variation

For large-quantity measurements, see page 609.

Ingredients	U.S.	Metric	%
Baking powder	0.1 oz (½ tsp plus ⅛ tsp)	3 g	2.5

For a more cakelike brownie, sift the above quantity of baking powder with the flour in step 4.

Cream Cheese Brownies

For large-quantity measurements, see page 610.

Yield: Three lb (1400 g) batter is enough for one 9 × 13 in. (23 × 33 cm) pan or two 8-in. (20 cm) square pans.

Ingredients	U.S.	Metric
Cream cheese	8 oz	225 g
Sugar	2 oz	55 g
Vanilla extract	½ tsp	2 mL
Egg yolks	1 yolk	20 g
Brownie batter without walnuts (p. 420), (1 recipe)	2 lb 9 oz	1190 g
Total weight:	*3 lb 3 oz*	*1492 g*

■ **P r o c e d u r e**

Mixing

1. In a mixer with the paddle attachment, work the cream cheese at low speed until smooth and creamy.
2. Add the sugar and vanilla and mix in at low speed until smooth.
3. Add the egg yolks and blend in.
4. Prepare the brownie batter according to the recipe.

Makeup

Sheet method. Grease and flour the pans or line them with parchment.

Spread about half the brownie batter into the pans. Deposit half the cream cheese mixture in pools on top of the brownie batter. Pour in the remaining brownie batter. Spread evenly in the pan. Drop the remaining cream cheese mixture in pools on top. Swirl the two batters together slightly, using a palette knife or a spoon handle.

Baking

325°F (190°C) for about 45 to 50 minutes
Cut into 2-in. (5 cm) square brownies.

Florentines

Ingredients	U.S.	Metric	%
Butter	7 oz	210 g	350
Sugar	10 oz	300 g	500
Honey	3 oz	90 g	150
Heavy cream	3 oz	90 g	150
Sliced almonds	12 oz	360 g	600
Ground almonds or hazelnuts	2 oz	60 g	100
Candied orange peel, chopped	4 oz	120 g	200
Bread flour	2 oz	60 g	100
For finishing			
Chocolate, melted	as needed	as needed	
Total weight:	*2 lb 11 oz*	*1290 g*	*2150%*

■ **P r o c e d u r e**

Mixing

1. Combine the butter, sugar, honey, and cream in a heavy saucepan. Bring to a strong boil, stirring constantly. Cook, stirring, until the mixture reaches 240°F (115°C).
2. Mix together the remaining ingredients and add to the sugar mixture. Mix well.

Makeup

Dropped method. Drop while the mixture is hot; it will get very stiff when cool. Drop ½-oz. (15 g) mounds on baking sheets lined with silicone paper or greased and floured. Allow at least 2 in. (5 cm) between cookies for spreading. Flatten the cookies with a fork.

Baking

375°F (190°C) until browned. As soon as the pans are removed from the oven, use a round cookie cutter to pull the cookies back together into a round shape. Let cool.

Finishing

Spread the flat sides of the cookies with melted chocolate. Mark grooves in the chocolate with an icing comb.

Swiss Leckerli

Ingredients	U.S.		Metric		%
Honey	10	oz	315	g	42
Sugar	6	oz	185	g	25
Baking soda	0.25	oz	8	g	1
Water	4	oz	125	g	17
Salt	0.17	oz (1 tsp)	5	g	0.7
Cinnamon	0.25	oz (4½ tsp)	8	g	1
Mace	0.06	oz (1 tsp)	1.5	g	0.2
Cloves, ground	0.06	oz (1 tsp)	1.5	g	0.2
Candied lemon peel, finely chopped	2	oz	60	g	8
Candied orange peel, finely chopped	2	oz	60	g	8
Blanched almonds, chopped	4	oz	125	g	17
Bread flour	1 lb		500	g	67
Cake flour	8	oz	250	g	33
Total weight:	*3 lb 5 oz*		*1644*	*g*	*220%*

■ P r o c e d u r e

Mixing

1. Heat the honey and sugar together until the sugar is dissolved. Cool.

2. Dissolve the baking soda in the water. Add to the honey mixture.

3. Add the remaining ingredients. Mix to a smooth dough.

Makeup

Sheet method. Roll out dough ¼ in. (6 mm) thick. Place on a well-greased baking sheet. Cut into small squares, but do not separate the squares until after they are baked.

Alternative method: Rolled method. Roll out ¼ in. (6 mm) thick and cut out with cutters, or cut into small squares. Place on greased, floured baking sheets.

Baking

375°F (190°C) for 15 minutes or more. Immediately after baking, while still hot, brush tops with flat icing.

Florentine Squares

For large-quantity measurements, see page 610.

Ingredients	U.S.		Metric		%
Butter	2.25	oz	65	g	65
Cake flour	3.5	oz	100	g	100
Salt	0.07	oz (⅓ tsp)	2	g	2
Sugar	1.5	oz	40	g	40
Egg yolk	0.75	oz	20	g	20
Lemon zest, grated	0.04	oz (½ tsp)	1	g	1
Vanilla extract	0.08	oz (½ tsp)	2	g	2
Heavy cream	4.5	oz	125	g	125
Sugar	6	oz	175	g	175
Butter	4.5	oz	125	g	125
Honey	6	oz	175	g	175
Glucose	2.5	oz	70	g	70
Raisins	3.5	oz	100	g	100
Mixed candied peel, chopped	3.5	oz	100	g	100
Glacé cherries	3.5	oz	100	g	100
Sliced almonds	10.5	oz	300	g	300
Total weight:	*3 lb 1 oz*		*1500*	*g*	*1500%*

■ P r o c e d u r e

1. Rub together the butter and flour to a sandlike consistency.

2. Make a well in the center and add the salt, sugar, yolk, lemon zest, and vanilla.

3. Mix to a smooth dough.

4. Roll the dough to a square or rectangle ⅛ in. (2 mm) thick. This recipe makes a 10-in. (25 cm) square. Dock well.

5. Bake at 325°F (165°C) for 10 minutes or until lightly golden.

6. Mix the cream, sugar, butter, honey, and glucose in a saucepan and cook to 248°F (120°C).

7. Add the remaining ingredients and stir well. Avoid overmixing, which breaks up the almonds.

8. Spread the hot mixture over the baked dough with a palette knife.

9. Place in the oven for 8 minutes at 230°F (110°C) so the mixture spreads evenly and is lightly colored.

10. Remove from the oven and allow to cool.

11. Cut into 1½-in. (4 cm) squares.

Biscotti

Ingredients	U.S.			Metric	%
Eggs		10	oz	300 g	35
Sugar	1 lb	2	oz	550 g	65
Salt		0.5	oz	15 g	2
Vanilla extract		0.3	oz (2 tsp)	8 g	1
Orange zest, grated		0.15	oz (2 tsp)	4 g	0.5
Pastry flour	1 lb	12	oz	850 g	100
Baking powder		0.7	oz	20 g	2.5
Blanched almonds		10	oz	300 g	35
Total weight:	*4 lb*	*3*	*oz*	*2047 g*	*241%*

Note These cookies are hard when cooled. They are traditionally dipped in a sweet wine when eaten.

■ Procedure

Mixing

Sponge method

1. Combine the eggs, sugar, and salt. Stir over hot water to warm the mixture, then whip until thick and light.

2. Fold in the vanilla and orange zest.

3. Sift together the flour and baking powder. Fold into the egg mixture.

4. Mix in the almonds.

Makeup

Bar method. Scale at 1 lb (500 g). Shape into logs about 2–2½ in. (6 cm) thick. Do not flatten the logs (the dough will be sticky and somewhat difficult to handle). Egg wash.

Baking

325°F (160°C) about 30–40 minutes, until light golden

Finishing

Let cool slightly. Slice diagonally ½ in. (12 mm) thick. Place cut side down on sheet pans. Bake at 275°F (135°C) until toasted and dry, about 30 minutes.

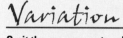

Omit the orange zest and flavor to taste with anise extract.

Espresso Biscotti

For large-quantity measurements, see page 611.

Ingredients	U.S.			Metric	%
Butter		4	oz	120 g	40
Sugar		6	oz	180 g	60
Salt		0.2	oz (1 tsp)	6 g	2
Eggs		3.33	oz (2 eggs)	100 g (2 eggs)	33
Water, hot		0.5	oz	15 g	5
Instant espresso powder		0.2	oz (2 tbsp)	6 g	2
Pastry flour		10	oz	300 g	100
Baking powder		0.25	oz (1½ tsp)	8 g	2.5
Blanched almonds		3.5	oz	105 g	35
Total weight:	*1 lb 11*		*oz*	*840 g*	*279%*

Note See discussion of biscotti, p. 339.

■ Procedure

Mixing

Creaming method. Dissolve the espresso powder in the hot water before adding to the creamed mixture. Mix in the almonds after adding the sifted dry ingredients.

Makeup, Baking, and Finishing

Same as Biscotti above

Chocolate Pecan Biscotti

For large-quantity measurements, see page 611.

Ingredients	U.S.		Metric		%
Butter	4	oz	120	g	40
Sugar	6	oz	180	g	60
Salt	0.1	oz (½ tsp)	3	g	1
Orange zest, grated	0.1	oz (1½ tsp)	3	g	0.5
Eggs	3.33	oz (2 eggs)	100	g (2 eggs)	33
Water	2	oz	60	g	20
Vanilla extract	0.16	oz (1 tsp)	5	g	1.5
Pastry flour	10	oz	300	g	100
Cocoa powder	1.5	oz	45	g	15
Baking powder	0.25	oz (1½ tsp)	8	g	2.5
Baking soda	0.08	oz (½ tsp)	2.5	g	0.8
Pecan pieces	2	oz	60	g	20
Small chocolate chips	2	oz	60	g	20
Total weight:	*1 lb 15*	*oz*	*946*	*g*	*314%*

Note   See discussion of biscotti, page 399

■ **P r o c e d u r e**

Mixing
Creaming method. Mix in the nuts and chocolate chips after adding the sifted dry ingredients.

Makeup, Baking, and Finishing
Same as Biscotti (p. 423)

▶ TERMS FOR REVIEW

spread	dropped	molded	sheet
one-stage method	bagged	icebox	stencil
creaming method	rolled	bar	double-panning
sponge method			

Batons Marechaux and Eponges

For large-quantity measurements, see page 611.

Ingredients	U.S.	Metric	%
Confectioners' sugar	3.33 oz	100 g	333
Cake flour	1 oz	30 g	100
Powdered almonds	2.5 oz	75 g	250
Egg whites	4 oz	120 g	400
Granulated sugar	1.33 oz	40 g	133
For finishing Batons Marechaux			
Chocolate, tempered	as needed	as needed	
For finishing Eponges			
Slivered almonds	as needed	as needed	
Raspberry jam	as needed	as needed	
Total weight:	*12 oz*	*365 g*	*1216%*

■ P r o c e d u r e

Mixing

Sponge method

1. Sift together the confectioners' sugar, flour, and almonds.

2. Whip the egg whites with the granulated sugar to make a common meringue.

3. Fold the sifted ingredients into the meringue.

Makeup for Batons Marechaux

Butter and flour sheet pans. Using a pastry bag with a plain tip (no. 8), pipe strips 2¼-in. (7 cm) long. Bake at 340°F (170°C) for 10 minutes. Remove from baking sheet and cool on rack. Dip the bottoms (flat sides) of the cookies in tempered chocolate and spread thin with a palette knife.

Makeup for Eponges

Butter and flour sheet pans. Using a pastry bag with a plain tip, pipe small mounds ¾ in. (2 cm) in diameter. Sprinkle with slivered almonds. You will need about 1 oz (30 g) of almonds for each 2 oz (60 g) of dough. Bake at 340°F (170°C) for 10 minutes. Remove from baking sheet and cool on rack. Sandwich together in pairs with a little raspberry jam spread on the bottoms.

▶ QUESTIONS FOR REVIEW

1. What makes cookies crisp? How can you keep them crisp after they are baked?

2. If you baked some cookies that were unintentionally chewy, how would you correct them in the next batch?

3. Describe briefly the difference between the creaming method and the one-stage method.

4. Besides cost control, why is accurate scaling and uniform sizing important when making up cookies?

16

Custards, Puddings, Mousses, and Souffl¢s

*T*his chapter discusses a variety of desserts not covered in earlier chapters. Although most of these items are not "baked goods" in the sense that breads, pastries, cakes, and cookies are, they are popular desserts that are important in food service. They include custards, puddings, creams, and frozen desserts.

Most of the items and techniques discussed are related to each other and to techniques discussed in earlier chapters. For example, many puddings, Bavarians and mousses, soufflés, and frozen desserts are based on two basic custards, crème anglaise and pastry cream, presented in chapter 8. Also, Bavarians, mousses, and soufflés depend on meringues (discussed in chapter 8) or whipped cream or both for their texture.

As you know, the art and science of baking and dessert preparation rely on a coherent set of principles and techniques that are applied over and over again to many kinds of products. The topics in this chapter are a further illustration of that fact.

CUSTARDS AND PUDDINGS

It is very difficult to come up with a definition of pudding that includes everything called by that name. The term is used for such different dishes as chocolate pudding, blood sausages (blood puddings), and steak-and-kidney pudding. In this chapter, however, we are considering only popular American dessert puddings.

Two kinds of puddings, starch-thickened and baked, are the most frequently prepared in food service kitchens. A third type, steamed pudding, is less often served, and then only in cold weather, because it is usually rather heavy and filling.

Because custards are the basis of so many puddings, we will begin with a general discussion of this type of preparation. A *custard* is a liquid thickened or set by the coagulation of egg protein. There are two basic kinds of custards: *stirred custard*, which is stirred as it cooks and remains pourable when cooked, and *baked custard*, which is not stirred and sets firm.

One basic rule governs the preparation of both types of custard: *Do not heat custards higher than an internal temperature of 185°F (85°C)*. This temperature is the point at which egg-liquid mixtures coagulate. If they are heated beyond this, they tend to curdle. An overbaked custard becomes watery because the moisture separates from the toughened protein.

Crème Anglaise, or vanilla custard sauce, discussed in detail in chapter 8 (p. 184), is a stirred custard. It consists of milk, sugar, and egg yolks stirred over very low heat until lightly thickened.

Pastry Cream, also discussed in chapter 8 (p. 185), is stirred custard that contains starch thickeners as well as eggs, resulting in a much thicker and more stable product. Because of the stabilizing effect of the starch, pastry cream is an exception to the rule of not heating custards over 185°F. In addition to being used as a component of many pastries and cakes, pastry cream is also the basis for cream puddings.

Baked custard, like custard sauce, consists of milk, sugar, and eggs—usually whole eggs for their thickening power. Unlike the sauce, it is baked rather than stirred over heat, so that it sets and becomes firm. Baked custard is used as a pie filling, as a dessert by itself, and as a basis for many baked puddings.

RANGETOP PUDDINGS

Most of the puddings in this category are thickened with starch, so they must be boiled in order to cook or gelatinize the starch. The first two types of pudding in the following list are of this type. The third type is bound with gelatin, so heating or cooking is necessary to dissolve the gelatin. This type of pudding may need only to be heated gently rather than simmered or boiled.

1. *Cornstarch pudding or blancmange* Cornstarch pudding consists of milk, sugar, and flavorings, and is thickened with cornstarch (or sometimes another starch). If enough cornstarch is used, the hot mixture may be poured into molds, chilled, and unmolded for service.

2. *Cream puddings* Cream puddings, as we have suggested, are the same as pastry cream. Puddings are usually made with less starch, however, and may contain any of several flavoring ingredients, such as coconut or chocolate. Butterscotch pudding is given its flavor by using brown sugar instead of white sugar.

If you look again at the recipes for pastry cream (p. 187–188), you will see that the only difference between cornstarch puddings and cream puddings is that the latter contain eggs. In fact, cream puddings may be made by stirring hot cornstarch pudding into beaten eggs and then heating the entire mixture to just below a simmer. Care must be taken to avoid curdling the eggs if this method is used.

Because these puddings are basically the same as pastry cream, which in turn is used for cream pie fillings, it is not necessary to give separate recipes here. *To prepare any of the following puddings, simply prepare the corresponding cream pie filling (pp. 220–221), but use only half the starch.* The following puddings can be made on this basis:

Vanilla pudding

Coconut cream pudding

Banana cream pudding (purée the bananas and mix with the pudding)

Chocolate pudding (two versions, using cocoa or melted chocolate)

Butterscotch pudding

3. ***Puddings bound with gelatin*** A pudding not thickened with starch or eggs must be bound or stabilized using another ingredient. Gelatin is often used for this purpose. One of the simplest and most popular desserts of this type is *panna cotta,* which is Italian for "cooked cream." In its most basic form, panna cotta is made by heating cream and milk with sugar, adding vanilla and gelatin, and chilling in molds until set. It is often served with fruits or caramel sauce.

Mousses and Bavarian creams, which owe their light texture to whipped cream or meringue, are often bound with gelatin. They are covered in detail later in this chapter.

Blancmange English-Style

Yield: About 2½ pt (1.25 L)

Ingredients	U.S.	Metric	%
		Milk at 100%	
Milk	2 lb (1 qt)	1000 mL	80
Sugar	6 oz	190 g	15
Salt	0.04 oz (¼ tsp)	1 g	0.1
Cornstarch	4 oz	125 g	10
Milk, cold	8 oz (½ pt)	250 mL	20
Vanilla or almond extract	0.25 oz	8 mL	0.6

Note French blancmange is very different from the English style. The French style is made from almonds or almond paste and gelatin.

■ P r o c e d u r e

1. Combine the milk, sugar, and salt in a heavy saucepan and bring to a simmer.

2. Mix the cornstarch and milk until perfectly smooth.

3. Pouring it in a thin stream, add about 1 cup (2.5 dL) of the hot milk to the cornstarch mixture. Stir this mixture back into the hot milk.

4. Stir over low heat until the mixture thickens and comes to a boil.

5. Remove from the heat and add desired flavoring.

6. Pour into half-cup molds. Cool and then chill. Unmold for service.

Variations

Blancmange or cornstarch pudding may be flavored in any way that cream puddings are. See the general discussion preceding this recipe.

For puddings that are to be served in dishes rather than unmolded, reduce the cornstarch to 2 oz (62 g).

Panna Cotta

Ingredients	U.S.	Metric
Milk	10 oz	300 g
Heavy cream	10 oz	300 g
Sugar	4 oz	125 g
Gelatin (see *note*)	1½ tsp–2¼ tsp	5–7 g (2½–3½ sheets)
Vanilla extract	1 tsp	5 g
Total weight:	*1 lb 8 oz*	*740 g*

Note The lower quantity of gelatin makes a soft, delicate dessert. Use this quantity if the room temperature is cool. The larger quantity makes a firmer dessert that can withstand more handling when unmolded.

■ P r o c e d u r e

1. Heat the milk, cream, and sugar until the sugar is dissolved.
2. Soften the gelatin in cold water (see p. 39). Add the softened gelatin to the hot milk mixture and stir until dissolved.
3. Stir in the vanilla.
4. Pour into 3- or 4-oz. (90 or 125 mL) molds. Chill until set.
5. Unmold to serve.

BAKED PUDDINGS

Many, if not most, baked puddings are custards that contain additional ingredients, usually in large quantities. Bread pudding, for example, is made by pouring a custard mixture over slices or cubes of bread arranged in a baking pan and placing it in the oven to bake. Rice pudding, made of cooked rice and custard, is another popular item.

Baked custard, a mixture of eggs, milk, sugar, and flavorings, is baked until the eggs coagulate and the custard sets. A good custard holds a clean, sharp edge when cut.

The amount of egg in a custard determines its firmness. A custard to be unmolded requires more egg than one that is to be served in its baking dish. Also, egg yolks make a richer custard with a softer texture than do whole eggs.

When baking custards, note in particular these points:

1. Scald the milk before beating it slowly into the eggs. This reduces cooking time and helps the product cook more evenly.
2. Remove any foam that would mar the appearance of the finished product.
3. Bake at 325°F (165°C). Higher temperatures increase the risk of overcooking and curdling.
4. Bake in a water bath so that the outside edges do not overcook before the inside is set.
5. To test for doneness, insert a thin-bladed knife about an inch or two from the center. If it comes out clean, the custard is done. The center may not be completely set, but it will continue to cook in its own heat after removal from the oven.

The procedure for making many baked puddings, such as bread pudding, is the same as that for making plain baked custard. A water bath may not be necessary if the starch content of the pudding is high.

Soft pie fillings, such as pumpkin, can also be considered baked puddings and can be served as such. These preparations are, strictly speaking, custards because they are liquids or semiliquids that are set by the coagulation of eggs. They may also contain small amounts of starch as a stabilizer.

It may surprise you to see recipes for cheesecake in this section. Technically, however, cheesecake is the same type of preparation as baked custard or pumpkin pie filling. It is a liquid mixture of milk, sugar, eggs, and cream cheese that becomes firm when the eggs coagulate. The fact that it happens to be called a cake has nothing to do with its composition. In fact, the same mixture is also used as a pie filling.

Baked Custard

Yield: 12 portions, 5 oz (150 g) each

Ingredients	U.S.		Metric		Milk at 100% %
Eggs	1 lb		500	g	40
Sugar		8 oz	250	g	20
Salt		0.08 oz (½ tsp)	2.5	g	0.2
Vanilla extract		0.5 oz	15	g	1.25
Milk	2 lb 8	oz (2½ pt)	1250	mL	100

■ P r o c e d u r e

1. Combine the eggs, sugar, salt, and vanilla in a mixing bowl. Mix until thoroughly blended, but do not whip.

2. Scald the milk in a double boiler or in a saucepan over low heat.

3. Gradually pour the milk into the egg mixture, stirring constantly.

4. Skim off all foam from the surface of the liquid.

5. Arrange custard cups in a shallow baking pan. Butter the insides of the cups if the custards are to be unmolded.

6. Carefully pour the custard mixture into the cups. If bubbles form during this step, skim them off.

7. Set the baking pan on the oven shelf. Pour enough hot water into the pan around the cups so that the level of the water is about as high as the level of the custard mixture.

8. Bake at 325°F (165°C) until set, about 45 minutes.

9. Carefully remove the custard from the oven and cool. Store covered in the refrigerator.

Variations

Crème Caramel
Cook 12 oz (375 g) sugar with 2 oz (60 mL) water until it caramelizes (see the section on sugar cooking (p. 176). Line the bottoms of the custard cups with this hot caramel. (Be sure the cups are clean and dry.) Fill with custard and bake as in a basic recipe.

Vanilla Pots de Crème
Pots de crème (pronounced "poh duh krem") are rich cup custards. Substitute 1 pt (500 mL) heavy cream for 1 pt (500 mL) of the milk in the basic recipe. Use 8 oz (250 g) whole eggs plus 4 oz (125 g) egg yolks.

Chocolate Pots de Crème
Follow the procedure for vanilla pots de crème above, but stir 12 oz (375 g) chopped sweet chocolate into the hot milk until melted and evenly blended. Reduce the sugar to 4 oz (125 g).

Crème Brûlée

Yield: 12 portions, about 5 oz (150 g) each

Ingredients	U.S.		Metric	
Brown sugar	8	oz	250	g
Egg yolks	12		12	
Granulated sugar	6	oz	180	g
Heavy cream, hot	3	pt	1.5	L
Vanilla extract	0.25 oz (1½ tsp)		8	mL
Salt	¾	tsp	3	g

■ P r o c e d u r e

1. Spread the brown sugar on a pan; dry out in a low oven. Cool, crush, and sift.

2. Mix together the egg yolks and granulated sugar until well combined.

3. Gradually stir in the hot cream. Add the vanilla and salt. Strain the mixture.

4. Set 12 shallow ramekins or gratin dishes, about 1 in. (2.5 cm) deep, on a towel in a sheet pan (the purpose of the towel is to insulate the bottoms of the ramekins from the strong heat). Divide the custard mixture equally among the dishes. Pour into the sheet pan enough hot water to come about halfway up the sides of the ramekins.

5. Bake at 350°F (175°C) until the custard is just set, about 25 minutes.

6. Cool, then refrigerate.

7. To finish, first dab any moisture from the tops of the custards. Sprinkle with an even layer of brown sugar. Caramelize the sugar under the broiler; place the custards very close to the heat so that the sugar caramelizes quickly before the custard warms up too much (alternatively, use a blowtorch). When it cools, the caramelized sugar will form a thin, hard crust. Serve within an hour or two. If the custards are held too long, the caramel tops will soften.

Variations

Granulated sugar may be used instead of brown sugar. It is not necessary to dry it (as in step 1), but it is slightly harder to brown.

For a deluxe version, flavor with vanilla beans instead of extract. Split 2 vanilla beans in half lengthwise and scrape out the tiny seeds. Simmer the pods and seeds with the heavy cream. Remove the pods and continue with the basic recipe.

Coffee Crème Brûlée
Flavor the hot cream to taste with coffee extract or instant coffee powder.

Cinnamon Crème Brûlée
Add 2 tsp (3.5 g) cinnamon to the hot cream.

Chocolate Crème Brûlée
Use half milk and half cream. Mix 8 oz (250 g) melted bittersweet chocolate with the hot cream and milk mixture.

Raspberry or Blueberry Crème Brûlée
Place a few berries in the ramekins before adding the custard mixture.

Raspberry Passion Fruit Crème Brûlée
Reduce the quantity of cream to 2¾ pt (1375 mL). Omit the vanilla. Add 4 oz (125 mL) strained passion fruit juice and pulp to the mixture just before straining. Continue as for Raspberry Crème Brûlée.

Bread and Butter Pudding

Yield: About 5 lb (2.5 kg)

Ingredients	U.S.		Metric
White bread, in thin slices	1 lb		500 g
Butter, melted	4	oz	125 g
Eggs	1 lb		500 g
Sugar	8	oz	250 g
Salt	0.08 oz ($\frac{1}{2}$ tsp)		2 g
Vanilla extract	0.5	oz	15 mL
Milk	2 lb 8	oz (1$\frac{1}{4}$ qt)	1250 mL
Cinnamon	as needed		as needed
Nutmeg	as needed		as needed

■ P r o c e d u r e

1. Cut each slice of bread in half. Brush both sides of each piece with melted butter.

2. Arrange the bread so that it overlaps in a buttered 10 × 12 in. (25 × 30 cm) baking pan. (To use a full size hotel pan, double the quantities.)

3. Mix together the eggs, sugar, salt, and vanilla until thoroughly combined. Add the milk.

4. Pour the egg mixture over the bread in the pan.

5. Let stand, refrigerated, for 1 hour or longer, so that the bread absorbs the custard mixture. If necessary, push the bread down into the pan once or twice after the mixture has had time to stand.

6. Sprinkle the top lightly with cinnamon and nutmeg.

7. Set the pan in a larger pan containing about 1 inch hot water.

8. Place in the oven preheated to 350°F (175°C). Bake about 1 hour until set.

9. Serve warm or cold with whipped cream or crème anglaise (p. 184), with a fruit purée, or with confectioners' sugar.

Variations

For a richer pudding, substitute cream for up to half of the milk.

Add 4 oz (125 g) raisins to the pudding, sprinkling them between the layers of bread.

Brandy or Whiskey Bread Pudding
Add 2 oz (60 mL) brandy or whiskey to the custard mixture.

Cabinet Pudding
Prepare in individual custard cups instead of a baking pan. Substitute diced sponge cake for the bread and omit the melted butter. Add about 1$\frac{1}{2}$ tsp (4 g) raisins to each cup before pouring in the custard mix.

Dried Cherry Bread Pudding
Add 4–6 oz (125–185 g) dried cherries to the bread pudding, sprinkling them between the layers of the bread. Substitute heavy cream for up to half of the milk.

Chocolate Bread Pudding

Yield: about 5 lb (2500 g)

Ingredients	U.S.		Metric
Heavy cream	1 lb	4 oz	625 g
Milk	1 lb	4 oz	625 g
Sugar		6 oz	180 g
Bittersweet chocolate, chopped		12 oz	350 g
Dark rum		2 oz	60 g
Vanilla extract		2 tsp	10 g
Eggs		8	8
White bread, in thick slices, crusts trimmed (see *note*)	1 lb		500 g

Note   A good-quality, rich white bread, such as challah (p. 74), is recommended for this recipe.

■ **P r o c e d u r e**

1. Combine the cream, milk, and sugar in a heavy saucepan. Heat, stirring, until the sugar is dissolved.

2. Remove the pan from the heat and let cool 1 minute. Then add the chocolate and stir until it is melted and completely blended in.

3. Add the rum and vanilla.

4. Beat the eggs in a bowl, then gradually beat in the warm chocolate mixture.

5. Cut the bread into large dice and place in a buttered half-size hotel pan or baking pan (10 × 12 in. or 25 × 30 cm). (Or use two 8-in. (20 cm) square pans.) Pour the chocolate mixture over the bread. If any bread is not coated with the chocolate mixture, push it down into the chocolate to coat it.

6. Bake at 350°F (175°C) until set, about 30–45 minutes.

Rice Pudding

Yield: About 4 lb 8 oz (2.25 kg)

Ingredients	U.S.	Metric
Rice, medium or long-grain	8 oz	250 g
Milk	3 lb (3 pt)	1500 mL
Vanilla extract	0.16 oz (1 tsp)	5 mL
Salt	0.04 oz (¼ tsp)	2 g
Egg yolks	3 oz	95 g
Sugar	8 oz	250 g
Light cream	8 oz (½ pt)	250 mL
Cinnamon	as needed	as needed

■ Procedure

1. Wash the rice well. Drain. (See *note*.)

2. Combine the rice, milk, vanilla, and salt in a heavy saucepan. Cover and simmer over low heat until the rice is tender, about 30 minutes. Stir occasionally to be sure the mixture doesn't scorch on the bottom. Remove from the heat when cooked.

3. Combine the egg yolks, sugar, and cream in a mixing bowl. Mix until evenly combined.

4. Ladle some of the hot milk from the cooked rice into this mixture and mix well. Then slowly stir the egg mixture back into the hot rice.

5. Pour into a buttered 10 × 12 in. (25 × 30 cm) baking pan. Sprinkle the top with cinnamon. (To use a full-size hotel pan, double the quantities.)

6. Bake in a water bath at 350°F (175°C) for 30–40 minutes until set. Serve warm or chilled.

Note In order to remove even more loose starch, some cooks prefer to blanch the rice in boiling water for 2 minutes, then drain and rinse it.

Variations

Raisin Rice Pudding
Add 4 oz (125 g) raisins to the cooked rice and milk mixture.

Rice Condé
Make the following adjustments:
  Increase the rice to 10.5 oz (325 g)
  Increase the egg yolks to 5 oz (150 g)
  Omit the cinnamon.

As soon as the egg yolks have been incorporated, pour the rice mixture into shallow individual buttered molds. Bake as in basic recipe, then chill until firm. Unmold onto serving dishes.

Rice Condé can be served plain, served with whipped cream or fruit sauce, or used as a base for poached fruit. Arrange the fruit on top of the unmolded rice; brush with apricot glaze (p. 117). Dishes made in this way are named after their fruit, such as Apricot Condé or Pear Condé.

Tapioca Pudding
This pudding is prepared like rice pudding through step 4 in the procedure. However, it is not baked. Instead, whipped egg whites are folded in and the mixture is chilled. To prepare, make the following adjustments in the recipe:
  Substitute 4 oz (125 g) of tapioca for the pound of rice. Do not wash the tapioca. Cook it in the milk until tender.
  Reserve 2 oz (60 g) of the sugar (from step 3) for the meringue.
  After the egg yolks are incorporated, return the pudding to low heat for a few minutes to cook the yolks. Stir constantly. Do not let the mixture boil.
  Whip 4 oz (125 g) egg whites with the reserved 2 oz (60 g) sugar to a soft meringue. Fold into the hot pudding. Chill.

Cream Cheesecake

Yield: Enough for four 10-in. (25 cm) cakes, five 9-in. (23 cm) cakes, or six 8-in. (20 cm) cakes

Ingredients	U.S.			Metric
Cream cheese	10 lb			4500 g
Sugar	3 lb	8	oz	1575 g
Cornstarch		3	oz	90 g
Lemon zest, grated		0.5	oz	15 g
Vanilla		1	oz	30 g
Salt		1.5	oz	45 g
Eggs	2 lb			900 g
Egg yolks		12	oz	340 g
Heavy cream	1 lb			450 g
Milk		8	oz	225 g
Lemon juice		2	oz	60 g
Short dough (p. 232) or sponge cake for lining pans				
Total weight:	18 lb	4	oz	8230 g

■ P r o c e d u r e

Cheesecake may be baked with or without a water bath. Baking in a water bath results in cakes with browned tops and unbrowned sides. Baking without a water bath results in browned sides and a lighter top. If you are not using a water bath, you may use either deep layer cake pans or springform pans (pans with removable sides). However, if you are using a water bath, you must use deep cake pans, not springform pans.

1. Prepare the pans by lining the bottoms with either a very thin layer of sponge cake or a thin layer of short dough. Prebake the short dough until it begins to turn golden.

2. Put the cream cheese in the mixing bowl and, with the paddle attachment, mix at low speed until smooth and lump free.

3. Add the sugar, cornstarch, lemon zest, vanilla, and salt. Blend in until smooth and uniform, but do not whip. Scrape down the sides of the bowl and the beater.

4. Add the eggs and egg yolks, a little at a time, blending them in thoroughly after each addition. Scrape down the bowl again to make sure the mixture is well blended.

5. With the machine running at low speed, gradually add the cream, milk, and lemon juice.

6. Fill the prepared pans. Scale as follows:

10-in. pans—4¹/₂ lb	25 cm pans—2050 g	
9-in. pans—3¹/₂ lb	23 cm pans—1600 g	
8-in. pans—3 lb	20 cm pans—1350 g	

7. To bake without a water bath, place the filled pans on sheet pans and set them in an oven preheated to 400°F (200°C). After 10 minutes, turn the oven down to 225°F (105°C) and continue baking until the mixture is set, about 1–1¹/₂ hours, depending on the size of the cake.

8. To bake with a water bath, set the filled pans inside another, larger pan. Fill the outer pan with water and bake at 350°F (175°C) until set.

9. Cool the cakes completely before removing from pans. To unmold a cake from a pan without removable sides, sprinkle the top of the cake with granulated sugar. Invert the cake onto a cardboard cake circle, then immediately place another circle over the bottom and turn it right-side up.

Variations

Cheesecake with Baker's Cheese

In place of the 10 lb of cream cheese, use 7¹/₂ lb (3400 g) baker's cheese plus either 3 lb (1350 g) butter or 2¹/₂ lb (1125 g) shortening. If desired, you may use all milk instead of part milk and part cream in step 5.

French Cheesecake

This cheesecake has a lighter texture achieved by incorporating whipped egg whites into the batter of either the cream cheese version or the baker's cheese version. To make French cheesecake, make the following adjustments in either recipe above:

Increase the cornstarch to 5 oz (150 g).

Reserve 1 lb (450 g) of the sugar and whip it with 2 lb 4 oz (1040 g) egg whites to make a soft meringue.

Fold the meringue into the cheese batter before filling the pans.

STEAMED PUDDINGS

Steamed puddings are primarily cold-weather fare. Their heavy, dense texture and richness make them warming, comforting desserts on winter nights. These same characteristics, however, make them inappropriate for year-round use.

The most famous steamed pudding is the English Christmas pudding, known in the United States as plum pudding. A Christmas pudding, well made and with good ingredients, is an unforgettable combination of flavors. The long list of ingredients makes the recipe look difficult, but once the ingredients are assembled and scaled, the pudding is simple to produce.

In addition to Christmas pudding, recipes for less complex steamed puddings are included to give you an idea of the range of possibilities. Many steamed puddings could be baked in a water bath, but steaming is more energy-efficient and helps to keep the pudding moist during the long cooking time.

If a compartment steamer is available, simply set the filled covered pudding molds in steamer pans and place them in the steamer. To steam on top of the stove, set the covered molds in large, deep pans and pour in enough hot water to come halfway up the sides of the molds. Bring the water to a boil, lower the heat to a gentle simmer, and cover the pan. Check the pan periodically and add more hot water as needed.

 ## Christmas Pudding

For large-quantity measurements, see page 612.

Ingredients	U.S.		Metric	
Dark raisins	8	oz	250	g
Light raisins	8	oz	250	g
Currants	8	oz	250	g
Dates, diced	4	oz	125	g
Almonds, chopped	3	oz	90	g
Candied orange peel, finely chopped	2	oz	60	g
Candied lemon peel, finely chopped	2	oz	60	g
Brandy	6	oz	190	mL
Bread flour	4	oz	125	g
Cinnamon	½	tsp	2	mL
Nutmeg	⅛	tsp	0.5	mL
Mace	⅛	tsp	0.5	mL
Ginger	⅛	tsp	0.5	mL
Cloves, ground	⅛	tsp	0.5	mL
Salt	0.13 oz (⅝ tsp)		4	g
Beef suet, finely chopped	6	oz	190	g
Brown sugar	4	oz	125	g
Eggs	4	oz	125	g
Fresh breadcrumbs	2	oz	60	g
Molasses	0.5	oz	15	g
Total weight:	*3 lb 13*	*oz*	*1915*	*g*

■ P r o c e d u r e

1. Soak the fruits and almonds in the brandy for 24 hours.

2. Sift the flour with the spices.

3. Combine the flour mixture, suet, sugar, eggs, crumbs, and molasses. Add the fruit and brandy and mix well.

4. Fill greased pudding molds, allowing a little room for expansion. Cover the pudding mixture with rounds of greased parchment cut to fit inside the molds. Then cover the molds with foil and tie with string so that steam does not get inside.

5. Steam for 4–6 hours, depending on size.

6. For storage, cool the puddings until just warm, then unmold. Wrap in cheesecloth and cool completely, then wrap again in plastic. These will keep a year or more if sprinkled with brandy or rum every 7–10 days.

7. Christmas pudding must be served warm. To reheat it, place it in molds and steam for 1–2 hours until heated through. Serve with hard sauce (p. 199).

Steamed Blueberry Pudding

For large-quantity measurements, see page 612.

Ingredients	U.S.		Metric	
Brown sugar	5	oz	150	g
Butter	2	oz	60	g
Salt	⅛	tsp	0.5	mL
Cinnamon	¾	tsp	4	mL
Eggs	2	oz	60	g
Bread flour	1	oz	30	g
Baking powder	0.18 oz (1 tsp)		6	g
Dry breadcrumbs	5	oz	150	g
Milk	4	oz	125	g
Blueberries, fresh or frozen, without sugar	4	oz	125	g
Total weight:	*1 lb 7*	*oz*	*706*	*g*

■ P r o c e d u r e

1. Cream together the sugar, butter, salt, and cinnamon.
2. Blend in the eggs, a little at a time. Cream until light.
3. Sift the flour with the baking powder, then mix with the breadcrumbs.
4. Add the dry ingredients to the sugar mixture alternately with the milk. Blend to a smooth batter.
5. Carefully fold in the blueberries.
6. Fill well-greased molds about two-thirds full. Cover tightly and steam for 1½–2 hours, depending on the size of the molds.
7. Unmold and serve hot with hard sauce (p. 199) or crème anglaise (p. 185).

Variations

Steamed Raisin Spice Pudding

Add 1 oz (30 g) molasses, ¼ tsp (1 mL) ginger, and ⅛ tsp (0.5 mL) mace to the sugar mixture. In place of the blueberries, use 3 oz (90 g) raisins, soaked and drained, and 2 oz (60 g) chopped nuts. Serve hot with hard sauce (p. 199), crème anglaise (p. 185), or lemon sauce (p. 194).

Steamed Chocolate Almond Pudding

Ingredients	U.S.		Metric	
Butter	4	oz	125 g	
Sugar	5	oz	150 g	
Salt	0.04 oz (¼ tsp)		1 g	
Unsweetened chocolate, melted	1.5	oz	45 g	
Egg yolks	3	oz	90 g	
Milk or dark rum	1	oz	30 g	
Powdered almonds	6	oz	190 g	
Dry breadcrumbs	1	oz	30 g	
Egg whites	5	oz	150 g	
Sugar	1.5	oz	45 g	
Total weight:	*1 lb 12*	*oz*	*856 g*	

■ P r o c e d u r e

1. Cream the butter, sugar, and salt until light. Blend in the chocolate.
2. Add the egg yolks in two or three stages, then blend in the milk or rum. Scrape down the bowl to eliminate lumps.
3. Blend in the almond powder and breadcrumbs.
4. Whip the egg whites and sugar to a soft meringue. Fold the meringue into the batter.
5. Butter the insides of molds and sprinkle with sugar. Fill three-fourths full with batter. Cover tightly and steam 1½ hours.
6. Unmold and serve hot with chocolate sauce (p. 195) or whipped cream.

BAVARIANS AND MOUSSES

Bavarians and mousses, along with soufflés, still-frozen desserts, and many other items discussed later in this chapter, have one thing in common: They all have a light, fluffy texture created by the addition of whipped cream, beaten egg whites, or both.

Bavarian creams are classic gelatin desserts containing custard and whipped cream. Chiffon pie fillings, discussed in chapter 9, are similar to Bavarians in that they are stabilized with gelatin and have a light, foamy texture. In the case of chiffons, however, this texture is due primarily to whipped egg whites; whipped cream may or may not be added. Chiffon pie fillings may also be served as puddings and chilled desserts.

Mousses may have a softer texture than Bavarians, although there is no exact dividing line between the two. Many desserts called mousses are made exactly like Bavarians. However, many mousses, especially chocolate mousses, are made without gelatin or with only a small amount. The light texture of mousses is created by adding whipped cream or meringue or both.

BAVARIANS

A Bavarian, also known as *Bavarian cream,* is made of three basic elements: custard sauce or crème anglaise (flavored as desired), gelatin, and whipped cream. That's all there is to it. Gelatin is softened in cold liquid, stirred into the hot custard sauce until dissolved, and chilled until almost set. Whipped cream is then folded in, and the mixture is poured into a mold until set. It is unmolded for service.

Accurate measuring of the gelatin is important. If not enough gelatin is used, the dessert will be too soft to hold its shape. If too much is used, the cream will be too firm and rubbery. The use of gelatin is discussed in detail in chapter 2 (p. 39) and in the section of chapter 9 pertaining to chiffon pie fillings (p. 222).

Fruit Bavarians can be made like regular custard-based Bavarian creams by adding fruit purées and flavorings to the custard base. They can also be made without a custard base by adding gelatin to a sweetened fruit purée and then folding in whipped cream. A separate recipe is included for basic fruit Bavarian creams. In addition, recipes for several modern specialty Bavarian creams are found this section.

Because they can be molded and decorated in many ways, Bavarian creams can be used to make elaborate, elegant desserts. They are the basis for a variety of desserts called cold *charlottes,* which are Bavarian creams molded in ring molds lined with various sponge cake products. Classic charlottes are usually decorated with whipped cream and fresh fruits, and are perhaps served with a fruit coulis. Procedures for assembling two famous charlottes from the classic pastry shop are included following the basic Vanilla Bavarian recipe.

Modern pastry chefs have created a whole new family of charlottes as a medium for displaying their decorative skills. This chapter includes several recipes of this type as examples of how flavorful and eye-appealing modern desserts can be created using classical techniques. These charlottes are made in large ring molds, but please note that they can also be made in single-portion sizes by using small ring molds 2¾ in. (7 cm) in diameter, just like several of the pastries in chapter 11. See page 283 for an illustration of the technique.

Procedure for Preparing Bavarian and Bavarian-Type Creams

1. Prepare the base, either crème anglaise (p. 185) or another base indicated in recipe.

2. Soften the gelatin in cold liquid and stir it into the hot base until dissolved. Or, if the base is not cooked, heat the gelatin and liquid until the gelatin is dissolved, then stir it into the base.

3. Cool the mixture until thick but not set.

4. Fold in the whipped cream.

5. Pour the mixture into prepared molds and chill until set.

This section also includes two other desserts that are made with the same techniques. Rice Impératrice, or empress rice, is an elegant molded rice pudding. The base is made somewhat like custard sauce (which is the base for Bavarian cream), except that rice is cooked in the milk before the egg yolks and gelatin are added. Whipped cream is then folded in. (Another way of arriving at the same result is to combine equal parts Rice Condé mixture, found on page 435, and Vanilla Bavarian Cream mixture, plus the candied fruit mixture indicated in the recipe on page 442.)

Cream cheese Bavarian is not made with a cooked custard base, but it contains gelatin and whipped cream. Thus it is similar in character and texture to other Bavarian creams. Similarly, three of the creams among the following recipes are based on pastry cream rather than crème anglaise like true Bavarian creams, although they belong in this section because of their gelatin and whipped cream content.

If a gelatin-based dessert is made in a bowl-shaped mold rather than a ring mold, unmold it by dipping the mold into hot water for 1 or 2 seconds. Quickly wipe the bottom of the mold and turn it over onto the serving plate (or invert the plate over the mold and flip the plate and mold over together). If it doesn't unmold after a gentle shake, repeat the procedure. Do not hold in the hot water for more than a few seconds or the gelatin will begin to melt.

MOUSSES

There are so many varieties of mousse that it is impossible to give a rule for all of them. In general, we could define a mousse as any soft or creamy dessert made light and fluffy by the addition of whipped cream, beaten egg whites, or both. Note that Bavarians and chiffons fit this description. In fact, they are often served as mousses, but with the gelatin reduced or left out so that the mousse is softer.

There are many kinds of bases for mousses. They may be nothing more than melted chocolate or puréed fresh fruit, or they may be more complex, like the bases for chiffons.

Some mousses contain both beaten egg whites and whipped cream. When this is the case, most chefs prefer to fold in the egg whites first, even though they may lose some volume. The reason is that if the cream is added first, there is more danger that it will be overbeaten and turn to butter during the folding and mixing procedure.

If egg whites are folded into a *hot* base, they will cook or coagulate, making the mousse firmer and more stable. Whipped cream should never be folded into hot mixtures because it will melt and deflate.

In addition to the chocolate mousse recipes included in this section and the additional recipes in chapter 8 (p. 193), you can also convert the chiffon pie filling recipes (p. 222) and the Bavarian cream recipes (p. 441) to mousses. Just reduce the quantity of gelatin to one-third or one-half the amount indicated in the recipe. For creamier mousses made from the chiffon recipes, substitute whipped cream for part of the meringue. (Some of the variations following the main recipes indicate this substitution.) By making these recipe adjustments, you can make a number of popular mousses—including raspberry, strawberry, lemon, orange, and pumpkin—without needing separate recipes.

The chocolate terrine on page 455 could be said to be a chocolate mousse that is thick enough to be sliced. Compare this recipe to the recipe for Chocolate Mousse I on page 193. You will see that the procedures are almost the same, although the ingredient proportions are different.

Vanilla Bavarian Cream

Yield: About 1½ qt (1.5 L)

Ingredients	U.S.		Metric
Gelatin	0.75	oz	22 g
Water, cold	5	oz	150 mL
Crème anglaise			
Egg yolks	4	oz	125 g
Sugar	4	oz	125 g
Milk	1 pt		500 mL
Vanilla	0.25	oz	8 mL
Heavy cream	1 pt		500 mL

■ P r o c e d u r e

1. Soak the gelatin in the cold water.

2. *Prepare the crème anglaise:* Whip the egg yolks and sugar until thick and light. Scald the milk and slowly stir it into the egg yolk mixture, beating constantly. Cook over a hot water bath, stirring constantly, until it thickens slightly. (Review page 184 for detailed discussion of making crème anglaise.)

3. Stir the gelatin mixture into the hot custard sauce until it is dissolved.

4. Cool the custard sauce in the refrigerator or over crushed ice, stirring occasionally to keep the mixture smooth.

5. Whip the cream until it forms soft peaks. Do not overwhip.

6. When the custard is very thick but not yet set, fold in the whipped cream.

7. Pour the mixture into molds or serving dishes.

8. Chill until completely set. If prepared in molds, unmold for service.

Variations

Chocolate Bavarian Cream
Add 6 oz (190 g) dark chocolate, chopped or grated, to the hot custard sauce. Stir until completely melted and blended in.

White Chocolate Bavarian Cream
Add 8 oz (250 g) white chocolate, chopped or grated, to the hot custard sauce. Stir until completely melted and blended in.

Coffee Bavarian Cream
Add 1½ tbsp (6 g) instant coffee powder to the hot custard sauce.

Strawberry Bavarian Cream
Reduce the milk to 8 oz (250 mL) and the sugar to 3 oz (90 g). Mash 8 oz (250 g) strawberries with 3 oz sugar (90 g), or use 12 oz (375 g) frozen, sweetened strawberries. Stir this purée into the custard sauce before adding the whipped cream.

Raspberry Bavarian Cream
Prepare like Strawberry Bavarian Cream, using raspberries.

Liqueur Bavarian Cream
Flavor to taste with a liqueur or spirit, such as orange, kirsch, maraschino, amaretto, or rum.

Praline Bavarian Cream
Mix 3 oz (95 g) praline paste with the hot custard sauce.

Diplomat Bavarian Cream
Moisten diced sponge cake (about 4 oz/125 g) and diced candied fruit (about 4 oz/125 g) with kirsch (about 1.5 oz/45 ml). Mix gently with Vanilla Bavarian mixture.

Orange Bavarian Cream
Proceed as in the basic recipe, except omit the vanilla and reduce the milk to 8 oz (250 mL). Flavor the custard sauce with the grated zest of 1 orange or with orange flavor. Before adding the whipped cream, stir 8 oz (250 mL) orange juice into the cold custard mixture.

Charlotte Russe
Line the bottom and sides of a charlotte mold with ladyfingers (p. 324). For the bottom, cut the ladyfingers into triangles and fit them in close together so that the points meet in the center. The ladyfingers must fit in tightly so that there is no space between them. Fill the mold with Bavarian cream mixture and chill until set. Before unmolding, trim the tops of the ladyfingers so that they are level with the cream, if necessary.

Another method for making Charlotte Russe, although not authentic, can make an attractive dessert. Mold some Bavarian cream mixture in an unlined charlotte mold. After unmolding, cover the top and sides with ladyfingers or langues de chat (p. 413), using a little melted Bavarian mixture to make them stick. Decorate with whipped cream.

Charlotte Royale
Line a round mold with thin slices of a small jelly roll. Fit them close together so that there is no space between them. Fill the mold with Bavarian mixture and chill until set. If desired, the charlotte may be glazed with apricot glaze (p. 117) after unmolding.

Fruit Bavarian

Yield: About 2½ pt (1.25 L)

Ingredients	U.S.		Metric
Fruit purée (see note)	8	oz	250 g
Extra-fine granulated sugar	4	oz	125 g
Lemon juice	1	oz	30 mL
Gelatin	0.5	oz	15 g
Water, cold	5	oz	150 mL
Heavy cream	12	oz	375 mL

Note Use 8 oz (250 g) unsweetened or lightly sweetened fresh, frozen, or canned fruit, such as strawberries, raspberries, apricots, pineapple, peaches, or bananas. To use heavily sweetened fruit, such as frozen, sweetened strawberries, use 10 oz (300 g) fruit and reduce the sugar to 2 oz (60 g).

■ P r o c e d u r e

1. Force the fruit purée through a fine sieve. Mix it with the sugar and lemon juice. Stir the mixture or let it stand until the sugar is completely dissolved.

2. Soften the gelatin in the cold water for 5 minutes. Heat the mixture gently until the gelatin is dissolved.

3. Stir the gelatin mixture into the fruit purée.

4. Chill the mixture until thickened but not set. *Note:* If the fruit purée is cold when the gelatin is added, it will start to set very quickly so that further chilling may not be needed.

5. Whip the cream until it forms soft peaks. Do not overwhip.

6. Fold the cream into the fruit mixture. Pour it into molds and chill.

Rice Impératrice

Yield: 1 qt (1 L)

Ingredients	U.S.		Metric	
Rice, long-grain	3	oz	90	g
Milk	1 pt		0.5	L
Vanilla	0.25	oz	8	mL
Egg yolks	2	oz	60	g
Sugar	3	oz	90	g
Gelatin	0.25	oz	8	g
Water, cold	2	oz	60	mL
Candied fruits, diced	3	oz	90	g
Kirsch	1	oz	30	mL
Heavy cream	6	oz	180	mL

Note A traditional way of preparing this dish is to line the bottoms of the molds with about ¼ in. (6 mm) red fruit gelatin. For the quantity in this recipe, you will need about ¼ pt (125 mL) gelatin mixture. Use either 1 oz (30 g) flavored gelatin mix dissolved in 4 oz (125 mL) water, or ¹⁄₁₆ oz (³⁄₈ tsp/2 g) plain gelatin dissolved in 4 oz (125 mL) sweetened red fruit juice. Pour it into molds and chill until set.

■ P r o c e d u r e

1. Rinse and drain the rice. Simmer it slowly in the milk, covered, until tender. Add the vanilla.

2. Whip the egg yolks and sugar together. Stir in a little of the hot milk from the rice mixture. Then stir the egg yolk mixture into the rice mixture. Cook very slowly for a few minutes, stirring constantly, until it is lightly thickened.

3. Soften the gelatin in the water. Stir the gelatin mixture into the hot rice mixture until the gelatin is dissolved. (*Note:* For buffet service or in hot weather, increase the gelatin to 0.4 oz (11 g).

4. Stir in the candied fruits, which have been soaked in the kirsch.

5. Chill the mixture until thick but not set.

6. Whip the heavy cream until it forms soft peaks. Fold it into the rice mixture.

7. Pour into molds (see *note*). Chill until set. Unmold onto serving plates. Decorate with candied fruits and whipped cream, if desired. Serve with Melba Sauce (p. 196).

Cream Cheese Bavarian

For large-quantity measurements, see page 613.

Yield: about 1¹/₂ qt (1.6 L)

Ingredients	U.S.			Metric	
Cream cheese	12	oz		375	g
Sugar	4	oz		125	g
Salt	0.12 oz (⁵/₈ tsp)			4	g
Lemon zest, grated	0.03 oz (³/₈ tsp)			1	g
Orange zest, grated	0.02 oz (¹/₄ tsp)			0.5	g
Vanilla extract	0.06 oz (³/₈ tsp)			2	g
Lemon juice	1	oz		30	g
Gelatin	0.25 oz			8	g
Water, cold	2	oz		60	g
Heavy cream	1 pt			500	mL
Total weight:	2 lb	3	oz	1105	g

■ P r o c e d u r e

1. Place the cream cheese in the bowl of a mixer and mix at low speed to soften it. Add the sugar, salt, and flavorings and blend until smooth. Scrape down the sides of the bowl to eliminate lumps.

2. Blend in the lemon juice.

3. Soften the gelatin in the water, then heat the water gently until the gelatin is dissolved.

4. Whip the cream until it forms soft, not stiff peaks. Do not overwhip.

5. Blend the warm gelatin mixture into the cream cheese mixture. Scrape down the bowl to make sure the gelatin is mixed in well.

6. Immediately fold in the cream. Do not let the cheese mixture stand after adding the gelatin, as it will set very quickly.

7. Pour the mixture into prepared molds or serving dishes. Chill until set.

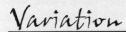

Variation

Icebox Cheesecake
Use one of the following methods:

1. Line the bottoms of cake pans or springform pans with thin sheets of sponge cake or with a crumb crust mixture. Pour in the Cream Cheese Bavarian mixture and chill until set. Unmold.

2. Follow the procedure for Bavarian Torte (p. 376), using the Cream Cheese Bavarian mixture.

One full recipe is enough for one 9-in. (23 cm) cake.

Orange Cheese Mousse

Ingredients	U.S.		Metric
Italian meringue			
Egg whites	4	oz	125 g
Sugar	4	oz	125 g
Water	2.5	oz	70 g
Gelatin	0.33	oz	9 g
Orange liqueur	1.33	oz	40 g
Cream cheese	8	oz	250 g
Orange zest, grated	1¾	tsp	4 g
Orange juice, strained	2	oz	60 g
Heavy cream	11	oz	350 g
Total weight:	*2 lb*	*1 oz*	*1033 g*

■ P r o c e d u r e

1. *Make the meringue:* Whip the egg whites to soft peaks. Make a syrup of the sugar and water and cook to 240°F (115°C). Gradually whip the hot syrup into the egg whites. Continue whipping until cold. Set aside.

2. Soften the gelatin in cold water (see p. 39).

3. Heat the orange liqueur. Add the gelatin and stir to dissolve.

4. In a mixer with the paddle attachment, blend the cream cheese with the zest and a little of the orange juice until smooth.

5. Mix in the gelatin and the remaining orange juice until smooth.

6. Whip the cream to soft peaks. Fold the meringue and the cream alternately into the cheese until smooth.

7. Fill molds and chill.

Unbaked Orange Cheesecake

Yield: one 7-in. (18 cm) charlotte

Ingredients	U.S.	Metric
Chocolate Sablé (p. 231)	one baked 7-in. circle, ⅛ in. thick	one baked 18-cm circle, 3 mm thick
Orange marmalade	1–1.33 oz	30–40 g
Chocolate Genoise (p. 319) or other chocolate sponge	one 7-in. circle, ¼ in. thick	one 18-cm circle, ½ cm thick
Dessert syrup flavored with orange liqueur	as needed	as needed
Orange Cheese Mousse (above)	1 lb	450–500 g
Decoration		
Crème Chantilly (p. 181)	as needed	as needed
Kumquat Compote (p. 503)	as needed	as needed
Marbled or wood-grain chocolate slab (p. 541)	as needed	as needed

■ P r o c e d u r e

1. Spread the chocolate sablé circle with orange marmalade. Top with the sponge circle; brush the sponge with syrup.

2. Place the sponge and sable inside a 7-in. charlotte ring on a cake card. Fill to the top with the mousse and smooth the top with a palette knife. Chill until set.

3. Remove the ring, using a blowtorch to gently warm the ring so that it releases.

4. Using a pastry bag with a star tip or a St Honoré tip, decorate the border of the cake with Crème Chantilly as desired. Fill the center with Kumquat Compote.

5. Break the sheet of chocolate into random-size pieces and use to cover the sides of the cake.

Three-Chocolate Bavarois

Yield: three 7-in. (18-cm) Bavarians

Ingredients	U.S.		Metric
Chocolate Sponge layers (p. 327), 6 in. (15 cm) in diameter	3		3
Cocoa Vanilla Syrup (p. 179)	4	oz	125 g
Crème anglaise			
Milk	8	oz	250 g
Heavy cream	8	oz	250 g
Egg yolks	5.5	oz	160 g
Sugar	3	oz	85 g
Gelatin	0.4	oz	12 g
Dark chocolate, finely chopped	2.75	oz	80 g
Milk chocolate, finely chopped	2.75	oz	80 g
White chocolate, finely chopped	2.75	oz	80 g
Heavy cream	1 pt 5	oz	600 g
Cocoa Jelly (p. 344)	10	oz	300 g
White chocolate for piping (p. 543)	as needed		as needed

■ P r o c e d u r e

1. Line each of three 6½-in. (16 cm) charlotte rings with an acetate strip.

2. Place the rings on cake cards. Place a sponge layer in the base of each ring. (The sponge layers should be slightly smaller than the rings so that there is a gap between the ring and sponge all the way around. If necessary, trim the sponge.)

3. Brush the sponge layers with the Cocoa Vanilla Syrup.

4. Prepare the crème anglaise according to the basic procedure on page 184.

5. Soften the gelatin in cold water (see p. 39). Add the gelatin to the hot crème anglaise and stir until dissolved.

6. Divide the crème anglaise into three equal portions. Add the dark chocolate to one bowl, the milk chocolate to the second, and the white chocolate to the third. Mix each one thoroughly to melt the chocolate.

7. Whip the cream into soft peaks. Divide the whipped cream into three equal portions.

8. Cool the dark chocolate Bavarian over a cold water bath until it is beginning to set. Fold in one-third of the whipped cream. Fill the charlotte ring and level the surface with an offset palette knife. Place in the refrigerator or freezer to set, approximately 20 minutes. The Bavarian should be firmly set before adding the next layer, or the layers will not be level.

9. Repeat step 7 with the milk chocolate, then with the white chocolate.

10. Place the finished layers in the freezer for at least 1 hour

11. Remove the charlottes from the freezer. Apply the Cocoa Jelly to the tops, running a palette knife across the top to smooth the glaze. Allow to set.

12. Decorate with piped white chocolate.

13. The ring molds may be removed at any time, but do not remove the acetate strips until ready to serve.

Almond Cream

Ingredients	U.S.		Metric
Crème anglaise			
Milk	10	oz	300 g
Vanilla bean, split (see *note*)	1		1
Sugar	2.5	oz	75 g
Egg yolks	2	oz	60 g
Marzipan	1.67	oz	50 g
Amaretto liqueur	1	oz	30 g
Gelatin	0.4	oz	12 g
Heavy cream	10	oz	300 g
Total weight:	*1 lb 11*	*oz*	*827 g*

Note   If vanilla beans are not available, add ½ tsp (2 mL) vanilla extract in place of 1 vanilla bean.

■ P r o c e d u r e

1. *Make the crème anglaise:* Heat the milk, vanilla bean, and half the sugar until simmering. Meanwhile whip the egg yolks with the remaining sugar. Gradually beat in the hot milk, then return to the heat and cook until just thickened enough to coat a spoon.

2. Stir in the marzipan in small pieces until smooth.

3. Soften the gelatin in cold water (see p. 39).

4. Mix in the amaretto and the softened gelatin. Stir until the gelatin is dissolved.

5. Cool the mixture over ice, stirring to make sure it stays smooth as it thickens.

6. Before the mixture sets, whip the cream to soft peaks and fold in. Pour the mixture into molds and chill until set.

Passion Fruit Bavarian

Ingredients	U.S.		Metric
Milk	7	oz	200 g
Sugar	3.5	oz	100 g
Egg yolks	6		6
Sugar	3.5	oz	100 g
Gelatin	0.5	oz	14 g
Passion fruit purée or juice	7	oz	200 g
Heavy cream	14	oz	400 g
Total weight:	*2 lb 10*	*oz*	*920 g*

■ P r o c e d u r e

1. Heat the milk and the first quantity of sugar in a pan.

2. Whip the yolks with the remaining second quantity of sugar.

3. When the milk mixture comes to a boil, temper the yolks with one-fourth of this mix and return all to the pan. Cook to 185°F (85°C), being careful not to exceed this temperature.

4. Strain through a fine china cap.

5. Soften the gelatin in cold water (see p. 39).

6. Bring the passion fruit pulp to a boil; add gelatin and stir to dissolve. Stir over a cold water bath until cooled to about 80°F (25–28°C). Combine with the milk mixture.

7. Whip the cream into soft peaks. Carefully fold in the whipped cream, working quickly before the gelatin sets.

8. Pour into molds and chill.

Mousse aux Cassis (Blackcurrant Mousse)

Ingredients	U.S.		Metric
Gelatin	0.33	oz	11 g
Sugar	1.67	oz	50 g
Water	1	oz	30 g
Blackcurrant (cassis) purée	10	oz	300 g
Heavy cream	8	oz	250 g
Total weight:	*1 lb 5*	*oz*	*641 g*

■ P r o c e d u r e

1. Soften the gelatin in cold water (see p. 39).
2. Heat the sugar and water until the sugar is dissolved. Remove from the heat and add the softened gelatin. Stir until dissolved.
3. Add the fruit purée to the gelatin mixture. Stir over ice until it begins to set.
4. Whip the cream to soft peaks and immediately fold into the fruit purée.
5. Fill molds and chill until set.

Variations

Passion Fruit Mousse
Substitute passion fruit purée for the blackcurrant purée in the main recipe. Omit the sugar and water syrup and instead use a syrup made of the following ingredients. Heat the water and sugar until dissolved. Remove from the heat and add the vodka.

Ingredients	U.S.		Metric
Sugar	1	oz	27 g
Water	1	oz	27 g
Vodka	0.5	oz	16 g

Charlotte aux Cassis

Yield: one 7-in. (18 cm) round charlotte

Ingredients	U.S.		Metric
Plain Genoise sponge (p. 319)	Half sheet pan, ¼ in. thick		Half sheet pan, ½ cm thick
Raspberry jam	3.5	oz	100 g
Sugar	1.67	oz	50 g
Water	1.67	oz	50 g
Crème de cassis liqueur	1	oz	30 g
Mousse aux Cassis (p. 447)	1 lb 4	oz	600 g
Fruit Glaçage (p. 345) made with blackcurrant (cassis) purée	2.5–3.5	oz	75–100 g
Berries and other soft fruits for decoration	as needed		as needed

■ P r o c e d u r e

1. Prepare the sponge for lining the mold. Cut out one 6-in. (15 cm) circle from one end of the sponge sheet and reserve. Trim the remaining sponge to make a square about 12 in. (30 cm) on a side. Cut this square into four small squares of equal size. Spread three of the squares with raspberry jam and layer them up. Top with the fourth sponge square. Press down lightly. Chill. (This makes enough for two charlottes; reserve the extra for later use.)

2. Line a 7-in. (18 cm) charlotte ring. (This is the same procedure as used for baumkuchen, illustrated on page 367). Cut the sponge square into strips whose width is two-thirds to three-fourths the height of the ring molds. The exact width is not important, as long as *all the strips are the same width.* Cut each of these strips crosswise into strips ¼ in. (5 mm) thick. Place the ring molds on cake cards. Arrange the strips of sponge around the inside of the ring molds, pressing them into place, so that the stripes of raspberry jam are vertical. Continue until the ring is compactly lined with sponge.

3. Make a syrup by boiling the sugar and water until dissolved. Remove from the heat and add the liqueur. (This small amount of syrup is enough for at least two or three charlottes.)

4. Place the sponge circle inside the ring to make a base. Brush with the syrup.

5. Fill the ring to the top with the Mousse aux Cassis. Level with a palette knife. Chill until set.

6. Spread the warm glaçage over the tops and level with a palette knife. Chill until set.

7. Remove the rings by warming them slightly with a blowtorch to release them, then lifting off.

8. Decorate as desired.

Variation

Passion Fruit Charlotte

Make the following changes to the recipe:

Line the mold with yellow-striped Ribbon Sponge (p. 327), as illustrated on page 366.

In place of the cassis syrup for soaking the sponge, use a simple dessert syrup.

Substitute Passion Fruit Mousse (p. 447) for the Blackcurrant Mousse.

Use passion fruit purée for the glaçage, and add the seeds from one-half fresh passion fruit to the glaçage before applying the charlotte.

The charlotte in the illustration is decorated with a bouquet of fruits and a free-form lattice made of piped choux pastry sprinkled with poppy seeds.

Nougatine Cream

Ingredients	U.S.			Metric	
Gelatin		0.25 oz		7.5	g
Pastry Cream II (p. 188)	11	oz		320	g
Sugar	3	oz		85	g
Crushed Nougatine (p. 562)	8.5	oz		250	g
Kirsch		1.25 oz		35	g
Heavy cream	2 lb 6	oz		1100	g
Total weight:	*3 lb 14*	*oz*		*1797*	*g*

■ **P r o c e d u r e**

1. Soften the gelatin in cold water (see p. 39).
2. Heat the pastry cream just until hot.
3. Add the softened gelatin and sugar. Stir until dissolved.
4. Add the nougatine.
5. When the temperature has dropped to about 85°F (30°C), stir in the kirsch.
6. Whip the cream into soft peaks and fold it into the mixture.
7. Pour into desired molds and chill.

Praline Cream I

Ingredients	U.S.			Metric	
Gelatin		0.12 oz		3	g
Pastry Cream II (p. 188), freshly made and warm	10	oz		250	g
Praline paste	2	oz		50	g
Heavy cream	8	oz		200	g
Total weight:	*1 lb 4*	*oz*		*503*	*g*

■ **P r o c e d u r e**

1. Soften the gelatin in cold water (see p. 39).
2. Add the gelatin to the pastry cream and stir until dissolved.
3. Add the praline paste and mix in.
4. Cool the mixture to about 75–80°F (25°C). Whip the cream into soft peaks and mix about one-fourth of it into the mixture.
5. Fold in the remaining whipped cream.
6. Pour into desired molds and chill.

Praline Cream II

Ingredients	U.S.			Metric	
Pastry Cream II (p. 188)	9	oz		225	g
Praline paste	3.5	oz		90	g
Gelatin		0.25 oz		6	g
Coffee liqueur		0.75 oz		20	g
Crushed Nougatine (p. 562)	3	oz		75	g
Heavy cream	8	oz		200	g
Total weight:	*1 lb 8*	*oz*		*616 g*	

■ **P r o c e d u r e**

1. Whip the pastry cream until it is smooth. Beat in the praline paste until well mixed in.
2. Soften the gelatin in cold water (see p. 39).
3. Heat the coffee liqueur. Add the gelatin and stir until dissolved, rewarming as necessary.
4. Beat the gelatin mixture into the pastry cream. Chill.
5. Beat in the crushed nougatine.
6. Whip the cream until it forms soft peaks. Fold in.

Banana Mousse

Ingredients	U.S.		Metric
Gelatin	0.33	oz	8 g
Banana pulp, fresh or frozen	12	oz	310 g
Lemon juice	1	oz	25 g
Sugar	1.33	oz	35 g
White rum	1	oz	25 g
Heavy cream	1 lb		420 g
Total weight:	*1 lb 15*	*oz*	*823 g*

▪ P r o c e d u r e

1. Soften the gelatin in cold water (see p. 39).

2. Heat a third of the banana pulp to 140°F (60°C). Add the gelatin and stir until dissolved.

3. Mix in the lemon juice and sugar. Stir to dissolve the sugar.

4. Add this mixture to the remaining banana pulp and mix in the rum.

5. Once this mixture has cooled to about 75°F (25°F), fold in the whipped cream.

6. Fill molds and chill.

Coconut Mousse with Tropical Fruit

Yield: about 1 lb 12 oz (800 g)

Ingredients	U.S.		Metric
Water	4	oz	120 g
Coconut milk (unsweetened)	4	oz	120 g
Sugar	7	oz	200 g
Mango, diced	5	oz	150 g
Pineapple, diced	5	oz	150 g
Gelatin	0.2	oz	6 g
Milk	1.67	oz	50 g
Sugar	1	oz	30 g
Coconut, grated	1	oz	30 g
Coconut milk (unsweetened), chilled	4.5	oz	140 g
Coconut-flavored liqueur	4	tsp	20 g
Heavy cream	8	oz	250 g

▪ P r o c e d u r e

1. For the fruit, heat together the water, coconut milk, and sugar to make a syrup. Add the diced mango and pineapple. Cover the surface with a round of parchment and poach the fruit for about 15 minutes until it is tender but still holding its shape. Do not overcook. Allow the fruit to cool in the syrup and then drain.

2. Soften the gelatin in cold water (see p. 39).

3. Heat the milk, sugar, and coconut in a saucepan to about 175°F (80°C). Let stand a few minutes to allow the coconut to infuse.

4. Remove from the heat and add the gelatin, stirring to dissolve.

5. Add the second quantity of coconut milk. When the temperature has cooled to about 75°F (25°C), stir in the liqueur.

6. Whip the cream to soft peaks and fold in.

7. Fold in the drained fruit.

8. Pour into molds and chill.

L'Exotique

Yield: one 6½-in. (16 cm) gâteau

Ingredients	U.S.		Metric
Ribbon Sponge (p. 327)	see step 1		see step 1
Hazelnut Coconut Sponge layers (p. 262) 6 in. (15 cm) in diameter	2		2
Coconut Mousse with Tropical Fruit (p. 451)	14	oz	400 g
Gelatin	0.13	oz	4 g
Mango pulp	4	oz	125 g
Sugar	0.4	oz (2¾ tsp)	12 g
Passion Fruit Ganache (p. 193), warm	6	oz	175 g
Decoration			
Chocolate for spraying	as needed		as needed
Mango wedges	as needed		as needed
Passion fruit seeds and pulp	as needed		as needed

L'Exotique
cut to show
the interior

■ **P r o c e d u r e**

1. Line a 6½-in. (16-cm) charlotte ring with a strip of acetate. Prepare a multicolored sheet of Ribbon Sponge with an abstract pattern, as shown on page 327. Cut a strip and line the charlotte ring as on page 366, making the strip slightly narrower than the height of the ring so that some of the filling shows above it.

2. Place the ring on a cake card and put one of the sponge layers in the bottom.

3. Fill about one-third full with the coconut mousse. Smooth the top and chill until set.

4. Soften the gelatin in cold water (see p. 39).

5. Heat about one quarter of the mango pulp to 140°F (60°C), then stir in the gelatin and sugar until they are dissolved. Add the remaining mango pulp and stir.

6. Spread the jellied mango pulp on top of the Coconut Mousse once the mousse has set. Place in the freezer to set.

7. Spread a thin layer of the Coconut Mousse (about ½ in./1 cm thick) on top of the mango.

8. Cover with the second layer of the sponge.

9. Finish with a third layer of the mousse, filling the mold to the top and leveling it. Place in the freezer to set.

10. Spread a ½-in. (1 cm) thick layer of the warm ganache over the frozen cake. (This depth is necessary because so much ganache is removed by the cake comb.) Before the ganache sets, quickly pass a cake comb over the top to make a design.

11. Return to the freezer for 15 minutes to set.

12. Spray the top with a chocolate sprayer (see p. 543) to leave a velvety finish.

13. Remove the ring. Decorate the top of a few wedges of mango and a few passion fruit seeds.

Chocolate Mousse III

Yield: about 2⅛ pt (1.12 L)

Ingredients	U.S.		Metric
Bittersweet chocolate	10	oz	300 g
Water	2.5	oz	75 g
Egg yolks	3	oz (9 yolks)	90 g (9 yolks)
Liqueur (see *note*)	1	oz	30 g
Egg whites	4.5	oz (9 whites)	135 g (9 whites)
Sugar	2	oz	60 g
Heavy cream	8	oz	250 mL
Total weight:	*1 lb 15*	*oz*	*950 g*

Note   Any appropriate liqueur or spirit, such as orange liqueur, amaretto, rum, or brandy, may be used. If you don't wish to use a liqueur, use 1 oz (30 mL) strong coffee or 1½ tsp (8 mL) vanilla plus 1½ tbsp (22 mL) water.

■ P r o c e d u r e

1. In a saucepan, add the chocolate to the water and melt it over low heat, stirring constantly so that the mixture is smooth.

2. Beat in the egg yolks. Whip the mixture over low heat for a few minutes until it thickens slightly.

3. Remove the mixture from the heat and stir in the liqueur or other liquid. Cool it completely.

4. Whip the egg whites with the sugar to form a firm meringue. Fold it into the chocolate mixture.

5. Whip the cream until it forms soft peaks. Fold it into the chocolate mixture.

6. Pour the mousse into serving bowls or individual dishes. Chill for several hours before serving.

Chocolate Mousse IV

Yield: about 2 pt (1 L)

Ingredients	U.S.		Metric
Bittersweet chocolate	1 lb		500 g
Butter	4	oz	125 g
Egg yolks	6	oz	180 g
Egg whites	8	oz	250 g
Sugar	2.5 oz		75 g
Heavy cream	8	oz	250 mL
Total weight:	*2 lb 12*	*oz*	*1378 g*

■ P r o c e d u r e

1. Melt the chocolate in a dry pan over a hot water bath.

2. Remove from the heat. Add the butter and stir until melted.

3. Add the egg yolks, mixing well.

4. Whip the egg whites with the sugar to form a soft meringue. Fold into the chocolate mixture.

5. Whip the cream until it forms soft peaks. Fold it into the chocolate mixture.

6. Transfer the mousse to serving bowls or individual dishes. Chill for several hours before serving.

Variations

The following variations are based on the above recipe, except that a few modifications are necessary due to the different composition and handling properties of milk chocolate and white chocolate.

Milk Chocolate Mousse
Substitute milk chocolate for the dark chocolate in the main recipe. Melt the chocolate with 4 oz (125 mL) water, stirring until smooth. Then remove from the heat and proceed with step 2 of the procedure. Reduce the quantity of yolks to 2 oz (60 g). Reduce the quantity of sugar to 2 oz (60 g).

White Chocolate Mousse
Substitute white chocolate for milk chocolate in the preceding variation.

Chocolate Mousse V (with Gelatin)

Ingredients	U.S.		Metric
Gelatin	0.2 oz		6 g
Sugar	1.67 oz		50 g
Water	1.67 oz		50 g
Glucose	0.33 oz		10 g
Egg yolks	2.67 oz (4 yolks)		80 g (4 yolks)
Dark chocolate couverture, melted	7.25 oz		225 g
Heavy cream	1 lb		500 g
Italian Meringue (p. 183)	6	oz	180 g
Total weight:	*2 lb 3*	*oz*	*1100 g*

■ P r o c e d u r e

1. Soften the gelatin in cold water (see p. 39).

2. Combine the sugar, water, and glucose and bring to a boil to make a syrup. Cook to 245°F (119°C).

3. Whip the egg yolks until thick and pale. Gradually beat in the hot syrup. Add the gelatin and beat until dissolved. Continue whipping until cold.

4. Fold the melted chocolate into the egg yolk mixture.

5. Whip the cream into soft peaks. Fold in.

6. Fold in the Italian meringue. Pour into molds and chill until set.

Chocolate Terrine

Yield: 1 lb 8 (735 g)

Ingredients	U.S.	Metric
Bittersweet chocolate	12 oz	375 g
Eggs	6	6
Orange liqueur	2 oz	60 mL
Cocoa powder	as needed	as needed
Total weight:	*1 lb 8 oz*	*735 g*

■ P r o c e d u r e

1. For each 12 oz of chocolate, prepare a 1-pt (500 mL) loaf pan by lining it with parchment. (For broader slices of the finished terrine, double the recipe and use a 1-qt (1 L) loaf pan.)

2. Chop the chocolate into small pieces. Melt the chocolate over warm water. Do not allow any water to get into the chocolate.

3. Separate the eggs.

4. Whip the egg whites until they form soft peaks. Set aside. (It is necessary to whip the egg whites before beginning to mix the chocolate because once you add the first liquid to the chocolate, you must continue the procedure without interruption.)

5. Add the orange liqueur to the chocolate and beat in. The chocolate will become very thick.

6. Beat the yolks into the chocolate, one or two at a time, until well blended.

7. Beat the egg whites into the chocolate mixture. Use a stiff whip to beat them in. Do not try to fold them in gently, as the mixture is too stiff.

8. In order to create the necessary smooth texture, force the mixture through a sieve to remove lumps of unblended chocolate or egg.

9. Pour some of the chocolate into the prepared pan(s) to fill them about halfway. Rap the pans on the bench sharply to remove air bubbles. Fill with the remaining chocolate, and again remove air bubbles.

10. Cover and refrigerate overnight.

11. Unmold onto a platter. Dust the top and sides lightly with cocoa powder. Slice about ¼ in. (6 mm) thick using a sharp, thin-bladed knife dipped into hot water and wiped dry before each slice. Serve small portions, as this dessert is very rich.

Variation

Substitute 3 oz (90 g) strong espresso for the orange liqueur.

Chocolate Indulgence

Yield: two gâteaux 7 in. (18 cm) in diameter

Ingredients	U.S.	Metric
To line mold		
Joconde Sponge Cake (p. 322)	one half-size sheet pan	one half-size sheet pan
Ganache I (recipe opposite)	as needed	as needed
Ganache II (recipe opposite)	as needed	as needed
Syrup		
Water	2 oz	60 g
Sugar	2 oz	60 g
Orange liqueur, such as Cointreau	2 oz	60 g
Chocolate Mousse V (p. 454)	2 lb (approx.)	900–1000 g
Ganache Icing (p. 344)	7 oz	200 g
Suggested decoration		
Chocolate fans (p. 543)	as needed	as needed
Cocoa powder	as needed	as needed
Fresh berries	as needed	as needed
Chocolate cigarettes (p. 542)	as needed	as needed

■ P r o c e d u r e

1. Prepare the Joconde Sponge Cake for lining the mold. Cut two 6-in. (15 cm) circles from one end of the sponge sheet and reserve. Trim the remaining sponge to make a square about 12 in. (30 cm) on a side. Cut this square into four small squares of equal size. Spread one with a thin layer of Ganache I. Top with a second square and spread with a layer of Ganache II. Top with a third square and spread with a layer of Ganache I. Top with the fourth sponge square. Press down lightly. Chill. (If you wish to simplify production, you could omit the Ganache II and use Ganache I for all three layers.)

2. Line two 7-in. (18 cm) charlotte rings. (This is the same procedure as used for Baumkuchen, illustrated on page 367). Cut the sponge square into strips whose width is two-thirds to three-fourths the height of the ring molds. The exact width is not important, as long as *all the strips are the same width.* Cut each of these strips crosswise into strips ¼ in. (5 mm) thick. Place the ring molds on cake cards. Arrange the strips of sponge around the inside of the ring molds, pressing them into place, so that the stripes of ganache are vertical. Continue until both rings are compactly lined with sponge.

3. Make a syrup by boiling the sugar and water until dissolved. Remove from the heat and add the liqueur.

4. Place one of the sponge circles inside each ring to make a base. Brush with the syrup.

5. Prepare the chocolate mousse and fill the rings to the top with the mousse. Level with a palette knife. Chill until set.

6. Spread the warm ganache icing over the tops and level with a palette knife. Chill until set.

7. Remove the rings by warming them slightly with a blowtorch to release them, then lifting off.

8. Decorate as desired.

Ganache I

Yield: 1 lb (450 kg)

Ingredients	U.S.	Metric
Dark chocolate, chopped	7 oz	200 g
Heavy cream	9 oz	250 g

■ **P r o c e d u r e**

Melt the chocolate in a water bath. Heat the cream and mix into the chocolate. Chill.

 Ganache II

Yield: 1 lb 4 oz (575 g)

Ingredients	U.S.	Metric
White chocolate, chopped	1 lb	450 g
Heavy cream	4.5 oz	125 g
Red coloring	few drops	few drops

■ **P r o c e d u r e**

Melt the white chocolate in a water bath. Heat the cream and mix in. Add a little red color to give a pale pink color. Chill.

SOUFFLÉS

Soufflés are lightened with beaten egg whites and then baked. Baking causes the soufflé to rise like a cake because the air in the egg foam expands when heated. Toward the end of the baking time, the egg whites coagulate, or become firm. However, soufflés are not as stable as cakes, and they fall shortly after they are removed from the oven. For this reason, they should be served immediately.

A standard soufflé consists of three elements:

1. *Base*   Many kinds of bases are used for dessert soufflés; most are heavy, starch-thickened preparations, such as pastry creams or sweetened white sauces. If egg yolks are used, they are added to the base.

2. *Flavoring ingredients*   These are added to the base and mixed in well. Popular flavorings include melted chocolate, lemon flavor, and liqueurs. Small quantities of solid ingredients such as dried candied fruits or finely chopped nuts may also be added.

   The base and flavor mixture may be prepared ahead of time and kept refrigerated. Portions can then be scaled to order and mixed with egg whites.

3. *Egg whites*   Whenever possible, egg whites should be whipped with some of the sugar. This makes dessert soufflés more stable.

   Butter soufflé dishes well and coat them with sugar. Fill dishes to about $\frac{1}{2}$ in. (1 cm) below the rim. When it is baked, the soufflé should rise 1-1$\frac{1}{2}$ in. above the rim.

Vanilla Soufflé

Yield: 10 to 12 portions

Ingredients	U.S.		Metric
Bread flour	3	oz	90 g
Butter	3	oz	90 g
Milk	1 pt		500 mL
Sugar	4	oz	120 g
Egg yolks	6	oz (8–9 yolks)	180 g (8–9 yolks)
Vanilla extract	0.33	oz (2 tsp)	10 mL
Egg whites	10	oz (10 whites)	300 g (10 whites)
Sugar	2	oz	60 g

■ P r o c e d u r e

1. Work the flour and butter together to form a paste.

2. Dissolve the sugar in the milk and bring to a boil. Remove from the heat.

3. With a wire whip, beat in the flour paste. Beat vigorously to make sure there are no lumps.

4. Return the mixture to the heat and bring it to a boil, beating constantly. Simmer for several minutes until the mixture is very thick and no starchy taste remains.

5. Transfer the mixture to a mixing bowl. Cover and let cool 5–10 minutes.

6. Beat in the egg yolks and vanilla.

7. Soufflés may be prepared ahead of time up to this point. Chill the mixture and scale portions of the base to order. Proceed with the following steps.

8. Prepare soufflé dishes by buttering the insides well and coating with granulated sugar. This recipe will fill ten to twelve single-portion dishes or two 7-in. (18 cm) dishes.

9. Whip the egg whites until they form soft peaks. Add the sugar and whip until the mixture forms firm, moist peaks.

10. Fold the egg whites into the soufflé base.

11. Pour the mixture into the prepared baking dishes and smooth the tops.

12. Bake at 375°F (190°C). Approximate baking times are 30 minutes for large dishes, 15 minutes for single-portion dishes.

13. *Optional step:* 3–4 minutes before soufflés are done, dust the tops generously with confectioners' sugar.

14. Serve as soon as removed from the oven.

Variations

Chocolate Soufflé
Melt together 3 oz (90 g) unsweetened chocolate and 1 oz (30 g) sweet chocolate. Add to the base after step 5.

Lemon Soufflé
Instead of vanilla, use the grated zest of 2 lemons for flavoring.

Liqueur Soufflé
Flavor with 2–3 oz (60–90 mL) of desired liqueur, such as kirsch or orange liqueur, added after step 5.

Coffee Soufflé
Flavor with 2 tbsp (15 g) instant coffee powder, or to taste, added to the milk in step 2.

Praline Soufflé
Blend 4–5 oz (125–150 g) praline paste with the base after step 5.

► TERMS FOR REVIEW

custard	cream pudding	Christmas pudding	rice impératrice
stirred custard	pot de crème	Bavarian cream	mousse
baked custard	panna cotta	charlotte	soufflé
cornstarch pudding			

► QUESTIONS FOR REVIEW

1. What is the internal temperature at which the eggs in custard mixtures become cooked or coagulated? What happens to stirred custards and baked custards if they are cooked beyond this point?

2. The basic techniques used to make crème anglaise and baked custard are also used for some of the following preparations. Identify which of the following desserts are made using a stirred custard (custard sauce) technique, which are made using a baked custard technique, and which are made without any custard.

Bread pudding	Apple cobbler
Christmas pudding	Charlotte Russe
Chocolate Bavarian	Chocolate pots de crème
Baked cheesecake	Apple charlotte

3. What is the main difference between cornstarch pudding and cream pudding?

4. In the production of Bavarian creams and other desserts that are stabilized with gelatin, why is it important to measure the gelatin carefully?

5. When making a Bavarian or chiffon pie filling, what difficulty would you encounter if you chilled the gelatin mixture too long before folding in the whipped cream or egg whites?

6. When making dessert soufflés, what is the advantage of adding part of the sugar to the whipped egg whites?

17
Frozen Desserts

$\mathcal{T}$he popularity of ice cream needs no explanation. Whether it is a plain scoop of vanilla ice cream in a dish or an elaborate assemblage of fruits, syrups, toppings, and numerous flavors of ice cream and sherbet, a frozen dessert appeals to everyone.

Until recently, few establishments made their own ice cream because of the labor involved, the equipment required, and the sanitation regulations and health codes that had to be followed. In addition, the convenience and high quality of commercially made ice creams make it unnecessary for many operations to make their own. But today, many restaurants find that serving their own homemade sorbets and ice creams is appealing to customers. In fact, in the finest restaurants, customers may expect the pastry chef to produce frozen desserts as well as pastries. Learning to make ice cream has become an important skill.

You will find that much of this chapter seems familiar. The base for ice cream, for example, is the same crème anglaise that you have used in many other preparations. Other techniques in this chapter, such as preparing syrups and whipping meringues, are used in many areas of the bakeshop.

CHURN-FROZEN DESSERTS

After reading this chapter, you should be able to:

■ Judge the quality of commercial ice creams.

■ Prepare ice creams and sorbets.

■ Prepare ice cream and sorbet desserts using commercial or homemade ice creams and sorbets.

■ Prepare still-frozen desserts, including bombes, frozen mousses, and frozen soufflés.

Ice cream and sherbet are churn-frozen, meaning that they are mixed constantly while being frozen. If they were not churned, they would freeze into solid blocks of ice. The churning keeps the ice crystals small and incorporates air into the dessert.

Ice cream is a smooth, frozen mixture of milk, cream, sugar, flavorings, and, sometimes, eggs. *Philadelphia-style* ice cream contains no eggs, and *French-style* ice cream contains egg yolks. The eggs add richness and help make a smoother product because of the emulsifying properties of the yolks.

Ice milk is like ice cream, but with a lower butterfat content. *Frozen yogurt* contains yogurt in addition to the normal ingredients for ice cream or ice milk.

Sherbets and *ices* are made from fruit juices, water, and sugar. American sherbets usually contain milk or cream and, sometimes, egg whites. The egg whites increase smoothness and volume. Ices, also called *water ices,* contain only fruit juice, water, sugar, and, sometimes, egg whites; they do not contain milk products. The French word *sorbet* (pronounced "sor-bay") is sometimes used for these products. *Granité* (pronounced "grah-nee-tay") is coarse, crystalline ice, made without egg whites. Italian versions of ice cream and sorbet are called *gelato* (plural: *gelati*) and *sorbetto* (plural: *sorbetti*).

PRODUCTION AND QUALITY

A basic ice cream mix is simply a crème anglaise or custard sauce mixed with 1 or 2 parts heavy cream for every 4 parts milk used in the sauce. This base is flavored, as desired, with vanilla, melted chocolate, instant coffee, sweetened crushed strawberries, and so on. Chill thoroughly, then freeze according to the instructions for your particular equipment.

When the mix has frozen, transfer it to containers and place these in a deep freeze at below 0°F (–18°C) to harden. (Soft-frozen or soft-serve ice creams are served directly as they come from the churn freezer, without being hardened.)

Whether you make ice cream or buy it, you should be aware of several quality factors:

1. **Smoothness** is related to the size of the ice crystals in the product. Ice cream should be frozen rapidly and churned well during freezing so that large crystals don't have a chance to form.

   Rapid hardening helps keep crystals small, as do eggs and emulsifiers or stabilizers added to the mix.

   Large crystals may form if ice cream is not stored at a low enough temperature (below 0°F/–18°C).

2. *Overrun* is the increase in volume due to incorporation of air when freezing ice cream. It is expressed as a percentage of the original volume of the mix. (For example, if it doubles in volume, then the amount of increase is equal to the original volume and the overrun is 100%.)

   Some overrun is necessary to give a smooth, light texture. If ice cream has too much overrun, it will be airy and foamy and will lack flavor. It was once thought that ice cream should have from 80% to 100% overrun and that less would make it heavy and pasty. This may be true for ice creams containing gums and other stabilizers. However, some high-quality manufacturers produce rich (and expensive) ice cream with as little as 20% overrun.

   Overrun is affected by many factors, including the type of freezing equipment, the length of churning time, the fat content of the mix, the percentage of solids in the mix, and how full the freezer is.

3. *Mouth feel* or body depends, in part, on smoothness and overrun as well as on other qualities. Good ice cream melts in the mouth to a smooth, not too heavy liquid. Some ice creams have so many stabilizers that they never melt to a liquid. Unfortunately, many people have become so accustomed to these products that an ice cream that actually does melt in the mouth strikes them as "not rich enough."

STORAGE AND SERVICE

1. Store ice creams and sherbets below 0°F (−18°C). This low temperature helps prevent the formation of large ice crystals.

2. To prepare for serving, temper frozen desserts at 8° to 15°F (−13° to −9°C) for 24 hours so that they will be soft enough to serve.

3. When serving, avoid packing the ice cream. The best method is to draw the scoop across the surface of the product so that the product rolls into a ball in the scoop.

4. Use standard scoops for portioning ice cream. Normal portions for popular desserts are as follows:

Parfait	3 No. 30 scoops
Banana split	3 No. 30 scoops
"À la mode" topping for pie or cake	1 No. 20 scoop
Sundae	2 No. 20 scoops
Plain dish of ice cream	1 No. 10, 12, or 16 scoop

5. Measure syrups, toppings, and garnishes for portion control. For syrups, use pumps that dispense measured quantities, or use standard ladles.

POPULAR ICE CREAM DESSERTS

Parfaits are made by alternating layers of ice cream and fruit or syrup in tall, narrow glasses. They are usually named after the syrup or topping. For example, a chocolate parfait has three scoops of vanilla or chocolate ice cream alternating with layers of chocolate syrup and topped with whipped cream and shaved chocolate.

Sundaes or *coupes* consist of one or two scoops of ice cream or sherbet placed in a dish or glass and topped with any of a number of syrups, fruits, toppings, and garnishes. They are quick to prepare, unlimited in variety, and as simple or as elegant as you wish—served in an ordinary soda fountain glass or in a silver cup or crystal champagne glass.

Coupes are often elegant, attractively decorated desserts. Many types have been handed down to us from the classic cuisine of years ago. The following are some classic coupes and similar desserts that are still popular today.

Coupe Arlesienne In the bottom of the cup, place a spoonful of diced candied fruits that have been soaked in kirsch. Add a scoop of vanilla ice cream, top with a poached pear half, and coat with apricot sauce.

Coupe Black Forest Place a scoop of chocolate ice cream in the cup and add sweet, dark cherries flavored with a little cherry brandy. If desired, add a few chopped walnuts. Decorate with rosettes of whipped cream and shaved chocolate.

Coupe Edna May Top vanilla ice cream with sweet cherries. Decorate with whipped cream mixed with enough raspberry purée to color it pink.

Coupe Gressac Top vanilla ice cream with three small almond macaroons that have been moistened with kirsch. Top with a small poached peach half, cut side up, and fill the center of the peach with red currant jelly. Decorate with a border of whipped cream.

Coupe Jacques Place a scoop each of lemon sherbet and strawberry ice cream in a cup. Top with a mixture of diced, fresh fruit flavored with kirsch.

Coupe aux Marrons Top vanilla ice cream with candied chestnuts (marrons glacés) and whipped cream.

Coupe Orientale Place diced pineapple in the bottom of the cup and add pineapple sherbet. Top with apricot sauce and toasted almonds.

Peach Melba Top vanilla ice cream with a poached peach half covered with Melba sauce (p. 196) and topped with slivered almonds.

Pear Belle Hélène Top vanilla ice cream with a poached pear half covered with chocolate sauce and garnished with toasted, sliced almonds.

Among other popular ice cream desserts mentioned earlier in this book are Meringues Glacés (p. 264) and Frozen Éclairs and Profiteroles (p. 249). The popular festive dessert called Baked Alaska is discussed in the following procedure. Although no one is surprised by it any more, one of the classic names for this dessert is Soufflé Surprise, so called because it looks like baked whipped eggs on the outside but is frozen inside.

Procedure for Making Baked Alaska

1. Pack softened ice cream into a dome-shaped mold of the desired size. Freeze solid.

2. Prepare a layer of sponge cake the same size as the flat side of the mold and about ½ in. (12 mm) thick.

3. Unmold the frozen ice cream onto the cake layer so that the cake forms the base for the ice cream.

4. With a spatula, cover the entire dessert with a thick layer of meringue. If desired, decorate with more meringue forced from a pastry bag.

5. Bake at 450°F (230°C) until the raised edges of the meringue decorations turn golden brown.

6. Serve immediately.

HOMEMADE ICE CREAMS AND SORBETS

The same quality factors that apply to commercially made frozen desserts, as discussed above, apply to those you make yourself.

The first two recipes that follow illustrate the basic procedures for making ice cream and sorbet. Using the procedures in these two recipes, you can make an unlimited variety of frozen desserts, as exemplified by the many variations that follow each main recipe. Following these basic recipes are additional recipes for specialty ice creams and sorbets.

As in other areas in the bakeshop, accurate measurement of ingredients is important. In the case of frozen desserts, proper measurement is important to ensure that the mix freezes properly. This is because the ratio of sugar weight to total weight has a strong effect on freezing. If an ice cream or sorbet mix contains too much sugar, it will not freeze enough to become firm. On the other hand, an ice cream with too little sugar will not be as smooth as one with the correct amount. For a basic vanilla ice cream, the weight of the sugar is usually 16–20% of the total weight. Adding other ingredients makes the calculation more complicated because many ingredients, such as fruits, contain sugar.

In addition, careful sanitation procedures are critical because ice cream mix is a good breeding ground for bacteria. Equipment should be made of stainless steel or other nonporous and noncorrosive material, and it should be properly cleaned and sanitized after every use.

Vanilla Ice Cream

Yield: about 2 qt (2 L), depending on overrun

Ingredients	U.S.	Metric
Egg yolks (12 yolks)	8 oz	250 g
Sugar	12 oz	375 g
Milk	2 pt	1 L
Heavy cream	1 pt	500 mL
Vanilla extract	2 tsp	10 mL
Salt	pinch	pinch

■ P r o c e d u r e

1. Vanilla ice cream mix is basically a custard sauce or crème anglaise with the addition of heavy cream. Review the guidelines for preparing crème anglaise on page 184.

2. Combine the egg yolks and sugar in a bowl. Whip until thick and light.

3. Scald the milk and gradually beat it into the egg mixture.

4. Heat over a hot water bath or in a double boiler, stirring constantly, until the mixture thickens enough to coat the back of a spoon. Immediately remove from the heat.

5. Stir in the cold cream to stop the cooking. Add the vanilla and salt. (*Note:* If you are not using freshly opened, pasteurized cream, it is best to scald and cool the cream or else to heat it with the milk in step 3. In this case, set the cooked custard in an ice-water bath as soon as it is cooked to stop the cooking.)

6. Chill the mixture thoroughly.

7. Freeze in an ice cream freezer according to the manufacturer's directions.

Variations

For a less rich ice cream, substitute milk for part of the cream. In addition, the quantity of egg yolks may be decreased to 6 (4 oz/125 g).

The quantity of sugar may be slightly increased or decreased, if desired.

Vanilla Bean Ice Cream

Split 1 or 2 vanilla beans, scrape out the seeds, and simmer the seeds and pods with the cream. Cool. Remove and discard the pods. Omit the vanilla extract from the basic recipe.

Chocolate Ice Cream

Reduce the sugar to 9 oz (280 g). Melt together 4 oz (125 g) unsweetened chocolate and 4 oz (125 g) bittersweet chocolate. When the custard has cooled to tepid, carefully stir it into the melted chocolate. Reduce the cream to 12 oz (375 ml).

Cinnamon Ice Cream

Add 1 tbsp (5 g) cinnamon to the egg mixture before cooking.

Coffee Ice Cream

Flavor the hot custard mix to taste with instant coffee powder or instant espresso powder.

Coconut Ice Cream

Reduce the number of egg yolks to 6 (4 oz/125 g). Reduce the sugar to 4 oz (125 g). Add 12 fl oz (375 mL) canned sweetened coconut cream to the yolks and sugar. Omit the heavy cream and vanilla. Stir the cooked mix over ice until cold to prevent the coconut fat from separating.

Caramel Ice Cream

Omit the vanilla. Caramelize the sugar, following the procedure in the recipe for Caramel Sauce (p. 196) but omitting the lemon. Add the 1 pint (500 mL) heavy cream from the basic recipe and simmer until the caramel is dissolved, again following the procedure in the caramel sauce recipe, steps 2–4. Beat the eggs, add the hot milk and caramel cream, make the custard, and finish the ice cream as in the basic recipe.

Almond, Hazelnut, or Macadamia Praline Ice Cream

Make a praline with any of the above nuts, following the recipe for Nougatine (p. 562). Crush 6 oz (185 g) of the praline and add it to chilled vanilla or caramel ice cream mix before freezing.

Cheesecake Ice Cream

Prepare the basic vanilla ice cream mix but use only 4 oz (125 g) egg yolks and substitute milk for half of the cream. In a mixer with the paddle attachment, blend 2 lb (1 kg) cream cheese, 7 oz (200 g) sugar, 1 tsp (3 g) each grated lemon zest and orange zest, and 1½ oz (50 mL) lemon juice until light and free of lumps. Gradually add the chilled custard and mix until smooth. Chill well. Freeze.

Strawberry Ice Cream

Reduce the number of yolks to 6 (4 oz/125 g). Mash 1½ lb (750 g) strawberries with 6 oz (185 g) sugar and refrigerate at least 2 hours. Mix the strawberries with the cold ice cream mix before freezing.

Raspberry Swirl Ice Cream

Reduce the number of yolks to 6 (4 oz/125 g). Mash 1 lb (500 g) raspberries with 4 oz (125 g) sugar. Refrigerate at least 2 hours. Make vanilla ice cream and freeze in an ice cream freezer. After the churn-freezing is finished but before hardening the ice cream, fold in the raspberries but do not mix in completely; leave it in swirls.

Mango Ice Cream

Reduce the number of yolks to 6 (4 oz/125 g). Combine 1½ lb (750 g) sieved mango purée, 3 oz (90 mL) lime juice, and 3 oz (90 g) sugar. Refrigerate at least 2 hours. Combine with cold custard mix and freeze.

Peach Ice Cream

Mash 2 lb (1 kg) sliced fresh peaches, 4 oz (125 g) sugar, and 1 oz (30 mL) lemon juice. Reduce the number of egg yolks to 6 (4 oz/125 g). Omit the milk, increase the cream to 2 pt (1 L), and make the custard with the cream. Mix the peaches with the cold custard and freeze.

Gingerbread-Spice Ice Cream

Ingredients	U.S.	Metric
Ginger	1½ tsp	2.8 g (7 mL)
Cinnamon	1 tsp	1.7 g (5 mL)
Cloves, ground	½ tsp	1 g (2 mL)
Nutmeg	¼ tsp	0.5 g (1 mL)
Molasses	2 oz	60 g

Add the spices to the egg mixture before cooking. Add the molasses to the mixture after cooking.

Lemon Ice Cream

Reduce the quantity of milk to 1 pt (500 mL) and the sugar to 8 oz (250 g). Scald the milk and cream together. Omit the vanilla. With these exceptions, make the ice cream mix as in the basic recipe. Separately, combine 2 tbsp (15 g) grated lemon zest and 1 oz (30 g) sugar. Work the zest and sugar together with the back of a spoon or with a mortar and pestle to make a coarse paste. Beat this lemon sugar with 3 egg yolks (2 oz/60 g). Add 12 oz (375 mL) lemon juice and beat over hot water until thick and creamy, as for making crème anglaise. Cool over ice. Combine with the custard and freeze.

Lime Ice Cream

Substitute lime zest and juice for the lemon in the preceding recipe.

Sorbet

Yield: variable

Ingredients	U.S.	Metric
Sugar	1 lb	500 g
Water	1 pt	500 mL
Fruit juice or pulp or other flavor ingredients	(see variations)	(see variations)
Water	(see variations)	(see variations)

■ P r o c e d u r e

1. Make a syrup by heating the sugar and first quantity of water to dissolve the sugar. Cool.

2. Prepare the desired flavor ingredients as indicated in the variations that follow. If additional water is required, mix it with the flavor ingredient.

3. Mix the syrup with the remaining ingredients. Chill well. Freeze in an ice cream freezer according to the manufacturer's instructions.

Variations

The following sorbet variations indicate the quantities of flavor ingredients and additional water to be used in the above recipe. If the ingredients require special preparation instructions, they are indicated. If no special directions are given, simply follow the basic procedure above. Note that most fruit sorbets require strained fruit purée for the smoothest texture. This refers to fruit pulp that has been puréed and then forced through a sieve.

Lemon or Lime Sorbet

Ingredients	U.S.	Metric
Lemon or lime zest, grated	1 tbsp	8 g
Lemon juice or lime juice	12 oz	375 mL
Water	1 pt	500 mL

Boil the zest with the syrup. Cool and strain.

Orange or Tangerine Sorbet

Ingredients	U.S.	Metric
Orange or tangerine juice	4 pt	2 L
Water	none	none

Raspberry, Strawberry, Melon, or Kiwi Sorbet

Ingredients	U.S.	Metric
Strained fruit purée	2 lb 4 oz	1125 g
Water	none	none

Taste the mix before freezing. Some fruit may be low in acidity, so a little lemon juice may improve the flavor of the mix.

Mango Sorbet

Ingredients	U.S.	Metric
Strained mango purée	2 lb 4 oz	1125 g
Lemon juice	2 oz	60 mL
Water	8 oz	250 mL

Pineapple Sorbet

Ingredients	U.S.	Metric
Fresh pineapple chunks	2 lb	1125 g
Water	12 oz	375 mL

Poach the pineapple in the syrup. Cool. Purée and force through a sieve. Add the water. Freeze.

Blueberry Sorbet

Ingredients	U.S.	Metric
Blueberries	3 lb	1500 g
Lemon juice	3 oz	90 g
Cinnamon	½ tsp	0.8 g (2 mL)
Water	none	none

Simmer the blueberries, lemon juice, and cinnamon in the syrup until the berries are tender. Strain through a fine sieve.

Banana Passion Fruit Sorbet

Ingredients	U.S.	Metric
Banana pulp, strained	1 lb	500 g
Passion fruit pulp or juice, strained	1 lb	500 g

Rhubarb Sorbet

Ingredients	U.S.	Metric
Rhubarb	2 lb 8 oz	1250 g
Water	1 pt	500 mL

Cut the rhubarb into 1-in. slices. Combine the syrup, rhubarb, and water in a stainless-steel saucepan. Bring to a simmer and cook until the rhubarb is tender, about 10 minutes. Let the mixture cool, then strain through a fine strainer. Do not press down on the rhubarb solids, but let the rhubarb stand in the strainer about 30 minutes to let all the flavored syrup drain off. This will keep the syrup clear. Measure the syrup and add enough cold water to bring the volume to 20 oz (625 mL). Freeze the syrup. Reserve the rhubarb for another use (for example, add sugar to taste to make a simple rhubarb compote).

White Wine or Champagne Sorbet

Ingredients	U.S.	Metric
White wine or champagne	3 pt	1.5 L
Water	none	none

Chocolate Sorbet

Ingredients	U.S.	Metric
Bittersweet or semisweet chocolate	6 oz	185 g
Water	none	none

Reduce the quantity of sugar in the syrup to 6 oz (185 g). Melt the chocolate and cool it, but do not let it harden. Carefully mix in the cooled syrup.

Mascarpone Sorbet

Ingredients	U.S.	Metric
Mascarpone (soft Italian cream cheese)	2 lb	1 kg
Lemon juice	2 oz	60 mL
Water	6 oz	185 mL

Be sure to chill the mixture thoroughly, and do not leave in the ice cream freezer too long. Overmixing in the churn-freezer may cause some milkfat to separate and form chunks of butter.

Honey Ice Cream

Yield: about 1 qt (1 L) depending on overrun

Ingredients	U.S.		Metric
Milk	8	oz	250 g
Vanilla bean, split	1		1
Honey	4.33	oz	130 g
Egg yolks	4	oz (6 yolks)	120 g (6 yolks)
Heavy cream	8	oz	250 g

■ P r o c e d u r e

1. Heat the milk and the vanilla bean to the scalding point.

2. Whip the honey and egg yolks until light. Slowly beat in the hot milk.

3. Return the mixture to the pan. Cook over low heat, stirring constantly, until thick enough to coat the back of a spoon. Remove from the heat and cool. Scrape out the seeds from the vanilla bean and return them to the mixture. Chill.

4. Add the heavy cream. Freeze in an ice cream freezer.

Dulce de Leche Ice Cream

Yield: about 3½ pt (1750 mL) depending on overrun

Ingredients	U.S.	Metric
Milk	1 pt 8 oz	750 g
Dulce de Leche (p. 198)	1 lb 2 oz	560 g
	(about 14 fl oz)	(about 425 mL)
Heavy cream	6 oz	185 g
Vanilla extract	¼ tsp	1 g
Salt	pinch	pinch

■ P r o c e d u r e

1. Heat the milk and the dulce de leche together until the dulce de leche is completely dissolved.

2. Remove from the heat and add the remaining ingredients.

3. Chill well and freeze in an ice cream freezer.

Bitter Chocolate Ice Cream

Yield: about 2 qt (2 L), depending on overrun

Ingredients	U.S.	Metric
Egg yolks	8 oz (12 yolks)	250 g (12 yolks)
Sugar	6 oz	190 g
Milk	2 pt 8 oz	1250 mL
Sugar	12 oz	375 g
Bittersweet chocolate	8 oz	250 g
Cocoa powder	8 oz	250 g
Heavy cream	8 oz	250 mL

■ P r o c e d u r e

1. Combine the egg yolks and the first quantity of sugar in a bowl. Whip until thick and light.

2. Combine the milk and the second quantity of sugar in a heavy saucepan. Bring to a simmer, stirring to dissolve the sugar.

3. Gradually beat the milk into the egg yolk mixture. Set over a hot water bath and heat, stirring constantly, until the mixture thickens enough to coat the back of a spoon. Immediately remove from the heat. Let cool until lukewarm.

4. Melt the chocolate and let cool slightly.

5. Gradually stir in the custard mixture.

6. Add the cocoa and beat with a whip until it is thoroughly mixed in.

7. Stir in the heavy cream.

8. Chill the mixture, then freeze in an ice cream freezer.

Coconut Sorbet

Yield: about 1¾ pt (850 mL), depending on overrun

Ingredients	U.S.		Metric
Frozen coconut purée, thawed (see variation)	1	lb	480 g
Confectioners' sugar	3.5	oz	100 g
Lime juice, fresh	1.75	oz	50 g
Coconut-flavored rum	2	oz	60 g

■ P r o c e d u r e

1. Mix together all ingredients.
2. Freeze in an ice cream freezer.

Variation

The coconut purée used in this recipe contains 20% sugar. If this product is not available, use canned, unsweetened coconut milk, and adjust the quantities as follows:

Ingredients	U.S.		Metric
Canned, unsweetened coconut milk	14	oz	400 g
Confectioners' sugar	6	oz	180 g
Lime juice	1.75 oz		50 g
Coconut-flavored rum	2	oz	60 g

Cider Apple Sorbet

Yield: about 1½ pt (700 mL)

Ingredients	U.S.		Metric
Sugar	4.5 oz		135 g
Water	4	oz	120 g
Cooking apples	7	oz	200 g
Fermented cider	5.5 oz		165 g

■ P r o c e d u r e

1. Heat the sugar and water until the sugar is dissolved.
2. Peel, core, and chop the apples. Add to the syrup and cook until tender.
3. Add the cider. Place in a blender and blend until smooth. Pass through a fine strainer.
4. Cool, then freeze in an ice cream freezer.

Cassata Italienne

Ingredients	U.S.	Metric
Common Meringue (p. 182)	3 oz	90 g
Vanilla Ice Cream (p. 466), softened	7 oz	200 g
Raspberry jam	1.5–2 oz	50 g
Raspberry Sorbet (p. 469), softened	7 oz	200 g
Total weight:	*1 lb 2 oz*	*540 g*

■ P r o c e d u r e

This procedure is for rectangular (loaf) molds approximately 6½ × 3½ in. (17 × 9 cm). It can be modified for any size or shape mold.

1. Using a pastry bag with a plain tip, pipe the meringue onto a parchment-lined sheet pan in a rectangle the same size as the top of the mold. Bake at 250°F (120°C) for 1 hour. Cool.

2. Line the mold with plastic film.

3. Using a pastry bag with a plain tip, pipe the ice cream into the bottom of the mold and smooth the surface (using a pastry bag makes it easier to avoid air bubbles). Freeze until firm.

4. Spread the raspberry jam onto the ice cream in an even layer. Freeze until firm.

5. Pipe the raspberry sorbet into the mold and smooth the surface.

6. Place the baked, cooled meringue on top of the sorbet and press down gently. Freeze until firm.

7. Unmold, remove the plastic film, and slice to serve.

STILL-FROZEN DESSERTS

The air that is mixed into ice cream by churn-freezing is important to its texture. Without this air, the ice cream would be hard and heavy rather than smooth and creamy. Desserts that are still-frozen—that is, frozen in a container without mixing—also must have air mixed into them in order to be soft enough to eat. In this case, the air is incorporated before freezing by mixing in whipped cream, whipped egg whites, or both.

Thus, still-frozen desserts are closely related to products such as Bavarians, mousses, and hot soufflés. These products are all given lightness and volume by adding whipped cream or an egg foam. In fact, many of the same mixtures used for these products are also used for frozen desserts. However, because freezing serves to stabilize or solidify frozen desserts, they don't depend as much on gelatin or other stabilizers.

Still-frozen desserts include bombes, frozen soufflés, and frozen mousses. In classical theory, each of these types is made with different mixes, but in actual practice today, many of these mixes are interchangeable.

A note on the use of alcohol in frozen desserts: Liqueurs and spirits are often used to flavor these items. However, even a small amount of alcohol lowers the freezing point considerably. If you find that liqueur-flavored parfaits, bombes, and mousses aren't freezing hard enough, you can add additional whipped cream. This will raise the freezing point. In future batches, you might try using less alcohol.

A high sugar concentration also inhibits freezing. It is important to avoid using too much sugar in these items so that they freeze properly.

PARFAITS AND BOMBES

In North America, the term *parfait* usually means an ice cream dessert consisting of layers of ice cream and topping in a tall, thin glass. The original parfait, however, is a still-frozen dessert frozen in a tall, thin mold and unmolded for service. (No doubt the ice cream parfait is so named because the glass it is served in is similar in shape to a parfait mold.) The mixture for parfaits consists of three elements: a thick, sweet egg-yolk foam, an equal volume of whipped cream, and flavorings.

The parfait mixture is also called a *bombe mixture* because it is used in the production of a dessert called a *bombe*. The bombe is one of the most elegant frozen desserts, and it is often elaborately decorated with fruits, whipped cream, petits fours secs, and other items after unmolding. It is made by lining a chilled mold (usually spherical or dome-shaped) with a layer of ice cream or sherbet and freezing it hard. The center is then filled with a bombe mixture of compatible flavor and then frozen again.

Mixtures for frozen mousses can also be used to fill bombes, as can regular ice cream or sherbet, but a special bombe mixture is most often used.

Two recipes are given below for bombe mixtures. The ingredients and final results are nearly the same, but the techniques differ. Note that the technique for the first mixture is the same as that used to make French buttercream (p. 336). The second recipe requires a sugar syrup of a specific strength; the recipe for this syrup is also provided.

A procedure for assembling bombes is given, followed by descriptions of a number of classic bombes that have been popular for many decades.

Basic Bombe Mixture I

Yield: 1½ qt (1.5 L)

Ingredients	U.S.	Metric
Sugar	8 oz	250 g
Water	2 oz	60 g
Egg yolks	4 oz (6 yolks)	125 g (6 yolks)
Flavoring (see variations following recipe for Basic Bombe Mixture II)		
Heavy cream	12 oz	375 mL

■ Procedure

1. Dissolve the sugar in the water over high heat and boil the mixture until it reaches 240°F (115°C). (See page 177 for information on boiling sugar.)

2. While the syrup is boiling, whip the egg yolks (using the whip attachment of the mixing machine) until light and foamy.

3. With the machine running, slowly pour the hot syrup into the egg yolks. Continue whipping until the mixture is cool. It should be very thick and foamy.

4. This mixture will keep, covered and refrigerated, for up to a week. When you are ready to assemble a dessert, proceed with the next steps.

5. Stir the desired flavorings into the egg yolk mixture.

6. Whip the cream until it forms soft, not stiff, peaks. Do not overwhip.

7. Fold the cream into the base mixture. Pour the result into prepared molds or other containers and freeze it until firm.

Syrup for Bombes

Yield: about 1½ qt (1.5 L)

Ingredients	U.S.	Metric
Sugar	3 lb	1.5 kg
Water	2 lb	1 kg

Note   Simple syrup of this concentration is used in the Basic Bombe Mixture II (opposite) and Frozen Mousse II (p. 479).

■ Procedure

1. Combine the water and sugar in a saucepan. Bring the mixture to a boil, stirring until the sugar is completely dissolved.

2. Remove the syrup from the heat and let it cool. Store it in a covered container in the refrigerator.

Basic Bombe Mixture II

Yield: 1½ qt (1½ L)

Ingredients	U.S.	Metric
Egg yolks	6 oz (9 yolks)	180 g (9 yolks)
Syrup for bombes (see recipe opposite)	8 oz	250 mL
Flavoring (see variations below)		
Heavy cream	12 oz	375 mL

■ P r o c e d u r e

1. Whip the egg yolks lightly in a stainless-steel bowl, then gradually beat in the syrup.

2. Set the bowl over hot water and whip the mixture with a wire whip until it is thick and creamy, about the consistency of a thick hollandaise sauce.

3. Remove it from the heat, set it over ice, and continue whipping the mixture until it is cold.

4. Add the desired flavoring.

5. Whip the cream until it forms soft peaks. Do not overwhip. Fold it into the egg yolk mixture.

6. Pour the mixture into molds or other containers. Freeze until firm.

Variations

To create bombes of different flavors, add the suggested flavorings to either of the egg yolk mixtures in the above two recipes before folding in the whipped cream.

Vanilla
Add 0.5–0.75 oz (15–22 mL) vanilla extract.

Chocolate
Melt 2 oz (60 g) unsweetened chocolate. Stir in a little stock syrup to make a thick sauce. Then fold this into the yolk mixture. (For a stronger chocolate flavor, melt 1–1.5 oz/30–45 g sweet chocolate with the 2 oz unsweetened chocolate.)

Liqueur
Add 1–1.5 oz (30–45 mL), or to taste, desired liqueur or spirit, such as orange liqueur, kirsch, or rum.

Coffee
Add ¼ oz (8 g) instant coffee dissolved in half an ounce (15 mL) of water.

Praline
Add 2.5 oz (75 g) praline paste, softened with a little water, to the yolk mixture.

Fruit (Raspberry, Strawberry, Apricot, Peach, etc.)
Add up to 8 oz (250 g) fruit purée.

Bombe or Parfait with Fruit
Instead of flavoring the bombe mixture with a fruit purée, add solid fruits cut in small dice to plain or liqueur-flavored bombe mixture.

Bombe or Parfait with Nuts, Sponge Cake, or Other Ingredients
Other solid ingredients besides fruit may be mixed with plain or flavored bombe mixture, including chopped nuts, crumbled almond macaroons, marrons glacés (candied chestnuts), and diced sponge cake or ladyfingers moistened with liqueur.

Procedure for Making Bombes

1. Place the bombe mold in the freezer until very cold.

2. Line the mold with a layer of slightly softened ice cream, using your hand to press it against the sides and smooth it. The ice cream layer should be about ³⁄₄ in. (2 cm) thick for small molds, up to 1¹⁄₂ in. (4 cm) for large molds.

    If the ice cream becomes too soft to stick to the sides, place it in the freezer to harden it, then try again.

3. Freeze the mold until the ice cream layer is hard.

4. Fill the mold with bombe mixture, cover, and freeze until firm.

5. To unmold, dip the mold in warm water for a second, wipe off the water from the outside of the mold, and turn out the bombe onto a cold serving plate. (*Note:* To keep the bombe from sliding around on the plate, turn it out onto a thin sheet of genoise, which acts as a base.)

6. Decorate with whipped cream and appropriate fruits or other items.

7. Serve immediately. Cut into wedges or slices so that all portions are uniform.

A Selection of Popular Bombes

Bombe Africaine
Coating: chocolate ice cream

Filling: apricot bombe mixture

Bombe Aida
Coating: Strawberry ice cream

Filling: kirsch-flavored bombe mixture

Bombe Bresilienne
Coating: pineapple sherbet

Filling: bombe mixture flavored with vanilla and rum and mixed with diced pineapple

Bombe Cardinale
Coating: raspberry sherbet

Filling: praline vanilla bombe mixture

Bombe Ceylon
Coating: coffee ice cream

Filling: rum-flavored bombe mixture

Bombe Coppelia
Coating: coffee ice cream

Filling: praline bombe mixture

Bombe Diplomat
Coating: vanilla ice cream

Filling: bombe mixture flavored with maraschino liqueur and mixed with candied fruit

Bombe Florentine
Coating: raspberry sherbet

Filling: praline bombe mixture

Bombe Formosa
Coating: vanilla ice cream

Filling: bombe mixture flavored with strawberry purée and mixed with whole strawberries

Bombe Moldave
Coating: pineapple sherbet

Filling: bombe mixture flavored with orange liqueur

Bombe Sultane
Coating: chocolate ice cream

Filling: praline bombe mixture

Bombe Tutti-Frutti

Coating: strawberry ice cream or sherbet

Filling: lemon bombe mixture mixed with candied fruits

Cassata Napoletana

Cassatas are Italian-style bombes lined with three layers of different ice creams and filled with Italian meringue mixed with various ingredients. The most popular, Cassata Napoletana, is made as follows. Line the mold first with vanilla, then with chocolate, and finally with strawberry ice cream. Fill with Italian Meringue (p. 183) flavored with vanilla, kirsch, or maraschino and mixed with an equal weight of diced candied fruits. A little whipped cream may be added to the meringue, if desired.

FROZEN MOUSSES AND FROZEN SOUFFLÉS

Frozen mousses are light frozen desserts containing whipped cream. Although they are all similar in character because of their whipped cream content, the bases for them are made in several ways. Three types of preparations are included here:

- Mousse with Italian meringue base

- Mousse with syrup and fruit base

- Mousse with custard base

The mixture for bombes and parfaits can also be used for mousses.

The simplest method for serving mousse is to pour the mixture into individual serving dishes and freeze them. The mixtures can also be poured into molds of various shapes. After unmolding, the mousse is cut into portions and decorated with whipped cream and appropriate fruits, cookies, or other items.

Frozen soufflés are simply mousse or bombe mixtures frozen in soufflé dishes or other straight-sided dishes. A band of heavy paper or foil is tied around the mold so that it extends 2 in. (5 cm) or more above the rim of the dish. The mousse or bombe mixture is poured in so that it comes within ½ in. (12 mm) of the top of this band. After the dessert is frozen, the band is removed. The dessert thus looks like a hot soufflé that has risen above its baking dish.

Other items may be incorporated in the frozen soufflé, such as sponge cake, ladyfingers, baked meringue, fruits, and so forth. For example, you might pour one-third of the mousse mixture into the prepared dish, place a japonaise disk (p. 261) on top, pour in another layer of mousse, add a second japonaise, then fill with the mousse mixture. This technique can also be used with thin sponge cake layers. For further variety, arrange a layer of fruit on top of each genoise layer before adding more mousse.

Frozen Mousse I (Meringue Base)

Yield: 1½ qt (1.5 L)

Ingredients	U.S.	Metric
Italian meringue		
Sugar	8 oz	250 g
Water	2 oz	60 mL
Egg whites	4 oz	125 g
Flavoring (see *note*)		
Heavy cream	12 oz	375 mL

Note Possible flavorings include fruit purées, liqueurs, and chocolate. Use up to 3 oz (90 mL) strong spirits (brandy or dark rum, for example) or 4 oz (125 mL) sweet liqueur. Use 4 oz (125 g) melted unsweetened chocolate or up to 8 oz (250 g) thick fruit purée. Specific flavors are suggested in the variations following the basic procedure.

■ P r o c e d u r e

1. *For the Italian meringue:* Dissolve the sugar in the water in a saucepan and boil the syrup until it reaches 250°F (120°C). Meanwhile, whip the egg whites until they form soft peaks. Whipping constantly, slowly pour the hot syrup into the egg whites. Continue to whip the meringue until it is completely cool (unless you are flavoring it with liqueur—see next step).

2. Stir or fold in flavoring ingredients. If you are using melted chocolate or a thick fruit purée, stir a little of the meringue into the flavoring, then fold this into the rest of the meringue. If you are using a liqueur or spirit, add it while the meringue is still warm, so that most of the alcohol evaporates.

3. Whip the cream until it forms soft peaks. Fold it into the meringue mixture. Freeze.

Variations

The following are a few of many possible flavors for frozen mousse.

Liqueur Mousse
Flavor with 3 oz (90 mL) brandy, dark rum, or Calvados, or with 4 oz (125 mL) sweet liqueur.

Chocolate Mousse
Melt 4 oz (125 g) unsweetened chocolate. Stir in a little Syrup for Bombes (p. 474) to make a thick sauce. Stir some of the meringue into this mixture, then fold the chocolate mixture into the rest of the meringue.

Apricot Mousse
Soak 6 oz (188 g) dried apricots in water overnight, then simmer until tender. Drain and purée in a food mill. Fold into the meringue. If desired, add 0.5 oz (15 mL) rum or kirsch.

Banana Mousse
Purée 8 oz (250 g) very ripe bananas with 0.5 oz (15 mL) lemon juice. Add to meringue.

Lemon Mousse
Add 3 oz (90 mL) lemon juice and the grated zest of 1 lemon to the meringue.

Chestnut Mousse
Soften 7 oz (220 g) chestnut purée by blending it with 1 oz (30 mL) dark rum until smooth. Add it to the meringue.

Raspberry or Strawberry Mousse
Force 8 oz (250 g) fresh or frozen (unsweetened) raspberries or strawberries through a sieve. Add to the meringue.

Frozen Mousse II (Syrup and Fruit Base)

Yield: about 2½ pt (1.25 L)

Ingredients	U.S.	Metric
Syrup for Bombes (p. 474)	8 oz	250 mL
Fruit purée	8 oz	250 mL
Heavy cream	1 pt	500 mL

■ P r o c e d u r e

1. Mix the syrup and fruit purée until uniformly blended.
2. Whip the cream until it forms soft peaks.
3. Fold the cream into the syrup mixture.
4. Pour the mixture into molds or dishes and freeze.

Frozen Mousse III (Custard Base)

Yield: about 1½ qt (1.5 L)

Ingredients	U.S.	Metric
Egg yolks	5 oz (7–8 yolks)	150 g (7–8 yolks)
Sugar	8 oz	250 g
Milk	8 oz	250 mL
Flavoring (see step 6)		
Heavy cream	1 pt	500 mL

■ P r o c e d u r e

1. Whip the egg yolks with *half* the sugar until they are light and foamy.
2. Meanwhile, bring the milk to a boil with the rest of the sugar.
3. Pour the milk over the yolks, whipping constantly.
4. Set the milk and egg mixture over a hot water bath and cook, stirring constantly, until the mixture thickens like crème anglaise (p. 184). Do not overcook, or the custard will curdle.
5. Cool the mixture, then chill it in the refrigerator or over ice.
6. Add the desired flavoring. The same flavorings and quantities may be used as in Frozen Mousse I (p. 478).
7. Whip the cream and fold it into the custard mixture.
8. Pour the mousse into molds or dishes and freeze.

White Chocolate Parfait with Flambéed Cherries

Yield: 10 parfaits, 3 oz (95 g) each

Ingredients	U.S.		Metric
Flambéed cherries			
Fresh cherries (see *note*)	10	oz	300 g
Sugar	2	oz	60 g
Vanilla extract	½	tsp	2 g
Port wine	5	oz	150 g
Baked disks of Chocolate Meringue (p. 260), 2½ in. (6 cm) in diameter	10		10
Sugar	3.67	oz	110 g
Water	2.5	oz	75 g
Egg yolks	4	oz	120 g
White chocolate, chopped	5	oz	150 g
Heavy cream	12	oz	375 g
Decoration			
Chocolate curls	as needed		as needed
Pistachios	as needed		as needed
Total weight of parfait mix:	*1 lb 9*	*oz*	*775 g*

Note Cherries packed in syrup may also be used. Morello cherries (griottes) are especially good in this preparation. Drain the cherries and proceed as in the basic recipe.

Procedure

1. *Prepare the cherries:* Pit them and place them and the sugar in a saucepan. Heat gently until liquid begins to cook out of the cherries. Continue to heat until the liquid is almost evaporated. Add the vanilla and the port. Place over high heat and flambé to burn off the alcohol. Continue to cook, lightly covered, over low heat until the juices are thick and syrupy. Drain the cherries for use in step 7. Reserve the syrup.

2. Set 2¾-in. (7 cm) ring molds on a tray. Place a disk of baked Chocolate Meringue in the base of each.

3. For the parfait, dissolve the sugar in the water and bring to a boil.

4. Whip the egg yolks until light and gradually whip in the hot syrup. Continue whipping until cool.

5. Melt the white chocolate over a hot water bath.

6. Quickly mix the chocolate into the egg yolk sabayon. Do not overmix, or the sabayon may fall.

7. Whip the cream and quickly fold in.

8. Without delay, fill the molds about two-thirds full. Place 6–8 cherries in each one, pushing some of them down into the mix. (Reserve the remaining cherries and syrup to serve with the parfaits.) Fill to the top with parfait mix and level the tops. Freeze for at least 1 hour or until firm.

9. To serve, unmold by lightly warming the mold and lifting off. Top with chocolate curls and pistachios and a few cherries. Spoon some of the cherry syrup and a few more cherries onto the plate.

Cointreau Iced Soufflé

Ingredients	U.S.	Metric
Milk	7 oz	200 g
Vanilla bean, split (see *note*)	½	½
Egg yolks	4 oz	120 g
Sugar	7 oz	200 g
Cointreau liqueur (see *note*)	2 oz	60 g
Heavy cream	14 oz	400 g
Mold preparation		
Almond Macaroons II (p. 415)	12	12
Cointreau liqueur	1.5–2 oz	50 g
For service		
Crème Chantilly (p. 181)	as needed	as needed
Candied Orange Zest (p. 505)	as needed	as needed
Additional Almond Macaroons	as needed	as needed
Total weight of soufflé mix:	*2 lb 2 oz*	*980 g*

Note If vanilla beans are not available, add ¼ tsp (1 g) vanilla extract to the cooked egg mixture.

Other orange liqueurs can be used, but the name of the recipe should be changed to reflect that.

■ P r o c e d u r e

1. *Make a crème anglaise:* Combine the milk and vanilla bean and bring to a simmer. Whip the egg yolks with sugar until light, then temper by beating in half the hot milk. Return this mixture to the pan with the rest of the milk and cook gently until slightly thickened. Cool over an ice bath.

2. Add the liqueur. Chill.

3. Whip the cream to soft peaks. Fold into the chilled custard mixture. Pour into prepared mold (see below) and level the top with a palette knife. Freeze.

Mold Preparation

1. Use a doubled sheet of parchment paper to tie a collar around a 5-in. (12.5 cm) soufflé dish, so that the collar extends 1½ in. above the rim. Secure with string.

2. Dip the Almond Macaroons in liqueur and arrange them in the bottom of the dish.

3. Fill with the soufflé mix.

Service

Remove the paper collar. Decorate the top with rosettes of Crème Chantilly around the edge. Arrange some Candied Orange Zest in the center. Top each cream rosette with a macaroon.

Poppy Seed Parfait

Ingredients	U.S.		Metric
Milk	8	oz	250 g
Poppy seeds	3.25	oz	100 g
Milk	4	oz	125 g
Egg yolks	2.67	oz (4 yolks)	80 g (4 yolks)
Sugar	3.75	oz	120 g
Vanilla extract	¼	tsp	1 g
Amaretto liqueur	1.25	oz	40 g
Heavy cream	13	oz	400 g
Total weight:	*2 lb 3*	*oz*	*1116 g*

■ P r o c e d u r e

1. Heat the first quantity of milk with the poppy seeds. Simmer for 10 minutes. Skim and cool.

2. *Make a crème anglaise:* Heat the remaining milk. Whip the egg yolks and sugar until pale. Temper the egg mixture with half the hot milk, then pour this mixture back into the pan with the remaining milk and cook gently until just thickened enough to coat the back of a spoon. Add the vanilla, the amaretto, and the poppy seeds and milk from step 1. Chill over ice.

3. Whip the cream to stiff peaks. (It is important to whip the cream until stiff to prevent the poppy seeds from sinking to the bottom of the parfait, but take care not to overwhip.) Fold the whipped cream into the chilled poppy seed mixture.

4. Pour into molds and freeze.

Iced Low-Fat Raspberry Parfait

Yield: about 3 pt (1.5 L)

Ingredients	U.S.		Metric
Italian meringue			
Sugar	3.5	oz	100 g
Water	2.25	oz	65 g
Egg whites	3	oz	90 g
Raspberries, fresh or frozen	7	oz	200 g
Plain low-fat yogurt	7	oz	200 g

■ P r o c e d u r e

1. *Make an Italian meringue:* Dissolve the sugar in the water and boil to 250°F (120°C). Whip the egg whites to soft peaks. While whipping constantly, slowly pour in the hot syrup. Continue whipping until the meringue is cool.

2. Purée the raspberries and force the purée through a sieve to remove the seeds.

3. Whip the yogurt until smooth and mix in the raspberry purée.

4. Fold the cold meringue, one-third at a time, into the yogurt mixture.

5. Pour into molds and freeze.

Variations

Other fruit purées can be substituted for the raspberries.

See page 518 for a serving suggestion.

▶ TERMS FOR REVIEW

ice cream	ice milk	overrun	bombe
Philadelphia-style ice cream	sherbet	coupe	frozen mousse
French-style ice cream	ice	parfait	frozen soufflé
	granité	Baked Alaska	

▶ QUESTIONS FOR REVIEW

1. Why do ice cream and sherbet have to be frozen in a special freezer that mixes the product while it is being frozen? Why is it possible to freeze frozen mousses and similar desserts without this kind of freezer?

2. How does sugar affect the freezing properties of frozen desserts?

3. How does alcohol affect the freezing properties of frozen desserts?

4. How are still-frozen desserts similar to Bavarians?

5. Describe the procedure for making a Baked Alaska or Soufflé Surprise.

6. Describe the basic procedure for making bombes.

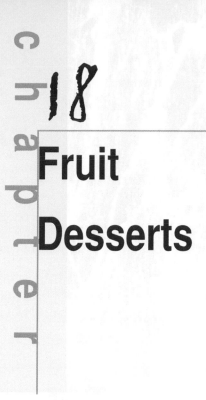

chapter 18

Fruit Desserts

Interest in desserts with less fat and fewer calories has stimulated interest in fruit desserts as alternatives to richer pastries and cakes. Fruits are, of course, important components of many pastries, cakes, and sauces, and many fruit desserts contain significant amounts of fat and sugar, including some in this chapter. Nevertheless, customers often perceive such desserts as more healthful, and this may account, in part, for their popularity. Another factor is the fresh, stimulating flavors of many fruit desserts.

In earlier chapters, we discussed fruit pies, fritters, pastries, tarts, cakes, and sauces. Many other types of fruit-based desserts, however, do not fit neatly into these categories. A representative sampling of recipes is included here, although, of course, they are only a small fraction of the many hundreds of recipes to be found elsewhere.

SELECTING AND PREPARING FRESH FRUITS

Advances in transportation and refrigeration have made fresh fruits widely available year-round. Even exotic tropical fruits are increasingly common in the market. Not long ago, most fresh fruits were available during limited seasons only. For example, strawberries were usually available for a short time in the spring, when they were in season. Now, however, almost everything is in season somewhere in the world, and it is easy to ship that crop to any market.

The following is a summary of the most commonly available fresh fruits. Emphasis is on what qualities to look for when purchasing them and on how to trim and prepare the fruit for use. In addition, identification information is included for certain exotic items. Nearly everyone knows what apples, bananas, and strawberries are, but not everyone can identify a persimmon or a passion fruit.

Apples Mature apples have a fruity aroma, brown seeds, and a slightly softer texture than unripe fruit. Overripe or old apples are soft and sometimes shriveled. Avoid apples with bruises, blemishes, decay, or mealy texture. Summer varieties (sold until fall) do not keep well. Fall and winter varieties keep well and are available for a longer period. Apples with a good acid content are usually better for cooking than bland eating varieties like Red Delicious. Granny Smith and Golden Delicious are widely used for cooking.

To prepare, wash; pare if desired. Quarter and remove core, or leave whole and core with special coring tool. Use stainless-steel knife for cutting. After paring, dip in solution of lemon juice (or other tart fruit juice) or ascorbic acid to prevent browning.

Apricots Only tree-ripened apricots have sufficient flavor, and they keep for only a week or less under refrigeration. They should be golden yellow, firm, and plump, not mushy. Avoid fruit that is too soft, blemished, or decayed.

Wash, split in half, and remove pit. Peeling is not necessary for most purposes.

Bananas Look for plump, smooth bananas without bruises or spoilage. All bananas are picked green, so you don't need to avoid unripe fruit. Avoid overripe fruit, however.

Ripen at room temperature for three to five days; fully ripe fruit is all yellow with small brown flecks and no green. Do not refrigerate, or fruit will discolor. Peel and dip in fruit juice to prevent browning.

Berries This category includes blackberries, blueberries, cranberries, black currants (cassis) and red currants, lingonberries, raspberries, and strawberries. Berries should be full, plump, and clean, with bright, fully ripe color. Watch for moldy or spoiled fruits. Wet spots on carton indicate damaged fruit.

Refrigerate in original container until ready to use in order to reduce handling. Except for cranberries, berries do not keep well. Sort out spoiled berries and foreign materials. Wash with gentle spray and drain well. Remove stems from strawberries. Red currants for garnishing are often left on the stem. Handle berries carefully to avoid bruising.

Cherries Look for plump, firm, sweet, juicy cherries. Bing or black cherries should be uniform dark red to almost black.

Refrigerate in original container until ready to use. Just before use, remove stems and sort out damaged fruit. Rinse and drain well. Pit with special pitting tool.

Coconuts Shake to hear liquid inside; fruits with no liquid are dried out. Avoid cracked fruits and fruits with wet "eyes."

Pierce eye with ice pick or nail and drain liquid. Crack with hammer and remove meat from shell (easier if placed in 350°F/175°C oven for 10–15 minutes). Peel brown skin with paring knife or vegetable peeler.

Figs Calimyrna figs, also called Smyrna figs, are light green; Black Mission figs and Black Spanish figs (also called Brown Turkey) are purple. All figs are sweet when ripe and soft and delicate in texture. They should be plump and soft, without spoilage or sour odor.

Keep refrigerated (although firm, unripe figs can be left at room temperature, spread in one layer, for a few days to ripen slightly). Rinse and drain, handling carefully. Trim off hard stem ends.

Grapefruit Select fruit that is heavy for its size and has a firm, smooth skin. Avoid puffy, soft fruits or those with pointed ends, which have low yield and a lot of rind. Cut and taste for sweetness.

For sections and slices, peel with a chef's knife, removing all white pith. Free sections from membrane with a small knife.

Grapes Look for firm, ripe, good-colored fruits in full bunches. Grapes should be firmly attached to stems and not fall off when shaken. Watch for rotting or shriveling at stem ends.

Refrigerate in original container. Wash and drain. Except for seedless varieties, cut in half and remove seeds with the point of a paring knife.

Kiwi fruit Kiwis are firm when unripe; they become slightly softer when ripe but do not change color significantly. Allow them to ripen at room temperature. Avoid fruits with bruises or soft spots.

Pare thin outer skin. Cut crosswise into slices.

Kumquats These look like tiny, elongated oranges, about the size of a medium olive. The skin and even the seeds can be eaten. In fact, the skin is sweet, while the flesh and juice are tart. Avoid soft or shriveled fruit. Kumquats keep well and are usually in good condition in the market.

Wash, drain well, and cut as desired.

Lemons and limes Look for firm, smooth skins. Colors may vary: Limes may be yellow and lemons may have some green on skin.

Cut in wedges, slices, or other shapes for garnish, or cut in half crosswise for juicing.

Litchis (or lychees) This Chinese fruit is about the size of a walnut or ping-pong ball. Its rough, leathery outer skin, which ranges from reddish to brown, is easily peeled away to reveal aromatic, juicy white flesh that surrounds an inedible pit. Look for heavy, plump fruit with good color.

Peel, cut in half, and remove the seed.

Mangoes The two main types of this tropical fruit are oval ones with a skin that ranges from green to orange to red and kidney-shaped fruit with skin that is a more uniform yellow when ripe. Mangoes have a thin but tough skin and yellow to yellow-orange flesh that is juicy and aromatic. Fruit should be plump and firm, with clear color and no blemishes. Avoid rock-hard fruit, which may not ripen properly.

Let ripen at room temperature until slightly soft. Peel and cut flesh away from center stone, or cut in half before peeling, working a thin-bladed knife around both sides of the flat stone.

Melons Look for the following characteristics when selecting melons. *Cantaloupes:* Smooth scar on stem end, with no trace of stem (called "full slip," meaning melon was picked ripe). Yellow rind, with little or no green. Heavy, with good aroma. *Honeydew:* Good aroma, slightly soft, heavy, creamy white to yellowish rind, not too green. Large sizes have best quality. *Crenshaw, Casaba, Persian, Canary, Santa Claus:* Heavy, with a rich aroma and slightly soft blossom end. *Watermelon:* Yellow underside, not white. Firm and symmetrical. Large sizes have best yield. Velvety surface, not too shiny. When cut, look for hard dark brown seeds and no "white heart" (hard white streak running through center).

To prepare hollow melons, wash, cut in half, and remove seeds and fibers. Cut into wedges and cut flesh from rind, or cut balls with ball cutter. For watermelon, wash, cut in half or into pieces, and cut balls with ball cutter, or cut flesh from rind and remove seeds.

Nectarines   See peaches and nectarines.

Oranges and mandarins (including tangerines)   To buy high-quality oranges, use the same guidelines as for grapefruit. Mandarins may feel puffy, but they should be heavy for their size. Unusual varieties include blood oranges, with dark red flesh and juice and intense flavor, and Seville oranges, with tart rather than sweet flesh. Seville oranges are prized for making marmalade.

Peel mandarins by hand and separate the sections. For juicing, cut oranges in half crosswise; for sections, see grapefruit.

Papayas   Papayas are pear-shaped tropical fruits with a mild, sweet flavor and slightly floral aroma. The flesh is yellow or pinkish, depending on the variety, and the center cavity holds a mass of round, black seeds. Papayas may weigh from less than one pound to several pounds (less than 500 g to more than 1 kg) each. Their skin is green when unripe, becoming yellow as they ripen. For best quality, select fruits that are firm and symmetrical, without bruises or rotten spots. Avoid dark green papayas, which may not ripen properly.

Let ripen at room temperature until slightly soft and nearly all yellow, with only a little green. Wash. Cut in half lengthwise and scrape out the seeds. Peel, if desired, or serve like cantaloupe.

Passion fruit   These are tropical fruits about the size of eggs, with a brownish purple skin that becomes wrinkled when ripe. (There is also a yellow-skinned variety.) They are mostly hollow when ripe, with juice, seeds, and a little flesh inside. The tart juice has an intense, exotic flavor and aroma that is greatly prized by pastry chefs. Select fruits that are large and heavy for their size. If they are smooth, let ripen at room temperature until the skin is wrinkled.

To use, cut in half, taking care not to lose any juice. Scrape out the seeds, juice, and pulp. Seeds can be eaten, so do not discard. If you need only the juice, it is much more economical to buy the frozen juice, as fresh fruits are expensive.

Peaches and nectarines   Peaches should be plump and firm, without bruises or blemishes. Avoid dark green fruits, which are immature and will not ripen well. Avoid fruits that have been refrigerated before ripening, as they may be mealy. Select freestone varieties of peaches. Clingstone varieties require too much labor (they are used primarily for canning).

Let ripen at room temperature, then refrigerate. Peel peaches by blanching in boiling water about 10 to 20 seconds, until skin slips off easily, and cool in ice water. (Nectarines do not need to be peeled.) Cut in half, remove pits, and drop into fruit juice, sugar syrup, or ascorbic acid solution to prevent darkening.

Pears   Pears should be clean, firm, and bright, with no blemishes or bruises.

Pears for eating raw should be fully ripe and aromatic. For cooking, they are better if slightly underripe, as fully ripe pears are too soft when cooked. Wash, pare, cut in halves or quarters, and remove core. To prevent browning, dip in fruit juice.

Persimmons   Persimmons are orange-red fruits available in two varieties. The most common is Hachiya, which is shaped somewhat like a large acorn (about 8 oz/250 g each). It is extremely tannic when unripe, making it nearly inedible until it ripens to a soft, jellylike mass. Ripe persimmons are sweet, juicy, and mild but rich in flavor. The other variety, Fuyu, is smaller and more squat in shape. It lacks the tannin content of Hachiya persimmons and can be eaten even when not fully ripe. Select plump persimmons with a good red color and stem cap attached.

Ripen at room temperature until very soft, then refrigerate. Remove stem cap, cut as desired, and remove seeds, if there are any.

Pineapple   Pineapples should be plump and fresh-looking, with an orange-yellow color and abundant fragrance. Avoid soft spots, bruises, and dark, watery spots.

Store at room temperature for a day or two to allow some tartness to disappear, then refrigerate. Pineapples may be cut in many ways. For slices, chunks, and dice, cut off top and bottom and pare the rough skin from the sides, using a stainless-steel knife. Remove all eyes. Cut into quarters lengthwise and cut out hard center core. Slice or cut as desired.

Plums   Look for plump, firm but not hard plums, with no bruises or blemishes.
Wash, cut in half, and remove pits.

Pomegranates   The pomegranate is a subtropical fruit about the size of a large apple. It has a dry red skin or shell enclosing a mass of seeds. Each seed is surrounded by small sphere of juicy, bright red pulp. Pomegranates are used mostly for their red, tart-sweet juice. The seeds with their surrounding pulp can also be used as an attractive garnish for desserts and even meat dishes. Look for heavy fruits without bruises. When squeezed, they should yield to gentle pressure; if they are too hard, they may be dried out.

To prepare, lightly score the skin without cutting into the seeds, and carefully break into sections. Separate the seeds from the membranes. Juicing is difficult. Some methods crush the seeds and make the juice bitter. This method makes a better juice. Roll the whole pomegranate on the countertop under the palm of the hand to break the juice sacs. Then pierce a hole in the side of the fruit and squeeze out the juice.

Prickly pears or cactus pears   This is a barrel-shaped fruit about the size of a large egg. Its skin color ranges from magenta to greenish red and it has a bright pinkish red, spongy interior with black seeds. The pulp is sweet and aromatic, but with a mild flavor. Good-quality fruits are tender but not mushy, with a good skin color, not faded. Avoid fruits with rotten spots.

If the fruit is firm, allow to ripen at room temperature, then refrigerate. As it is the fruit of a cactus, thorns grow on the skin. These are removed before shipping, but small, hard-to-see thorns may remain. To avoid getting stung, hold the fruit with a fork while you slice off the top and bottom. Still holding it with a fork, pare the sides with a knife and discard the peels without touching them. Cut or slice the pulp as desired, or force it through a sieve to purée it and remove the seeds.

Quince   Quinces grow in temperate climates and were once very popular in Europe and North America. Many old, neglected quince trees remain in New England and elsewhere. The fruit resembles a large, yellow, lumpy pear with either a smooth or slightly downy skin. The raw fruit is never eaten—it is dry and hard. When cooked (usually stewed or poached in a sugar syrup), it becomes aromatic, flavorful, and sweet, and the color of the flesh turns slightly pink. The fruit keeps well. Select fruit with good color and free of bruises or blemishes.

Cut, pare, and core like apples or pears, then cook.

Rhubarb   Rhubarb is a stem, not a fruit, but it is used like a fruit. Buy firm, crisp, tender rhubarb with thick stalks, not thin and shriveled.

Cut off all traces of leaf, which is poisonous. Trim root end, if necessary. Peel with a vegetable peeler if desired, or omit this step if the skin is tender. Cut into desired lengths.

FRUIT DESSERTS

SIMPLE FRUIT SALADS AND COOKED FRUITS

After a rich meal, a piece of fresh fruit can be a light and refreshing dessert. Most diners, however, are happier with something that requires a little more effort from the kitchen. Serving fresh fruit, such as berries, with cream or a sauce such as sabayon, crème anglaise, or coulis often satisfies these desires. (See chapter 8 for a selection of dessert sauces.) A simple fruit salad can be an attractive alternative. Marinating fresh fruit in a flavored syrup adds a new dimension to the fruit and also allows the pastry chef to make an attractive mixture of colorful, carefully cut seasonal items.

A simple and versatile category of fruit dessert is the *compote,* which can be defined as cooked fruit, usually small fruits or cut fruit, served in its cooking liquid. Mixed fruit compotes are versatile because they can be seasoned and sweetened as desired, and the combination of fruits is infinitely variable. Cooking mediums range from light syrups to concentrated spiced caramel, honey, or liqueur mixtures.

There is no clear dividing line between fresh fruit salads and lightly cooked fruit compotes. If a boiling syrup is poured over a mixture of fruit and the fruit is marinated without additional cooking, it could be called either a compote or a fresh fruit salad.

Hard fruits and mixtures of dried fruits are usually cooked longer, until they are tender. Larger, whole fruits cooked in syrup are not usually called compotes, but the cooking procedure is the same. Pears poached in wine is a classic dessert that remains popular and can be found on the menus of many restaurants.

This chapter contains two types of compotes. The first part of the recipe section includes light mixtures of fresh fruit in syrup that are served as desserts. Later in the chapter you will find sweeter, more intensely flavored compotes that are not served by themselves but are used as sauces, condiments, and ingredients in pastries and other preparations.

Many fruits can also be sautéed for serving as desserts. This procedure is similar to sautéing vegetables, except that sugar is added to the fruit and butter in the pan. The sugar caramelizes and forms a rich sauce as it combines with the juices that are drawn out of the fruit. Apples, apricots, bananas, pears, peaches, pineapples, plums, and cherries are especially suited to this style of preparation. For examples of this type of preparation, see the recipe for Caramelized Pears (p. 493) and the variations that follow.

TRADITIONAL AND SPECIALTY FRUIT DESSERTS

This chapter also includes a selection of recipes ranging from the old-fashioned and rustic to the stylishly modern. Traditional North American favorites include *cobblers,* which are like fruit pies made in large baking pans, but without bottom crusts, *crisps,* which are like cobblers but with brown sugar streusel topping instead of a pastry crust, and *betties,* which have alternating layers of rich cake crumbs and fruit. These homey desserts are, for the most part, easy to prepare.

At the other end of the range of difficulty is the Caramelized Pear Charlotte, perhaps the most complex recipe in this chapter. Before preparing this dessert, you may need to review the information on Bavarians, mousses, and charlottes in chapter 16.

FRUIT PRESERVES, CONDIMENTS, AND GARNISHES

Finally, you will find at the end of the chapter a variety of preparations that are not served as desserts but are used as elements or ingredients in other dishes. These include jams and marmalades, sweet compotes used as sauces or garnishes, and specialty items such as fruit crisps and candied citrus zests that add appeal to plated desserts and petit four trays.

Poached Fruit (Fruit Compote)

Yield: about 3 lb (1.5 kg), plus syrup

Ingredients	U.S.	Metric	
Water	1 qt	1	L
Sugar (see *note*)	1–2 lb	0.5–0.75	kg
Vanilla extract (see *note*)	2 tsp	10	mL
Prepared fruit (see individual variations)	3 lb	1.5	kg

Note The amount of sugar used depends on the desired sweetness of the dessert and the natural sweetness of the fruit. Other flavoring may be used in place of the vanilla. A popular alternative is to add 2 or 3 strips of lemon peel and 1 oz (30 mL) lemon juice to the syrup.

■ Procedure

1. Combine the water and sugar in a saucepan. Bring to a boil, stirring until the sugar is dissolved.
2. Add the vanilla.
3. Add the prepared fruit to the syrup or, if using tender fruit, place the fruit in a shallow pan and pour the syrup over it.
4. Cook very slowly, just below a simmer, until the fruit is just tender.
5. Let the fruit cool in the syrup. When cool, refrigerate in the syrup until needed.

Variations

Poached Apples, Pears, or Pineapple
Peel, quarter, and core the fruit. For pineapple, cut into small wedges. Poach as in basic recipe.

Pears in Wine
Substitute red or white table wine for the water. Omit the vanilla. Add ½ sliced lemon to the syrup. Peel the pears but leave them whole.

Poached Peaches
Peel the peaches by blanching them in boiling water for a few seconds and slipping off the skins. Cut in half and remove the stones. Poach as in the basic recipe.

Peaches in Wine
Prepare the peaches as above. Poach as for pears in wine, flavoring the syrup with lemon.

Poached Apricots, Plums, or Nectarines
Cut the fruits in half and remove the stones. (Nectarines may be peeled like peaches, if desired.) Poach as in the basic recipe.

Poached Cherries
Pit the cherries with a cherry pitter. Poach as in the basic recipe.

Poached Dried Fruit
Soak dried fruit in water overnight. Use the soaking liquid for making the syrup. Poach as in the basic recipe, adding 1 oz (30 mL) lemon juice to the syrup.

Tropical Fruit Compote
Prepare the syrup as in the basic recipe, flavoring it with lemon and orange zest in addition to the vanilla and substituting white wine for half the water. Prepare a mixture of kiwi fruit, peeled and sliced crosswise; papayas, peeled, seeded, and cut into thin wedges or slices; mangoes, peeled, pitted, and sliced; orange wedges; and strawberries, trimmed and halved. While the syrup is still hot, pour it over the fruit. Cool, cover, and refrigerate overnight. If desired, top each portion with toasted or untoasted shredded coconut.

Fresh Fruit Salad
This is an uncooked version of fruit compote. Prepare the syrup as in the basic recipe. Cool it completely. Prepare a mixture of fresh fruits; dice large fruits or cut them into bite-size pieces. Combine the fruits and cold syrup and let them stand several hours or overnight in the refrigerator.

Fruit Salad

Yield: about 2 lb 8 oz (1100 g), including syrup

Ingredients	U.S.	Metric
Apple	1	1
Pear	1	1
Orange	1	1
Peach	1	1
Strawberries	10	10
Raspberries	10	10
Red plum	1	1
Passion fruit	1	1
Sugar	11 oz	300 g
Water	14 oz	400 g
Cinnamon sticks	2	2
Vanilla bean	1	1
Bay leaves	2	2

■ **P r o c e d u r e**

1. Prepare all the fruit as necessary (wash, peel, pit, core, and so on, depending on the fruit). Cut all the fruit, except the passion fruit, into large bite-size pieces and place in a bowl. Add the pulp, juice, and seeds from the passion fruit to the bowl.

2. Heat the sugar, water, cinnamon sticks, vanilla bean, and bay leaves gently until the sugar has dissolved. Bring to a boil. Remove from the heat and pour over the prepared fruit.

3. Let the mixture steep and infuse for 2–3 hours.

4. Drain or serve with a slotted spoon. Reserve the syrup for other uses, if desired.

Marinated Tropical Fruits

Yield: about 4 lb (2 kg), including syrup

Ingredients	U.S.		Metric
Mangoes	3		3
Large pineapple	1		1
Kiwi fruits	5		5
Water	7	oz	200 g
Sugar	7	oz	200 g
Cinnamon stick	1		1
Orange rind, in strips	0.3 oz		8 g
Lemon	½		½
Cloves, whole	4		4
Mint sprig	1		1
Vanilla bean	1		1

■ **P r o c e d u r e**

1. Peel the fruit. Core the pineapple and remove the pit from the mangoes. Cut into large cubes (about 1 in./2.5 cm). Place the fruit in a saucepan.

2. Combine the remaining ingredients, stirring to dissolve the sugar. (If desired, the spices may be tied in a cheesecloth bag so that they can be removed easily before serving.)

3. Pour the boiling syrup over the fruit, cover with a round of parchment, and simmer 5 minutes. Cool and then chill the fruit in the syrup.

Caramelized Pears

Yield: 8 portions

Ingredients	U.S.	Metric
Pears, ripe	8	8
Butter	2 oz	60 g
Granulated sugar	4 oz	125 g

■ P r o c e d u r e

1. Peel, core, and quarter the pears.

2. Heat the butter in a sauté pan. Add the pears and sugar. Cook over moderate heat; the pears will give off some juice, which will combine with the sugar to form a syrup. Continue to cook, turning and basting the pears, until the syrup reduces and thickens and the pears are lightly caramelized. The syrup will become light brown; do not try for a dark brown color or the fruit will overcook.

3. Serve warm. A small scoop of vanilla ice cream is a good accompaniment.

Variations

Cut the pears into halves instead of quarters. To serve, place them cut-side down on a plate, slice crosswise, and fan the slices. For a more caramelized surface, sprinkle the top of the fruit with sugar and caramelize under a salamander or broiler, being careful not to let it scorch. The following fruits can be prepared using the same basic method. Adjust the quantities of butter and sugar according to taste and according to the sweetness of the fruit.

Caramelized Apples
Peel, core, and slice the apples. Use white or brown sugar, depending on desired flavor. If desired, season with cinnamon and nutmeg, with vanilla, or with lemon zest.

Caramelized Peaches
Blanch and skin the peaches. Cut in half and remove the pits. Slice or cut into wedges.

Caramelized Pineapple
Peel, slice crosswise, and remove the core from each slice using a small, round cutter. Use white or brown sugar, as desired.

Caramelized Bananas
Peel; quarter by cutting in half crosswise and then lengthwise. Use brown sugar. Because bananas release little juice, you may add a little orange juice or pineapple juice. Flavor with cinnamon and nutmeg or mace.

Apple Crisp

Yield: One pan 12 × 20 in. (30 × 50 cm)
48 portions, 4 oz (120 g) each

Ingredients	U.S.		Metric
Peeled, sliced apples	8 lb		4000 g
Sugar	4	oz	125 g
Lemon juice	2	oz	60 mL
Butter	1 lb		500 g
Brown sugar	1 lb 8	oz	750 g
Cinnamon	0.12 oz (2 tsp)		4 g
Pastry flour	1 lb 8	oz	750 g

■ P r o c e d u r e

1. Toss the apples gently with the sugar and lemon juice. Spread evenly in a 12 × 20 in. (30 × 50 cm) baking pan.

2. Rub the butter, sugar, cinnamon, and flour together until well blended and crumbly.

3. Sprinkle evenly over the apples.

4. Bake at 350°F (175°C) for about 45 minutes, until top is browned and apples are tender.

Variation

Peach, Cherry, or Rhubarb Crisp
Substitute peaches, cherries, or rhubarb for the apples. If rhubarb is used, increase the sugar in step 1 to 12 oz (375 g).

Fruit Cobbler

Yield: One pan 12 × 20 in. (30 × 50 cm)
48 portions, 5 oz (150 g) each

Ingredients	U.S.	Metric
Fruit pie filling	12–15 lb	5.5–7 kg
Flaky Pie Dough (p. 204)	2 lb	1 kg

■ P r o c e d u r e

1. Place fruit filling in a 12 × 20 in. (30 × 50 cm) baking pan.

2. Roll out the pastry to fit the top of the pan. Place on top of the filling and seal the edges to the pan. Pierce small holes in the pastry to allow steam to escape.

3. Bake at 425°F (220°C) for about 30 minutes, until top is browned.

4. Cut the dessert in six rows of 8, or 48 portions. Serve warm or cold.

Variation

In place of the pie pastry, use biscuit dough. Roll out the dough ¼ in. (6 mm) thick and cut it into 1½-in. rounds. Place the round on top of the fruit filling.

Apple Betty

Yield: One pan 12 × 20 in. (30 × 50 cm)
48 portions, 4 oz (120 g) each

Ingredients	U.S.		Metric
Peeled, sliced apples	8 lb		4000 g
Sugar	1 lb 8	oz	750 g
Salt		0.25 oz (1½ tsp)	7 g
Nutmeg		0.08 oz (1 tsp)	2 g
Lemon zest, grated		0.12 oz (1½ tsp)	3 g
Lemon juice	2	oz	60 mL
Yellow or white cake crumbs	2 lb		1000 g
Butter, melted	8	oz	250 g

■ P r o c e d u r e

1. Combine the apples, sugar, salt, nutmeg, zest, and lemon juice in a bowl. Toss gently until well mixed.
2. Place one-third of the apple mixture in an even layer in a well-buttered 12 × 20 in. (30 × 50-cm) baking pan.
3. Top with one-third of the cake crumbs.
4. Continue until all the apples and crumbs have been used. You will have three layers of fruit and three layers of crumbs.
5. Pour the butter evenly over the top.
6. Bake at 350°F (175°C) for about 1 hour, until fruit is tender.

Apple Charlotte

Yield: One 1-qt (1 L) mold

Ingredients	U.S.		Metric	
Tart cooking apples	2 lb		900	g
Butter	1	oz	30	g
Lemon zest, grated		0.08 oz (1 tsp)	2	g
Cinnamon		0.01 oz (¼ tsp)	0.4	g
Puréed apricot jam	2	oz	60	g
Sugar	1–2	oz	30–60	g
Firm white bread, trimmed of crusts	12 slices		12 slices	
Butter, melted	4	oz	110	g

Note Apple charlottes should normally not be made in sizes larger than 1 qt, or they are likely to collapse after unmolding. Also, to avoid collapse, the apple mixture must be cooked until it is quite thick. The bread should be firm, and the charlotte should be baked long enough to brown the bread well.

■ P r o c e d u r e

1. Peel, core, and slice the apples. Combine them with the butter, zest, and cinnamon in a broad, shallow pan. Cook over moderate heat until soft. Mash the apples lightly with a spoon and continue to cook until they form a thick purée. Some lumps of apple are OK.
2. Stir in the apricot jam. Add sugar to taste, depending on the sweetness of the apples.
3. Line a 1-qt (1 L) charlotte mold, two 1-pt (500 mL) charlotte molds, or other straight-sided molds in the following manner: Dip bread slices in melted butter and line the mold with the buttered side against the inside of the mold. The bottom may be lined with one round slice or with wedges of bread cut to fit. Line the sides with half slices of bread overlapping each other shingle-fashion.
4. Fill with the apple purée and top with the remaining bread.
5. Bake at 400°F (200°C) for 30–40 minutes.
6. Cool for 20 minutes, then carefully unmold. Serve warm or cold.

Strawberries Romanoff

Yield: 8 to 12 portions

Ingredients	U.S.		Metric
Strawberries, fresh	2	qt	2 L
Confectioners' sugar	2	oz	60 g
Orange juice	4	oz	125 mL
Orange liqueur, such as curaçao	2	oz	60 mL
Heavy cream	12	oz	400 mL
Confectioners' sugar	0.75 oz (3 tbsp)		20 g
Orange liqueur, such as curaçao	0.75 oz (1½ tbsp)		20 mL

■ P r o c e d u r e

1. Trim the stems from the strawberries. Cut the berries in half if they are large.

2. Combine the berries with the first quantities of sugar, orange juice, and liqueur. Let stand for 1 hour, refrigerated.

3. Prepare whipped cream flavored with orange liqueur, following the procedure on page 180.

4. To serve, put the berries and juices in a serving bowl or individual dessert dishes. Put the whipped cream in a pastry bag fitted with a star tube. Pipe the cream decoratively over the berries to cover them completely.

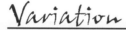

Place a small scoop of orange sorbet in each dessert dish and cover it with the marinated berries. Cover with whipped cream as in the basic recipe.

Raspberry or Cherry Gratin

Ingredients per portion	U.S.		Metric
Genoise layer (p. 319) (see step 2)			
Raspberries or sweet, pitted cherries	3	oz	90 g
Pastry cream (pp. 187–188)	2	oz	60 g
Whipped cream	1	oz	30 g
Optional flavoring			
Kirsch, orange liqueur, or raspberry or cherry brandy	to taste		to taste
Sliced almonds	0.25 oz		7 g
Butter, melted	0.25 oz		7 g
Confectioners' sugar			

■ P r o c e d u r e

1. Select a shallow gratin dish or other heatproof dish large enough to hold the fruit in a shallow layer.

2. Cut a thin slice of genoise (about ⅜ in./1 cm thick) to cover the bottom of the dish.

3. Arrange the fruit on top of the genoise. (If desired, marinate the fruit ahead of time in fruit brandy or liqueur and a little sugar. Drain and use the liquid in step 4.)

4. Combine the pastry cream, whipped cream, and flavoring. Spread the mixture over the fruit to cover completely.

5. Mix the almonds and butter and sprinkle over the pastry cream. Dredge the top heavily with confectioners' sugar.

6. Place under a broiler or in the top of a hot oven for a few minutes to brown the top.

7. Serve hot.

Gratin de Fruits Rouges (Red Fruit Gratin)

Yield: 5 portions, 5 oz (150 g) each

Ingredients	U.S.	Metric
Sponge layers (see step 1)	5	5
Dessert syrup flavored with kirsch (p. 178)	as needed	as needed
Strawberries	7 oz	200 g
Blackberries	3.5 oz	100 g
Raspberries	3.5 oz	100 g
Red currants	2.5 oz	75 g
Sabayon I (p. 197)	5 oz (about 15 fl oz)	150 g (about 450 mL)
Raspberry Sauce (p. 196)	3.5 oz	100 g
Additional fruit for garnish	as needed	as needed

■ P r o c e d u r e

1. Cut 5-in. (12 cm) circles of sponge ¼ in. (6 mm) thick (Sponge Roll I, p. 318, is recommended, but Genoise, p. 319, or other sponges can be used.)

2. Place the circles of sponge on serving plates. Brush with the syrup.

3. Clean the fruit as necessary, and cut the strawberries into halves or quarters, depending on size. Arrange the fruit on top of the sponge.

4. With a spoon, cover the fruit with a layer of sabayon at least ⅛ in. (3 mm) thick.

5. Place under a hot salamander or broiler until lightly browned.

6. Pour a ribbon of raspberry sauce around each gratin and serve immediately.

Baked Apples Tatin-Style

Yield: 6 apples, about 4½ oz (130 g) each

Ingredients	U.S.		Metric
Puff pastry	6	oz	150 g
Stuffing			
Brown sugar	2	oz	50 g
Butter	2	oz	50 g
Almonds, chopped	2	oz	50 g
Pecans, chopped	1	oz	25 g
Raisins	2	oz	50 g
Prunes, chopped	2	oz	50 g
Armagnac or brandy	0.5	oz	15 g
Cinnamon	1	tsp	2 g
Topping			
Sugar	5	oz	150 g
Vanilla bean (see *note*)	½		½
Butter	3	oz	70 g
Sliced almonds, toasted	0.75	oz	20 g
Pecans, chopped	0.75	oz	20 g
Pine nuts	0.75	oz	20 g
Raisins	0.75	oz	20 g
Pistachios	0.75	oz	20 g
Granny Smith apples	6		6
Butter, melted	2	oz	50 g
Crème Anglaise (p. 185)	12	oz	300 g
Calvados	2	oz	50 g

Note If vanilla beans are not available, add ¼ tsp (1 g) vanilla extract to the caramel in step 4.

■ P r o c e d u r e

1. Roll out the pastry until it is very thin. Dock and chill. Cut six circles 4½ in. (11 cm) in diameter. Return to the refrigerator until needed.

2. Butter 6 pudding molds about 3 inches in diameter on top, or large enough to hold an apple. Set aside.

3. *Prepare the stuffing:* Cream the butter and sugar. Mix in the remaining stuffing ingredients.

4. *Prepare the topping:* Cook the sugar to the caramel stage. Keeping the pan over moderate heat, add the vanilla and butter and stir constantly until the butter is incorporated into the caramel (see p. 197 for information on butter caramel). Pour a little of the caramel into the bottoms of the pudding molds, using about one-fourth of the caramel in all. Add the remaining topping ingredients to the caramel and keep warm.

5. Peel and core the apples. Brush with melted butter.

6. Place the apples in the pudding molds and fill the cores with the stuffing mixture. Press down well.

7. Cover with foil and bake at 350°F (180°C) until the apples start to soften, about 15 minutes. Remove from the oven and allow to cool slightly.

8. Place a disk of puff pastry on top of each apple and tuck in the sides.

9. Bake at 400°F (200°C) until the pastry is browned.

10. Mix the crème anglaise with the Calvados. Ladle pools of this sauce onto serving plates. Turn out the apples onto the pools with the puff pastry on the bottom. Spoon a little of the topping over the apples.

Pear and Apple Gratin

Yield: 6 portions

Ingredients	U.S.		Metric
Apples	4		4
Pears	4		4
Sugar	10	oz	300 g
Butter	5	oz	150 g
Vanilla extract	½	tsp	2 g
Calvados brandy	1	oz	30 g
Flour	1.33	oz	40 g
Ground almonds	1.33	oz	40 g
Extra-fine granulated sugar	3.5	oz	100 g
Egg whites	3.5	oz	100 g
Butter	3.5	oz	100 g
Confectioners' sugar for dusting	as needed		as needed
Apple Crisps (p. 506)	12		12
Cider Apple Sorbet (p. 471)	6 small scoops or quenelles		6 small scoops or quenelles

■ P r o c e d u r e

1. Peel and core the apples and pears. Chop into bite-size pieces.

2. Heat the sugar to a golden caramel. Add the butter, then the apples, pears, and vanilla. Cook gently until the fruit is tender. Add the calvados. Remove the fruit with a slotted spoon and reserve.

3. Sift the flour with the ground almonds into a bowl. Add the sugar and mix. Make a well in the center.

4. Froth the egg whites lightly with a fork and pour into the well. Heat the butter until it is browned and pour into the well. Draw the ingredients to form a paste. Place this mixture in a pastry bag with a small plain tip.

5. Lightly butter six ovenproof serving plates. Arrange the fruit on the plates, leaving the centers empty.

6. Pipe the almond mixture over the fruit in a random pattern. Dust with confectioners' sugar.

7. Clean the edges of the plates. Bake at 350°F (180°C) until golden brown.

8. Place an apple crisp in the center of each plate. Top with a small quenelle of sorbet, then another apple crisp. If desired, decorate with a sprig of mint. Serve immediately.

Variation

In place of the cooked pears and apples, use uncooked berries.

Crème Brûlée Sophia

Yield: 6 portions

Ingredients	U.S.		Metric
Grapefruits	2		2
Peaches, fresh or canned, drained and chopped	8	oz	250 g
Sugar	1.75	oz	50 g
Milk	9	oz	280 g
Heavy cream	3	oz	90 g
Whole eggs	5	oz	150 g
Egg yolks	1.33	oz	40 g
Sugar	3.5	oz	100 g
Vanilla extract	½	tsp	2 g
Peach schnapps	2	oz	60 g
Extra-fine granulated sugar	3.5	oz	100 g

■ Procedure

1. Segment the grapefruits. If any segments are thick, cut them in half horizontally to make thinner segments. Drain on absorbent paper until thoroughly dry to the touch.

2. Cook the peach flesh with the sugar over low heat until soft, then purée. Divide the purée among six shallow 5-oz (150 mL) ramekins, spreading it evenly on the bottom.

3. Bring the milk and cream to a scalding point.

4. Whip the eggs, yolks, and sugar until light. Temper with half of the hot milk, then stir this back into the remaining milk mixture. Add the vanilla.

5. Strain through a fine china cap.

6. Add the peach schnapps. Pour carefully into the ramekins so as not to stir the peach purée.

7. Place in a hot water bath and bake at 215°F (100°C) until just set.

8. Cool completely.

9. Arrange the grapefruit wedges on top in a pinwheel pattern. Just before serving, dust with sugar and caramelize the tops with a blowtorch.

Figs in Port Wine

Yield: about 1 lb 4 oz (600 g) figs in sauce, depending on size of figs

Ingredients	U.S.		Metric
Sugar	3.75	oz	100 g
Butter	1.5	oz	40 g
Red wine	3	oz	80 g
Port wine	3	oz	80 g
Vanilla extract	½	tsp	2 g
Blackcurrant purée	2	oz	50 g
Fresh, whole figs	8		8

■ Procedure

1. Cook the sugar to a golden caramel.

2. Keeping the pan over moderate heat, add the butter and stir constantly until the butter is incorporated into the caramel (see p. 197 for information on butter caramel).

3. Add the red wine, port, and vanilla extract. Simmer until the caramelized sugar is dissolved.

4. Add the blackcurrant purée and reduce by one-third.

5. Trim the hard stem ends of the figs and cut the figs in half lengthwise.

6. Place the figs in a baking dish and pour the caramel-wine syrup over them.

7. Bake at 350°F (180°C) until the figs are slightly puffed, 10–20 minutes, longer if the figs are not ripe.

8. Serve the figs with the sauce. See page 528 for serving idea.

Caramelized Pear Charlotte

Yield: 3 cakes, 7 in. (18 cm) each

Ingredients	U.S.		Metric
Caramelized pears			
Sugar	10	oz	270 g
Water	4	oz	110 g
Heavy cream	11	oz	310 g
Vanilla bean, split (see *note*)	1		1
Pears, peeled, cored, and quartered	6		6
Syrup			
Sugar	2	oz	60 g
Water	2	oz	60 g
Poire Williams	3.33	oz	100 g
Assembly			
Baumkuchen (p. 326)	see step 3		see step 3
Genoise layer (p. 319)	see step 3		see step 3
Mousse			
Milk	7.5	oz	220 g
Egg yolks	3	oz	90 g
Sugar	4	tsp	20 g
Gelatin, softened in water	0.5	oz	14 g
Caramel from the pears	8	oz	240 g
Heavy cream	1 lb 7	oz	650 g
Glaçage			
Gelatin	0.25	oz	6 g
Caramel from the pears	4	oz	120 g
Glucose	1	oz	30 g
Poire Williams	1	oz	30 g
Decoration			
Italian Meringue (p. 183)	as needed		as needed
Chocolate cigarettes (p. 542)	as needed		as needed
Red currants or other berries	as needed		as needed
Mint leaves	as needed		as needed

Note   If vanilla beans are not available, add ½ tsp (2 g) vanilla extract to the caramel in step 1.

■ P r o c e d u r e

1. *For the pears:* Make a syrup with the sugar and water and cook to a golden caramel. Carefully add the cream and vanilla bean. Stir and simmer until the caramel is dissolved. Add the pears. Cover with a round of parchment and simmer until tender. Drain and reserve both the caramel and the pears. Scrape the seeds from the vanilla bean and add them to the caramel. There should be about 7 oz (200 g) of caramel.

2. *For the syrup:* Heat the water and sugar until the sugar is dissolved. Remove from heat and add the Poire Williams.

3. Line three 7-in. (18 cm) charlotte rings with baumkuchen, as shown on page 367. Place the rings on cake cards. Cut six thin layers from the genoise and place one in the bottom of each ring. (Reserve the other three layers for step 8.) Brush the genoise with the syrup.

4. Reserve three pear quarters for decorating the charlottes and chop the remaining pears into bite-size pieces, retaining any juices they release when cut. Add these juices to the caramel. Place the chopped pears on top of the genoise layers.

5. *For the mousse:* Heat the milk to the scalding point. Whip the egg yolks and sugar until light, then whip in half the milk. Return this mixture to the pan with the remaining milk and heat until thick enough to coat the back of a spoon.

6. Add the gelatin and two-thirds of the reserved caramel from the pears. Stir until the gelatin is dissolved.

7. Cool the mixture by stirring over ice. Before it sets, whip the cream to soft peaks and fold in.

8. Fill the rings three-fourths full with the mousse mixture and level the tops. Place a layer of genoise on top and press down gently. Brush with syrup.

9. Fill the rings to the top with the remaining mousse and level the tops with a palette knife. Chill until set.

10. *For the glaçage:* Soften the gelatin in cold water (see p. 39). Heat the remaining caramel with the glucose. Stir in the gelatin until dissolved. Add the Poire Williams. Cool slightly.

11. Spoon the glaçage over the mousse. Smooth with a palette knife and chill.

12. Remove the charlotte rings by warming them slightly with a blowtorch and lifting them off.

13. Decorate the tops with a few scrolls of Italian meringue, piped with a star or plain tip, a fanned quartered pear, some chocolate cigarettes, berries, and mint leaves.

Spiced Pineapple

Yield: about 2 lb (950 g) pineapple and sauce

Ingredients	U.S.		Metric
Baby pineapples (see *note*)	4		4
Sugar	7	oz	200 g
Butter	3.5 oz		100 g
Star anise, whole	2		2
Cloves, whole	2		2
Cinnamon sticks	2		2
Rum	1.5 oz		40 g
Vanilla extract	½	tsp	2 g
Heavy cream	3.5 oz		100 g

Note   Baby pineapples weigh about 8 oz (250 g) each and yield about 5 oz (150 g) flesh. If they are not available, substitute 20 oz (600 g) peeled, cored fresh pineapple, in large pieces.

■ P r o c e d u r e

1. Peel, core, and eye the pineapples.

2. Cook the sugar to a golden caramel. Keeping the pan over moderate heat, add the butter and spices. Stir constantly until the butter is incorporated into the caramel (see p. 197 for information on butter caramel).

3. Roll the pineapple in the caramel and transfer the fruit to a baking dish.

4. Add the rum and vanilla to the caramel and flambé. Pour this mixture over the pineapple.

5. Bake at 350°F (180°C), basting regularly, until the pineapple is tender, about 35 minutes.

6. Slice the pineapples and serve warm. Heat the caramel sauce, add the cream, and strain. Pour the sauce over the pineapple. See page 529 for serving suggestion.

Raspberry Jam

For large-quantity measurements, see page 613.

Yield: 7½ oz (240 g)

Ingredients	U.S.		Fruit at 100% Metric	%
Sugar	3	oz	94 g	75
Water	1	oz	30 g	25
Raspberries, fresh	4	oz	125 g	100
Glucose	0.4	oz	12 g	10
Sugar	0.6	oz	18 g	15
Pectin	0.33 oz		10 g	8

■ P r o c e d u r e

1. Place the first quantity of sugar and water in a saucepan and bring to a boil, dissolving the sugar.

2. Add the raspberries and glucose. Boil until the fruit has broken down and the consistency is thick.

3. Mix together the pectin and the remaining sugar. Add to the cooked fruit. Mix well and simmer another 3 minutes.

4. Pour into a clean glass jar and seal. Keep refrigerated.

Variations

Other soft fruits may be prepared in the same way.

Strawberry Marmalade

For large-quantity measurements, see page 613.

Yield: 13 oz (400 g)

Ingredients	U.S.		Metric	%
			Fruit at 100%	
Strawberries	8	oz	250 g	100
Sugar	8	oz	250 g	100
Pectin	0.17	oz	5 g	2
Lemon juice	0.5	oz	15 g	3

■ P r o c e d u r e

1. If the strawberries are large, cut them into halves or quarters. Otherwise, leave them whole.

2. Mix the berries with the sugar. Refrigerate overnight.

3. Bring the sugared fruit to a simmer and cook until a purée consistency is obtained.

4. Remove from the heat. Sprinkle the pectin over the fruit and stir in. Return to the heat and cook 3 to 4 minutes.

5. Add the lemon juice and mix in.

6. Pour into clean glass jars and seal. Refrigerate.

Apple Marmalade

For large-quantity measurements, see page 613.

Yield: 2 lb 2 oz (1060 g)

Ingredients	U.S.	Metric	%
		Fruit at 100%	
Apples, peeled and cored	2 lb	1000 g	100
Water	4 oz	125 g	12.5
Sugar	10 oz	300 g	30

■ P r o c e d u r e

1. Chop the apples.

2. Place all ingredients in a saucepan and cook over low heat until very soft and of a purée consistency.

3. Force through a sieve or food mill.

4. Pour into clean glass jars. Refrigerate.

Caramelized Apricots

For large-quantity measurements, see page 613.

Yield: 12 oz (300 g)

Ingredients	U.S.	Metric
Sugar	4 oz	100 g
Water	1 oz	25 g
Honey	2 oz	50 g
Butter	1 oz	25 g
Canned apricots, drained	12 oz	300 g

■ P r o c e d u r e

1. Combine the sugar, water, and honey, and cook to the caramel stage.

2. Keeping the pan over moderate heat, add the butter and stir constantly until the butter is incorporated into the caramel (see p. 197 for information on butter caramel).

3. Add the apricots to the caramel mixture. Heat until the apricots are well coated with the caramel.

4. Remove the apricots from the caramel mixture and place on a tray or sheet pan. Cover with plastic film and cool.

Apricot Compote

For large-quantity measurements, see page 613.

Yield: 9.5 oz (240 g)

Ingredients	U.S.	Metric
Sugar	4.5 oz	112 g
Water	0.6 oz	15 g
Apricots, fresh or canned, halved and pitted	5 oz	125 g
Pectin	0.4 oz	10 g
Glucose	0.5 oz	12 g

■ P r o c e d u r e

1. Combine the sugar and water in a saucepan and bring to a boil to dissolve the sugar and make a syrup. Cook to 221°F (105°C).

2. Cut up the apricot halves into halves or thirds, depending on size. Add to the syrup. Cook an additional 15–17 minutes if the apricots are fresh, about 3 minutes if canned.

3. Add the pectin and glucose and mix in well. Cook an additional 3 minutes.

Apricot and Almond Compote

For large-quantity measurements, see page 613.

Ingredients	U.S.	Metric
Whole blanched almonds	2 oz	50 g

Add the almonds to the apricots at the same time as the pectin and glucose.

Plum Compote

Yield: 2 lb 4 oz (1000 g)

Ingredients	U.S.	Metric
Sugar	7 oz	200 g
Butter	2 oz	50 g
Star anise, whole	2	2
Vanilla bean (see *note*)	1	1
Red or black plums, stoned and quartered	2 lb 4 oz	1000 g
Lemon juice	1 oz	30 g
Lemon zest, grated	1 tsp	2 g
Port wine, warmed	2 oz	50 g

■ P r o c e d u r e

1. Melt the sugar in a heavy saucepan. Cook to a pale caramel.

2. Remove from heat; cool slightly.

3. Add the butter, star anise, plums, lemon juice, zest, wine, and vanilla.

4. Bring to a boil, then reduce to a simmer. Cook until the fruit is tender but the pieces remain intact. Cool.

Note If desired, omit the vanilla bean and add ½ tsp (2 mL) vanilla extract to the simmering fruit in step 4.

Pineapple Kumquat Compote

For large-quantity measurements, see page 614.

Yield: 11 oz (270 g)

Ingredients	U.S.	Metric
Sugar	4.5 oz	112 g
Water	0.6 oz	15 g
Vanilla bean (see *note*)	½	½
Glucose	0.5 oz	12 g
Canned pineapple, drained and diced	5 oz	125 g
Kumquats, sliced and blanched	2 oz	50 g
Pistachios	0.4 oz	10 g

Note   If vanilla beans are not available, flavor the finished compote with vanilla extract to taste.

■ P r o c e d u r e

1. Place the sugar, water, and vanilla bean in a saucepan. Bring to a boil. Cook to 238°F (120°C).

2. Add the fruit and nuts to the syrup.

3. Cook over high heat for 2–3 minutes. Remove the vanilla bean.

4. Pour into clean glass jars and seal. Refrigerate.

Variation

Kumquat Compote

For large-quantity measurements, see page 614.

Ingredients	U.S.	Metric
Sugar	4.5 oz	112 g
Water	0.6 oz	15 g
Glucose	0.5 oz	12 g
Kumquats, halved or sliced, blanched	5 oz	125 g
Pistachios	0.75 oz	20 g

Follow the procedure in the basic recipe, but omit the pineapple and vanilla and adjust the quantities as listed above.

Candied Orange or Lemon Zest

Yield: variable

Ingredients	U.S.	Metric
Oranges or lemons	4	4
Water	as needed	as needed
Sugar	7 oz	200 g
Water	7 oz	200 g

■ P r o c e d u r e

1. Peel the zest from the oranges in strips, using a vegetable peeler. Using a small, sharp knife, remove white pith. Square off the strips and then cut them into julienne.

2. Boil the zest in a generous quantity of water until tender. Drain and discard the water.

3. Boil the sugar and water to make a syrup.

4. Poach the zest in the syrup until tender and translucent. Cool.

5. The zest can be stored in the syrup and drained as needed. Alternatively, drain and pat off excess syrup with absorbent paper. Then roll in extra-fine granulated sugar and shake in a sieve to remove excess sugar.

Apple Crisps

Yield: variable, depending on size of apple and thickness of cuts

Ingredients	U.S.	Metric
Sugar	7 oz	200 g
Water	7 oz	200 g
Green apple, peeled	2	2

■ Procedure

1. Heat the sugar and water until the sugar is dissolved.

2. Cut the apple crosswise into paper-thin slices, preferably using a slicing machine or a mandoline. Immediately drop the slices into the syrup and heat gently for 2 minutes.

3. Allow the fruit to cool in the syrup

4. Carefully remove the slices from the syrup and arrange on a silicone mat on a sheet pan. Dry in an oven at 175°F (80°C) until dry and crisp.

5. Use as a garnish for fruit desserts (see, for example, p. 498).

Variations

Other fruits, such as oranges, pineapple, pears, and large strawberries, may be prepared in the same way.

 Applesauce

Yield: about 1 qt (1 L)

Ingredients	U.S.	Metric
Apples	4 lb	2 kg
Sugar	as needed	as needed
Flavoring (see step 5)		
Lemon juice	to taste	to taste

■ Procedure

1. Cut the apples into quarters and remove the cores. Skins may be left on because they will be strained out later. (Red peels will color the applesauce pink.) Coarsely dice the apples.

2. Place the apples in a heavy saucepan with about 2 oz (60 ml) water. Cover.

3. Set the pan over a low heat and cook the apples until very soft. Stir occasionally.

4. Remove the cover. Add sugar to taste. The amount depends on the desired sweetness of the sauce and the sweetness of the apples.

5. Add desired flavoring to taste, such as grated lemon zest, vanilla or cinnamon. Add lemon juice to taste, especially if the apples lack tartness. Simmer for a few minutes to blend in flavors.

6. Pass the sauce through a food mill.

7. If the sauce is too thin or watery, let it simmer uncovered until thickened.

▶ TERMS FOR REVIEW

compote	fruit crisp	apple charlotte
fruit cobbler	fruit betty	fruit gratin

▶ QUESTIONS FOR REVIEW

1. Briefly describe each of the following fruits.

   kumquat

   litchi

   mango

   papaya

   passion fruit

   persimmon

   pomegranate

   prickly pear

   quince

2. *True or false:* Berries should be removed from their containers and washed as soon as possible after delivery or purchase. Explain.

3. For the following fruits, describe how to select produce of good quality.

   apples

   apricots

   bananas

   coconuts

   grapefruit

   grapes

   peaches

   pineapples

4. Describe in general terms how to sauté a fruit for a dessert.

5. Describe the procedure for preparing pears poached in red wine.

19

Dessert
Presentation

In recent years, chefs have devoted more of their creativity to the arrangement of food on the plate. This is something of a change from earlier decades, when much of the plating of foods in elegant restaurants was done by the dining room staff at tableside. This trend has extended to the service of desserts as well. A piece of pastry or a wedge of cake that was at one time served by itself on a small dessert plate is now likely to be served on a large plate with a sauce and one or more items of garnish.

A pastry chef may devote as much attention to the appearance of a plated dessert as he or she gives to the decoration of a cake or the assembly of a large pastry for the display case or retail counter. The purpose of this section is to present guidelines and general suggestions for the presentation of individual desserts. The chapter concludes with a list of specific suggestions that employ recipes from throughout this book.

After reading this
chapter, you should be
able to:

■ Plate and serve attractive
presentations of desserts with
appropriate sauces and
garnishes.

GENERAL GUIDELINES

For the purpose of explanation, dessert presentations can be divided into two basic categories, based on the number of main items on the plate: simple and complex. Simple presentations are those with one portion of one item, plus any garnishes and sauces. Complex presentations are those with two or more main items.

SIMPLE PRESENTATIONS

A single portion of a simple dessert can be plated in four basic ways:

1. ***The dessert alone.*** This is, obviously, the simplest and most elemental way to serve a dessert. A portion of dessert—such as a wedge of pie or cake, a piece of pastry, or a scoop or two of ice cream—is placed on an appropriate dish or in a bowl or cup and served unadorned. This presentation is usually used for simple, home-style desserts or, at the opposite extreme, for elegant pastries or gâteaux that are beautiful on their own and need no added elements.

2. ***The dessert plus garnish.*** Although the term *garnish* may be used to refer to a purely decorative item, such as a sprig of mint, we use it here to mean an edible item that complements the main item. Following are some examples. The first two of these are, perhaps, the most versatile because they include the greatest variety of items and possible presentations.

   Fruit is a suitable garnish for a great variety of pastries, cakes, and other desserts. Nearly any appropriate fresh or poached fruit can be used. Depending on size and shape, they may be left whole (as in the case of berries) or cut into slices, wedges, dice, or other shape.

   A scoop or spoonful of *ice cream* or *sorbet* complements many desserts. For home-style desserts such as pies, the ice cream is usually served with a standard scoop. For more elegant desserts, the ice cream is often shaped into a small, oval *quenelle*. To shape a quenelle, first make sure that the ice

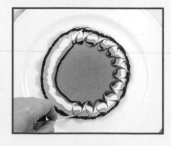

cream or sorbet is tempered to a soft consistency; this will not work if it is too hard. Scoop a portion of ice cream with a tablespoon dipped in water. With a second spoon, scoop the ice cream out of the first spoon. This shapes the ice cream into a neat oval shape about the size of the bowl of the spoon. Repeat the scooping action with the first spoon if necessary to make a neat oval.

A dollop of *whipped cream,* applied with a spoon or a pastry bag, is a classic garnish for pastries, pies, and cakes.

A small *cookie (petit four sec)* or two goes well with frozen desserts.

Fruit crisps (p. 494) are used to decorate fruit desserts of a corresponding flavor. For example, one or more apple crisps can garnish a plating of baked apple with apple sorbet.

Chocolate decorations of many types, including curls, cigarettes, cutouts, and piped lacework, go well with many kinds of desserts, not only chocolate desserts. Decorative chocolate work is discussed in chapter 20.

A *choux lattice* is used in the photo of a decorated slice of Passion Fruit Charlotte (p. 530). This decoration is made as follows: Draw lattice designs on a sheet of parchment, then turn the parchment over (the drawing should show through). Using a paper cone (p. 351), pipe pâte à choux over the outlines. Use the point of a small knife to make the joints neat, as necessary. Sprinkle with poppy seeds and bake at 375°F (190°C) until golden, 4–7 minutes.

Stencil paste or *Tuile batter* (pp. 323 and 418) can be piped in designs in the same way as choux paste, then baked until crisp. Alternatively, use the stencil method of cookie makeup (p. 399) to make wafers in decorative shapes for dressing up dessert presentations.

Sugar spirals, spun sugar, and other forms of decorative *sugar work,* as well as caramelized or toasted nuts, are other items used to garnish appropriate desserts. Sugar work is discussed in chapter 21.

3. ***The dessert plus a sauce.*** Dessert sauces enhance desserts both by their flavor and by their appearance, just as savory sauces enhance meats, fish, and vegetables. The most popular and useful dessert sauces are discussed in chapter 8. Crème anglaise variations, chocolate sauce, and the

Decorating with Sauces

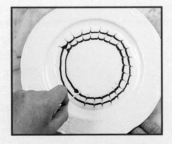
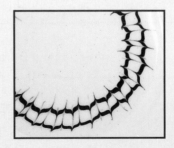
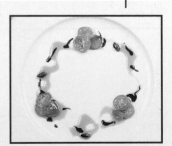

many fruit sauces or sweetened fruit purées are the most versatile. One or another of these complement nearly any dessert.

Except for some home-style desserts and frozen desserts, sauces are usually not ladled over a dessert because this would mar its appearance by covering it up. Sauces are usually plated as a small pool, either around the dessert portion or to the side of the dessert. Another way to serve a sauce is to drizzle it in a ribbon or in a random pattern onto the plate.

Desserts served in a pool are often marbled or feathered, as shown on the previous two pages. This is done by piping lines or dots of a sauce of a contrasting color and then drawing a pick or skewer through the piped sauce to make a pattern. For this technique to work properly, the piped sauce must be of about the same weight and consistency as the sauce in the pool. The easiest way to pipe a sauce is to use a small squeeze bottle.

For dark-colored sauces, such as raspberry purée or chocolate sauce, a white sauce such as that on page 199 is a good choice for piping. Crème anglaise or other light sauces can be decorated with chocolate crème anglaise or other dark sauces. Contrasting fruit sauces can also be used to decorate each other.

4. ***The dessert plus garnish and sauce.***   This method of plating combines all three elements discussed above.

COMPLEX PRESENTATIONS

A complex presentation is one that includes two or more desserts on one plate. A complex presentation may also include one or more sauces, garnishes, or both. Naturally, the portion size of each component is smaller so that the total dessert portion is not too large.

Especially elegant dessert presentations in fine restaurants often consist of several distinct desserts on a plate, along with appropriate garnish and sauces. Example of such presentations are included in the last section of this chapter. The desserts must complement and harmonize with one another. The number of elements on the plate creates a feeling of abundance, even though the portion size of each item is usually quite small. To avoid crowding the various elements together, it is best to use a large dinner plate.

Elaborate desserts should usually be served on simple plates without a complex design that might detract from the presentation. Simple desserts, on the other hand, may be enhanced by an attractive design on the plate.

The distinction between simple and complex desserts is not exact and is made only for the purpose of discussion. For example, a wedge of fruit tart accompanied by a spoonful of sorbet might be considered a simple dessert plus a garnish or a complex dessert combining two main items, depending on the amount of sorbet.

MATCHING ELEMENTS

As we have discussed, a dessert presentation consists of one or more desserts plus any garnish and sauce, arranged attractively on a plate. All these items must go together—that is, they must be carefully selected so that they complement and enhance each other. They may go well together because they have similar flavors. Some typical examples include the following:

A chocolate soufflé served with a chocolate sauce

A medley of chocolate desserts

A fruit dessert, such as a tart, served with a sorbet made of the same fruit

On the other hand, they may have contrasting flavors that emphasize one another, such as the following combinations:

A pastry with a creamy filling served with a slightly tart raspberry purée

Poached pear with vanilla ice cream and chocolate sauce

A hot dessert, such as a fruit fritter or a warm fruit compote, served with ice cream or other frozen dessert

Because there are countless possible combinations, it is impossible to give a set of rules that covers them all. Additional specific examples can be found in the following section.

EXAMPLES OF DESSERT PRESENTATIONS

The techniques and recipes presented in other chapters of this book and in the first part of this chapter give you the tools to prepare an unlimited variety of modern, stylish desserts.

This section follows a format similar to the one used to explain the procedures for preparing gâteaux and torten, beginning on page 370. In other words, no new recipes are required; individual components—as prepared from recipes elsewhere in this book—are assembled and arranged as indicated.

The following presentations are merely a few suggestions, selected to provide a sampling of ideas using different types of desserts and a variety of styles of arrangement. The list begins with the simplest presentations—for example, ideas for plating a slice of cake—and proceeds to more elaborate arrangements, ending with medleys of three or more desserts on a plate. The list includes both homey, rustic desserts and elegant desserts.

Each procedure begins with a list of the components required for the presentation. Page numbers refer to recipes or procedures elsewhere in this book. Where no page number is given, there may be two or more recipes, any one of which is suitable; refer to the index for page numbers.

Mocha Torte

Components

Mocha Torte (p. 371)

Chocolate Sauce (p. 195)

Crème Anglaise (p. 185)

■ P r o c e d u r e

1. Place a wedge of Mocha Torte in the center of a plate.

2. Spoon a small pool of chocolate sauce on one side of the cake. Spoon a small pool of crème anglaise on the other side of the cake.

3. If desired, marble the chocolate sauce with a little crème anglaise, and marble the crème anglaise with a little chocolate sauce (see p. 571).

Panna Cotta with Caramel and Fresh Berries

Components

Caramel for Cages (p. 570)

Panna Cotta (p. 430)

Clear Caramel Sauce (p. 196)

Assorted fresh berries

■ P r o c e d u r e

1. *Prepare the caramel decorations:* Drizzle the caramel onto a silicone mat or an oiled sheet pan into desired shapes or patterns. Allow to cool and harden.

2. Unmold a portion of panna cotta onto a broad soup plate or other suitable plate.

3. Ladle a little caramel sauce around the panna cotta.

4. Distribute the mixed berries around the panna cotta on top of the caramel sauce.

5. Top with the caramel decoration immediately before serving. Do not let it stand, or the caramel decoration may begin to dissolve in the moisture from the dessert.

Apple Walnut Turnover

Components

Apple Walnut Pie Filling (p. 215)

Puff Pastry (pp. 236–237)

Sabayon (p. 197)

Walnuts

■ P r o c e d u r e

1. Prepare the pie filling as directed, but chop the apples into fairly small pieces.

2. Prepare and bake turnovers (p. 240), using a generous amount of filling for each.

3. Cut a warm turnover in half and spread open on a plate to display the filling.

4. In the space between the two cut surfaces, spoon a pool of sabayon. Sprinkle the sauce with walnut pieces.

Variation

Instead of sabayon, use Créme Anglaise (p. 185) flavored with cinnamon.

 ## Peach Napoleon

Components

3 phyllo layers for napoleons, one of which is caramelized (p. 257)

Pastry Cream (p. 185) flavored with amaretto

Caramelized peach slices (p. 493)

Clear Caramel Sauce (p. 196)

Peach Ice Cream (p. 467)

■ P r o c e d u r e

1. Place a plain phyllo layer just to one side of the center of a plate. Cover with caramelized peach slices.

2. Place a small spoonful of pastry cream on the peaches and spread gently over the center with the back of a spoon.

3. Top with another phyllo layer and additional peaches and pastry cream.

4. Top with the caramelized phyllo layer.

5. Drizzle caramel sauce onto the plate around the napoleon.

6. Place a quenelle (see p. 510) of ice cream next to the napoleon. Serve at once.

Variations

Instead of the peach ice cream, use Caramel Ice Cream (p. 467), Cinnamon Ice Cream (p. 467), or whipped cream flavored with amaretto.

Strawberry Cream Cake

Components

Strawberry Cream Cake (p. 374; see step 1 of procedure)
Strawberry sauce (p. 194)
Cream Sauce for Piping (p. 199)

■ **P r o c e d u r e**

1. Prepare the cake following the procedure for Orange Cream Cake but using strawberries instead of oranges and kirsch to flavor the syrup and cream.

2. Place a wedge of cake on one side of a plate.

3. On the other half of the plate, spoon a pool of strawberry sauce.

4. Pipe two or three lines of cream sauce onto the strawberry sauce and draw a pick through the lines to marble them.

Lemon Tart

Components

Lemon Tart (p. 273)
Whipped cream
Fruit, as desired
Sprig of mint

■ **P r o c e d u r e**

1. Place a wedge of tart slightly to the left of center of the plate with the point toward you.

2. To the right of the tart wedge, pipe a rosette or shell of whipped cream using a pastry bag with a large star tube.

3. As garnish, place a colorful piece of fruit and a mint sprig next to the cream.

Apple Crisp with Caramel Sauce or Butterscotch Sauce

Components

Caramel Sauce or Butterscotch Sauce (p. 176)
Apple Crisp (p. 494)
Vanilla ice cream

■ **P r o c e d u r e**

1. Spoon a pool of sauce in the center of a plate.

2. With a large serving spoon, place a generous spoonful of apple crisp on the pool of sauce slightly to one side of the center of the plate.

3. Garnish with a small scoop of vanilla ice cream.

Variation

Substitute a generous spoonful of whipped cream for the ice cream.

Fattigman with Lingonberries

Components

Fattigman (p. 162)

Lingonberry preserves

Vanilla ice cream

Mint

■ P r o c e d u r e

1. Arrange three to five fattigman on one side of a dessert plate.

2. Place a spoonful of lingonberries next to the fattigman.

3. In the space remaining on the plate, place a scoop of vanilla ice cream.

4. Decorate with a sprig of mint.

Charlotte au Cassis

Components

Charlotte au Cassis (p. 448)

Chocolate fan (p. 543)

Fresh berries

Candied Orange Zest (p. 505)

Mint

Crème Chantilly (p. 181)

Sauces (see step 4)

■ P r o c e d u r e

1. Place a wedge of charlotte toward the back of a plate.

2. In front of the charlotte, place a chocolate fan and fill it with berries. Garnish with a few pieces of candied orange zest and a sprig of mint.

3. Make a quenelle of crème chantilly and place it next to the chocolate fan. Alternatively, pipe a rosette of the cream with a star tip.

4. Spoon a band of sauce around the plate and marble it with a sauce of a contrasting color. (The sauces in the photograph are syrup from kumquat compote and raspberry coulis.)

Brownie Cherry Cheesecake Ice Cream Sandwich

Components

Two 2-inch Cream Cheese Brownies (p. 421)

1½–2 oz Cheesecake Ice Cream (p. 467)

1 oz Cherry Pie Filling (p. 213)

Whipped cream

Chocolate shavings or other chocolate decorations

■ P r o c e d u r e

1. Place one brownie slightly off center on a plate. Top with the ice cream, which has been flattened slightly.

2. Place the second brownie on top.

3. Spoon the cherry pie filling onto the plate next to the brownie sandwich.

4. Decorate with whipped cream and chocolate decorations.

Iced Low-Fat Raspberry Parfait with Almond Macaroons

Components

Iced Low-Fat Raspberry Parfait (p. 482)

Italian Meringue (p. 183)

Raspberry Sauce (p. 196)

Fresh raspberries and other berries

Almond Macaroons II (p. 415)

■ P r o c e d u r e

1. Freeze the parfait in a gutter mold lined with plastic film.

2. Unmold onto a tray and remove the plastic film. Using a pastry bag with a star tip, coat the top and sides of the parfait with Italian meringue. Brown lightly with a blowtorch.

3. For each portion, cut a slice of the parfait 1¼–1½ in. (3–4 cm) thick and stand on one side of a plate. Spoon a crescent of raspberry sauce on the other side of the plate. Top the pool of sauce with a bouquet of fruit and with two or three macaroons.

Tricolor Fruit Mousse

Components

Ingredients for strawberry, pineapple, and raspberry Bavarians (p. 442)

Peach sauce, made by puréeing fresh or canned peaches (p. 194)

■ Procedure

1. Prepare the strawberry Bavarian, *using half the quantity of gelatin indicated in the recipe.* Pour the mixture into a flat-bottomed, straight-sided mold so that the mousse is about ³/₄ in. (2 cm) thick. Chill until set.

2. Prepare pineapple Bavarian, using canned or poached pineapple (raw pineapple does not work with gelatin). Use only half the indicated quantity of gelatin. Pour a layer of pineapple Bavarian on top of the strawberry layer. Chill until set.

3. Repeat with the raspberry Bavarian, again using half the gelatin.

4. Pour a pool of peach purée sauce onto a plate.

5. Remove a spoonful of the tricolor mousse by holding a tablespoon vertically and inserting it into the mousse so that each spoonful contains all three layers. Place several spoonfuls of the mousse onto the sauce.

Cream Cheese Bavarian with Fruit Compote

Components

Genoise (p. 319)

Cream Cheese Bavarian (p. 443)

Toasted, sliced almonds

Fruit compote (p. 491) made with a mixture of colorful fresh fruit

■ Procedure

1. Select a round, straight-sided, flat-bottomed mold 3–4 in. (8–10 cm) in diameter. Cut a layer of genoise as thin as possible and line the bottom of the mold.

2. Prepare the Bavarian and pour a layer into the mold about 1¹/₂ in. (4 cm) thick. Sprinkle the top with a few almonds. Chill until set.

3. Unmold the Bavarian and place in the center of a plate.

4. Spoon the fruit compote around the Bavarian.

Pumpkin Profiteroles

Components

4 unfilled profiteroles (cream puffs) about 1½–2 in. (4–5 cm) in diameter

Pumpkin Cream Chiffon (p. 224) made with half the gelatin

Crème Anglaise (p. 185)

Whipped cream

■ **P r o c e d u r e**

1. Cut the tops off the profiteroles. Fill with the pumpkin chiffon, using a pastry bag with a star tube, and replace the tops. Dust with confectioners' sugar.

2. Ladle a pool of crème anglaise onto a plate.

3. Arrange three of the profiteroles in a triangle in the center of the plate.

4. Pipe a rosette of whipped cream in the center of the triangle.

5. Place the fourth profiterole on the center of the whipped cream.

Steamed Chocolate Almond Pudding with Caramel Sauce

Components

Steamed Chocolate Almond Pudding (p. 438)

Caramel Sauce (p. 196)

Praline ice cream (p. 467)

■ **P r o c e d u r e**

1. The pudding may be prepared in single-serving molds or in large molds and then sliced or broken coarsely into portions, depending on whether an elegant appearance or a home-style, rustic appearance is desired.

2. Ladle a pool of caramel sauce onto a plate.

3. Place a portion of pudding on the sauce.

4. Garnish with a small scoop or spoonful of ice cream placed next to the pudding.

Bombe Bresilienne

Components

Bombe Bresilienne (p. 476)

Whipped cream

Caramelized Pineapple (p. 493)

■ **P r o c e d u r e**

1. Cut a wedge of bombe and place it on its side on a plate so that the thick part of the wedge is against the rim of the plate and the point of the wedge lies across the center of the plate.

2. Using a pastry bag with a small star tube, pipe a row of whipped cream rosettes along the thin edge of the bombe.

3. In the remaining space on the plate, arrange a few pieces of caramelized pineapple and their juices.

4. If desired, decorate the pineapple with a few fresh berries, a little toasted coconut, or some candied orange zest.

Chocolate Mousse Trio

Components

Crème Anglaise (p. 185)

White Chocolate Mousse (p. 454)

Milk Chocolate Mousse (p. 454)

Dark Chocolate Mousse (p. 454)

Toasted sliced almonds

■ P r o c e d u r e

1. Ladle a pool of crème anglaise onto a plate.

2. Place a spoonful of each mousse on the sauce.

3. Garnish the tops of the mousses with a few toasted sliced almonds.

Variation

Use three different nuts, one to garnish each mousse.

Trio of Fruit Sorbets

Components

Fruit purée sauces (p. 194): raspberry, kiwi, mango, strawberry

Three fruit sorbets (p. 468) of contrasting colors, such as lemon, melon, and raspberry

■ P r o c e d u r e

1. Spoon pools of the sauces onto a dinner plate, using about 1 oz (30 mL) of each. Tap the plate gently so that the pools run together and cover the entire center of the plate. With a fork or other utensil, swirl the sauces together to make an attractive pattern.

2. Place a spoonful of each of three sorbets in the center of the plate.

Raspberry Millefeuille

Components

Almond Tuile batter (p. 418)

Fresh raspberries

Whipped cream flavored with orange liqueur

Raspberry Sauce (p. 196)

Optional: Cream Sauce for Piping (p. 199)

■ P r o c e d u r e

1. Bake tuile wafers about 3 in. (7 cm) in diameter, but leave them flat; do not bend or mold them.

2. Place one wafer in the center of a plate. Arrange a ring of berries on the wafer lining the outside edge. Using a pastry bag, fill the space in the center of the berry ring with the flavored whipped cream.

3. Top with a second wafer and repeat with the berries and cream.

4. Dredge a third wafer generously with confectioners' sugar (optional). Carefully place it on top of the dessert.

5. Spoon a ring of raspberry sauce onto the plate around the pastry. If desired, marble the raspberry sauce with the cream sauce for piping. Serve at once, while the wafers are crisp.

Variations

Garnish with a spoonful of raspberry or orange sorbet (p. 469).

Apple-Filled Brioche with Berries

Components

Brioche (p. 111)

Pastry Cream Mousseline (p. 187)

Applesauce (p. 506; see procedure)

Crème Anglaise (p. 185)

Assorted fresh berries

■ P r o c e d u r e

1. Slice off the top of the brioche. Hollow out the brioche and toast lightly in the oven.

2. Prepare an applesauce that is sweet, not too tart, and well flavored with vanilla. Leave it slightly chunky; do not force it through a food mill.

3. Spoon a little pastry cream mousseline into the bottom of the brioche case. Fill almost to the top with the applesauce. Place a little more pastry cream on top and replace the top of the brioche.

4. Ladle a pool of crème anglaise onto a plate. Place the filled brioche in the center of the plate. Scatter some fresh berries around the brioche.

French-Toasted Challah with Cheesecake Ice Cream

Components

Challah (p. 74)

Batter for French toast (mixture of beaten eggs, milk, a little sugar, cinnamon)

Confectioners' sugar

Cheesecake Ice Cream (p. 467)

Melba Sauce (p. 196)

■ P r o c e d u r e

1. Slice the bread. Soak in the egg batter and pan fry in butter to make French toast.

2. Place two or three slices of French toast, overlapping, on one side of a plate. Dust heavily with confectioners' sugar.

3. Place a scoop of ice cream in the center of the plate.

4. Spoon a pool of melba sauce on the other side of the plate.

5. *Optional:* Garnish with a few rosettes of whipped cream.

Savarin with Berries

Components

Small (single-portion size) Savarin (p. 109)

Sabayon (p. 197)

Fresh berries

■ P r o c e d u r e

1. Ladle a pool of sabayon onto a plate.

2. Place a savarin in the center of the plate.

3. Fill the savarin with berries.

Warm Tropical Fruit Compote with Coconut Ice Cream

Components

Tropical Fruit Compote (p. 491)

Coconut Ice Cream (p. 467)

Toasted coconut

■ P r o c e d u r e

1. If the compote is not warm, heat it.

2. Spoon the compote into a soup plate or shallow bowl.

3. Place a scoop of the ice cream in the center.

4. Sprinkle lightly with toasted coconut.

5. If the compote is not colorful, sprinkle with a few pomegranate seeds or fresh berries.

Apple Fritters with Mascarpone Sorbet

Components

Apple fritters (p. 159)

Confectioners' sugar

Raspberry Sauce (p. 196)

Mascarpone Sorbet (p. 469)

A strawberry or a few raspberries for garnish

■ P r o c e d u r e

1. Place two fritters on one side of a plate. Dust with confectioners' sugar.

2. On the other side of the plate, spoon a pool of raspberry sauce.

3. Place a spoonful of the sorbet on the pool of sauce.

4. Garnish the plate with a fresh strawberry or a few raspberries.

Poached Pear with Wine Sorbet

Components

Small pear, such as Seckel
Ingredients for Pears in Wine (p. 491)
White Wine Sorbet (p. 469)
Sabayon (p. 197)

■ P r o c e d u r e

1. Peel the pear and core it from the blossom end, but leave the stem in. Poach it in red wine, as directed by the recipe.

2. Slice the cooled poached pear vertically but leave the slices attached at the stem end; do not slice all the way through. Carefully fan out the pear and place slightly off center on a plate.

3. Place a spoonful of wine sorbet next to the pear.

4. Place a spoonful of sabayon in front of the pear and sorbet.

Poppy Seed Parfait

Components

Poppy Seed Parfait (p. 482)
Genoise or Chocolate Genoise (p. 319)
Crème Chantilly (p. 181)
Kumquat Compote (p. 505)
Chocolate cigarettes (p. 542)

■ P r o c e d u r e

1. Fill a loaf-shaped mold nearly to the top with the parfait mixture. Top with a thin slice of genoise. Freeze until solid.

2. Unmold the parfait so that the genoise forms the base.

3. Cut three slices, about 1½ oz (45 g) each. Overlap the slices off center on a cold plate.

4. Decorate with rosettes of crème chantilly.

5. On the empty side of the plate, spoon 2–3 oz (60–90 g) Kumquat Compote.

6. Lay two or three chocolate cigarettes across the plate.

Hot and Cold Banana Split

Components

Strawberries, lightly sugared
Caramelized Bananas (p. 493)
Crème Anglaise (p. 165)
Raspberry Sauce (p. 196)
Strawberry sauce (p. 194)
Chocolate Sauce (p. 195)
Chocolate Ice Cream (p. 467)
Strawberry Ice Cream (p. 467)
Peach Ice Cream (p. 467)
Vanilla Ice Cream (p. 466)
Whipped cream (*optional*)

■ P r o c e d u r e

1. Place a small mound of strawberries in the center of a plate.

2. Arrange four caramelized banana quarters, cut-side up, on the plate like spokes of a wheel, with the strawberries as the hub, so that they divide the plate into four quadrants. The round ends of the banana should be toward the outside and the cut or square ends against the strawberries.

3. In each quadrant, between the banana pieces, spoon a small pool of one of the four sauces.

4. Place a small scoop of the chocolate ice cream on the crème anglaise, vanilla ice cream on the chocolate sauce, strawberry ice cream on the raspberry sauce, and peach ice cream on the strawberry sauce. Use no more than about 1 oz (30 g) of each ice cream, or the dessert will be too big.

5. If desired, decorate the dessert with a few rosettes of whipped cream.

Meringue Glacé with Macédoine of Fresh Fruit

Components

Vanilla ice cream

Whipped cream

Crisp, baked meringues (p. 260) made in the shape of whipped cream rosettes

Mixture of diced fresh fruit (such as kiwi, strawberries, mango, papaya, melon, apple, pear)

Chocolate Sauce (p. 195)

■ P r o c e d u r e

1. Place a scoop of ice cream in the center of a dish.

2. Surround the ice cream with crisp meringues alternating with rosettes of whipped cream, piped so that the whipped cream rosettes look just like the meringues.

3. Spoon the fruit mixture over the dessert.

4. Serve the chocolate sauce in a small pitcher on the side.

Cornucopia of Fresh Fruit with Lemon Ice Cream

Components

Florentine batter (p. 421)

Whipped cream flavored with orange liqueur

Raspberry Sauce (p. 196)

Assorted fresh fruit

Lemon Ice Cream (p. 467)

■ P r o c e d u r e

1. Prepare florentines as directed in the recipe, but while the baked cookies are still hot and pliable, bend them into cones.

2. Fill a florentine cone two-thirds full of the flavored whipped cream. Place it on a plate so that the point of the cone is at the back rim of the plate and the open end is near the center. (To keep it from rolling, stick it in place with a dab of whipped cream.)

3. Spoon the raspberry sauce onto the plate so that it appears to have spilled out of the cone and spread across the front of the plate.

4. Arrange a colorful assortment of fresh fruit on top of the sauce, so that it appears to have spilled out of the cone.

5. Place an oval spoonful of lemon ice cream on each side of the cone.

Variations

In place of the florentine horn, use tulipe or almond tuile cookies bent into cones, or puff pastry horns.

French Doughnuts, Presentation 1

Components

3 French Doughnuts, fried by method 1 (p. 160)

2-2½ oz (70 g) Praline Cream II (p. 450)

3 oz (90 g) Apricot and Almond Compote (p. 504)

Crushed Nougatine (p. 562)

Red currants

Sugar spirals (p. 569)

Mint sprig

■ Procedure

1. On one side of a plate, arrange three doughnuts alternating with two quenelles of praline cream.

2. Place the Apricot and Almond Compote on the other side of the plate.

3. Garnish with a few pieces of nougatine and the currants, sugar spirals, and mint sprig.

French Doughnuts, Presentation 2

Components

2 French Doughnuts, fried by method 2 (p. 160)

Confectioners' sugar

2 oz (60 g) Coconut Sorbet (p. 471)

Toasted coconut

Blanched pineapple leaves (*optional*)

2½-3 oz (80 g) Pineapple Kumquat Compote (p. 505)

Pistachios

Red currants

■ Procedure

1. Dust the doughnuts lightly with confectioners' sugar.

2. Place one doughnut on one side of a plate. Top with a scoop of sorbet and then with the second doughnut.

3. Sprinkle a little toasted coconut around the doughnuts and, if desired, decorate with three blanched pineapple leaves.

4. Place the Pineapple Kumquat Compote on the other side of the plate and decorate with a few pistachios and red currants.

Pear Pecan Tart, Chocolate Ganache Torte, and Raspberry Sorbet

Components

Pastry for pear tart (see step 1)

Caramel Sauce (p. 196)

Chopped pecans

Caramelized pear half (p. 493)

Apricot glaze (p. 117)

Chocolate genoise, dessert syrup, and
  ganache for Chocolate Ganache Torte
  (p. 375; see procedure for assembly)

Tulipe (p. 418)

Raspberry sorbet

■ P r o c e d u r e

1. *Prepare the pastry for the tart:* Bake a thin, round disk of pastry about 2½–3 inches (7 cm) in diameter, using puff pastry, phyllo pastry, short dough, or enriched pie pastry, as desired.

2. Brush or spread the baked pastry with a thin layer of caramel sauce. Sprinkle with chopped pecans. Slice a caramelized pear half and fan it out on the pastry base. Brush the top with apricot glaze.

3. Prepare a Chocolate Ganache Torte as a sheet cake, but without the meringue layer and buttercream; you will have an uniced cake consisting of three thin layers of chocolate genoise, flavored with rum or vanilla syrup, and two layers of ganache. Cut the cake into 2-in. (5 cm) squares, then cut each square in half diagonally to make two triangles. If desired, dust the top of the cake with confectioners' sugar.

4. Place a spoonful of raspberry sorbet in a tulipe.

5. Arrange a tart, a cake triangle, and a sorbet-filled tulipe on a plate.

Winter Dessert Medley with Frozen Banana and Chocolate Mousse Cake

Components

Crisp meringue, chocolate meringue, or japonaise disks
  to fit inside 7-in. (18 cm) cake pan or springform pan

Frozen Banana Mousse mixture (p. 478)

Bananas

Frozen Chocolate Mousse mixture (p. 478)

Orange Bavarian (p. 441) prepared in 2-oz (60 mL) molds

Whipped cream

Raspberry sauce (p. 196)

Segments (free of membranes) from small, sweet orange,
  blood orange, or tangerine

■ P r o c e d u r e

1. *Prepare the frozen mousse cake:* Place one meringue disk in the bottom of a 7-in. (18 cm) cake pan. Add a layer ½ in. (12 mm) thick of the banana mousse mixture. Cut bananas in half lengthwise and again crosswise. Arrange them at intervals (that is, not touching each other) in the pan and push them down into the mousse. Add a layer about ¾ in. (2 cm) thick of chocolate mousse mixture. Top with another meringue disk and press down gently. Freeze.

2. Unmold the mousse cake and cut into wedges. Place a wedge on one side of a plate.

3. Unmold an orange Bavarian and place on the plate, leaving at least one third of the plate empty. Decorate the Bavarian with whipped cream.

4. Ladle a pool of raspberry sauce onto the remaining space on the plate. Arrange orange segments in a star pattern on top of the sauce.

Spiced Pineapple with Coconut Sorbet and Coconut Tuile

Components

Spiced Pineapple (p. 502)

Coconut Tuile (p. 420), shaped as a cup or tulipe

Coconut Sorbet (p. 471)

Pistachios

Pine nuts

Red currants, dusted with confectioners' sugar

Toasted coconut

■ P r o c e d u r e

1. Rewarm the pineapple if it was prepared in advance, and finish the sauce with the cream as in the basic recipe. Strain it, reserving the spices. Slice the pineapple and arrange the slices on one side of a plate. Pour the sauce over the pineapple.

2. Place a coconut tuile cup on the other side of the plate. Place one or more scoops of coconut sorbet in the tuile.

3. Garnish the plate with some of the spices from the sauce, and garnish the pineapple with a few pistachios and pine nuts.

4. Decorate the sorbet with a small cluster of red currants.

5. Finish the plate by sprinkling with a little toasted coconut.

Figs in Port Wine with Honey Ice Cream and Sesame Tuile

Components

Figs in Port Wine (p. 499)

Sesame Tuile (p. 419)

Honey Ice Cream (p. 470)

Caramelized almonds

Mint sprig

■ P r o c e d u r e

1. If the figs were prepared ahead of time, re-heat them in the oven with the syrup.

2. Spoon the syrup onto a plate.

3. Stand a sesame tuile on its side on the plate.

4. In the broad curve of the tuile, arrange three or four fig halves.

5. On the other side of the tuile, place a scoop of honey ice cream. (Optionally, pipe the ice cream using a star tip, as in the illustration.)

6. Place a few caramelized almonds in front of the figs.

7. Garnish the ice cream with a sprig of mint.

 ## Passion Fruit Charlotte

Components

Passion Fruit Charlotte (p. 449)

Kumquat Compote (p. 505)

Red currants

Choux pastry lattice (p. 250)

Crème anglaise

Confectioners' sugar

■ P r o c e d u r e

1. Place a wedge of the charlotte toward the back of a plate.

2. Place a spoonful of Kumquat Compote in front of the char-lotte wedge and garnish with a few red currants or other small red berries to add color.

3. Prop a piece of choux pastry lattice in front of the compote so that it leans against the wedge of charlotte.

4. Spoon a little crème anglaise on the plate in a decorative fashion.

5. Dust the pastry lattice lightly with confectioners' sugar.

Caramel Medley

Components

Crème Brûlée (p. 432) in small dish

Tarte Tatin (p. 274)

Clear Caramel Sauce (p. 196)

Tulipe (p. 418)

Caramel Ice Cream (p. 467)

■ P r o c e d u r e

1. Place the Crème Brûlée on a dinner plate large enough so that only a third of the plate is covered.

2. Place a thin wedge of Tarte Tatin next to the Crème Brûlée.

3. In the remaining space on the plate, drizzle caramel sauce in a lattice pattern. Place a tulipe on the sauce, and place a scoop of Caramel Ice Cream in the tulipe.

Chocolate Medley

Components

Chocolate Mousse (p. 193)

Crisp chocolate meringue disk, 2 in. (5 cm) in diameter

Chocolate shavings

Chocolate Ice Cream (pp. 467, 470) or Chocolate Sorbet (p. 469)

Tulipe (p. 418) or Almond Tuile (p. 418)

Raspberries

White Chocolate Bavarian (p. 441) prepared in 2-oz (60 mL) mold

Tempered chocolate

Chocolate Sauce (p. 195)

Chocolate Ganache (p. 192), soft but not whipped

Crème Anglaise

■ P r o c e d u r e

This dessert consists of five separate elements—in small quantities—arranged on a large plate:

1. Chocolate mousse, piped in a mound onto a chocolate meringue disk, coated with chocolate shavings

2. Chocolate ice cream or sorbet in a tulipe or tuile, garnished with a few raspberries placed next to the ice cream

3. White chocolate Bavarian on a pool of chocolate sauce. Decorate the top of the Bavarian with a piped chocolate decoration (see p. 543).

4. A quenelle of chocolate ganache

5. A pool of crème anglaise marbled with chocolate sauce. (This is a separate element on the plate, with nothing placed on it.)

▶ TERMS FOR REVIEW

simple presentation   complex presentation   garnish   quenelle

▶ QUESTIONS FOR REVIEW

1. What are the four basic ways in which a single portion of a single dessert can be presented on a plate?

2. What is a quenelle of ice cream? Describe how to make it.

3. Name four types of items that can be used as garnish for a dessert.

4. Describe how to marble or feather a sauce.

20
Chocolate

*C*hocolate is not only one of the world's most popular confections, it is also a wonderful medium for decorative work, ranging from simple garnishes for desserts to elaborate showpieces. Many pastry chefs make a specialty of chocolate work and become well known for their imaginative and skillful pieces.

Because of its composition, chocolate is difficult to work with. It is sensitive to temperature and moisture. Melting and cooling must be done with accurate temperature control. Unless a liquid is to be added for any reason, chocolate must be protected from moisture. A single drop of water will ruin its texture and make it unusable for dipping or molding.

This chapter provides an introduction to fine chocolate work. The fundamentals of handling chocolate are discussed, followed by procedures for simple decorative work and molding. A brief look at chocolate confections closes the chapter.

HANDLING CHOCOLATE

After reading this chapter, you should be able to:

■ Temper chocolate couverture.

■ Use tempered chocolate for dipping and molding.

■ Produce a variety of chocolate decorations.

■ Make chocolate truffles.

Chocolate is produced from the seeds of a tropical tree called the *cocoa* or *cacao* tree. As with coffee, the quality of cocoa is sensitive to growing conditions, so cocoa from the best growing regions commands the highest prices. Cocoa trees produce large pods full of seeds called *cocoa beans.* After the pods are harvested, the beans are quickly removed and allowed to ferment until they lose most of their moisture. There are several ways of doing this, but the traditional method is to spread them between layers of banana leaves and leave them for several days, turning them often so that they ferment evenly.

The chemical changes that take place during fermentation turn the beans from yellowish to brown and begin to develop the flavor. The fermented beans are next dried in the open air, because they still contain a great deal of moisture. The dried beans are now ready to be shipped to processors.

Cocoa processors clean the dried beans thoroughly and then roast them. The true flavor of the cocoa develops during roasting, and the temperature and degree of roasting are important factors in the quality of the finished chocolate. After roasting, the beans are cracked and the shells are removed. The broken particles of cocoa that result are called *nibs.* Nibs contain more than 50% fat, in the form of cocoa butter, and very little moisture.

Grinding the nibs produces a paste and releases the cocoa butter from inside the cell walls. This paste is called *chocolate liquor* and is the basis of chocolate production. When chocolate liquor cools, it sets into a hard block.

The next stage of manufacturing is to separate the cocoa powder from the cocoa butter. This is done with powerful hydraulic presses that squeeze out the melted fat, leaving hard cakes that are then ground into cocoa powder. Meanwhile, the cocoa butter is purified to remove odor and color.

To manufacture chocolate, the cocoa powder is blended with sugar and, in the case of milk chocolate, milk solids. These ingredients are ground and blended together. At this point comes the critical procedure called *conching.* This is a two-stage process that first removes additional moisture and refines the flavor. During the second stage of conching, cocoa butter is added back and the liquid mass is ground and mixed for hours or even days to develop a fine, smooth texture. In general, higher-quality, more expensive chocolates derive their superior texture from longer conching. Finally, the liquid chocolate is tempered, as explained below, and molded into blocks for sale as couverture.

COUVERTURE

The basic types of chocolate are introduced in chapter 2. Please review pages 42–45 and, in particular, note the difference between *couverture* and *coating chocolate* or *baking chocolate.* Genuine couverture contains cocoa butter and no other fat. Coating chocolate is chocolate that had part or most of the cocoa butter replaced with other fats in order to make it easier to handle and in order to reduce the cost. In this chapter, we are concerned entirely with couverture, also known as *confectioners' chocolate.*

There are three main ingredients of dark couverture:

* Cocoa solids
* Sugar
* Cocoa butter

In addition, it may also contain small quantities of vanilla (a flavoring) and lecithin (an emulsifier). On the packaging of a block of professional couverture, you may see a series of numbers such as the following: 65/35/38. The first two numbers refer to the ratio of cocoa solids to sugar—in this case, 65% cocoa solids to 35% sugar. The last number is the total fat content (38% in the example) and indicates the viscosity or thickness of the chocolate. The higher the fat content, the thinner the chocolate will be when melted. Couverture must contain at least 31% cocoa butter.

The quantities of cocoa solids and sugar determine whether the couverture is referred to as semisweet, bitter, or extra bitter. The higher the percentage of cocoa solids, the lower the sugar content will be. Semisweet chocolate couverture contains 50–60% cocoa solids. Chocolates with more cocoa solids (and, therefore, less sugar) are called bitter and extra-bitter. The highest practical percentage of cocoa is 75–76%.

Milk chocolate couverture contains milk solids in addition to cocoa solids and sugar. It usually contains about 36% cocoa solids and no more than 55% sugar. *White couverture* cannot be called chocolate because it contains no cocoa solids, only cocoa butter, sugar, milk solids, and flavoring.

In this chapter, the term *couverture,* when used by itself, always refers to dark chocolate. Milk chocolate couverture or white couverture is specified if those types are intended.

TEMPERING

For most chocolate work, couverture will not handle properly if simply melted. It will take too long to set, and when it does set, it will not have the desired shine or the proper texture. The process of preparing couverture for dipping, coating, molding, and other purposes is called *tempering.*

The reason for tempering can be explained as follows: Cocoa butter consists of several fats. Some of these melt at low temperatures and others melt at high temperatures. The fats that melt at high temperatures are, of course, the first ones to solidify as the melted chocolate is cooled. These high-melt-point fats give high-quality chocolate its shine and its snap (high-quality chocolate that has been properly tempered and cooled breaks with a clean, sharp snap). The objective of tempering is to create a very fine fat-crystal structure in the chocolate. In a melted, tempered chocolate, the high-melt-point fats have begun to solidify into fine crystals that are distributed throughout the melted chocolate. When the chocolate is left to cool, the chocolate sets or solidifies quickly because the fine crystals act as seeds around which the rest of the chocolate crystallizes.

To summarize, tempered chocolate sets quickly and has a good texture and shine. Melted, untempered chocolate takes a long time to set. Its texture will not be as good. Its surface will be cloudy because some of the cocoa butter floats to the surface and makes a whitish coating called *bloom.*

The actual process of melting and tempering chocolate consists of three steps. The proper temperatures for each of these three stages depend on the type of chocolate and its exact composition. The table on page 536 indicates the range of temperatures appropriate to the basic chocolate types. The manufacturer or the supplier should be able to indicate the exact temperatures that are best for each of its products.

1. ***Melting*** The chocolate is placed in a pan or bowl and set over hot water to melt. It should not be set over direct heat because the chocolate is easily burned, which destroys both the texture and the flavor. Stir constantly while the chocolate is melting.

The chocolate must be brought to a temperature high enough to completely melt all the fats, including the high-melt-point fats. Refer to the table below.

2. *Tempering (cooling or precrystallizing)* When the chocolate is melted, it is removed from the heat. All or part of the chocolate is then cooled until it is thick and pasty. At this point, fine fat crystals have formed.

3. *Rewarming* At this point, the chocolate is too thick for dipping, molding, or most other uses and must be warmed slightly before it is ready to be used. Set it over warm water and stir it until it is the proper temperature and thickness to be used.

This step must be done carefully. Do not let the chocolate get warmer than the recommended temperature. If this happens, too many of the fat crystals melt and the chocolate is no longer tempered, making it necessary to repeat the whole procedure. If the chocolate is too thick at the proper temperature, thin it with a little melted cocoa butter. Do not thin it by heating it.

Critical Temperatures for Tempering Chocolate

Proces	Dark Chocolate Couverture	Milk Chocolate and White Couverture
Melting	122°–131°F (50°–55°C)	113°–122°F (45°–50°C)
Tempering (cooling)	80°–84°F (27°–29°C)	78°–82°F (26°–28°C)
Rewarming	86°–89°F (30°–32°C)	84°–86°F (29°–30°C)

Manufacturers and large processors use precise thermostatically controlled equipment to automatically heat, cool, and rewarm the chocolate to the exact temperatures required. In the pastry shop, however, two other methods are used for tempering small quantities of couverture. The first method below is quick to do and is, perhaps, the most popular.

Tools for Chocolate
Clockwise from top left, grooved scraper, wood-grain tool, molds for truffles and small chocolates, dipping forks, plastic mat for textured cutouts, cotton wool for polishing molds and acetate, and inexpensive molds for larger pieces.

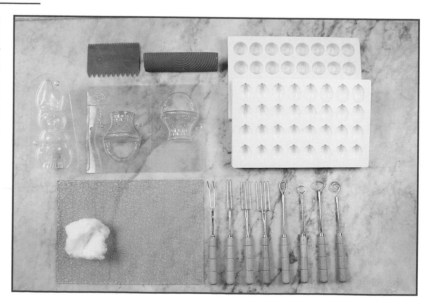

Procedures for Tempering Chocolate

Method 1: Tablage

1. In all stages of this procedure, do not let even a trace of moisture come in contact with the chocolate.

2. With a heavy knife, chop the chocolate into small pieces. Place the pieces in a dry stainless-steel bowl.

3. Set the bowl in a pan of warm water. Stir the chocolate constantly so that it melts uniformly.

4. Continue stirring until the chocolate is completely melted and reaches the proper temperature, as indicated in the table on page 536.

5. Remove the bowl from the water bath. Wipe all traces of moisture from the bottom of the bowl to avoid contaminating the chocolate.

6. Pour about two-thirds of the chocolate onto a marble slab (a). With a metal scraper and a spatula, spread out the chocolate and quickly scrape it back together, continuing to mix the chocolate so that it cools uniformly (b).

7. When the chocolate cools to the proper temperature (78°–84°F or 26°–29°C, as indicated in the table on page 536), it will become thick and pasty. Quickly scrape it back into the bowl with the remaining melted chocolate (c).

8. Mix and reheat the chocolate over hot water to the proper rewarming temperature (84°–89°F or 29°–32°C, depending on the chocolate). Do not warm it above the recommended temperature. The chocolate is now ready for use.

Procedure variation

Instead of working the chocolate on a marble slab in step 6, some chefs prefer to set the entire bowl over ice water and stir until the chocolate cools to the proper temperature. Then they rewarm the chocolate as in step 8. This method may not produce chocolate with as good a temper, and it adds the risk of getting water in the chocolate. However, it has the advantage of speed.

Method 2: Seeding or Injection

1. Chop the chocolate to be melted into small pieces as in method 1.

2. Cut fine shreds or shavings from a block of tempered chocolate and set them aside.

3. Melt the chopped chocolate as in method 1.

4. Remove the melted chocolate from the water bath. Stir in some of the shaved chocolate.

5. When these shavings are nearly all melted, add a few more shavings. Continue adding and stirring until the melted chocolate is cooked down to the proper tempering point and all the added shavings are melted. Do not add the shavings too fast or they may not all melt.

6. Rewarm the chocolate as in method 1.

a.

b.

c.

Once the chocolate is tempered, it is ready for molding, dipping, and other uses. The following sections describe procedures for a variety of chocolate work.

For all work with tempered chocolate, the work area should be at a temperature between 65° and 77°F (18° and 25°C). If it is colder, the chocolate will set up too quickly and will be difficult to handle. If warmer, the chocolate will take too long to set; in addition, the marble slab will be too warm for some techniques to work.

MOLDING CHOCOLATE

Molding is made possible by the fact that chocolate contracts when it sets. Thus, it pulls away from the mold and can be easily removed. Molds are made of metal or plastic. They must be kept clean and dry, and the insides must be kept shiny and free of scratches. If they are scratched, chocolate will stick to them.

To be sure that the molds are completely clean and smooth, hold them briefly over steam, then polish the inside surfaces with cotton wool. Be sure that they are completely dry before proceeding to mold the chocolate.

Procedures for molding chocolate truffles and other candies are covered in the last part of this chapter. The following discussion deals with molding decorative chocolates as well as display pieces.

Molding chocolate eggs is one of the simpler molding procedures; it also illustrates the techniques used in other types of molds. The following procedures explain in detail how to mold eggs. Next is a more general discussion of other types of molds and how to use them.

These procedures explain molding single-color chocolates. You can also use two contrasting colors of chocolate for decorative effects. This is done by decorating the inside of the mold with one color and then coating it with another color. Use the same techniques as described in the discussion of chocolate cutouts, below.

Two-part molds are used to make hollow chocolate items. There are two kinds: completely enclosed molds and molds with open bottoms. The first step for using either kind of mold is to paint the inside surfaces with a thin layer of tempered chocolate, using a soft brush. This step is frequently omitted, but it is recommended because it eliminates small air bubbles that might otherwise mar the surface of the chocolate. When the chocolate is set but not hard, continue with one of the following procedures.

To use two-part molds with open bottoms, clip the two parts together. Pour tempered chocolate into the opening until the mold is nearly full. Tap the mold with a wooden stick to release air bubbles. After a few moments, invert the mold over the chocolate pot and pour out the chocolate, leaving a layer of chocolate coating the mold. Set the mold, open-end down, on a sheet of parchment. Additional melted chocolate will run down the inside and seal the open end. Leave the filled mold in a cool place until set, then open it and remove the chocolate.

If you are using plastic molds, you can easily see when the chocolate has set and pulled away from the mold. With metal molds, however, you just have to let the molds stand long enough until you are certain the chocolate is set.

To use enclosed molds, pour enough tempered chocolate into one half of the mold to completely coat the insides of both halves. Place the second half of the mold on top and clip it in place. Turn the mold over and over so that the inside is completely coated with chocolate. Tap the mold several times while rotating it in order to release air bubbles. Let the chocolate stand until set, then unmold.

Procedures for Molding Chocolate Eggs

Method 1

1. Polish the insides of the molds with cotton wool.

2. Using a clean, dry brush, brush the inside of the mold with tempered chocolate. Be sure to cover the inside of the mold completely with an even layer.

3. Let the mold stand until the chocolate is partially set. It should be firm but not hard.

4. Using a metal scraper, scrape off the excess chocolate from the top of the mold, so that the half egg has a smooth, sharp edge.

5. Let stand in a cool place until the chocolate is completely set and hard.

6. Turn the mold over and tap it gently to unmold the egg.

7. To avoid getting fingerprints on the shiny surface of the unmolded chocolate, handle it with disposable plastic gloves.

8. To glue two halves together to make a whole, hollow egg, use one of two methods:

    Using a paper cone filled with tempered chocolate, pipe a fine line of chocolate onto the edge of one of the halves, then press the two halves together.

    Place one of the halves open-side down on a warm baking sheet for just an instant to melt the edge slightly, then fasten the two halves together.

9. Use the point of a small knife to trim excess chocolate from the seam.

Method 2

1. Polish the inside of the molds with cotton wool.

2. Fill the mold with tempered chocolate until it runs over the top.

3. Invert the chocolate over the container of tempered chocolate to dump out the chocolate, leaving a coating on the insides of the molds.

4. Prop the molds upside down over two sticks set on a sheet of parchment or clean sheet pan to allow the excess to drip out.

5. Continue with step 3 of method 1.

CHOCOLATE DECORATIONS

Tempered chocolate can be used to make a variety of decorations for cakes, pastries, and other items. The most popular of these are described here.

Mix dark and white couverture very lightly to marble, and spread onto acetate.

When the chocolate clouds over and is set but not hard, cut out desired shapes with a sharp knife or cutter.

Broken pieces of dark chocolate streaked with white and cutouts of marbled white and milk chocolate

CHOCOLATE CUTOUTS

Polish a sheet of acetate with cotton wool. Pour tempered chocolate onto the acetate and spread into a thin layer with a palette knife. Let the chocolate stand until it clouds over and becomes firm but not hard. Cut with a small, sharp knife, cutting straight through to the acetate, or use a metal cutter, slightly warmed, to cut out desired shapes. Do not attempt to remove the cutouts at this point. Let stand until the chocolate is hard and the acetate peels away easily from the chocolate.

For decorative effects, the acetate can be coated with two colors of chocolate, making attractive patterns. The following are some of the easiest and most popular techniques:

1. Flick or spatter streaks of one color of chocolate—for example, white couverture. Let the chocolate set, and then coat the acetate with a contrasting color of chocolate.

2. With a paper cone, pipe a latticework design of fine stripes with one color of chocolate. Let the chocolate set, and then coat the acetate with a contrasting color.

3. With a paper cone, pipe large dots of chocolate at regular intervals. Let the chocolate set, and then coat the acetate with a contrasting color.

4. Spread with one color of chocolate, then scrape with a comb scraper, using the same technique as for ribbon sponge (p. 323). Then cover with another color.

5. Brush the inside of the mold very lightly with one color of chocolate so that it is coated only in streaks or splotches. Let the chocolate set, and then coat the acetate with a contrasting color.

6. To marble chocolate, add a little tempered white couverture to tempered dark couverture and mix just until the white shows streaks against the dark (top left). Then coat the acetate.

CHOCOLATE STRIPS

Strips of acetate can be coated with decorative chocolate in the same way as sheets. Strips have many uses, such as ribbons and bows for show pieces (p. 541) and liners for charlotte molds. The procedure for coating a strip of acetate with tempered chocolate is similar to coating a large sheet, as described above. Use a palette knife to spread the chocolate in an even layer to cover the strip. Then carefully lift the strip and run your fingers along the edges of the strip to remove excess chocolate and make a neat, straight edge.

Chocolate strips may be decorated with patterns of chocolate in two colors, using the same techniques as above. An additional technique, which creates a pattern with the appearance of wood grain, requires a special tool shown on page 536.

a.

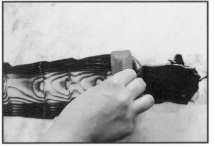

b.

c.

d.

1. Drizzle a little tempered dark chocolate onto an acetate strip and, with a palette knife, spread it into a thin layer covering the strip (a).

2. Scrape the wood-grain tool down the length of the strip, rocking it back and forth to make the grain pattern (b). Let stand a few minutes to allow the chocolate to set.

3. Spread the strip with a layer of tempered white couverture (c).

4. Lift the acetate strip and run your fingers along both edges to remove excess chocolate (d).

5. The acetate side of the strip shows the pattern (e).

6. Fit the strip into a ring mold and allow it to set (f). This mold is to be used to make a Julianna cake (p. 383). For a freestanding chocolate ring, such as the one used for the candy box on page 539, spread the chocolate more thickly so that the ring will be sturdier.

Chocolate Bows

For chocolate bows, cut strips of acetate to the desired size. Spread with tempered chocolate, either in a single color or in a pattern of two colors. Allow the chocolate to cloud and partially set, then bend into a teardrop shape and fasten the ends together with a paper clip. If necessary, pipe a little tempered chocolate with a paper cone into the joint between the ends of the chocolate in order to strengthen the seam. Let set until hardened.

Peel the acetate from the bows after they are completely set. Cut the ends to points so that they will fit together on the box (a). To hold the bows in place, pipe a little tempered chocolate with a paper cone (b). Fit the bow in place. Hold steady until the chocolate sets (c).

Chocolate strips made into teardrops (like bows, but larger) are used for plating presentations of desserts such as chocolate mousse. Place the teardrop on the plate and fill with mousse using a pastry bag.

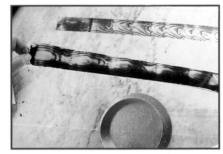

e.

f.

a.

b.

c.

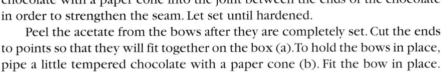
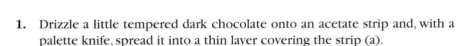

CHOCOLATE CIGARETTES AND CURLS

Melted chocolate can be used for these decorations. Tempered chocolate may also be used but is not necessary. For cigarettes, spread the chocolate in a long strip on a slab of marble. Allow the chocolate to set. It should be completely set but not hard and brittle. If it becomes too hard, warm it slightly by rubbing it with the palm of the hand. Hold a metal scraper and push it forward so that the chocolate curls up ahead of the metal edge (a).

For curls and shavings, score the strip of chocolate with the point of a knife (b) and then scrape up the curls with the knife (c).

a.

b.

c.

CHOCOLATE STRIPS AND FANS

Chocolate strips are used for coating cakes and pastries (see Pralinette, p. 287, and Feuille d'Automne, p. 377). Chocolate fans are used as decorations for various cakes and pastries. As in the case of chocolate strips, chocolate does not have to be tempered for this procedure. Melted, untempered chocolate may be used.

Heat a clean half-size sheet pan at 325°F (160°C) for 4 minutes. The tray should be warm but not too hot to handle. (The purpose of warming the pan is to enable you to spread a thinner coat of chocolate; be careful, however, not to get the pan too hot. Some chefs prefer to use cold trays.) Turn the sheet upside down and spread melted chocolate in a thin, even layer on the bottom of the pan. Let stand until the chocolate looks cloudy, then refrigerate until set. Remove from the refrigerator and let warm to room temperature.

To make chocolate strips, push the scraper against the tray and, with the other hand, lift off the strip of chocolate as it is released by the scraper (a). Handle the strip of chocolate very lightly (b). After coating the sides of the cake, make more strips for the top (c). Arrange the strips on the top (d). Finish the cake with coiled strips, touching them as little as possible to prevent melting (e). (The cake pictured here is a Feuille d'Automne.)

a.

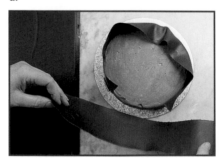

b.

c.

d.

e.

To make chocolate fans, scrape the chocolate as for strips, except hold your thumb against one corner of the scraper so that the strip bunches or gathers on one side (a). Carefully neaten the ruffles or folds of the fan as necessary (b).

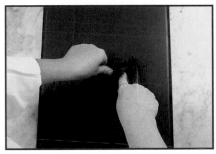

a.

b.

PIPING CHOCOLATE

With the use of a paper cone as described in chapter 13, tempered chocolate can be used to make decorations for cakes, pastries, and other desserts. It can be piped directly onto the dessert or piped onto parchment paper in small designs and left to harden. After they are set, the decorations can be removed from the paper and placed on the desserts. In this way, decorations can be made during slack hours and stored until needed.

Ordinary tempered chocolate is adequate for small, fine decorations, such as those for petits fours (see p. 253), but it is too thin for most other piped decorations. To make piping chocolate, add a very little warm simple syrup to the tempered chocolate. This will thicken the chocolate immediately. Stirring constantly, add more syrup very slowly until the chocolate is thinned out to piping consistency.

MODELING CHOCOLATE

Modeling chocolate is a thick paste that can be molded by hand to make a variety of shapes, just as you might use marzipan. Simply combine melted chocolate with half its weight of glucose (corn syrup) that has been warmed to the temperature of the chocolate. Mix them together well. Place them in an airtight container and let stand for an hour or more. Knead the mixture until it forms a workable paste.

SPRAYING CHOCOLATE

A standard paint sprayer can be used to spray liquid chocolate. The sprayed chocolate creates a velvety coating on cakes, pastries, and showpieces.

In order to thin the chocolate enough to pass through the sprayer, thin it with melted cocoa butter. It is not possible to give exact quantities, as the cocoa butter content of couverture varies considerably.

A chocolate sprayer being used to stencil a pattern on a dessert

CHOCOLATE TRUFFLES AND CONFECTIONS

Chocolate truffles get their name because of their resemblance to black truffles, the aromatic underground fungus that is prized by gourmets.

In their simplest form, chocolate truffles are simply balls of chocolate ganache, the thick mixture of chocolate and cream that was introduced in chapter 8. Ganache can be made not only with dark chocolate but also milk chocolate and white couverture. Many flavorings and other ingredients can also be added to create a variety of confections. Review the discussion of ganache on page 192.

The simplest way of finishing truffles, and one of the most popular, is simply to coat the balls of ganache with cocoa powder. This technique is used in the first recipe in this section, Dark Chocolate Truffles.

For more elaborate presentations, the truffles may be coated with chocolate by dipping or molding.

DIPPING CHOCOLATES

For candy makers, the techniques for dipping and molding candies are basic. There are two basic procedures for dipping small items such as truffles, other candy centers, and nuts.

For the first method, place the items one at a time on the surface of the tempered chocolate. With a dipping fork, turn them over to cover them completely, then lift them out. Tap the fork holding the chocolate on the edge of the bowl to even the coating. Draw the fork holding the coated chocolate over the edge of the bowl to wipe off excess chocolate from the bottom of the fork, then set the item on a sheet of parchment. To mark the chocolate, touch the top of the item lightly with the dipping fork. Each kind of fork will leave its own distinctive pattern, so you can mark different flavors with different patterns. Let stand until hardened.

The second dipping method is hand-dipping. To hand-dip plain truffles, pipe bulbs of ganache onto a parchment sheet (a). Using plastic gloves, hand-roll the truffles with a little cornstarch to round them (b). Still wearing plastic gloves, coat the truffles with a thin layer of tempered chocolate by hand-rolling them in tempered chocolate (c). Drop into a bowl of cocoa powder (d).

a.

b.

c.

d.

MOLDING CHOCOLATES

Small molds for individual candies are lined with chocolate using the same techniques as for larger molds, as discussed on page 539. Either of the two methods above may be used. The procedure described here is an example of the first method. It shows how to make white couverture molds decorated with dark chocolate brush strokes. Other decorative techniques, as described on page 540, can be applied to this molding method as well.

First prepare the molds by holding them over steam, then brushing with cotton wool to make sure they are clean, smooth, and dry (a). Brush the insides lightly with tempered dark couverture to create a marbled or stippled effect (b). Coat with tempered white couverture (c). Let set. Repeat this step to make a thicker coating, if desired. After each layer, it is essential to remove excess chocolate by scraping the flat top of the mold with a metal scraper. This should be done before the chocolate becomes too hard. Failure to do this will mar the appearance of the finished chocolates and may make it impossible to seal them properly.

Pipe in the ganache filling (d). Do not fill the molds too full, and do not get any filling on the top edge of the chocolate. Doing so will make it impossible to seal the candies with the final layer of chocolate.

With a paper cone, cover with tempered couverture (e). Scrape off excess chocolate (f). If the filling is soft, it is necessary to use the paper cone for this step. For firmer fillings, scrape a layer of tempered couverture back and forth over the top of the mold until the chocolates are sealed.

To unmold the candies, turn the mold over onto a sheet of parchment. Most of them should fall out easily. If necessary, tap the mold lightly on the work surface to release remaining chocolates.

a.

b.

c.

d.

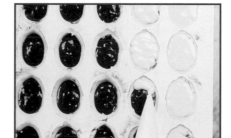

e.

f.

Dark Chocolate Truffles

Yield: about 75 truffles, ⅓ oz (10 g) each

Ingredients	U.S.	Metric
Ganache		
Heavy cream	7 oz	225 g
Vanilla extract	½ tsp	2.5 g
Dark chocolate couverture, chopped	1 lb	500 g
Butter	2 oz	60 g
Coating		
Cocoa powder	as needed	as needed

■ P r o c e d u r e

1. Heat the cream and vanilla to a simmer.
2. Pour over the chopped chocolate in a bowl. Stir until the chocolate is completely melted and blended in. Cool the mixture until it is just slightly warm to the touch.
3. Stir in the butter until it is melted and completely blended in.
4. Let the mixture stand until it starts to thicken, then put it in a pastry bag fitted with a medium plain tip.
5. Pipe the mixture into small mounds about 2 teaspoons (10 mL) each on sheets of parchment paper. Chill until firm.
6. One by one, roll between the palms of the hands to round the pieces of ganache; drop them into a bowl of cocoa powder.
7. Remove the truffles from the cocoa and shake in a sieve to remove excess cocoa.

Banana Truffles

Yield: about 120 truffles, ⅓ oz (9 g) each

Ingredients	U.S.		Metric
Ganache centers			
Banana pulp	5	oz	150 g
Rum	4	tsp	20 g
Heavy cream	3.33	oz	100 g
Butter	4	tsp	20 g
Honey	3.33	oz	100 g
Milk chocolate couverture	4	oz	125 g
Dark chocolate couverture	3.33	oz	100 g
Coating			
Dark chocolate couverture, tempered	7	oz	200 g
White couverture, tempered	1 lb 5	oz	600 g

Note The quantity of chocolate needed for the coating is approximate. Because you need enough for the molding procedure, you must temper more chocolate than will actually be used up.

■ P r o c e d u r e

1. Mash the bananas with the rum until smooth.
2. Heat the cream, butter, and honey to the boiling point. Remove from heat.
3. Melt the milk and dark chocolates and stir into the cream mixture.
4. Mix in the bananas. Let stand until completely cold.
5. Prepare polycarbonate molds by holding them over steam and polishing with cotton wool.
6. Brush the inside of the molds very lightly with tempered dark chocolate, allow to set, and then brush with white couverture to give a marbled effect. Scrape the top surface level. (If desired, brush a second time with white couverture for a thicker coating.)
7. Put the ganache mixture into a piping bag with a small plain tip and fill the molds three-quarters full.
8. Seal the molds by piping additional white chocolate over the filling, using a paper cone. Scrape off excess chocolate and chill before unmolding.

Orange Truffles

Yield: about 125 truffles, ⅓ oz (9 g) each

Ingredients	U.S.		Metric
Heavy cream	4	oz	120 g
Orange juice, strained	1	oz	30 g
Orange liqueur	3	oz	90 g
Butter	2	oz	60 g
Egg yolks	1.67	oz	50 g
Sugar	1.67	oz	50 g
Dark chocolate, chopped	7	oz	215 g
Coating			
Dark chocolate couverture, tempered	1 lb 4	oz	600 g

Note The quantity of chocolate needed for the coating is approximate. Because you need enough for the molding procedure, you must temper more chocolate than will actually be used up.

■ P r o c e d u r e

1. Combine the cream, juice, liqueur, and butter in a saucepan and bring to a boil.

2. Whip the egg yolks with the sugar until light.

3. Gradually beat the hot liquid into the egg mixture.

4. Return this mixture to the heat and bring quickly to a boil, then remove from heat.

5. Strain the liquid over the chopped chocolate in a bowl. Stir until all the chocolate is melted and the mixture is evenly blended.

6. Let the mixture stand until it starts to thicken. This may take an hour or longer, depending on the room temperature. If necessary, the mixture can be chilled briefly, but do not let it become too hard. Then put it in a pastry bag fitted with a medium plain tip.

7. Pipe the mixture into small mounds about 2 teaspoons (10 mL) each on sheets of parchment paper. Chill until firm.

8. One by one, roll between the palms of the hands to round the pieces of ganache. Place them back onto the parchment.

9. Coat the truffles in one of two ways:

   Drop them a few at a time in a bowl of tempered chocolate, then remove with a dipping fork and place on a parchment-lined tray.

   Roll in tempered chocolate in the palms of the hands while wearing disposable plastic gloves, as shown on page 544, then place on a parchment-lined tray.

Let stand until the chocolate is completely set.

Rocher with Almonds

For large-quantity measurements, see page 614.

Ingredients	U.S.	Metric
Dark chocolate	4 oz	100 g
Praline paste	6 oz	150 g
Ice cream wafers (pailletine), finely crushed	2 oz	50 g
Dark chocolate	6 oz	150 g
Almonds, toasted and chopped	1 oz	25 g
Total weight:	*1 lb 3 oz*	*475 g*

■ P r o c e d u r e

1. Melt the first quantity of dark chocolate over a hot water bath.

2. Add the praline paste and mix quickly.

3. Add the crushed wafers and mix.

4. As soon as the mixture starts to thicken but before it starts to solidify, use a spoon to drop 1-tbsp (12 g) pieces onto a parchment-lined sheet pan. If desired, roll between palms to shape into balls.

5. Allow to set at room temperature for 2–3 hours.

6. Temper the remaining dark chocolate and add the chopped almonds.

7. Dip each ball into the tempered chocolate and retrieve using a chocolate fork.

8. Place onto a parchment-lined baking sheet and allow to harden.

Lemon Truffles

Yield: about 110 truffles, ½ oz (14 g) each

Ingredients	U.S.		Metric
Ganache centers			
Milk	4	oz	125 g
Heavy cream	4	oz	125 g
Glucose	1.67	oz	50 g
White couverture, chopped	1 lb		500 g
Lemon juice	3.25	oz	100 g
Coating			
White couverture, tempered	1 lb 10	oz	800 g

Note The quantity of chocolate needed for the coating is approximate. Because you need enough for the molding and dipping procedure, you must temper more chocolate than will actually be used up.

■ P r o c e d u r e

1. Heat the milk, cream, and glucose until the mixture is warm and the glucose is dissolved.

2. Add the white couverture and stir until it is melted and uniformly blended with the cream mixture.

3. Stir in the lemon juice.

4. Let the mixture cool completely. Place the ganache in a pastry bag fitted with a small, plain tip.

5. Prepare hemispherical polycarbonate truffle molds by holding them over steam and polishing with cotton wool.

6. Brush the insides of the molds with tempered white chocolate. Scrape off the top surface. Repeat if a thicker coating is desired. Let stand until the chocolate has hardened.

7. Fill to the top with the ganache filling. Unmold. For each truffle, stick two half-spheres together to make a round ball.

8. Dip in tempered white chocolate, remove with a dipping fork, and place on a wire rack. To create a textured surface, allow to set a few moments, then roll along the rack to give a spiked coating to the truffle. Allow to harden completely before removing from the rack.

Alternative procedure: Use ready-made chocolate shells. Fill them using a pastry bag with a small plain tip and seal the opening by covering it with tempered couverture using a paper cone. Dip as in the basic procedure above.

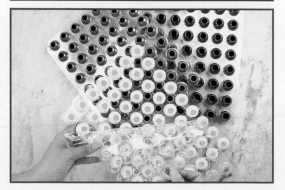

Muscadines

Yield: about 45 truffles, ⅓ oz (10 g) each

Ingredients	U.S.		Metric
Ganache			
Milk chocolate couverture	6.75	oz	200 g
Praline paste	1	oz	30 g
Water, boiling	1	oz	30 g
Butter, softened	4	tsp	20 g
Orange liqueur, such as Cointreau	1	oz	30 g
Coating			
Confectioners' sugar	as needed		as needed
Milk chocolate couverture	8	oz	250 g
Cocoa butter, melted	3.25	oz	100 g

■ P r o c e d u r e

1. Melt the first quantity of chocolate and stir in the praline paste.

2. Add the water and stir until evenly mixed.

3. Mix in the butter and liqueur. Chill over an ice water bath until the mixture is thick enough to hold its shape.

4. Place in a piping bag with a large star tip (approximately ½ in./1 cm wide at the opening). Pipe long logs of the mixture onto a baking sheet lined with parchment paper. Cut the logs into 1½-in. (4 cm) lengths. Chill.

5. Sift confectioners' sugar onto a tray or sheet pan until it is about ½ in. (1 cm) deep.

6. Temper the milk chocolate and stir in the cocoa butter.

7. Dip each piece of chilled ganache into the chocolate, remove with a dipping fork, and tap off the excess chocolate. Place in the confectioners' sugar. Shake the tray to cover the chocolates in sugar. Allow to set before removing.

▶ TERMS FOR REVIEW

chocolate liquor	cocoa butter	white couverture	seeding
conching	dark chocolate	tempering	chocolate truffle
couverture	milk chocolate	tablage	

▶ QUESTIONS FOR REVIEW

1. Why is it necessary to temper chocolate for making chocolate molds?

2. Briefly explain two methods for tempering chocolate.

3. If tempered chocolate is at the correct temperature for molding but is too thick, how should you thin it?

4. Why is "white chocolate" an inaccurate term?

5. Why are chocolate molds polished with cotton wool before use?

6. Describe one procedure for molding chocolate eggs.

7. Describe five techniques for making decorative patterns using two colors of chocolate for cutouts.

8. Describe the procedure for making chocolate fans, starting with melted chocolate.

9. What are chocolate truffles? Give as complete an answer as you can, describing various types and forms.

21

Decorative Work: Marzipan, Nougatine, and Pastillage

*T*hese last two chapters are an introduction to the pastry chef's art of making decorative items out of sugar and other materials. Although all the ingredients used for these pieces are edible, and many of these items are used to decorate cakes and other desserts, they are, in many cases, made as showpieces, such as centerpieces for dessert buffet tables, and are not intended to be eaten.

In hotels and other food service and retail operations, such showpieces can be useful and even profitable. They serve to draw the customers' attention to the skill and artistry of the pastry chef and, thus, indirectly lead to greater sales of desserts. Perhaps even more important, from a pastry chef's point of view, they are an enjoyable outlet for creative skills.

Some of the items in these two chapters are comparatively easy to make, while others, such as pulled sugar, require a great deal of practice before you can expect to achieve good results. The text and the many photographs that illustrate the techniques provide an introduction but, for the most part, the only effective way to learn these skills is with the guidance of an instructor.

MARZIPAN

After reading this
chapter, you should be
able to:

■ Make and handle marzipan and
mold decorative items from it.

■ Make pastillage and use it to create decorative items.

■ Make nougatine and shape it into
simple decorative items.

Marzipan is a paste made of almonds and sugar that is worked to a plastic consistency. Its texture allows it to be rolled out with a rolling pin like dough or to
be modeled into the shapes of fruits, animals, flowers, and so forth.

Pastry chefs and confectioners once had to grind almonds in order to
make marzipan, but today the ready availability of almond paste makes the job
much easier. As you can see in the accompanying recipe, making marzipan
involves moistening the almond paste and blending it with confectioners'
sugar. Recipes may vary slightly, but the principle behind them is the same.
Some recipes call for more or less sugar or use different moistening agents,
such as fondant or egg whites.

In order to preserve the color of the marzipan, be sure that all equipment,
including bowls, mixer attachments, and work surfaces, is very clean. Use stainless steel rather than aluminum mixing bowls because aluminum discolors
marzipan.

Marzipan dries quickly when exposed to air and forms a crust on the surface. To avoid this when you are working with marzipan, keep unused portions
in a bowl covered with a damp cloth. To store marzipan, keep it wrapped or
covered in an airtight container. It keeps indefinitely if protected from air. If left
uncovered, it eventually becomes hard as a rock.

When marzipan is kneaded and worked, the oil content (from the
almonds) comes to the surface and makes the marzipan sticky. To avoid this,
dust the work surface lightly with confectioners' sugar. Keep a pan of confectioners' sugar handy for dusting as needed.

MARZIPAN SHEETS AND CUTOUTS

Marzipan can be rolled out into sheets with a rolling pin in the same way that
you roll out short dough. Confectioners' sugar is used for dusting the workbench and rolling pin. Make sure that the bench and the pin are completely
clean.

Marzipan sheets are useful for covering cakes and petits fours, as
explained in chapter 13. They may be left smooth or textured with a ribbed
roller or basketweave roller (see p. 369).

Colored patterns, such as stripes or polka dots, can be made on marzipan
sheets as follows. Roll out a sheet of marzipan partway, so that it is about twice
as thick as desired. Roll out another small piece of marzipan in a contrasting
color until it is ⅛ in. (3 mm) thick. Cut out small circles or strips and arrange
them carefully on top of the thick sheet. Now continue to roll out this sheet to
the desired thickness. Be very careful to roll it evenly in all directions in order
to keep the design uniform.

Using round or fancy cutters, cut out small shapes from the marzipan
sheets and use them to decorate cakes and desserts. For additional effect,
spread the sheet of marzipan with tempered chocolate and texture it with an
icing comb. Make cutouts before the chocolate hardens completely. Another
variation is made by texturing the marzipan with ribbed rollers and then spin-
ning fine lines of chocolate over the sheet, using a paper cone with a very
small opening.

Note that the Easter plaque on the chocolate egg pictured on page 539 is
made of a textured marzipan sheet.

Marzipan petits fours can be made to look like fancy icebox cookies. Using
two colors of marzipan instead of icebox cookie dough, make a checkerboard
of pinwheel slices using the procedures for the icebox cookies (p. 403). (Do
not bake the slices.)

Marzipan

Ingredients	U.S.	Metric
Almond paste	1 lb	500 g
Glucose or corn syrup	3 oz	90 g
Confectioners' sugar, sifted	1 lb	500 g
Total weight:	*2 lb 3 oz*	*1090 g*

■ Procedure

1. In a clean stainless-steel bowl, blend the almond paste and glucose, using the paddle attachment, until smooth.

2. Add the sifted sugar, a little at a time, just as fast as it is absorbed. Stop adding sugar when the desired consistency is reached. The marzipan should be stiff but workable and not too dry.

3. If colored marzipan is desired, add a small amount of color and work it in.

MODELING WITH MARZIPAN

Fruits, vegetables, animals, flowers, and many other shapes can be molded out of marzipan. Small marzipan fruits, served as petits fours or candies, are perhaps the most popular items.

Fruits and Flowers

To make small fruits, first divide the paste into equal portions. For example, to make ¾-oz (22 g) pieces, flatten 1½ lb (700 g) marzipan into a fairly thick rectangle of uniform thickness. With a knife, carefully cut the rectangle into four rows of eight to make 32 equal pieces.

Begin by rolling each piece between the palms of the hands into a round ball that is perfectly smooth and free of seams and cracks (bananas are an exception—begin by rolling the pieces into smooth sausage shapes). Then start modeling the balls with the fingers into the shapes of pears, apples, and other fruits. The best way to make realistic-looking fruits is to use real fruits as models. Imitate the shapes of the real fruits as closely as possible.

Special effects can be made with ordinary tools or with special modeling tools. For example, make the crease on the sides of peaches, apricots, plums, and cherries with the back of a knife. Texture the surfaces of strawberries by poking them lightly with a toothpick. Imitate the rough surface of lemons and oranges by rolling them lightly on a cheese grater.

Let the fruits dry overnight before coloring. Coloring can be done in two ways:

1. Start with tinted marzipan—green for apples and pears, yellow for bananas, peaches, and lemons, and so on. Apply food color with a brush to color in highlights and markings, such as the brown streaks and dots on bananas, the red blush on apples and peaches, and so on.

2. Start with untinted marzipan. Color the finished fruits with background colors, using either a brush or a sprayer. Let the color dry, then color in the highlights.

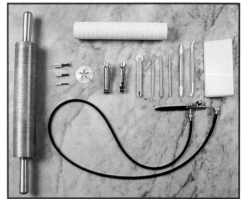

Marzipan Tools
Top: basketweave roller.
Middle row: metal rolling pin,
small cutters with release plungers,
strawberry leaf cutter, nippers,
modeling tools, smoother
for covering cakes with
sheets of marzipan.
Bottom: color sprayer.

Flowers such as carnations and roses are useful items to make because they can be used to decorate cakes as well as display pieces.

Marzipan rose, carnation, strawberry, and oranges

Procedure for Making a Marzipan Strawberry

1. Roll the ball of marzipan into a strawberry shape with the palms of the hands.
2. Indent the stem end of the strawberry with an appropriate modeling tool.

3. Roll the strawberry in sugar to simulate the textured surface of the real berry.
4. Cut out a leaf shape for the stem end and fasten it in place using an appropriate modeling tool.

Procedure for Making a Marzipan Carnation

1. Flatten a strip of marzipan on the workbench so that the edges are paper thin. Feather the edge with the point of a knife.
2. Release the strip of marzipan by sliding a knife under it. Gather it together into a carnation shape.

Procedure for Making a Marzipan Rose

1. Taper a ball of marzipan to serve as the base of the rose.
2. Mold the ball with the tapered end pointing up to serve as the center of the flower.

3. For the petals, roll a log of marzipan and cut pieces of equal size. Flatten these pieces into small disks.
4. With the back of the spoon, flatten the disks, using a circular motion to taper the edges to paper thinness.

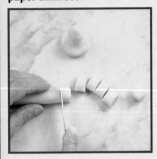 

5. Wrap the petal around the base, leaving one edge free so the second petal can be inserted under it.
6. Attach the second petal.
7. Continue adding petals in the same fashion until the rose is the desired size. With a sharp knife, cut the rose from the base

Other Items

The variety of objects that can be modeled from marzipan is limited only by the imagination and talent of the pastry cook. Vegetables such as carrots, asparagus, potatoes, and peas in the pod can be made in the same way as fruits. Marzipan snowmen and holly leaves are often used to decorate the Bûche de Noël (p. 387). Animals such as dogs, pigs, and frogs are popular subjects. Features such as eyes, nose, and tongue can be applied with royal icing, chocolate, or fondant.

Frames for chocolate paintings on pastillage (p. 557) are generally made of marzipan. Roll marzipan into long, round strips of perfectly uniform thickness and fasten them around the pastillage plaque. With assorted marzipan nippers and modeling tools, texture the marzipan to look like a carved frame. The raised details can then be highlighted by very carefully browning them with a blowtorch.

PASTILLAGE

Pastillage (pronounced "pahss-tee-yahzh") is a sugar paste that is used for modeling decorative items. Unlike marzipan and other modeling pastes, it is rarely, if ever, intended to be eaten. Although it is made entirely of edible items, pastillage is as hard and brittle as plaster of Paris when it dries, and nearly as tasteless. It is used primarily for making display pieces, such as centerpieces for dessert buffet tables, or small baskets or boxes to hold petits fours and candies. Pastillage is normally left pure white, although it may be colored in pastel shades.

The formula given here is a simple and popular one using readily available ingredients: confectioners' sugar, cornstarch (as a drying agent), water, cream of tartar (to help preserve whiteness), and gelatin (as a stiffening and stabilizing agent). Pastillage is sometimes called *gum paste,* although that term is more correctly used when a vegetable gum (usually gum tragacanth) is used instead of gelatin.

MAKING AND HANDLING PASTILLAGE

Many of the same precautions must be taken in the production of pastillage as in the production of marzipan. Great care is essential to preserve the pure white color. Make sure all equipment is scrupulously clean, and use a stainless-steel bowl, not aluminum, for mixing (aluminum imparts a grayish color to the paste). Likewise, the work surface, rolling pin, and molds must be clean and dry.

Pastillage Tools
Ribbed roller, molds, and cutters

Pastillage dries and crusts over even faster than marzipan, so it must be kept covered at all times. While working with pastillage, keep unused portions in a bowl covered with a damp cloth. Work quickly and without pause until your products are formed and ready for drying.

Most pastillage pieces are made of thin sheets of the paste that are cut to shape with the aid of paper patterns. The pieces are left flat or curved around molds and allowed to dry, then assembled by gluing them together with royal icing. A marble slab is ideal for rolling out pastillage because it gives the paste a smooth surface. Use cornstarch to dust the work surface. Be careful not to use more starch than is necessary to keep the paste from sticking. Excessive starch dries the surface of the paste quickly and causes it to crust over and crack.

For the most attractive, delicate pieces, the pastillage sheets should be rolled thin (about ⅛ in./3 mm thick). Thick sheets make heavy, clumsy-looking pieces. Have paper patterns ready, and as soon as the pastillage is rolled out, place the patterns on it and cut cleanly and accurately with a sharp knife or cutter.

Pastillage

Ingredients	U.S.			Sugar at 100% Metric	%
Gelatin		0.5	oz	12 g	1.25
Water, cold		5.5	oz	140 g	14
Confectioners' sugar (10X)	2 lb	8	oz	1000 g	100
Cornstarch		5	oz	125 g	12.5
Cream of tartar		0.04 oz (½ tsp)		1 g	0.1
Total weight:	*3 lb*	*3*	*oz*	*1278 g*	*127%*

■ P r o c e d u r e

1. Stir the gelatin into the water. Let stand 5 minutes, then heat until the gelatin is dissolved.

2. Sift together the sugar, starch, and cream of tartar.

3. Place the gelatin mixture in a stainless-steel mixer bowl. Fit the mixing machine with the dough hook.

4. With the machine running at low speed, add the sugar mixture just as fast as it is absorbed. Mix to a smooth, pliable paste.

5. Keep the paste covered at all times.

Techniques for creating this pastillage showpiece are illustrated on pages 558–559.

For pieces to be molded, have the molds clean, dry, and dusted with cornstarch. For example, to make a pastillage bowl, you can use the outside of another bowl, placed upside down on the workbench, as your mold. Carefully fit the sheet of paste outside or inside the mold, gently fitting it to the shape of the mold with your hands.

When the pastillage is partially dry and firm, turn it over to allow the bottom to dry. Continue turning it over from time to time so that it dries evenly. Pastillage that does not dry evenly tends to curl or distort out of shape. Drying time depends on the size and thickness of the pieces and may take from 12 hours to several days.

Dried pastillage may be lightly sanded with extra-fine sandpaper until it is very smooth. This also helps to smooth down the cut edges, which may be rough or sharp. Finally, assemble the pieces using royal icing as cement. Use very little icing; any excess is likely to squeeze out at the seams, which spoils the appearance of the piece.

The procedure below illustrates most of the steps discussed above. In the photos, the pastry chef is making and assembling the display piece pictured on this page. The flowers are tinted with food colors using the sprayer depicted on page 553.

Because of its pure white, smooth surface, pastillage makes an ideal canvas for chocolate painting. Make a round, oval, or rectangular plaque of pastillage, let it dry, and sand it smooth. Using an artist's brush, draw a picture using melted unsweetened chocolate. Create light and dark shades by diluting the chocolate with varying proportions of melted cocoa butter. For fine detail, etch lines in the chocolate with a sharp wooden pick. After the chocolate has set, the painting can be finished off with a marzipan frame (p. 555).

Techniques for Creating a Showpiece from Pastillage

The techniques shown here are used to create the showpiece pictured on page 557.

1. Roll out the pastillage on a work surface, preferably marble, dusted lightly with cornstarch.

2. Check the thickness.

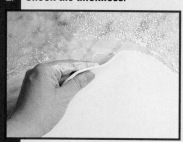

3. Lift the rolled-out pastillage by draping it over a rolling pin. Always dust off excess cornstarch.

4. Create a textured surface with a ribbed roller.

5. Cut out desired shapes. Working on a tray allows you to remove the pieces from the workbench for drying without disturbing them. The tray should be dusted with cornstarch.

6. Some shapes can be cut freehand with a knife.

7. Small cutters are used to cut additional pieces.

8. For the sides of the box, cut a strip of pastillage and fit it inside a ring mold. Trim the ends so the joint fits smoothly.

9. Trim excess from the top.

10. For leaves and petals, cut appropriate shapes and press in a mold.

11. Fit the petals into a mold lined with a little square of parchment to prevent sticking.

12. To make the center of the flower, press a ball of pastillage into a sieve.

13. Set the center of the flower in place.

14. To use this type of cutter/molder, stamp out a piece of pastillage, press it in to mold it, and push it out with the spring-loaded plunger.

15 For the feet of the box, press balls of pastillage into a chocolate mold. Pass a scraper over the top of the mold to remove excess and flatten the tops.

16. Once the pastillage has dried, sand it with fine sandpaper to achieve a smooth surface.

17. Fasten pieces together with royal icing.

18. Fasten the dried top of the box, textured with a ribbed roller, in place.

19 Fasten the side pieces in place.

20. The decorative lacework is made by coloring royal icing and piping it using a paper cone.

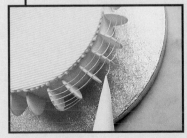

NOUGATINE

Nougatine is a candy made of caramelized sugar and almonds. It looks somewhat like peanut brittle but is more attractive because of the sliced almonds. The caramelized sugar should be a clear amber, not cloudy. Because the sugar is soft and pliable when it is hot, it can be cut and molded into various shapes to make decorative pieces.

PRODUCTION AND SHAPING

As can be seen in the following recipe, the cooking of nougatine involves two fairly simple steps: caramelizing the sugar and adding the almonds. The glucose inverts some of the sugar (see p. 23), thus preventing unwanted crystallization. Cream of tartar or lemon juice are sometimes used instead of glucose.

Nougatine can be cut into many shapes and is often cut freehand. If your display piece requires precise shapes, however, it is best to cut patterns out of sheets of parchment. Lay the patterns on top of the sheet of nougatine to guide your cutting. Have all your patterns ready before starting to make the nougatine.

Techniques for Working with Nougatine

1. Pour out the hot nougatine mixture onto a silicone mat.

2. With a spatula or with the hands (using rubber gloves), fold the mass over on itself as it cools so that it cools evenly.

3. While it is still hot and soft, roll out the nougatine with a rolling pin to the desired thickness.

4. This nougatine is to be used as the base of a centerpiece. It is molded to shape in a lightly oiled cake tin.

When the nougat is ready, pour it out onto silicone mat or an oiled tray or marble slab. It will cool quickly, so you have to work fast. When the sheet has begun to set, flip it over with a spatula so that it cools evenly. Have your paper pattern ready. Flatten the sheet with an oiled rolling pin to even out the thickness. Place the patterns on the sheet and quickly cut out shapes with a heavy, oiled knife. Because of the oiled surface, the patterns shouldn't stick, but don't press them down or leave them on the nougat too long.

Molds should be prepared ahead of time by oiling them lightly. For example, to make a nougat bowl, you can use the bottom of a stainless-steel bowl, placed upside-down on the bench and rubbed with oil. Place the soft, cut nougat over the bowl and carefully press it into shape.

If the nougat cools and hardens before you can shape it, place it on an oiled baking sheet and place it in a hot oven for a moment to soften it. You can even stick two sheets together by placing them next to each other and heating them. However, every time you reheat nougat it darkens a little more. Several shades of nougat in a display piece detract from its appearance.

When the molded nougat pieces have cooled and hardened, cement them together as necessary, using either royal icing or a hot sugar syrup boiled to 310° F (190° C). Nougat pieces can also be decorated with royal icing.

5. | **Trim off excess with a chef's knife.**

6. | **Thinly rolled nougatine can be cut into shapes for decorating cakes (such as the top layer of Brasilia, p. 380) and pastries. Bend cutouts to desired shape while still hot, or rewarm until pliable.**

OTHER USES OF NOUGATINE

Unlike some decorative materials, such as pastillage, nougatine is a tasty confection. Thin nougatine sheets can be cut into fancy shapes and used to decorate cakes and other desserts.

Hard nougatine can be crushed and used like chopped nuts for masking the sides of cakes. Finely ground and sifted, or ground to a paste, it makes an excellent flavoring for creams and icings. This product is similar to praline paste, except that praline generally contains hazelnuts.

Nougatine

Yield: about 2 lb 8 oz (1220 g)

Ingredients	U.S.		Metric	Sugar at 100% %
Sliced almonds	12	oz	375 g	50
Sugar	1 lb 8	oz	750 g	100
Glucose	9.5	oz	300 g	40
Water	6.5	oz	200 g	27

■ Procedure

1. Place the almonds on a heated baking sheet in a 320°F (160°C) oven, mixing occasionally until light golden in color.

2. Cook the water, sugar, and glucose to a blond caramel.

3. Add the almonds to the caramel all at once and mix in carefully. Do not overmix or the almonds will break into small pieces.

4. Pour the mixture onto an oiled baking sheet or silicone mat.

5. Spread the nougatine in small quantities and use a metal rolling pin to make an even layer.

6. Work the nougatine near the opening of the oven, as this will keep it pliable much longer. The nougatine should not stick to the rolling pin or table. If it does, allow the nougatine to cool a little before continuing, returning to the oven to achieve the correct consistency.

7. Trimmings may be used again after gentle reheating, but be careful not to use nougatine once it has become dark in color and the almonds are broken to a fine powder.

► TERMS FOR REVIEW

marzipan   pastillage   gum paste   nougatine

► QUESTIONS FOR REVIEW

1. What precaution must be taken when mixing marzipan in order to preserve its color?

2. Suppose you wanted to cover a strawberry-filled Swiss roll with white marzipan decorated with pink polka dots. How would you make the marzipan sheet?

3. Describe the procedure for making a marzipan carnation.

4. What procedure is used to make sure that pastillage dries properly?

5. How are dried pieces of pastillage fastened together?

6. Describe the procedure for making, cutting, and molding nougatine.

7. What are some uses for leftover nougatine trimmings?

22

Decorative Work: Sugar Techniques

Many pastry chefs consider sugar work the pinnacle of their decorative art. One reason is surely the sheer beauty of skillfully made pulled and blown sugar pieces, which can be elaborate constructions of multicolored sugar flowers in blown sugar vases, large sprays of sugar flowers cascading down the side of a wedding cake, or sugar baskets filled with sugar fruit, set on sugar pedestals wrapped with sugar ribbons and bows.

Another reason is, no doubt, the difficulty of decorative work. Becoming proficient at this art requires dedication and hours, even years, of practice and study, so chefs who have mastered it have earned the respect that this accomplishment brings them. Students are often irresistibly drawn to the challenge of learning these techniques when they see what results are possible.

This chapter is an introduction to sugar work, beginning with the simpler techniques of spun sugar and sugar cages and proceeding to the more difficult pulled and blown sugar.

After reading this
chapter, you should be
able to:

■ Boil sugar syrups correctly for
decorative sugar work.

■ Make spun sugar, sugar cages,
and poured sugar.

■ Pull sugar and use it to make
simple pulled and blown sugar
decorative items.

BOILING SYRUPS FOR SUGAR WORK

In chapter 8, we discussed the boiling of sugar syrups for use in various desserts. When syrups are boiled until nearly all the water is evaporated, the sugar becomes solid when it cools. This process enables us to make decorative pieces out of sugar that is boiled to 300°F (149°C) or more and shaped while still hot.

As you learned in chapter 2 (p. 23), sugar that is boiled in a syrup undergoes a chemical change called *inversion,* in which a molecule of double sugar (sucrose) combines with a molecule of water and changes into two molecules of simple sugar (dextrose and levulose). Invert sugar, you remember, resists crystallization, and plain sucrose (granulated sugar) crystallizes easily. The amount of sugar that is inverted depends on the amount of acid present. This principle is used in the production of fondant icing (p. 334): Just enough cream of tartar or glucose is added to the syrup to create a mass of extremely fine sugar crystals that give fondant its pure white color.

This technique is also used for the sugar work discussed in this section, especially in pulled sugar. If too much cream of tartar or glucose is used, too much sugar is inverted, so that the sugar is too soft and sticky to work and doesn't harden enough when cool. If not enough cream of tartar or glucose is used, too little sugar is inverted and the sugar is hard, so that it is difficult to work and easily broken.

As long as it is kept within limits, the exact amount of tartar or glucose to be used depends largely on the preferences of the pastry chef or confectioner. Some artists prefer to work with a harder sugar, while some prefer a softer one. Consequently, you will see many different recipes. Your instructor may have his or her own favorite to substitute for those in this book.

The temperature to which syrup is boiled is also important. The higher the temperature, the harder the sugar will be. The temperature range recommended in this book is 311°–320°F (155°–160°C), and the actual temperature used for the pulled and blown sugar items shown in the illustrations was 320°F (160°C). Nevertheless, you may see slightly different temperatures used in other books, because all chefs have their own preferred procedures.

Cooking the sugar to a higher temperature makes it harder and more brittle and thus more difficult to work. Cooking to a lower temperature makes a softer sugar that is easier to work, but the pieces may not hold up as well, especially in a humid climate. Inexperienced cooks may want to start with temperatures at the lower end of the range, not worrying about the keeping qualities of their pieces, until they develop some familiarity with sugar work.

Two more precautions are necessary regarding temperature and the addition of tartaric acid (cream of tartar). First, boiled invert sugar discolors more rapidly than pure sucrose. Therefore, the acid should not be added until near the end of the boiling process. In the recipes in this book, the tartaric acid is not added to the syrup until it has reached 275°F (135°C). Second, the syrup should be boiled rapidly over moderately high heat. Boiling slowly gives the syrup more time to discolor and it will not be clear white.

If color is added to the syrup during boiling (for poured or pulled sugar), it should be added partway through the cooking, at about 260°F (125°C). If it is added earlier, it has more time to discolor, but it must be added early enough for the alcohol or water to cook off.

Slightly different syrups are used for each of the techniques in this chapter. Follow the specific recipes in each section, keeping these guidelines in mind:

1. Use pure white granulated cane sugar.

2. Place the sugar and water in a clean, heavy pan. Place the mixture over low heat and stir gently until the sugar is dissolved.

3. When the sugar is dissolved, raise the heat to moderately high and do not stir any more. To prevent crystallization, use a clean pastry brush dipped in hot water to wash any sugar crystals down the side of the pan. Do not let the brush touch the syrup.

4. Always use a sugar thermometer.

5. Add coloring and tartaric acid solution at the temperatures specified in the recipes.

6. Liquid colors in an acid solution should not be used. For best results, use powdered colors and dissolve them in a little water or alcohol. Good-quality paste colors can also be used.

SPUN SUGAR AND CARAMEL DECORATIONS

SPUN SUGAR

Spun sugar is a mass of threadlike or hairlike strands of sugar used to decorate cakes and show pieces. Gateau St-Honoré (p. 278) is often decorated with spun sugar.

Spun sugar should be made just before it is needed because it does not keep well. It gradually absorbs moisture from the atmosphere and becomes sticky. Eventually, this absorbed moisture causes the sugar to dissolve.

Prepare a work station by propping a lightly oiled wooden rod or rolling pin on the edge of a table so that it projects horizontally beyond the edge of the table by 1–2 ft (30–60 cm). Place plenty of paper on the floor below to catch drippings. To spin the sugar, you will need a wire whip with the ends cut off.

Tools for Sugar Work
Top: sugar lamp.
Bottom, left to right: sugar thermometer, rubber gloves, leaf molds, blowpipe, cut-off wire whip for spun sugar.

Procedure for Making Spun Sugar

1. Prepare the syrup as in the recipe on page 570. When the correct temperature is reached, remove the pan from the heat and allow the syrup to stand for a few minutes until it is slightly cooled and thickened.

2. Dip the cut-off wire whip in the syrup and tap lightly to remove excess. Wave or flick the whip vigorously over the wooden rod so that the sugar is thrown off in fine, long threads.

3. Repeat until the desired amount of spun sugar is hanging from the rod. Carefully lift the mass from the rod.

4. Coil the sugar, or shape as desired for decoration.

5. If the syrup cools too much to spin, simply rewarm it over low heat.

CARAMEL CAGES AND OTHER SHAPES

Sugar cages are delicate, lacy sugar domes made of caramelized sugar. Their decorative effect can be impressive and elegant. Sugar cages can be made large enough to cover whole cakes, bombes, Bavarian creams, and other desserts, or small enough to decorate individual portions.

Bowls of the desired size can be used as molds for large cages. Ladles are usually used for small, single-portion cages. Lightly oil the bottom of the ladle or other mold so that the sugar can be removed when it is hard.

Procedure for Making Caramel Cages

1. Prepare a syrup as in the recipe on page 570. Testing with a sugar thermometer is the most accurate way to determine the stage of the boiled syrup.

2. Cool the syrup slightly. Holding the mold in one hand, dip a spoon in the sugar and drizzle it in a random, lacy pattern over the mold, turning the mold so that all sides receive some of the syrup.

3. Trim off excess, let the sugar cool until hard, and carefully lift off.

Other shapes can be made by piping or drizzling the sugar onto a silicone mat or oiled work surface. To create fine, even lines of sugar, use a paper cone, as in the recipe. Wear rubber gloves to protect your hands from the heat. For a rougher or more casual look, dip a spoon in the sugar and drizzle it onto the mat. The caramel shape decorating the panna cotta dessert pictured on page 516 was made this way.

Sugar spirals make elegant garnishes for some plated desserts (see, for example, the photo on p. 527). These are made using the following procedure.

Procedure for Making a Sugar Spiral

1. Prepare a syrup as for making caramel cages (p. 570).
2. Wind a strand of hot syrup around a lightly oiled pencil or thin wooden rod.
3. Slip the spiral off the pencil when the sugar has hardened.

Spun Sugar

Yield: about 12 oz (360 g)

Ingredients	U.S.	Sugar at 100% Metric	%
Sugar	10 oz	300 g	100
Water	5 oz	150 g	50
Glucose	2 oz	60 g	20
Coloring, if desired			

■ P r o c e d u r e

1. Make a syrup of the sugar, water, and glucose. See page 176 for guidelines on cooking sugar syrups.
2. Boil to 255°F (125°C) and add coloring, if desired.
3. Continue to boil to 320°F (160°C), then stop the cooking immediately by plunging the base of the pan into cold water. Remove from the cold water and allow to stand for 2–3 minutes to thicken slightly.
4. Lightly oil a rolling pin or metal pole and suspend it horizontally. Place sheets of paper on the floor under the pole to catch drips.
5. Dip a cut-off wire whip in the syrup and flick it over the pole, as in the illustrations. Continue until the desired quantity is made.
6. Lift the spun sugar from the pole and shape as desired.

Caramel for Cages and Other Shapes

Yield: about 10 oz (300 g)

Ingredients	U.S.	Sugar at 100% Metric	%
Sugar	10 oz	300 g	100
Water	10 oz	300 g	100
Glucose	1.33 oz	40 g	13

■ P r o c e d u r e

1. Make a syrup of the sugar, water, and glucose. See page 176 for guidelines on cooking sugar syrups.
2. Boil to 320°F (160°C), then stop the cooking immediately by plunging the base of the pan into cold water. Remove from the cold water and allow to stand for 2–3 minutes to thicken slightly.
3. Wear rubber gloves to protect the hands from the hot syrup. Pour the syrup into a paper cone. Snip off the tip and pipe desired shapes onto a silicone mat or oiled work surface. Allow to cool. Remove and store in an airtight container until use.
4. For cages, lightly oil the bottom of a ladle. Dip a spoon in the syrup (or, for more delicate sugar, dip the point of a knife in the syrup) and drizzle it in a lace pattern over the bottom of the ladle. Trim off excess with scissors. Let stand for 2 minutes, then carefully lift off.

POURED SUGAR

Poured sugar, also called *cast sugar,* is boiled sugar that is allowed to harden in various shapes. Usually it is cast in flat sheets like glass, although, like nougatine, it can be bent and shaped while it is hot and pliable. The syrup can also be colored before it finishes cooking.

There are several ways of preparing molds for casting the sugar. For round shapes, simply use a flan ring or charlotte ring. Metal molds in other shapes (like large cookie cutters) can also be used. For other shapes, bend a strip of metal into the desired shape. An easy way to make a mold of any shape is to roll heat-resistant plasticine (a type of modeling clay) into a rope and work it to the desired shape on an oiled marble slab or silicone mat. Whatever mold you use, it should be lightly oiled to prevent the sugar from sticking.

Procedure for Pouring Sugar

1. Prepare the syrup as in the recipe on page 572. Color the syrup as desired, as indicated in the recipe.

2. When the syrup reaches the proper temperature, briefly plunge the base of the saucepan into cold water to stop the cooking. Let stand for a moment.

3. Place a lightly oiled mold on a sheet of parchment. Pour the hot syrup—in this case, colored black—into the mold to the desired thickness.

4. Before the sugar cools, it can be marbled with another color—here, a little white coloring.

Once the edges of the sugar shape have hardened enough, remove the mold. When the entire shape has hardened enough, slide a palette knife under it to detach it from the work surface. (This is not necessary if you are using a silicone mat, which will peel away easily.)

To bend cast sugar, remove it from the work surface while it is still soft enough to be pliable. If it gets too hard, simply place it on an oiled baking sheet and heat it in an oven just until it is pliable. Then bend as desired or use an oiled mold to shape it as you would nougatine (p. 560).

Another item that can be made by simply pouring sugar onto a surface is sugar lace. Sugar lace can be seen in the display piece pictured on page 576. The base of this piece is made with poured sugar.

Procedure for Making Sugar Lace

1. Pour a small pool of boiled sugar onto a square of silicone paper. Quickly spread it to a thin layer with a palette knife.

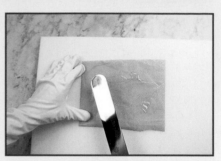

2. Before the sugar hardens, crinkle the paper to shape the sugar.

Poured Sugar

Yield: about 2 lb 6 oz (1200 g)

Ingredients	U.S.	Sugar at 100%	
		Metric	%
Sugar	2 lb	1000 g	100
Water	1 lb	500 g	50
Glucose	6.5 oz	200 g	20
Coloring, as desired			

■ Procedure

1. *Prepare molds for the desired shape:* Brush metal rings with oil or roll heat-resistant plasticine to desired shape, then brush it with oil. Place molds on a silicone mat or an oiled or parchment-covered marble slab.

2. Make a syrup of the sugar, water, and glucose. See page 176 for guidelines on cooking sugar syrups.

3. Boil to 255°F (125°C) and add coloring, if desired.

4. Continue to boil to 330°F (165°C). If desired, a few drops of another color could be added at this point without mixing to create a marbled effect.

5. Stop the cooking immediately by plunging the base of the pan into cold water. Remove from the cold water and allow to stand for 2–3 minutes to thicken slightly.

6. Pour into desired mold until approximately ¼ in. (5 mm) thick.

7. Once edges have set enough, remove rings. Score lightly with an oiled knife, if desired.

8. Use a little reheated sugar as glue to attach pieces together.

PULLED SUGAR AND BLOWN SUGAR

Pulled sugar and blown sugar are, perhaps, the most difficult of the pastry chef's decorative art forms. This section explains the basic procedure for making pulled sugar. Several techniques for making ribbons, flowers, leaves, and blown fruits are illustrated in detail, and a number of other techniques are explained in the text. Once you are comfortable with the basic techniques, you might want to consult any of a number of advanced books on decorative work, some of which are listed in the bibliography on page 629. The variety of shapes that can be made with sugar is limited only by the imagination and skill of the chef.

Before beginning work, assemble your equipment. The following tools are the most important items you will need, depending on what pieces you are making:

- Sugar thermometer, for accurate control of the temperature of the boiling syrup

- Sugar lamp or other warmer to keep the stock of sugar warm and soft

- Scissors and knife, lightly oiled, for cutting the sugar

- Alcohol lamp for melting sugar in order to fasten pieces together

- Blowpipe for blowing sugar; a pipe with a bulb for inflating is easier to use than one that is blown with the mouth

- Silicone mat or oiled marble slab for pouring out the cooked syrup

- Fan or hair dryer for cooling sugar items

- Rubber gloves to protect from burns when handling hot sugar (some experienced chefs prefer to work without gloves)

Prepare the syrup according to the recipe on page 580. Note the need for liquid tartaric acid, which is a solution of equal weights of cream of tartar and water, prepared as indicated in the recipe.

Once the pulled sugar is prepared, it can be used at once, or it can be cooled and stored in an airtight container for later use. To use stored sugar for pulled or blown items, first reheat it in an oven set at 170°F (75°C). After it has been heated to the proper temperature, it must again be pulled and folded as in step 7 of the recipe (p. 580) until it is cooled to a workable temperature and even in texture. Test the sugar by pulling a bit from the edge of the ball with the thumb and forefinger and attempting to break it off. If it breaks off cleanly, the sugar is ready. This pulling and folding procedure is sometimes called *pearling*. If this is not done, it will not be possible to work the sugar properly.

RIBBONS

A ribbon of a single color is made by simply pulling a piece of sugar out into a thin ribbon shape. This sounds easy, but making a thin, delicate ribbon of perfectly even thickness and width takes a great deal of practice and skill. Be sure that the piece of sugar is uniformly warm and that all parts of the strip stretch the same amount.

Procedure for Making Pulled Sugar

1. Pour the cooked sugar onto a silicone mat. If a color is desired and was not added during cooking, add the color now with a eyedropper.

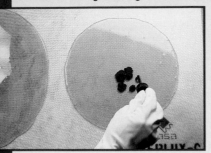

2. As the sugar cools, fold the edges toward the center so that it cools evenly.

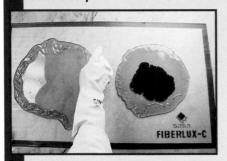

3. When the color is blended in, pick up the mass of sugar and begin to stretch and fold it.

4. Pull and fold the sugar until it has a silky or pearly appearance and makes a faint clicking sound when stretched.

5. Store the lumps of sugar under the sugar lamp as you work them in order to keep them at the proper temperature.

To make a two-colored ribbon, start with two pieces of sugar in contrasting colors. Shape them into strips of the same size and shape. Press them together side by side, then stretch them into a ribbon. For multiple stripes, cut the two-colored strip in half when it is partly stretched. Place the two pieces together side by side so that you have four alternating stripes. Finish stretching them out into a ribbon shape.

A ribbon of three or more colors can be made with the same technique.

To make a bow, cut off a length of ribbon with scissors and bend it into a loop. Cool the loop in front of a fan so that it holds its shape. Make as many loops as desired. Fasten them together into a bow by heating one end of each loop over a gas flame to soften the sugar and then pressing the heated ends together.

Procedure for Making Pulled Sugar Ribbons

1. Make equal-size ropes of the selected colors and place them side by side under the sugar lamp.

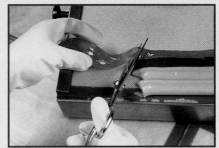

2. Pull or stretch to begin to form the ribbon.

3. Fold the ribbon so that the two ends are side by side; snip in half with an oiled scissor.

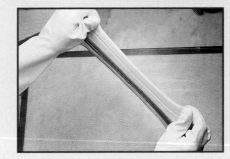

4. Repeat this pulling and doubling procedure until you have a ribbon of the desired pattern and width.

5. Before the sugar hardens, bend it into folds to resemble a slightly crinkled ribbon and snip into desired lengths with a lightly oiled scissor.

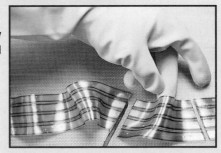

FLOWERS AND LEAVES

The basic techniques for making simple flowers is detailed in the procedure on page 577. The illustrations show the production of a lily and a leaf. Note the mold used to mark the veins in the leaf. If a mold is not available, you can mark the pattern of veins using the back of a knife.

Another popular flower to make with pulled sugar is, of course, the rose. Rose petals are made using the same basic technique as for lily petals, except the petal is pulled into a round shape rather than being stretched into a long shape. Roll the first petal into a tight cone shape. Then curl additional petals around the center cone just as you would for a marzipan rose (p. 555). Make the outer petals a little larger than the inner ones, and curl back the edges to resemble the petals of a real rose.

An alternative method is to make all the petals first without assembling them. Heat the bottom edges of the petals over the flame of an alcohol lamp so that they stick together, and assemble them to make the flower.

To make a stem that will support the weight of a flower, pull a strong piece of wire through warm pulled sugar so that it is completely coated. While the sugar is still soft, bend the covered wire to the desired shape.

Parts of the sugar display piece before assembly

SIMPLE BASKETS

Roll out a piece of pulled sugar with a rolling pin into a thin sheet. Mold it over an oiled bowl or large tin can, just as you would mold nougatine. A handle can also be attached.

WOVEN BASKETS

A woven pulled-sugar basket filled with pulled-sugar flowers or fruit is one of the most impressive of all display pieces. To make the basket, you need a base board into which an uneven number of holes has been drilled. The holes should be evenly spaced and should form a circle, oval, or square. In addition, you need wooden pegs that fit loosely into these holes. The holes should be drilled at an angle so that the pegs tilt outward. This makes the basket wider at the top than at the bottom. Oil the pegs and board lightly before weaving the basket.

Take a ball of soft pulled sugar and start to pull a rope or cord of sugar from the ball. Starting at the inside edge of one of the pegs, weave the sugar cords in and out around the pegs, pulling out more of the sugar as you go. Be careful to keep the thickness of the cord uniform. Continue weaving the sugar around the pegs until the basket is as high as desired.

Make pulled sugar rods the same size and number as the wooden pegs. One by one, pull out the pegs and replace them with the pulled sugar rods. If necessary, trim the tops of the rods with a hot knife or scissors.

Make a base for the basket with poured sugar (p. 571) or with pulled sugar rolled out with a rolling pin. Attach it to the basket with hot boiled syrup.

To finish off the top and bottom edges, twist two cords of pulled sugar together to make a rope. Coil the rope around the top and bottom edges of the basket and seal the ends together. A handle for the basket can be made by shaping heavy wire and then weaving a rope of sugar around it.

Finished sugar display piece

Procedure for Making a Pulled Sugar Lily

1. Stretch one side of a ball of pulled sugar to make a thin edge.

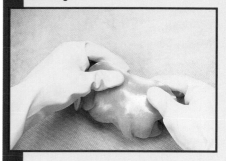

2. Grasp this thin edge and pull outward to make a pointed petal.

3. Snip off the petal with an oiled scissor. Repeat to make additional petals.

4. Attach the petals together into the shape of a lily.

5. For the inside of the flower, stretch pulled sugar into thin strands.

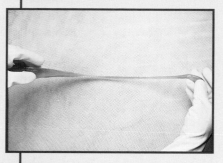

6. Fold two pieces of this sugar strand as shown and insert in the flower.

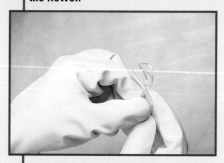

7. To make leaves, pull sugar as for the petals, but make the piece wider to resemble a leaf.

8. Press the piece of sugar in a mold to give it the texture of a leaf. The finished flowers are shown on page 576.

BLOWN SUGAR

Hollow sugar fruits and other items are blown from pulled sugar in much the same way that glass is blown. Traditionally, sugar was blown with the mouth, using a length of tube, and many chefs still prefer this method. Today, however, the use of a blowpipe inflated with a squeeze bulb (see p. 567) has become common and makes the work a little easier. Especially for the beginner, this type of blowpipe is easier to control than a tube blown with the mouth.

The shape of the sugar piece depends on how it is manipulated and supported with the hands and on how it is cooled or warmed. To make round objects, such as apples, hold the blow pipe and sugar upward at an angle, so that the weight of the sugar does not cause it to elongate. For long, thin objects such as bananas, stretch the sugar gently as you blow.

If the sugar on one side becomes too thin, cool that side slightly with a fan so that it hardens. By watching demonstrations and practicing, you can learn to control the temperature of the piece on all sides in order to shape it as you want. The best sugar pieces have a thin, delicate wall of sugar that is of even thickness all around.

Procedure for Blowing Sugar

1. Make a depression in a lump of hot pulled sugar and insert the end of the blowpipe.

2. Press the sugar firmly around the pipe to seal.

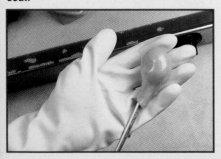

3. For a pear, inflate the bulb of sugar slowly, shaping the fruit as it is blown up.

4. Continue to inflate the sugar, shaping it with the fingers. When the desired shape and size are achieved, harden the sugar by cooling it with a fan.

More complex pieces, such as animals, birds, and fish, can be made with practice. For example, make a long-necked bird by blowing the sugar into the shape of a vase and stretching out the neck to form the long neck of the bird. An animal's head and body may be blown separately and attached. Parts such as wings and fins are made separately from pulled sugar.

When the blown sugar has hardened, add additional coloring to make the fruit more realistic. If the pieces were blown from colored pulled sugar, you may need to add only a few highlights and markings with an artist's brush. An alternative method is to use uncolored sugar for blowing and then a sprayer for adding layers of color to give a more blended effect. If done skillfully, this can give the fruit a more natural look. For spraying, dissolve powdered color in alcohol. If a dull rather than a shiny surface is appropriate for the item, dust the finished piece with cornstarch.

The procedure below illustrates the major steps in making blown sugar fruits.

5. | Heat the neck of the pipe over a flame and detach the pear from the pipe. Mold the stem end with the fingers.

6. | Mold other fruit in a similar fashion, such as bananas.

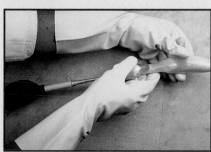

7. | . . . and apples.

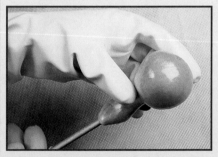

8. | These finished fruits have been colored with a sprayer (see p. 553) and highlighted with a small paintbrush.

Pulled Sugar and Blown Sugar

Yield: about 2 lb 6 oz (1200 g)

Ingredients	U.S.	Metric	Sugar at 100% %
Sugar	2 lb	1000 g	100
Water	9.5 oz	300 g	30
Glucose	6.5 oz	200 g	20
Color	as desired	as desired	
Tartaric acid solution (see *note*)	8 drops	8 drops	

Note   To prepare tartaric acid solution, use equal weights of cream of tartar and water. Bring the water to a boil, remove from the heat, and add the cream of tartar. Let cool.

■ P r o c e d u r e

1. Make a syrup of the sugar, water, and glucose. See p. 176 for guidelines on cooking sugar syrups.

2. Boil to 255°F (125°C) and add coloring, if desired. (Color can also be added when the sugar is poured out in step 5.)

3. Continue to boil to 275°F (135°C) and add the tartaric acid.

4. Continue boiling. When the temperature reaches 320°F (160°C), or whatever final temperature is desired (see p. 566), stop the cooking immediately by plunging the base of the pan into cold water. Remove from the cold water and allow to stand for 2–3 minutes to thicken slightly.

5. Pour out onto an oiled marble slab or, preferably, onto a silicone mat. If color was not added in step 2, it can be added now, as on p. 574.

6. Let cool slightly, but before the sugar begins to harden around the outside edges, fold the edges into the center. Repeat until the sugar mass can be picked up off the table.

7. Begin stretching the sugar and folding back onto itself. Repeat until the mixture is cooler and makes a faint crackling or clicking sound when pulled. Do not attempt to pull when the sugar becomes too cool, as it could start to crystallize. Cut the sugar into smaller pieces with a scissors and place under a sugar lamp to keep them at workable temperature. Pull and fold the pieces one at a time so that they will have a uniform texture and temperature. The sugar will take on a silky or pearled appearance after about 12 to 20 folds. Do not pull too much, or the sugar will lose this pearled appearance and become less shiny.

8. The sugar is now ready to be made into blown or pulled sugar decorations.

▶ TERMS FOR REVIEW

inversion	sugar cage	pulled sugar
spun sugar	poured sugar	blown sugar

▶ QUESTIONS FOR REVIEW

1. When boiling sugar for pulled sugar, why is it important to boil it rapidly?

2. Describe the procedure for making spun sugar (assuming you have already boiled the syrup).

3. Explain the importance of the final cooking temperature when cooking a syrup for pulled sugar.

4. Discuss the effect of tartaric acid in the production of pulled sugar. Include in your discussion the time it is added and the total quantity added.

5. Describe the procedure making a pulled sugar ribbon using two alternating colors of sugar.

6. If pulled sugar is made in advance and stored, what must be done to make it workable?

Large-Quantity Measurements

Hard Rolls (p. 67)

Ingredients	U.S.	Metric
Water	3 lb	1400 g
Yeast, fresh	3 oz	90 g
Bread flour	5 lb 8 oz	2500 g
Salt	2 oz	55 g
Sugar	2 oz	55 g
Shortening	2 oz	55 g
Egg whites	2 oz	55 g
Total weight:	*9 lb 3 oz*	*4210 g*

Vienna Bread (p. 67)

Ingredients	U.S.	Metric
Water	3 lb	1400 g
Yeast, fresh	3 oz	90 g
Bread flour	5 lb 8 oz	2500 g
Salt	2 oz	55 g
Sugar	2.5 oz	75 g
Malt syrup	1 oz	25 g
Oil	2.5 oz	75 g
Eggs	3.5 oz	100 g
Total weight:	*9 lb 6 oz*	*4320 g*

Italian Bread (p. 68)

Ingredients	U.S.	Metric
Water	4 lb	1700 g
Yeast, fresh	3 oz	80 g
Bread flour	7 lb	3000 g
Salt	2 oz	50 g
Malt syrup	0.5 oz	15 g
Total weight:	*11 lb 5 oz*	*4845 g*

Variation

Whole Wheat Italian Bread
Use the following proportions of flour in the above formula.

Ingredients	U.S.	Metric
Whole wheat flour	3 lb	1300 g
Bread flour	4 lb	1700 g

Increase the water to 59–60% to allow for the extra absorption by the bran. Mix 8 minutes.

French Bread (Straight Dough) (p. 69)

Ingredients	U.S.		Metric
Water	4 lb		1700 g
Yeast, fresh	3	oz	80 g
Bread flour	7 lb		3000 g
Salt	2	oz	50 g
Malt syrup	0.5	oz	15 g
Sugar	2	oz	50 g
Shortening	2	oz	50 g
Total weight:	*11 lb 9*	*oz*	*4945 g*

Variation

Whole Wheat French Bread
Use the following proportions of flour in the above formula.

Ingredients	U.S.	Metric
Whole wheat flour	3 lb	1300 g
Bread flour	4 lb	1700 g

Increase the water to 59–60% to allow for the extra absorption by the bran. Mix 8 minutes.

French Bread (Sponge) (p. 69)

Ingredients	U.S.		Metric
Sponge			
Bread flour	2 lb		1000 g
Water	2 lb		1000 g
Yeast, fresh	2	oz	60 g
Malt syrup	1	oz	30 g
Dough			
Bread flour	4 lb		2000 g
Water	1 lb 10	oz	810 g
Salt	1.75	oz	52 g
Total weight:	*9 lb 14*	*oz*	*4952 g*

Variation

Country-Style French Bread
Use the following proportions of flour and water in the dough stage of the above formula.

Ingredients	U.S.	Metric
Clear or bread flour	1 lb 8 oz	740 g
Whole wheat flour	2 lb 8 oz	1260 g
Water	1 lb 13 oz	900 g

Make up the dough into round loaves.

Baguette (p. 70)

Ingredients	U.S.		Metric
Bread flour	6 lb 6	oz	3000 g
Salt	2	oz	60 g
Yeast, fresh	2.25	oz	75 g
Water	3 lb 12	oz	1800 g
Total weight:	*10 lb 6*	*oz*	*4935 g*

Cuban Bread (p. 70)

Ingredients	U.S.	Metric
Water	3 lb 12 oz	1860 g
Yeast, fresh	4 oz	120 g
Bread flour	6 lb	3000 g
Salt	2 oz	60 g
Sugar	4 oz	120 g
Total weight:	*10 lb 6 oz*	*5160 g*

Ciabatta (p. 71)

Ingredients	U.S.		Metric
Sponge			
Water	4 lb 4 oz		1920 g
Yeast, fresh		4 oz	120 g
Bread flour	4 lb		1800 g
Virgin olive oil	1 lb 8 oz		720 g
Dough			
Salt		2 oz	60 g
Bread flour	2 lb		880 g
Total weight:	*12 lb 2 oz*		*5550 g*

White Pan Bread (p. 72)

Ingredients	U.S.		Metric
Water	3 lb		1200 g
Yeast, fresh		3 oz	75 g
Bread flour	5 lb		2000 g
Salt		2 oz	50 g
Sugar		3 oz	75 g
Nonfat milk solids		4 oz	100 g
Shortening		3 oz	75 g
Total weight:	*8 lb 15 oz*		*3575 g*

Variation

Whole Wheat Bread
Use the following proportions of flour in the above formula.

Ingredients	U.S.	Metric
Bread flour	2 lb	800 g
Whole wheat flour	3 lb	1200 g

White Pan Bread (Sponge) (p. 72)

Ingredients	U.S.		Metric
Sponge			
Flour	4 lb		2000 g
Water	2 lb 12	oz	1350 g
Yeast, fresh		2.5 oz	75 g
Malt syrup		0.5 oz	15 g
Dough			
Flour	2 lb		1000 g
Water		14 oz	450 g
Salt		2 oz	60 g
Nonfat milk solids		3 oz	90 g
Sugar		5 oz	150 g
Shortening		3 oz	90 g
Total weight:	*10 lb 10*	*oz*	*5280 g*

Soft Rolls (p. 73)

Ingredients	U.S.		Metric
Water	3 lb		1425 g
Yeast, fresh		3 oz	90 g
Bread flour	5 lb 4	oz	2500 g
Salt		1.5 oz	45 g
Sugar		8 oz	240 g
Nonfat milk solids		4 oz	120 g
Shortening		4 oz	120 g
Butter		4 oz	120 g
Total weight:	*9 lb 12*	*oz*	*4660 g*

Egg Bread and Rolls (p. 73)

Ingredients	U.S.			Metric
Water	2 lb 10		oz	1250 g
Yeast, fresh	3		oz	90 g
Bread flour	5 lb 4		oz	2500 g
Salt		1.5	oz	45 g
Sugar		8	oz	240 g
Nonfat milk solids		4	oz	120 g
Shortening		4	oz	120 g
Butter		4	oz	120 g
Eggs		8	oz	240 g
Total weight:	*9 lb 14*		*oz*	*4725 g*

100% Whole Wheat Bread (p. 73)

Ingredients	U.S.		Metric
Water	4 lb		1860 g
Yeast, fresh	3	oz	90 g
Whole wheat flour	6 lb 8 oz		3000 g
Sugar	2	oz	60 g
Malt syrup	2	oz	60 g
Nonfat milk solids	3	oz	90 g
Shortening	4	oz	120 g
Salt	2	oz	60 g
Total weight:	*11 lb 8 oz*		*5340 g*

Challah (p. 74)

Ingredients	U.S.		Metric
Water	2 lb		800 g
Yeast, fresh	3	oz	80 g
Bread flour	5 lb		2000 g
Egg yolks	1 lb		400 g
Sugar	6	oz	150 g
Malt syrup	0.5	oz	10 g
Salt	1.5	oz	38 g
Vegetable oil	8	oz	250 g
Total weight:	*9 lb 3*	*oz*	*3728 g*

Milk Bread (Pain au Lait) (p. 74)

Ingredients	U.S.			Metric
Bread flour	6 lb 12		oz	3000 g
Sugar	10		oz	300 g
Salt		2.25	oz	60 g
Yeast, fresh	3		oz	90 g
Eggs	10		oz	300 g
Milk	3 lb 6		oz	1500 g
Butter or margarine	15		oz	450 g
Malt syrup	1		oz	30 g
Total weight:	*12 lb 11*		*oz*	*5730 g*

Light American Rye Bread and Rolls (p. 75)

Ingredients	U.S.		Metric
Water	3 lb		1400 g
Yeast, fresh	3	oz	90 g
Light rye flour	2 lb		1000 g
Bread or clear flour	3 lb		1400 g
Salt	1.5	oz	45 g
Shortening	2	oz	60 g
Molasses or malt syrup	2	oz	60 g
Caraway seeds (*optional*)	1	oz	30 g
Rye flavor	1	oz	30 g
Total weight:	*8 lb 10*	*oz*	*4115 g*

Onion Rye (p. 75)

Ingredients	U.S.		Metric
Water	3 lb		1200 g
Yeast, fresh	3	oz	75 g
Light rye flour	1 lb 12	oz	700 g
Clear flour	3 lb 4	oz	1300 g
Dried onions, scaled, soaked in water, and well drained	4	oz	100 g
Salt	1.5	oz	40 g
Caraway seeds	1	oz	25 g
Rye flavor	1	oz	25 g
Malt syrup	2	oz	50 g
Total weight:	*8 lb 12*	*oz*	*3515 g*

Variation

Onion Pumpernickel (Nonsour)
Use the following proportions of flour in the above formula.

Ingredients	U.S.	Metric
Rye meal (pumpernickel flour)	1 lb	400 g
Medium rye flour	12 oz	300 g
Clear flour	3 lb 4 oz	1300 g

Dough may be colored with caramel color or cocoa powder.

Basic Yeast Starter (p. 77)

Ingredients	U.S.		Metric
Bread flour	3 lb 12	oz	1800 g
Water	2 lb 4	oz	1080 g
Yeast, fresh	0.12	oz	4 g
Salt	1.2	oz	36 g
Total weight:	*6 lb 1*	*oz*	*2920 g*

Rye Sour I (p. 77)

Ingredients	U.S.	Metric
Rye flour	5 lb	2000 g
Water	3 lb 12 oz	1500 g
Yeast, fresh	4 oz	10 g
Onion, halved (*optional*)	1	1
Total weight:	*9 lb*	*3600 g*

Rye Sour III (p. 78)

Ingredients	U.S.		Metric
Rye flour	4 lb		2000 g
Water, warm (85-90°F or 30-35°C)	4 lb		2000 g
Yeast, fresh	1	oz	30 g
Total weight:	*8 lb*		*4030 g*

Sour Rye Bread (p. 80)

Ingredients	U.S.		Metric
Water	3 lb		1200 g
Yeast, fresh	1	oz	25 g
Fermented rye sour	3 lb 8	oz	1440 g
Clear flour	6 lb		2400 g
Salt	2	oz	50 g
Total weight:	*12 lb 11*	*oz*	*5115 g*
Optional			
Caraway seeds	up to 1.5 oz		up to 35 g
Molasses or malt syrup	up to 3 oz		up to 70 g
Caramel color	up to 1.5 oz		up to 35 g

Pumpernickel (p. 80)

Ingredients	U.S.			Metric
Water	3 lb			1500 g
Yeast, fresh		1	oz	30 g
Fermented rye sour	2 lb	8	oz	1260 g
Rye meal (pumpernickel)	1 lb	4	oz	600 g
Clear flour	4 lb	12	oz	2400 g
Salt		2	oz	60 g
Malt syrup		1	oz	30 g
Molasses		2	oz	60 g
Caramel color (*optional*)		1.5	oz	45 g
Total weight:	*11 lb*	*15*	*oz*	*5985 g*

French Rye (p. 81)

Ingredients	U.S.		Metric
Rye Sour III (p. 78)	6 lb		3000 g
Bread flour	1 lb		500 g
Salt	1.25 oz		40 g
Total weight:	*7 lb 1*	*oz*	*3540 g*

Pain de Campagne (Country-Style Bread) (p. 81)

Ingredients	U.S.			Metric
Rye Sour III (p. 78)	1 lb	2	oz	600 g
Bread flour	4 lb	8	oz	2400 g
Rye flour	1 lb	2	oz	600 g
Salt		1.75	oz	60 g
Yeast, fresh		1.5	oz	45 g
Water	3 lb	12	oz	1950 g
Lard or goose fat (*optional*)		1.75	oz	60 g
Total weight:	*10 lb*	*13*	*oz*	*5675 g*

English Muffins (p. 85)

Ingredients	U.S.		Metric
Water (see mixing instructions)	3 lb		1500 g
Yeast, fresh		1 oz	30 g
Bread flour	4 lb		2000 g
Salt		1 oz	30 g
Sugar		1 oz	30 g
Nonfat milk solids		1.5 oz	45 g
Shortening		1 oz	30 g
Total weight:	*7 lb 5*	*oz*	*3665 g*

Bagels (p. 86)

Ingredients	U.S.		Metric
Water	2 lb		1000 g
Yeast, fresh		2 oz	60 g
High-gluten flour	4 lb		2000 g
Malt syrup		4 oz	120 g
Salt		1 oz	30 g
Oil		0.5 oz	16 g
Total weight:	*6 lb 7*	*oz*	*3226 g*

Olive Focaccia (p. 86)

Ingredients	U.S.			Metric
Water	3 lb	10	oz	1800 g
Yeast, fresh		1.5	oz	45 g
Bread flour	6 lb			3000 g
Salt		1	oz	30 g
Olive oil		3.5	oz	100 g
Chopped, pitted oil-cured black olives	2 lb			1000 g
Total weight:	*12 lb*			*5975 g*

 Herb Focaccia (Sponge Method) (p. 87)

Ingredients	U.S.			Metric
Sponge				
Flour	2 lb			925 g
Water	1 lb	8	oz	675 g
Yeast, fresh		0.5	oz	15 g
Flour	5 lb			2275 g
Water	3 lb	8	oz	1600 g
Yeast, fresh		0.5	oz	15 g
Salt		2	oz	60 g
Olive oil		4	oz	125 g
Rosemary and salt (see Makeup)				
Total weight:	*12 lb*	*7*	*oz*	*5690 g*

 Chestnut Bread (p. 87)

Ingredients	U.S.			Metric
Water	2 lb	4	oz	1080 g
Yeast, fresh		3.5	oz	100 g
High-gluten flour	2 lb	13	oz	1350 g
Chestnut flour		15	oz	450 g
Salt		1.5	oz	45 g
Butter		1.75	oz	54 g
Total weight:	*6 lb*	*6*	*oz*	*3079 g*

 Prosciutto Bread (p. 88)

Ingredients	U.S.		Metric
Water	1 lb	11 oz	855 g
Yeast, fresh		1 oz	30 g
Bread flour	3 lb		1500 g
Salt		1 oz	30 g
Rendered lard or prosciutto fat		3 oz	90 g
Basic Yeast Starter (p.77) or fermented dough		10 oz	300 g
Prosciutto, chopped or diced into small pieces		10 oz	300 g
Total weight:	*6 lb*	*4 oz*	*3105 g*

Olive Bread (p. 88)

Ingredients	U.S.			Metric	
Water	3 lb	2	oz	1480	g
Yeast, fresh		1.2	oz	36	g
Bread flour	3 lb	12	oz	1800	g
Whole wheat flour		8	oz	240	g
Rye flour		12	oz	360	g
Salt		1.5	oz	50	g
Olive oil		4	oz	120	g
Basic Yeast Starter (p. 77) or fermented dough		8	oz	240	g
Pitted black olives, whole or halved	1 lb	8	oz	720	g
Total weight:	*10 lb*	*8*	*oz*	*5046*	*g*

Crumpets (p. 89)

Ingredients	U.S.			Metric	
Water, warm	3 lb	12	oz	1650	g
Yeast, fresh		3	oz	90	g
Bread flour	3 lb	6	oz	1500	g
Salt		1	oz	30	g
Sugar		0.4	oz	10	g
Baking soda		0.16	oz	4.5	g
Water, cold		15	oz	420	g
Total weight:	*8 lb*	*5*	*oz*	*3704*	*g*

Sweet Roll Dough (p.106)

Ingredients	U.S.		Metric
Water	2 lb		800 g
Yeast, fresh		6 oz	150 g
Butter, margarine, or shortening	1 lb		400 g
Sugar	1 lb		400 g
Salt		1 oz	25 g
Nonfat milk solids		4 oz	100 g
Eggs		12 oz	300 g
Bread flour	4 lb		1600 g
Cake flour	1 lb		400 g
Total weight:	*10 lb*	*7 oz*	*4175 g*

Rich Sweet Dough (p. 107)

Ingredients	U.S.		Metric
Milk, scalded and cooled	2 lb		800 g
Yeast, fresh		4 oz	100 g
Bread flour	2 lb	8 oz	1000 g
Butter	2 lb		800 g
Sugar	1 lb		400 g
Salt		1 oz	25 g
Eggs	1 lb	4 oz	500 g
Bread flour	2 lb	8 oz	1000 g
Total weight:	*11 lb 9 oz*		*4625 g*

Variations

Stollen

Ingredients	U.S.	Metric
Almond extract	0.5 oz	10 g
Lemon rind, grated	0.5 oz	10 g
Vanilla extract	0.5 oz	10 g
Raisins (light, dark, or a mixture)	1 lb	600 g
Mixed glacéed fruit	1 lb 12 oz	700 g

Add almond extract, lemon rind, and vanilla extract to the butter and sugar during the blending stage. Knead raisins and mixed glacéed fruit into the dough.

Babka

Ingredients	U.S.	Metric
Vanilla extract	0.5 oz	10 g
Cardamom	0.25 oz	5 g
Raisins	1 lb	400 g

Add vanilla and cardamom to the butter during blending. Knead raisins into the dough.

Hot Cross Buns (p.108)

Ingredients	U.S.			Metric
Sweet Roll Dough (p. 106)	10 lb			5000 g
Dried currants	1 lb			1250 g
Golden raisins			8 oz	625 g
Mixed candied peel, diced			4 oz	300 g
Ground allspice			4 tsp	10 g
Total weight:	*11 lb 12 oz*			*7185 g*

Baba/Savarin Dough (p.109)

Ingredients	U.S.			Metric
Milk	1 lb			500 g
Yeast, fresh		2	oz	60 g
Bread flour		10	oz	300 g
Eggs	1 lb	4	oz	600 g
Bread flour	1 lb	14	oz	900 g
Sugar		1	oz	30 g
Salt		0.5 oz		15 g
Butter, melted	1 lb			500 g
Total weight:	*5 lb 15*		*oz*	*2905 g*

Brioche (p. 111)

Ingredients	U.S.			Metric
Milk		8	oz	250 g
Yeast, fresh		2	oz	60 g
Bread flour		8	oz	250 g
Eggs	1 lb	4	oz	600 g
Bread flour	2 lb			950 g
Sugar		2	oz	60 g
Salt		0.5 oz		15 g
Butter, softened	1 lb	12	oz	850 g
Total weight:	*6 lb*	*4*	*oz*	*3035 g*

Danish Pastry Dough (Brioche-Style) (p. 114)

Ingredients	U.S.			Metric
Milk	1 lb	6	oz	675 g
Yeast, fresh		4	oz	120 g
Bread flour	4 lb	14	oz	2400 g
Eggs		10	oz	300 g
Butter, melted		4.5 oz		150 g
Salt		1	oz	30 g
Sugar		4.5 oz		150 g
Milk		7.5 oz		225 g
Butter, softened	3 lb			1500 g
Total weight:	*11 lb 3*		*oz*	*5550 g*

Croissants (p. 115)

Ingredients	U.S.	Metric
Milk	2 lb	900 g
Yeast, fresh	2 oz	60 g
Sugar	2 oz	60 g
Salt	1 oz	30 g
Butter, softened	6 oz	160 g
Bread flour	3 lb 8 oz	1600 g
Butter	2 lb	900 g
Total weight:	*8 lb 3 oz*	*3710 g*

Danish Pastry (p. 115)

Ingredients	U.S.		Metric
Water	2 lb		800 g
Yeast, fresh	5	oz	125 g
Butter	10	oz	250 g
Sugar	12	oz	300 g
Nonfat milk solids	4	oz	100 g
Salt	1	oz	25 g
Cardamom or mace (*optional*)	0.16 oz (2 tsp)		4 g
Whole eggs	1 lb		400 g
Egg yolks	4	oz	100 g
Bread flour	4 lb		1600 g
Cake flour	1 lb		400 g
Butter (for rolling in)	2 lb 8	oz	1000 g
Total weight:	*12 lb 12*	*oz*	*5104 g*

Cinnamon Sugar (p. 116)

Ingredients	U.S.		Metric
Sugar	2 lb		1000 g
Cinnamon	1	oz	30 g
Total weight:	*2 lb 1 oz*		*1030 g*

Streusel or Crumb Topping (p. 116)

Ingredients	U.S.		Metric
Butter and/or shortening	1 lb		500 g
Granulated sugar	10	oz	300 g
Brown sugar	8	oz	250 g
Salt	0.16 oz (1 tsp)		5 g
Cinnamon or mace	0.08-0.16 oz (1-2 tsp)		2.5-5 g
Pastry flour	2 lb		1000 g
Total weight:	*4 lb 2*	*oz*	*2060 g*

Apricot Glaze I (p. 117)

Yield: 3 lb 4 oz (3760 g)

Ingredients	U.S.		Metric
Apricots, canned	2 lb		1000 g
Apples	2 lb		1000 g
Sugar	3 lb 12	oz	1900 g
Water	2	oz	50 g
Sugar	4	oz	100 g
Pectin	1.33 oz		40 g

Apricot Glaze II (p. 117)

Yield: 1 lb 12 oz (880 g)

Ingredients	U.S.	Metric
Apricot preserves	2 lb	1000 g
Water	8 oz	250 g

Lemon Cheese Filling (p. 117)

Ingredients	U.S.		Metric
Cream cheese	1 lb 4	oz	600 g
Sugar	4	oz	120 g
Grated lemon zest	0.4 oz (5 tsp)		12 g
Total weight:	*1 lb 8*	*oz*	*732 g*

Date, Prune, or Apricot Filling (p. 118)

Yield: about 6 lb (3000 g)		
Ingredients	**U.S.**	**Metric**
Dates, prunes (pitted), or dried apricots	4 lb	2000 g
Sugar	12 oz	400 g
Water	2 lb	1000 g

 ### Almond Filling I (Frangipane) (p. 118)

Ingredients	**U.S.**	**Metric**
Almond paste	2 lb	1000 g
Sugar	2 lb	1000 g
Butter and/or shortening	1 lb	500 g
Pastry or cake flour	8 oz	250 g
Eggs	8 oz	250 g
Total weight:	*6 lb*	*3000 g*

 ### Almond Cream (Crème d'Amande) (p. 119)

Ingredients	**U.S.**		**Metric**
Butter	12	oz	360 g
Fine granulated sugar	12	oz	360 g
Grated lemon zest	0.12 oz (1½ tsp)		4 g
Whole egg	6.67 oz (4 eggs)		200 g
Egg yolk	2.67 oz (4 yolks)		80 g
Vanilla extract	8	drops	8 drops
Powdered almonds	12	oz	360 g
Cake flour	4	oz	120 g
Total weight:	*3 lb*		*1480 g*

 ### Apple Compote Filling (p. 119)

Yield: about 4 lb (2 kg) or 2 lb 4 oz (1100 g) drained		
Ingredients	**U.S.**	**Metric**
Apples, peeled and cored	2 lb 4 oz	1100 g
Butter	10 oz	300 g
Sugar	1 lb	480 g
Water	8 oz	240 g

 ### Cinnamon Raisin Filling (p. 119)

Ingredients	**U.S.**		**Metric**
Powdered almonds	14	oz	400 g
Sugar	8	oz	240 g
Maple syrup	4	oz	120 g
Egg whites	8	oz	240 g
Cinnamon	1.33	oz	40 g
Raisins, golden	7	oz	200 g
Total weight:	*2 lb 10*	*oz*	*1240 g*

Pecan Maple Filling (p. 120)

Ingredients	**U.S.**		**Metric**
Powdered hazelnuts	14 oz		400 g
Sugar	8 oz		240 g
Egg whites	8 oz		240 g
Maple syrup	4 oz		120 g
Pecans, finely sliced or chopped	8 oz		240 g
Total weight:	*2 lb 10 oz*		*1240 g*

Hazelnut Filling (p.120)

Ingredients	U.S.		Metric
Hazelnuts, toasted and ground	1 lb		500 g
Sugar	2 lb		1000 g
Cinnamon		0.5 oz	15 g
Eggs		6 oz	190 g
Cake crumbs	2 lb		1000 g
Milk	1-2 lb		500-1000 g
Total weight:	*6 lb 6 oz*		*3205 g*
	to 7 lb 6 oz		*to 3705 g*

 ## Chocolate Filling (p. 121)

Ingredients	U.S.		Metric
Sugar	1 lb		400 g
Cocoa		6 oz	150 g
Cake crumbs	3 lb		1200 g
Eggs		4 oz	100 g
Butter, melted		6 oz	150 g
Vanilla		1 oz	25 g
Water (*as needed*)		12 oz	300 g
Total weight:	*5 lb 13 oz*		*2425 g*

 ## Honey Pan Glaze (For Caramel Rolls) (p.121)

Ingredients	U.S.		Metric
Brown sugar	2 lb	8 oz	100 g
Butter, margarine, or shortening	1 lb		400 g
Honey		10 oz	250 g
Corn syrup (or malt syrup)		10 oz	250 g
Water (*as needed*)		4 oz	100 g
Total weight:	*5 lb*		*2000 g*

 ## Cranberry Scones (p. 144)

Ingredients	U.S.			Metric
Butter	1 lb	2	oz	550 g
Sugar		15	oz	450 g
Salt		1.25	oz	25 g
Egg yolks		4	oz (6 yolks)	120 g
Milk	2 lb	10	oz	1300 g
Pastry flour	4 lb	8	oz	2250 g
Baking powder		4.5	oz	135 g
Dried cranberries		12	oz	375 g
Total weight:	*7 lb*	*14*	*oz*	*3905 g*

 ## Chocolate Cake Doughnuts (p. 157)

Ingredients	U.S.		Metric
Shortening		6 oz	180 g
Sugar	1 lb		500 g
Salt		0.5 oz	15 g
Nonfat milk solids		3 oz	90 g
Vanilla extract		1 oz	30 g
Whole eggs		6 oz	180 g
Egg yolks		2 oz	60 g
Water	2 lb	2 oz	1060 g
Cake flour	2 lb	8 oz	1500 g
Bread flour	1 lb	8 oz	500 g
Cocoa powder		5 oz	155 g
Baking powder		2 oz	60 g
Baking soda		0.4 oz (2⅔ tsp)	13 g
Total weight:	*8 lb 11 oz*		*4343 g*

Rich Vanilla Spice Doughnuts (p. 158)

Ingredients	U.S.			Metric
Bread flour	1 lb	8	oz	750 g
Cake flour	1 lb	8	oz	750 g
Baking powder		1.5	oz	45 g
Nutmeg		0.4	oz (2 tbsp)	12 g
Cinnamon		0.12	oz (2 tsp)	4 g
Salt		0.6	oz (1 tbsp)	18 g
Whole eggs		10	oz	310 g
Egg yolks		2	oz	60 g
Sugar	1 lb	4	oz	630 g
Milk	1 lb	3	oz	600 g
Vanilla extract		1.5	oz	45 g
Butter, melted		6	oz	190 g
Total weight:	*6 lb 13*		*oz*	*3414 g*

French Doughnuts (Beignets Soufflés) (p. 160)

Ingredients	U.S.			Metric
Milk	1 lb	14	oz	750 g
Butter		12	oz	300 g
Salt		0.5	oz	15 g
Sugar		0.5	oz	15 g
Bread flour	1 lb	2	oz	450 g
Eggs	1 lb	8	oz	600 g
Total weight:	*5 lb 5*		*oz*	*2130 g*

Fritter Batter I (p. 160)

Ingredients	U.S.			Metric
Pastry flour	2 lb	4	oz	1000 g
Sugar		2	oz	60 g
Salt		0.5	oz	15 g
Baking powder		0.5	oz	15 g
Eggs, beaten	1 lb	2	oz	500 g
Milk	2 lb			900 g
Oil		2	oz	60 g
Vanilla extract		0.33	oz (2 tsp)	10 g
Total weight:	*5 lb 11*		*oz*	*2560 g*

Fritter Batter II (p. 161)

Ingredients	U.S.			Metric
Bread flour	1 lb 8		oz	750 g
Cake flour		8	oz	250 g
Salt		0.5	oz	15 g
Sugar		1	oz	30 g
Milk	2 lb 4		oz	1125 g
Egg yolks, beaten		4	oz	125 g
Oil		4	oz	125 g
Egg whites		8	oz	250 g
Total weight:	*5 lb 5*		*oz*	*2670 g*

Beignets de Carnival (p. 161)

Ingredients	U.S.		Metric
Bread flour	1 lb 5	oz	600 g
Sugar		1.5 oz	45 g
Salt		0.5 oz	15 g
Egg yolks	6	oz	180 g
Light cream	6	oz	180 g
Kirsch		1.5 oz	45 g
Rose water	1	oz	30 g
Total weight:	*2 lb 5*	*oz*	*1095 g*

Viennoise (p. 162)

Ingredients	U.S.	Metric
Brioche Dough (p. 111)	5 lb	2400 g
Egg wash	as needed	as needed
Red currant jelly	14 oz	400 g

Cannoli Shells (p. 163)

Ingredients	U.S.		Metric
Bread flour	1 lb 8	oz	700 g
Pastry flour	1 lb 8	oz	700 g
Sugar	4	oz	120 g
Salt	0.15 oz (⅔ tsp)		4 g
Butter	8	oz	240 g
Egg, beaten	6.5	oz	200 g
Dry white wine or Marsala	1 lb		500 g
Total weight:	*5 lb 2*	*oz*	*2464 g*

Ricotta Cannoli Filling (p. 163)

Ingredients	U.S.	Metric
Ricotta impastato (see p. 31)	4 lb	2000 g
Confectioners' sugar	2 lb	1000 g
Cinnamon extract	1 oz	30 g
Candied citron, candied citrus peel, or candied pumpkin, finely diced	6 oz	180 g
Sweet chocolate, finely chopped, or tiny chocolate bits	4 oz	120 g
Total weight:	*6 lb 11 oz*	*3530 g*

Vanilla Syrup (p. 178)

Ingredients	U.S.	Metric
Water	1 lb 12 oz	800 g
Sugar	1 lb 8 oz	720 g
Vanilla bean, split	2	2
Total weight:	*3 lb 4 oz*	*1520 g*
	(about	*(about*
	2¼ pt)	*1300 mL)*

Cocoa Vanilla Syrup (p. 179)

Ingredients	U.S.	Metric	
Water	1 lb	500	g
Sugar	1 lb	500	g
Vanilla bean	2	2	
Cocoa powder	4 oz	125	g
Total weight:	*2 lb 4 oz*	*1125 g*	
	(about	*(about*	
	30 fl.oz)	*1 L)*	

Coffee Rum Syrup (p. 179)

Ingredients	U.S.		Metric
Sugar	10	oz	260 g
Water	10	oz	260 g
Ground coffee	0.67	oz	20 g
Rum	14	oz	360 g
Total weight:	*2 lb 2*	*oz (29–31 fl. oz)*	*900 g (770–800 mL)*

Variations

Coffee Syrup

Ingredients	U.S.	Metric
Coffee liqueur	6.5 oz	160 g

Omit the rum in the basic recipe and add the coffee-flavored liqueur:

Rum Syrup

Ingredients	U.S.	Metric
Water	12 oz	300 g
Sugar	10.5 oz	260 g
Dark rum	2 oz	60 g

Omit the coffee in the basic recipe and adjust the ingredient quantities as listed above.

Crème Chantilly (p. 181)

Ingredients	U.S.	Metric
Heavy cream or crème fraîche	2 pt	1000 g
Confectioners' sugar	5 oz	155 g
Vanilla extract	2 tsp	10 mL
Total weight:	*2 lb 5 oz*	*1165 g*

Vanilla Crème Diplomat (p. 191)

Ingredients	U.S.		Metric
Milk	1 pt 8	oz	750 g
Vanilla bean, split	1		1
Egg yolks	4	oz	120 g
Fine granulated sugar	3	oz	90 g
Cake flour	2	oz	60 g
Cornstarch	1.5	oz	45 g
Orange liqueur, such as Grand Marnier	3	oz	90 g
Crème Chantilly (p. 181)	1 lb 4	oz	600 g
Total weight:	*3 lb 9*	*oz*	*1755 g*

Variations

Chocolate Crème Diplomat

Ingredients	U.S.	Metric
Dark chocolate, finely chopped	7 oz	210 g

Omit the orange liqueur from the basic recipe. Stir dark chocolate into the hot pastry cream in step 4. Stir until the chocolate is completely melted and well mixed.

Passion Fruit Ganache (p. 193)

Ingredients	U.S.	Metric
Heavy cream	12 oz	360 g
Passion fruit juice	12 oz	360 g
Butter	6 oz	180 g
Egg yolks	5 oz	150 g
Sugar	6 oz	180 g
Dark chocolate, chopped	1 lb 5 oz	645 g
Total weight:	*3 lb 14 oz*	*1875 g*

Chocolate Mousse II (p. 193)

Ingredients	U.S.	Metric
Egg yolks	4.5 oz	120 g
Fine granulated sugar	4 oz	105 g
Water	3 oz	90 g
Dark chocolate, melted	1 lb 2 oz	480 g
Heavy cream	2 lb	900 g
Total weight:	*3 lb 13 oz*	*1695 g*

Caramel Sauce (p. 196)

Yield: 1½ qt (1.5 L)

Ingredients	U.S.	Metric
Sugar	2 lb	1 kg
Water	8 oz	250 mL
Lemon juice	1 tbsp	15 mL
Heavy cream	1.5 pt	750 mL
Milk	1 pt	500 mL

Pie Dough (p. 204)

Ingredients	Flaky Pie Dough U.S.	Flaky Pie Dough Metric	Mealy Pie Dough U.S.	Mealy Pie Dough Metric
Pastry flour	5 lb	2000 g	5 lb	2000 g
Shortening, regular	3 lb 8 oz	1400 g	3 lb 4 oz	1300 g
Water, cold	1 lb 8 oz	600 g	1 lb 4 oz	500 g
Salt	1.5 oz	40 g	1.5 oz	40 g
Sugar (*optional*)	4 oz	100 g	4 oz	100 g
Total weight:	*10 lb 5 oz*	*4140 g*	*9 lb 13 oz*	*3940 g*

Enriched Pie Pastry (p. 205)

Ingredients	U.S.	Metric
Pastry flour	3 lb	1500 g
Sugar	8 oz	250 g
Butter	1 lb 8 oz	750 g
Egg yolks	4 oz	120 g
Water, cold	12 oz	375 g
Salt	0.5 oz	15 g
Total weight:	*6 lb*	*3010 g*

Raisin Pie Filling (p. 214)

Yield: About 10½ lb (4.8 kg)
   Six 8-in. (20 cm) pies
   Five 9-in. (23 cm) pies
   Four 10-in. (25 cm) pies

Ingredients	U.S.		Metric
Raisins	4 lb		1800 g
Water	4 pt		2000 mL
Water, cold	8	oz	250 mL
Cornstarch	2.5	oz	75 g
or			
Modified starch (waxy maize)	2	oz	60 g
Sugar	1 lb 4	oz	570 g
Salt	0.33 oz (2 tsp)		10 g
Lemon juice	3	oz	90 mL
Grated lemon zest	0.1	oz (1 tsp)	3 g
Cinnamon	0.06	oz (1 tsp)	2 g
Butter	3	oz	90 g

Peach Sour Cream Pie Filling (p. 216)

Yield: 6 lb (5000 g)
   Five 8-in. (20 cm) pies
   Four 9-in. (23 cm) pies
   Three 10-in. (25 cm) pies

Ingredients	U.S.	Metric
Sour cream	2 lb	1000 g
Sugar	1 lb	500 g
Cornstarch	2 oz	60 g
Eggs, beaten	8	8
Vanilla extract	2 tsp	8 mL
Nutmeg	½ tsp	2 mL
Fresh peaches, sliced	5 lb	2500 g
Streusel (p. 116)	1 lb 8 oz	720 g

Custard Pie Filling (p. 218)

Yield: 8 lb (3.7 kg)
   Five 8-in. (20 cm) pies
   Four 9-in. (23 cm) pies
   Three 10-in. (25 cm) pies

Ingredients	U.S.	Metric
Eggs	2 lb	900 g
Sugar	1 lb	450 g
Salt	0.17 oz (1 tsp)	5 g
Vanilla extract	1 oz	30 mL
Milk	5 pt	2400 mL
Nutmeg	1–2 tsp	2–3 g

Fresh Apple Pie Filling I (p. 215)

Yield: about 12 lb (5300 g)
*   Six 8-in. (20 cm) pies*
*   Five 9-in. (23 cm) pies*
*   Four 10-in. (25 cm) pies*

Ingredients	U.S.			Metric
Apples, peeled and sliced	10 lb			4500 g
Butter		5	oz	150 g
Sugar		15	oz	450 g
Water, cold		10	oz	300 g
Cornstarch		5	oz	150 g
or				
Modified starch (waxy maize)		4	oz	120 g
Sugar	1 lb			500 g
Salt		0.3	oz (1 tsp)	5 g
Cinnamon		0.3	oz (5 tsp)	5 g
Nutmeg		0.15	oz (1¼ tsp)	2.5 g
Lemon juice		1.67 oz		50 g
Butter		1.25 oz		35 g

Variations

Fresh Apple Pie Filling II

Ingredients	U.S.	Metric
Water	1 lb	500 g

Omit the first quantity of butter. Instead, simmer the apples in water and the first quantity of sugar as in the basic cooked fruit method, using the quantity of water listed above.

Apple Ginger Pie Filling

Ingredients	U.S.	Metric
Ground ginger	0.15 oz (1¼tsp)	2.5 g
Candied ginger, finely chopped	3.5 oz	100 g

Prepare as for Fresh Apple Pie Filling I or II, but omit the cinnamon and instead add ground and candied ginger.

Apple Walnut Pie Filling

Ingredients	U.S.	Metric
Chopped walnuts	12 oz	375 g

Mix walnuts into Fresh Apple Pie Filling I or II:

Rhubarb Pie Filling

Ingredients	U.S.	Metric
Fresh rhubarb	7 lb	3200 g

Substitute rhubarb, cut into 1-in. (2.5 cm) pieces, for the apples. Omit the cinnamon, nutmeg, and lemon juice.

Pumpkin Pie Filling (p. 219)

Yield: About 17 lb (8 kg)
  Ten 8-in. (20 cm) pies
  Eight 9-in. (23 cm) pies
  Six 10-in. (25 cm) pies

Ingredients	U.S.	Metric
Pumpkin purée	6 lb 10 oz (one No. 10 can or four No. 2½ cans)	3000 g
Pastry flour	4 oz	120 g
Cinnamon	0.5 oz	15 g
Nutmeg	0.08 oz (1 tsp)	2 g
Ginger	0.08 oz (1 tsp)	2 g
Cloves	0.04 oz (½ tsp)	1 g
Salt	0.5 oz	15 g
Brown sugar	2 lb 8 oz	1150 g
Eggs	1 lb 8 oz	700 g
Corn syrup or half corn syrup and half molasses	8 oz	240 g
Milk	6 pt	3000 mL

 ## Pecan Pie Filling (p. 219)

Yield: 8 lb (3.6 kg) filling plus 1 lb 4 oz (570 g) pecans
  Five 8-in. (20 cm) pies
  Four 9-in. (23 cm) pies
  Three 10-in. (25 cm) pies

Ingredients	U.S.	Metric
Granulated sugar (see *note*)	2 lb	900 g
Butter	8 oz	230 g
Salt	0.25 oz	7 g
Eggs	2 lb	900 g
Dark corn syrup	3 lb 8 oz (about 2½ pt)	1600 g
Vanilla extract	1 oz	30 g
Pecans	1 lb 4 oz	570 g

 ## Key Lime Pie Filling (p. 220)

Yield: 6 lb (3000 g)
  Five 8-in. (20 cm) pies
  Four 9-in. (23 cm) pies
  Three 10-in. (25 cm) pies

Ingredients	U.S.	Metric
Egg yolks	16	16
Sweetened condensed milk	3 lb 8 oz	1600 g
Freshly squeezed key lime juice	1 lb 4 oz	600 g

Vanilla Cream Pie Filling (p. 220)

Yield: About 2¼ qt (2.25 L) or 6 lb 4 oz (3.1 kg)
Five 8-in. (20 cm) pies
Four 9-in. (23 cm) pies
Three 10-in. (25 cm) pies

Ingredients	U.S.	Metric
Milk	4 pt	2000 mL
Sugar	8 oz	250 g
Egg yolks	5 oz (8 yolks)	150 g (8 yolks)
Whole eggs	7 oz (4 eggs)	220 g (4 eggs)
Cornstarch	5 oz	150 g
Sugar	8 oz	250 g
Butter	4 oz	125 g
Vanilla extract	1 oz	30 mL

Variations

Chocolate Cream Pie Filling I

Ingredients	U.S.	Metric
Unsweetened chocolate	4 oz	125 g
Sweet chocolate	4 oz	125 g

Melt together unsweetened and sweet chocolate and mix into hot vanilla cream filling.

Chocolate Cream Pie Filling II

Ingredients	U.S.	Metric
Milk	3 lb 8 oz (3½ pt)	1750 mL
Sugar	8 oz	250 g
Egg yolks	5 oz (8 yolks)	150 g (8 yolks)
Whole eggs	7 oz (4 eggs)	220 g (4 eggs)
Cold milk	8 oz	250 g
Cornstarch	5 oz	150 g
Cocoa	3 oz	90 g
Sugar	8 oz	250 g
Butter	4 oz	125 g
Vanilla extract	1 oz	30 mL

This variation uses cocoa instead of chocolate. The cocoa is sifted with the starch. Some of the milk must be included with the eggs in order to provide enough liquid to make a paste with the starch and cocoa. Follow the procedure in the basic recipe, but use the above ingredients.

Butterscotch Cream Pie Filling

Ingredients	U.S.	Metric
Brown sugar	2 lb	1000 g
Butter	10 oz	300 g

Combine brown sugar and butter in a saucepan. Heat over low heat, stirring, until the butter is melted and the ingredients are blended. Prepare the basic vanilla cream filling recipe, but omit all the sugar and increase the starch to 6 oz (180 g). As the mixture comes to a boil in step 5, gradually stir in the brown sugar mixture. Finish as in the basic recipe.

Lemon Pie Filling

Ingredients	U.S.	Metric
Water	4 pt	2000 mL
Sugar	1 lb	500 g
Egg yolks	5 oz (8 yolks)	150 g (8 yolks)
Whole eggs	7 oz (4 eggs)	220 g (4 eggs)
Cornstarch	6 oz	180 g
Sugar	8 oz	250 g
Lemon zest, grated	0.5 oz	15 g
Butter	4 oz	125 g
Lemon juice	8 oz	250 mL

Follow the procedure for vanilla cream filling, but use the above ingredients. Note that the lemon juice is added after the filling is thickened.

Strawberry Rhubarb Pie Filling (p. 222)

Yield: 10 lb 8 oz (5000 g)
Five 8-inch (20-cm) pies
Four 9-inch (23-cm) pies
Three 10-inch (25-cm) pies

Ingredients	U.S.	Metric
Rhubarb, fresh or frozen, in 1-in. (2.5 cm) pieces	2 lb 8 oz	1200 g
Sugar	1 lb 8 oz	720 g
Water	8 oz	240 g
Egg yolks	8	8
Heavy cream	8 oz	240 g
Cornstarch	3 oz	90 g
Fresh strawberries, hulled and quartered	2 lb	1000 g

 ## Pâte Brisée (p. 230)

Ingredients	U.S.	Metric
Pastry flour	1 lb 8 oz	800 g
Salt	0.6 oz	20 g
Sugar	0.6 oz	20 g
Butter, chilled	12 oz	400 g
Eggs	8 oz	260 g
Water	1.2 oz	40 g
Vanilla extract	8 drops	8 drops
Lemon zest, grated	0.25 oz	8 g
Total weight:	*2 lb 14 oz*	*1548 g*

 ## Pâte Sablée (p. 231)

Ingredients	U.S.	Metric
Butter, softened	1 lb 8 oz	600 g
Confectioners' sugar	12 oz	300 g
Lemon zest, grated	0.12 oz	4 g
Vanilla extract	8 drops	8 drops
Eggs, beaten	4 oz	100 g
Pastry flour	2 lb 4 oz	900 g
Total weight:	*4 lb 12 oz*	*1904 g*

Variation

Chocolate Sablée

Ingredients	U.S.	Metric
Butter	1 lb 8 oz	600 g
Confectioners' sugar	12 oz	300 g
Grated orange zest	0.33 oz	8 g
Eggs, beaten	8 oz	200 g
Pastry flour	1 lb 12 oz	700 g
Cocoa powder	4 oz	120 g

Substitute the above ingredients and follow the basic procedure. Sift the flour with the cocoa.

Pâte Sucrée (p. 231)

Ingredients	U.S.		Metric
Butter, softened	15	oz	500 g
Sugar	6	oz	200 g
Salt	0.12 oz (¾ tsp)		4 g
Lemon zest, grated	0.12 oz (1½ tsp)		4 g
Vanilla extract	8 drops		8 drops
Eggs, beaten	6	oz	200 g
Pastry flour	1 lb 8	oz	800 g
Total weight:	*3 lb 3*	*oz*	*1708 g*

 Short Dough I (p. 232)

Ingredients	U.S.		Metric
Butter *or* butter and shortening	2 lb		1000 g
Sugar	12	oz	375 g
Salt	0.25 oz		8 g
Eggs	9	oz	280 g
Pastry flour	3 lb		1500 g
Total weight:	*6 lb 5*	*oz*	*3163 g*

 Almond Short Dough (p. 232)

Ingredients	U.S.		Metric
Butter	2 lb		800 g
Sugar	1 lb 8	oz	600 g
Salt	0.4 oz (2½ tsp)		10 g
Powdered almonds	1 lb 4	oz	500 g
Eggs	6.5	oz	165 g
Vanilla extract	0.2 oz (1¼ tsp)		5 g
Pastry flour	2 lb 8	oz	1000 g
Total weight:	*7 lb 11*	*oz*	*3080 g*

 *Variation*

Linzer Dough

Ingredients	U.S.	Metric
Cinnamon	0.25 oz (4½ tsp)	6 g
Nutmeg	0.04 oz (½ tsp)	1 g

Use ground hazelnuts, ground almonds, or a mixture of the two. Mix in the cinnamon and nutmeg with the salt in the first step.

 Short Dough II (p. 232)

Ingredients	U.S.		Metric
Butter	1 lb 4	oz	600 g
Sugar	14	oz	400 g
Salt	0.25 oz		8 g
Vanilla powder	0.25 oz		8 g
Powdered almonds	4	oz	120 g
Eggs	7	oz	200 g
Pastry flour	2 lb 2	oz	1000 g
Total weight:	*4 lb 15*	*oz*	*2336 g*

 Classic Puff Pastry (Pâte Feuilletée Classique) p. (236)

Ingredients	U.S.		Metric
Bread flour	3 lb		1500 g
Salt	1 oz		30 g
Butter, melted	8 oz		225 g
Water	1 lb 8 oz		750 g
Butter, for rolling in	1 lb 12 oz		900 g
Total weight:	*6 lb 13 oz*		*3405 g*

Ordinary Puff Pastry (p. 237)

Ingredients	U.S.	Metric
Bread flour	3 lb	1500 g
Cake flour	1 lb	500 g
Butter, softened	8 oz	250 g
Salt	1 oz	30 g
Water, cold	2 lb 4 oz	1125 g
Butter	4 lb	2000 g
Bread flour	8 oz	250 g
Total weight:	*11 lb 5 oz*	*5655 g*

 ## Almond Meringues (p. 261)

Ingredients	U.S.	Metric
Egg whites	1 lb	500 g
Fine granulated sugar	1 lb	500 g
Powdered almonds	1 lb	500 g
Total weight:	*3 lb*	*1500 g*

 ## Succès (p. 263)

Ingredients	U.S.	Metric
Egg whites	1 lb 2 oz	540 g
Granulated sugar	12 oz	360 g
Powdered almonds	12 oz	360 g
Confectioners' sugar	12 oz	360 g
Cake flour	3 oz	90 g
Total weight:	*3 lb 9 oz*	*1710 g*

 ## Chocolate Butter Cake (p. 309)

Ingredients	U.S.		Metric
Butter	2 lb		1000 g
Sugar	3 lb 8	oz	1725 g
Salt	0.75	oz	22 g
Unsweetened chocolate, melted	1 lb		500 g
Eggs	1 lb 8	oz	750 g
Cake flour	3 lb		1500 g
Baking powder	2	oz	60 g
Milk	1 lb 8	oz	750 g
Vanilla extract	1	oz	30 g
Total weight:	*12 lb 11*	*oz*	*6337 g*

 ## Yellow Butter Cake (p. 310)

Ingredients	U.S.		Metric
Butter	2 lb 4	oz	1100 g
Sugar	3 lb		1450 g
Salt	0.5	oz	15 g
Eggs	1 lb 11	oz	810 g
Cake flour	3 lb 12	oz	1800 g
Baking powder	2.5	oz	72 g
Milk	2 lb 8	oz	1200 g
Vanilla extract	1	oz	30 g
Total weight:	*13 lb 7*	*oz*	*6477 g*

Variations

Pan Spread
For one sheet pan:

Ingredients	U.S.	Metric
Brown sugar	1 lb	450 g
Granulated sugar	6 oz	170 g
Corn syrup or honey	4 oz	120 g
Water (as needed)		

Cream together the first three ingredients. Add enough water to thin out to spreading consistency.

Sacher Mix II (p. 315)

Ingredients	U.S.			Metric
Butter, softened		13.5	oz	400 g
Fine granulated sugar		11	oz	330 g
Egg yolks		12	oz	360 g
Egg whites	1 lb	2	oz	540 g
Fine granulated sugar		6	oz	180 g
Cake flour		4	oz	120 g
Cocoa powder		4	oz	120 g
Powdered almonds, toasted		5.5	oz	165 g
Total weight:	*4 lb 10*		*oz*	*2215 g*

White Cake (p. 316)

Ingredients	U.S.			Metric
Cake flour	3 lb			1500 g
Baking powder		3	oz	90 g
Salt		1	oz	30 g
Emulsified shortening	1 lb	8	oz	750 g
Sugar	3 lb	12	oz	1875 g
Skim milk	1 lb	8	oz	750 g
Vanilla extract		0.75 oz (4½ tsp)		20 g
Almond extract		0.36 oz (2¼ tsp)		10 g
Skim milk	1 lb	8	oz	750 g
Egg whites	2 lb			1000 g
Total weight:	*13 lb 9*		*oz*	*6775 g*

Devil's Food Cake (p. 317)

Ingredients	U.S.			Metric
Cake flour	3 lb			1500 g
Cocoa		8	oz	250 g
Salt		1	oz	30 g
Baking powder		1.5	oz	45 g
Baking soda		1	oz	30 g
Emulsified shortening	1 lb	12	oz	870 g
Sugar	4 lb			2000 g
Skim milk	2 lb			1000 g
Vanilla extract		0.75 oz (4½ tsp)		20 g
Skim milk	1 lb	8	oz	750 g
Eggs	2 lb			1000 g
Total weight:	*15 lb*			*7495 g*

Genoise Mousseline (p. 319)

Ingredients	U.S.	Metric
Whole eggs	1 lb 14 oz	900 g
Egg yolks	4 oz (6 yolks)	120 g (6 yolks)
Sugar	1 lb 2 oz	540 g
Cake flour, sifted	1 lb 2 oz	540 g
Total weight:	*4 lb 6 oz*	*2100 g*

Milk and Butter Sponge (p. 320)

Ingredients	U.S.		Metric
Sugar	2 lb 8	oz	1250 g
Whole eggs	1 lb 8	oz	750 g
Egg yolks	8	oz	250 g
Salt	0.5 oz		15 g
Cake flour	2 lb		1000 g
Baking powder	1	oz	30 g
Skim milk	1 lb		500 g
Butter	8	oz	250 g
Vanilla extract	1	oz	30 g
Total weight:	*8 lb 2*	*oz*	*4075 g*

Joconde Sponge Cake (Biscuit Joconde) (p. 322)

Ingredients	U.S.		Metric
Powdered almonds	14	oz	340 g
Confectioners' sugar	12	oz	300 g
Cake flour	4	oz	100 g
Whole eggs	1 lb 3	oz	480 g
Egg whites	13	oz	320 g
Sugar	1.6	oz	40 g
Butter, melted	5	oz	120 g
Total weight:	*4 lb 5*	*oz*	*1700 g*

Marjolaine Sponge Cake (p. 325)

Ingredients	U.S.	Metric
Confectioners' sugar	12 oz	360 g
Powdered almonds	12 oz	360 g
Egg yolks	10 oz	300 g
Egg whites	6 oz	180 g
Egg whites	15 oz	450 g
Sugar	9 oz	270 g
Pastry flour, sifted	9 oz	270 g
Total weight:	*4 lb 9 oz*	*2190 g*

Hazelnut Sponge Cake (p. 325)

Ingredients	U.S.		Metric
Butter, softened	14	oz	400 g
Sugar	11	oz	330 g
Egg yolks	12	oz	360 g
Egg whites	1 lb 2	oz	540 g
Sugar	6	oz	180 g
Cake flour	4	oz	120 g
Cocoa powder	4	oz	120 g
Ground hazelnuts, toasted	5.5 oz	165 g
Total weight:	*4 lb 10*	*oz*	*2215 g*

Almond Chocolate Sponge (p. 327)

Ingredients	U.S.	Metric
Marzipan	13 oz	390 g
Egg yolks	8 oz	240 g
Egg whites	12 oz	360 g
Sugar	5 oz	150 g
Cake flour	4 oz	120 g
Cocoa powder	4 oz	120 g
Butter, melted	4 oz	120 g
Total weight:	*3 lb 2 oz*	*1500 g*

Chocolate Sponge
Layers (p. 327)

Ingredients	U.S.		Metric
Egg whites	1 lb	4 oz	600 g
Sugar	1 lb		480 g
Egg yolks		14 oz	400 g
Cake flour		14 oz	400 g
Cocoa powder		4 oz	120 g
Total weight:	*4 lb*	*4 oz*	*2000 g*

 Chocolate Velvet Cake
(Moelleux) (p. 328)

Ingredients	U.S.		Metric
Almond paste	7.5	oz	225 g
Confectioners' sugar	5	oz	150 g
Egg yolks	6	oz	180 g
Egg whites	6	oz	180 g
Sugar	2.5	oz	75 g
Cake flour	4	oz	120 g
Cocoa powder	1	oz	30 g
Butter, melted	2	oz	60 g
For baking			
Almonds, chopped	3	oz	90 g
Total dough weight:	*2 lb 2*	*oz*	*1020 g*

 Lemon Madeleines (p. 329)

Ingredients	U.S.		Metric
Egg yolks	6	oz	180 g
Demerara sugar (see *note*)	1	oz	30 g
Lemon zest, grated	0.4 oz (4½ tsp)		12 g
Honey	1.5	oz	45 g
Egg whites	6	oz	180 g
Extra-fine granulated sugar	7.5	oz	225 g
Salt	0.1 oz (½ tsp)		3 g
Baking powder	0.3 oz (1½ tsp)		9 g
Cake flour	9	oz	270 g
Butter, melted	9	oz	270 g
Total weight:	*2 lb 8*	*oz*	*1224 g*

Variation

Chocolate and Orange Madeleines

Ingredients	U.S.		Metric
Egg yolks	6	oz	180 g
Demerara sugar	1	oz	30 g
Orange zest, grated	0.75 oz		24 g
Honey	1.5	oz	45 g
Egg whites	6	oz	180 g
Extra-fine granulated sugar	7.5	oz	225 g
Salt	0.1	oz (½ tsp)	3 g
Baking powder	0.4	oz (2¼ tsp)	12 g
Cocoa powder	2.5	oz	75 g
Cake flour	6	oz	180 g
Butter, melted	9	oz	270 g

Follow the basic procedure, but make change the ingredients as listed above.

French Buttercream
(p. 336)

Yield: 5 lb 8 oz (2750 g)

Ingredients	U.S.		Metric
Sugar	2 lb		1000 g
Water	8	oz	250 mL
Egg yolks	12	oz	375 g
Butter, softened	2 lb 8	oz	1250 g
Vanilla extract	0.5 oz		15 mL

Simple Buttercream (p. 337)

Ingredients	U.S.		Metric
Butter	2 lb		1000 g
Shortening	1 lb		500 g
Confectioners' sugar	4 lb		2000 g
Egg whites	5	oz	150 g
Lemon juice	0.33 oz (2 tsp)		10 g
Vanilla extract	0.5	oz	15 g
Water (*optional*)	4	oz	125 g
Total weight:	7 lb 9	oz	3800 g

Meringue-Type Buttercream
(p. 338)

Yield: 5 lb 12 oz (2900 g)

Ingredients	U.S.		Metric
Italian meringue			
Sugar	2 lb		1000 g
Water	8	oz	250 mL
Egg whites	1 lb		500 g
Butter	2 lb		1000 g
Emulsified shortening	8	oz	250 g
Lemon juice	0.33 oz (2 tsp)		10 mL
Vanilla extract	0.5	oz	15 mL

Praline Buttercream
(p. 338)

Yield: 3 lb 6 oz (1650 g)

Ingredients	U.S.		Metric
Water	4 oz		120 g
Sugar	12 oz		360 g
Egg yolks	10 oz		300 g
Butter, softened	1 lb 2 oz		540 g
Praline paste	15 oz		450 g

Vanilla Cream (p. 338)

Ingredients	U.S.		Metric
Pastry Cream II (p. 188)	2 lb 8	oz	1125 g
Gelatin	0.5	oz	16 g
Rum	1.75 oz		50 g
Butter, softened	1 lb 2	oz	500 g
Total weight:	3 lb 12	oz	1690 g

Caramel Buttercream
(p. 339)

Yield: 4 lb (2000 g)

Ingredients	U.S.		Metric
Water	4	oz	100 g
Sugar	1 lb 10	oz	740 g
Water	7	oz	200 g
Heavy cream	5	oz	140 g
Coffee extract	0.75 oz		20 g
Egg yolks	8	oz	240 g
Butter, softened	1 lb 11	oz	760 g

Light Praline Cream (p. 339)

Ingredients	U.S.		Metric
Butter, softened	2 lb		1000 g
Praline paste	1 lb		500 g
Cognac	6 oz		200 g
Italian Meringue (p. 183)	3 lb 6 oz		1700 g
Total weight:	6 lb 12 oz		3400 g

Flat Icing (p. 342)

Ingredients	U.S.		Metric
Confectioners' sugar	4 lb		2000 g
Water, hot	12	oz	375 mL
Corn syrup	4	oz	125 g
Vanilla extract	0.5	oz	15 g
Total weight:	*5 lb*		*2500 g*

Opera Glaze (p. 344)

Ingredients	U.S.		Metric
Coating chocolate (p. 43)	1 lb 8	oz	750 g
Dark chocolate couverture	10.5	oz	300 g
Peanut oil	4	oz	120 g
Total weight:	*2 lb 6*	*oz*	*1170 g*

Variation

If only couverture is used instead of part coating chocolate and part couverture, the quantity of oil must be increased so that the icing has the proper texture and can easily be cut with a cake knife.

Ingredients	U.S.	Metric
Dark chocolate couverture	1 lb 2.5 oz	1050 g
Peanut oil	2 oz	180 g

Cocoa Jelly (p. 344)

Ingredients	U.S.		Metric
Water	1 lb		450 g
Fondant	1 lb 8	oz	675 g
Glucose	8	oz	225 g
Gelatin	1	oz	30 g
Cocoa powder	4.75	oz	135 g
Total weight:	*3 lb 5*	*oz*	*1515 g*

Coffee Marble Glaze (p. 345)

Yield: 2 lb (1000 g)

Ingredients	U.S.	Metric
Gelatin	1 oz	24 g
Water	1 lb 8 oz	750 g
Sugar	4 oz	120 g
Glucose	4 oz	120 g
Vanilla bean, split	2	2
Coffee liqueur	2 oz	60 g
Coffee extract	1 oz	30 g

Diamonds (p. 410)

Ingredients	U.S.		Metric
Butter, cut in small pieces	1 lb 4	oz	560 g
Cake flour	1 lb 12	oz	800 g
Confectioners' sugar	8	oz	240 g
Salt	0.16 oz (¾ tsp)		4 g
Grated orange zest	0.3 oz (4 tsp)		8 g
Vanilla extract	0.3 oz (2 tsp)		8 g
For rolling			
Crystal sugar	7	oz	200 g
Total dough weight:	*3 lb 15 oz*		*1620 g*

Almond Macaroons II (p. 415)

Ingredients	U.S.		Metric
Powdered almonds	8	oz	240 g
Confectioners' sugar	1 lb		500 g
Egg whites	8	oz	240 g
Fine granulated sugar	3.5 oz		100 g
Vanilla extract	8 drops		8 drops
Total weight:	*2 lb 3 oz*		*1080 g*

Cocoa Almond Macaroons
Prepare as in the basic recipe, using the following ingredients and quantities. Process the cocoa and cake flour with the almonds and sugar in step 1.

Ingredients	U.S.		Metric
Powdered almonds	12	oz	300 g
Confectioners' sugar	1 lb		400 g
Cocoa powder	4	oz	100 g
Cake flour	3.5	oz	80 g
Egg whites	1 lb 3	oz	480 g
Fine granulated sugar	8	oz	200 g

Almond Tuiles I (p. 418)

Ingredients	U.S.		Metric
Butter	12 oz		360 g
Confectioners' sugar	1 lb		480 g
Egg whites	12 oz		360 g
Cake flour	14 oz		420 g
Garnish			
Sliced almonds	10 oz		300 g
Batter weight:	*3 lb 6 oz*		*1620 g*

Coconut Tuiles (p. 420)

Ingredients	U.S.		Metric
Confectioners' sugar	1 lb		520 g
Egg, lightly beaten		12 oz	400 g
Dessicated coconut	1 lb		520 g
Butter, melted		3 oz	100 g
Total weight:	*2 lb 15 oz*		*1540 g*

Brownies (p. 420)

Yield: One large recipe (about 10 lb or 4600 g) fills one full-size sheet pan (18 × 26 in./46 × 66 cm), two half-size sheet pans, four 9 × 13 in. (23 × 33 cm) pans, or six 9-in. (23 cm) square pans.

Ingredients	U.S.		Metric
Unsweetened chocolate	12	oz	340 g
Bittersweet chocolate	1 lb 4	oz	560 g
Butter	2 lb 8	oz	1125 g
Eggs	1 lb 8	oz	675 g
Sugar	2 lb 4	oz	1015 g
Salt		0.25 oz	7 g
Vanilla extract	1	oz	30 mL
Bread flour	1 lb		450 g
Walnuts or pecans, chopped	1 lb		450 g
Total weight:	*10 lb 5 oz*		*4652 g*

Variation

Ingredients	U.S.	Metric
Baking powder	0.4 oz	11 g

For a more cakelike brownie, sift the above quantity of baking powder with the flour in step 4.

Cream Cheese Brownies (p. 421)

Yield: One large recipe (about 10 lb or 4600 g) fills one full-size sheet pan (18 × 26 in./46 × 66 cm), two half-size sheet pans, four 9 × 13 in. (23 × 33 cm) pans, or six 9-in. (23 cm) square pans.

Ingredients	U.S.		Metric
Cream cheese	2 lb		900 g
Sugar		8 oz	225 g
Vanilla extract		2 tsp	7 mL
Egg yolks		2.7 oz (4 yolks)	80 g
Brownie batter without walnuts (above), (1 recipe)	10 lb 5 oz		4650 g
Total weight:	*12 lb 15 oz*		*5862 g*

Florentine Squares (p. 422)

Yield: This recipe fills a half-size sheet pan.

Ingredients	U.S.		Metric
Butter	7	oz	195 g
Cake flour	10.5	oz	300 g
Salt	0.2	oz (1 tsp)	6 g
Sugar	4	oz	120 g
Egg yolk	2	oz	60 g
Lemon zest, grated	0.12 oz (1½ tsp)		3 g
Vanilla extract	0.25 oz (1½ tsp)		6 g
Heavy cream	13	oz	375 g
Sugar	1 lb 2	oz	525 g
Butter	13	oz	375 g
Honey	1 lb 2	oz	525 g
Glucose	7.5	oz	210 g
Raisins	10.5	oz	300 g
Mixed candied peel, chopped	10.5	oz	300 g
Glacé cherries	10.5	oz	300 g
Sliced almonds	2 lb		900 g
Total weight:	*9 lb 12 oz*		*4500 g*

Espresso Biscotti (p. 423)

Ingredients	U.S.		Metric
Butter	12	oz	360 g
Sugar	1 lb 2	oz	540 g
Salt	0.6	oz	18 g
Eggs	10	oz	300 g
Water, hot	1.5	oz	45 g
Instant espresso powder	0.6	oz	18 g
Pastry flour	1 lb 14	oz	900 g
Baking powder	0.75	oz	24 g
Blanched almonds	11	oz	315 g
Total weight:	*5 lb 2*	*oz*	*2520 g*

 ## Chocolate Pecan Biscotti (p. 424)

Ingredients	U.S.		Metric
Butter	12	oz	360 g
Sugar	1 lb		540 g
Salt	0.3	oz	9 g
Orange zest, grated	0.3	oz	9 g
Eggs	10	oz	300 g
Water	6	oz	180 g
Vanilla extract	0.5	oz	15 g
Pastry flour	1 lb 14	oz	900 g
Cocoa powder	4.5	oz	135 g
Baking powder	0.75	oz	24 g
Baking soda	0.25	oz	8 g
Pecan pieces	6	oz	180 g
Small chocolate chips	6	oz	180 g
Total weight:	*5 lb 12*	*oz*	*2840 g*

 ## Batons Marechaux and Eponges (p. 425)

Ingredients	U.S.		Metric
Confectioners' sugar	10	oz	300 g
Cake flour	3	oz	90 g
Powdered almonds	7.5	oz	225 g
Egg whites	12	oz	360 g
Granulated sugar	4	oz	120 g
For finishing Batons Marechaux			
Chocolate, tempered	as needed		as needed
For finishing Eponges			
Slivered almonds	as needed		as needed
Raspberry jam	as needed		as needed
Total weight:	*2 lb 4*	*oz*	*1095 g*

Christmas Pudding (p. 437)

Ingredients	U.S.		Metric
Dark raisins	2 lb		1000 g
Light raisins	2 lb		1000 g
Currants	2 lb		1000 g
Dates, diced	1 lb		500 g
Almonds, chopped		12 oz	375 g
Candied orange peel, finely chopped		8 oz	250 g
Candied lemon peel, finely chopped		8 oz	250 g
Brandy	1 pt	8 oz	750 mL
Bread flour	1 lb		500 g
Cinnamon		0.12 oz (2 tsp)	4 g
Nutmeg		0.03 oz (½ tsp)	1 g
Mace		0.03 oz (½ tsp)	1 g
Ginger		0.03 oz (½ tsp)	1 g
Cloves, ground		0.03 oz (½ tsp)	1 g
Salt		0.5 oz	15 g
Beef suet, finely chopped	1 lb	8 oz	750 g
Brown sugar	1 lb		500 g
Eggs	1 lb		500 g
Fresh breadcrumbs		8 oz	250 g
Molasses		2 oz	60 g
Total weight:	*15 lb*	*7 oz*	*7700 g*

Steamed Blueberry Pudding (p. 438)

Ingredients	U.S.		Metric
Brown sugar	1 lb	4 oz	625 g
Butter		8 oz	250 g
Salt		0.08 oz (½ tsp)	3 g
Cinnamon		0.17 oz (1 tbsp)	5 g
Eggs		8 oz	250 g
Bread flour		4 oz	125 g
Baking powder		0.75 oz	22 g
Dry breadcrumbs	1 lb	4 oz	625 g
Milk	1 lb		500 g
Blueberries, fresh or frozen, without sugar	1 lb		500 g
Total weight:	*5 lb*	*13 oz*	*2905 g*

Cream Cheese Bavarian (p. 443)

Yield: about 6 qt (6.5 L)

Ingredients	U.S.		Metric	
Cream cheese	3 lb		1500	g
Sugar	1 lb		500	g
Salt	0.5	oz	15	g
Lemon zest, grated	0.12 oz (1½ tsp)		4	g
Orange zest, grated	0.08 oz (1 tsp)		2.5	g
Vanilla extract	0.25 oz (1½ tsp)		8	g
Lemon juice	4	oz	125	g
Gelatin	1	oz	30	g
Water, cold	8	oz	250	g
Heavy cream	4 pt		2000	mL
Total weight:	*8 lb 13*	*oz*	*4434*	*g*

Raspberry Jam (p. 502)

Yield: 1 lb 14 oz (950 g)

Ingredients	U.S.		Metric
Sugar	12	oz	375 g
Water	1	oz	125 g
Raspberries, fresh	1 lb		500 g
Glucose	1.6	oz	50 g
Sugar	2.5	oz	75 g
Pectin	1.33	oz	40 g

Strawberry Marmalade (p. 503)

Yield: 3 lb 4 oz (1600 g)

Ingredients	U.S.		Metric
Strawberries	2 lb		1000 g
Sugar	2 lb		1000 g
Pectin	0.67	oz	20 g
Lemon juice	2	oz	30 g

Apple Marmalade (p. 503)

Yield: 8 lb 8 oz (4240 g)

Ingredients	U.S.	Metric
Apples, peeled and cored	8 lb	4000 g
Water	1 lb	500 g
Sugar	2 lb 8 oz	1200 g

Caramelized Apricots (p. 503)

Yield: 2 lb 8 oz (1200 g)

Ingredients	U.S.		Metric
Sugar	1 lb		400 g
Water	4	oz	100 g
Honey	8	oz	200 g
Butter	4	oz	100 g
Canned apricots, drained	2 lb 8 oz		1200 g

Apricot Compote (p. 504)

Yield: 2 lb 6 oz (960 g)

Ingredients	U.S.		Metric
Sugar	1 lb 2	oz	450 g
Water	2.5	oz	60 g
Apricots, fresh or canned, halved and pitted	1 lb 4	oz	500 g
Pectin	1.5	oz	40 g
Glucose	2	oz	50 g

Variation

Apricot and Almond Compote

Ingredients	U.S.	Metric
Whole blanched almonds	8 oz	200 g

Add the almonds to the apricots at the same time as the pectin and glucose.

Pineapple Kumquat Compote (p. 505)

Yield: 2 lb 12 oz (1080 g)

Ingredients	U.S.		Metric
Sugar	1 lb 2	oz	450 g
Water	2.5	oz	60 g
Vanilla bean	1		1
Glucose	2	oz	48 g
Canned pineapple, drained and diced	1 lb 4	oz	500 g
Kumquats, sliced and blanched	8	oz	200 g
Pistachios	1.5	oz	40 g

Variation

Kumquat Compote

Ingredients	U.S.		Metric
Sugar	1 lb 2	oz	450 g
Water	2.5	oz	60 g
Glucose	2	oz	48 g
Kumquats, halved or sliced, blanched	1 lb 4	oz	500 g
Pistachios	3	oz	80 g

Follow the procedure in the basic recipe, but omit the pineapple and vanilla and adjust the quantities as listed above.

Rocher with Almonds (p. 547)

Ingredients	U.S.		Metric
Dark chocolate	1 lb		450 g
Praline paste	1 lb	8 oz	675 g
Ice cream wafers (pailletine), finely crushed		8 oz	225 g
Dark chocolate	1 lb	8 oz	675 g
Almonds, toasted and chopped		4 oz	112 g
Total weight:	*4 lb 12 oz*		*2137 g*

Appendix 2
Metric Conversion Factors

WEIGHT

1 ounce equals 28.35 grams

1 gram equals 0.035 ounce

1 pound equals 454 grams

1 kilogram equals 2.2 pounds

VOLUME

1 fluid ounce equals 29.57 milliliters

1 milliliter equals 0.034 fluid ounce

1 cup equals 237 milliliters

1 quart equals 946 milliliters

1 liter equals 33.8 fluid ounces

LENGTH

1 inch equals 25.4 millimeters

1 centimeter equals 0.39 inch

1 meter equals 39.4 inches

TEMPERATURE

To convert Fahrenheit to Celsius: Subtract 32, then multiply by $\frac{5}{9}$.

Example: Convert 140°F to Celsius.

$$140 - 32 = 108$$
$$108 \times \tfrac{5}{9} = 60°C$$

To convert Celsius to Fahrenheit: Multiply by $\frac{9}{5}$, then add 32.

Example: Convert 150°C to Fahrenheit.

$$150 \times \tfrac{9}{5} = 270$$
$$270 + 32 = 302° F$$

Note: The metric measurements in the recipes in this book are not equivalent to the corresponding U.S. measurements. See page 8 for a complete explanation.

Appendix 3

Decimal Equivalents of Common Fractions

Fraction	Rounded to 3 places	Rounded to 2 places
$\frac{5}{6}$	0.833	0.83
$\frac{4}{5}$	0.8	0.8
$\frac{3}{4}$	**0.75**	**0.75**
$\frac{2}{3}$	**0.667**	**0.67**
$\frac{5}{8}$	0.625	0.63
$\frac{3}{5}$	0.6	0.6
$\frac{1}{2}$	**0.5**	**0.5**
$\frac{1}{3}$	**0.333**	**0.33**
$\frac{1}{4}$	**0.25**	**0.25**
$\frac{1}{5}$	0.2	0.2
$\frac{1}{6}$	0.167	0.17
$\frac{1}{8}$	**0.125**	**0.13**
$\frac{1}{10}$	0.1	0.1
$\frac{1}{12}$	0.083	0.08
$\frac{1}{16}$	0.063	0.06
$\frac{1}{25}$	0.04	0.04

Appendix

Approximate Volume Equivalents of Dry Foods

The following equivalents are rough averages only. Actual weight varies considerably. For accurate measurement, all ingredients should be weighed.

Following common practice, volume measures in this chart are represented as common fractions rather than as decimals.

Bread flour, sifted
1 lb = 4 cups
1 cup = 4 oz

Bread flour, unsifted
1 lb = 3⅓ cups
1 cup = 4.75 oz

Cake flour, sifted
1 lb = 4¼ cups
1 cup = 3.75 oz

Cake flour, unsifted
1 lb = 3½ cups
1 cup = 4.5 oz

Granulated sugar
1 lb = 2¼ cups
1 cup = 7 oz

Confectioners' sugar, sifted
1 lb = 4 cups
1 cup = 4 oz

Confectioners' sugar, unsifted
1 lb = 3½ cups
1 cup = 4.5 oz

Cornstarch, sifted
1 lb = 4 cups
1 cup = 4 oz
1 oz = 4 tbsp = ¼ cup
1 tbsp = 0.25 oz

Cornstarch, unsifted
1 lb = 3½ cups
1 cup = 4.5 oz
1 oz = 3½ tbsp
1 tbsp = 0.29 oz

Cocoa, unsifted
1 lb = 5 cups
1 cup = 3.2 oz
1 oz = 5 tbsp
1 tbsp = 0.2 oz

Gelatin, unflavored
1 oz = 3 tbsp
¼ oz = 2¼ tsp
1 tbsp = 0.33 oz
1 tsp = 0.11 oz

Baking powder (phosphate type and sodium aluminum sulfate type)
1 oz = 2 tbsp
¼ oz = 1½ tsp
1 tbsp = 0.5 oz
1 tsp = 0.17 oz

Baking soda
(same as for Baking Powder)

Cream of tartar
1 oz = 4 tbsp
¼ oz = 1 tbsp
1 tsp = 0.08 oz

Salt
1 oz = 5 tsp
¼ oz = 1¼ tsp
1 tsp = 0.2 oz

Cinnamon
1 oz = 17 tsp
¼ oz = 4¼ tsp
1 tsp = 0.06 oz

Ground spices (except cinnamon)
1 oz = 14 tsp
¼ oz = 3½ tsp
1 tsp = 0.07 oz

Grated lemon zest
1 oz = 4 tbsp
1 tsp = 0.08 oz

Appendix 5

Temperature Calculations for Yeast Doughs

In chapter 3 (p. 60), a simple formula is presented to enable you to calculate what the water temperature should be in order to get a mixed dough of a specified temperature. This formula is sufficient for most straight doughs made in small batches. However, some other calculations may sometimes be required. These are detailed here.

MACHINE FRICTION

Machine friction depends on many factors, including the type of mixer, amount of dough, stiffness of dough, and mixing time. This friction may be determined for each dough prepared, assuming a constant batch size.

ICE CALCULATION

If your tap water is warmer than the water temperature you need for a batch of dough, you can cool the water with crushed ice. A simple formula can be used to calculate how much crushed ice to use.

This formula is based on the fact that it requires 144 BTUs of heat energy to melt 1 pound of ice. A BTU (British Thermal Unit) is the amount of heat needed to raise the temperature of 1 pound of water 1°F. Therefore, it takes 144 BTUs to melt a pound of ice, but only one more BTU to heat that pound of melted ice from 32° to 33°F.

You can use the following formula without having to understand how it is derived. However, if you wish to know where the formula comes from, an explanation fol-

Procedure for Determining Machine Friction

1. Prepare a batch of dough, first measuring the room temperature, flour temperature, and water temperature. Add these three figures.

2. Measure the temperature of the dough as it comes from the mixer. Multiply this figure by 3.

3. Subtract the result of step 1 from the result of step 2. This is the machine friction.

4. Use this factor when calculating the water temperature required for subsequent batches of this particular dough, as explained on page 60.

   Example: Room temperature = 72°F
   Flour temperature = 65°F
   Water temperature = 75°F
   Dough temperature = 77°F

   1. $72 + 65 + 75 = 212$
   2. $77 \times 3 = 231$
   3. $231 - 212 = 19$
      Machine friction = 19°F

lows the formula and sample calculation. Please note that this formula is more accurate than many of the formulas you will see elsewhere. Many other formulas allow for the heat energy needed to melt the ice, but they don't allow for the fact that the melted ice is also warmed up to the final water temperature.

Also, please remember that the ice counts as part of the water for the dough.

Procedure for Determining Ice Requirement

1. **Measure the temperature of the tap water. Subtract the water temperature needed for your dough from the tap water temperature. This number is the temperature decrease needed.**

   Tap water temperature

   − desired water temperature

   = temperature decrease

2. **Calculate the weight of ice needed by using the following formula.**

$$\text{Ice weight} = \frac{\text{Total water} \times \text{temperature decrease}}{\text{Tap water temperature} + 112}$$

   "Total water" is the weight of water needed for the dough recipe.

3. **Subtract the ice weight from the total water needed to get the weight of the tap water needed.**

   Total water − ice = tap water

   Example: For a batch of bread, you need 16 lb water at 58°F. Your tap water is 65°F. How much tap water and how much ice should you use?

$$\text{Ice} = \frac{16\ \text{lb} \times (65 - 58)}{65 + 112} = \frac{16\ \text{lb} \times 7}{177}$$

$$= \frac{112\ \text{lb}}{177} = 0.63\ \text{lb} = 10\ \text{oz}$$

   Tap water = 16 lb − 10 oz = 15 lb 6 oz

   You need 10 oz ice plus 15 lb 6 oz tap water.

The above formula is based on the fact that the number of BTUs needed to bring the ice up to the desired water temperature equals the number of BTUs lost by the tap water when it is cooled to the desired temperature.

This can be expressed as follows:

BTUs to melt ice *plus*
BTUs to heat melted ice to } = BTUs lost by tap water
desired temperature

Remember, as explained earlier, that 144 BTUs are needed to melt a pound of ice, and that 1 BTU is needed to heat a pound of water 1°F.

Therefore, the three BTU values in the above equation can each be expressed mathematically:

BTUs to melt ice = Ice weight (in pounds) *times* 144

BTUs to heat melted ice to temperature = Ice weight *times* degrees of temperature rise

or

Ice weight *times* (desired temperature *minus* 32°F)

BTUs lost by tap water = weight of tap water *times* degrees of temperature drop

or

(total water *minus* ice) *times* (tap water temperature *minus* desired temperature)

In order to make the calculations easier to read, we adopt the following abbreviations. Then we substitute them in our basic equation and proceed to simplify it mathematically.

$$I = \text{ice weight}$$
$$W = \text{tap water weight}$$
$$W + I = \text{total water required in recipe}$$
$$T = \text{tap water temperature}$$
$$D = \text{desired temperature}$$

BTUs to melt ice *plus*
BTUs to heat melted ice to } = BTUs lost by
desired temperature   tap water

$$(I \times 144) + (I \times (D - 32)) = ((W + I) - I) \times (T - D)$$

$$I \times (144 + D - 32) = ((W + I) \times (T - D)) - (I \times (T - D))$$

$$(I \times (144 + D - 32)) + (I \times (T - D)) = (W + I) \times (T - D)$$

$$I \times (144 + D - 32 + T - D) = (W + I) \times (T - D)$$

$$I \times (112 + T) = (W + I) \times (T - D)$$

$$I = \frac{(W + I) \times (T - D)}{112 + T}$$

$$\text{Ice} = \frac{\text{Total water} \times \text{temperature decrease}}{\text{Tap water temperature} + 112}$$

Appendix 6

Equipment Checklist

*T*he following is a list of the basic equipment found in a small bakeshop. These items are used in preparing baked goods and desserts of the types discussed in this book. Most large, specialized equipment and automatic machinery used in large bakeries—such as dough molders, overhead proofers, and automatic droppers—are omitted. Special tools for chocolate, marzipan, pastillage, and sugar work are illustrated in chapters 20, 21, and 22.

STATIONARY EQUIPMENT AND OTHER LARGE EQUIPMENT

COOKING AND BAKING EQUIPMENT

Revolving ovens or reel ovens are large chambers containing many shelves or trays on a Ferris-wheel type arrangement. These ovens eliminate the problem of hot spots or uneven baking because the mechanism rotates the foods throughout the oven.

Deck ovens are conventional ovens in which items are placed directly on the oven deck rather than on wire shelves. A supply of steam is important in such ovens for baking crisp-crusted breads and some other products.

Convection ovens contain fans that circulate the air and distribute the heat rapidly throughout the interior. The forced air may deform some soft items; cake batters, for example, may develop ripples.

Cookstoves or cooktops are needed for cooking such items as syrups, sauces, stirred custards, and poached fruits.

Trunnion kettles are small, tilting, steam-jacketed kettles, which are convenient for cooking larger quantities of such items as pastry cream and pie fillings. These foods could also be cooked in saucepans on a cook top, but a trunnion kettle is easier to use for larger quantities.

Fryers are needed for doughnuts and other fried items. Small operations often use standard deep fryers (or even stovetop kettles), but larger doughnut fryers are best if you make doughnuts in quantity. They should be used in conjunction with screens for lowering the doughnuts into the fat and for removing them when fried.

MIXERS AND OTHER DOUGH EQUIPMENT

Vertical mixers do most of the mixing work in small bakeshops. *Bench-model mixers* range from 5- to 20-qt capacity. *Floor models* are available as large as 140 qt. Adapter rings enable several sizes of bowls to be used on one machine. Most mixers have three, or sometimes four, operating speeds. (Large commercial bakeries use horizontal mixers for making bread doughs.)

Agitator attachments are of three major types. The *paddle* is a flat blade used for general mixing. The *wire whip* is used for whipping eggs, cream, and similar items. The *dough arm* is used for mixing and kneading yeast doughs. Additional specialized attachments, including wing whips, pastry knives, and sweet-dough arms, are also available.

Dough dividers cut scaled dough presses into small, equal units for rolls. See page 54 for more information. *Divider-rounders* automatically round the small units after they are divided.

Dough rollers and sheeters are available in many models, each operating somewhat differently. Pairs of adjustable rollers sheet out dough to specifications. Dough is fed to the rollers by gravity from hoppers or by canvas belts. Some types also curl sheeted bread dough into loaves.

Dough fermentation troughs are used to hold mixed yeast doughs during fermentation. Small operations might simply use large *mixing bowls on stands* instead.

Proof boxes are enclosed boxes with controlled temperature and humidity, used to proof trays of made-up yeast goods. They come in all variations and sizes, are operated by steam or electricity, and have manual or automatic controls.

Retarder-proofers combine the functions of freezers, retarders, and proofers; see page 61 for an explanation of this equipment.

STORAGE, HOLDING, AND MISCELLANEOUS LARGE EQUIPMENT

Refrigerators, for ingredient storage

Retarders, for dough storage

Flour and ingredient bins

Tray racks

Work tables

Two- or three-compartment sink

Hand sink

Pan washer, for larger operations

PANS AND CONTAINERS

Sheet pans or baking sheets come in standard full size (18 × 26 in./46 × 66 cm) and half size (18 × 13 in./46 × 33 cm). For hearth-type breads and rolls, *perforated pans* allow better circulation of hot air.

Baking pans and molds come in an immense variety of shapes and sizes. Most commonly used are:

Round layer cake pans in various diameters and 1½, 2, and 3 in. deep

Loaf pans, for bread, pound cake, etc.

Center-tube pans, also called simply *tube pans,* for angel food cake and some sweet breads

Pie pans

Tart or *quiche pans*

Brioche tins

Muffin and cupcake tins

Stainless-steel *hotel pans or bake pans,* 12 × 20 × 2½ in., sometimes used for such items as rice pudding, especially for counter service

Various other pans and fancy molds are used for specialty items, such as charlottes, Bavarians, gelatin-type desserts, individual baked custards, and soufflés.

Mixing bowls are usually round-bottomed, stainless-steel bowls in various sizes and are used for mixing various ingredients by hand and for holding ingredients, sauces, icings, etc. They are also used for items warmed or stirred over hot water.

Saucepans, double boilers, icing warmers, etc. are used for cooking and heating items on the cookstove.

Volume measures for liquids have lips for easy pouring. Sizes are pints, quarts, half gallons, and gallons. Each size is marked off into fourths by ridges on the sides.

HAND TOOLS AND OTHER SMALL TOOLS

KNIVES AND CUTTERS

French knife (heavy)

Utility knife

Paring knife

Vienna knife or *razor,* for cutting tops of proofed breads

Long serrated slicer

Cookie cutters and biscuit cutters

Wheel knife

Roller cutters for biscuits, doughnuts, croissants, etc.

Roller docker, for docking sheets of puff pastry and other doughs

DECORATING AND FINISHING TOOLS

Note: Many of the following are discussed on pages 349–350.

Cake turntable

Pastry bag and tubes

Icing screens or grates

Icing comb

Sugar dredger

Jelly pump

MISCELLANEOUS TOOLS

Rolling pins: ball-bearing type for puff pastry Danish dough, etc.; *broom-handle type* for pie crusts and small items

Pastry brushes, for glazing and applying washes

Bench brushes, for brushing flour

Bench scrapers, rectangular pieces of steel with a wooden handle on one edge, for scraping the workbench and dividing pieces of dough

Plastic *bowl scraper*

Palette knife, bowl knife, or metal spatula, used mostly for applying and spreading batters and icings. Both straight and offset blades are available.

Wire whips, for whipping and mixing by hand

Spoons, metal and wood

Sieves and strainers, for sifting flour and for straining and puréeing foods

Thermometers: dough thermometer, fat thermometer, and candy or sugar thermometer

Peel, a broad, flat wooden shovel for inserting and removing hearth breads from the oven

Silicone mat, a flexible nonstick mat, that withstands high heat. It is used for sugar work and, in place of parchment paper, as a baking pan liner

Balance scale, discussed on page 9

Digital scale, for small-quantity work, discussed on page 9.

Glossary

Note: Many culinary terms in common use are taken from French. Phonetic guides for difficult words are included here, using English sounds. However, exact renderings are impossible in many cases because French has a number of sounds that don't exist in English.

Air Cell: A tiny bubble of air, created by creaming or foaming, that assists in leavening a dough or batter.

Allumette: Any of various puff pastry items made in thin sticks or strips (French word for "matchstick").

Almond Paste: A mixture of finely ground almonds and sugar.

Angel Food Cake: A type of cake made of meringue (egg whites and sugar) and flour.

Angel Food Method: A cake-mixing method involving folding a mixture of flour and sugar into a meringue.

Apple Charlotte: A dessert of apples cut up and baked in a mold lined with bread slices.

Baba: A type of yeast bread or cake that is soaked in syrup.

Babka: A type of sweet yeast bread or coffee cake.

Bagel: A ring-shaped lean yeast dough product made from a very stiff dough.

Bagged: A cookie makeup method in which the dough is shaped and deposited with a pastry bag.

Baked Alaska: A dessert consisting of ice cream on a sponge cake base, covered with meringue and browned in the oven.

Baked Custard: A custard that is baked without being disturbed so that it sets into a solid.

Baked Meringue: Any of various meringue mixtures that are baked until dry.

Baking Ammonia: A leavening ingredient that releases ammonia gas and carbon dioxide.

Baklava: A Greek or Middle Eastern dessert made of nuts and phyllo dough and soaked with syrup.

Bar: A cookie makeup method in which the dough is shaped into flattened cylinders, baked, and sliced crosswise into individual cookies; a cookie made by this method.

Batter: A semiliquid mixture containing flour or other starch, used for the production of such products as cakes and breads and for coating products to be deep fried.

Baumkuchen (*bowm koo khen*): A cake made by adding one thin layer of batter at a time to a pan and browning lightly under a broiler after each addition, repeating until the cake is the desired thickness.

Bavarian Cream: A light, cold dessert made of gelatin, whipped cream, and custard sauce or fruit.

Beignet Soufflé (*ben yay soo flay*): A type of fritter made with éclair paste, which puffs up greatly when fried.

Biscuit Method: A mixing method in which the fat is mixed with the dry ingredients before the liquid ingredients are added.

Black Forest Torte: A chocolate sponge layer cake filled with whipped cream and cherries.

Blancmange (*bla mahnge*): (1) An English pudding made of milk, sugar, and cornstarch. (2) A French dessert made of milk, cream, almonds, and gelatin.

Blitz Puff Pastry: A type of pastry that is mixed like a very flaky pie dough, then rolled and folded like puff pastry.

Bloom: A whitish coating on chocolate, caused by separated cocoa butter.

Blown Sugar: Pulled sugar that is made into thin-walled, hollow shapes by being blown up like a balloon.

Boiled Icing: Italian meringue used as a cake icing.

Bombe: A type of frozen dessert made in a dome-shaped mold.

Boston Cream Pie: A sponge cake or other yellow cake filled with pastry cream and topped with chocolate fondant or confectioners' sugar.

Bran: The hard outer covering of kernels of wheat and other grains.

Bran Flour: Flour to which bran flakes have been added.

Bread Flour: Strong flour, such as patent flour, used for breads.

Brioche: Rich yeast dough containing large amounts of eggs and butter; a product made from this dough.

Brown Sugar: Regular granulated sucrose containing various impurities that give it a distinctive flavor.

Buttercream: An icing made of butter and/or shortening blended with confectioners' sugar or sugar syrup and, sometimes, other ingredients.

Cabinet Pudding: A baked custard containing sponge cake and fruit.

Cake Flour: A fine, white flour made from soft wheat.

Cannoli: Fried Italian pastries made in tube shapes, generally with a sweet cream or cheese filling (singular form is "cannolo").

Caramelization: The browning of sugars caused by heat.

Cassata: An Italian-style bombe, usually with three layers of different ice creams, plus a filling of Italian meringue.

Cast Sugar: Sugar that is boiled to the hard crack stage and then poured into molds to harden. Also called *poured sugar.*

Celsius Scale: The metric system of temperature measurement, with 0°C at the freezing point of water and 100°C at the boiling point of water.

Centi-: Prefix in the metric system meaning "one-hundredth."

Challah: A rich egg bread, often made as a braided loaf.

Charlotte: (1) A cold dessert made of Bavarian cream or other cream in a special mold, usually lined with ladyfingers or other sponge products. (2) A hot dessert made of cooked fruit and baked in a special mold lined with strips of bread.

Charlotte Ring: A metal ring used as a mold for charlottes and other desserts.

Chemical Leavener: A leavener such as baking soda, baking powder, or baking ammonia, which releases gases produced by chemical reactions.

Chiffon Cake: A light cake made by the chiffon method.

Chiffon Method: A cake-mixing method involving the folding of whipped egg whites into a batter made of flour, egg yolks, and oil.

Chiffon Pie: A pie with a light, fluffy filling containing egg whites and, usually, gelatin.

Chocolate Liquor: Unsweetened chocolate, consisting of cocoa solids and cocoa butter.

Chocolate Truffle: A small ball of chocolate ganache, served as a confection.

Christmas Pudding: A dark, heavy steamed pudding made of dried and candied fruits, spices, beef suet, and crumbs.

Ciabatta: A type of Italian bread made from a very slack dough deposited on pans with minimal shaping.

Clear Flour: A tan-colored wheat flour made from the outer portion of the endosperm.

Coagulation: The process by which proteins become firm, usually when heated.

Cobbler: A fruit dessert similar to a pie but without a bottom crust.

Cocoa: The dry powder that remains after cocoa butter is pressed out of chocolate liquor.

Cocoa Butter: A white or yellowish fat found in natural chocolate.

Common Meringue: Egg whites and sugar whipped to a foam; also called *French meringue.*

Complex Presentation: A style of plating a dessert consisting of an arrangement of two or more desserts plus sauces and garnishes.

Compote: Cooked fruit served in its cooking liquid, usually a sugar syrup.

Conching: A step in the manufacturing of chocolate, the purpose of which is to create a fine, smooth texture.

Confectioners' Sugar: Sucrose that is ground to a fine powder and mixed with a little cornstarch to prevent caking.

Cooked Fruit Method: A method for making pie fillings in which the fruit is cooked and thickened before being placed in the pie crust.

Cooked Juice Method: A method for making pie fillings in which the fruit juices are cooked, thickened, and mixed with the fruit.

Cornstarch Pudding: A sweetened liquid, usually milk and flavorings, that is boiled with cornstarch to thicken it.

Coulis: A sweetened fruit purée, used as a sauce.

Coupe: A dessert consisting of one or two scoops of ice cream or sherbet placed in a dish or glass and topped with any of a number of syrups, fruits, toppings, and garnishes; a sundae.

Couverture: Natural, sweet chocolate containing no added fats other than natural cocoa butter; used for dipping, molding, coating, and similar purposes.

Creaming: The process of beating fat and sugar together to blend them uniformly and to incorporate air.

Creaming Method: A mixing method that begins with the blending of fat and sugar; used for cakes, cookies, and similar items.

Cream Pie: An unbaked pie containing a pastry-cream-type filling.

Cream Pudding: A boiled pudding made of milk, sugar, eggs, and starch.

Crème Anglaise (*krem awng glezz*): A light vanilla-flavored custard sauce made of milk, sugar, and egg yolks.

Crème Brûlée: A rich custard with a brittle top crust of caramelized sugar (French name means "burnt cream").

Crème Caramel: A custard baked in a mold lined with caramelized sugar, then unmolded.

Crème Chantilly (*krem shawn tee yee*): Sweetened whipped cream flavored with vanilla.

Crème Chiboust: A cream filling made of pastry cream, gelatin, meringue, and flavorings.

Crème Fraîche (*krem fresh*): A slightly aged, cultured heavy cream with a slightly tangy flavor.

Crêpe (*krep*): A very thin French pancake, often served rolled around a filling.

Crêpes Suzette: French pancakes served in a sweet sauce flavored with orange.

Croissant (*krwah sawn*): A flaky, buttery yeast roll shaped like a crescent and made from a rolled-in dough.

Crumb Crust: A pie crust made of cookie crumbs, butter, and sugar.

Crystallize: To form crystals, as in the case of dissolved sugar.

Custard: A liquid that is thickened or set by the coagulation of egg protein.

Dark Chocolate: Sweetened chocolate that consists of chocolate liquor and sugar.

Deci-: Prefix in the metric system meaning "one-tenth."

Demerara Sugar: A type of crystalline, brown sucrose.

Dessert Syrup: A flavored sugar syrup used to flavor and moisten cakes and other desserts.

Devil's Food Cake: A chocolate cake made with a high percentage of baking soda, which gives the cake a reddish color.

Diastase: Various enzymes, found in flour and in diastatic malt, that convert starch into sugar.

Disaccharide: A complex or "double" sugar, such as sucrose.

Dobos Torte: A Hungarian cake made of seven thin layers filled with chocolate buttercream and topped with caramelized sugar.

Docking: Piercing or perforating pastry dough before baking in order to allow steam to escape and to avoid blistering.

Double-Acting Baking Powder: Baking powder that releases some of its gases when it is mixed with water and the remaining gases when it is heated.

Double-Panning: Placing a baking sheet or pan on or in a second pan to prevent scorching the bottom of the product being baked.

Drained Weight: The weight of solid canned fruit after draining off the juice.

Dredge: To sprinkle thoroughly with sugar or another dry powder.

Drop Batter: A batter that is too thick to pour but will drop from a spoon in lumps.

Dropped: A cookie makeup method in which portions of dough are measured with a scoop or spoon and dropped onto a baking pan.

Dutch Process Cocoa: Cocoa that has been processed with an alkali to reduce its acidity.

Éclair Paste: A paste or dough made of boiling water or milk, butter, flour, and eggs; used to make éclairs, cream puffs, and similar products.

Egg-Foam Cake: A cake leavened primarily by whipped eggs; it usually has a low percentage of fat.

Emulsified Shortening: Shortening containing emulsifiers so that it can be used for high-ratio cakes.

Emulsion: A uniform mixture of two or more unmixable substances.

Endosperm: The starchy inner portion of grain kernels.

English Muffin: A yeast dough product made in the shape of a disk and cooked on a griddle.

Extract: A flavoring ingredient consisting of flavorful oils or other substances dissolved in alcohol.

Extraction: The portion of the grain kernel that is separated into a particular grade of flour. Usually expressed as a percentage.

Fermentation: The process by which yeast changes carbohydrates into carbon dioxide gas and alcohol.

Flaky Pie Crust: A pie crust that has a flaky texture due to layers of fat sandwiched between layers of dough.

Flat Icing: A simple icing made of confectioners' sugar and water, usually used for Danish pastries and sweet rolls.

Flour-Batter Method: A cake-mixing method in which the flour is first mixed with the fat.

Foaming: The process of whipping eggs, with or without sugar, to incorporate air.

Focaccia: A flat Italian bread similar to a thick pizza dough.

Fondant: A type of icing made of boiled sugar syrup that is agitated so that it crystallizes into a mass of extremely small white crystals.

Fougasse: A regional French bread made in the shape of a trellis or ladder.

Four-Fold: A technique used to increase the number of layers in puff pastry or Danish pastry by folding the dough in fourths.

Frangipane: A type of almond-flavored cream.

French Doughnut: A fried pastry made of choux paste.

French Meringue: Egg whites and sugar whipped to a foam; also called *common meringue.*

French Pastry: Any of a variety of small fancy cakes and other pastries, usually in single-portion sizes.

French-Style Ice Cream: Ice cream containing egg yolks.

Fritter: A deep-fried item made of or coated with a batter or dough.

Frozen Mousse: A still-frozen dessert containing whipped cream.

Fruit Betty: A baked dessert consisting of layers of fruit and cake crumbs.

Fruit Cake: A loaf cake containing a high percentage of dried and candied fruits and, usually, nuts.

Fruit Cobbler: A baked fruit dessert with a pastry topping or top crust.

Fruit Crisp: A baked fruit dessert with a streusel topping.

Fruit Gratin: A dessert consisting of fruit plus a topping, browned under a broiler.

Fruit Pie: A baked single- or double-crust pie with a fruit filling.

Fruit Torte: A layer cake topped with a decorative arrangement of fruit.

Ganache (*gah nahsh*): A rich cream made of sweet chocolate and heavy cream.

Garnish: An edible item added to another food as a decoration or accompaniment.

Gâteau (*gah toe*): French word for "cake."

Gâteau St-Honoré: A pastry consisting of a base made of short pastry and pâte à choux and a cream filling, usually crème chiboust or crème diplomat.

Gaufre (*go fr'*): French word for "waffle."

Gelatin: A water-soluble protein extracted from animal tissue, used as a jelling agent.

Gelatinization: The process by which starch granules absorb water and swell in size.

Gelato: Italian ice cream.

Genoise: A sponge cake made by whipping whole eggs with sugar and folding in flour and, sometimes, melted butter.

Germ: The plant embryo portion of a grain kernel.

Glacé (glah say): (1) Glazed; coated with icing. (2) Frozen.

Glaze: (1) A shiny coating, such as a syrup, applied to a food. (2) To make a food shiny or glossy by coating it with a glaze or by browning it under a broiler or in a hot oven.

Gliadin: A protein in wheat flour that combines with another protein, glutenin, to form gluten.

Glucose: A simple sugar available in the form of a clear, colorless, tasteless syrup.

Gluten: An elastic substance, formed from proteins present in wheat flours, that gives structure and strength to baked goods.

Glutenin: See Gliadin.

Gram: The basic unit of weight in the metric system; equal to about one-thirtieth of an ounce.

Granité (*grah nee tay*): A coarse, crystalline frozen dessert made of water, sugar, and fruit juice or another flavoring.

Granulated Sugar: Sucrose in a fine crystalline form.

Gum Paste: A type of sugar paste or pastillage made with vegetable gum.

Hard Sauce: A flavored mixture of confectioners' sugar and butter; often served with steamed puddings.

Hard Wheat: Wheat high in protein.

Hearth Bread: A bread that is baked directly on the bottom of the oven, not in a pan.

Heavy Pack: A type of canned fruit or vegetable with very little added water or juice.

High-Fat Cake: A cake with a high percentage of fat; distinguished from a sponge or egg-foam cake.

High-Ratio: (1) Term referring to cakes and cake formulas mixed by a special method and containing more sugar than flour. (2) The mixing method used for these cakes. (3) Term referring to certain specially formulated ingredients used in these cakes, such as shortening.

High-Ratio Method: See Two-Stage Method.

Homogenized Milk: Milk that has been processed so that the cream does not separate out.

Hot Milk and Butter Sponge: A sponge cake batter in which a mixture of warm milk and melted butter is mixed into the batter.

Hydrogenation: A process that converts liquid oils to solid fats (shortenings) by chemically bonding hydrogen to the fat molecules.

Ice: A frozen dessert made of water, sugar, and fruit juice.

Icebox: A cookie makeup method in which the dough is shaped into cylinders, refrigerated, and sliced.

Ice Cream: A churn-frozen mixture of milk, cream, sugar, flavorings, and, sometimes, eggs.

Ice Milk: A frozen dessert similar to ice cream but with a lower fat content.

Icing Comb: A plastic triangle with toothed or serrated edges; used for texturing icings.

Instant Starch: A starch that thickens a liquid without cooking because it has been precooked.

Inversion: A chemical process in which a double sugar splits into two simple sugars.

Invert Sugar: A mixture of two simple sugars, dextrose and levulose, resulting from the breakdown of sucrose.

Italian Meringue: A meringue made by whipping a boiling syrup into egg whites.

Japonaise (*zhah po nez*): A baked meringue flavored with nuts.

Kernel Paste: A nut paste, similar to almond paste, made of apricot kernels and sugar.

Kilo-: Prefix in the metric system meaning "one thousand."

Kirsch: A clear alcoholic beverage distilled from cherries.

Kirschtorte: A torte made of genoise, meringue disks, and buttercream and flavored with kirsch.

Kugelhopf: A type of rich, sweet bread or coffee cake, usually made in a tube-type pan.

Ladyfinger: A small, dry, finger-shaped sponge cake or cookie.

Langue de Chat (*lahng duh shah*): A thin, crisp cookie. The French name means "cat's tongue," referring to the shape of the cookie.

Lattice Crust: A top crust for a pie made of strips of pastry in a criss-cross pattern.

Lean Dough: A dough that is low in fat and sugar.

Leavening: The production or incorporation of gases in a baked product to increase volume and to produce shape and texture.

Linzertorte: A tart made of raspberry jam and a short dough containing nuts and spices.

Liter: The basic unit of volume in the metric system; equal to slightly more than one quart.

Macaroon: A cookie made of eggs (usually whites) and almond paste or coconut.

Malt Syrup: A type of syrup containing maltose sugar, extracted from sprouted barley.

Marble: To partly mix two colors of cake batter or icing so that the colors are in decorative swirls.

Margarine: An artificial butter product made of various hydrogenated fats and flavorings.

Marron: French word for "chestnut."

Marshmallow: A light confection, icing, or filling made of meringue and gelatin (or other stabilizers).

Marshmallow Icing: Boiled icing with the addition of gelatin.

Marzipan: A paste or confection made of almonds and sugar and often used for decorative work.

Meal: Coarsely ground grain.

Mealy Pie Crust: A pie crust in which the fat has been mixed in thoroughly enough so that the dough does not have a flaky texture.

Melba Sauce: A sweet sauce made of puréed raspberries and, sometimes, red currants.

Meringue: A thick, white foam made of whipped egg whites and sugar.

Meringue Chantilly (*shawn tee yee*): Baked meringue filled with whipped cream.

Meringue Glacée: Baked meringue filled with ice cream.

Meter: The basic unit of length in the metric system; slightly longer than one yard.

Metric System: A measurement system based entirely on decimals.

Milk Chocolate: Sweetened chocolate containing milk solids.

Millefeuille (*mee foy*): French term for napoleon; literally, "thousand leaves." Also used for various layered desserts.

Milli-: Prefix in the metric system meaning "one-thousandth."

Modeling Chocolate: A thick paste, made of chocolate and glucose, that can be molded by hand into decorative shapes.

Modified Straight Dough Method: A mixing method similar to the straight dough method, except that the fat and sugar are mixed together first to ensure uniform distribution; used for rich doughs.

Molasses: A heavy brown syrup made from sugar cane.

Molded: A cookie makeup method in which the dough is shaped into cylinders, cut into equal portions, and shaped as desired.

Monosaccharide: A simple or single sugar such as glucose and fructose.

Mousse: A soft or creamy dessert that is made light by the addition of whipped cream, egg whites, or both.

Muffin Method: A mixing method in which the mixed dry ingredients are combined with the mixed liquid ingredients.

Napoleon: A dessert made of layers of puff pastry filled with pastry cream.

Natural Starter: A type of sourdough starter containing natural yeasts. See also Sourdough.

Net Weight: The weight of the total contents of a can or package.

No-Time Dough: A bread dough made with a large quantity of yeast and given no fermentation time, except for a short rest after mixing.

Nougatine: A mixture of caramelized sugar and almonds or other nuts, used in decorative work and as a confection and flavoring.

Old Dough: A dough that is overfermented.

One-Stage Method: A cookie-mixing method in which all ingredients are added to the bowl at once.

Opera Cake: A layer cake made of thin sponge layers, coffee-flavored buttercream, and chocolate ganache.

Othello: A small (single-portion size), spherical sponge cake filled with cream and iced with fondant.

Oven Spring: The rapid rise of yeast goods in the oven due to the production and expansion of trapped gases caused by the oven heat.

Overrun: The increase in volume of ice cream or frozen desserts due to the incorporation of air while freezing.

Pain de Campagne: French country-style bread.

Pain d'Épice (*pan day peece*): A type of gingerbread (French name means "spice bread").

Palmier (*palm yay*): A small pastry or petit four sec made of rolled, sugared puff pastry cut into slices and baked.

Panna Cotta: An Italian pudding made of cream, gelatin, and flavorings; literally, "cooked cream."

Pannetone: An Italian sweet bread made in a large loaf, generally containing dried and candied fruits.

Parfait: (1) A type of sundae served in a tall, thin glass. (2) A still-frozen dessert made of egg yolks, syrup, and heavy cream.

Paris-Brest: A dessert consisting of a ring of baked éclair paste filled with cream.

Pasteurized: Heat-treated to kill bacteria that might cause disease or spoilage.

Pastillage: A sugar paste, used for decorative work, that becomes very hard when dry.

Pastry Cream: A thick custard sauce containing eggs and starch.

Pastry Flour: A weak flour used for pastries and cookies.

Pâte à Choux (*pot ah shoo*): Éclair paste.

Pâte Brisée: A type of rich pastry dough used primarily for tarts.

Pâte Feuilleté (*pot foo ya tay*): French name for puff pastry.

Patent Flour: A fine grade of wheat flour milled from the inner portions of the kernel.

Peasant Tart: A baked tart with a custard filling containing prunes.

Pectin: A soluble plant fiber, used primarily as a jelling agent for fruit preserves and jams.

Peel: A flat wooden shovel used to place hearth breads in an oven and to remove them.

Petit Four: A delicate cake or pastry small enough to be eaten in one or two bites.

Petit Four Glacé: An iced or cream-filled petit four.

Petit Four Sec: An uniced or unfilled petit four ("sec" means "dry"), such as a small butter cookie or palmier.

Philadelphia-Style Ice Cream: Ice cream containing no eggs.

Phyllo (*fee lo*): A paper-thin dough or pastry used to make strudels and various Middle Eastern and Greek desserts.

Piping Jelly: A transparent, sweet jelly used for decorating cakes.

Pithiviers (*pee tee vyay*): A cake made of puff pastry filled with almond cream.

Pot de Crème (*poh duh krem*): A rich baked custard.

Pound Cake: (1) A cake made of equal weights of flour, butter, sugar, and eggs. (2) Any cake resembling this.

Pour Batter: A batter that is liquid enough to pour.

Poured Sugar: Sugar that is boiled to the hard crack stage and then poured into molds to harden. Also called *cast sugar*.

Praline: A confection or flavoring made of nuts and caramelized sugar.

Press: A scaled piece of dough that is divided into small, equal units in a dough divider.

Profiterole: A small puff made of éclair paste. Often filled with ice cream and served with chocolate sauce.

Puff Pastry: A very light, flaky pastry made from a rolled-in dough and leavened by steam.

Pulled Sugar: Sugar that is boiled to the hard-crack stage, allowed to harden slightly, then pulled or stretched until it develops a pearly sheen.

Pullman Loaf: A long, rectangular loaf of bread.

Pumpernickel Flour: A coarse, flaky meal made from whole rye grains.

Punching: A method of expelling gases from fermented dough.

Purée: A food made into a smooth pulp, usually by being ground or forced through a sieve.

Quenelle (*kuh nell*): A small oval portion of food.

Regular Shortening: Any basic shortening without emulsifiers, used for creaming methods and for icings.

Retarder-Proofer: An automated, timer-controlled combination of retarder/freezer and proofer, used for holding and proofing yeast products.

Retarding: Refrigerating a yeast dough to slow its fermentation.

Reversed Puff Pastry: A type of puff pastry made with the dough enclosed between layers of butter.

Ribbon Sponge: A thin sponge cake layer with a decorative design made of stencil paste.

Rice Condé: A thick, molded rice pudding, usually topped with fruit.

Rice Impératrice: A rich rice pudding containing whipped cream, candied fruits, and gelatin.

Rich Dough: A dough high in fat, sugar, and/or eggs.

Rolled: A cookie makeup method in which the dough is rolled out into a sheet and cut into shapes with cutters.

Rolled-in Dough: Dough in which a fat has been incorporated in many layers by using a rolling and folding procedure.

Rounding: A method of molding a piece of dough into a round ball with a smooth surface or skin.

Royal Icing: A form of icing made of confectioners' sugar and egg whites; used for decorating.

Rye Blend: A mixture of rye flour and hard wheat flour.

Rye Meal: Coarse rye flour.

Sabayon: A foamy dessert or sauce made of egg yolks whipped with wine or liqueur.

Sachertorte: A rich chocolate cake from Vienna.

Sacristain (*sak ree stan*): A small pastry made of a twisted strip of puff paste coated with nuts and sugar.

St-Honoré: (1) A dessert made of a ring of cream puffs set on a short dough base and filled with a type of pastry cream. (2) The cream used to fill this dessert, made of pastry cream and whipped egg whites.

Savarin: A type of yeast bread or cake that is soaked in syrup.

Scaling: Weighing, usually of ingredients or of doughs or batters.

Scone: A type of biscuit or biscuitlike bread.

Scone Flour: A mixture of flour and baking powder that is used when very small quantities of baking powder are needed.

Seeding: A technique for tempering chocolate by adding grated tempered chocolate to melted chocolate to cool it.

Sfogliatelle (*sfo lee ah tell eh*): A Southern Italian flaky turnover pastry with a sweet cheese filling.

Sheet: A cookie makeup method in which the dough is baked in sheets and cut into portions.

Sherbet: A frozen dessert made of water, sugar, fruit juice, and, sometimes, milk or cream.

Short: Having a high fat content, which makes the product (such as a cookie or pastry) very crumbly and tender.

Shortbread: A crisp cookie made of butter, sugar, and flour.

Short Dough: A pastry dough, similar to a basic cookie dough, made of flour, sugar, and fat. See also Short.

Shortening: (1) Any fat used in baking to tenderize the product by shortening gluten strands. (2) A white, tasteless, solid fat that has been formulated for baking or deep frying.

Simple Presentation: A style of plating a dessert consisting of a portion of one dessert plus optional sauces and garnishes.

Simple Syrup: A syrup consisting of sucrose and water in varying proportions.

Single-Acting Baking Powder: Baking powder that releases gases as soon as it is mixed with water.

Soft Pie: A single-crust pie with a custard-type filling—that is, a filling that sets or coagulates due to its egg content.

Soft Wheat: Wheat low in protein.

Solid Pack: A type of canned fruit or vegetable with no water added.

Sorbet (*sor bay*): French word for "sherbet."

Sorbetto: Italian word for "sherbet."

Soufflé: (1) A baked dish containing whipped egg whites, which cause the dish to rise during baking. (2) A still-frozen dessert made in a soufflé dish so that it resembles a baked soufflé.

Sour: Sourdough starter; a sponge that is fermented until it is noticeably acidic.

Sourdough: (1) A yeast-type dough made with a sponge or starter that has fermented so long that it has become very sour or acidic. (2) A bread made with such a dough.

Sponge: A batter or dough of yeast, flour, and water that is allowed to ferment and is then mixed with more flour and other ingredients to make a bread dough.

Sponge Cake: A type of cake made by whipping eggs and sugar to a foam, then folding in flour.

Sponge Method: A cake-mixing method based on whipped eggs and sugar.

Sponge Roll: See Swiss Roll.

Spread: The tendency of a cookie to spread out and flatten when baked.

Spun Sugar: Boiled sugar made into long, thin threads by dipping wires into the sugar syrup and waving them so that the sugar falls off in fine streams.

Staling: The change in texture and aroma of baked goods due to the loss of moisture by the starch granules.

Stencil: A pattern cut from plastic or cardboard, used for depositing batter for thin cookies made in decorative shapes.

Stencil Paste: A type of thin cookie or wafer dough used to make cookies in decorative shapes and for making decorative patterns in ribbon sponge.

Stirred Custard: A custard that is stirred while it is cooked so that it thickens but does not set.

Stollen: A type of sweet yeast bread with fruit.

Straight Dough Method: A mixing method for yeast goods in which all ingredients are mixed together at once.

Straight Flour: Flour made from the entire wheat kernel minus the bran and germ.

Streusel (*stroy sel*): A crumbly topping for baked goods, consisting of fat, sugar, and flour rubbed together.

Strong Flour: Flour with a high protein content.

Strudel: (1) A type of dough that is stretched until paper thin. (2) A baked item consisting of a filling rolled up in a sheet of strudel dough or phyllo dough.

Sucrose: The chemical name for regular granulated sugar and confectioners' sugar.

Sugar Cage: A lacy dome of hard or caramelized sugar.

Swiss Meringue: Egg whites and sugar warmed, usually over hot water, and then whipped to a foam.

Swiss Roll: A thin sponge cake layer spread with a filling and rolled up.

Syrup Pack: A type of canned fruit containing sugar syrup.

Tablage: A technique for tempering chocolate by cooling it on a marble slab.

Tart: A flat, baked item consisting of a pastry and a sweet or savory topping or filling; similar to a pie but usually thinner.

Tarte Tatin: An upside-down apple tart.

Tempering: The process of melting and cooling chocolate to specific temperatures in order to prepare it for dipping, coating, or molding.

Three-Fold: A technique used to increase the number of layers in puff pastry or Danish pastry by folding the dough in thirds.

Tiramisu: An Italian dessert made of ladyfinger sponge flavored with espresso coffee and a creamy cheese filling.

Torte: German word for various types of cakes, usually layer cakes.

Tulipe: A thin, crisp cookie molded into a cup shape.

Tunneling: A condition of muffin products characterized by large, elongated holes; caused by overmixing.

Turntable: A pedestal with a flat, rotating top, used for holding cakes while they are being decorated.

Two-Stage Method: A cake-mixing method, beginning with the blending of flour and high-ratio shortening, followed by the addition of liquids. Also called the *high-ratio method*.

Vacherin (*vah sher ran*): A crisp meringue shell filled with cream, fruits, or other items.

Wash: (1) A liquid brushed onto the surface of a product, usually before baking. (2) To apply such a liquid.

Water Pack: A type of canned fruit or vegetable containing the water used to process the item.

Weak Flour: Flour with a low protein content.

White Couverture: A confection consisting of cocoa butter, milk solids, and sugar. Sometimes erroneously called "white chocolate."

Whole Wheat Flour: Flour made by grinding the entire wheat kernel, including the bran and germ.

Yeast Starter: A type of sourdough starter made with a cultivated yeast.

Young Dough: A dough that is underfermented.

Zabaglione: An Italian dessert or sauce made of whipped egg yolks and Marsala wine.

Zest: The colored outer portion of the peel of citrus fruits.

Bibliography

Amendola, Joseph. *The Bakers' Manual for Quantity Baking and Pastry Making.* 4th ed. New York: John Wiley & Sons, 1993.

Amendola, Joseph, and Donald E. Lundberg. *Understanding Baking.* 2nd ed. New York: John Wiley & Sons, 1992.

Bilheux, Roland, and Alain Escoffier. *Professional French Pastry Series.* 4 vols. New York: John Wiley & Sons, 1988.

Bilheux, Roland, et al. *Special and Decorative Breads.* 2 vols. New York: John Wiley & Sons, 1989.

Boyle, Peter T. *Sugar Work.* New York: John Wiley & Sons, 1988.

Boyle, Tish, and Timothy Moriarty. *Grand Finales: The Art of the Plated Dessert.* New York: John Wiley & Sons, 1997.

Clayton, Bernard. *Bernard Clayton's New Complete Book of Breads.* New York: Fireside, 1995.

Clayton, Bernard. *The Breads of France.* Indianapolis: Bobbs-Merrill, 1978.

D'Ermo, Dominique. *The Modern Pastry Chef's Guide to Professional Baking.* New York: Harper & Row, 1962.

Duchêne, Laurent, and Bridget Jones. *Le Cordon Bleu Dessert Techniques.* New York: William Morrow, 1999.

Escoffier, A. *The Escoffier Cook Book.* New York: Crown, 1969.

Fance, Wilfred J., ed. *The New International Confectioner.* 5th ed. London: Virtue, 1981.

Friberg, Bo. *The Professional Pastry Chef.* 3rd ed. New York: John Wiley & Sons, 1996.

Hanneman, L. J. *Baker: Bread and Fermented Goods.* London: Heinemann, 1980.

Hanneman, L. J. *Pâtisserie.* London: Heinemann, 1977.

Lenôtre, Gaston. *Lenôtre's Desserts and Pastries.* Woodbury, N.Y.: Barron's, 1977.

Lenôtre, Gaston. *Lenôtre's Ice Creams and Candies.* Woodbury, N.Y.: Barron's, 1979.

Matz, S. A. *Bakery Technology and Engineering.* 3rd ed. Pan-Tech International, 1999.

MacLauchlan, Andrew. *The Making of a Pastry Chef.* New York: John Wiley & Sons, 1999.

Pyler, E. J. *Baking Science and Technology.* 2nd ed. 2 vols. Chicago: Siebel, 1973.

Roux, Michel. *Michel Roux's Finest Desserts.* New York: Rizzoli, 1995.

Schünemann, Claus, and Günter Treu. *Baking: The Art and Science.* Calgary, Alberta: Baker Tech, 1986.

Sultan, William J. *The Pastry Chef.* New York: Van Nostrand Reinhold, 1983.

Sultan, William J. *Practical Baking.* 5th ed. New York: John Wiley & Sons, 1989.

Teubner, Christian. *The Chocolate Bible.* New York: Penguin, 1997.

Recipe Index

Subject Index